MICHELIN®

ROAD ATLAS

Europe

First published in Great Britain 1988 by
Paul Hamlyn, an imprint of Reed Consumer Books Limited
Michelin House, 81 Fulham Road, London SW3 6RB
and Auckland, Melbourne, Singapore and Toronto

Fifth edition 1994
First impression 1994

A catalogue record for this book is available from the
British Library.

ISBN Spiral bound 0 600 58313 9

Printed in Great Britain

MICHELIN®
ROAD ATLAS
Europe

MICHELIN®
Touring Services

PAUL HAMLYN

Michelin

MICHELIN tyres and road maps have a reputation unsurpassed throughout Europe for quality and technical excellence in their respective fields.

It is appropriate, since the twelve member states of the European Community have formed a single European market, that Michelin should provide a new **Road Atlas of Europe**, compiled from their authoritative cartography, designed to meet the needs of the professional driver and holidaymaker alike.

There are over a hundred pages of mapping in this Atlas, showing the road network from North Cape to Gibraltar and from the Atlantic to the Black Sea. A full range of symbols show road categories and widths, towns and cities and places of interest as well as numerous other details, in keeping with Michelin's reputation for accuracy, legibility and up-to-date information.

Seventy one town plans are included to help the driver negotiate built-up areas and the 'Driving in Europe' section provides details of national motoring regulations which are useful to know when crossing national frontiers. The comprehensive index locates about 30 000 towns and features.

The map showing 'Climates in Europe' will assist travellers in deciding which is the best season to visit a particular country.

The indispensable road mapping can be used in conjunction with other Michelin publications which provide complementary information on accommodation and sightseeing. The Red Guides, in particular the 'Europe' volume which contains a selection of hotels and restaurants in major European cities, and the Green Guides to the various countries of Europe are ideal companions for this Atlas.

Michelin are always happy to receive suggestions and comments from readers of their publications; taking these into account when preparing new editions can only improve their service to the public.

Thank you in advance and have a good journey!

MICHELIN maps and guides complement one another: use them together!

Contents

Inside front cover
Key to symbols

IV Michelin
VI **Route Planning**
X **Distances in Europe**
XII **Driving in Europe**

1 **Key to symbols**
2 **Western Europe** at a scale of 1: 1 000 000
78 **Greece** at a scale of 1: 700 000
94 **Scandinavia** at a scale of 1: 1 500 000
110 **Eastern Europe** at a scale of 1: 3 000 000

116 **Index of place names**
Channel Tunnel
133 Calais Terminal
142 Folkestone Terminal

Inside back cover
Climates in Europe

Plans of cities and principal towns

118 ● Amsterdam
120 ● Antwerpen
86 ● Athina
122 ● Barcelona
123 ● Basel
124 ● Belfast
125 ● Berlin
126 ● Bern
127 ● Birmingham
126 ● Bologna
128 ● Bonn
129 ● Bordeaux
46 ● Bremen
130 ● Brugge
131 ● Bruxelles-Brussel
130 ● Budapest
137 ● Den Haag

136 ● Dijon
138 ● Dublin
138 ● Düsseldorf
139 ● Edinburgh
140 ● Essen
141 ● Firenze
143 ● Frankfurt a. M.
145 ● Genève
145 ● Genova
144 ● Gent
146 ● Glasgow
147 ● Göteborg
46 ● Hamburg
149 ● Hannover
107 ● Helsinki
151 ● Istanbul
153 ● København
154 ● Köln

156 ● Lausanne
157 ● Liège
158 ● Lille
159 ● Lisboa
162 ● Liverpool
160 ● London
164 ● Luxembourg
163 ● Lyon
165 ● Madrid
166 ● Manchester
33 ● Marseille
167 ● Milano
168 ● Monaco
169 ● München
172 ● Nantes
65 ● Napoli
173 ● Nice
174 ● Nürnberg

175 ● Oslo
69 ● Palermo
178 ● Paris
182 ● Porto
183 ● Praha
62 ● Roma
186 ● Rotterdam
190 ● Salzburg
193 ● Sevilla
194 ● Stockholm
195 ● Strasbourg
196 ● Stuttgart
198 ● Torino
199 ● Toulouse
201 ● Valencia
202 ● Venezia
205 ● Wien
207 ● Zürich

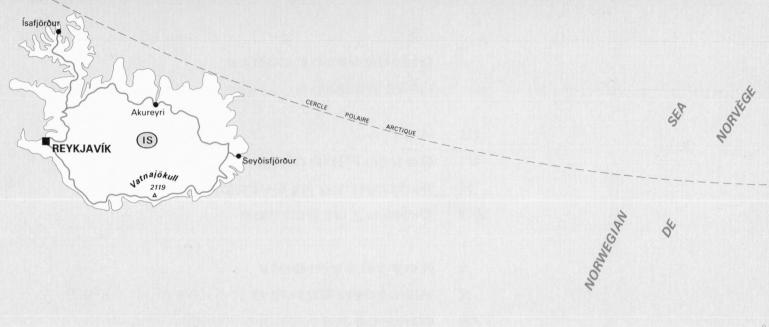

Jan Mayen

Ísafjörður

Akureyri

IS

REYKJAVÍK

Seyðisfjörður

Vatnajökull
2119

CERCLE POLAIRE ARCTIQUE

SEA

NORVÈGE

NORWEGIAN

DE

MER

Hitra

Kristiansund

Ålesund

2 470
Jotunheimen

Bergen

N

Skien

Stavanger

Kristiansand

Skagerrak

Føroyar

Shetland

OCEAN

ATLANTIQUE

Orkney

Thurso

Hebrides

Skye

Inverness
Loch Ness

1 344
Ben Nevis

Aberdeen

Dundee

Glasgow

Edinburgh

NORTH   SEA

DK

ATLANTIC

OCÉAN

Londonderry

Stranraer

Carlisle

Newcastle

MER   DU   NORD

Esbjerg

Belfast

Galway

IRL

Man

IRISH   SEA

York

Groningen

DUBLIN

Shannon

Leeds

Liverpool

Manchester

Sheffield

NL

Bremen

Limerick

St. George's Channel

GB

Nottingham

Ijsselmeer

Cork

Birmingham

Coventry

Norwich

AMSTERDAM

Hannover

Cardiff

Oxford

Cambridge

Den Haag

Rotterdam

LONDON

Thames

Waal

Dortmund

Essen

Southampton

Dover

Brugge

Kassel

Portsmouth

Calais

Gent

Antwerpen

Düsseldorf

Plymouth

B

Aachen

Köln

Land's End

ENGLISH CHANNEL

LA MANCHE

Lille

BRUSSEL

Bonn

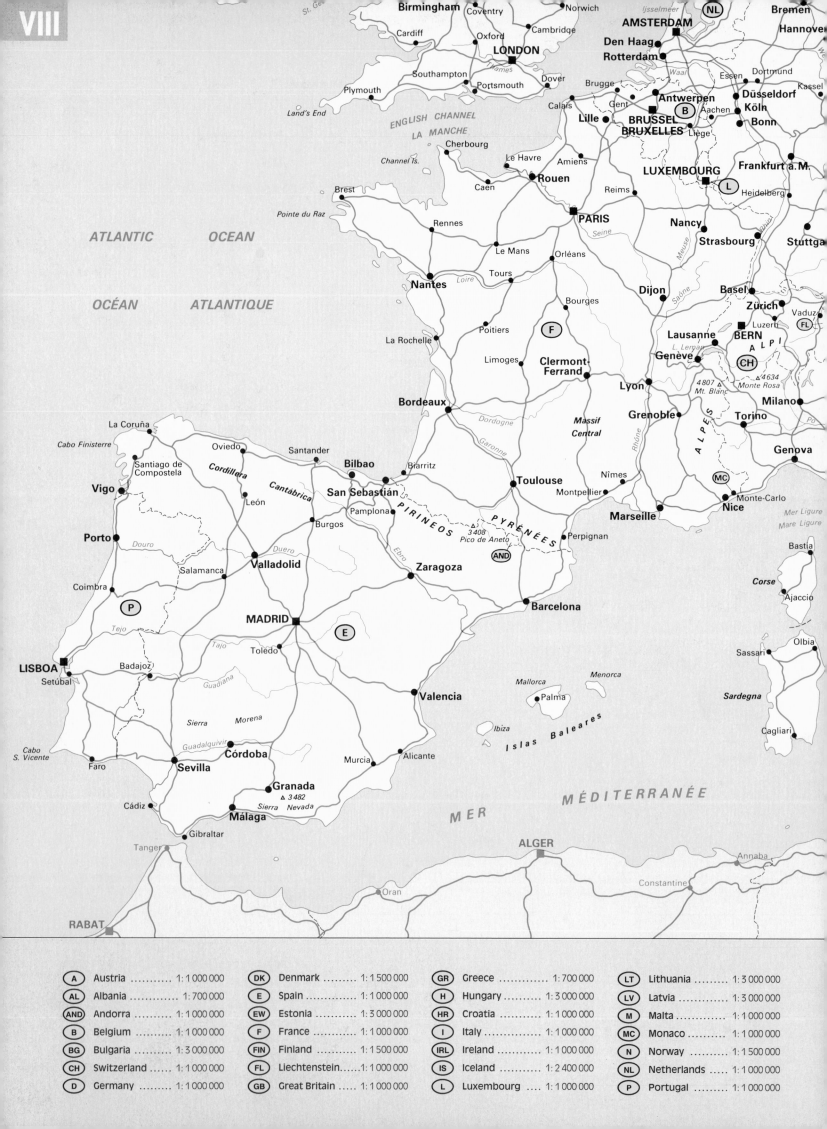

MER MÉDITERRANÉE

	Austria 1:1 000 000		Denmark 1:1 500 000		Greece 1:700 000		Lithuania 1:3 000 000
(A)	Austria 1:1 000 000	(DK)	Denmark 1:1 500 000	(GR)	Greece 1:700 000	(LT)	Lithuania 1:3 000 000
(AL)	Albania 1:700 000	(E)	Spain 1:1 000 000	(H)	Hungary 1:3 000 000	(LV)	Latvia 1:3 000 000
(AND)	Andorra 1:1 000 000	(EW)	Estonia 1:3 000 000	(HR)	Croatia 1:1 000 000	(M)	Malta 1:1 000 000
(B)	Belgium 1:1 000 000	(F)	France 1:1 000 000	(I)	Italy 1:1 000 000	(MC)	Monaco 1:1 000 000
(BG)	Bulgaria 1:3 000 000	(FIN)	Finland 1:1 500 000	(IRL)	Ireland 1:1 000 000	(N)	Norway 1:1 500 000
(CH)	Switzerland 1:1 000 000	(FL)	Liechtenstein..... 1:1 000 000	(IS)	Iceland 1:2 400 000	(NL)	Netherlands 1:1 000 000
(D)	Germany 1:1 000 000	(GB)	Great Britain 1:1 000 000	(L)	Luxembourg 1:1 000 000	(P)	Portugal 1:1 000 000

Magdeburg
BERLIN
Poznań
Oder
Odra
WARSZAWA
Brest
Cernihiv
PL
Łódź
Lublin
KYÏV
Poltava
D
Erfurt
Leipzig
Dresden
Wrocław
Częstochowa
UKR
Žytomir
Kremenčuc'k
Vodoschovyš
Nürnberg
Plzeň
PRAHA
CZ
Brno
Kraków
L'viv
Vinnycja
Kryvyj Rih
Main
Regensburg
Tatry
△ 2 655
K A R P A T Y
Dnister
Pivdennyj Buh
Donau
Košice
Černivci
Dnipro
Augsburg
SK
Tisza
MOL
Cherson
München
Linz
WIEN
BRATISLAVA
BUDAPEST
Cluj-Napoca
CHIŞINĂU
Iaşi
Odesa
Salzburg
Graz
H
Carpaţii
Innsbruck
△ Großglockner
3 797
A
Duna
Balaton
Braşov
Sibiu
Moldoveanu
2 543
MER   NOIRE
ALPEN
2 863 △ Triglav
SLO
Timişoara
RO
Carpaţii Meridionali
BUCUREŞTI
Constanţa
Bolzano
LJUBLJANA
ZAGREB
Pécs
Dráva
Novi Sad
Sava
Ruse
Padova
Trieste
HR
Tisa
Dunărea
BLACK   SEA
Verona
Venezia
Rijeka
Sava
BEOGRAD
Dunav
Varna
Parma
Adige
BH
Drina
Stara   Planina
Veliko Târnovo
Bologna
Ravenna
SARAJEVO
2 376
Botev
Burgas
RSM
Firenze
YU
SOFIA
BG
Pisa
Siena
Kota
Dalmatska
Split
Plovdiv
Edirne
İstanbul
Perugia
ADRIATIC   SEA
Dubrovnik
Podgorica
Rodopi
Gran Sasso △
Pescara
MER   ADRIATIQUE
Drin
2 764
Korab
SKOPJE
MKD
TR
Marmara
Denizi
V
ROMA
I
Durrës
TIRANË
Bursa
Bari
Thessaloníki
Napoli
1277
△ Vesuvio
AL
Ólimbos
△
2917
Izmir
Taranto
TYRRHENIAN   SEA
Kérkira
Pindes
Lárissa
Vólos
AEGEAN   SEA
Lésvos
MER
ÉGÉE
Dodekánissa
MER   TYRRHÉNIENNE
Igoumenitsa
Iónia
GR
Évia
Palermo
Messina
IONIAN   SEA
Pátra
ATHÍNA
Reggio
di Calabria
3 340
M. Etna △
Catania
MER   IONIENNE
Nissiá
Kórinthos
Pelopónissos
Kikládes
Ródos
Sicilia
TUNIS
M E D I T E R R A N E A N   S E A
Iráklio
M
Valletta
Kriti

Distances between European cities (km)

Amsterdam
2836 · Athina
1547 3090 · Barcelona
1971 2621 1792 · Bari
745 2466 1029 1226 · Basel
1341 3874 2046 2690 1508 · Belfast
1718 1118 1972 1503 1348 2756 · Beograd
1817 4017 3178 3244 2187 3112 2899 · Bergen
669 2584 1853 1811 862 1906 1466 1463 · Berlin
1424 3422 607 2124 1174 1755 2304 3196 1990 · Bilbao
782 3316 1487 2131 950 535 2198 2554 1348 1196 · Birmingham
1081 3240 633 1942 831 1412 2122 2853 1647 334 853 · Bordeaux
1098 3501 1242 2278 1096 1244 2383 2870 1664 965 686 627 · Brest
204 2792 1365 1777 551 1150 1674 1969 781 1229 591 886 903 · Brussel/Bruxelles
2221 1238 2611 2142 1987 3259 639 3200 1711 2943 2701 2761 2886 2177 · Bucuresti
1393 1510 1952 1482 1073 2431 392 2372 883 2283 1873 2041 2058 1349 828 · Budapest
902 2752 648 1485 477 1337 1634 2636 1311 706 779 365 808 706 2273 1614 · Clermont-Ferrand
1053 3586 1758 2402 1220 165 2468 2824 1618 1467 247 1124 956 862 2971 2143 1049 · Dublin
2024 1265 2049 1580 1425 2892 525 3204 1771 2381 2333 2199 2480 1970 1164 787 1711 2604 · Dubrovnik
1289 3823 1994 2638 1457 251 2705 3061 1855 1703 484 1360 1193 1098 3208 2380 1286 416 2840 · Edinburgh
1391 2115 1075 720 646 2099 997 2664 1231 1407 1539 1225 1686 1197 1636 976 883 1810 1074 2046 · Firenze
446 2396 1318 1553 327 1549 1278 1864 566 1502 991 1159 1176 402 1781 953 776 1261 1583 1498 973 · Frankfurt A. M.
885 2446 770 1203 259 1492 1328 2446 1121 1102 934 682 1081 703 1967 1307 310 1204 1405 1441 611 586 · Genève
1005 3205 2366 2432 1375 2300 2087 812 651 2384 1742 2041 2058 1157 2388 1560 1824 2012 2392 2249 1852 1052 1634 · Göteborg
441 2780 1802 2007 811 1736 1662 1384 289 1820 1178 1477 1494 593 2026 1198 1260 1448 1967 1685 1427 488 1070 572 · Hamburg
386 2637 1659 1864 668 1623 1519 1527 288 1707 1065 1364 1381 498 2022 1194 1117 1335 1824 1572 1284 345 927 715 151 · Hannover
1204 2540 2388 2346 1397 2441 1422 1186 505 2525 1883 2182 2199 1316 1858 1030 1846 2153 1893 2390 1766 1101 1656 662 776 823 · Helsinki
2665 1171 2919 2450 2295 3703 947 3846 2413 3251 3145 3069 3330 2621 692 1339 2581 3415 1326 3652 1944 2225 2275 3034 2609 2466 2369 · İstanbul
2017 2311 3114 2644 2187 3254 1336 2844 1383 3338 2696 2995 3012 2129 1073 1162 2636 2966 1861 3203 2138 1914 2339 2032 1670 1636 1146 489 · Kyïv
738 2938 2099 2165 1108 2033 1820 1079 384 2117 1475 1774 1791 890 2121 1293 1557 1745 2125 1982 1585 785 1367 267 305 448 795 2767 1765 · København
264 2579 1342 1714 488 1361 1461 1802 575 1440 803 1097 1114 211 1964 1136 802 1073 1766 1310 1314 189 747 990 426 292 1110 2408 1923 723 · Köln
1637 2973 2821 2779 1830 2874 1855 1619 938 2958 2316 2615 2632 1749 2625 1463 2279 2586 2326 2823 2199 1534 2089 1095 1209 1256 433 2041 1552 1228 1543 · (Leningrad) St. Peterburg
283 2910 1308 1836 610 1046 1792 2055 849 1139 487 799 716 116 2295 1467 645 758 2088 994 1256 520 669 1243 679 566 1384 2739 2197 976 329 1817 · Lille
2322 4320 1285 3022 2072 2653 3202 4094 2888 907 2094 1232 1863 2127 3841 3181 1604 2365 3279 2601 2305 2400 2000 3282 2718 2605 3423 4149 4236 3015 2338 3856 2037 · Lisboa

971 3504 1676 2320 1138 416 2386 2742 1536 1385 165 1042 874 780 2889 2061 967 167 2522 365 1728 1179 1122 1930 1366 1253 2071 3333 2884 1663 991 2504 676 2283 **Liverpool**
719 3252 1424 2068 886 722 2134 2490 1284 1133 196 790 622 528 2637 1809 715 434 2270 612 1476 927 870 1678 1114 1001 1819 3081 2632 1411 739 2252 424 2031 **London**
391 2637 1148 1560 334 1338 1519 1994 767 1290 779 947 964 218 1993 1165 608 1050 1758 1286 980 248 486 1182 618 484 1302 2466 2115 915 193 1735 334 2188 **Luxembourg**
917 2559 630 1292 400 1415 1441 2548 1223 962 857 538 1018 735 2080 1421 172 1127 1518 1364 690 688 151 1736 1172 1029 1758 2388 2548 1469 711 2191 682 1860 **Lyon**
1812 3760 686 2462 1562 2143 2642 3584 2378 397 1584 722 1353 1617 3281 2622 1094 1855 2719 2091 1745 1890 1440 2772 2208 2095 2913 3589 3726 2505 1828 3346 1527 658 **Madrid**
2360 4086 1012 2788 2025 2691 2968 4132 2849 945 2132 1270 1901 2165 3607 2948 1644 2403 3045 2639 2071 2314 1766 3320 2756 2643 3384 3915 4110 3053 2376 3817 2075 634 **Málaga**
1228 2621 493 1323 710 1727 1503 2859 1534 825 1168 648 1218 1046 2142 1483 417 1439 1580 1675 606 999 452 2047 1483 1340 2069 2450 2645 1780 1023 2502 992 1723 **Marseille**
1088 2128 973 878 343 1810 1010 2493 1040 1305 1251 1123 1398 894 1649 989 629 1522 1087 1758 298 670 323 1681 1117 974 1575 1957 2151 1414 831 2008 953 2203 **Milano**
2463 3169 3630 3306 2639 3700 2194 2313 1829 3784 3142 3441 3458 2575 1931 1918 3088 3412 2705 3649 2800 2360 2898 1789 2116 2082 1127 1347 638 2211 2369 924 2643 4682 **Moskva**
837 2063 1370 1224 399 1794 945 2018 585 1615 1236 1272 1421 769 1506 678 918 1506 1184 1743 644 397 599 1206 781 638 1120 1892 1744 939 580 1553 887 2513 **München**
887 3290 945 1923 847 1168 2172 2659 1453 669 609 325 302 692 2675 1847 465 880 2125 1116 1331 965 726 1847 1283 1170 1988 3119 2801 1580 903 2421 604 1567 **Nantes**
1878 2602 1562 261 1133 2585 1484 3151 1718 1894 2026 1712 2173 1684 2123 1463 1370 2297 1561 2533 490 1460 1098 2339 1914 1771 2253 2431 2625 2072 1621 2686 1743 2792 **Napoli**
1387 2434 656 1136 658 1886 1316 2808 1355 988 1327 808 1377 1205 1955 1295 577 1598 1393 1834 419 985 478 1996 1432 1289 1890 2263 2457 1729 1146 2323 1152 1886 **Nice**
666 2171 1427 1391 436 1715 1053 1867 434 1668 1157 1325 1342 622 1556 728 885 1427 1351 1664 811 226 695 1055 610 467 969 2000 1759 788 409 1402 740 2566 **Nürnberg**
1321 3521 2682 2748 1691 2616 2403 496 967 2700 2058 2357 2374 1473 2704 1876 2140 2328 2708 2565 2168 1368 1950 316 888 1031 690 3350 2348 583 1306 1123 1559 3598 **Oslo**
2599 3322 2283 691 1853 3305 2204 3872 2439 2614 2747 2432 2893 2404 2843 2184 2091 3017 2281 3254 1210 2180 1818 3060 2635 2492 2974 3151 3346 2793 2341 3407 2464 3512 **Palermo**
504 2912 1091 1735 553 965 1794 2275 1069 922 407 579 597 308 2297 1469 426 677 1937 914 1143 587 538 1463 899 786 1604 2741 2417 1196 520 2037 221 1820 **Paris**
2143 4141 1167 2843 1893 2474 3023 3915 2709 728 1915 1053 1684 1948 3662 3002 1425 2186 3100 2422 2126 2221 1821 3103 2539 2426 3244 3970 4057 2836 2159 3677 1858 314 **Porto**
950 2154 1711 1596 720 1999 1036 1839 350 1952 1441 1609 1626 906 1361 533 1169 1711 1261 1948 1016 510 979 1027 665 603 859 1983 1389 760 859 1292 1024 2850 **Praha**
1665 2389 1349 449 920 2372 1271 2938 1505 1681 1813 1499 1960 1471 1910 1250 1157 2084 1348 2320 277 1247 885 2126 1701 1558 2040 2218 2412 1859 1408 2473 1530 2579 **Roma**
2483 4683 3844 3910 2853 3778 3565 2824 2129 3862 3220 3519 3536 2635 3866 3038 3302 3490 3870 3727 3330 2530 3112 1528 2050 2193 837 4512 2557 1745 3288 1005 2721 4760 **Rovaniemi**
980 1932 1539 1172 536 1952 814 2161 728 1772 1393 1429 1578 927 1363 535 1076 1664 1052 1900 660 540 736 1349 924 781 1263 1761 1601 1082 723 1696 1045 2670 **Salzburg**
2295 4117 1043 2819 2056 2626 2999 4067 2880 880 2067 1205 1836 2100 3638 2979 1577 2338 3076 2574 2102 2345 1797 3255 2691 2578 3415 3946 4141 2988 2311 3848 2010 417 **Sevilla**
2104 818 2358 1889 1734 3142 386 3285 1852 2690 2584 2508 2769 2060 420 778 2020 2854 765 3091 1383 1664 1714 2473 2048 1905 1808 561 1493 2206 1847 2241 2178 3588 **Sofia**
1368 3568 2729 2795 1738 2663 2450 1021 1014 2747 2105 2404 2421 1520 2751 1923 2187 2375 2755 2612 2215 1415 1997 497 935 1078 165 3397 2395 630 1353 598 1606 3645 **Stockholm**
634 2438 1110 1371 145 1450 1320 2076 751 1264 892 918 1080 439 1881 1053 563 1162 1559 1399 791 216 404 1264 700 557 1286 2267 2076 997 377 1719 549 2162 **Strasbourg**
622 2302 1258 1404 267 1592 1184 2046 631 1413 1034 1070 1219 558 1745 917 716 1304 1423 1541 824 204 526 1234 670 527 1166 2131 1956 967 365 1599 676 2311 **Stuttgart**
2350 511 2604 2135 1980 3388 632 3531 2098 2936 2830 2754 3015 2306 727 1024 2266 3100 779 3337 1629 1910 1960 2719 2294 2151 2054 660 1800 2452 2093 2487 2424 3834 **Thessaloniki**
1154 2263 779 997 .409 1699 1145 2596 1157 1110 1140 864 1287 905 1784 1124 492 1411 1222 1647 395 736 252 1784 1220 1077 1692 2092 2286 1517 897 2125 961 2008 **Torino**
1199 2994 388 1696 933 1611 1876 3082 1757 447 1053 244 870 1003 2515 1856 384 1323 1953 1560 977 1222 675 2270 1706 1563 2292 2823 3018 2003 1246 2725 923 1345 **Toulouse**
3041 5241 4402 4468 3411 4336 4123 1893 2687 4420 3778 4077 4094 3193 4424 3596 3860 4048 4428 4285 3888 3088 3670 2570 2608 2751 1367 5070 3087 2303 3026 1535 3279 5318 **Tromsø**
1865 4065 3226 3292 2235 3160 2947 717 1511 3244 2602 2901 2918 2017 3248 2420 2684 2872 3252 3109 2712 1912 2494 1394 1432 1575 949 3894 2892 1127 1850 1382 2103 4142 **Trondheim**
1892 3435 361 2137 1374 2391 2317 3523 2198 606 1832 771 1402 1710 2956 2297 993 2103 2394 2339 1420 1663 1115 2711 2147 2004 2733 3264 3459 2444 1687 3166 1653 924 **Valencia**
1283 1878 1229 760 605 2072 760 2512 1079 1561 1513 1379 1660 1156 1399 739 891 1784 837 2020 254 891 585 1700 1275 1132 1614 1707 1901 1433 1026 2047 1215 2459 **Venezia**
1223 2188 2390 2066 1399 2460 1070 2050 589 2544 1902 2201 2218 1335 1506 678 1848 2172 1465 2409 1560 1120 1658 1238 876 842 352 2017 794 971 1129 785 1403 3442 **Warszawa**
1150 1862 1833 1341 830 2188 744 2131 642 2141 1630 1798 1815 1106 1071 243 1370 1900 969 2137 835 710 1030 1319 957 951 924 1691 1309 1052 893 1357 1224 3039 **Wien**
1337 1499 1591 1122 967 2375 381 2518 1085 1923 1817 1741 2002 1293 1020 350 1253 2087 618 2324 616 897 947 1706 1281 1138 1287 1328 1512 1439 1080 1720 1411 2821 **Zagreb**
831 2416 1058 1176 86 1594 1298 2267 852 1260 1036 917 1182 637 1816 988 597 1306 1375 1543 596 412 287 1455 891 748 1387 2245 2054 1188 573 1820 696 2158 **Zürich**

Distances in Europe

Distances are calculated from centres and along the best roads from a motoring point of view - not necessarily the shortest

Example: **Luxembourg – Warszawa** 1321 km

1321

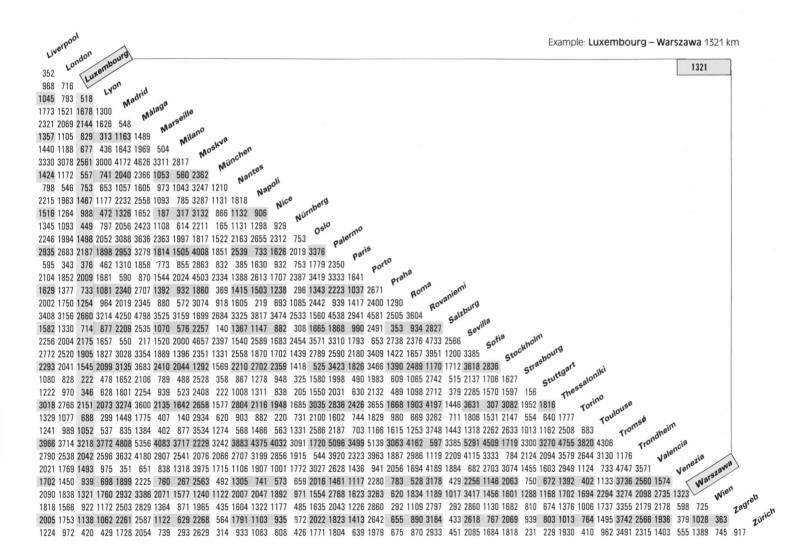

Liverpool
London
Luxembourg
Lyon
Madrid
Málaga
Marseille
Milano
Moskva
München
Nantes
Napoli
Nice
Nürnberg
Oslo
Palermo
Paris
Porto
Praha
Roma
Rovaniemi
Salzburg
Sevilla
Sofia
Stockholm
Strasbourg
Stuttgart
Thessaloniki
Torino
Toulouse
Tromsø
Trondheim
Valencia
Venezia
Warszawa
Wien
Zagreb
Zürich

```
352
968  716
1045  793  518
1773 1521 1678 1300
2321 2069 2144 1626  548
1357 1105  829  313 1163 1489
1440 1188  677  436 1643 1969  504
3330 3078 2561 3000 4172 4626 3311 2817
1424 1172  557  741 2040 2366 1053  560 2362
 798  546  753  653 1057 1605  973 1043 3247 1210
2215 1963 1467 1177 2232 2558 1093  785 3287 1131 1818
1516 1264  988  472 1326 1652  187  317 3132  866 1132  906
1345 1093  449  797 2056 2423 1108  614 2211  165 1131 1298  929
2246 1994 1498 2052 3088 3636 2363 1997 1817 1522 2163 2655 2312  753
2935 2683 2187 1898 2953 3279 1814 1505 4008 1851 2539  733 1626 2019 3376
 595  343  376  462 1310 1858  773  855 2863  832  385 1630  932  753 1779 2350
2104 1852 2009 1681  590  870 1544 2024 4503 2334 1388 2613 1707 2387 3419 3333 1641
1629 1377  733 1081 2340 2707 1392  932 1860  369 1415 1503 1238  296 1343 2223 1037 2671
2002 1750 1254  964 2019 2345  880  572 3074  918 1605  219  693 1085 2442  939 1417 2400 1290
3408 3156 2660 3214 4250 4798 3525 3159 1699 2684 3325 3817 3474 2533 1560 4538 2941 4581 2505 3604
1582 1330  714  877 2209 2535 1070  576 2257  140 1367 1147  882  308 1665 1868  990 2491  353  934 2827
2256 2004 2175 1657  550  217 1520 2000 4657 2397 1540 2589 1683 2454 3571 3310 1793  653 2738 2376 4733 2566
2772 2520 1905 1827 3028 3354 1889 1396 2351 1331 2558 1870 1702 1439 2789 2590 2180 3409 1422 1657 3951 1200 3385
2293 2041 1545 2099 3135 3683 2410 2044 1292 1569 2210 2702 2359 1418  525 3423 1826 3466 1390 2489 1170 1712 3618 2836
1080  828  222  478 1652 2106  789  488 2528  358  867 1278  948  325 1580 1998  490 1983  609 1065 2742  515 2137 1706 1627
1222  970  346  628 1801 2254  939  523 2408  222 1008 1311  838  205 1550 2031  630 2132  489 1098 2712  379 2285 1570 1597  156
3018 2766 2151 2073 3274 3600 2135 1642 2658 1577 2804 2116 1948 1685 3035 2836 2426 3655 1668 1903 4197 1446 3631  307 3082 1952 1816
1329 1077  688  299 1449 1775  407  140 2934  620  903  882  220  731 2100 1602  744 1829  980  669 3262  711 1806 1531 2147  554  640 1777
1241  989 1052  537  835 1384  402  877 3534 1274  568 1466  563 1331 2586 2187  703 1166 1615 1253 3748 1443 1318 2262 2633 1013 1162 2508  683
3966 3714 3218 3772 4808 5356 4083 3717 2229 3242 3883 4375 4032 3091 1720 5096 3499 5139 3063 4162  597 3385 5291 4509 1719 3300 3270 4755 3820 4306
2790 2538 2042 2596 3632 4180 2907 2541 2076 2066 2707 3199 2856 1915  544 3920 2323 3963 1887 2986 1119 2209 4115 3333  784 2124 2094 3579 2644 3130 1176
2021 1769 1493  975  351  651  838 1318 3975 1715 1106 1907 1001 1772 3027 2628 1436  941 2056 1694 4189 1884  682 2703 3074 1455 1603 2949 1124  733 4747 3571
1702 1450  939  698 1899 2225  760  267 2563  492 1305  741  573  659 2016 1461 1117 2280  783  528 3178  429 2256 1146 2063  750  672 1392  402 1133 3736 2560 1574
2090 1838 1321 1760 2932 3386 2071 1577 1240 1122 2007 2047 1892  971 1554 2768 1623 3263  620 1834 1189 1017 3417 1456 1601 1288 1168 1702 1694 2294 3274 2098 2735 1323
1818 1566  922 1172 2503 2829 1364  871 1965  435 1604 1322 1177  485 1635 2043 1226 2860  292 1109 2797  292 2860 1130 1682  810  674 1376 1006 1737 3355 2179 2178  598  725
2005 1753 1138 1062 2261 2587 1122  629 2268  564 1791 1103  935  672 2022 1823 1413 2642  655  890 3184  433 2618  767 2069  939  803 1013  764 1495 3742 2566 1936  379 1028  363
1224  972  420  429 1728 2054  739  293 2629  314  933 1083  608  426 1771 1804  639 1979  675  870 2933  451 2085 1684 1818  231  229 1930  410  962 3491 2315 1403  555 1389  745  917
```

Driving in Europe

Introduction

The information panels which follow give the principal motoring regulations in force when this atlas was prepared for press (1.7.93); an explanation of the symbols is given below, together with some additional notes.

🔧 The name, address and telephone number of the national motoring organisation or organisations; the initials FIA and AIT indicate membership of the international touring associations, the Fédération Internationale de l'Automobile and the Alliance Internationale de Tourisme

🕓 Speed restrictions in kilometres per hour applying to:

🏟 motorways
🛣 dual carriageways
🅰 single carriageways
🏙 urban areas

Where restrictions for 'trailers' or 'towing' are given, it may be assumed that these apply to both trailers and caravans

🍷 The maximum permitted level of alcohol in the bloodstream. This should not be taken as an acceptable level; it is NEVER sensible to drink and drive

💺 Whether the wearing of seat belts is compulsory

👶 Restrictions applying to children

△ Whether a warning triangle must be carried

🔲 Whether a first aid kit must be carried

💡 Whether a spare bulb kit must be carried

🪖 Whether crash helmets are compulsory for motorcyclists

🏟 Whether tolls are payable on motorways and/or other parts of the road network

⛽ Whether petrol concessions or restrictions apply

⊖ The minimum age for drivers

▤ Documentation required; note that while insurance for driving at home usually provides the legally required minimum third party cover abroad, it will not provide cover against damage, fire, theft or personal accident; for this reason, an International Motoring Certificate (Green Card) is recommended for all countries and essential where 'Green Card required' is given

★ In this section are given any other regulations not falling into the categories above

Andorra

🔧 **Automobil Club d'Andorra FIA,** Babot Camp 13, Andorra-la-Vella Tel: 20-8-90

🕓   90   70   40 km/h

🍷 0.08%

💺

👶 Children under 10 years of age not allowed in front seats

△ Recommended (compulsory if vehicle exceeds 3000 kg)

🔲 Recommended

💡 Compulsory

🪖 Compulsory for motorcyclists and passengers

🏟

⛽

⊖ 18

▤ Valid driving licence; Vehicle registration document or Vehicle on hire certificate; Green Card recommended; National vehicle identification plate

Austria

🔧 **Österreicher Automobil-, Motorrad- und Touring Club (ÖAMTC),** FIA & AIT, Schubertring 1-3, 1010 Wien 1 Tel: (01) 711990

🕓 100-130   100   50 km/h
If towing trailer over 14.5 cwt:
100   80   50 km/h
If towing trailer under 14.5 cwt:
100   100   100   50 km/h

🍷 0.08%

💺 Compulsory if fitted for driver and front and rear seat passengers

👶 Children under 12 years of age not allowed in front seats

△ Compulsory

🔲 Compulsory

💡

🪖 Compulsory for motorcyclists and passengers

🏟 Tolls payable on motorways for Brenner (A13), Tauern (part of the A10), and a section of the A9 north of Graz, as well as on certain roads (especially trans-alpine routes) and tunnels

⛽

⊖ 18

▤ Valid driving licence; Vehicle registration document or Vehicle on hire certificate; Green Card compulsory; National vehicle identification plate

★ Towing is forbidden on certain alpine routes

Belgium

🔧 **Royal Automobile Club de Belgique (RACB),** FIA, 53 rue d'Arlon, 1040 Bruxelles Tel: (02) 287 09 00

Touring Club Royal de Belgique (TCB), AIT, 128 av. Carton de Wiart 1090 Bruxelles   Tel: (070) 344 777

Vlaamse Automobilistenbond (VTB-VAB) Sint-Jacobs Markt 45, 2000 Antwerpen   Tel: (03) 253 63 63

🕓 120   90-120   90   50 km/h

🍷 0.05%

💺 Compulsory if fitted for driver and front and rear seat passengers

👶 Children under 12 years of age not allowed in front seats unless they are using an approved child's safety seat

△ Compulsory

🔲 Recommended

💡

🪖 Compulsory for motorcyclists

🏟 Toll payable on the Liefkenshoektunnel

⛽

⊖ 18

▤ Valid driving licence; Vehicle registration document or Vehicle on hire certificate; Green Card recommended; National vehicle identification plate

Bulgaria

🔧 **Union of Bulgarian Motorists (SBA)** FIA & AIT, 3 Place Pozitano, Sofia 1090 B.P.257   Tel: (02) 86151

🕓 120   80   80   60 km/h

🍷 0.0%

💺 Compulsory if fitted for driver and front seat passengers

👶 Children under 10 years of age not allowed in front seats

△ Compulsory

🔲 Compulsory

💡

🪖 Compulsory for motorcyclists

🏟

⛽ Foreign motorists must buy fuel with coupons available in unlimited quantities at border posts and within Bulgaria

⊖ 18

▤ Valid driving licence or International Driving Permit; Vehicle registration document or Vehicle on hire certificate; Green Card required; National vehicle identification plate

Czech Republic

✦ **Ústřední Automotoklub ČSFR**, AIT & FIA, Na rybníčku 16, 120 76 Praha 2 Tel: 24 911 830

🏛	🅰	🄰	🏭
🕧 110	110	90	60 km/h

🍷 0.0% any alcohol found in the bloodstream may result in prosecution

🚗 Compulsory if fitted for driver and front and back seat passengers

👶 Children under 12 years of age not allowed in front seats

△ Compulsory

[ ] Compulsory

🔦 Compulsory

🪖 Crash helmets and goggles compulsory for drivers of motorcycles over 50cc; crash helmets only for passengers

🏛
🛢
⊖ 18

🪪 Valid driving licence; Vehicle registration document or Vehicle on hire certificate; Green Card valid for the Czech Republic recommended; National vehicle identification plate

Estonia

✦ **Automobile Club: AUTOM Pikk**, 41 EE001 Tallinn Tel: 601-215

🏛	🅰	🄰	🏭
🕧	90	90	50 km/h

🍷 0.0%

🚗 Compulsory

👶 Children under 12 years of age not allowed in front seats

△ Compulsory

[ ] Compulsory

🔦 Recommended

🪖 Compulsory

🏛
🛢
⊖ 18

🪪 Driving licence; Vehicle registration document or Vehicle on hire certificate; Green Card recommended

France

✦ **Automobile Club de France**, (FIA), 6 Place de la Concorde, 75008 Paris Tel: (01) 42 65 34 70

Automobile Club National, (FIA) (AIT), 5 rue Auber, 75 009 Paris Tel: (01) 44 51 83 99

🏛	🅰	🄰	🏭
🕧 110-130	110	90	50 km/h

If wet:
| 100-110 | 100 | 80 | 50 km/h |

🍷 0.08% or 0.40 mg per litre of air exhaled

🚗 Compulsory if fitted for driver and front and rear seat passengers

👶 Children under 10 years of age not allowed in front seats

△ Compulsory unless hazard warning lights are fitted; triangle and lights compulsory for cars pulling caravans or trailers and for vehicles greater than 3.5 tons

[ ] Recommended

🔦 Recommended

🪖 Compulsory for motorcyclists and passengers

🏛 Tolls payable on most motorways although short urban sections of motorway around Paris and some other major cities are free; tolls also payable on some major bridges and in some tunnels

🛢
⊖ 18

🪪 Valid driving licence; Vehicle registration document or Vehicle on hire certificate; Green Card recommended; National vehicle identification plate

Great Britain

✦ **Automobile Association (AA)**, FIA & AIT, Fanum House, Basingstoke, Hampshire RG21 2EA Tel: (0256) 20123

Royal Automobile Club (RAC), FIA & AIT, RAC House, Bartlett Street, South Croydon CR2 6XW Tel: (081) 686 0088

🏛	🅰	🄰	🏭
🕧 112	112	96	48 km/h

If towing:
| | 96 | 96 | 80 | 48 km/h |

🍷 0.08%

🚗 Compulsory if fitted for driver and front and rear seat passengers

👶 Children under 1 year of age travelling in front seat must be strapped in or placed in an approved child's safety seat

△

[ ] Recommended

🔦

🪖 Compulsory for motorcyclists and passengers

🏛 Tolls payable on certain major bridges and tunnels

🛢
⊖ 17

🪪 Valid driving licence; Vehicle registration document or Vehicle on hire certificate; Green Card recommended; National vehicle identification plate

★ Drive on the left!

Denmark

✦ **Forenede Danske Motorejere (FDM)**, AIT, Firskovvej 32, 2800 Lyngby Tel: (45) 93 08 00

🏛	🅰	🄰	🏭
🕧 110	80	80	50 km/h

If towing:
| 70 | 70 | 70 | 50 km/h |

🍷 0.08%

🚗 Compulsory in front and in back

👶 Children under 3 need not use seat belt. Between 3 and 7 they may use a child's safety seat or booster cushion and seat belt

△ Compulsory

[ ] Recommended

🔦

🪖 Compulsory for motorcyclists and passengers

🏛
🛢
⊖ 18

🪪 Valid driving licence; Vehicle registration document or Vehicle on hire certificate; Green Card recommended; National vehicle identification plate

★ Fire extinguisher recommended; dipped headlights compulsory at all times

Finland

✦ **Autoliitto (Automobile and Touring Club of Finland) (ATCF)**, FIA & AIT, Hämeentie 105 00550 Helsinki 10 Tel: (90) 6940022

🏛	🅰	🄰	🏭
🕧 100-120		80-100	50 km/h

Towing if trailer has brakes:
| 80 | | 80 | 50 km/h |

Towing if trailer unbraked:
| 60 | | 60 | 50 km/h |

🍷 0.05%

🚗 Compulsory if fitted for driver and front and rear seat passengers

👶 People under 1.50m tall must travel with a safety belt in a special child's seat

△ Compulsory

[ ] Recommended

🔦 Recommended

🪖 Compulsory for motorcyclists and passengers

🏛
🛢
⊖ 18

🪪 Valid driving licence; Vehicle registration document or Vehicle on hire certificate; Green Card recommended; National vehicle identification plate

★ Compulsory use of headlights at all times outside built-up areas

Germany

✦ **ADAC - Allgemeiner Deutscher Automobil-Club**, FIA & AIT, Am Westpark 8, 81373 München 70 Tel: (089) 76760

Automobil-Club von Deutschland (AvD), FIA, Lyonerstraße 16, 60528 Frankfurt am Main 71 Tel: (069) 66060

🏛	🅰	🄰	🏭
🕧 130*	130*	100	50 km/h

If towing:
| 80 | 80 | 80 | 50 km/h |
*recommended

🍷 0.08%

🚗 Compulsory for driver and front and rear seat passengers

👶 Children under 12 years of age not allowed in front seats unless strapped in or placed in a child's safety seat

△ Compulsory

[ ] Compulsory

🔦

🪖 Compulsory for motorcyclists and passengers

🏛
🛢
⊖ 18

🪪 International Driving Permit required if 'pink' EC licence not held; Vehicle registration document or Vehicle on hire certificate; Green Card recommended; National vehicle identification plate

Greece

✦ **The Automobile and Touring Club of Greece (ELPA)**, FIA & AIT, 2-4 Messogion, 115 27 Athína Tel: (01) 779 1615

Hellenic Touring Club, AIT, 12 Politehniou, 104 33 Athína Tel: (01) 524 0854

🏛	🅰	🄰	🏭
🕧 120	100	80	50 km/h

🍷 0.05%

🚗 Compulsory for driver and front seat passengers

👶 Children under 10 years of age not allowed in front seats

△ Compulsory

[ ] Compulsory

🔦

🪖 Compulsory for motorcyclists

🏛 Tolls payable on most 'national' roads

🛢
⊖ 18

🪪 Valid international driving licence, EC licence accepted; Vehicle registration document or Vehicle on hire certificate; Green Card required; National vehicle identification plate

★ Fire extinguisher compulsory

Hungary

🔧 **Magyar Autóklub (MAK)**, FIA & AIT, Rómer Flóris utca 4a, 1024 Budapest
Tel: (01) 115 2040

🏛	🛣	Ⓐ	🏘
120	100	80	50 km/h

If towing:
| 80 | 70 | 70 | 50 km/h |

🍷 0.0%   if the alcohol test changes colour, the driver is taken to a hospital for a blood test and his driving licence confiscated

💺 Compulsory if fitted for driver and front seat passengers

👶 Children under 6 years of age not allowed in front seats

△ Compulsory

[ ] Compulsory

🔦 Compulsory

🦺 Compulsory for motorcyclists and passengers

🏛

⛽

⊖ 18

🪪 Valid driving licence; Vehicle registration document or Vehicle on hire certificate; Green Card strongly recommended; National vehicle identification plate

★ Headlights compulsory at all times

Ireland

🔧 **Automobile Association (AA)**, FIA & AIT, 23 Suffolk Street, Dublin 2
Tel: (01) 8779481

Royal Automobile Club (RAC), FIA & AIT, 34 Dawson Street, Dublin 2
Tel: (01) 8775141

🏛	🛣	Ⓐ	🏘
88	88	64-88	48 km/h

If towing:
| 56 | 56 | 56 | 48 km/h |

🍷 0.10%

💺 Compulsory if fitted for driver and front seat passengers

👶 Children under 12 years of age not allowed in front seats unless strapped in or placed in a child's safety seat

△ Recommended

[ ] Recommended

🔦 Recommended

🦺 Compulsory for motorcyclists and passengers

🏛 Toll payable on two bridges over River Liffey in Dublin

⛽

⊖ 17

🪪 Valid driving licence; Vehicle registration document or Vehicle on hire certificate; Green Card recommended; National vehicle identification plate

★ Drive on the left!

Latvia

🔧 **Transporta Ministrija** Brivibas iela 58, Rīga   Tel: 226 922

🏛	🛣	Ⓐ	🏘
	100	100	60 km/h

🍷 0.05%

💺 Compulsory if fitted for driver and front seat passengers

👶 Children under 12 years of age not allowed in front seats

△

[ ] Compulsory

⛽

🔦

🏛

⛽

⊖ 18

🪪 Driving licence; Vehicle registration document

Luxembourg

🔧 **Automobile Club du Grand Duché de Luxembourg (ACL)**, FIA & AIT, 54 route de Longwy, 8007 Bertrange
Tel: 45 00 45

🏛	🛣	Ⓐ	🏘
120	90	90	60 km/h

If towing:
| 90 | 75 | 75 | 60km/h |

🍷 0.08%

💺 Compulsory if fitted for driver and front and rear seat passengers

👶 Children under 10 years of age allowed in front seats if vehicle is equipped with child's safety seat

△ Compulsory

[ ] Recommended

⛽

🔦 Compulsory

🏛

⛽ The purchasing, selling and transporting of petrol in drums or jerrycans is prohibited

⊖ 18

🪪 Valid driving licence; Vehicle registration document or Vehicle on hire certificate; Green Card recommended; National vehicle identification plate

Iceland

🔧 **Felag Islenskra Bifreidaeigenda (FIB)**, FIA & AIT, Borgatun 33, 105 Reykjavik
Tel: (01) 62 99 99

🏛	🛣	Ⓐ	🏘
	80-90	80-90	50 km/h

🍷 0.05%

💺 Compulsory for driver and front seat passengers; rear seat belts recommended

👶 Children in rear seats must be strapped in or placed in a child's safety seat

△ Compulsory

[ ] Recommended

🔦 Recommended

🦺 Compulsory for motorcyclists and passengers

🏛

⛽

⊖ 17

🪪 Driver's passport; Valid driving licence; Vehicle registration document or Vehicle on hire certificate; Green Card, valid for Iceland, required; Temporary importation permit; National vehicle identification plate

★ Headlights compulsory at all times; vehicles with diesel engines are subject to a special charge on entry to Iceland

Italy

🔧 **Automobile Club d'Italia (ACI)**, FIA & AIT, Via Marsala 8, 00185 Roma
Tel: (06) 49981

Touring Club Italiano (TCI), AIT, Corso Italia 10, 20122 Milano   Tel: (02) 85261

🏛	🛣	Ⓐ	🏘
130	110	90	50 km/h

If towing:
| 80 | 70 | 70 | 50 km/h |

🍷 Severe penalties for drinking and driving

💺 Compulsory in front (and in back if installed)

👶 Children under 12 not allowed in front unless seat is fitted with child restraint system

△ Compulsory

[ ] Recommended

⛽ Compulsory

🦺 Compulsory for motorcyclists and passengers

🏛 Tolls payable on most motorways

⛽

⊖ 18

🪪 Valid driving licence (translation in Italian recommended); Vehicle registration document; Green Card recommended; National vehicle identification plate

Lithuania

🔧 **Lietuvos Automobilininku Sajunga**, Lvovo 9, 2005 Vilnius
Tel: (370-2) 35 21 86

🏛	🛣	Ⓐ	🏘
110	100	90	60 km/h

🍷 0.00%

💺 Compulsory if fitted for driver and front and rear seat passengers

👶 Children under 12 years of age not allowed in front seats

△ Compulsory

[ ] Compulsory

⛽ Compulsory

🦺 Compulsory

🏛

⛽

⊖ 18

🪪 Valid driving licence; Visa; Passport; Vehicle registration document; Green Card (insurance must be taken out at frontier if no Green Card); National identification plate

Netherlands

🔧 **Koninklijke Nederlandse Automobiel Club (KNAC)**, FIA, Westvlietweg 118, Leidschendam
Tel: (070) 399 74 51

Koninklijke Nederlandse Toeristenbond (ANWB), AIT, Wassenaarseweg 220, Den Haag
Tel: (070) 314 71 47

🏛	🛣	Ⓐ	🏘
120	100	80	50 km/h

If towing:
| 80 | 80 | 80 | 50 km/h |

🍷 0.05%

💺 Compulsory if fitted for driver and front and rear seat passengers

👶 Children under 12 years of age and under 1,50 m tall allowed in front if seat is fitted with child restraint system; in the back children between 3 and 12 years must wear a seat belt if there is no child's safety seat or booster cushion

△

[ ] Recommended

⛽

🦺 Compulsory for motorcyclists and passengers

🏛 Tolls payable on: Kiltunnel (from Dordrecht to Hoekse Waard) and Prins Willem Alexander Brug

⛽

⊖ 18

🪪 Valid driving licence; Vehicle registration document; Green Card recommended; National vehicle identification plate

Norway

🔧 **Kongelig Norsk Automobilklub (KNA)**, FIA, Drammensveien 20c, 0201 Oslo 2 Tel: 22 56 19 00

Norges Automobil-Forbund (NAF), AIT, Storgata 2, 0155 Oslo 1 Tel: 22 34 14 00

🚦	🛣	🛣	🏭
80-90	80-90	80-90	50 km/h

If towing trailer with braking system:
80 80 80 50 km/h

If towing trailer without braking system:
60 60 60 50 km/h

🍷 0.05%

🚗 Compulsory if fitted for driver and front and rear seat passengers

🧒 Children are allowed in front if seat is fitted with child restraint system and seat and belt can be adapted to their size

△ Compulsory

[ ] Recommended

🔦 Recommended

🪖 Compulsory for motorcyclists and passengers

🛣 Tolls payable on some new major roads

⛽

⊖ 18 or 20 depending on the type of vehicle

🪪 Valid driving licence; Vehicle registration document or Vehicle on hire certificate; Green Card recommended; National vehicle identification plate

★ Dipped headlights compulsory at all times

Portugal

🔧 **Automóvel Club de Portugal (ACP)**, FIA & AIT, Rua Rosa Araújo 24, 1200 Lisboa Tel: (01) 3563931

🚦	🛣	🛣	🏭
120	90	90	60 km/h

If towing:
100 70 70 50 km/h

🍷 0.05%

🚗 Compulsory for driver and front seat passengers

🧒 Children under 12 years of age not allowed in front seat

△ Compulsory

[ ] Recommended

🔦 Recommended

🪖 Compulsory for motorcyclists

🛣 Tolls payable on some motorways and bridges

⛽

⊖ 18

🪪 Valid driving licence; Vehicle registration document or Vehicle on hire certificate; Green Card required; National vehicle identification plate

Slovakia

🔧 **Ústředni Automotoklub Slovenska**, AIT & FIA, Wolkrova 4, 85001 Bratislava Petržalka Tel: (07) 123

🚦	🛣	🛣	🏭
110	90	90	50 km/h

🍷 0.0% any alcohol found in the bloodstream may result in prosecution

🚗 Compulsory if fitted for driver and front and back seat passengers

🧒 Children under 12 years of age not allowed in front seats

△ Compulsory

[ ] Compulsory

🔦 Compulsory

🪖 Crash helmets and goggles compulsory for drivers of motorcycles over 50cc; crash helmets only for passengers

🛣

⛽

⊖ 18

🪪 Valid driving licence; Vehicle registration document or Vehicle on hire certificate; Green Card valid for Slovakia recommended; National vehicle identification plate

Spain

🔧 **Real Automóvil Club de España (RACE)**, FIA & AIT, José Abascal 10, 28003 Madrid Tel: (91) 447 3200

🚦	🛣	🛣	🏭
120	120	90-100	50 km/h

If towing:
80 80 70-80 50 km/h
these limits are increased by 20 km/h for overtaking

🍷 0.08%

🚗 Compulsory for driver and passengers

🧒 Children under 12 years of age not allowed in front seats

△ Compulsory

[ ] Recommended

🔦 Compulsory

🪖 Compulsory for motorcyclists

🛣 Tolls payable on motorways and Cadi tunnel

⛽

⊖ 18

🪪 International Driving Permit required if 'pink' EC licence not held; Vehicle registration document or Vehicle on hire certificate; Green Card required; Bail Bond strongly recommended; National vehicle identification plate

Poland

🔧 **Polski Zwiazek Motorowy (PZM)**, FIA & AIT, 66 ul. Kazimierzowska, 02-518 Warszawa Tel: (022) 49 93 61/ 49 92 12

Auto Assistance, P BOX 470, 19 ul. Sandomierska, 00-950 Warszawa Tel: (022) 49 25 36/ 49 76 57 (02) 628 62 55

🚦	🛣	🛣	🏭
110	90	90	60 km/h

If towing:
70 70 70 60 km/h

🍷 0.02%

🚗 Compulsory for driver and front seat passengers; compulsory if fitted in the back

🧒 Children under 10 years of age not allowed in front seats

△ Compulsory

[ ] Recommended

🔦 Recommended

🪖 Compulsory for motorcyclists and passengers

🛣

⛽ In exchange for zlotys (PLZ) in currency

⊖ 17

🪪 Valid driving licence or International Driving Permit; Vehicle registration document or Vehicle on hire certificate; Green Card, valid for Poland, required; National vehicle identification plate

★ Between 1/11 and 1/3 dipped headlights compulsory at all times; fire extinguisher compulsory

Romania

🔧 In the event of breakdown or accident contact **Automobile-Club roumain**, FIA & AIT Strada Tache Ionescu 27, Bucureşti Tel: (400) 155510

🛣	🛣	🛣	🏭
70-90*	60-90*	60-90*	60 km/h

*according to cylinder capacity

🍷 0.0% any alcohol found in the bloodstream may result in immediate imprisonment

🚗 Compulsory if fitted

🧒 Children under 14 years of age not allowed in front seats

△ Compulsory

[ ] Compulsory

🔦 Recommended

🪖 Compulsory for motorcyclists and passengers

🛣 Tolls payable on some major routes (Bucharest-Constanta)

⛽

⊖ 18

🪪 Valid driving licence; Vehicle registration document or Vehicle on hire certificate; Green Card, valid for Romania, required; National vehicle identification plate

Slovenia

🔧 **Zveza Slovenije (AMZS)** Dunajska 128, 61 113 Ljubljana Tel: 38 61 / 18 11 11

🚦	🛣	🛣	🏭
80-120	80-100	80	60 km/h

If towing:
80 80 80 60 km/h

🍷 0.05%

🚗 Compulsory if fitted for driver and front and rear seat passengers

🧒 Children under 12 years of age not allowed in front seats

△ Compulsory

[ ] Compulsory

🔦 Compulsory

🪖 Compulsory for motorcyclists and passengers

🛣 Tolls on major motorways and the Karavanke tunnel

⛽

⊖ 18

🪪 Valid driving licence; Vehicle registration document or Vehicle on hire certificate; Green Card required; National vehicle identification plate

Sweden

🔧 **Motormännens Riksförbund (M)**, AIT, Sturegatan 32, Stockholm Tel: (08) 7 82 38 00

🚦	🛣	🛣	🏭
90-110	70-110	70-110	50 km/h

If towing with braking device:
70 70 70 50 km/h

If towing with no braking device:
40 40 40 40 km/h

🍷 0.02%

🚗 Compulsory if fitted for driver and front and rear seat passengers

🧒 Special safety seats compulsory for children under 8 years of age

△ Compulsory

[ ] Recommended

🔦

🪖 Compulsory for motorcyclists and passengers

🛣

⛽

⊖ 18

🪪 Valid driving licence; Vehicle registration document or Vehicle on hire certificate; Green Card required (for certain countries only); National vehicle identification plate

★ Dipped headlights compulsory at all times

Switzerland

🔧 **Automobile Club de Suisse (ACS)**, FIA, Wasserwerkgasse 39, 3000 Bern 13 Tel: (031) 22 47 22

Touring Club Suisse (TCS), AIT, 9 rue Pierre-Fatio, 1211 Genève 3 Tel: (022) 737 12 12

🚅 120	🛣 100	🛤 80	🏭 50 km/h

If towing – up to 20 cwt trailer:
80	80	80	50 km/h

If towing – over 20 cwt trailer:
60	60	60	50 km/h

🍷 0.08%

💺 Compulsory if fitted for driver and front seat passengers

🧒 Children under 7 years of age not allowed in front seats

△ Compulsory

[ ]

🔦

🔧 Compulsory for motorcyclists and passengers

🏛 Vignette compulsory: obtainable from frontier posts, post offices or garages; separate vignette required for trailer or caravan

🔧

⊖ 18

📖 Valid driving licence; Vehicle registration document or Vehicle on hire certificate; Green Card; National vehicle identification plate

Turkey

🔧 **Turkiye Turing ve Otomobil Kurumu (TTOK)**, FIA & AIT, Halaskargasi Cad. 364, 80222 Sisli, Istanbul   Tel: (01) 231 46 31

🚅	🛣 90	🛤 90	🏭 50 km/h

If towing:
	70	70	40 km/h

🍷 0.05%

💺 Compulsory if fitted for driver and front seat passengers

🧒 Children under 12 years of age not allowed in front seats

△ Two must be carried – one to place in front of the vehicle, one behind

[ ] Compulsory

🔦

🔧 Compulsory for motorcyclists

🏛 Tolls payable on some roads

🔧

⊖ 18

📖 Passport; Valid driving licence; International Driving Permit advised, compulsory if driving Turkish vehicle (obtainable at frontier with 2 photos and 267 000 Turkish Lire); Vehicle registration document or Vehicle on hire certificate; Green Card required – must cover European and Asian regions; National vehicle identification plate

★ Fire extinguisher, chock and towrope compulsory

Belorussia, Moldavia, Russia, Ukraine

🔧 In the event of breakdown or accident contact officer of State Automobile Inspection or nearest office of Intourist (obliged to give tourists assistance)

🚅 90	🛣 90	🛤 90	🏭 60 km/h

🍷 0.0%

💺 Compulsory if fitted for driver and front seat passengers

🧒 Children under 12 years of age not allowed in front seats

△ Compulsory

[ ] Compulsory

🔦 Recommended

🔧 Compulsory

🏛 Road tax payable on entry to these states though some foreign cars exempt

🔧 Petrol coupons recommended; obtainable at border posts

⊖ 18

📖 Valid driving licence meeting requirements of International Convention on Road Traffic; Vehicle registration document or Vehicle on hire certificate; Car insurance obtainable on entry to these states at Ingosstrakh offices or at Intourist offices; Itinerary card, service coupons and motor routes map issued by Intourist; Customs obligation to take the car out of the country on departure; National vehicle identification plate

★ Fire extinguisher compulsory

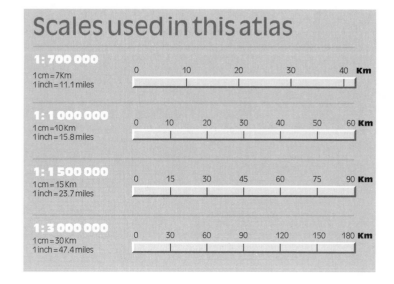

Scales used in this atlas

1: 700 000
1 cm = 7 Km
1 inch = 11.1 miles

| 0 | 10 | 20 | 30 | 40 **Km** |

1: 1 000 000
1 cm = 10 Km
1 inch = 15.8 miles

| 0 | 10 | 20 | 30 | 40 | 50 | 60 **Km** |

1: 1 500 000
1 cm = 15 Km
1 inch = 23.7 miles

| 0 | 15 | 30 | 45 | 60 | 75 | 90 **Km** |

1: 3 000 000
1 cm = 30 Km
1 inch = 47.4 miles

| 0 | 30 | 60 | 90 | 120 | 150 | 180 **Km** |

Signos convencionales

Para más información ver el interior de la cubierta anterior

Importancia de los itinerarios

Autopista con calzadas separadas
con calzada única
Autovía con calzadas separadas
❸ ❸ Número de acceso
Accesos: completo – medio acceso
parcial – sin precisión
Carretera de comunicación internacional o nacional asfaltada:
calzadas separadas
4 carriles – 3 carriles
2 carriles anchos – 2 carriles
Carretera de comunicación interregional asfaltada:
calzadas separadas
2 carriles o más – 2 carriles estrechos
Sin asfaltar: transitable, con macadán
Otra carretera asfaltada – sin asfaltar
Autopista, carretera en construcción
(en su caso: fecha de entrada en servicio)

Distancias en kilómetros (totales o parciales)

12 en autopista:
tramo de peaje
5 12 7
tramo libre
5 7
12 en carretera
5 7
14 10
GB e IRL: en millas
24
39 en kilómetres

Transporte

Línea férrea – Tren-coche
Ⓑ Barcaza
Enlace marítimo: permanente – de temporada
✈ Aeropuerto

Zeichenerklärung

Vollständige Zeichenerklärung siehe Umschlaginnenseite

Verkehrsbedeutung der Straßen

Autobahn mit getrennten Fahrbahnen
mit nur einer Fahrbahn
Schnellstraße mit getrennten Fahrbahnen
❸ ❸ Nummer der Anschlußstelle
Anschlußstellen: Autobahnein- und/oder
-ausfahrt – ohne Angabe
Internationale bzw. nationale Hauptverkehrsstraße mit Belag:
getrennte Fahrbahnen
4 Fahrspuren – 3 Fahrspuren
2 breite Fahrspuren – 2 Fahrspuren
Überregionale Verbindungsstraße mit Belag:
getrennte Fahrbahnen
2 u. mehr Fahrspuren – 2 schmale Fahrspuren
Ohne Belag: befahrbar, mit Makadam
Sonstige Straßen: mit Belag, ohne Belag
Autobahn, Straße im Bau
(ggf. Datum der Verkehrsfreigabe)

Entfernungsangaben in Kilometern (Gesamt- und
Teilentfernungen)

12 auf der Autobahn:
gebührenpflichtiger Abschnitt
5 12 7
gebührenfreier Abschnitt
5 7
12 auf anderen Straßen
5 7
14 10
in GB und IRL: in Meilen
24
39 in Kilometern

Transport

Bahnlinie – Autoreisezug
Ⓑ Fähre
Schiffsverbindung: ganzjährig – während der Saison
✈ Flughafen

Légende

Voir la légende complète à l'intérieure de la couverture

Importance des itinéraires

Autoroute à chaussées séparées
à une seule chaussée
Double chaussée de type autoroutier
❸ ❸ Numéro d'échangeur
Echangeurs: complet – demi-échangeur
partiel – sans precision
Route de liaison internationale ou nationale revêtue:
chaussées séparées
4 voies – 3 voies
2 voies larges – 2 voies
Route de liaison interrégionale revêtue:
chaussées séparées
2 voies et plus – 2 voies étroites
Non revêtue: carrossable, en macadam
Autre route revêtue – non revêtue
Autoroute, route en construction
(le cas échéant: date de mise en service)

Distances en kilomètres (totalisées et partielles)

12 sur autoroute:
section à péage
5 12 7
section libre
5 7
12 sur route
5 7
14 10
GB et IRL: en miles
24
39 en kilomètres

Transport

Voie ferrée –Train-auto
Ⓑ Bac
Liaison maritime: permanente – saisonnière
✈ Aéroport

Segni convenzionali

Vedere la legenda completa all'interno della copertina

Importanza degli itinerari

Autostrada a carreggiate separate
a carreggiata unica
Doppia carreggiata di tipo autostradale
❸ ❸ Numero dello svincolo
Svincoli: completo – semi-svincolo
parziale – non precisato
Strada di comunicazione internazionale o nazionale rivestita:
a carreggiate separate
a 4 corsie – a 3 corsie
a 2 corsie larghe – a 2 corsie
Strada di comunicazione interregionale rivestita:
a carreggiate separate
a 2 corsie e più – a 2 corsie strette
Non rivestita: carrozzabile, in macadam
Altre strade con rivestimento – senza rivestimento
Autostrada, strada in costruzione
(se del caso: data di apertura prevista)

Distanze in chilometri (totali e parziali)

12 su autostrada:
tratto a pedaggio
5 12 7
tratto esente da pedaggio
5 7
12 su strada
5 7
14 10
GB e IRL: in miglia
24
39 in chilometri

Trasporti

Ferrovia – trasporto automobili per ferrovia
Ⓑ Su chiatta
Collegamento via-traghetto: tutto l'anno – stagionale
✈ Aeroporto

Verklaring der tekens

Zie voor de volledige verklaring der tekens de binnenzijde van het omslag

Belang van het wegennet

Autosnelweg met gescheiden rijbanen
met één rijbaan
Dubbele rijbaan van het type autosnelweg
❸ ❸ Nummer knooppunt/aansluiting
Knooppunten/aansluitingen: volledig – half
gedeeltelijk – niet nader aangegeven
Internationale of nationale verharde verbindingsweg:
gescheiden rijbanen
4 rijstroken – 3 rijstroken
2 brede rijstroken – 2 rijstroken
Regionale verharde verbindingsweg:
gescheiden rijbanen
2 of meer rijstroken – 2 smalle rijstroken
Onverhard: berijdbaar, macadamweg
Andere weg: verhard – onverhard
Autosnelweg, weg in aanleg
(indien van toepassing: datum openstelling)

Afstanden in kilometers (totaal en gedeeltelijk)

12 op de autosnelweg:
gedeelte met tol
5 12 7
tolvrij gedeelte
5 7
12 op de weg
5 7
14 10
GB en IRL: in mijlen
24
39 in kilometers

Vervoer

Spoorweg – Autotrein
Ⓑ Veerpont
Scheepvaartverbinding : permanent – alleen in het seizoen
✈ Luchthaven

Key to symbols

A full key to symbols appears inside the front cover

Road classification

Motorway: dual carriageway
single carriageway
Dual carriageway with motorway characteristics
❸ ❸ Interchange number
Interchange: complete – half
limited – unspecified
International and national surfaced road network:
dual carriageway
four lanes – three lanes
two wide lanes – two lanes
Interregional surfaced road network:
dual carriageway
two lanes or more – two narrow lanes
Unsurfaced: suitable for vehicles, macadam
Other surfaced road – unsurfaced
Motorway, road under construction
(where available: with scheduled opening date)

Distances in kilometres (total and intermediate)

12 on motorway:
toll section
5 12 7
free section
5 7
12 on other roads
5 7
14 10
GB and IRL: in miles
24
39 kilometres

Transportation

Railway – Motorail
Ⓑ Ferry
Car ferry: all the year – seasonal
✈ Airport

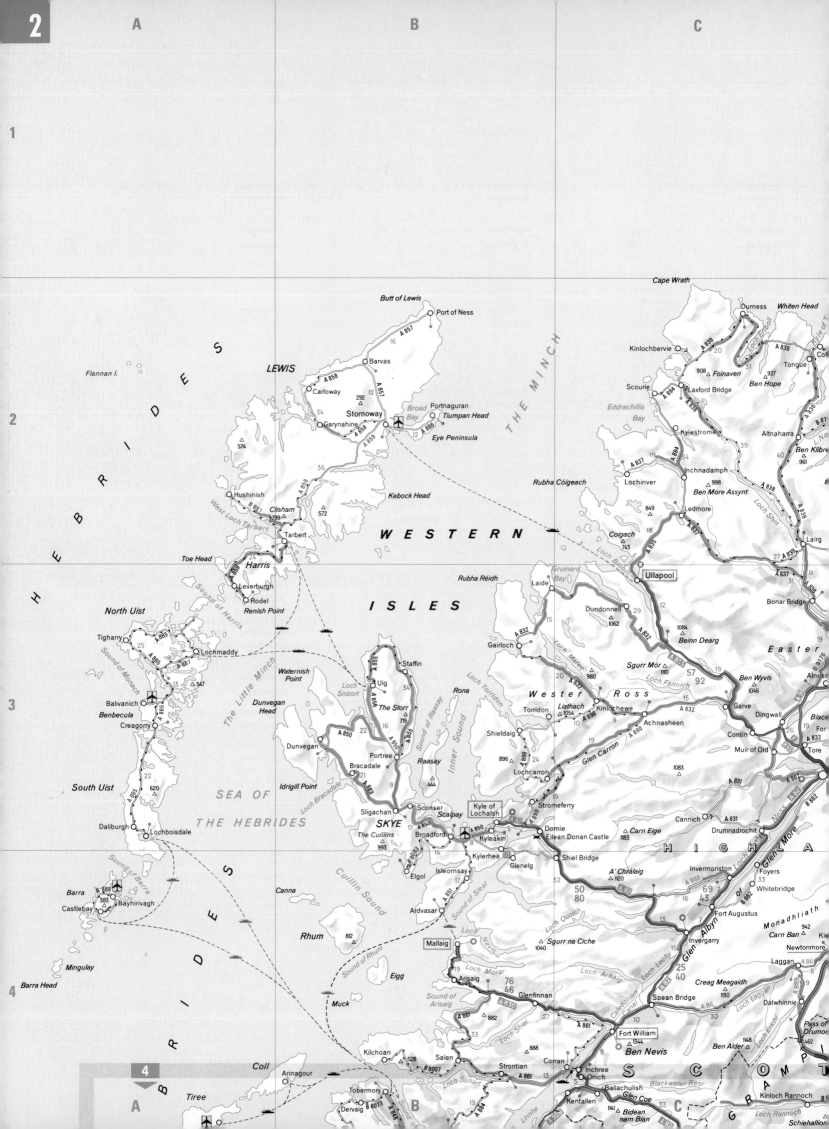

12

Inishkea · Bangor · Inishcrone · Stranfull · L 132 · Sligeach · Sligo · 69 · N16 · 43

A · Blacksod Bay · N 59 · 140 · 12 · 17 · Ballina · Beal an Átha · The Ox Mountains · 543 · Ballysadare · L 117 · L 54 · Dowra · L 50 · 26

Ballycroy · 670 · 720 · 19 · Crossmolina · L 136 · 10 · L. Conn · N 133 · SLIGO · 16 · Drumkeeran · Lough Allen · **B**

Keel · Nephin Beg Range · 698 · Nephin · 804 · Pontoon · 140 · Foxford · Moy · Swinford · Tobercurry · 20 · Ballymote · Boyle / Mainistir na Búille · Keadew · Drumshanbo

Achill Island · 521 · Corraun · Mulrany · N 41 · Castlebar · Caisleán an Bharraigh · N 5 · 40 · Charlestown · L. Gara · Gorteen · L. Key · 26 · LEIT

Clare Island · Newport · Clew Bay · N 59 · N 60 · N 58 · 25 · Connaught · Ballaghaderreen · Carrick-on-Shannon · Cora Droma Rúisc · T 52 · Mohill

1 · Louisburgh · T 39 · 14 · 763 · Westport · Cathair na Mart · Kiltamagh · 21 · Frenchpark · 49 · 79 · Castlerea · Elphin · Lon · Lon

Inishturk · Croagh Patrick · L 100 · 52 · Ballintober · Claremorris · Ballyhaunis · ROSCOMMON · Castlerea · Tulsk · Strokestown · (Edgewo)

Inishbofin · Mweelrea Mts · 817 · N 59 · Partry Mountains · Ballinrobe · Kilmaine · 96 · 60 · Dunmore · Ballymoe · N 60 · Roscommon · Glennamaddy · Ros Comáin · Lanesborough

Inishshark · Rinvyle Pt · Killary Harbour · Letterfrack · Leenane · 681 · Lough Mask · Clonbur · Cong · 4 · Tuam / Tuaim · N 63 · Ballyforan · Lough Ree

Slyne Head · The Twelve Pins · 728 · 701 · Maumturk Mts · L 100 · Headford · N 84 · Mount Bellew · Athlone / Baile Átha Luain · Moat · **WEST**

Clifden · An Clochán · N 59 · Connemara · Maam Cross · 49 · Oughterard · N 59 · GALWAY · N 63 · Ballinasloe / Béal Átha na Sluaighe · Clonmacnoise · 54

Roundstone · Gortmore · Carna · L 102 · Lough Corrib · Spiddal · Galway / Gaillimh · Oranmore · Athenry · N 6 · Ferbane

Lettermullan · L 100 · Barna · Galway Bay · Craughwell · T 4 · N 65 · Loughrea · 89 · 55 · Clonfert · Grand Ca

2 · Gorumna Island · Aran Islands · Inishmore · Kilronan · Black Head · Ardrahan · N 18 · Kinvarra · L 54 · Portumna · L 41 · Birr · Kinnitty · 23

Inishmaan · Inisheer · Ballyvaughan · 25 · Gort · 15 · L 55 · Banagher · Kilcormac · L 52

Cliffs of Moher · Lisdoonvarna · Kilfenora · L 53 · L 55 · 103 · 64 · Slieve Bloom · L 116

Lahinch · Ennistimon · Corrofin · 19 · N 18 · Lough Derg · N 65 · 24 · Borrisokane · Roscrea · Mour

Spanish Point · Milltown Malbay · L 55 · 16 · L 63 · CLARE · Tulla · T 41 · Scarriff · 52 · Nenagh / An tAonach · Moneygall · 111 · 69 · T 214 · N 7 · 88 · Rathd

Ennis / Inis · L 31 · Broadford · 531 · Killaloe · 1 · Dolla · Templemore · T 31 · 58 · 93

Creegh · N 67 · L 52 · Knappogue Castle · Kilmurry · L 182 · Milestone · T 19 · Thurles / Durlas · N 75

Kilkee · L 54 · N 68 · 27 · Newmarket on Fergus · 23 · Shannon · Bunratty Castle · L 124 · Newport · TIPPERARY · Holy Cross Abbey · Urling

3 · Loop Head · Kilbaha · Kilrush · 6 · Killimer · Labasheeda · River Shannon · N 69 · LIMERICK / LUIMNEACH · N 7 · 63 · 39 · Milford · Cashel / Caiseal

Mouth of the Shannon · Ballybunnion · Tarbert · Askeaton · Adare · 21 · Croom · 63 · 39 · L 119 · Rock of Cashel · Killenaule · 153

Kerry Head · Ballyduff · L 106 · Listowel · L 10 · Rathkeale · N 21 · LIMERICK · N 24 · Tipperary / Tiobraid Árann · Fethard

Ballyheige · L 105 · L 104 · Feale · T 36 · Newcastle West · 26 · Hospital · N 74 · Slievenamon · 719

Brandon Head · 951 · Tralee Bay · Abbeyfeale · N 21 · Dromcolliher · L 70 · Kilmallock · Galty Mountains · Caher · Clonmel / Cluain Meala · N 24 · 63 · 39

Sybil Head · Brandon Mountain · 825 · Tralee / Trá Lí · 65 · 105 · T 38 · 408 · Rath Luirc (Charleville) · 917 · R. Suir

Clogher Head · Dingle · Castleisland · 438 · Newmarket · Buttevant · Kildorrery · 74 · Mitchelstown · Knockmealdown Mts · Comeragh Mts · 789

Great Blasket I · 516 · Dingle · Anascaul · Slieve Mish Mts · 850 · 108 · 67 · L 70 · Kanturk · 93 · 58 · 74 · 46 · Lismore · 753 · WAT

Slea Head · T 68 · Castlemaine · L 103 · KERRY · Boherboy · Mallow / Mala · Fermoy · R. Blackwater · Dungarvan · Dún Garbhán

Dingle Bay · Killorglin · Killarney / Cill Airne · Rathmore · N 72 · CORK · Cappoquin · N 72

4 · Doulus Head · 689 · Ring of Kerry · Muckross House · L. Leane · Millstreet · Blackwater · 644 · N 25 · 119 · 74 · Helvick

Knight's Town · Carrantuohill · 1038 · Macgillycuddy's Reeks · Mangerton Mountain · 838 · Derrynasaggart Mts · Macroom · Blarney · CORK / CORCAIGH · Midleton · Youghal / Eochaill · Ardmore

Valencia Island · Cahersiveen · 772 · Iveragh · 87 · 54 · Coachford · 29 · N 25 · Cobh / An Cóbh · Youghal Bay

St. Finan's Bay · Waterville · 90 · L. Currane · Sneem · Kilgarvan · L 41 · Lee · Ringaskiddy · Ballycotton

Bolus Head · Ring of Kerry · Kenmare · L 62 · Pass of Keimaneigh · Dunmanway · Bandon · Crosshaven · Swansea

Skellig · Lauragh · Glengarriff · L 58 · L 64 · Kinsale · le Havre

Castletownbere · Beara · Caha Mts · 684 · Bantry / Beanntraí · Timoleague · Old Head of Kinsale

Dursey Island · Bantry Bay · Skull · Rosscarbery · Clonakilty

Mizen Head · Sheep's Head · Dunmanus Bay · N 71 · Skibbereen · Galley Head

Roaringwater Bay · Toe Head

A · **B** · **C**

A B C

CÔTES-D'ARMOR

Moncontour · Combourg · Ambrières-les-Vallées · Lassay · Pré-en-Pail · M^t des Avaloirs
Plœuc · Évran · Tinténiac · **Fougères** · Gorron · D33 · Javron · Villaines-la-Juhel
Uzel · Collinée · Broons · Caulnes · Bécherel · St Aubin-d'Aubigné · St Aubin-du-Cormier · Ernée · **Mayenne** · Bais · Fresnay
Mur-de-Bretagne · Plouguenast · St Méen · Montauban · Liffré · Champeaux · Chailland · Montsûrs · Evron · Silté-Guillaume · Ste Suzanne · Conlie
Loudéac · la Chèze · la Trinité-Porhoët · Montfort · **RENNES** · Châteaubourg · **Vitré** · Argentré-du-Plessis · **Laval** · Meslay · Vaiges · St Denis d'Orques
Rohan · Josselin · Plélan-le-Grd · Mordelles · St Jacques · Châteaugiron · Janzé · Cossé-le-Vivien · Craon · Château-Gontier
Vannes · **Auray** · Ploërmel · N24 · Guichen · Retiers · la Guerche-de-B. · Renazé · Segré · Bierné · Sablé · Solesmes
St Jean-Brévelay · Grd Champ · Malestroit · Maure · Bain-de-Bretagne · Martigné-Ferchaud · Pouancé · Châteauneuf-s-S · **la Flèche**
Ste Anne d'A. · Elven · Pipriac · Rougé · Châteaubriant · St Julien-de-Vouvantes · Candé · Tiercé · Durtal · Baugé
Locmariaquer · Questembert · Allaire · **Redon** · Derval · Moisdon · St Mars-la-Jaille · le Lion-d'A · Seiches
Port-Navalo · St Gildas-de-Rhuys · Sarzeau · Rochefort-en-T. · Guéméné-Penfao · Nozay · St Florent · **ANGERS** · Beaufort-en-V. · les Rosiers
Houat · Damgan · Pénestin · la Roche-Bernard · St Gildas-des-B. · Blain · Nort · Riaillé · le Louroux · Brissac-Quincé · Gennes · Cunault
Hædic · Piriac · la Turballe · Herbignac · Pontchâteau · Savenay · Ancenis · Varades · Ingrandes · Montjean · Chalonnes · Doué · **Saumur**
le Croisic · Batz · **la Baule** · Guérande · Donges · Paimbœuf · St Étienne-de-Montluc · Carquefou · Champtoceaux · St Georges · les Ponts-de-Cé · Thouarcé
le Pouliguen · Pornichet · **St NAZAIRE** · St Brevin · St Père-en-R. · le Pellerin · **NANTES** · Vallet · Beaupréau · Chemillé · Villiers
Pnte de St Gildas · Mindin · Bouaye · St Philbert · Clisson · Montfaucon · **Cholet** · Montreuil-B.
Pornic · Bourgneuf-en-Retz · Machecoul · Aigrefeuille-s-M. · Montaigu · Mortagne-s-S. · Argenton-Chau · les Trois-Moutiers
Île de Noirmoutier · Noirmoutier · Beauvoir · Rocheservière · St Laurent · Mauléon · Thouars
Fromentine · Challans · Legé · Palluau · les Herbiers · St Fulgent · Cerizay · Bressuire · St Jouin-de-Marnes · St Varent · Airvault
St Jean-de-Monts · St Gilles-Croix-de-Vie · Aizenay · le Poiré · les Essarts · St Michel Mont-Mercure · Pouzauges · Moncoutant · St Loup-Lamairé · Thénezay
Île d'Yeu · Port-Joinville · la Mothe-Achard · **la Roche-s-Yon** · Chantonnay · Mouilleron-en-Pareds · la Châtaigneraie · **Parthenay** · Secondigny
VENDÉE · St Hermine · Mareuil · l'Hermenault · Vouvant · St Hilaire-des-Loges · Mazières-en-Gâtine · Champdeniers · Ménigoute
les Sables-d'Olonne · Talmont · Moutiers-les-Mauxfaits · Luçon · les Chemins · **Fontenay-le-Comte** · Goulonges · St Maixent-l'École
Jard · Chaillé · Maillezais · Coulon · DEUX-SÈVRES · Brioux
la Tranche · l'Aiguillon · St Michel-en-l'Herm · Marans · **Niort** · Prahecq · Celles · Melle · Sauzé-Vaussais
Île de Ré · St Martin · Ars · Courçon · Mauzé · Beauvoir · Loulay
LA ROCHELLE · la Pallice · Aigrefeuille-d'Aunis · Surgères · Chef-Boutonne
Châtelaillon-Plage · St Denis · I. d'Aix · Loulay · Aulnay · Villefa
Fouras · Tonnay-Charente · St Jean-d'Angély · Matha
Rochefort · le Château · St Agnant · St Savinien · St Hilaire-de-Villefranche · Burie · Rouillac
Île d'Oléron · Brouage · St Trojan · Pont-d'Oléron · St Porchaire · CHARENTE-MARITIME · Aigre
Marennes · la Tremblade · Ronce

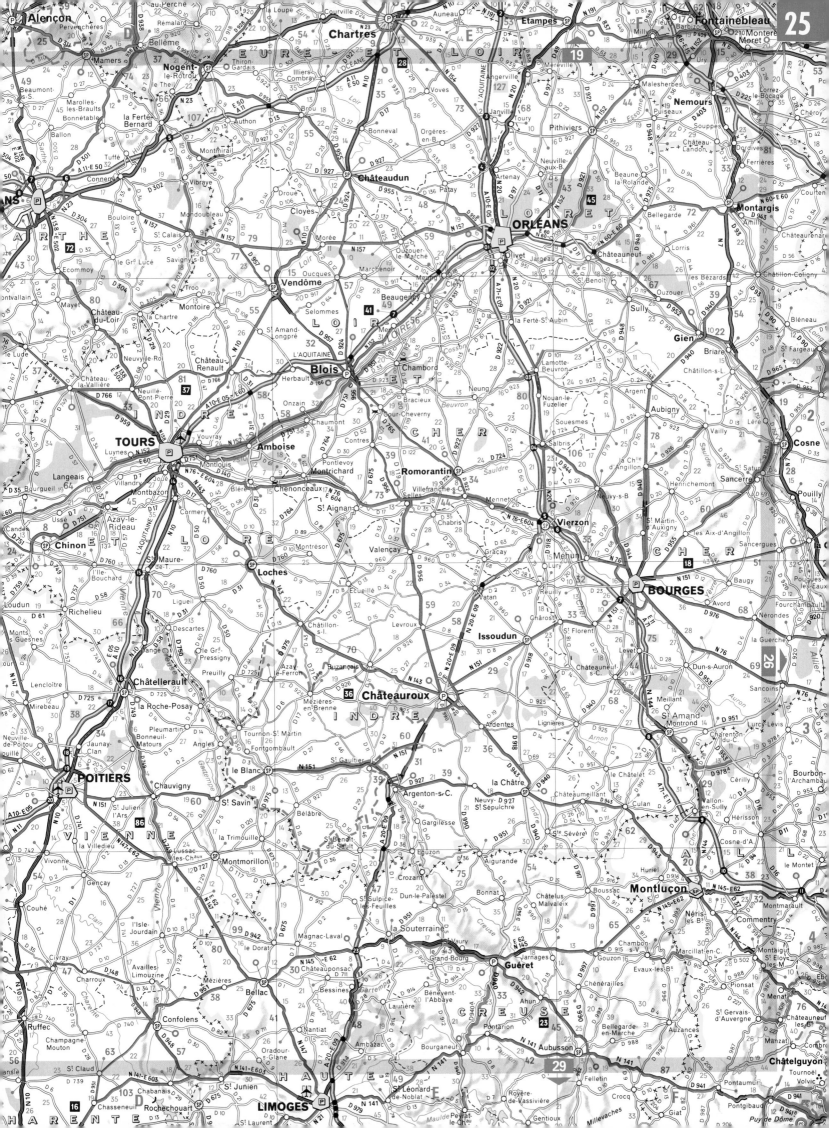

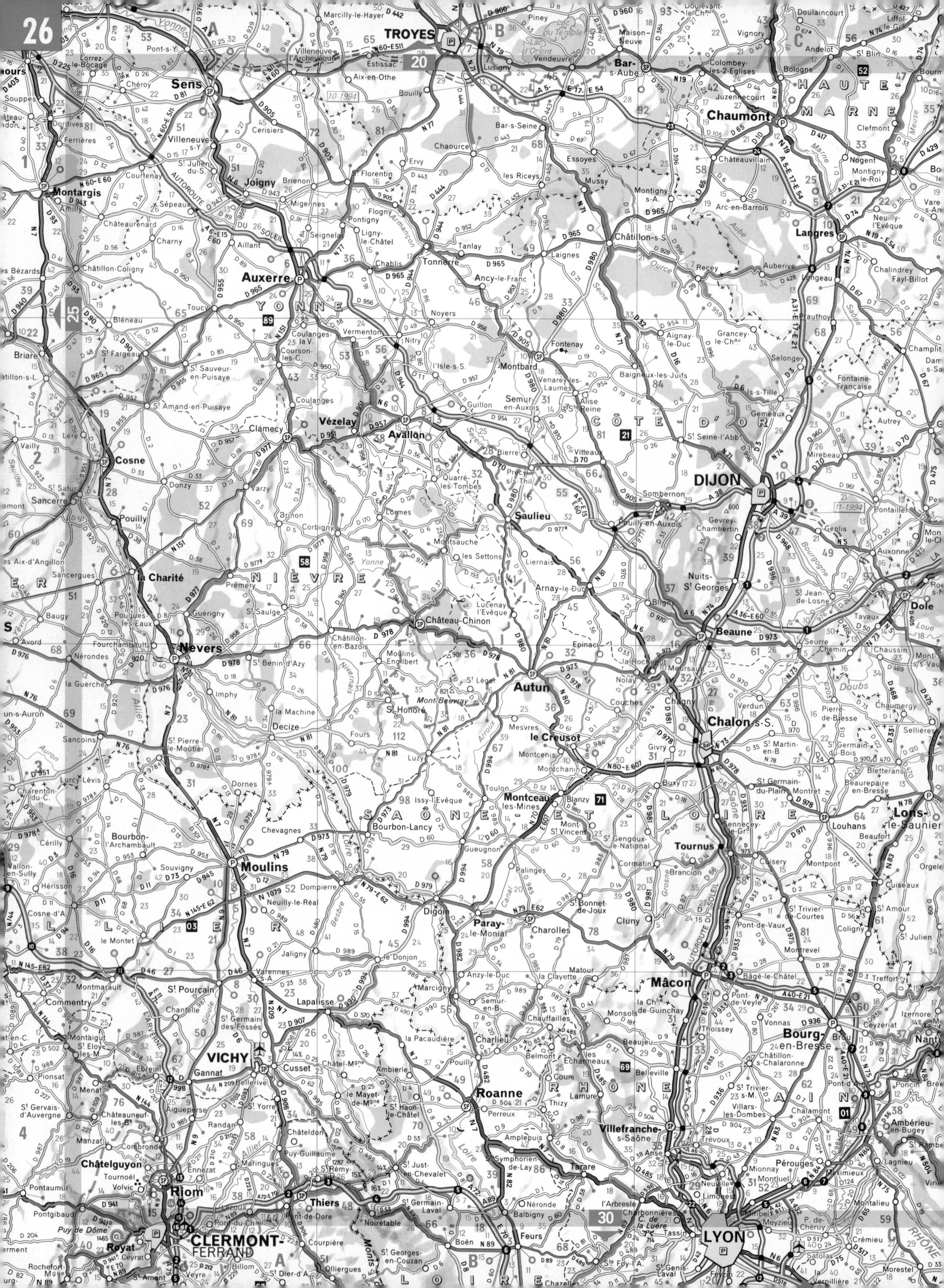

TROYES

Sens

Chaumont

HAUTE-MARNE

Montargis

Joigny

Auxerre

Langres

CÔTE-D'OR

Cosne

Vézelay

Avallon

Saulieu

DIJON

la Charité

NIÈVRE

Château-Chinon

Beaune

Nevers

Autun

Chalon-s.-S.

le Creusot

Montceau-les-Mines

SAÔNE-ET-LOIRE

Bourbon-Lancy

Moulins

Digoin

Paray-le-Monial

Charolles

Tournus

Lons-le-Saunier

ALLIER

Mâcon

Bourg-en-Bresse

AIN

VICHY

Roanne

Villefranche-s-Saône

RHÔNE

Châtelguyon

Riom

Thiers

LOIRE

CLERMONT-FERRAND

LYON

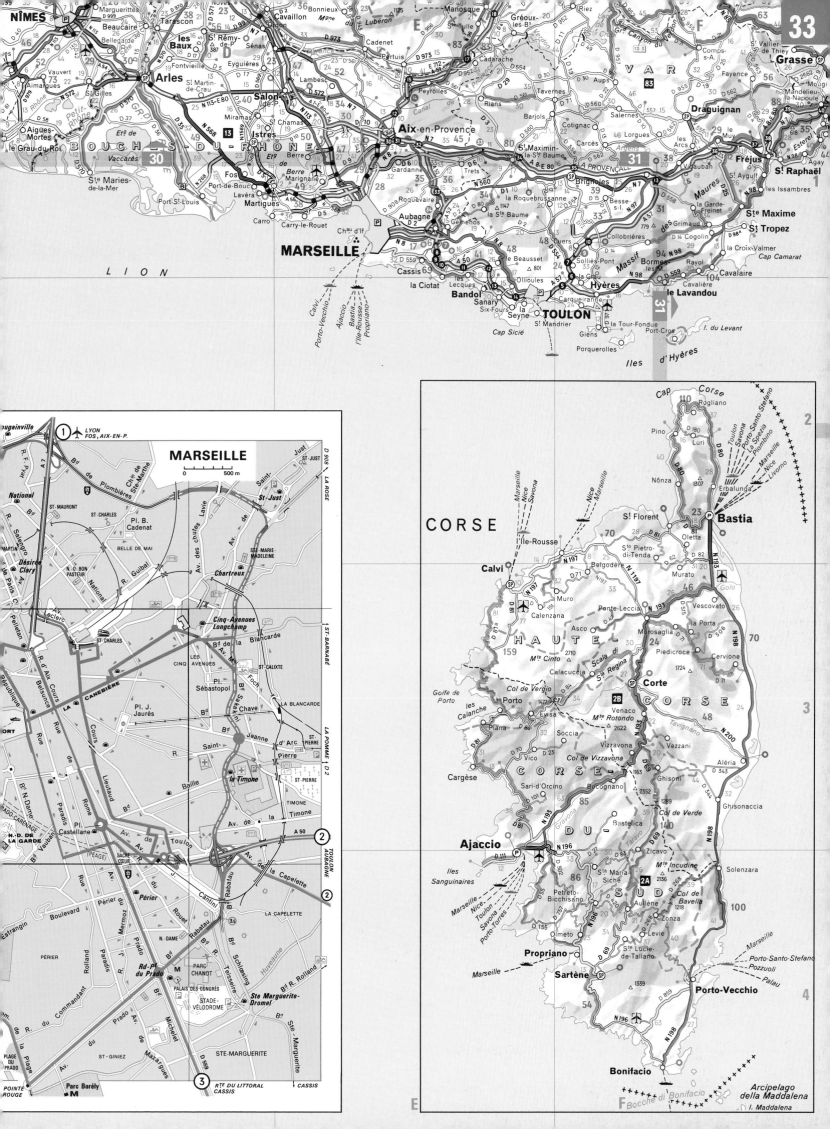

A   B   C

Ferrol
A CORUÑA / LA CORUÑA
SANTIAGO DE COMPOSTELA
Lugo
Pontevedra
VIGO
Ourense / Orense
Ponferrada
Viana do Castelo
Bragança
Braga
Guimarães
Vila Real
PORTO
Espinho
Póvoa de Varzim
Vila do Conde

GALICIA
MINHO
TRÁS - OS - MONTES
DOURO

Cabo Prior
Cabo de S. Adrián
Cabo Vilán
Camariñas
Muxía
Corcubión
Carnota
Islas Cíes
Isla de Ons
I. de Sálvora
I. de Arousa
Cabo Silleiro

Ribadeo
Navia
Viveiro
Burela
Foz
Mondoñedo
Villalba
Baamonde
Sarriá
Monforte de Lemos
Chantada
Becerreá
Pedrafita do Cebreiro
Villafranca del Bierzo
Cacabelos
Carracedelo
O Barco
A Rúa
Quiroga
Puebla de Trives
A Gudiña
Verín
Chaves
Mirandela
Vidago
Vila Flol
Alijó
Pêso da Régua
Lamego
Amarante
Penafiel
Betanzos
Pontedeume
Padrón
Cambados
Vilagarcía de Arosa
Caldas de Reis
Redondela
Tui
Valença do Minho
Porriño
Ponteareas
Ribadavia
Celanova
Xinzo de Limia
Bande
Caminha
Ponte de Lima
Barcelos
Esposende

N 642
N VI
N 540
N 547
N 525
N 120
N 550
N 541
N 554
N 103
N 232
N 634
N 640
N 641

Río Miño
Río Sil
Río Eume
Embalse de Belesar
Embalse de Las Portas
Embalse de Salime
Embalse de Arbón
Río Duero
Río Tâmega
Río Sabor

A B C

1 2 3 4

Espinho
Aveiro
Viseu
Guarda
COIMBRA
Figueira da Foz
Covilhã
Leiria
Batalha
Nazaré
Alcobaça
Fátima
Tomar
Castelo Branco
Abrantes
Santarém
Portalegre
Marvão
Torres Vedras
Mafra
Sintra
Estoril
Cascais
LISBOA
Setúbal
Almada
Barreiro
Évora
Estremoz
Elvas
Vendas Novas
Montemor-o-Novo
Ponte de Sor

RIO DOURO
RIO TEJO
RIO MONDEGO
SERRA DA ESTRELA
PORTUGAL

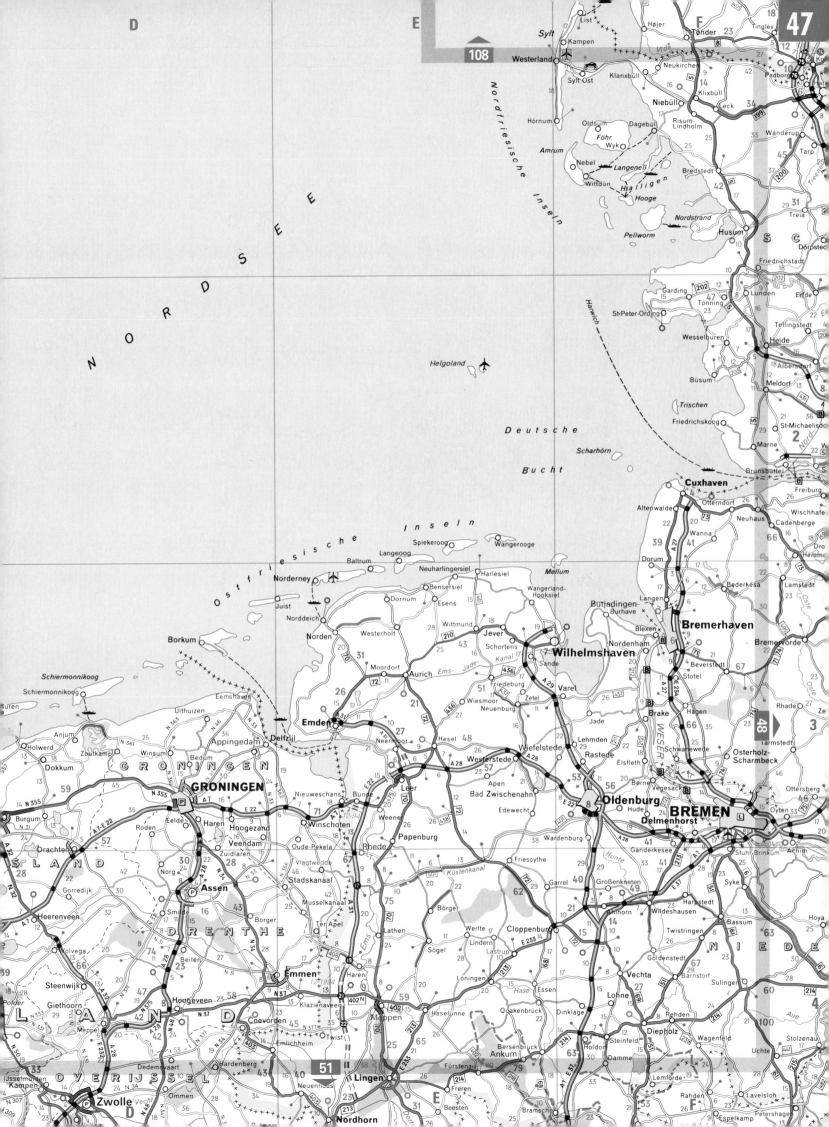

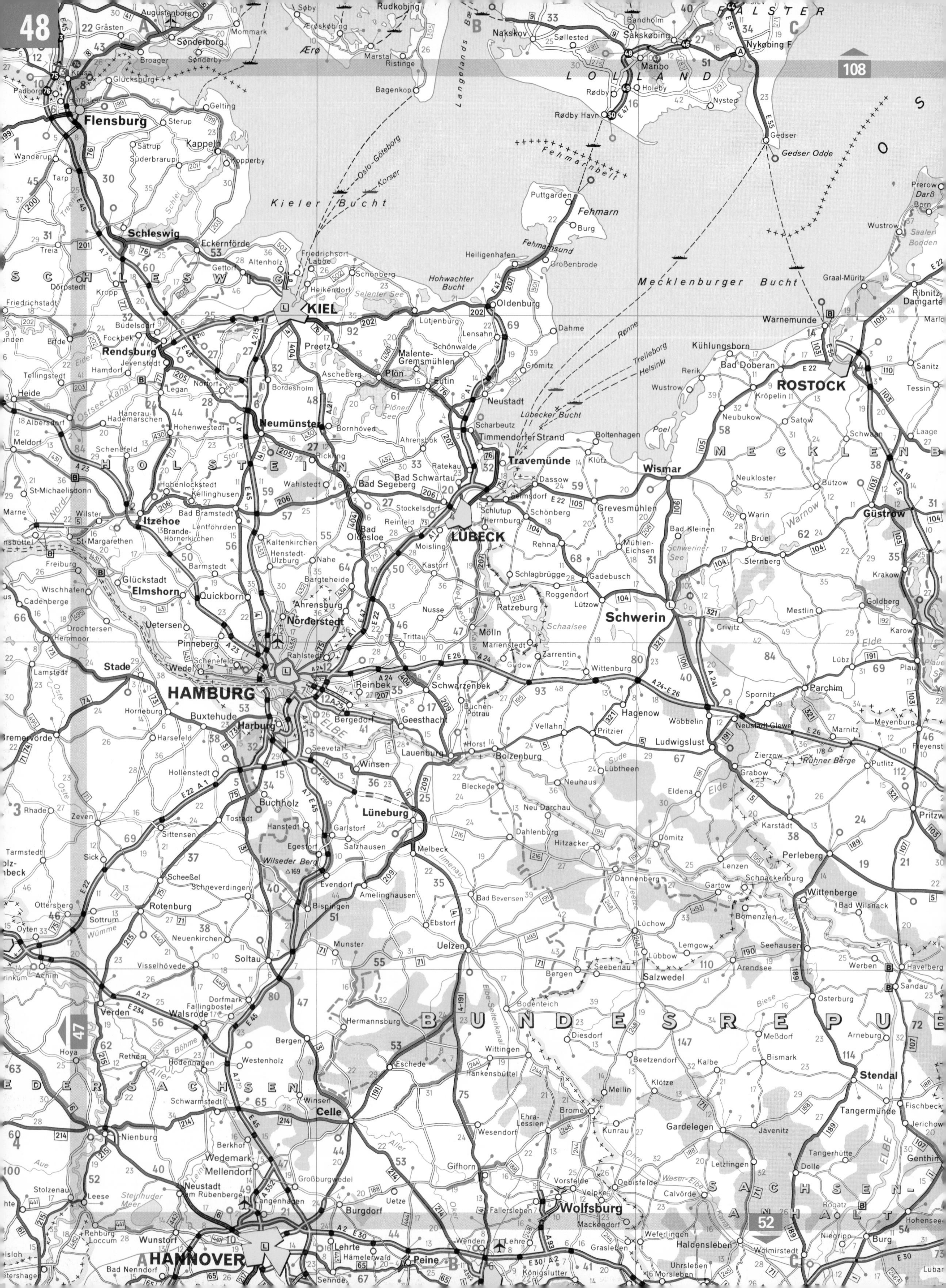
FALSTER
LOLLAND
Nakskov
Maribo
Rødby
Rødby Havn
Nykøbing F
Gedser
Gedser Odde
Ærø
Marstal
Rudkøbing
Søby
Ærøskøbing
Augustenborg
Sønderborg
Gråsten
Broager
Glücksburg
Flensburg
Padborg
Harrislee
Gelting
Sterup
Kappeln
Satrup
Süderbrarup
Wanderup
Tarp
Schleswig
Eckernförde
Kieler Bucht
Oslo-Göteborg
Korsør
Fehmarnbelt
Puttgarden
Fehmarn
Burg
Heiligenhafen
Fehmarnsund
Großenbrode
Hohwachter Bucht
Oldenburg
Dahme
Mecklenburger Bucht
Rønne
Trelleborg
Helsinki
KIEL
Friedrichsort
Laboe
Schönberg
Selenter See
Heikendorf
Lütjenburg
Lensahn
Preetz
Malente-Gremsmühlen
Schönwalde
Plön
Eutin
Grömitz
Neustadt
Lübecker Bucht
Rendsburg
Büdelsdorf
Fockbek
Jevenstedt
Hamdorf
Nortorf
Heide
Albersdorf
Meldorf
Hohenwestedt
Neumünster
Bordesholm
Bornhöved
Ascheberg
Scharbeutz
Timmendorfer Strand
Travemünde
Boltenhagen
Poel
Wismar
Klütz
Dassow
Kühlungsborn
Bad Doberan
Rerik
Wustrow
Warnemünde
ROSTOCK
Kröpelin
Neubukow
Satow
Graal-Müritz
Ribnitz-Damgarten
Sanitz
Tessin
Laage
Schwaan
Bützow
Güstrow
Neukloster
Warin
Brüel
Sternberg
Krakow
Goldberg
Mestlin
Karow
Lübz
Plau
Prerow
Darß
Born
Saaler Bodden
SCHLESWIG
HOLSTEIN
Itzehoe
Kellinghusen
Wilster
St-Michaelisdonn
Marne
Glückstadt
Elmshorn
Uetersen
Pinneberg
Wedel
Stade
Barmstedt
Quickborn
Bad Bramstedt
Kaltenkirchen
Henstedt-Ulzburg
Norderstedt
Ahrensburg
Bad Segeberg
Bad Oldesloe
Bad Schwartau
Stockelsdorf
Reinfeld
LÜBECK
Ratzeburg
Mölln
Gadebusch
Rehna
Schönberg
Grevesmühlen
Schwerin
Crivitz
Zarrentin
Schaalsee
Wittenburg
Hagenow
Ludwigslust
Parchim
Neustadt Glewe
Grabow
Marnitz
Meyenburg
Putlitz
Pritzwalk
HAMBURG
Reinbek
Bergedorf
Geesthacht
Schwarzenbek
Buxtehude
Harburg
Seevetal
Winsen
Lauenburg
Boizenburg
Lübtheen
Neuhaus
Bleckede
Dömitz
Hitzacker
Dannenberg
Lenzen
Karstädt
Perleberg
Wittenberge
Bad Wilsnack
Havelberg
Sandau
Lüneburg
Buchholz
Tostedt
Zeven
Rotenburg
Sittensen
Wilseder Berg
Soltau
Munster
Uelzen
Bad Bevensen
Ebstorf
Bispingen
Amelinghausen
Salzwedel
Lüchow
Gartow
Arendsee
Osterburg
Seehausen
Stendal
Tangermünde
Verden
Walsrode
Fallingbostel
Bergen
Hermannsburg
Eschede
Celle
Wittingen
Gifhorn
Wolfsburg
Gardelegen
Kalbe
Klötze
Haldensleben
Wolmirstedt
Nienburg
Neustadt am Rübenberge
Langenhagen
Burgdorf
Lehrte
Peine
HANNOVER
BUNDESREPUBLIK
NIEDERSACHSEN
SACHSEN-ANHALT
MECKLENBURG
ELBE

108
47
52

52 A B 48

HANNOVER · **BRAUNSCHWEIG** · **MAGDEBURG**

Stolzenau · Leese · Neustadt am Rübenberge · Großburgwedel · Vorsfelde · Velpke · Oebisfelde · Calvörde · Rogatz · Niegripp

Steinhuder Meer · Langenhagen · Uetze · Wolfsburg · Mackendorf · Weferlingen · Haldensleben · Wolmirstedt

Wunstorf · Lehrte · Burgdorf · Fallersleben · Lehre · Graslebe · Uhrsleben · Morsleben

Minden · Stadthagen · Barsinghausen · Rethen · Sehnde · Peine · Königslutter · Helmstedt · Marienborn · Irxleben · **MAGDEBURG** · Möcke

Bad Nenndorf · Springe · Sarstedt · **BRAUNSCHWEIG** · Schöningen · Seehausen · Gommern

Bückeburg · Lauenau · Bad Münder · **Salzgitter** Lebenstedt · Wolfenbüttel · Schöppenstedt · Hamersleben · Oschersleben · Wanzleben · Schönebeck

Rinteln · Hess. Oldendorf · Hachmühlen · **Hildesheim** · Salzgitter-Bad · Osterwieck · Dardesheim · Gröningen · Förderstedt

Bad Salzuflen · Lemgo · Bad Pyrmont · Bodenwerder · Alfeld · Rhüden · Langelsheim · Vienenburg · **Halberstadt** · Kroppenstedt · Staßfurt · Bernburg

Lage · Barntrup · Blomberg · Polle · **Goslar** · Ilsenburg · Wernigerode · Derenburg · Blankenburg · Quedlinburg · Aschersleben

Detmold · Schieder-Schwalenberg · Stadtoldendorf · Einbeck · Seesen · Lautenthal · Bad Harzburg · **Brocken** · Thale · Gernrode · Ballenstedt · Hettstedt

Höxter · Holzminden · Dassel · Clausthal-Zellerfeld · Altenau · Braunlage · Hasselfelde · Harzgerode · Mansfeld · Wettin

Paderborn · Brakel · Beverungen · Uslar · Northeim · Osterode · Herzberg · Bad Lauterberg · Bad Sachsa · Ellrich · Stolberg · Eisleben

Bad Lippspringe · Bad Driburg · Godelheim · Neuhaus im Solling · Katlenburg-Duhm · Nörten-Hardenberg · Gieboldehausen · Mackenrode · Sangerhausen · Riestedt

Warburg · Hofgeismar · Trendelburg · Hardegsen · **Göttingen** · Duderstadt · Günterode · Worbis · Nordhausen · Berga · Kelbra · Allstedt · Querfurt

Scherfede · Hann.-Münden · Friedland · Hohengandern · Heiligenstadt · Leinefelde · Bleicherode · Sondershausen · Bad Frankenhausen · Heldrungen · Artern

KASSEL · Witzenhausen · Bad Sooden-Allendorf · Dingelstädt · Ebeleben · Greußen · Weißensee · Sömmerda · Eckartsberga · Naumburg

Niederelsungen · Burghasungen · Lutterberg · Geismar · Wanfried · Diedorf · Schlotheim · **Mühlhausen** · Bad Tennstedt · Straußfurt · Buttstädt · Bad Sulza

Wolfhagen · Hessisch Lichtenau · Helsa · Eschwege · Treffurt · Bad Langensalza · Gebesee · Apolda · **Weimar**

Korbach · Fritzlar · Melsungen · Waldkappel · Rittmannshausen · Creuzburg · **ERFURT** · Gotha · Buchenwald · **Jena**

Bad Wildungen · Spangenberg · Sontra · Herleshausen · Wartha · **Eisenach** · Waltershausen · Arnstadt · Mellingen · Bad Berka

Frankenberg · Homberg · Rotenburg · Bebra · Berka · Ruhla · Friedrichroda · Ohrdruf · Stadtilm · Blankenhain · Kahla

Münchhausen · Schwalmstadt-Ziegenhain · Hauenstein · Hönebach · Dorndorf · Bad Liebenstein · Oberhof · Crawinkel · Ilmenau · Bad Blankenburg · Schwarza

Marburg · Neustadt · Treysa · Kirchheim · **Bad Hersfeld** · Vacha · Bad Salzungen · Barchfeld · Schmalkalden · Gr. Beerberg · Gehren · Königsee · Rudolstadt · Saalfeld

Kirchhain · Alsfeld · Niederaula · Sorga · Dermbach · Wasungen · Zella-Mehlis · Gr.breitenbach · Neuhaus · Leutenberg

Marburg · Homberg · Schlitz · Rasdorf · Geisa · Meiningen · Rohr · **Suhl** · Schleusingen · Themar · Ludwigstadt · Probstzella

Gießen · Lauterbach · Bad Salzschlirf · Hünfeld · Tann · Kaltennordheim · Steinbach-Hallenberg · Hildburghausen · Eisfeld · Steinach · Nordhalben

Grünberg · Herbstein · **Fulda** · Wasser-Kuppe · Fladungen · Henneberg · Ehrenberg · Eußenhausen · Neustadt · Neuhaus-Schierschnitz · Burggrub

Schotten · Vogelsberg · Gersfeld · Ostheim · Mellrichstadt · Römhild · Rottenbach · Rodach · Sonneberg · Wallenfels

Bad Nauheim · Gedern · Schlüchtern · Bad Brückenau · Bad Königshofen · Linden · Trappstadt · Neustadt · Kronach

Butzbach · Münzenberg · Wächtersbach · Steinau · Bad Orb · Bad Neustadt · Oberessfeld · Heldburg · **Coburg** · Lichtenfels

Bad Homburg · Gr. Feldberg · Friedberg · Nidderau · Büdingen · Bad Soden-Salmünster · Gelnhausen · Münnerstadt · Ebern · Weismain

Oberursel · Bad Vilbel · Altenstadt · Burgjoß · Burgsinn · Hammelburg · Poppenhausen · Staffelstein · Scheßlitz · Hollfeld

FRANKFURT A.M. · Hanau · Alzenau · Frammersbach · Gemünden · **Bad Kissingen** · Hofheim · Haßfurt · Ebrach · Ebermannstadt

Offenbach · Seligenstadt · Goldbach · Lohr · Karlstadt · Werneck · **Schweinfurt** · Breitengüßbach · Eltmann · **Bamberg**

Rüsselsheim · Langen · Babenhausen · Mespelbrunn · Rohrbrunn · Marktheidenfeld · Dettelbach · Volkach · Gerolzhofen · Pommersfelden · Gößweinstein

Darmstadt · Dieburg · Aschaffenburg · Weibersbrunn · **Würzburg** · Wiesentheid · Streitberg · Behringersmühle

51 · 52 · 55 · 12-1994

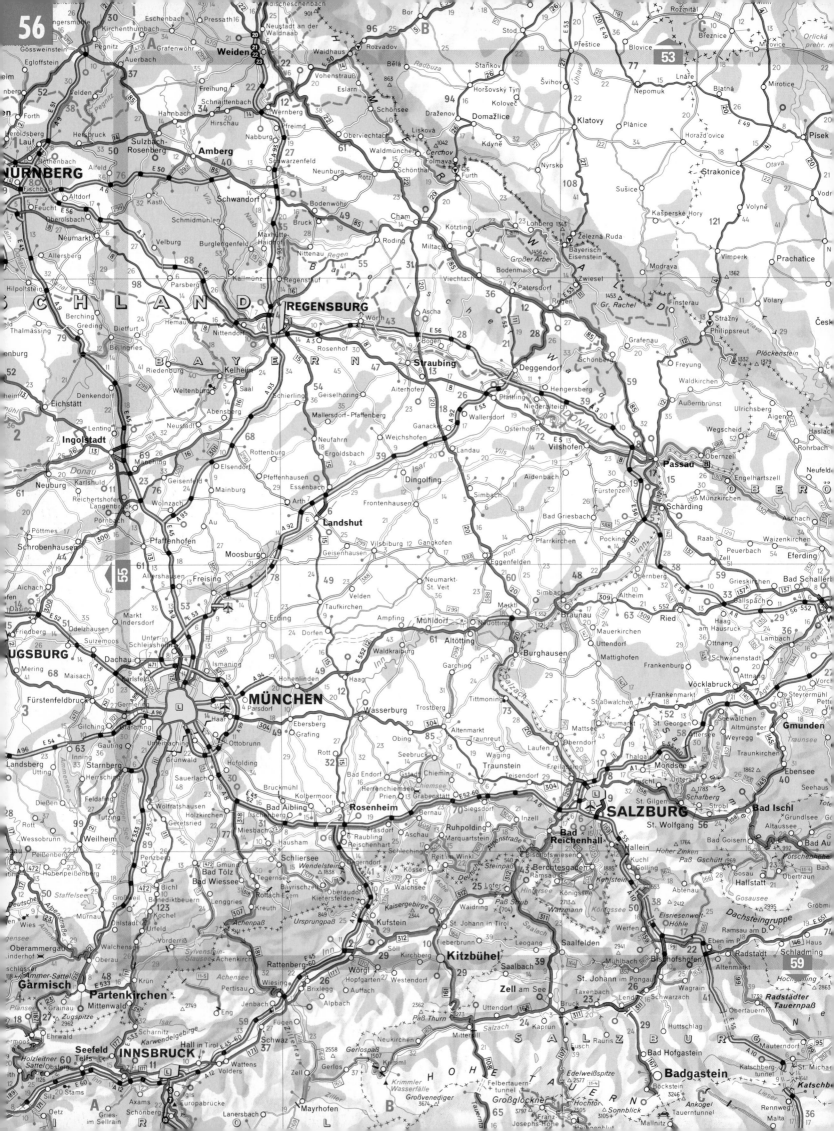

Milevsko · Mladá Vožice · Pacov · E 551 · E 50 · E 65 · Křižanov · Tišnov · Blansko · Vyškov · F

Tábor · Pelhřimov · Jihlava · E · Velké Meziříčí · Velká Bíteš · Kuřim · BRNO · D1 · Bučovice · E 50

Sezimovo-Ústí · 112 · Oslava · Náměšť · Rosice · Ivančice · Slavkov u Brna · Kyjov

Bernartice · Kamenice · Třešť · Telč · Třebíč · Židlochovice · Hodonín

Soběslav · Javořice · Jaroměřice · Moravský Krumlov · Pohořelice · Hustopeče · Čejč · Dubňany

Veselí · Jindřichuv Hradec · Dačice · Jemnice · Moravské Budějovice · Jevišovice · Drnholec · Mikulov · Břeclav · Holíč

Tyn · Nová Bystřice · Slavonice · Vranovská přehr. n. · Znojmo · Dyje · Hrušovany · Poštorná · Morava

Třeboň · Gmünd · Litschau · Dobersberg · Drosendorf Stadt · Hardegg · Retz · Hatě · Laa an der Thaya · Bernhardsthal · Kúty

České Budějovice · Neunagelberg · Schrems · E 49 · Heidenreichstein · Waidhofen · Gr.-Siegharts · Kleinhaugsdorf · Jetzelsdorf · Poysdorf · Hohenau · D2

Halámky · Trhové Sviny · České Velenice · Weitra · Thaya · Allentsteig · Neupölla · Horn · Eggenburg · Pulkau · Mistelbach · Zistersdorf · Dürnkrut · Malacky

Kaplice · Gmünd · Zwettl · Rastenfeld · Gföhl · Gars · Maissau · Hollabrunn · Ernstbrunn · Angern · Marchegg · Stupava

Dolní Dvořiště · Karlstift · Groß Gerungs · Langenlois · Kirchberg · Ziersdorf · Göllersdorf · Stockerau · Wolkersdorf · Gänserndorf · E 65

Wullowitz · Freistadt · Arbesbach · Ottenschlag · Weißenkirchen · Krems · Stein · Hadersdorf · Korneuburg · Deutsch-Wagram · BRATISLAVA

Vyšší Brod · Bad Leonfelden · Unterweißenbach · Königswiesen · Spitz · Dürnstein · Traismauer · Tulln · Klosterneuburg · Leopoldsdorf · Großenzersdorf · Hainburg · Berg

Zwettl · Pregarten · Mönchdorf · Laimbach · Pöggstall · Aggsbach-Markt · Dorf · Judenau · WIEN · Orth · Bad Deutsch Altenburg · Kittsee

Gallneukirchen · Mauthausen · Maria Taferl · Pöchlarn · Melk · St. Pölten · Neulengbach · Pressbaum · Schönbrunn · Schwechat · Fischamend Markt · Parndorf

LINZ · Urfahr · Asten · Enns · Strengberg · Ybbs · Loosdorf · Obergrafendorf · St. Christophen · Mödling · Brück · Neusiedl · Nickelsdorf · Hegyeshalom

Traun · Enns · Amstetten · Wieselburg · Mank · Wilhelmsburg · Altlengbach · Alland · Baden · Bad Vöslau · Leobersdorf · Mannersdorf · Purbach

Neuhofen an der Krems · Haag · Aschbach Markt · St. Peter in der Au · Purgstall · Lilienfeld · Traisen · Hainfeld · Pottenstein · Berndorf · Pernitz · Ebenfurth · Eisenstadt · Rust · Mörbisch

Kremsmünster · Steyr · Sierninghofen · Seitenstetten · Gresten · Scheibbs · Kirchberg a.d. Pielach · Hohenberg · Gutenstein · Wöllersdorf · Wiener Neustadt · Mattersburg · Klingenbach · Sopron

Bad Hall · Waidhofen · Gaming · Türnitz · St. Aegyd · Annaberg · Puchberg · Schneeberg · Neunkirchen · Ternitz · Pamhagen · Fertőszentmiklós

Grünburg · Losenstein · Weyer-Markt · Göstling · Lunz · Mariazell · Zellerrain · Heukuppe · Reichenau · Gloggnitz · Deutschkreutz · Nagycenk · Győr

Kirchdorf · Michdorf · Großraming · Altenmarkt · Gr. Ötscher · Preiner Gscheid · Semmering · Semmering-P. · Aspang · Kirchschlag · Oberpullendorf · Lutzmannsburg · Bük

Windischgarsten · St. Gallen · Aflenzer Seeberg · Seewiesen · Mürzsteg · Mürzzuschlag · Wechsel · Mönichkirchen · Bernstein · Lockenhaus · Kőszeg

Hinterstoder · Spital · Hieflau · Leopoldsteinersee · Wildalpen · Hochschwab · Aflenz Kurort · Krieglach · Langenwang · Friedberg · Pinkafeld · Rechnitz · Bucsu

Liezen · Admont · Gesäuse · Eisenerz · Kindberg · Ratten · Vorau · Oberwart · Bad Tatzmannsdorf · Szombathely

Rottenmann · Eisenerzer Alpen · Präbichl · Erzberg · Vordernberg · Kapfenberg · Birkfeld · Pöllau · Hartberg · Großpetersdorf · Rábafüzes

Irdning · Trieben · Schoberpaß · Mautern · Donawitz · Leoben · Bruck an der Mur · Anger · Weiz · Fürstenfeld · Güssing · Körmend

Donnersbachwald · Hohentauern · Hochreichart · St. Michael · Frohnleiten · Kateroch · Kaindorf · Stegersbach · Hegyhátsál

Oberzeiring · Seckau · Gaaldorf · Gleinalmtunnel · Gleisdorf · Riegersburg · BURGENLAND · Moschendorf

Sölkerpaß · Fohnsdorf · Knittelfeld · Speikkogel · Schöckl · Gratkorn · GRAZ · Feldbach · Jennersdorf · Szentgotthárd

Oberwölz · Zeltweg · Weißkirchen · Judenburg · Köflach · Voitsberg · Kalsdorf · Kirchbach · Bad Gleichenberg · Gornji Petrovci

Murau · Neumarkt · Obdach · Zirbitzkogel · Obdacher Sattel · Stainz · Fehring · Gasztony · Zalalövő

St. Lambrecht · Packsattel · Bad St. Leonhard · Wildon · Bad Radkersburg · Murska

Metnitz · Friesach · Twimberg · Deutschlandsberg · Leibnitz · Mureck · Dobrovnik

Turracherhöhe · Straßburg · Hüttenberg · Wolfsberg · Mačkovci · Szilvágy

WÜRTTEMBERG

Villingen-Schwenningen · Tuttlingen · Donaueschingen · Schaffhausen · Singen · Konstanz · Friedrichshafen · Ravensburg · Memmingen · Kaufbeuren · Kempten · Garmisch · Partenkirchen

ZÜRICH · Winterthur · Baden · Frauenfeld · St. Gallen · Bregenz · Dornbirn · Lindau · Feldkirch · VORARLBERG · Bludenz · St. Anton · Landeck

LUZERN · Zug · Einsiedeln · Glarus · Schwyz · LIECHTENSTEIN · Vaduz · Arlbergpaß · Sölden · Obergurgl

SVIZZERA · GRAUBÜNDEN · Chur · Davos · Arosa · Klosters · Silvrettagruppe · Scuol (Schuls) · Mals

Andermatt · Disentis/Mustér · Thusis · St-Moritz · Pontresina · Livigno · Bormio · Parco Nazionale dello Stelvio

TICINO · Bellinzona · Locarno · Chiavenna · Sondrio · Edolo · Madonna di Campiglio

Domodossola · LUGANO · Bellagio · Lecco · Como · BRESCIA

Varese · Bergamo · MILANO

Bodensee · Lago Maggiore · Lago di Como · Lago d'Iseo · Lago di Garda

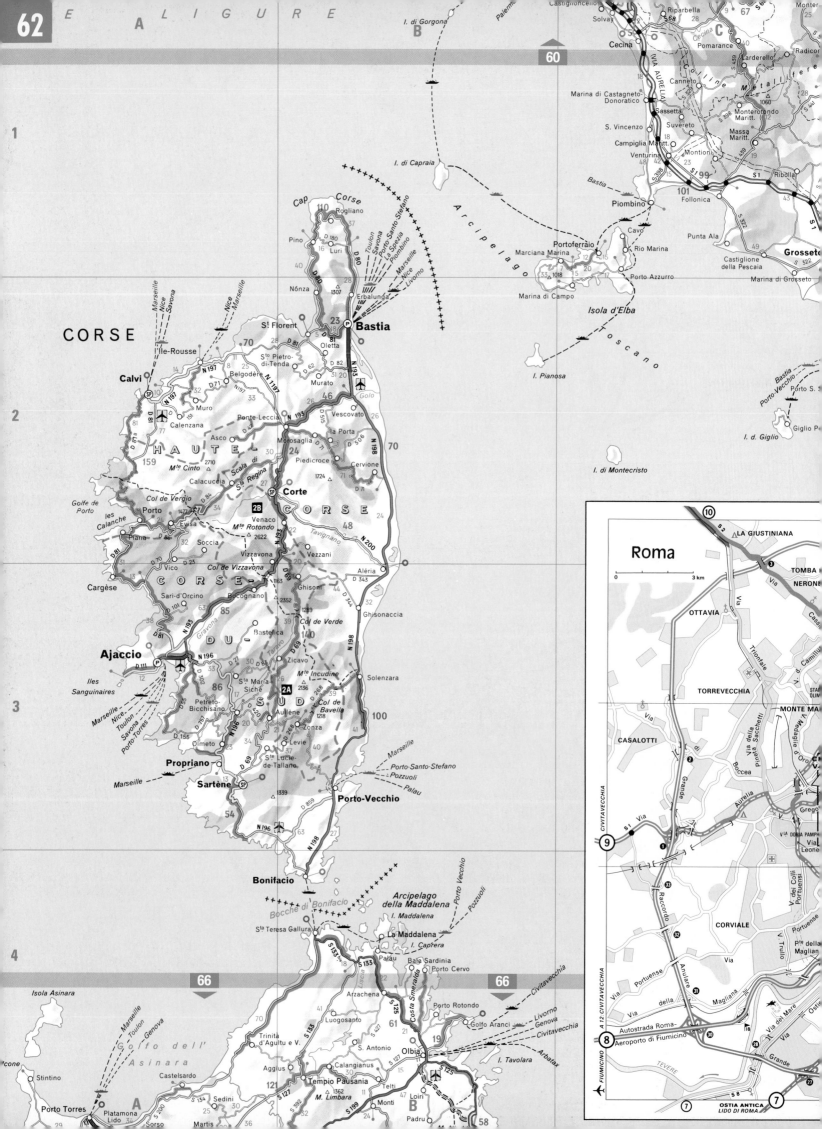

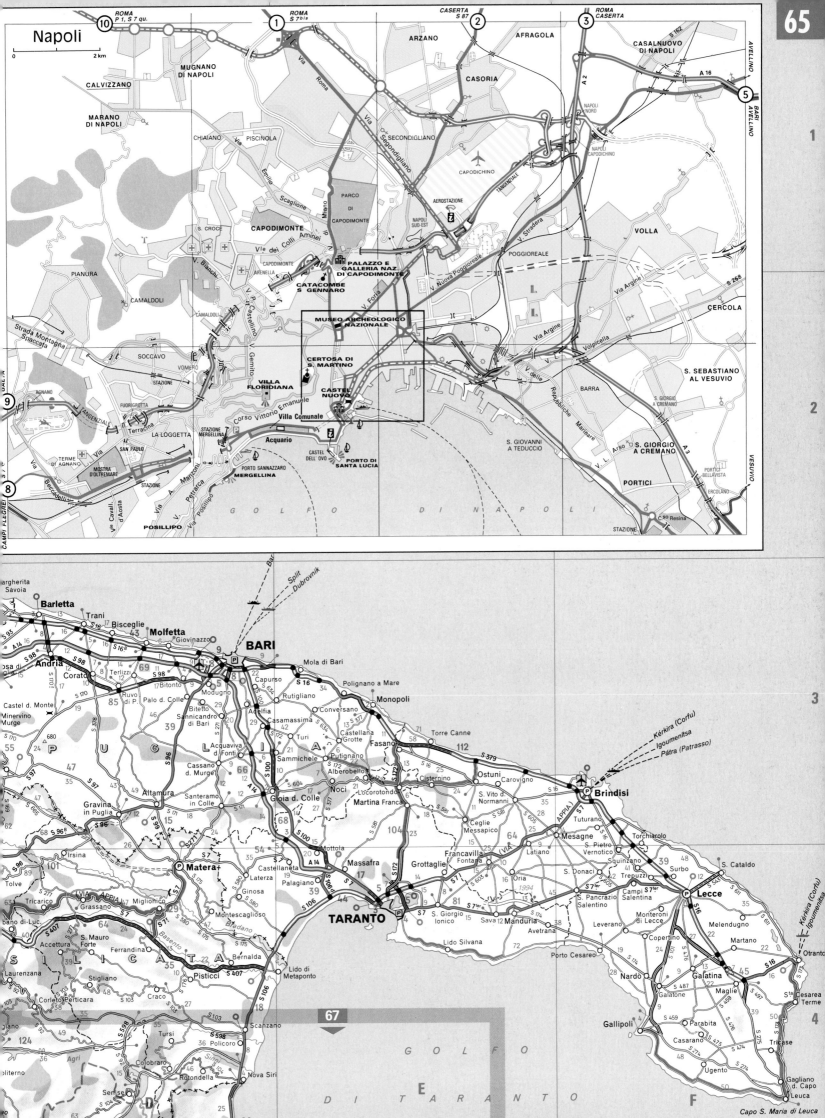

A · B · C

1

2

MARE TIRRENO

I. di Ustica

Isole

I. Filicudi

I. Alicudi

SICILIA

Cagliari
Genova
Livorno
Napoli
Ustica

Capo Gallo
Mondello
Sferracavallo
M. Pellegrino
PALERMO
Punta Raisi · 6 · 30 · A 29 · 606
Capaci
S. Vito lo Capo · Torre d. Impiso · Cinisi · 17 · Carini · Solunto
Golfo di · 17 · S 113 · 7 · **Bagheria**
Castellammare · **63** · Monreale · Casteldaccia
· 46 · S 186 · 8 · Misilmeri · 14 · Altavilla · 24 · S 113 · **Termini** · Cefalù · S. Stefano
Castellammare · 22 · Piana · S 121 · Trabia · **Imerese** · di Camastra
d. Golfo · Partinico · 30 · d. Albanesi · Buonfornello · 93 · Mistretta
Erice · 34 · Marineo · Caccamo · Collesano · Castelbuono
Trapani · S 187 · **41** · Alcamo · S. Cipirello · 34 · S 118 · Montemaggiore · P.ta Carbonara · Petralia · Gangi
I. di · S 113 · 19 · Fulgatore · 12 · Segesta · 24 · S 624 · R.ca Busambra · Villafrati · Belsito · 1979 · C. del Contrasto
Levanzo · Paceco · 41 · 18 · 28 · △ 1613 · S 285 · 42 · Caltavuturo · 1107
Isole Egadi · **42** · **50** · Calatafimi · 46 · Roccapalumba · 50 · Alia · Resuttano · Nicosia
I-Maréttimo · 38 · Salemi · 43 · Corleone · S 121 · 126 · **66** · Leonforte
I. Favignana · 50 · 41 · A 29 · 28 · Lercara · 25 · 56
Birgi · S 115 · 12 · 57 · S.ta Ninfa · Friddi · 132
Marsala · 38 · Partanna · S.ta Margherita · Chiusa Sclafani · 126 · S.ta Caterina · ** Enna**
· 19 · di Belice · Prizzi · Villarmosa · **35**
Castelvetrano · Sambuca · S. Stefano · Mussomeli · **Caltanissetta** · 14
Tunisi · S 115 · 22 · A 29 · di Sicilia · Quisquina · S. Cataldo · Valguarnere
Pantelleria · 24 · Menfi · Alessandria · Casteltermini · Serradifalco · Aidone · **Piazza Armerina**
Mazara d. Vallo · d. Rocca · 62 · Montedoro · Pietraperzia · S 117
Campobello · Caltabellotta · S. Biagio Platani · 83 · Delia · Barrafranca
di Mazara · Selinunte · Ribera · Aragona · 58 · Sommatino · Mazzarino · 65
Marinella · **93** · Sciacca · Raffadali · Canicattì · Riesi
· 41 · Favara · Campobello · Ravanusa · Butera · 81
Agrigento · di Licata · Niscemi
S 115 · 8 · Naro · 72
Porto Empedocle · Palma · **Gela**
Linosa · di Montechiaro · Licata

MARE

Trapani

Pantelleria · Tracino
△ 836
I. di Pantelleria

I. di Linosa

Isole

Pelagie

Porto Empedocle

I. di Lampedusa
Lampedusa

Gozo
Victoria · Nadur
Mgarr · *Comino*
Mellieha · *Siracusa*
Mosta · Sliema
MALTA · Rabat · **Valletta**
Dingli · Vittoriosa
△ 249 · Zejtun
Zurrieq · Birzebugga
Filfola

A · B · C

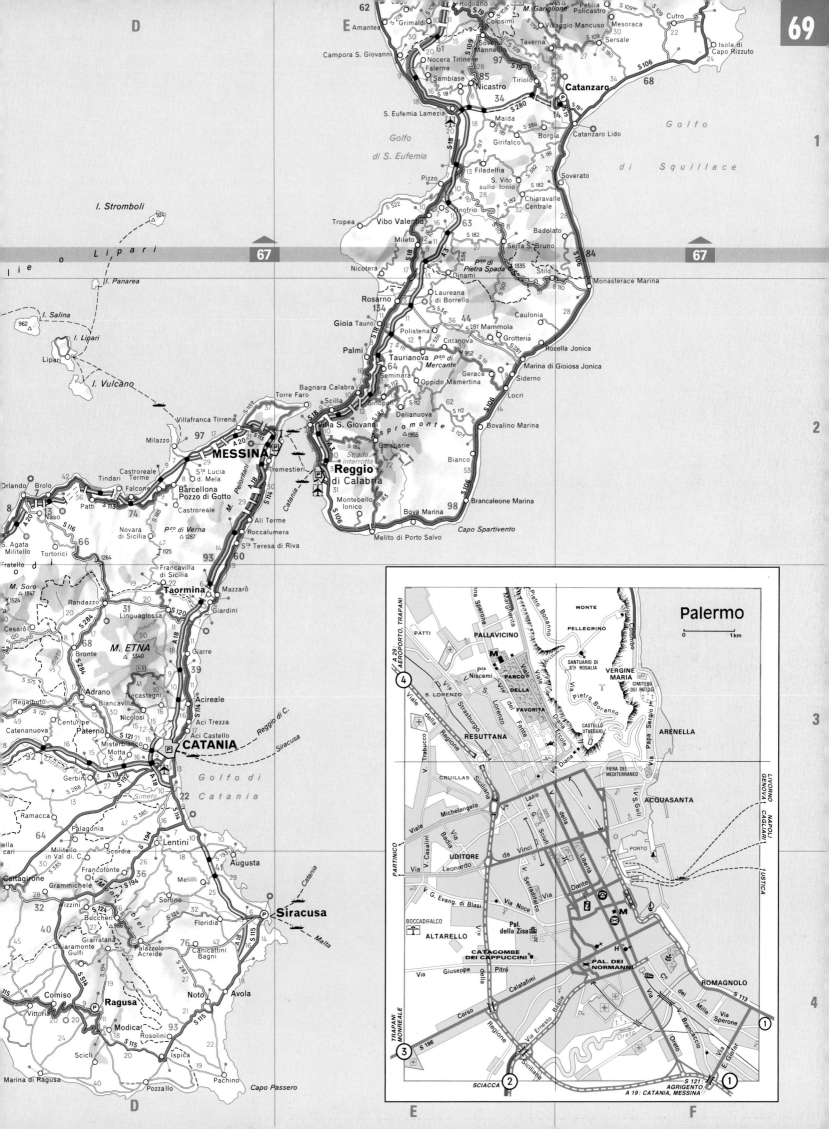

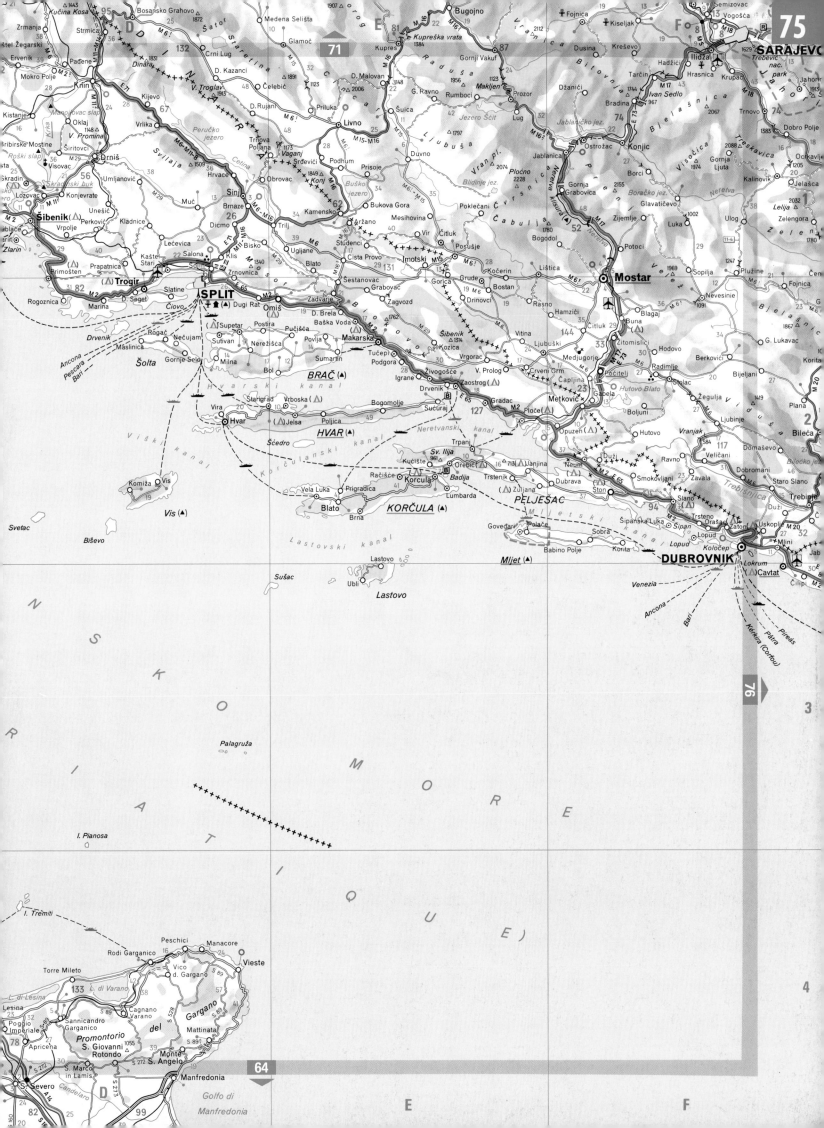

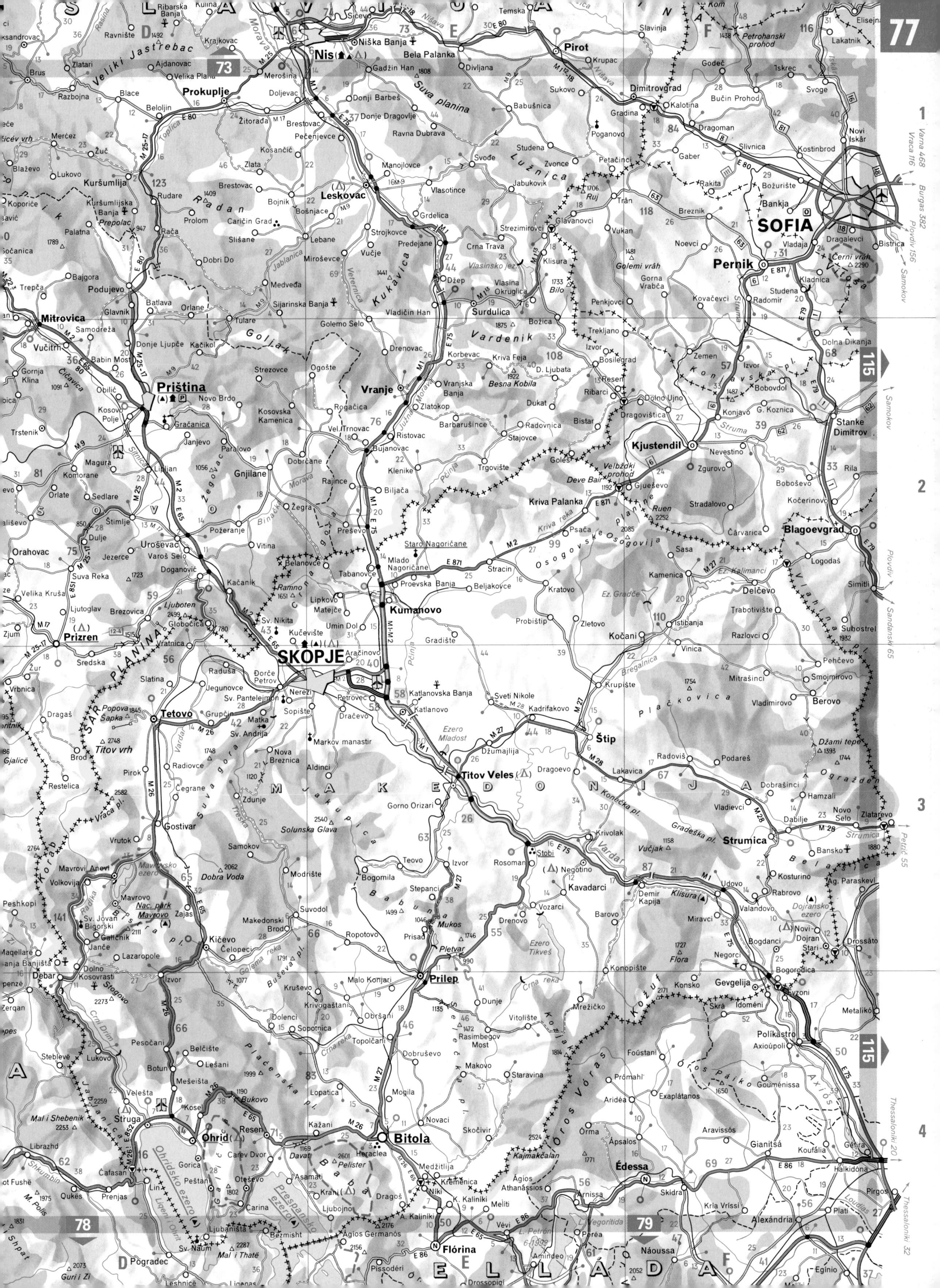

SOFIA

Pernik

Pirot

Niš

Niška Banja
Bela Palanka

Dimitrovgrad

Prokuplje

Leskovac

Vranje
Vranjska Banja

Surdulica

Kjustendil

Blagoevgrad

Kriva Palanka

Kumanovo

SKOPJE

Prishtina

Mitrovica

Prizren

Tetovo

Gostivar

Titov Veles

Štip

Strumica

Prilep

Kavadarci

Negotino

Gevgelija

Bitola

Ohrid

Struga

Édessa

Flórina

Políkastro

Debar

Stanke Dimitrov

Sandanski 65

Manastir
Zagražden
Davidkovo
Dolno Prahovo
Stremci
Dolni Glavanak
Gorata
Ormênio
Ορμένιο
Petrotá
Petrotá
Dikéa
Δίκαια
Dilofos
Δίλοφος
Kapikule
Marássia
Μαράσια
Kastaniés
Καστανιές

Prespa
2000
Bjal Izvor
Kárdžali
Jaz. Kárdžali
Arda
Kobiljane
Ardino
Potočnica
Madžarovo
Spílaio
Σπήλαιο
Pentálofos
Πεντάλοφος
Plátí
Πλάτι
Komara
Κόμαρα
Rizia
Ρίζια
N. Vissa
N. Βύσσα
Orestiáda
Ορεστιάδα

Ustovo
Srednogorci
Madan
Rudozem
Čepinci
Madan
Dolno Glavanak
Momčilgrad
Orešari
Jaz. Studen Kladenec
Jaz Ivajlovgrad
Ivajlovgrad
Milia
Μηλιά
Filatio
Φυλάκιο
Valtos
Βάλτος
Neohóri
Νεοχώρι
Kavíli
Καβύλη
Thoúrio
Θούριο
Ambelákia
Αμπελάκια
Máni
Μάνη
Elinohóri
Ελληνοχώρι
Prangío
Πράγγιο
Didimótiho
Διδυμότειχο

Žalti djal
Nedelino
Dobromirci
Podkova
Krumovgrad
Popsko
Perunika
Metaxades
Μεταξάδες
Vrysiká
Βρυσικά
Mavroklíssio
Μαυροκκλήσιο
Asvestádes
Ασβεστάδες
Amório
Αμόριο
Lávara
Λάβαρα
Meríç

Zlatograd
Thérmes
Θέρμες
Medoussa
Μέδουσα
Tokačka
Rodopi
Iztočni
Avren
Mikr. Dério
Μικρ. Δέρειο
Roússa
Ρούσσα
Kornofoléa
Κορνοφωλέα
Kiriakí
Κυριακή
Protoklíssio
Πρωτοκκλήσιο
Mándra
Μάνδρα

Koúla
Κούλα
Melivia
Μελίβοια
Ehínos
Εχίνος
Míki
Μύκη
Sátres
Σάτρες
Papíkio
Παπίκιο
Nimféa
Νυμφαία
Orgáni
Οργάνη
Smigáda
Σμιγάδα
Méga Dério
Μέγα Δέρειο
Kéhros
Κέχρος
Gianoúli
Γιαννούλη
Souflí
Σουφλί
Meríç

Prossílio
Προσήλιο
Oréo
Ωραίο
Xánthi
Ξάνθη
Kimméria
Κιμμέρια
Sélero
Σέλερο
Sóstis
Σώστης
Gratiní
Γρατινή
Fillira
Φυλλύρα
Plagiá
Πλαγιά
Silo
Σήλω
Kotroniá
Κοτρονιά
Dadiá
Δαδιά
Kornofoléa
Likófos
Λυκόφως
Küplü

Polissito
Πολύσιτο
Iasmos
Ίασμος
Komotini
Κομοτηνή
Roditis
Ροδίτης
Áratos
Άρατος
Arianá
Αρριανά
N. Sánda
N. Σάντα
Leptokariá
Λεπτοκαρυά
Provatónas
Προβατώνας
Laginá
Λαγυνά
Tihero
Τυχερό

Vafeika
Βαφέικα
Paládio
Παλλάδιο
Pagoúria
Παγούρια
Kósmio
Κόσμιο
M. Doúkato
M. Δουκάτο
Arísvi
Αρίσβη
Kizário
Κιζάριο
Essími
Αίσύμη
Lefkími
Λευκίμη
Trifíli
Τριφύλλι
Thimariá
Θυμαριά
Ibriktepe

Gizéla
Γκιζέλα
Mélissa
Μέλισσα
Koutsó
Κουτσό
Pezoúla
Πεζούλα
Pórpi
Πόρπη
Xilagani
Ξυλαγανή
Véna
Βέννα
Lofário
Λοφάριο
Sápes
Σάπες
Kírki
Κίρκη
Áva
Άβα
Nípsa
Νίψα
Piléa
Πυλαία
Kípi
Κήποι

Évlalo
Εύλαλο
Mángana
Μάγγανα
Lagós
Λαγός
Pórpi
Messi
Μέσση
Díoni
Διώνη
Sikoráhi
Συκορράχη
Mésti
Μέστη
Ardánio
Αρδάνιο
Péplos
Πέπλος
Ipsala

Gení Erásmio
Dassohóri
Δασοχώρι
Fanári
Φανάρι
Arogí
Αρωγή
Ímeros
Ίμερος
Marónia
Μαρώνεια
Pal. Krovíli
Παλ. Κρωβύλη
Pláka
Πλάκα
Palagia
Παλαγία
Ánthia
Άνθεια
Féres
Φέρες

Áv̇dira
Άβδηρα
Ág. Harálambos
Αγ. Χαράλαμπος
Messimvría
Μεσημβρία
Díkela
Δίκελλα
Makri
Μάκρη
N. Híli
N. Χιλή
Loutrós
Λουτρός
Monastiráki
Μοναστηράκι

Akr. Maronías
Ακρ. Μαρωνείας
Alexandroúpoli
Αλεξανδρούπολη

Enez

THRAKIKÓ PÉLAGOS
ΘΡΑΚΙΚΟ ΠΕΛΑΓΟΣ

Panagía
Παναγία
Skála Potamiás
Σκάλα Ποταμιάς
Kinira
Κοίνυρα
N. THÁSSOS
N. ΘΑΣΟΣ
Akr. Stavrós
Ακρ. Σταυρός

Karahisar

Suluca

İbrice

Mecidiye

Paleópoli
Παλαιόπολη
Thérma
Θέρμα
Kamariótissa
Καμαριώτισσα
N. SAMOTHRÁKI
N. ΣΑΜΟΘΡΑΚΗ
Akr. Makrígialos
Ακρ. Μακρύγιαλος
Samothráki
Σαμοθράκη
Lákoma
Λάκκωμα
Akr. Kípos
Ακρ. Κήπος

Saros Körfezi

Findikli

Tayfur

Gelibolu Yarımadası

Kokaçimen T.

Kemalyeri

Ariburnu

Kaleköy
Kuzu Limanı
Çinarlı
Deréköy
Kefaloz
Kefalo Br.
GÖKÇE ADASI
Ayagalip
İlyas Br.
Abide
Kumkale

Eceabat
Kilitbahir
Çanakkale
Dardanos
Truva
İntepe
Kumkale

N. Sergítai
N. Σεργίται
Kólpos Pourniás
Κόλπος Πουρνιάς
Akr. Pláka
Ακρ. Πλάκα
Pláka
Πλάκα

Akr. Moúrdzeflos
Ακρ. Μούρτζεφλος
Kavírio-Hlói
Καβίριο-Χλόι
Panagía
Παναγία
Ifestia
Ηφαιστία

Káspakas
Κάσπακας
Kátalako
Κατάλακο
Atsikí
Ατσική
Dáfni
Δάφνη
Kondopoúli
Κοντοπούλι

Mírina
Μύρινα
Kondiás
Κοντιάς
Livadohóri
Λιβαδοχώρι
Kamínia
Καμίνια
Moúdros
Μούδρος
N. LÍMNOS
N. ΛΗΜΝΟΣ

Tavşan Adaları

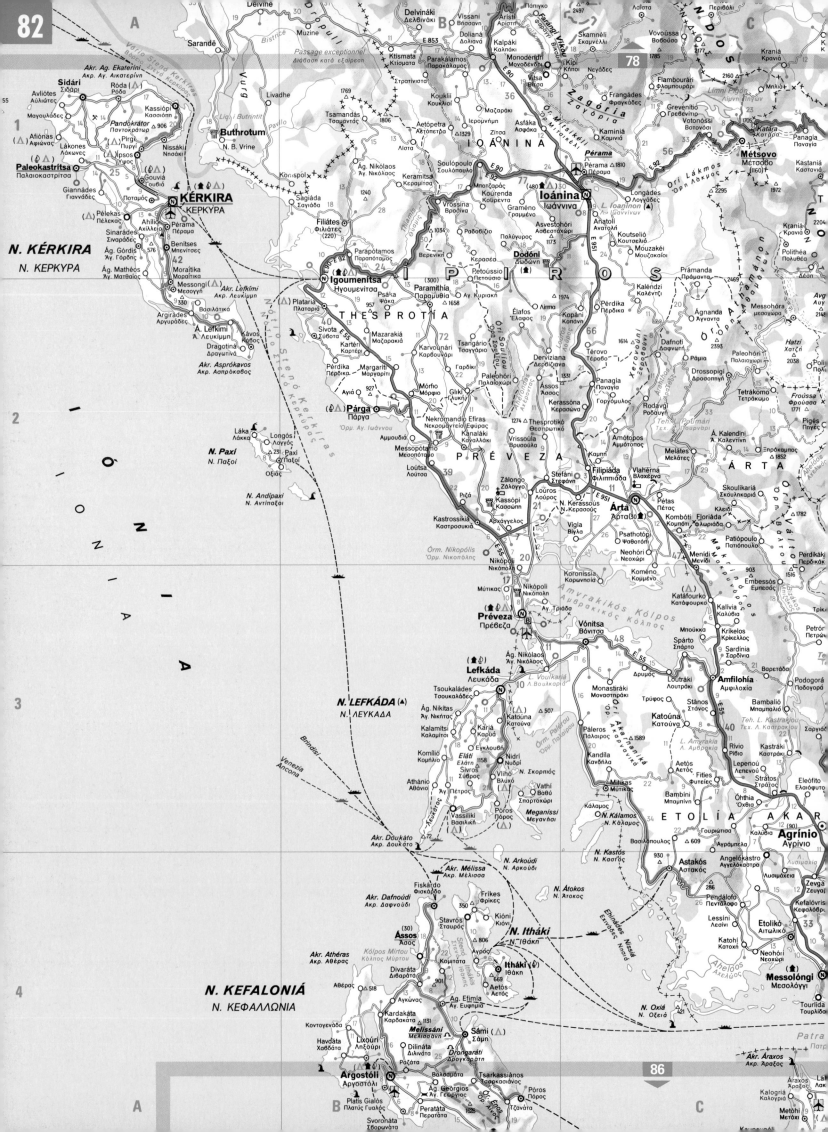

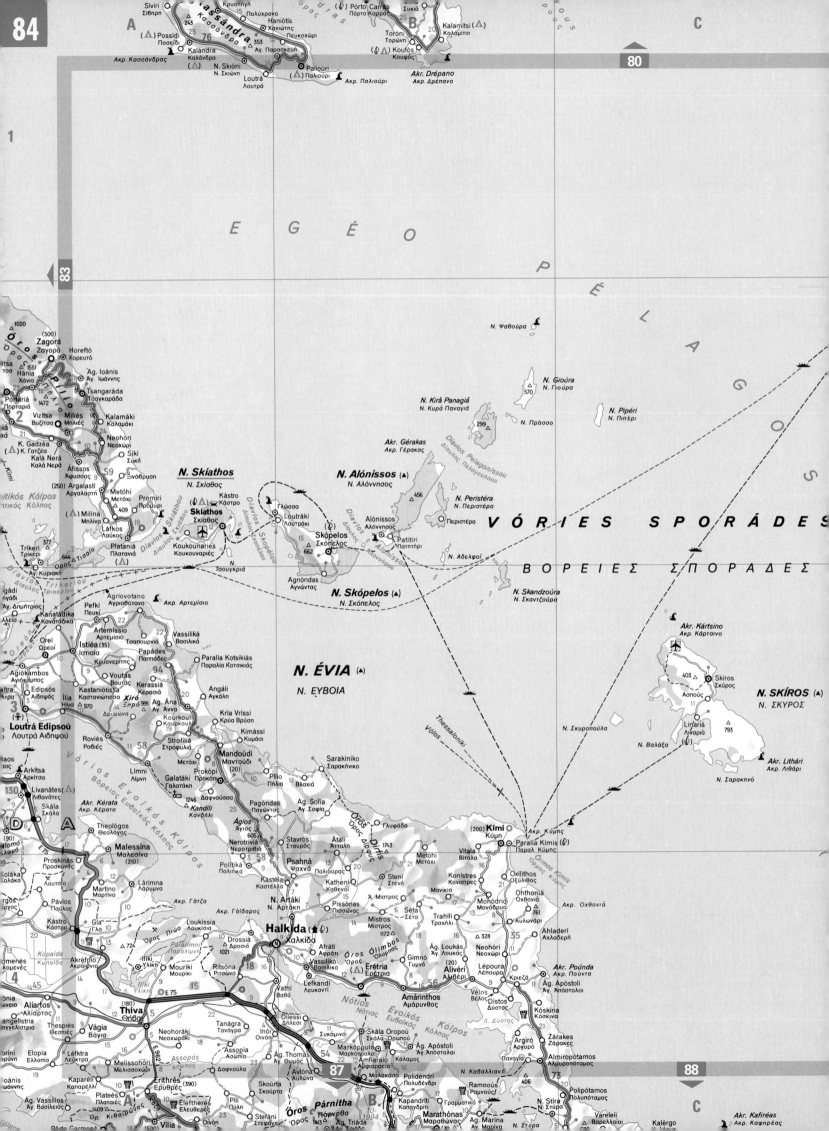

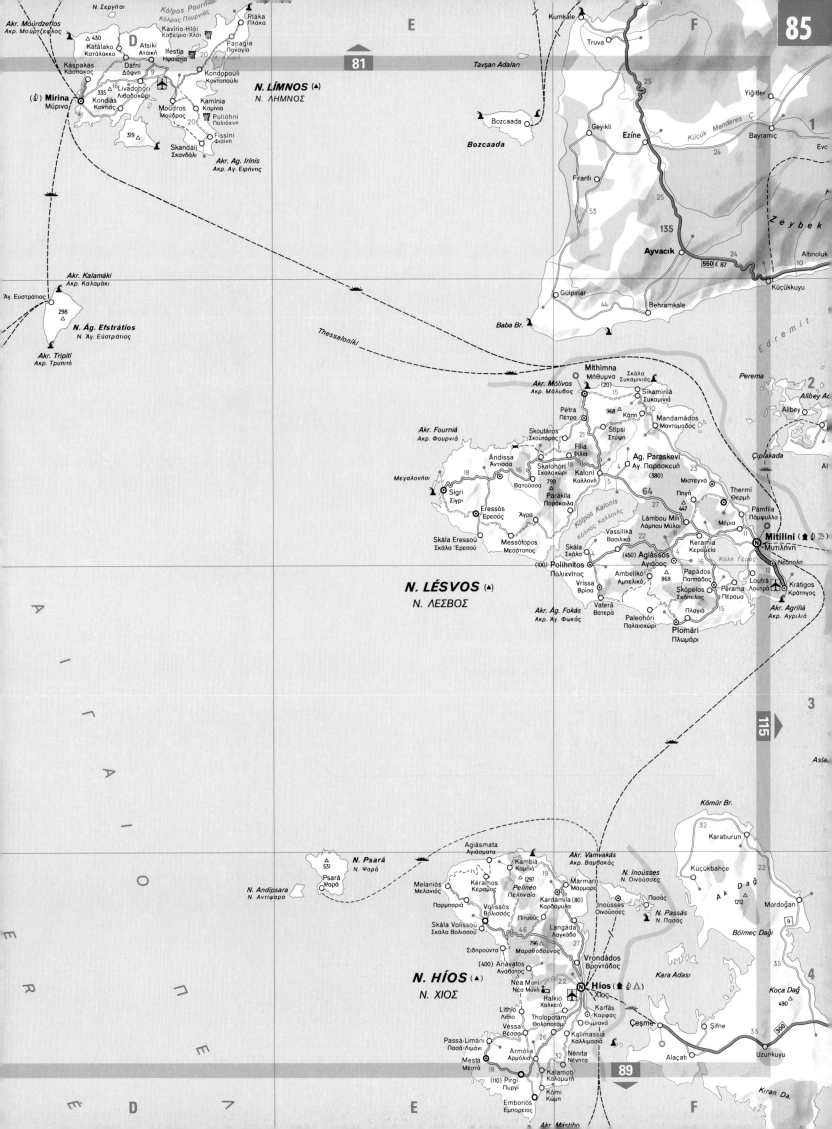

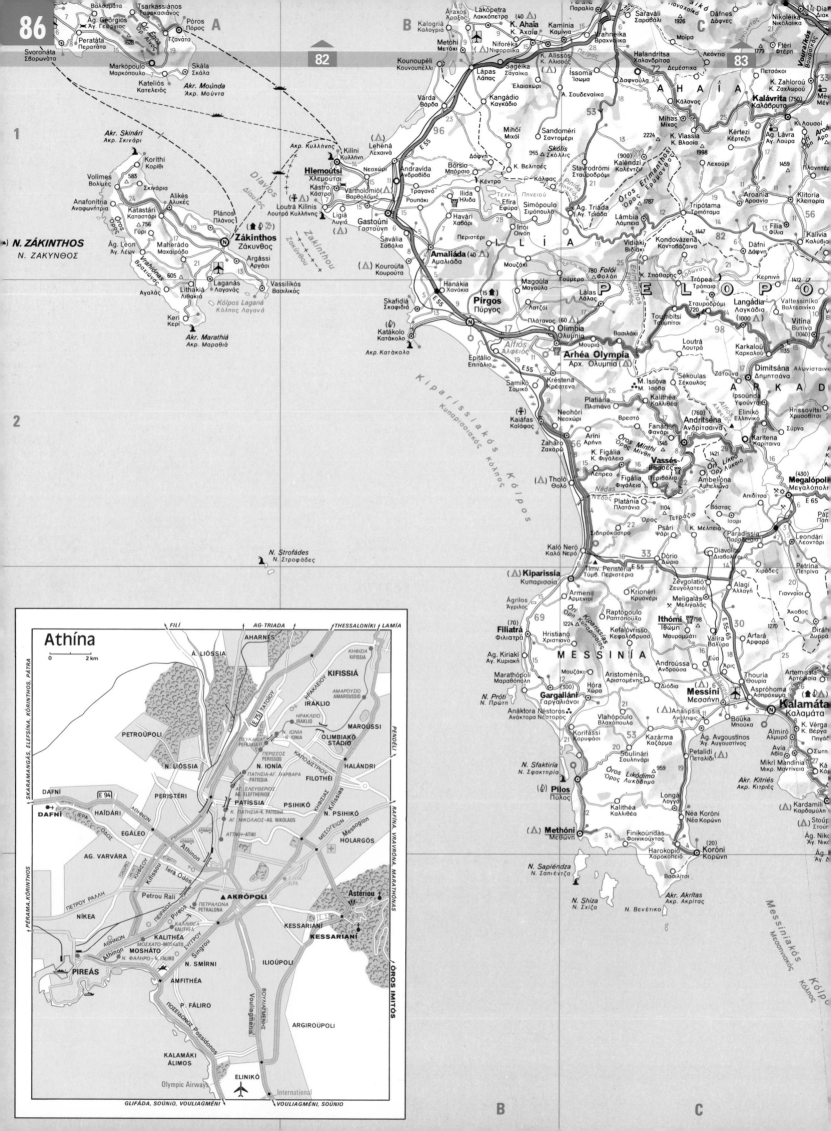

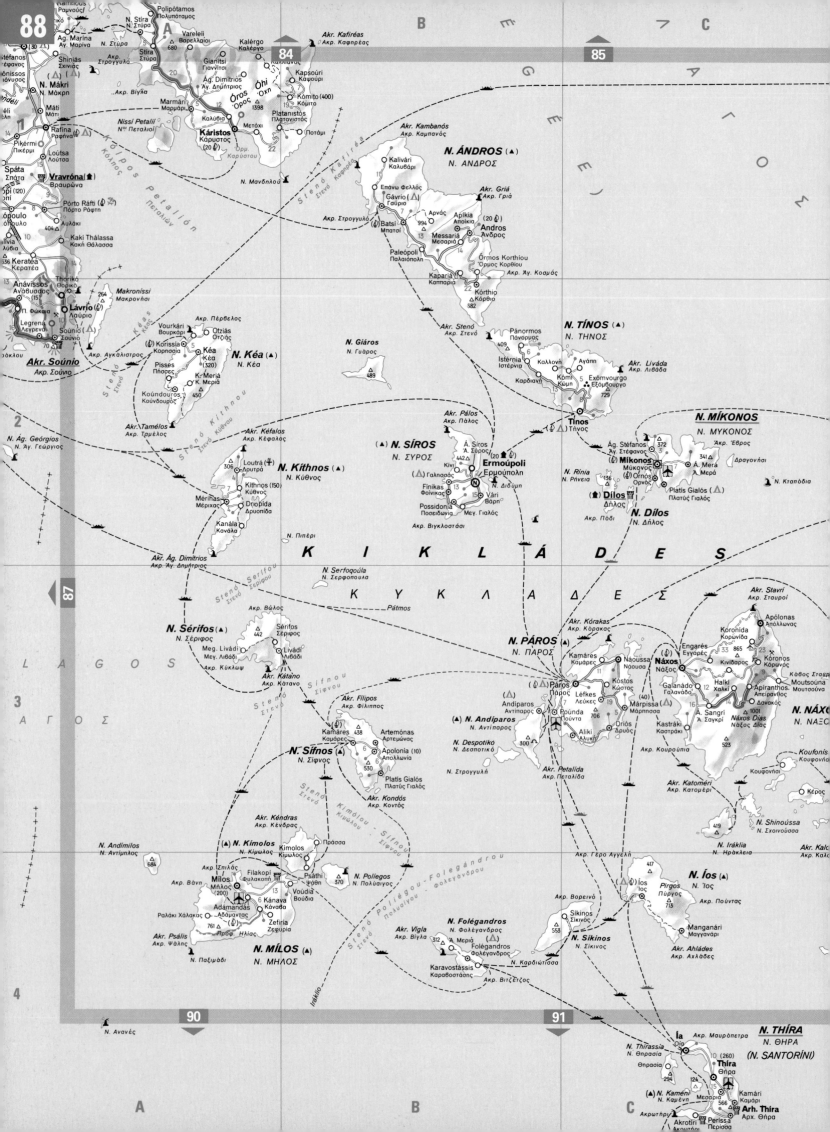

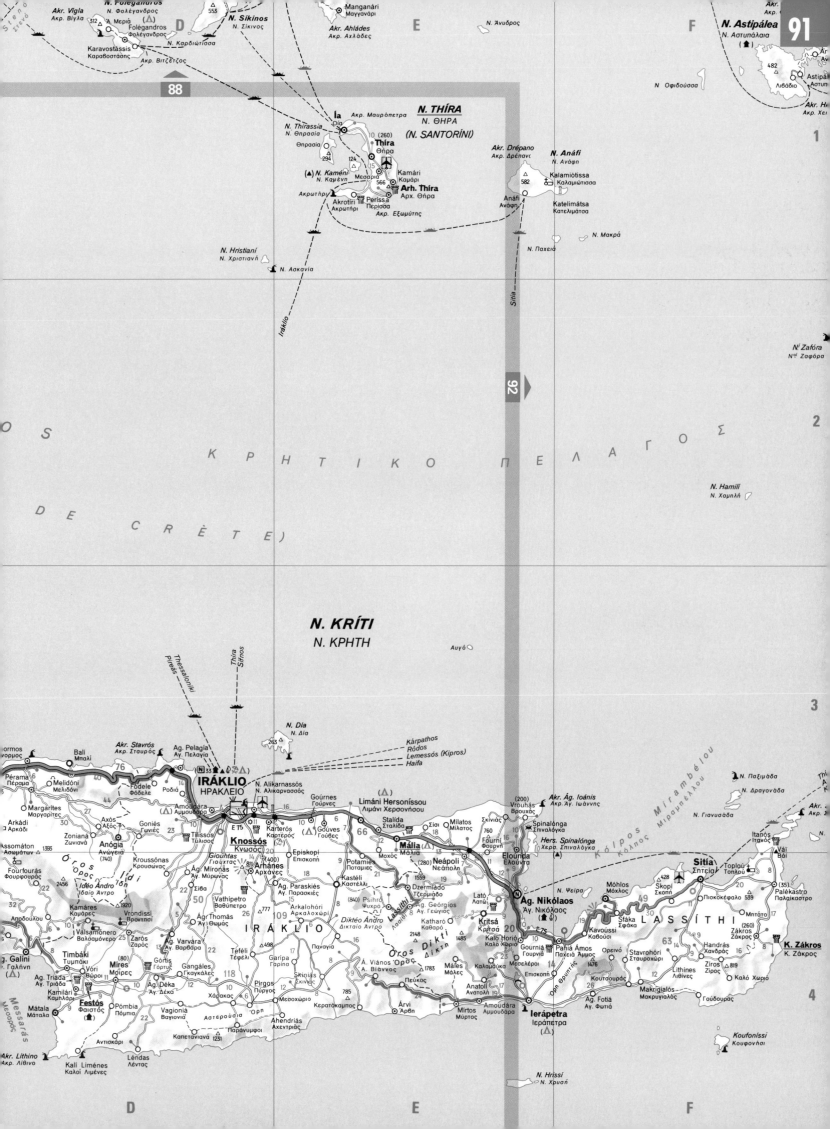

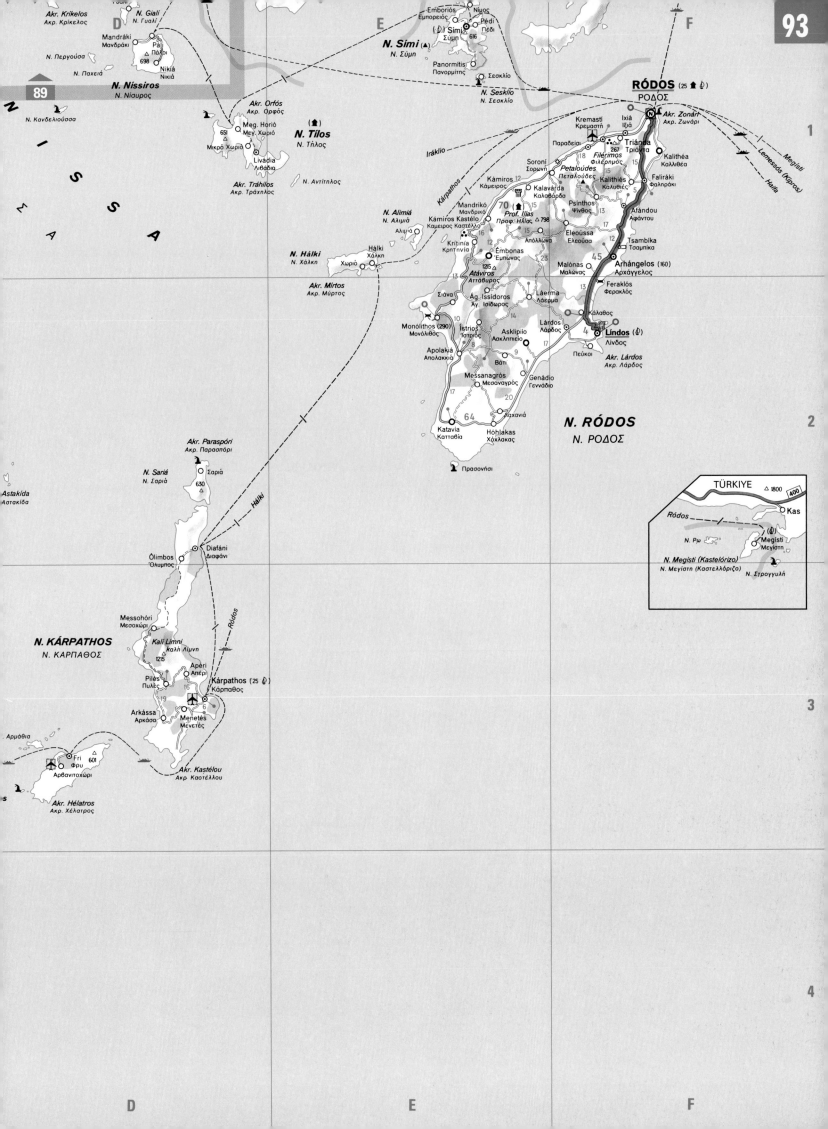

A   B   C

Cercle polaire arctique   Norðurheimskautsbaugur   Grímsey   66°33

1

Hornbjarg
Reykjafjörður
Jökulfirðir
Bolungarvík
Ísafjörður
18
Drangajökull
925
Norðurfjörður
Raufarhöfn
85
Kópasker
78
29
Þórshöfn
Bakkaflói
Bakkafjörður
pingeyri
62
60
61
184
96
Húsavík
867
36
38
70
Bíldudalur
41
Gláma
68
120
843
37
Hólmavík
Krafla
818
Skagaströnd
122
Siglufjörður
Ólafsfjörður
Hrísey
Dettifoss
864
Vopnafjörður
Patreksfjörður
48
62 44
Brjánslækur
Hofsós
Dalvík
Árskógssandur
Reykjahlíð
62
Borgarfjörður
Látrabjarg
48
Húnaflói
Sauðárkrókur
44
46
54
62
71
Flatey
Reykhólar
Skagafjörður
115
Krafla
40
274
107
Tórsh
Hvammstangi
Varmahlíð
Akureyri
Mývatn
Eiðar
Breiðafjörður
83
24
22
89
Goðafoss
54
Fellabær
Egilsstaðir
25
Seyðisfjörður
Laugar
99
590
59
33
425
Laugarbakki
5
Hrafnagil
Neskaups
Hallormsstaður
31
Stykkishólmur
Búðardalur
86
86
93
F 82
Óðáðahraun
Askja
Reyðarfjörður
40
Eskifjörður
Grundarfjörður
67
110
57
76
48
Laugafell
135
Dreki
190
75
96 102
Fáskrúðsfjörður
Ólafsvík
20
Snæfellsnes
22
Í   **S**   **L**   **A**   **N**   **D**
123
Nýidalur
68
241
Breiðdalsvík
1448
Búðir
37
62
1675
Hofsjökull
45
Sprengisandur
2000
1570
Djúpivogur

2

37
Reykholt
Húsafell
Hveravellir
1765
Langjökull
105
V   **A**   **T**   **N**   **A**   **J**   **Ö**   **K**   **U**   **L**   **L**
Nesjahverfi
Borgarnes
52
102
Hvítárnes
F 37
98
23
Faxaflói
157
Geysir
Gullfoss
130
Höfn
Akranes
914
Þingvellir
Laugarvatn
461
219
REYKJAVÍK
36
Pingvallavatn
46 63
Flúðir
96
Skaftafell
Garður
57
Hveragerði
78
110
Sandgerði
50
30
Hekla
95
Eldgjá
Keflavík
25
44 30
Selfoss
1491
Landmannalaugar
Kirkjubæjarklaustur
Skeiðarársandur
Fagurhólsmýri
Grindavík
34
Þorlákshöfn
Hella
204
Hvolsvöllur
Mýrdals-
3
135
249
jökull
Seljalandsfoss
Þórsmörk
Skógar
50
Skógafoss
Vestmannaeyjar
Vík

1 / 2 400 000
0   50 km

ATLANTSHAF   ATLANTSHAF

FØROYAR
FÆRØERNE
(DK)
Seyðisfjörður
NORÐOYAR
Viðareiði
Eiði
882
Gjógv
Kunoy
Viðoy
Tjørnuvík
Oyndarfjörður
Svínoy
790
Borðoy
Streymoy
Hvalvík
Eysturoy
Leirvík
Klaksvík
Mykines
Vestmanna
18
Mýkines
722
Vágar
20
58
Sørvágur
Tóftir
Tórshavn
Kirkjubøur
Skopun
Sandoy
Skopun
479
Sandur
Skálavík
Lerwick - Bergen
Hanstholm · Esbjerg
Suðuroyarfjörður

Lerwick - Bergen
Hanstholm · Esbjerg

4
Hvalba
610
Tvøroyri
Fámjin
Suðuroy
Vágur
Sumba

0   30 km

Hurtigrute
Sør-Flatanger
Osen
Roan
Harsvik
66
NORSKEHAVET

OULUJÄRVI

Manamansalo
Paltaniemi
Vuokatti
Kuhmo
Kestilä (△) D
Vorna
Pulkkila
Kajaani
Sotkamo
Tuhkakylä
Tipasoja
Reboly
Piippola
Vuolijoki
Otanmäki
Lehtovaara
Kiekinkoski
Haapavesi
Pyhäntä
Nissilä
Sukeva
Maanselkä
Valtimo
Tulivaara
Kärsämäki
Remeskylä
Vieremä
Sonkajärvi
Jyrkkä
Nurmes
Nurmijärvi
Lendery
Nuttupera
Luupuvesi
Soinlahti
Koirakoski
Rautavaara
Palomäki
Kylänlahti
Pankakoski
Hattuvaara
Pyhäsalmi
Kiuruvesi
Iisalmi
Peltosalmi
Juminen
Lieksa
Pyhäjärvi
Runni
Varpaisjärvi
Hankamäki
Juuka
Pielinen
Haapamäki
Lapinlahti
Tahkvuori
Säyneinen
Koli
Naarva
Pihtipudas
Kärväskylä
Alapitkä
Nilsiä
Martonvaara
Uimaharju
Kinnula
Suopelto
Pielavesi
Maaninka
Juankoski
Polvijärvi
Eno
Möhkö
Keitele
Talluskylä
Siilinjärvi
Toivala
Kaavi
Maarianvaara
Kontiolahti
Ilomantsi
Viitasaari
Hirvilahti
Juurusvesi
Kaavinjärvi
POHJOIS-KARJALAN LÄÄNI
Ruuponsaari
Tervo
KUOPIO
Riistavesi
Paakkila
Outokumpu
JOENSUU
Kannonkoski
Vesanto
Karttula
Ritoniemi
Vehmersalmi
Kuusjärvi
Viinijärvi
Ylamylly
Heinävaara
Kovero
Pyha-Häkki
Hakkila
Kerkonkoski
Iisvesi
Rasala
Kosula
Palokki
Liperi
Pyhäselkä
Hammaslahti
Tikkala
Saarijärvi
Sumiainen
Rautalampi
Suonenjoki
Oravikoski
Heinävesi
Rääkkylä
Tohmajärvi
Vartsilä (△)
Äänekoski
Konnevesi
Haapakoski
Leppävirta
Savonranta
Kitee
Korkeakangas
Suolahti
Jäppilä
Kangaslampi
Orivesi
Puhos
Hankasalmi
Varkaus
Könönpelto
Enonkoski
Villala
Kesälahti
JYVÄSKYLÄ
Laukaa
Pieksämäki
Juvola
Kerimäki
Multia
Vaajakoski
Lievestuore
Joroinen
Virtasalmi
Rantasalmi
Ruokojärvi
Sortavala
Petäjävesi
Säynätsalo
Toivakka
Haukivuori
Narila
Kallislahti
Punkaharju
Uukuniemi
Mänttä
Muurame
Kangasniemi
Juva
Savonlinna
Saari
Korpilahti
Leivonmäki
MIKKELIN LÄÄNI
Sulkava
Jämsä
Joutsa
Luhanka
Hartola
Mikkeli
Puumala
Rautjärvi
Kuhmoinen
Sysmä
Ristiina
Imatra
Priozërsk
Padasjoki
Heinola
Savitaipale
Taipalsaari
Joutseno
Svetogorsk
Asikkala
Vierumäki
Jaala
Luumäki
Lappeenranta
Vyborg
LAHTI
Hollola
Valkeala
KYMEN LÄÄNI
Nastola
Kuusankoski
Kouvola
Riihimäki
Orimattila
Anjalankoski
Hyvinkää
Mäntsälä
Kotka
Järvenpää

(F) Lorsqu'un nom figure plusieurs fois dans l'index, une précision est ajoutée entre parenthèses pour permettre de l'identifier plus facilement: pays, région ou ville la plus proche, élément géographique d'après les abréviations ci-dessous.

(NL) Bij namen die meermalen in het register voorkomen, staat tussen haakjes een aanduiding ter verklaring: het land, de streek, de dichtstbijgelegen stad of een geografisch gegeven (zie de afkortingen hieronder).

(GB) Where there are two or more identical place names, the name of the distinguishing country or region or nearest large town is given in brackets; geographical features are indicated by the abbreviations below.

(E) Para poder localizar más fácilmente un nombre que figura varias veces en el índice, se añade entre paréntesis el país, la región o ciudad más cercana, o un elemento geográfico, con las abreviaturas siguientes.

(D) Tritt ein Name mehrfach im Register auf, wird er durch eine in Klammern gesetzte nähere Bestimmung genauer definiert. Sie finden folgende Zusätze: Land, Region oder nächstgelegene Stadt, geographische Gegebenheiten, ggf. abgekürzt

(I) Quando un nome figura più volte nell'indice, una precisazione viene aggiunta tra parentesi per permettere d'identificarlo più facilmente: nazione, regione o città la più vicina, elemento geografico come da abbreviazioni qui di seguito.

Akr	Akra, Akrotírion
B	Bay, Baie, Bucht, Bahía, Baía, Bukt(en), Bugt, Bukhta
Bgem	Barragem
C	Cape, Cap, Cabo, Capo
Co	County
Ch	Chaîne
Chan	Channel
Dépt	Département
Emb	Embalse
Ez	Ezero
G	Gulf, Golfe, Golfo
Gges	Gorges
I(s), I(s)	Isles(s), Island(s), Ile(s), Ilha(s), Isla(s), Isola(e)
Jez	Jezoro, Jezioro
K	Kanal, Kanaal
L, L	Lake, Loch, Lough, Llyn, Lac, Laguna, Lago, Limni

Liq	Liquen
Meg	Méga, Megál, -a, -i, -o
Mikr	Mikr-í, -ón
Mgne(s)	Montagne(s)
M, Mte(s)	Maj, Maj'e, Monte(s)
Mt(s), Mt(s)	Mount(s), Mountain(s), Mont(s)
Mti	Monti, Muntii
Nac	Nacional(e)
Nat	National
Naz	Nazionale
N	Nissi, Nissos
Ni	Nissiá, Nissi
Os	Ostrov(a)
Ot	Otok(i), Otoci
Oz	Ozero(a)
P	Pass
Pal	Paleós, á, ó

Pen	Peninsula, Penisola
Pk	Park
Pl	Planina
Pque	Parque
Prov	Province
Pso	Passo
Pt(e)	Point(e)
Rib	Ribeirão
R, R	River, Rivière, Rio, Ria, Rijeka
Reg	Region, Région
Res	Reservoir, Reservoire
Sa	Sierra, Serra
Sd	Sound, Sund
St	Saint, Sankt, Sint
Ste(s)	Sainte(s)
Teh L	Tehnití Limni
V	Valley, Vale, Vallée, Val, Valle, Vall

A

Aachen	51	D3
Aalen	55	E2
Aalsmeer	16	C2
Aalst	50	B3
Aalten	17	D3
Aalter	50	B3
Äänekoski	103	D2
Aapajärvi	95	F4
Aarau	27	E2
Aarberg	27	E2
Aarburg	27	F2
Aare	58	A3
Aargau	27	F2
Aarlen	21	D2
Aarschot	50	C3
Aavasaksa	98	C2
Abades	40	A1
Abadiño	36	B1

A Baiuca	34	A1
Abanilla	45	D2
Abano Terme	61	D1
Abbadia San Salvatore	63	D1
Abbasanta	66	B3
Abbazia di Casamari	63	F3
Abbazia di Fossanova	63	F3
Abbazia di Montecassino	64	A3
Abbazia San Clemente a Casauria	64	A2
Abbeville	19	E2
Abbeyfeale	14	B3
Abbeyleix	12	C4
Abbey Town	5	D4
Abbiategrasso	60	A1
Abborrträsk	98	B3
Abbots Bromley	6	C3

Abbotsbury	9	D3
Abcoude	16	C2
Abejar	36	B3
Abejuela	41	E3
Abela	42	A1
Abelvær	97	D4
Abenberg	55	E2
Abenójar	39	F4
Åbenrå	108	A4
Abensberg	55	F2
Aberaeron	8	C1
Aberdar	8	C2
Aberdare	8	C2
Aberdaron	6	A3
Aberdaugleddau	8	B2
Aberdeen	3	E4
Aberdovey	6	A3
Aberfeldy	4	C1
Aberfoyle	4	C2
Abergavenny	9	D2
Abergele	6	B2

Abergwaun	8	B1
Aberhonddu	8	C1
Aberlady	5	D2
Aberpennar	8	C2
Aberporth	8	B1
Abersoch	6	A3
Abertawe	8	C2
Aberteifi	8	B1
Abertillery	9	D2
Aber-Wrac'h, l'	22	A2
Aberystwyth	8	C1
Abetone	60	C3
Abiego	37	E3
Abingdon	9	E2
Abington	5	D3
Abisko	94	B3
Abisko (Nat park)	94	B4
Abla	44	B3
Ablis	19	E4
Åbo	107	D2
Abondance	27	E3

Abony	112	B4
Aboyne	3	E4
Abrantes	38	B3
Abreschviller	21	E4
Abrets, les	30	C1
Abriès	31	E2
Abruzzo	63	F2
Abruzzo, Parco Nazionale d'	64	A2
Abstadt-Tailfingen	55	D3
Abtenau	59	E1
Åby	105	F4
Åbybro	108	B2
A Caniza	34	A3
Acceglio	31	E2
Accettura	65	D4
Acciaroli	67	D1
Accous	37	D1
Accrington	6	C2
Acebo	39	D2

Acedo	36	B2
Acehuche	39	D3
Acerno	64	B4
Acerra	64	B4
Aceuchal	39	D4
Ache	59	E1
Achenkirch	59	D1
Achenpaß	56	A4
Achensee	59	D1
Achern	54	C3
Acheux	19	F2
Achill I	12	A2
Achim	17	F1
Achnacroish	4	B1
Achnasheen	2	C3
A'Chràlaig	2	C4
Aci Castello	69	D3
Acipayam	115	F4
Acireale	69	D3
Aci Trezza	69	D3
Acle	7	F3
A Coruña	34	B1
Acqualagna	61	E4
Acquapendente	63	D1
Acquasanta Terme	63	F1
Acquasparta	63	E1
Acquaviva delle Fonti	65	D3
Acqui-Terme	60	A2
Acri	67	E2
Ada	72	C1
Adaja, R	39	F2
Adak	98	A3
Ådalsel	104	C2
Adamandás	88	A4
Adamclisi	115	E1
Adamello	58	C3
Adamello Brenta, Parco Naturale	58	C3
Adamello, Mont'	58	C3
Adamuz	43	F2
Adanero	39	F1
Adapazarı	115	F3
Adare	14	B3
Adaševci	72	B3
Adda	60	B2
Adelboden	27	E3
Adelfia	65	D3
Adelsheim	55	D1
Ademuz	41	D3
Adenau	51	E4
Ádendro	79	F3
Adéres, Óros	87	E2
Adiça, Sa da	42	C1
Adige	61	D1
Adjud	113	E4
Admont	57	D3
Adolfström	97	F3
Adorf	53	D3
Adour	28	B4
Adra	44	B4
Adradas	36	B4
Adrall	32	A3
Adrano	69	D3
Adria	61	D2
Adriatic Sea	114	A3
Adzaneta	41	E3
Adzaneta de Albaida	45	E1
Aegean Sea	115	E4
Aenona	74	C1
Aerinó	83	F2
Ærø	108	B4
Ærøskøbing	108	B4
Aetópetra	82	B1
Aetós (Kefaloniá)	82	B4
Aetós (Makedonia)	79	D3
Aetós (Stereá Eláda)	82	C4
Aetsä	107	D2
Afándou	93	F1
Åfarnes	100	B2
Aféa	87	F2
Affi	60	C1
Afiónas	82	A1

Áfissos	83	F2
Áfitos	80	B4
Afjord	100	C1
Åfjorden	104	A1
Aflenzer Seeberg	57	E3
Aflenz Kurort	57	E3
Afráti	84	B4
Afsluitdijk	16	C1
A Garda	34	A3
Agathonissi	89	E2
Agay	31	E4
Agazzano	60	B2
Agde	30	A4
Agdenes	100	C1
Agen	28	C3
Åger	37	F3
Ager	56	C3
Ageranós	87	D4
Agerbæk	108	A3
Agger	17	E4
Aggius	66	B1
Aggsbach-Dorf	57	E2
Aggsbach-Markt	57	E2
Agiá	83	F1
Agiá, Akr	83	F4
Agia Ana (Évia)	84	A3
Agía Ana (Viotía)	83	F4
Agía Efimía	82	B4
Agía Efthimía	83	E4
Agía Ekateríni, Akr	82	A1
Agía Fotiá	91	F4
Agía Galini	91	D4
Agía Kiriakí (Makedonía)	78	C3
Agía Kiriakí (Pelopónissos)	86	B3
Agía Kiriakí (Sámos)	89	E2
Agía Lávra	86	C1
Agía Marina (Égina)	87	F2
Agía Marina (Kríti)	90	B3
Agía Marina (Léros)	89	E2
Agía Marina (Stereá Eláda)	83	E3
Agía Marina (Stereá Eláda)	88	A1
Agía Paraskeví (Lésvos)	85	F2
Agía Paraskeví (Makedonía)	80	C2
Agía Paraskiés	91	E4
Agía Pelagia (Kíthira)	90	A1
Agía Pelagía (Kríti)	91	D4
Agía Rouméli	90	B4
Agiasma	80	C2
Agiásmata	85	E4
Agía Sofía (Évia)	84	B3
Agía Sofía (Pelopónissos)	87	D2
Agía Sotíra	87	E1
Agiássos	85	F2
Agía Triáda (Kríti)	91	D3
Agia Triáda (Makedonía)	79	F3
Agía Triáda (Pelopónissos)	86	C1
Agia Triáda (Stereá Eláda)	87	F1
Agía Varvára	91	D4
Agiófilo	83	D1
Agiókambos (Évia)	83	F3
Agiókambos (Thessalía)	83	F1
Agionóri	87	E2
Ágio Óros	80	C4
Agiopigi	83	D2
Ágios	84	A3
Ágios Anárgiri (Pelopónissos)	87	D3
Ágios Anárgiri (Thessalía)	83	E2
Ágios Andónios	80	A3
Ágios Andréas (Arkadía)	87	D2

Ágios Andréas (Lakonía) 87 E4
Ágios Apóstoli (Évia) 84 B4
Ágios Apóstoli (Pelopónissos) 87 E4
Ágios Apóstoli (Stereá Eláda) 84 B4
Ágios Athanássios (Dráma) 80 C2
Ágios Athanássios (Péla) 79 D2
Ágios Avgoustinos . . 86 C3
Ágios Déka 91 D4
Ágios Dimítrios, Akr 88 A3
Ágios Dimítrios (Évia) 88 A1
Ágios Dimítrios (Lakonía) 87 D3
Ágios Dimítrios (Makedonía) 79 E4
Ágios Dimítrios (Messinía) 87 D4
Ágios Dimítrios (Stereá Eláda) 83 D3
Ágios Dioníssios . . . 79 D4
Ágios Efstrátios, N . 85 D2
Ágios Fokás 89 F3
Ágios Fokás, Akr . . . 85 F3
Ágios Geórgios (Évia) 83 F3
Ágios Geórgios, N . . 87 F2
Ágios Geórgios (Lassíthi) 91 E4
Ágios Geórgios (Stereá Eláda) 83 D3
Ágios Geórgios (Zákinthos) 86 A1
Ágios Georgíou, Órmos 87 E3
Ágios Germanós . . . 79 D2
Ágios Górdis 82 A1
Ágios Harálambos 81 E2
Ágios Ioánis, Akr . . . 91 F3
Ágios Ioánis (Dodekánissa) 89 F4
Ágios Ioánis (Pelopónissos) 87 E2
Ágios Ioánis (Stereá Eláda) 83 F4
Ágios Ioánis (Thessalía) 83 F3
Ágios Ioánis (Thessalía) 83 F2
Ágios Irínis, Akr . . . 85 D1
Ágios Issídoros 93 E2
Ágios Kírikos 89 D2
Ágios Konstandínos (Stereá Eláda) 83 F3
Ágios Konstandínos (Thessalía) 83 E2
Ágios Kosmás (Grevená) 79 D4
Ágios Kosmás (Kavála) 80 C2
Ágios Léon 86 A1
Ágios Loukás 84 B4
Ágios Mámas 80 A4
Ágios Márkos 80 A2
Ágios Mathéos 82 A2
Ágios Mironas 91 D4
Ágios Nikítas 82 B3
Ágios Nikólaos (Etolía-Akarnanía) 82 B3
Ágios Nikólaos (Fokída) 83 E4
Ágios Nikólaos (Fthiótida) 83 F3
Ágios Nikólaos (Hers.Methánon) . . 87 E2
Ágios Nikólaos (Ípiros) 82 B1
Ágios Nikólaos (Kríti) 91 E4
Ágios Nikólaos (Lakonía) 87 D3
Ágios Nikólaos (Makedonía) 80 B4
Ágios Nikólaos (Messinía) 86 C3
Ágios Pandeleímonos . . . 79 D3

Ágios Pángalos, Akr 83 E4
Ágios Paraskeví (Ípiros) 78 C4
Ágios Paraskeví (Makedonía) 79 F2
Ágios Pávlos 80 A3
Ágios Pétros 87 D2
Ágios Pnévma 80 B2
Ágios Pródromos . . 80 A3
Ágios Sóstis 83 E3
Ágios Stéfanos (Kikládes) 88 C2
Ágios Stéfanos (Stereá Eláda) 87 F1
Ágios Theódori (Makedonía) 79 D4
Ágios Theódori (Pelopónissos) . . 87 E1
Ágios Theódori (Thessalía) 83 F3
Ágios Thomás (Kríti) 91 D4
Ágios Thomás (Stereá Eláda) 84 B4
Ágios Vassílios (Makedonía) 80 A3
Ágios Vassílios (Stereá Eláda) 84 A4
Ágios Vissários 83 E2
Agiou Órous, Kólpos 80 C4
Agira 68 C3
Agly 32 B2
Agnanda 82 C2
Agnanderó 83 D2
Agnandi 83 F3
Agnóndas 84 B3
Agnone 64 B2
Agnoúnda 87 E2
Agoitz 36 C2
Agon-Coutainville . . 18 B3
Agorá 80 C2
Agordo 59 D3
Agost 45 E1
Agout 29 D4
Agrafiótis 83 D2
Agramunt 37 F3
Agrate Br. 60 A1
Agreda 36 C3
Agreliá 83 D1
Agri 65 D4
Agriá 83 F2
Agrigento 68 B4
Agriliá 82 C4
Agriliá, Akr. 85 F3
Ágrilos 86 B3
Agrínio 82 C4
Agriovótano 83 F3
Agrópoli 64 B4
Agskaret 97 E2
Aguadulce (Almería) 44 B4
Aguadulce (Sevilla) 43 E3
Aguas Vivas, R. . . . 37 D4
Aguaviva 41 E2
A Gudiña 34 C3
Agudo 39 F4
Agueda 38 B1
Agueda, R. 39 D2
Aguiar 42 B1
Aguiar da Beira . . . 38 C1
Aguilafuente 40 A1
Aguilar 43 F2
Aguilar de Campóo 35 F2
Aguilar del Alfambra 41 E2
Aguilar, Emb de . . . 35 F2
Águilas 44 C3
Ahaΐa 86 C1
Aharnés 87 F1
Ahaus 17 E3
Åheim 100 A3
Ahelóos 82 C4
Ahendriás 91 E4
Ahérondas 82 B2
Ahigal 39 D2
Ahílio (Kérkira) 82 A1
Ahílio (Thessalía) . . 83 E2
Ahinós 80 B2
Ahjärvi 103 F3
Ahladerí 84 B4

Ahládes, Akr 88 C4
Ahladohóri 80 B1
Ahlainen 102 B3
Ahlbeck 49 E2
Ahlen 17 E3
Ahlhorn 17 F1
Ahrensbök 48 B2
Ahrensburg 48 B2
Ahrweiler 51 E4
Ähtäri 102 C2
Ähtärinjärvi 102 C2
Ahtävänjoki 102 C2
Ahun 25 E4
Åhus 109 D3
Ahvenanmaa 106 C3
Ahvenselkä 99 E1
Aichach 55 F3
Aidenbach 56 B2
Aidone 68 C3
Aigen 56 C2
Aigle 27 E3
Aigle, Bge de l' 29 E1
Aigle, l' 19 D4
Aignan 28 C4
Aignay-le-Duc 26 C2
Aigoual, Mt 29 F3
Aigre 24 C4
Aigrefeuille-d'Aunis 24 B4
Aigrefeuille-sur-Maine 24 B3
Aigua Blava 32 C3
Aiguebelette 30 C1
Aiguebelle 31 D1
Aigueperse 26 A4
Aigues 30 C3
Aigues-Mortes 30 B4
Aigües Tortes, Parque Nac de . . 37 F2
Aiguilles 31 E2
Aiguillon 28 C3
Aiguillon, l' 24 B4
Aigurande 25 E4
Ailefroide 31 D2
Aillant 26 A1
Ailly-le-Haut-locher 19 E2
Ailly-sur-Noye 19 F2
Ailsa Craig 4 B3
Aimargues 30 B4
Aime 31 D1
Ain 27 D3
Ain (Dépt) 26 C4
Ainhoa 28 A4
Ainsa 37 E2
Ainsdale 6 B2
Ainzón 36 C3
Airaines 19 E2
Airasca 31 E2
Airdrie 4 C2
Aire R 7 D2
Aire 19 F1
Aire, l del 45 F2
Aire, Sa de 38 B3
Aire-sur-l'Adour . . . 28 B4
Airisto 107 D3
Airolo 58 A3
Airvault 24 C3
Aisne 20 A3
Aisne (Dépt) 20 A2
Aitana 45 E1
Aiterhofen 56 B2
Aitrach 55 E3
Aitzgorri 36 B1
Aiud 112 C4
Aix-d'Angillon, les . 26 A2
Aixe 29 D1
Aix-en-Othe 26 B1
Aix-en-Provence . . . 30 C4
Aix, l d' 24 B4
Aix-les-Bains 27 D4
Aizenay 24 B3
Aizkraukle 110 C3
Ajaccio 33 E4
Ajaureforsen 97 F3
Ajdanovac 77 D1
Ajdovščina 70 A2
Ajka 112 A4
Ajo 35 F1
Ajo, C de 36 A1
Ajos 99 D3
Ajtos 115 E2
Akarnaniká, Óri 82 C3

Äkäsjokisuu 95 D4
Äkäskero 95 D4
Akáslompolo 95 D4
Akçakoca 115 F3
Aken 53 D1
Åkersberga 106 B3
Åkershus 105 D3
Åkers styckebruk . . 106 B4
Akhisar 115 F4
Åkirkeby 109 D4
Akkajaure 94 B4
Akkerhaugen 104 C3
Akku 95 E3
Akranes 96 A1
Akráta 87 D1
Akréfnio 83 F4
Åkrehamn 104 A3
Akrestrømmen 100 C3
Akritas 79 D2
Akritas, Akr 86 C4
Akrogiáli 80 B3
Akropótamos 80 B3
Akrotíri 91 E1
Akrovoúni 80 C2
Akti Apólona 87 F2
Akujärvi 95 F3
Akureyri 96 B1
Ål 104 C2
Ala 60 C1
Alacant 45 E2
Ala di Stura 31 E1
Alá dei Sardi 66 B2
Alaejos 35 E4
Alagi 86 C3
Alagna Valsesia . . . 27 F4
Alagnon 29 F2
Alagón 37 D3
Alagón, R 39 D2
Alagonía 86 C3
Alahärmä 102 C2
Ala-Honkajoki 102 B3
Alaior 45 F2
Alajärvi 102 C2
Alakylä 99 D1
Alalkomenés 83 F4
Alamedilla 43 F3
Alameda 43 F3
Alamillo 43 F1
Alanás 101 F1
Åland 48 C3
Åland 106 C3
Alandroal 38 C4
Alange 39 D4
Alange, Emb de . . . 39 D4
Alanís 43 E2
Alapitkä 103 E2
Alaraz 39 E1
Alarcón 40 C3
Alarcón, Emb de . . . 40 C3
Alar del Rey 35 F3
Alaşehir 115 F4
Alassio 31 F3
Alastaro 107 D2
Alatoz 41 D4
Alatri 63 F3
Alavieska 102 C1
Ala-Vuokki 99 F4
Alavus 102 C2
Alba 31 F2
Alba Adriatica 64 A1
Albacete 40 C4
Albacken 101 F2
Alba de Tormes . . . 39 E1
Ålbæk 108 B1
Albaida, Pto de . . . 45 E1
Alba Iulia 114 C1
Albaladejo 44 B1
Albalate de Cinca . . 37 E3
Albalate del Arzobispo 37 D4
Albalate de las Nogueras 40 C2
Alban 29 E3
Albánchez 44 C3
Albano di Lucania . . 65 D4
Albano Laziale 63 E3
Albarca 37 F4
Albarella, I. 61 D1
Albares 35 D2
Albarracín 41 D2
Albarracín, Sa de . . 41 D2
Albatana 45 D1
Albatera 45 D2

Albena 115 E2
Albenga 31 F3
Albens 27 D4
Alberche, R 39 F2
Alberga 105 F4
Albergaria-a-Velha 38 B1
Alberique 41 E4
Albernoa 42 B1
Alberobello 65 E3
Albersdorf 48 A2
Albert 19 F2
Albert Kanaal 50 C3
Albertville 27 D4
Albestroff 21 E3
Albi 29 E3
Albiano 31 F1
Albinia 63 D2
Albisola Marina . . . 60 A3
Albocàcer 41 F2
Albolodúy 44 B3
Albolote 44 A3
Albo, M 66 C2
Alborea 41 D4
Ålborg 108 B2
Ålborg Bugt 108 B2
Albox 44 C3
Alburno, Mte 64 C4
Alburquerque 38 C3
Alby (F) 27 D4
Alby (S) 101 E3
Alcácer do Sal 42 A1
Alcáçovas 42 A1
Alcadozo 44 C1
Alcafozes 38 C2
Alcains 38 C2
Alcalá de Chivert . . 41 F2
Alcalá de Guadaira . 43 D3
Alcalá de Henares . 40 B2
Alcalá de la Selva . . 41 E2
Alcalá del Júcar . . . 41 D4
Alcalá de los Gazules 43 D4
Alcalá del Río 43 D2
Alcalá la Real 44 A3
Alcamo 68 B3
Alcampel 37 E3
Alcanadre, R 37 E3
Alcanar 41 F2
Alcanede 38 A3
Alcanena 38 B3
Alcanhões 38 B3
Alcañices 34 C4
Alcañiz 37 E4
Alcántara 39 D3
Alcántara, Emb de 39 D3
Alcantarilha 42 A2
Alcantarilla 45 D2
Alcaracejos 43 E1
Alcaraz 44 B1
Alcaraz, Sa de 44 C1
Alcaria do Cume . . 42 B2
Alcaria Ruiva 42 B2
Alcarrache, R 42 C1
Alcarràs 37 E4
Alcaudete 43 F3
Alcaudete de la Jara 39 F3
Alcázar de San Juan 40 B4
Alceda 35 F2
Alcester 9 E1
Alcoba 39 F4
Alcobaça 38 A3
Alcoba de los Montes 39 F4
Alcobendas 40 B2
Alcochete 38 A4
Alcoi 45 E1
Alcolea 43 F2
Alcolea de Cinca . . 37 E3
Alcolea del Pinar . . 36 B4
Alcolea del Río 43 E2
Alconchel 42 C1
Alcora 41 E3
Alcorisa 41 E2
Alcorlo, Emb de . . . 40 B1

Alcossebre 41 F3
Alcoutim 42 B2
Alcover 37 F4
Alcoy 45 E1
Alcubierre 37 D3
Alcubierre, Sa de . . 37 D3
Alcubilla de Avellaneda 36 A3
Alcublas 41 E3
Alcudia 45 F2
Alcudia de Guadix . 44 B3
Alcuéscar 39 D4
Aldeacentenera . . . 39 E3
Aldeadávila, Emb de 34 C4
Aldea del Cano 39 D3
Aldea del Fresno . . 40 A2
Aldea del Rey 44 A1
Aldeanueva de Ebro 36 C3
Aldeanueva de la Vera 39 E2
Aldeanueva del Camino 39 E2
Aldeburgh 11 E1
Alderney 18 A2
Aldershot 9 F3
Aldinci 77 E3
Aldocer 40 C2
Aledo 44 C2
Aleksandrovac (Srbija) 73 D3
Aleksandrovac (Srbija) 77 D1
Aleksa Šantić 72 B1
Aleksinac 73 E4
Alençon 23 F3
Alenquer 38 A3
Alentejo 42 B1
Alepohóri (Pelopónissos) 87 D2
Alepohóri (Stereá Eláda) 87 E1
Aléria 33 F3
Alès 30 B3
Ales 66 B3
Alesd 112 C4
Alessandria 60 A2
Alessandria d. Rocca 68 B3
Ålestrup 108 A2
Ålesund 100 A2
Aletschhorn 27 F3
Alexandria (GB) 4 C2
Alexándria (GR) . . . 79 F3
Alexandria (RO) . . . 115 D2
Alexandroúpoli 81 E2
Alf 51 E4
Alfajarín 37 D3
Alfambra (E) 41 D2
Alfambra (P) 42 A2
Alfambra, R 41 E2
Alfândega da Fé . . . 34 C4
Alfaro 36 C3
Alfarràs 37 E3
Alfaz del Pi 45 E1
Alfedena 64 C4
Alfeizerão 38 A3
Alfeld (Bayern) 55 F1
Alfeld (Niedersachsen) . . 52 B1
Alfiós 86 B2
Alfonsine 61 D2
Alfonso XIII, Emb de 44 C2
Alford (Grampian) . . . 3 E4
Alford (Lincs) 7 E3
Alfreton 7 D3
Alfta 101 F4
Algaida 45 F2
Algar 43 D4
Ålgård 104 A3
Algar de Palancia . . 41 E3
Algarinejo 43 F3
Algarrobo 43 F4
Algarve 42 B2
Algatocin 43 E4
Algeciras 43 D4
Algemesi 41 E4
Alghero 66 A2
Alginet 41 E4

Algodonales 43 E3
Algodor, R 40 A3
Algora 40 C1
Algorta 36 B1
Algoz 42 A2
Alhama de Almería 44 B3
Alhama de Aragón . 36 C4
Alhama de Granada 43 F3
Alhama de Murcia . . 45 D2
Alhambra 40 B4
Alhamilla, Sa 44 B4
Alhaurín el Grande . 43 E4
Alhóndiga 40 B2
Alía (E) 39 E3
Alia (I) 68 C3
Aliaga 41 E2
Aliaguilla 41 D3
Aliákmona, L 79 E4
Aliákmonas 79 E4
Aliartos 83 F4
Alibunar 73 D2
Alicante 45 E2
Alicudi, I 68 C3
Alicún de Ortega . . 44 B2
Alife 64 B3
Alijó 34 B4
Alikés 86 A1
Alikianós 90 B3
Aliki (Kikládes) 88 C3
Aliki (Thássos) 81 D3
Alimiá, N 93 E3
Alingsås 108 C1
Alinyà 32 A3
Alise-Ste-Reine . . . 26 B2
Aliste, R 35 D4
Alistráti 80 B2
Alì Terme 69 D2
Alivéri 84 B4
Aljezur 42 A2
Aljibe 43 D4
Aljucén 39 D4
Aljustrel 42 B1
Alkionidon, Kólpos . 87 E1
Alkmaar 16 C2
Allaire 23 D4
Allaman, M 76 C4
Allanche 29 E2
Alland 57 E3
Allariz 34 B3
Alleen 104 B4
Alleghe 59 D3
Allègre 29 F2
Allen, L 12 C2
Allensbach 55 D4
Allentsteig 57 E2
Allepuz 41 E2
Aller 48 A4
Allersberg 55 F1
Allershausen 55 F3
Alleuze 29 F2
Allevard 31 D1
Allier (Dépt) 26 A3
Allier R 26 A3
Allinge-Sandvig . . . 109 D4
Allo 36 C2
Alloa 5 D2
Allonnes 23 F4
Allos 31 D3
Allos, Col d' 31 D3
Alloza 41 E1
Allstedt 52 C2
Almacelles 37 E3
Almáchar 43 F3
Almada 38 A4
Almadén 39 F4
Almadén de la Plata 43 D2
Almadenejos 39 F4
Almagro 40 A4
Almajano 36 B3
Almansa 45 D1
Almansil 42 B3
Almanza 35 E2
Almanzora, R 44 B3
Almanzor, Pico 39 E2
Almaraz 39 E3
Almargen 43 E3
Almarza 36 B3
Almazán 36 B4
Almedinilla 43 F3

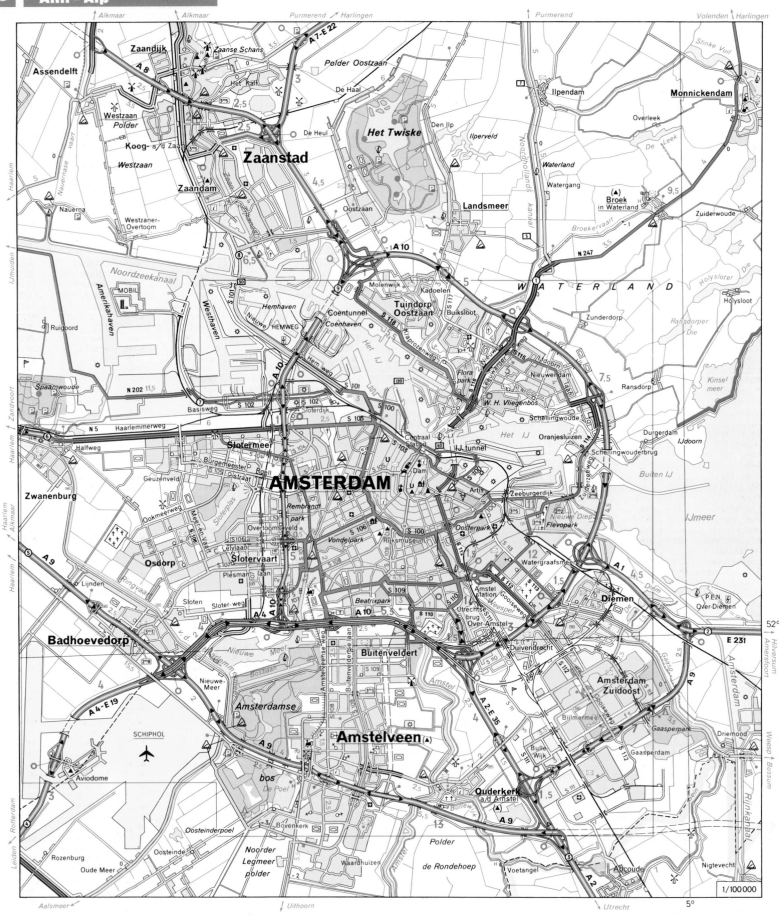

Almeida (E) 35 D4	Almendra, Emb de . . 35 D4	Almijara, Sa de 44 A3	Almodóvar del Pinar 40 C3	Almonacid de Toledo 40 A3	Almsee 56 C3	Alónissos, N 84 B2
Almeida (P) 39 D1	Almendral 38 C4	Almiri 87 E1			Almudébar 37 D3	Alora 43 E3
Almeirim 38 B3	Almendralejo 39 D4	Almiró 86 C3	Almodóvar del Río 43 E2	Almonacid de Zorita 40 B2	Almuñécar 44 A4	Alorines, Pto de . . . 45 D1
Almelo 17 D2	Almere-Stad. 16 C2	Almiropótamos 84 B4			Almuradiel 44 A1	Alosno 42 C2
Almenar 37 E3	Almeria 44 B4	Almirós 83 F2	Almogia 43 F3	Almonaster la Real . 42 C2	Alness 2 C3	Alost 50 B3
Almenara 41 E3	Almeria, G de 44 B4	Almiróu, Órmos 90 C3	Almoguera 40 B2	Almonte 42 C3	Alnö 101 F3	Alozaina 43 E4
Almenaras 44 B1	Almerimar 44 B4	Almodóvar 42 B2	Almoharin 39 D4	Almoradi 45 D2	Alnwick 5 E3	Alp 32 A3
Almenara, Sa de la . . 44 C3	Almese 31 E1	Almodóvar del Campo 43 F1	Almonacid de la Sierra 36 C4	Almorox 40 A2	Alónia 79 F3	Alpalhão 38 C3
Almenar de Soria . . . 36 B3	Älmhult 109 D2			Almourol 38 B3	Alónissos 84 B2	Alpbach 59 D1

Alpe-d'Huez, l' 31 D1
Alpedrinha 38 C2
Alpera 41 D4
Alpes-de-Haute-Provence 31 D3
Alpes-Maritimes 31 E3
Alpe Veglia 58 A3
Alphen aan den Rijn 16 C3
Alpi Apuane 60 B3
Alpiarça 38 B3
Alpignano 31 E1
Alpi Orobie 58 B3
Alpirsbach 54 C3
Alpua 99 D4
Alqueva 42 B1
Alqueva, Bgem de 42 B1
Alquézar 37 E3
Als 108 B2
Als (Reg) 108 B4
Alsasua 36 B2
Alsdorf 17 D4
Alsen 101 E2
Alsfeld 52 A3
Alstahaug 97 D3
Alston 5 E4
Alta 95 D2
Altaelva 95 D2
Altafjorden 95 D2
Altamura 65 D3
Alta, Sa 41 D2
Altastenberg 17 F4
Altaussee 56 C3
Altavilla 68 B3
Altdöbern 53 E1
Altdorf (CH) 58 A2
Altdorf (D) 55 F1
Altea 45 E1
Altedo 61 D2
Altena 17 E4
Altenau 52 B2
Altenberg 53 E3
Altenberge 17 E3
Altenburg 53 D3
Altenholz 48 A1
Altenhundem 17 F4
Altenkirchen (Mecklenburg-Vorpommern) 49 D1
Altenkirchen (Rheinland-Pfalz) 51 E3
Altenmarkt (D) 56 B3
Altenmarkt (Salzburg) 59 F1
Altenmarkt (Steiermark) 57 D3
Altenstadt 55 E3
Altensteig 54 C3
Altentreptow 49 D2
Altenwalde 47 F2
Alte Oder 49 E3
Alter do Chão 38 C3
Altglashütten 54 C4
Altheim 56 C3
Althofen 70 B1
Altkirch 27 E1
Altlandsberg 49 E4
Altlengbach 57 E2
Altmühl 55 F2
Altmühlsee 55 E2
Altmünster 56 C3
Altnaharra 2 C2
Alto Campó 35 F2
Alto Cruz 36 C4
Alto de Allariz 34 B3
Alto de Barazar 36 B1
Alto de Covelo 34 C3
Alto de Estividas 34 B3
Alto de Fumaces 34 B3
Alto del Couso 34 B3
Alto del Portalé 37 E4
Alto del Rodicio 34 B3
Alto de Santo Domingo 34 B2
Alto del Cañizo 34 C3
Alto Laza 37 D2
Alto Lindoso, Bgem do 34 B3
Altomira 40 B2
Alton 9 F3

Altopascio 60 C3
Alto Rabagão, Bgem do 34 B3
Altorricon 37 E3
Altotero 36 A2
Altötting 56 B3
Altrincham 6 C2
Alt Ruppin 49 D3
Altshausen 55 D4
Altstätten 58 B2
Altura 41 E3
Alustante 41 D2
Alva 4 C2
Alvaiázere 38 B2
Alvalade 42 A1
Alvão, Sa de 34 B4
Alva, R. 38 B2
Alvdal 100 C3
Älvdalen 101 E4
Alvelos, Sa de 38 B2
Alverca do Ribatejo 38 A4
Alvesta 109 D2
Alvignac 29 D2
Ålvik 104 B2
Alvito 42 B1
Alvito, Bgem do 42 B1
Älvkarleby 106 B2
Alvor 42 A2
Älvros 101 E3
Älvsborgs Län 108 C1
Älvsbyn 98 B3
Alyth 5 D1
Alytus 110 C4
Alz 56 B3
Alzenau 52 A4
Alzey 54 C1
Alzira 41 E4
Alzola 36 B1
Alzon 29 F3
Alzonne 32 B1
Amadora 38 A4
Åmål 105 E4
Amalfi 64 B4
Amaliáda 86 B1
Amaliápoli 83 F2
Amálo 89 D2
Amance 27 D1
Amancey 27 D2
Amandola 61 F4
Amantea 67 E3
Amárandos (Ípiros) 78 C4
Amárandos (Thessalia) 83 D2
Amarante 34 B4
Amareleja 42 C1
Amares 34 A4
Amárinthos 84 B4
Amatrice 63 F1
Amay 50 C4
Amaya 35 F3
Ambarès-et-Lagrave 28 B2
Ambasaguas 35 E2
Ambazac 25 E4
Ambelákia (Thessalia) 83 E1
Ambelákia (Thráki) 81 F1
Ambelia 83 E2
Ambelikó 85 F3
Ambelióna 86 C2
Ambelónas 83 E1
Amberg 55 F1
Ambérieu-en-Bugey 26 C4
Ambert 29 F1
Ambès 28 B2
Ambierle 26 B4
Amble 5 E3
Ambleside 5 D4
Amblève 51 D4
Amboise 25 D2
Ambra 61 D4
Ambrières-les-Vallées 18 C4
Ameixial 42 B2
Ameland 16 C1
Amelia 63 E2
Amélie-les-Bains-Palalda 32 B3
Amelinghausen 48 B3
Amer 32 B3

A Merca 34 B3
Amerongen 16 C3
Amersfoort 16 C3
Amersham 9 F2
Amesbury 9 E3
A Mezquita 34 C3
Amfiaraío 84 B4
Amfíklia 83 E3
Amfilohía 82 C3
Amfípoli 80 B2
Ámfissa 83 E4
Amiata, Mont' 63 D1
Amiens 19 F2
Amigdaleónas 80 C2
Amigdaliá 83 E4
Amíndeo 79 D3
Åmli 104 B4
Amlwch 6 A2
Ammanford 8 C2
Ämmänsaari 99 E3
Ammarfjället 97 F3
Ammarnäs 97 F3
Ammel 56 A4
Ammersattel 55 F4
Ammersee 56 A3
Amohóri 79 D3
Amoliani 80 B4
Amorbach 55 D1
Amorebieta 36 B1
Amorgós 89 D3
Amorgós, N 89 D3
Amório 81 F1
Åmot (Buskerud) 104 C3
Åmot (S) 105 F2
Åmot (Telemark) 104 B3
Åmotfors 105 D3
Amótopos 82 C2
Amou 28 B4
Amoudára 91 D3
Amoudára 91 E4
Amoúdia 89 D2
Ampezzo 59 E3
Ampfing 56 B3
Amphion 27 D3
Amplepuis 26 B4
Amposta 41 F2
Ampthill 9 F2
Ampudia 35 E4
Ampuero 36 A1
Amriswil 58 B1
Amrum 47 F1
Amsele 98 B4
Amstelveen 16 C2
Amsterdam 16 C2
Amstetten 57 D3
Amungen 101 E4
Amurrio 36 B1
Amusco 35 F3
Amvrakia, L. 82 C3
Amvrakikós Kólpos 82 C3
Anadia 38 B1
Anáfi 91 E1
Anáfi, N 91 F1
Anafonítria 86 A1
Anagni 63 F3
Anáktora Néstoros 86 B3
Análipsi 83 F4
Análipsi 92 C1
Análipsis 86 C3
Anan'iv 113 E3
Anaráhi 79 D3
Anárgiri 79 D3
Anáscaul 14 A3
Åna Sira 104 A4
Anatolí (Ípiros) 82 C1
Anatolí (Kríti) 91 E4
Anatolí (Thessalia) 83 F1
Anatolikó 79 D3
Anatolikí Rodópi 81 D2
Anättijärvi 99 F4
Anávatos 85 E4
Anávissos 87 F2
Anávra (Karditsa) 83 E2
Anávra (Magnissia) 83 E3
An Cabhán 13 C3
Ancares, Sa de 34 C2
Ancenis 23 D4
Ancerville 20 C4
Anchuras 39 F3
An Clochán 12 A3

An Cóbh 14 C4
Ancona 61 F3
Ancy-le-Franc 26 B1
Anda 100 A3
Andalo 58 C3
Åndalsnes 100 B3
Andalucía 43 E2
Andarax, R. 44 B3
Andartikó 79 D2
Andebu 104 C3
Andelot 26 C1
Andelys, les 19 E3
Andenes 94 A3
Andenne 50 C4
Anderlues 50 B4
Andermatt 58 A3
Andernach 51 E4
Andernos 28 A2
Anderstorp 109 D2
Andfjorden 94 B3
Andigonos 79 D3
Andikira 83 E4
Andikiras, Kólpos 83 E4
Andikithira, N. 90 A2
Andimáhia 89 F3
Andímilos, N 88 A4
Andinitsa 83 E3
Andiparos 88 B3
Andiparos, N 88 B3
Andipaxi, N. 82 B2
Andipsara, N 85 E4
Andírio 83 D4
Ándissa 85 E2
Andoain 36 C1
Andorno Micca 31 F1
Andorra 41 E1
Andorra la Vella 32 A2
Andosilla 36 C2
Andover 9 E3
Andøya 94 A3
Andratx 45 E3
Andravída 86 B1
Andretta 64 C3
Andrézieux-Bouthéon 30 B1
Andria 65 D3
Andrijevica 76 C2
Andrítsena 86 C2
Andros 88 B1
Ándros, N. 88 B1
Androússa 86 C3
Andselv 94 B3
Andújar 43 F2
Anduze 30 B3
Aneby 109 D1
Ånes 100 B3
Anet 19 E4
Aneto, Pico de 37 E2
Angáli 84 A3
Ånge (Jämtlands Län) 101 E2
Ånge (Västernorrlands Län) 101 E3
Ängelholm 108 C3
Angeli 95 E3
Angelohóri 79 E3
Angelókastro (Pelopónnissos) 87 E2
Angelókastro (Stereá Eláda) 82 C4
Anger 57 E4
Angera 58 A4
Ängermanälven 101 F2
Angermünde 49 E3
Angern 57 F2
Angers 23 E4
Angerville 25 E1
Angístis, Stathmós 80 B2
Angístri 87 E2
Angístri, N. 87 E2
Angístro 80 B1
Angitis 80 B2
Angle 25 D3
Anglès (E) 32 B3
Anglès (F) 32 B1
Anglesey, I of 6 A2
Anglesola 37 F3
Anglet 28 A4
Anglure 20 B4
Angoulême 28 C1

Angri 64 B4
Ängsö 106 C3
Angüés 37 E3
Anguiano 36 B2
Anguillara Veneta 61 D1
Angvik 100 B2
Anholt 108 C2
Aniane 30 A4
Aniche 20 A1
Anina 63 F2
Anixi 79 D4
Anizy-le-Château 20 A3
Anjalankoski 107 F2
Anjum 47 D3
Ankaran 70 A3
Ankarsrum 109 E1
Anklam 49 E2
Ankogel 59 E2
An Longfort 12 C3
An Muileann gCearr 13 D3
Ånn 101 D2
Ånn L. 101 D2
Annaberg 57 D3
Annaberg-Buchholz 53 E3
Annaburg 53 E1
Annan 5 D3
Annan R. 5 D3
Anndalsvågen 97 D3
Annecy 27 D4
Annemasse 27 D4
Annevoie-Rouillon 50 C4
Annonay 30 B1
Annone Veneto 59 E4
Annot 31 D3
Annweiler 54 C2
Áno Drossini 81 E2
Áno Hóra 83 D4
Anógia 87 D3
Anógia 91 D3
Anoia, R. 32 A4
Áno Kalendíni 82 C2
Áno Kaliniki 79 D2
Áno Kómi 79 E4
Áno Lefkími 82 A2
Áno Melás 79 D3
Áno Merá 88 C3
Anópoli 90 C4
Áno Polidéndri 83 F1
Áno Poróïa 80 A2
Áno Rodákino 90 C4
Áno Sangrí 88 C3
Áno Siros 88 B2
Añover de Tajo 40 A3
Áno Viános 91 E4
Áno Vrondoú 80 B1
Áno Zervohóri 79 E3
Ansbach 55 E1
Anse 26 C4
Ansedonia 63 D2
Ansião 38 B2
Ansnes 100 C1
Ansó 37 D2
Anstruther 5 D2
Antas 44 C3
Antegnate 60 B1
Antemil 34 A1
Antequera 43 F3
Anterselva 59 D2
Ånthia 81 E2
Ánthili 83 E3
Antholz 59 D2
Anthótopos 83 E2
Antibes 31 E4
Antifer, Cap d' 19 D3
An tInbhear Mór 15 E3
Antnäs 98 C3
Antraigues 30 B2
Antrain 18 B4
Antrim 13 E2
Antrim Coast 13 E1
Antrim Mts 13 E1
Antrodoco 63 F2
Anttola 103 E3
Antwerpen 50 B3
Antwerpen (Prov) 50 B3
An Uaimh 13 D3
Anvers 50 B3
Anzano di Puglia 64 C3

Anzio 63 E3
Anzola d'Ossola 58 A4
Anzy-le-Duc 26 B4
Aóos 78 C4
Aosta 27 E4
Aoste 27 E4
Apatin 72 B2
Apatovac 71 D2
Apecchio 61 E4
Apeldoorn 17 D2
Apen 47 E3
Apéri 93 D3
Aphrodísias 115 F4
Apidiá 87 D3
Apíkia 88 B1
Apolakiá 93 E2
Apolitáres, Akr. 90 A2
Apólonas 88 C3
Apolonía (Kikládes) 88 B3
Apolonía (Makedonía) 80 B3
A Pontenova Villaodriz 34 C1
Apóstoli 90 C4
Äppelbo 105 E2
Appenweier 54 C3
Appenzell 58 B2
Appiano 59 D3
Appingedam 47 D3
Appleby 5 D4
Aprica 58 C3
Apricena 64 C2
Aprilia 63 E3
Apt 30 C3
Áptera 90 C3
Aquileia 59 F3
Aquitaine, L' 25 C2
Arabba 59 D3
Aracena 42 C2
Aracena, Emb de 43 D2
Aracena, Sa de 42 C2
Aračinovo 77 E3
Arada, Sa de 38 B1
Aragona 68 B4
Aragón, R 36 C2
Aragón 37 D3
Arahnéo, Óros 87 E2
Árahova (Etolía-Akarnanía) 83 D4
Árahova (Viotía) 83 E4
Arákinthos, Óros 83 D4
A Ramallosa 34 A3
Aramits 37 D1
Aran I 12 C1
Aran Is 12 A4
Aranjuez 40 B2
Arantzazu 36 B1
Aran, Vall d' 37 F2
Araquil, R. 36 C2
Aras de Alpuente 41 D3
Arasluokta 97 F1
Árahthos 82 C2
Áratos 81 E2
Aravaca 40 A2
Aravis, Col des 27 D4
Aravissós 79 E2
Arazede 38 B2
Arba, R. 36 C3
Arbatax 66 C3
Arbeca 37 F4
Arbesbach 57 D2
Arboga 105 F3
Arbois 27 D3
Arbón, Emb de 34 C1
Arborea 66 B3
Arbório 31 F1
Arbrå 101 E4
Arbresle, l' 26 B4
Arbroath 5 E1
Arbúcies 32 B4
Arbus 66 B3
Arc 31 D1

Arcachon 28 A2
Arce 64 A3
Arcen 17 D3
Arc-en-Barrois 26 C1
Arceniega 36 A1
Arcevia 61 E4
Archena 45 D2
Arches 27 D1
Archiac 28 B1
Archidona 43 F3
Arcidosso 63 D1
Arcipelago Toscano 62 B1
Arcis 20 B4
Arco 58 C4
Arco de Baúlhe 34 B4
Arcos 35 F3
Arcos de Jalón 36 B4
Arcos de la Frontera 43 D3
Arcos de Valdevez 34 A3
Arcouest, Pte de l' 22 C2
Arcs, les (Savoie) 31 D1
Arcs, les (Var) 31 D4
Arcusa 37 E2
Arcyz 113 E4
Arda 115 E3
Ardales 43 E3
Årdalstangen 104 B1
Ardánio 81 F2
Ardara 12 C1
Árdas 81 F1
Ardbeg 4 B2
Ardèche (Dépt) 30 B2
Ardèche R. 30 B2
Ardèche, Gges de l' 30 B3
Ardee 13 D3
Ardennes (Dépt) 20 B3
Ardennes, Canal des 20 C3
Ardentes 25 E3
Ardentinny 4 C2
Ardes 29 F1
Ardez 58 B2
Ardglass 13 E2
Ardila, R. 42 C1
Ardila, Rib de 42 C1
Ardisa 37 D3
Ardlussa 4 B1
Ardmore 14 C4
Ardrahan 12 B4
Ardres 19 E1
Ardrishaig 4 B2
Ardrossan 4 C2
Ards Pen 13 E2
Arduaine 4 B1
Ardvasar 2 B4
Åre 101 D2
Arenas de Cabrales 35 E2
Arenas de Iguña 35 F2
Arenas de San Juan 40 B4
Arenas de San Pedro 39 F2
Arendal 104 C4
Arendonk 50 C3
Arendsee 48 C3
Arenos, Emb de 41 E3
Arenys de Mar 32 B4
Arenzano 60 A3
Areópoli 87 D4
Arès 28 A2
Ares (Galicia) 34 B1
Ares (Valencia) 41 E2
Ares, Col des 37 F2
Ares, Pto de 32 B3
Åreskutan 101 D2
Aréthoussa 80 B3
Aretí 80 A3
Arévalo 39 F1
Arez 38 C3
Arezzo 61 D4
Arfará 86 C3
Argalastí 83 F2
Argamasilla de Alba 40 B4
Argamasilla de Calatrava 44 A1
Arganda 40 B2
Arganil 38 B2
Arga, R. 36 C2

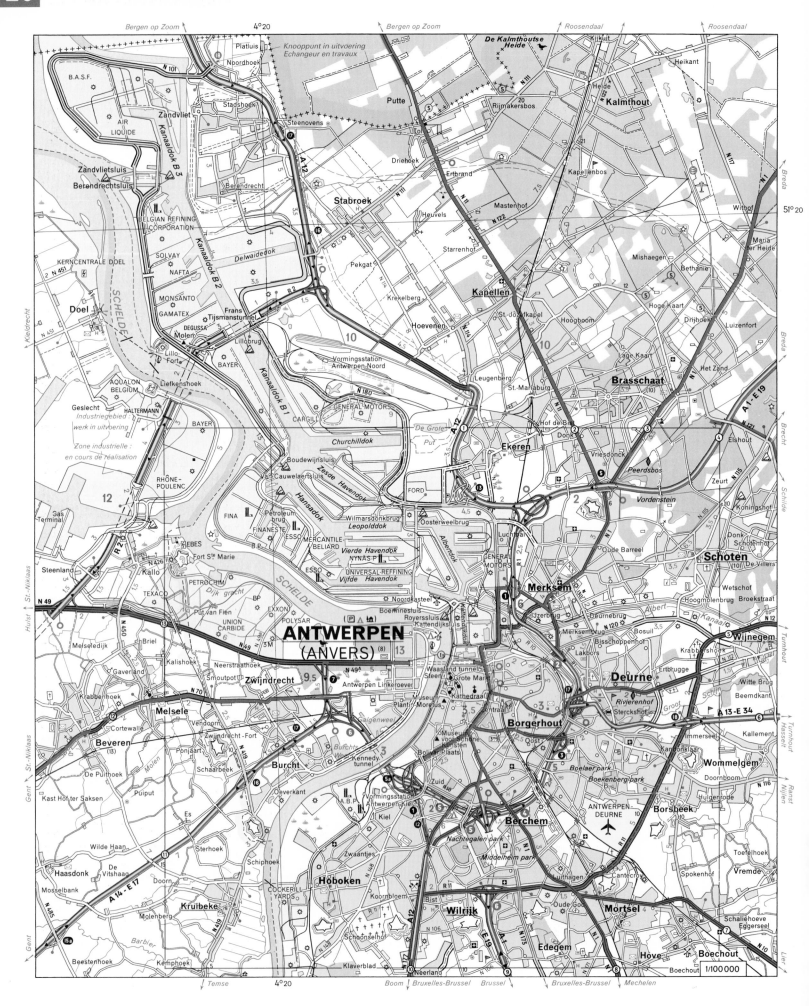

Argássi 86 A2
Argelès 32 B2
Argelès-Gazost . . . 37 E1
Argens 31 D4
Argent 25 F2
Argenta 61 D2
Argentan 19 D4
Argentario, Mte 63 D2
Argentat 29 D2
Argente 41 D2
Argentera 31 E3
Argentière 27 E4
Argentière-la-
  Bessée, l' 31 D2
Argentona 32 B4
Argenton-
  Château 24 C3
Argenton-sur-
  Creuse 25 E3
Argentré-du-
  Plessis 23 E3
Arginónda 89 F3
Argirádes 82 A2
Argiró 84 B4
Argiropoúlio 83 E1
Argiroúpoli 90 C3
Argithéa 83 D2
Argolida 87 E2
Argolikós Kólpos . . . 87 E2
Árgos 87 D2
Árgos Orestikó 79 D3
Argos, R 44 C2
Argostóli 82 B4
Arguedas 36 C3
Argueil 19 E3
Arguellite 44 B1
Arguis 37 D2
Argyll 4 B1
Argyll Forest Park . . 4 C2
Arhánes 91 D4
Arhángelos
  (Makedonia) . . . 79 E2
Arhángelos
  (Ródos) 93 F1
Arhéa Epidavros . . . 87 E2
Arhéa Kleonés 87 D1
Arhéa Kórinthos . . . 87 E1
Arhéa Neméa 87 D1
Arhéa Olympía 86 C2
Arhéa Thíra 91 E1
Århus 108 B3
Arianá 81 E2
Ariano Irpino 64 B3
Ariano nel
  Polesine 61 D2
Aridéa 79 E2
Ariège (Dépt) 32 A2
Ariège R 32 A2
Arija 35 F2
Arild 108 C3
Arilje 72 C4
Arinagour 2 B4
Arini 86 C2
Ariño 37 D4
Arinthod 27 D3
Arisaig 2 B4
Arisaig, Sd of 2 B4
Aristi 78 C4
Aristoménis 86 C3
Arisvi 81 E2
Aritzo 66 B3
Arive 36 C2
Ariza 36 B4
Årjäng 105 D3
Arjeplog 98 A3
Arjona 44 A2
Arkádi 91 D3
Arkadía 86 C2
Arkaig, L 2 C4
Arkalohóri 91 E4
Arkássa 93 D3
Arkessíni 89 D3
Arkí, N 89 E2
Arkitsa 83 F3
Arklow 15 E3
Arkona, Kap 49 D1
Arkoúdi, N 82 B4

Arlaban, Pto de 36 B1
Arlanc 29 F1
Arlanda 106 B3
Arlanza, R 36 A3
Arlanzón 36 A2
Arlanzón, R 35 F3
Arlber**gpaß** 58 B2
Arlberg-
  Straßentunnel . . . 58 B2
Arlempdes 30 A2
Arles (Bouches-du-
  Rhône) 30 B4
Arles (Pyrénées-
  Orientales) 32 B3
Arlesheim 27 E2
Arlon 21 D2
Arlsleben 52 C2
Armação
  de Pêra 42 A3
Armadale 5 D2
Arma di Taggia 31 F3
Armagh 13 D2
Armagh (Co) 13 D2
Armamar 34 B4
Arméni 90 C3
Armenii 86 C3
Armenistís 89 D3
Armentières 19 F1
Armilla 44 A3
Armólia 85 E4
Armunia 35 D3
Árna 87 D3
Arnac-
  Pompadour 29 D1
Arnay-le-Duc 26 B2
Arnéa 80 B2
Arneburg 48 C4
Arnedillo 36 B3
Arnedo 36 C3
Arnes 41 F2
Årnes 105 D3
Arnhem 17 D3
Arni 60 B3
Árnissa 79 D3
Arno 60 C4
Arnoldstein 59 F2
Arnon 25 F3
Arnøy 94 C2
Arnsberg 17 F3
Arnstadt 52 C3
Arnstein 52 B4
Aroania, Óri 86 C1
Aroche 42 C2
Aroche Mt 42 C1
Arogi 81 D2
Arolsen 52 A2
Arona 58 A4
Aroniádika 90 A1
Aronkylä 102 B3
Åros 104 C3
Arosa 58 B2
Arouca 38 B1
Arousa, I de 34 A2
Årøysund 104 C3
Arpajon 19 F4
Arpela 99 D3
Arquata del
  Tronto 63 F1
Arques (Pas-de-
  Calais) 19 F1
Arques (Seine-
  Maritime) 19 E2
Arquillos 44 A2
Arrabal 34 A3
Arrábida, Sa da 38 A4
Arracourt 21 D4
Arraiolos 38 B4
Arran 4 B2
Arras 19 F2
Arrasate-
  Mondragon 36 B1
Arreau 37 E2
Arrecife 42 C4
Arredondo 36 A1
Arrée, Mts d' 22 B2
Arrens 37 E2
Arrifana 38 C1

Arrigorriaga 36 B1
Arriondas 35 E1
Arrochar 4 C2
Arromanches 18 C3
Arronches 38 C4
Arroux 26 B3
Arrow, L 12 C2
Arroyo de la Luz . . . 39 D3
Arroyo del Ojanco . . 44 B1
Arroyo de San
  Serván 39 D4
Arroyomolinos de
  León 43 D1
Arroyomolinos de
  Montánchez 39 D4
Arruda dos Vinhos . . 38 A3
Års 108 A2
Ars (Charente-
  Maritime) 24 B4
Ars (Moselle) 21 D3
Arsiè 59 D3
Arsiero 59 D4
Års Kógssanður . . . 96 B1
Arsunda 106 B2
Arsy 19 F3
Artà 45 F2
Árta 82 C2
Artajona 36 C2
Árta (Nomos) 82 C2
Arta Terme 59 E3
Arteaga, G de 36 B1
Artemíssia 86 C3
Artemíssio (Évia) . . 83 F3
Artemísio
  (Pelopónissos) . . 87 D2
Artemónas 88 B3
Artena 63 F3
Artenay 25 E1
Artern 52 C2
Artesa de Segre . . . 37 F3
Artessianó 83 D2
Artfjället 97 E3
Arth (CH) 58 A2
Arth (D) 56 B2
Arthurstown 15 D4
Arties 37 F2
Artjärvi 107 F2
Artotína 83 D3
Artruix, C de 45 F2
A Rúa 34 C3
Arucas 42 B4
Arudy 37 D1
Arundel 9 F3
Arve 27 E4
Árvi 91 E4
Arvidsjaur 98 A3
Árvik 100 A2
Arvika 105 E3
Árviksand 94 C2
Arzachena 66 B1
Arzacq-Arraziguet . . 28 B4
Arzano 22 B3
Arzano 75 E1
Arzberg 53 D4
Arzignano 60 C1
Árzos 81 F1
Arzúa 34 B2
As 50 C3
Aš 53 D4
Åsa 108 C2
Asamati 77 D4
Åsarna 101 E2
Åsarp 109 D1
Ascain 28 A4
Ascha 56 B2
Aschach 56 C2
Aschaffenburg 52 A4
Aschau 56 B3
Ascheberg (Nordrhein-
  Westfalen) 17 E3
Ascheberg (Schleswig-
  Holstein) 48 B2
Aschendorf 17 E1
Aschersleben 52 C2
Asciano 61 D4
Ascione, Colle d' . . . 67 F3

Asco 33 F3
Ascó 37 E4
Ascoli Piceno 63 F1
Ascoli Satriano 64 C3
Ascona 58 A3
Åse 94 A3
Åseda 109 E2
Åsele 101 F1
Åsen 101 D1
Asenovgrad 115 D3
Åseral 104 B4
Asfáka 82 B1
Asfeld 20 B3
Åsgårdstrand 104 C3
Ashbourne (GB) . . . 6 C3
Ashbourne (IRL) . . . 13 D3
Ashburton 8 C4
Ashby de la Zouch . . 6 C3
Ashford 11 D3
Ashington 5 E3
Ashton-under-
  Lyne 6 C2
Asiago 59 D4
Asikkala 107 F2
Asín 37 D3
Asinara, G dell' 66 B1
Asinara, I 66 A1
Ask 105 D3
Askainen 107 D2
Askeaton 14 B3
Askersund 105 F4
Askífou 90 C3
Askim 105 D3
Áskio, Óros 79 D3
Askja 96 C2
Asklipiío
  (Dodekánissa) . . 89 F3
Asklipiío (Ródos) . . . 93 E2
Askola 107 F2
Askós 80 A3
Askøy 104 A2
Askvoll 104 A1
Asmunti 99 D3
Asnæs 108 B3
Asnen 109 D2
As Neves 34 A3
Asola 60 B1
Asolo 59 D4
Aspang 57 F3
Aspatria 5 D4
Aspe 45 D2
Aspe, Gave d' 37 D1
Asperg 55 D2
Aspet 37 F2
Aspin, Col d' 37 E2
As Ponte de Garcia
  Rodriguez 34 B1
Áspra Spítia 83 E4
Aspres 30 C2
Áspro 79 E3
Aspróhoma 86 C3
Asprókavos, Akr . . . 82 A2
Aspromonte 67 E4
Asprópirgos 87 F1
Asprovålta 80 B3
Asse 50 B3
Assemini 66 B4
Assen 17 D1
Assens 108 B3
Assergi 63 F2
Assini 87 E2
Assisi 63 E1
Aßmannshausen . . 51 F4
Assomáton 91 D3
Assopía 84 A4
Assopós
  (Korinthía) 87 D1
Assopós
  (Lakonía) 87 E4
Assopós R 87 E1
Ássos (Ípiros) 82 B2
Ássos (Kefaloniá) . . 82 B4
Astaffort 28 C3
Astafjorden 94 B3
Astakída, N 93 D2
Astakós 82 C4
Asten 57 D3

Asti 31 F2
Astipálea 92 C1
Astipálea, N 92 C1
Astorga 35 D3
Åstorp 108 C3
Ástros 87 D2
Astudillo 35 F3
Asturias 34 C2
Asvestádes 81 F1
Asvestohóri 82 B1
Asvestópetra 79 D3
Atalaia 38 A3
Ataländi 83 F3
Atalaya de la
  Calzada 44 A1
Atalayassa 45 D4
Átali 84 B3
Ataquines 39 F1
Atarfe 44 A3
Atáviros 93 E2
Ateca 36 C4
Atella 64 C3
Atessa 64 B2
Ath 50 B4
Athamánon, Óri . . . 82 C2
Athánio 82 B3
Athboy 13 D3
Athenry 12 B3
Athéras 89 D2
Athéras, Akr 82 B4
Atherstone 9 E1
Athína 87 F1
Athinai 79 F2
Athlone 12 C3
Áthos 80 C4
Athy 13 D4
Atienza 36 B4
Atikí-Piréas 87 F1
Atina 64 A3
Atokos, N 82 C4
Atouguia da Baleia . . 38 A3
Ätran 108 C2
Ätran R 108 C2
Atri 64 A1
Atsikí 85 D1
Attendorn 17 F4
Attersee 56 C3
Attersee L 56 C3
Attigliano 63 E2
Attigny 20 B3
Attleborough 11 D1
Attnang 56 C3
Åtvidaberg 109 E1
Au 55 F2
Aub 55 E1
Aubagne 30 C4
Aubange 21 D2
Aube 20 B4
Aube (Dépt) 20 B4
Aubenas 30 B2
Aubenton 20 B2
Auberive 26 C1
Aubeterre 28 C1
Aubigny (Cher) 25 F2
Aubigny (Pas-de-
  Calais) 19 F2
Aubin 29 E3
Aubisque, Col d' . . . 37 E1
Aubonne 27 D3
Aubrac 29 F2
Aubrac, Mts d' 29 F2
Aubusson 25 F4
Auch 28 C4
Auchencairn 4 C3
Auchterarder 5 D1
Auchtermuchty 5 D1
Aude (Dépt) 32 B2
Aude R 32 B1
Audenge 28 A2
Audeux 27 D2
Audierne 22 A3
Audincourt 27 E2
Audlem 6 C3
Audruicq 19 F1
Audun-le-Roman . . 21 D3
Audun-le-Tiche 21 D3
Aue 53 D3
Aue R 48 A4

Aue 53 D3
Auer 59 D3
Auerbach (Bayern) . . 55 F1
Auerbach (Sachsen) . . 53 D3
Auffach 59 D1
Aughnacloy 13 D2
Aughrim 13 D4
Augsburg 55 F3
Augusta 69 D4
Augustenborg 108 B4
Augustów 110 C3
Augustusburg 53 E3
Aukan 100 B2
Aukra 100 B2
Aulanko 107 E2
Auletta 64 C4
Aulla 60 B3
Aullène 33 F4
Aulnay 24 C4
Aulne 22 B3
Aulnoye-Aymeries . . 20 B2
Aulus-les-Bains . . . 37 F2
Auma 53 D3
Aumale 19 E2
Aumetz 21 D3
Aumont-Aubrac . . . 29 F2
Aunay-sur-Odon . . 18 C3
Auneau 19 E4
Auneuil 19 E3
Auning 108 B2
Aups 31 D4
Aura 107 D2
Aurajoki 107 D2
Auray 22 C4
Aurdal 104 C2
Aure 100 B2
Aurich 47 E3
Aurignac 37 F1
Aurillac 29 E2
Aurland 104 B2
Auron 31 E3
Auronzo di
  Cadore 59 E2
Auros 28 B3
Aursjøen 100 B3
Aursuden 101 D2
Ausonia 64 A3
Außernbrünst 56 C2
Ausso Corno 59 F3
Aust-Agder 104 B4
Austbygd 104 C3
Austvågøy 94 A3
Auterive 37 F1
Authie 19 F2
Autol 36 C3
Autrans 30 C1
Autrey 26 C2
Auttoinen 107 E1
Autun 26 B3
Auvézère 28 C2
Auvillar 28 C3
Auxerre 26 A1
Auxi-le-Château . . . 19 E2
Auxonne 26 C2
Auzances 25 F4
Auzon 29 F1
Availles-
  Limouzine 25 D4
Avala 73 D3
Avaldsnes 104 A3
Avallon 26 B2
Avaloirs, Mt des . . . 23 E3
Ávas 81 E2
Avaviken 98 A3
Ávdira 81 D2
Avebury 9 E2
Aveiras de Cima . . . 38 A3
Aveiro 38 B1
Aveiro, R de 38 B1
Avellino 64 B4
Aven Armand 29 F3
Aven d'Orgnac 30 B3
Averøya 100 B2
Aversa 64 B4

Avesnes 20 B2
Avesnes-le-Comte . . 19 F2
Avesta 105 F3
Avetrana 65 E4
Aveyron 29 D3
Aveyron (Dépt) 29 E3
Avezzano 63 F2
Avgerinós 79 D4
Avgó 82 C2
Avía 86 C3
Aviano 59 E3
Aviémonas 90 A2
Aviemore 3 D4
Aviés 79 E4
Avigliana 31 E1
Avigliano 64 C4
Avignon 30 B3
Ávila 39 F2
Ávila, Sa de 39 F2
Avilés 35 D1
Aviño 34 B1
Avintes 34 A4
Avión 34 B2
Avioth 20 C3
Avis 38 B4
Avisio 59 D3
Avize 20 B3
Avláki 89 E1
Avlí 80 C2
Avliótes 82 A1
Avlóna 84 B4
Avlum 108 A2
Avola 69 D4
Avon (Co) 9 D2
Avon R (Hants) 9 E1
Avon R (Warw) 9 E3
Avonmouth 9 D2
Avord 25 F3
Avoriaz 27 E4
Avranches 18 B4
Avre 19 D4
Avtovac 76 A2
Awe, L 4 B1
Axams 59 D2
Axat 32 B2
Axiohóri 79 F2
Axiós 79 F2
Axioúpoli 79 F2
Ax-les-Thermes . . . 32 A2
Axminster 9 D3
Axós 91 D3
Ay 20 B3
Ayamonte 42 B2
Ayedo 36 B3
Ayerbe 37 D3
Aylesbury 9 F2
Ayllón 36 A4
Ayllón, Sa de 36 A4
Aylsham 7 F3
Ayna 44 C1
Ayora 41 D4
Ayr 4 C3
Ayre, Pt of 6 A1
Ayvacık 115 E4
Ayvalık 115 E4
Aywaille 51 D4
Azáceta, Pto de . . . 36 B2
Azaila 37 D4
Azambuja 38 A3
Azanja 73 D3
Azaruja 38 B4
Azay-le-Ferron 25 E3
Azay-le-Rideau 25 D2
Azinheira dos
  Barros 42 A1
Azkoitia 36 B1
Aznalcázar 43 D3
Aznalcóllar 43 D2
Azpeitia 36 B1
Azuaga 43 E1
Azuara 37 D4
Azuer, R 40 A4
Azuqueca de
  Henares 40 B2
Azután, Emb de . . . 39 F3
Azzano Decimo . . . 59 E3

B

Baad	58 B2	Bački Brestovac	72 B2
Baal	17 D4	Bački Monoštor	72 B2
Baamonde	34 B1	Bački Petrovac	72 B2
Baarle-Nassau	16 C4	Backnang	55 D2
Baarn	16 C2	Bačko Gradište	72 C2
Baba	77 E4	Bačko Novo Selo	72 B2
Babadag	113 E4	Bačko Petrovo	
Babajevo	111 E1	Selo	72 C1
Babelsberg	49 D4	Bačkovo	115 D3
Babenhausen		Bacoli	64 A4
(Bayern)	55 E3	Bacqueville	19 D2
Babenhausen		Baczyna	49 F3
(Hessen)	52 A4	Bad Aibling	56 B3
Babina Greda	71 F3	Badajoz	38 C4
Babin Kal	73 E4	Badalona	32 B4
Babin Most	77 D2	Bad Aussee	56 C3
Babino Polje	75 F2	Bad Bentheim	17 E2
Babin Potok	70 C4	Bad Bergzabern	54 C2
Babljak	76 B2	Bad Berka	52 C3
Babuna	77 E3	Bad Berleburg	17 F4
Babušnica	77 E1	Bad Berneck	53 D4
Bač	72 B2	Bad Bertrich	51 E4
Bački Breg	72 B1	Bad Bevensen	48 B3
Bacău	113 D4	Bad Bibra	52 C2
Baccarat	21 E4	Bad Blankenburg	52 C3
Bæccegæhal'di	94 C2	Bad Brambach	53 D4
Baceno	58 A3	Bad Bramstedt	48 A2
Bacharach	51 E4	Bad Brückenau	52 B4
Bächistock	58 A2	Bad Buchau	55 D3
Bachmač	113 F1	Bad Camberg	51 F4
Băcina	73 E4	Bad Deutsch	
Bačka Palanka	72 B2	Altenburg	57 F2
Bäckaskog	109 D3	Bad Doberan	48 C2
Bačka Topola	72 B1	Bad Driburg	52 A2
Backe	101 F1	Bad Düben	53 D2
Bäckebo	109 E2	Bad Dürkheim	54 C1
Bäckefors	105 D4	Bad Dürrenberg	53 D2
Bački Breg	71 F1	Bad Dürrheim	54 C3
		Bad Elster	53 D4
		Bad Ems	51 E4
		Baden (A)	57 F3

Baden (CH)	27 F2	Bad Krozingen	54 C4
Baden-Baden	54 C2	Bad Laasphe	17 F4
Bad Endorf	56 B3	Bad Langensalza	52 B3
Badenweiler	54 C4	Bad Lauchstädt	53 D2
Baden-		Bad Lausick	53 D2
Württemberg	55 D3	Bad Lauterberg	52 B2
Baderna	70 A3	Bad Leonfelden	57 D2
Bad Essen	17 F2	Bad Liebenstein	52 B3
Bad Frankenhausen	52 C2	Bad Liebenwerda	53 E2
Bad Freienwalde	49 E3	Bad Liebenzell	54 C2
Bad Friedrichshall	55 D2	Bad Lippspringe	17 F3
Bad Gandersheim	52 B1	Badljevina	71 D2
Badgastein	59 E2	Bad Meinberg	52 A2
Bad Gleichenberg	57 F4	Bad Mergentheim	55 D1
Bad Godesberg	51 E3	Bad Mitterndorf	56 C4
Bad Goisern	56 C3	Bad Münder	52 A1
Bad Gottleuba	53 E3	Bad Münster am Stein-	
Bad Griesbach	56 C2	Ebernburg	54 B1
Bad Grund	52 B2	Bad Münstereifel	51 E4
Bad Hall	57 D3	Bad Muskau	53 F1
Bad Harzburg	52 B1	Bad Nauheim	52 A4
Bad Herrenalb	54 C2	Bad Nenndorf	52 A1
Bad Hersfeld	52 B3	Bad Neuenahr-	
Bad Hofgastein	56 C4	Ahrweiler	51 E4
Bad Homburg	51 F4	Bad Neustadt	52 B4
Bad Honnef	51 E3	Bad Oeynhausen	17 F2
Bad Honnigen	51 E4	Bad Oldesloe	48 B2
Badia Polesine	61 D2	Bad Orb	52 A4
Badia Tedalda	61 D3	Badonviller	21 E4
Bad Iburg	17 F2	Badovinci	72 B3
Badija	75 E2	Bad Peterstal-	
Bad Ischl	56 C3	Griesbach	54 C3
Bad Karlshafen	52 A2	Bad Pyrmont	52 A1
Bad Kissingen	52 B4	Bad Radkersburg	70 C1
Bad Kleinen	48 C2	Bad Ragaz	58 B2
Bad		Bad Rappenau	55 D2
Kleinkirchheim	59 F2	Bad Reichenhall	56 B3
Bad König	55 D1	Bad Rippoldsau-	
Bad Königshofen	52 B4	Schapbach	54 C3
Bad Kösen	52 C2	Bad Rothenfelde	17 F2
Bad Kreuznach	54 B1	Bad Saarow-	
		Pieskow	49 E4
		Bad Sachsa	52 B2
		Bad Säckingen	54 C4
		Bad St Leonhard	57 D4
		Bad Salzdetfurth	52 B1

Bad Salzschlirf	52 B3	Bad Urach	55 D3
Bad Salzuflen	17 F2	Bad Vibel	52 A4
Badolato	67 F3	Bad Vöslau	57 F3
Badolatosa	43 F3	Bad Waldsee	55 D4
Bad Salzungen	52 B3	Bad Wiessee	56 A4
Bad Schallerbach	56 C3	Bad Wildungen	52 A3
Bad Schandau	53 F2	Bad	
Badonville	21 E4	Schmiedeberg	53 D1
Bad Orb	52 A4	Bad Schönborn	54 C2
Bad Schönborn	54 C2	Bad Wilsnack	48 C3
Bad Peterstal-		Bad Wimpfen	55 D2
Badl		Bad Windsheim	55 E1
Schussenried	55 D3	Bad Wörishofen	55 E3
Bad Pyrmont	52 A1	Bad Wurzach	55 D4
Bad Schwalbach	51 F4	Bad Zwischenahn	47 F3
Bad Schwartau	48 B2	Bae Colwyn	6 B2
Bad Segeberg	48 B2	Baena	43 F2
Bad Soden	51 F4	Baeza	44 A2
Bad Soden-		Bagà	32 A3
Salmünster	52 A4	Bâgé-le-Châtel	26 C4
Bad Sooden-		Bagenalstown	15 D3
Allendorf	52 B2	Bagenkop	108 B4
Bad Sulza	52 C2	Bagheria	68 B3
Bad Sülze	49 D2	Bagnacavallo	61 D2
Bad Tatzmannsdorf	57 F4	Bagnara Calabra	67 E4
Bad Tennstedt	52 C2	Bagnères-	
Bad Tölz	56 A4	de-Bigorre	37 E1
Badules	36 C4		

Barcelona

0   2 km

TERRASSA/TARRASA
MATARÓ
GIRONA/GERONA
PUIGCERDÀ VICH/VIC

N 150   A 18   A 17   N 152   Besòs
VALLBONA
STA COLOMA DE GRAMENET
NOU BARRIS
BADALONA
A 19   N II

S. ANDREU
S. ADRIÀ DE BESÒS

TERRASSA/TARRASA
S. CUGAT DEL VALLÈS
VELODROM
HORTA
LA VALL D'HEBRON
TIBIDABO (532)
Pas. de Valldaura
Meridiana
Sagrera
Santander
Prim
Maragall
VALLVIDRERA
Llobregós   Pas. de
TÚNEL DE LA RABIRA
Parc Güell
Gràcia
Indústria
Corts
Pere IV
Prim
Guipúscoa
Catalanes
PI. de Lesseps
SAGRADA FAMÍLIA
PI. de les Glòries Catalanes
ST. GERVASI
Muntaner   Balmes
G^l Mitre   V. Augusta
PI. Travessera   Pas.
DIAGONAL
PI. de Joan Carles I
Aragó
Lepant
Padilla
MONASTIR DE PEDRALBES
SARRIÀ
Ronda   Av. de Pedralbes
Av. de Sarria
PI. Francesc Macià
Balmes
Pas. de Gràcia
Sant   Aragó
Zamora
PLAÇA BRAUS MONUMENTAL
PI. de Tetuàn
PARC ZOOLÒGIC
França
MAR MEDITERRÁNEO
ESPLUGUES DE LLOBREGAT
S. JUST DESVERN
Carret. Reial
Laureà
Comte
AV.
Corts
Av. de Roma
Aragó
d'Urgell
PI. de Catalunya
CATEDRAL
BARRI GÒTIC
Pas. de Colom
PLATJA
N 340   A 2
LLEIDA/LÉRIDA TARRAGONA
RONDA DE DALT
Carret. de Cornellà
Miró
DIAGONAL
Collblanc
Sants
Travess. de les Corts
Sants
PI. d'Espanya
FERIA
E
W
ESTACIÓ MARÍTIMA
MAR MEDITERRANIA
CASTELLDEFELS
Carret. d'Esplugues
L'HOSPITALET DE LLOBREGAT
COLLBLANC
Gran   Badal
Sta Eulàlia
la   Gran Via
MONTJUÏC
de l'Estadi
ESTADI OLÍMPIC
Parc d'Atraccions
CASTELL DE MONTJUÏC
C 245
CORNELLÀ DE LLOBREGAT
Av.   del
Carrilet
PI. Cerdà
Pas. de la Zona Franca
C 246
CASTELLDEFELS SITGES
BALEARES GENOVA

Bagnères-
de-Luchon **37** E2
Bagni del Masino . . **58** B3
Bagni di Lucca **60** C3
Bagno a Ripoli **61** D3
Bagno di
Romagna **61** D3
Bagnoles-
de-l'Orne **18** C4
Bagnoli
del Trigno **64** B2
Bagnolo Mella **60** B1
Bagnols-les-Bains . . **29** F3
Bagnols-sur-Cèze . . **30** C3
Bagnoregio **63** E1
Bagolino **58** C4
Bagrationovsk **110** B4
Bagrdan **73** E4
Baia Mare **112** C3
Baiano **64** B4
Baião **34** B4
Baiersbronn **54** C3
Baignes-Ste-
Radegonde **28** B1
Baigneux-
les-Juifs **26** C2
Baile Átha Cliath . . . **13** E4
Baile Átha Luain . . . **12** C3
Băile Herculane . . . **114** C1
Bailên **44** A2
Băile Tușnad **113** D4
Bailieborough **13** D3
Bailleul **19** F1
Bain-de-Bretagne . . **23** D3
Bains-les-Bains **27** D1
Baio **34** A1
Baiono **34** A3
Bais **23** E3
Baise **28** C3
Baïse-Darrê **37** E1
Baja **114** B1
Baja Sardinia **66** B1
Bajgora **77** D1
Bajina Bašta **72** C4
Bajmok **72** B1
Bajram Curri **76** C2
Bajša **72** B1
Bajzë **76** B3
Bakar **70** B3
Bakarac **70** B3
Bakewell **6** C3
Bakio **36** B1
Bakkaflói **96** C1
Bakony **112** A4
Bakvattnet **101** E1
Bala **6** B3
Balaguer **37** F3
Balanegra **44** B4
Balaruc **30** A4
Balassagyarmat . . . **112** B3
Balaton **112** A4
Balatonfüred **112** B4
Balatonkeresztúr . . **112** A4
Balazote **40** C4
Balbigny **26** B4
Balbriggan **13** E3
Balčik **115** E2
Balderschwang **55** E4
Baldock **9** F2
Baldo, Mte **58** C4
Bale **70** A4
Baleal **38** A3
Baleizão **42** B1
Balerma **44** B4
Balestrand **100** A3
Bali **91** D3
Balikesir **115** E4
Bälinge **106** B3
Balingen **55** D3
Balivanich **2** A3
Ballachulish **2** C4
Ballaghaderreen . . . **12** C3
Ballangen **94** B3
Ballantrae **4** B3
Ballao **66** B3
Ballater **3** D4
Ballaugh **6** A1
Ballenstedt **52** C2
Balleroy **18** C3
Ballerup **108** C3
Ballina **12** B2
Ballinamore **12** C3
Ballinasloe **12** C3
Ballingarry **14** C3

Ballinrobe **12** B3
Ballintober **12** B3
Ballobar **37** E4
Ballon **23** F3
Ballon d'Alsace **27** E1
Ballstad **97** E1
Ballybay **13** D2
Ballybofey **12** C1
Ballybunnion **12** A4
Ballycastle (IRL) . . . **12** B2
Ballycastle (N Ire) . . **13** E1
Ballyclare **13** E2
Ballyconnell **12** C2
Ballycotton **14** C4
Ballycroy **12** B2
Ballyduff **14** B3
Ballyforan **12** C3
Ballygawley **13** D2
Ballyhaunis **12** B3
Ballyheige **14** A3
Ballyjamesduff **13** D3
Ballymahon **12** C3
Ballymena **13** E2
Ballymoe **12** C3
Ballymoney **13** E1
Ballymore **12** C3
Ballymote **12** C2
Ballynahinch **13** E2
Ballysadare **12** C2
Ballyshannon **12** C2
Ballyvaughan **12** B4
Balmaseda **36** A1
Balme **31** E1
Balmoral Castle **3** D4
Balneario de
Panticosa **37** E2
Balsareny **32** A3
Balsfjorden **94** B2
Balsicas **45** D2
Balsorano **63** F2
Bålsta **106** B3
Balsthal **27** E2
Balta **113** E3
Baltanás **35** F4
Baltar **34** B3
Bălţi **113** E3
Baltic Sea **110** B2
Baltijsk **110** B4
Baltinglass **13** D4
Baltrum **47** E3
Bambaló **82** C3
Bamberg **52** C4
Bambini **82** C3
Bamburgh **5** E3
Bampton **8** C3
Banagher **12** C4
Banat **114** C1
Banatska Palanka . . **73** D2
Banatska Topola . . . **72** C1
Banatski
Brestovac **73** D3
Banatski Dvor **72** C2
Banatski Karlovac . . **73** D2
Banatsko
Aranđđelovo **72** C1
Banatsko
Karaddorđđevo . . **72** C2
Banatsko Novo
Selo **73** D2
Banbridge **13** E2
Banbury **9** E1
Banchory **3** E4
Bande **34** B3
Bandak **104** B3
Bandırma **115** E3
Bandol **30** C4
Bandon **14** B4
Bandon R. **14** B4
Bañeres **45** E1
Banff **3** E3
Bangor (IRL) **12** B2
Bangor (N Ire) **13** E2
Bangor (Wales) **6** A2
Bangsund **97** D4
Banie **49** E3
Banja (Srbija) **73** E4
Banja (Srbija) **76** B1
Banja Koviljača **72** B3
Banja Luka **71** E3
Banjani **72** C3
Banja Vrućica **71** F3
Banjska **76** C1
Bankeryd **109** D1
Bann (N Ire) **13** D1

Bann (Wexford) **15** D3
Bannalec **22** B3
Banon **30** C3
Bañón **41** D2
Baños de Cerrato . . **35** F4
Baños de la Encina . **44** A2
Baños de
la Fuensanta **44** C2
Baños de Molgas . . . **34** B3
Baños de
Montemayor **39** E2
Baños de
Fuensanta **35** E1
Banova Jaruga **71** D2
Banovići **71** F4
Banque de Fraiture . **51** D4
Banque Michel **51** D4
Bansin **49** E2
Banská-Bystrica . . . **112** B3
Banská-Štiavnica . . **112** B3
Bansko **77** F3
Bantry **14** B4
Bantry B **14** A4
Bañuela **43** F1
Banyalbufar **45** E2
Banyoles **32** B3
Banyuls **32** C3
Bao, Emb de **34** C3
Bapaume **19** F2
Bar (UKR) **113** D3
Bar (Crna Gora) . . . **76** B3
Baracaldo **36** B1
Barači **71** E4
Baradla **112** B3
Barahona **36** B4
Barajas **40** B2
Barajas de Melo . . . **40** B3
Barajevo **73** D3
Baralla **34** C2
Barane **76** C2
Baranoviči **111** D4
Baraqueville **29** E3
Barasona, Emb de . . **37** E3
Barbadillo del
Mercado **36** A3

Barban **70** A3
Barbarano
Vicentino **61** D1
Barbarušince **77** E2
Barbastro **37** E3
Barbat **70** B4
Barbate de Franco . **43** D4
Barbate, Emb de . . **43** D4
Barbazan **37** F2
Barberino
di Mugello **60** C3
Barbezieux **28** B1
Barbizon **19** F4
Barbotan **28** B3
Barby **52** C1
Barca de Alva **39** D1
Barca, Emb de la . . . **35** D1
Barcarrota **42** C1
Barcellona Pozzo di
Gotto **69** D2
Barcelona **32** B4
Barcelonnette **31** D2
Barcelos **34** A4
Barcena, Emb de . . . **34** C2
Barchfeld **52** B3
Barcis **59** E3
Barcones **36** B4
Barcs **114** A1
Bardal **101** D1
Bardejov **112** B3
Bardi **60** B2
Bardineto **31** F3
Bardolino **60** C1
Bardonecchia **31** D1
Bardu **94** B3
Bardufoss **94** B3
Bare **76** B1
Barèges **37** E2
Barentin **19** D3
Barenton **18** C4
Bares, Estaca de . . . **34** B 1
Barfleur **18** B2
Barfleur, Pte de . . . **18** B2
Bargas **40** A3
Bargoed **9** D2

Bargteheide **48** B2
Bari **65** D3
Barič Draga **70** C4
Barisciano **63** F2
Barjac **30** B3
Barjols **31** D4
Barlby **7** D2
Bar, le **31** E3
Bar-le-Duc **20** C4
Barletta **65** D3
Barlinek **49** F3
Barlovento **42** A4
Barmouth **6** A3
Barmstedt **48** A2
Barna **12** B3
Barnard Castle **5** E4
Bärnau **53** D4
Barneveld **16** C3
Barneville **18** B3
Barnsley **7** D2
Barnstaple **8** C3
Barnstorf **17** F1
Barntrup **52** A1
Barovo **77** E3
Barqueiro **38** B2
Barr **21** E4
Barra **2** A4
Barracas **41** E3
Barrachina **41** D2
Barraco **39** F2
Barrafranca **68** C4
Barra Head **2** A4
Barrancos **42** C1
Barranco Velho **42** B2
Barranda **44** C2
Barra, Sd of **2** A4
Barrax **40** C4
Barrea **64** A2
Barre-des-
Cévennes **29** F3
Barreiro **38** A4
Barrême **31** D3
Barrhead **4** C2
Barrhill **4** C3
Barri **9** D2

Barrow **13** D4
Barrow-
in-Furness **6** B1
Barrow, R **15** D3
Barruecopardo **39** D1
Barruelo de
Santullán **35** F2
Barry **9** D2
Barsinghausen **52** A1
Bar-sur-Aube **26** B1
Bar-sur-Seine **26** B1
Barth **49** D1
Barthe-de-Neste,
la **37** E1
Barton-upon-
Humber **7** D2
Barumini **66** B3
Baruth **53** E1
Barvas **2** B2
Barycz **112** A2
Barzio **58** B4
Bašaid **72** C1
Bàscara **32** B3
Baschi **63** E1
Basconcillos
del Tozo **35** F2
Basel **27** E2
Baselga di Pinè **59** D3
Bas-en-Basset **30** B1
Basento **65** D4
Basildon **11** D2
Basilicata **65** D4
Basingstoke **9** E3
Baška **70** B3
Bæskades **95** D3
Baška Voda **75** E2
Baške Oštarije **70** C4
Baslow **6** C3
Basovizza **59** F4
Bas-Rhin **21** E4
Bassano del
Grappa **59** D4
Bassée, la **19** F1
Bassella **37** F3
Bassens **28** B2

Bassum **17** F1
Båstad **108** C3
Bastasi **71** D4
Bastelica **33** F3
Bas'tevarri **95** D3
Bastia **33** F2
Bastide-de-
Sérou, la **37** F2
Bastogne **20** C2
Bastunäsfjället **97** E4
Bastuträsk **98** B4
Bataille, Col de la . . **30** C2
Batajnica **72** C3
Batak **115** D3
Batalha **38** B3
Batea **41** F1
Bath **9** D2
Bathgate **5** D2
Bâtie-Neuve, la **31** D2
Batina **72** B1
Batlava **77** D1
Batočina **73** D3
Båtsfjord **95** F1
Batsi **88** B1
Battaglia Terme . . . **61** D1
Battenberg **17** F4
Battice **51** D3
Battipaglia **64** B4
Battle **11** D3
Batz (Finistère) **22** B2
Batz (Loire-
Atlantique) **24** A2
Baud **22** C3
Baugé **23** E4
Baugy **26** A2
Baule, la **24** A2
Baume, Cirque de . . **27** D3
Baume-les-
Dames **27** D2
Baumholder **54** B1
Bauska **110** C3
Bautzen **53** F2
Baux, les **30** B3
Bavanište **73** D2
Bavay **20** B1

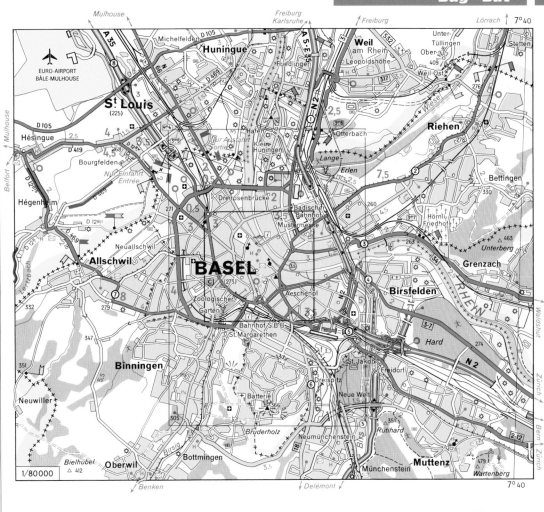

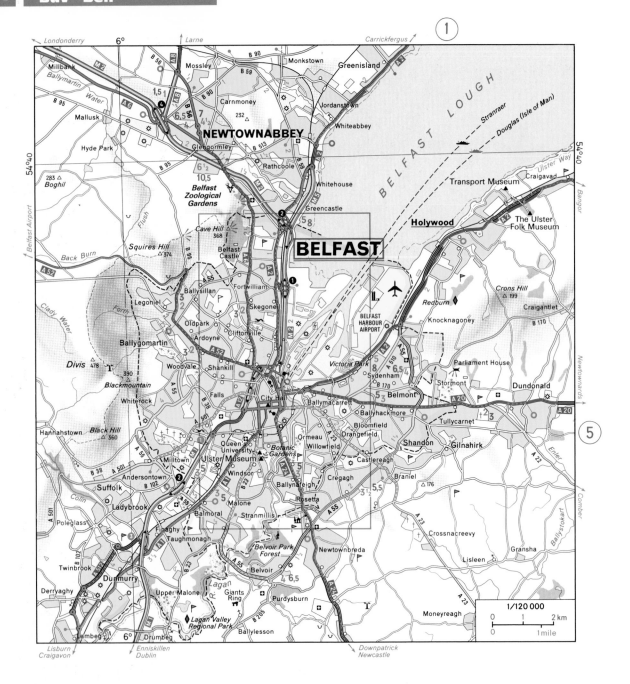

Belgodère 33 F3
Belianes 37 F4
Belice 68 B3
Beli Drim 76 C2
Beli Manastir 71 F2
Belin-Béliet 28 B3
Beli Potok 73 F4
Belišče 71 F2
Beli Timok 73 F4
Beljakovce 77 E2
Beljanica 73 E3
Beljina 73 D3
Bellac 25 D4
Bellagio 58 B4
Bellano 58 B4
Bellaria 61 E3
Bellcaire d'Urgell 37 F3
Belledonne,
   Chaîne de 31 D1
Belleek 12 C2
Bellegarde (Ain) 27 D4
Bellegarde (Gard) . . . 30 B3
Bellegarde (Loiret) . . 25 F1
Bellegarde-en-
   Marche 25 F4
Belle-Ile 22 B4
Belle-Isle-en-Terre . . 22 B2
Bellême 23 F3
Bellencombre 19 E2
Bellerive 26 A4
Belleville 26 C4
Belley 27 D4
Bellinzona 58 A3
Bell-Iloc d'Urgell 37 F3
Bello 41 D1
Bellpuig 37 F4
Belluno 59 E3
Bellver 45 E3
Bellver de
   Cerdanya 32 A3
Bèlmez 43 E1
Belmont (F) 26 B4
Belmont (GB) 3 F1
Belmonte
   (Asturias) 35 D1
Belmonte (Castilla-la-
   Mancha) 40 C3
Belmonte (P) 38 C2
Belmont-sur-
   Rance 32 B1
Belmullet 12 A2
Belo Brdo 76 C1
Belogradčik 114 C2
Belo jez 72 C2
Beloljin 77 D1
Beloœil 50 B4
Belo Polje 76 C2
Belorado 36 A2
Belpech 32 A2
Belper 6 C3
Belsay 5 E3
Belsh 76 C2
Beltinci 70 C1
Belturbet 13 D2
Belušić 73 E4
Belvedere
   Marittimo 67 E2
Belver 37 E3
Belvès 28 C2
Belvis de la Jara 39 F3
Belyj 111 E2
Belz 22 C4
Belzig 53 D1
Bembézar, Emb de . 43 E2
Bembézar, R. 43 E2
Bembibre 35 D2
Bemposta 38 B3
Bemposta,
   Bgem da 34 C4
Benabarre 37 E3
Benaguasil 41 E3
Benahadux 44 B3
Ben Alder 2 C4
Benalmádena 43 F4
Benalúa
   de las Villas 44 A3
Benamargosa 43 F3
Benamaurel 44 B2
Benameji 43 F3
Benamocarra 43 F4
Benaoján 43 E4
Ben Armine 3 D2
Benasal 41 E2
Benasque 37 E2

Bavella, Col de 33 F4
Båven 106 B4
Baveno 58 A4
Bawtry 7 D2
Bayard, Col 31 D2
Bayerisch
   Eisenstein 56 C1
Bayerischer Wald . . . 56 B2
Bayern 55 F2
Bayeux 18 C3
Bayhirivagh 2 A4
Bayındır 115 F4
Bayon 21 D4
Bayonne 28 A4
Bayreuth 52 C4
Bayrischzell 56 B4
Baza 44 B3
Bazas 28 B3
Baza, Sa de 44 B3
Bazoches-sur-
   Hoëne 19 D4
Bazzano 60 C2
Beachy Head 10 C3
Beaconsfield 9 F2
Béal an Átha 12 B2
Béal Átha
   na Sluaighe 12 C3
Beaminster 9 D3
Beanntraí 14 B4
Beara 14 A4

Beariz 34 B2
Beas 42 C2
Beasain 36 C1
Beas de Segura 44 B2
Beattock 5 D3
Beaucaire 30 B3
Beaufort (Jura) 26 C3
Beaufort (Savoie) . . . 27 E4
Beaufort-en-
   Vallée 23 E4
Beaugency 25 E2
Beaujeu 26 C4
Beaulieu (Alpes-
   Maritime) 31 E3
Beaulieu
   (Corrèze) 29 D2
Beaulieu (GB) 9 E3
Beaumaris 6 A2
Beaumesnil 19 D3
Beaumetz-lès-
   Loges 19 F2
Beaumont (B) 50 B4
Beaumont
   (Dordogne) 28 C2
Beaumont
   (Manche) 18 B2
Beaumont
   (Val d'Oise) 19 F3
Beaumont-de-
   Lomagne 28 C3

Beaumont-le-
   Roger 19 D3
Beaumont-sur-
   Sarthe 23 F3
Beaune 26 C2
Beaune-la-
   Rolande 25 F1
Beaupréau 24 C2
Beauraing 50 C4
Beaurepaire 30 C1
Beaurepaire-en-
   Bresse 26 C3
Beausset, le 31 D4
Beauvais 19 E3
Beauvoir (Deux-
   Sèvres) 24 C2
Beauvoir
   (Vendée) 24 A3
Bebington 6 B2
Bebra 52 B3
Beccles 11 E1
Becedas 39 E2
Beceite 41 F2
Bečej 72 C2
Becerreá 34 C2
Bec-Hellouin, le 19 D3
Bécherel 23 D3
Bechet 115 D2
Bechhofen 55 E2
Bečići 76 B3

Becilla de
   Valderaduey 35 E3
Beckenried 58 A2
Beckington 9 D3
Beckum 17 F3
Bečov 53 E4
Bedale 6 C1
Bédarieux 30 A4
Beddgelert 6 A3
Bederkesa 47 F3
Bedford 9 F1
Bedfordshire 9 F1
Bedlington 5 E3
Bedmar 44 A2
Bednja 70 C1
Bedonia 60 B3
Bedum 47 D3
Bedwas 9 D2
Bedworth 9 E1
Beeford 7 E2
Beelitz 49 D4
Beerfelden 55 D1
Beeskow 49 E4
Beetzendorf 48 B4
Bégard 22 C2
Begejci 72 C2
Begejski kanal 72 C2
Beg-Meil 22 B3
Begna 104 C2
Begov Han 71 F4

Bégude-de-Mazenc,
   la 30 C2
Begues 32 A4
Begur 32 C3
Behalúa de Guadix . . 44 B3
Behobia 28 A4
Behringersmühle . . . 55 F1
Beiarn 97 E2
Beilen 17 D1
Beilngries 55 F2
Beinn a'Ghlò 3 D4
Beinn an Oir 4 B2
Beinn Bheigeir 4 B2
Beinn Dearg 2 C3
Beira Alta 38 B1
Beira Baixa 38 C2
Beira Litoral 38 B1
Beisfjord 94 B3
Beith 4 C1
Beitostølen 104 C1
Beitstadfjorden 101 D1
Beiuş 112 C4
Beja 42 B1
Béjar 39 E2
Béjar, Pto de 39 E2
Békés 112 C4
Békéscsaba 112 C4
Bel 41 F2
Bělá 56 B1
Bélâbre 25 E3

Bela Crkva (Srbija) . . 72 C3
Bela Crkva
   (Vojvodina) 73 D2
Belalcázar 43 E1
Belanovce 77 E2
Belanovica 73 D3
Bela Palanka 77 E1
Belarus' 111 D4
Belasica 77 F3
Belcaire 32 A2
Belchen 54 C4
Belchite 37 D4
Belčišče 77 D4
Belcoo 12 C2
Belec 70 C2
Belecke 17 F3
Belegiš 72 C2
Belej 70 B4
Beleña, Emb de 40 B1
Belesar, Emb de 34 B2
Belev 111 F3
Bele Vode 76 C1
Belfast 13 E2
Belfast L 13 E2
Belford 5 E3
Belfort 27 E2
Belforte all'Isauro . . . 61 E3
Belgern 53 E2
België 16 B3
Belgique 50 B4

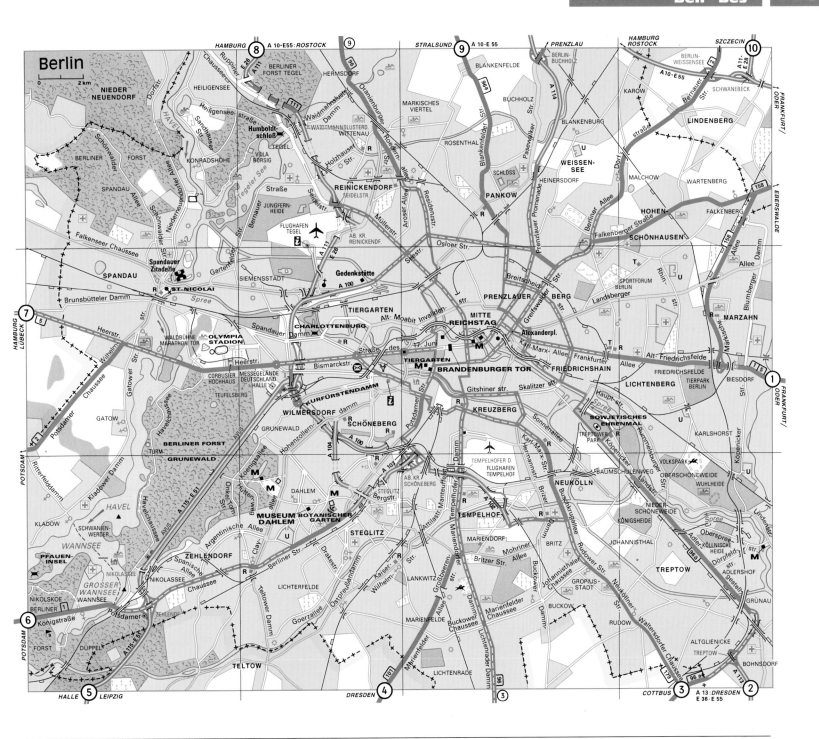

Benavente (E) 35 D3	Benifaió 41 E4	Beočin 72 C2	Berg (S) 101 E2	Bergnäset 98 C3	Berlebeck 17 F3	Bernkastel-Kues 54 B1
Benavente (P) 38 A4	Beninar, Emb de .. 44 B3	Beograd 73 D3	Berg (Troms) 94 B2	Bergneustadt 17 E4	Berlenga, I. 38 A3	Bernsdorf 53 F2
Benavides 35 D3	Benissa 45 E1	Berane 76 C2	Berga (D) 52 C2	Bergö 102 B2	Berlevåg. 95 F1	Bernstein. 57 F3
Benbecula 2 A3	Benítses 82 A1	Bérarde, la 31 D2	Berga (E) 32 A3	Berg-	Berlin 49 E4	Beroun. 53 F4
Ben Chonzie........ 4 C1	Ben Klibreck 2 C2	Berat. 114 C3	Bergama 115 E4	Rudolphstein ... 53 D3	Bermejales, Emb .. 43 F3	Berounka. 53 F4
Ben Cruachan...... 4 B1	Benkovac 74 C1	Berbegal. 37 E3	Bergamo 60 B1	Bergsjö 101 F3	Bermeja, Sa 43 E4	Berovo 77 F3
Benderi............ 113 E4	Ben Lawers 4 C1	Berberana 36 B1	Bergara 36 B1	Bergsviken 98 B3	Bermeo 36 B1	Ber'oza 112 C4
Bendorf 51 E4	Ben Lomond. 4 C1	Berceto 60 B3	Bergby 106 B2	Bergues 19 F1	Bermillo 35 D4	Berra 61 D2
Benediktbeuern.... 56 A4	Ben Macdui 3 D4	Berching. 55 F2	Bergedorf 48 B3	Bergum 47 D3	Bern. 27 E2	Berre 30 C4
Benešov	Ben More	Berchtesgaden 56 C4	Bergen (B) 50 B4	Bergün 58 B3	Bernalda 65 D4	Berre, Etang de ... 30 C4
(Severočeský) ... 53 F3	(Grampian) 4 C1	Berck-Plage 19 E1	Bergen (D) 49 D1	Beringel 42 B1	Bernardsthal 57 F1	Beršad'. 113 E3
Benešov	Ben More (Mull) .. 4 B1	Berdyčiv 113 E2	Bergen (N) 104 A2	Beringen 50 C3	Bernartice. 57 D1	Bersenbrück 17 E2
(Středočeský) ... 53 F4	Ben More Assynt .. 2 C2	Bereguardo 60 A2	Bergen	Berja 44 B4	Bernau (Baden-	Bertamirans 34 A2
Bénévent-	Benneckenstein ... 52 B2	Berehove 112 C3	(Niedersachsen) .. 48 A4	Berka 52 B3	Württemberg) ... 54 C4	Bertinoro 61 D3
l'Abbaye 25 E4	Ben Nevis 2 C4	Bere I 14 A4	Bergen	Berkåk 100 C2	Bernau (Bayern) .. 56 B3	Bertrix 20 C2
Benevento 64 B3	Bénodet 22 B3	Berek 71 D2	(Niedersachsen) .. 48 B3	Berkel 17 D2	Bernau	Berwang. 58 C1
Benfeld 21 E4	Benquerencia	Bere Regis 9 D3	Bergen (NL) 16 C2	Berkhamsted 9 F2	(Brandenburg) .. 49 E4	Berwick-upon-
Benfleet 11 D2	de la Serena ... 43 E1	Beret 37 E2	Bergen aan Zee .. 16 C2	Berkheim. 55 E3	Bernaville. 19 F2	Tweed 5 E2
Bengtsfors 105 D4	Bensberg. 17 E4	Berettyóújfalu..... 112 C4	Bergen op Zoom .. 16 B4	Berkhof 48 A4	Bernay 19 D3	Berwyn 6 B3
Ben Hope 2 C2	Bensersiel 47 E3	Berezina 111 E4	Bergerac 28 C2	Berkovica 114 C2	Bernburg 52 C1	Berzocana 39 E3
Beničanci 71 E2	Bensheim 54 C1	Berezino 111 D4	Berggießhübel 53 F2	Berkovići 75 F2	Berndorf 57 E3	Berzosa. 39 D1
Benicarló 41 F2	Bentley 7 D2	Berezivka 113 F3	Berghamn	Berkshire 9 E2	Berne 47 F3	Besalú 32 B3
Benicasim 41 F3	Ben Vorlich 4 C1	Berg (A) 57 F2	fjärden 107 D3	Berlaimont 20 A2	Bernesga, R 35 D2	Besançon 27 C2
Benicàssim 41 F3	Ben Wyvis 2 C3	Berg (Nordland) .. 97 D3	Bergheim 17 D4	Berlanga 43 D1	Bernina, Piz 58 B3	Besande. 35 E2
Benidorm 45 E1	Bény-Bocage, le .. 18 C3	Berg (Nordland) .. 97 D3	Bergisch Gladbach . 17 E4	Berlanga de Duero . 36 B4	Bernina, Pso del .. 58 B3	Besaya, R 35 F2

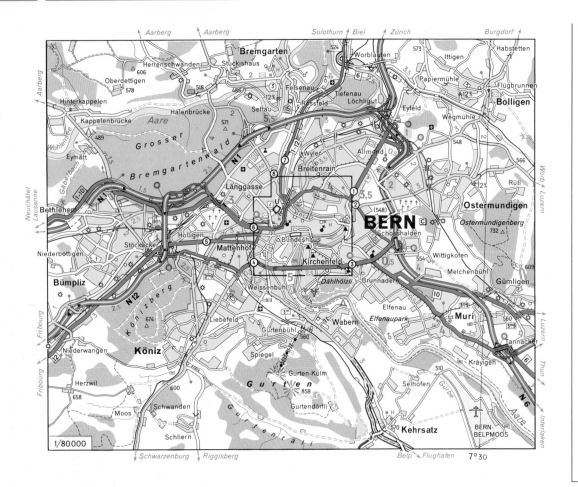

Besbre	26 B3	Beynat	29 D2
Besigheim	55 D2	Bežanija	72 C3
Beška	72 C2	Bézards, les	26 A1
Besna Kobila	77 E2	Bezas	41 D2
Besse	29 E4	Bezdan	72 B1
Bessèges	30 B3	Bezdrep	57 D1
Besse-sur-Issole	31 D4	Bežeck	111 F1
Bessines	25 E4	Béziers	30 A4
Betancuria	42 C4	Bezmisht	77 D4
Betanzos	34 B1	Béznar	44 A3
Betelu	36 C1	Biała Podlaska	112 C1
Bètera	41 E3	Białowieska	112 C1
Beteta	40 C2	Białystok	112 C1
Bétharram, Grottes de	37 E1	Biancavilla	69 D3
Bethesda	6 A2	Bianco	67 E4
Béthune	19 F1	Bianco, M.	27 E4
Béthune R	19 E2	Biandrate	31 F1
Bettna	106 A4	Biar	45 D1
Bettola	60 B2	Biarritz	28 A4
Bettolle	61 D4	Biasca	58 A3
Bettyhill	3 D2	Bibbiena	61 D4
Betws-y-Coed	6 A3	Biberach	54 C3
Betz	19 F3	Biberach an der Ri.	55 E3
Betzdorf	51 F3	Bibinje	74 C1
Beuil	31 E3	Bibione	59 F4
Beura	58 A4	Bibury	9 E2
Beuron	55 D3	Bicaj	76 C3
Beuvray, Mont	26 B3	Bicaz	113 D4
Beuvron	25 E2	Bicester	9 E2
Beuzeville	19 D3	Bichl	56 A4
Bevagna	63 E1	Bidache	28 A4
Beveren-Waas	50 B3	Bidart	28 A4
Beverley	7 D2	Bidasoa, R.	36 C1
Beverstedt	47 F3	Biddendon	11 D3
Beverungen	52 A2	Bidean nam Bian	4 C1
Beverwijk	16 C2	Bideford	8 C3
Bewdley	9 D1	Biebelried	55 E1
Bex	27 E3	Biedenkopf	17 F4
Bexhill	11 D3	Biel	27 E2
Beynac	29 D2	Bielefeld	17 F4
		Bielerhöhe	58 B2

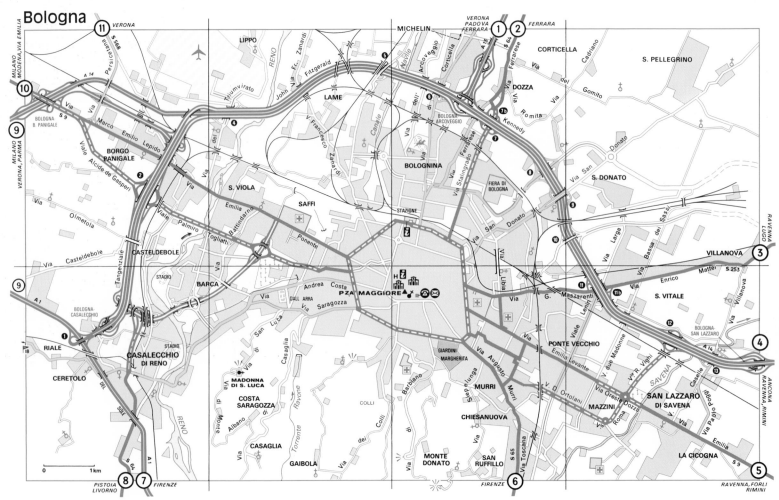

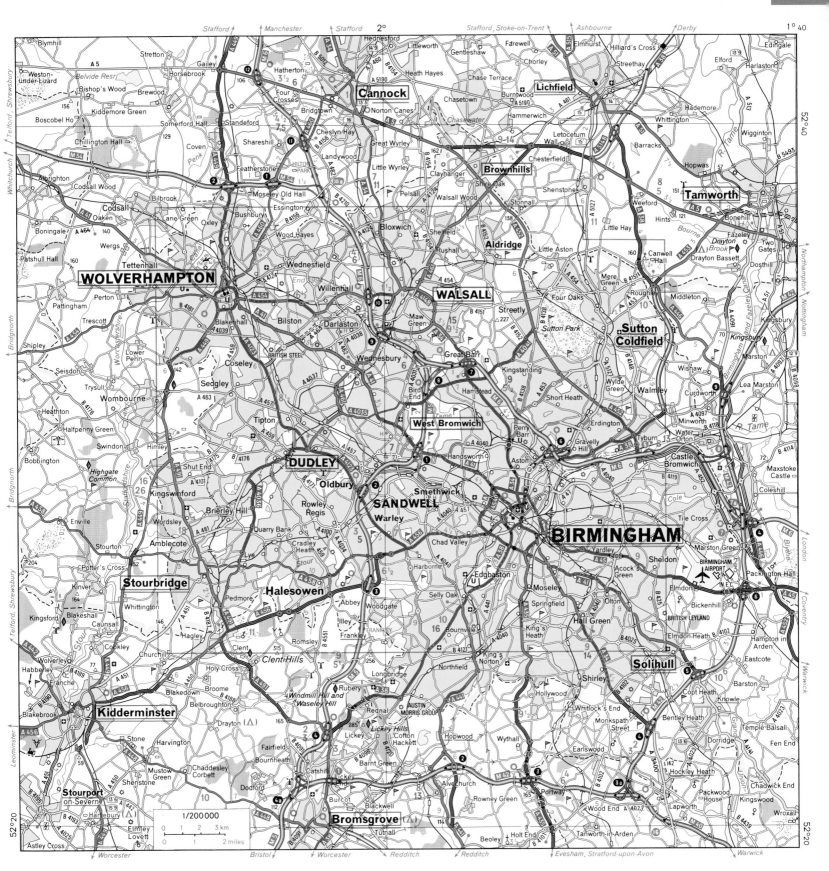

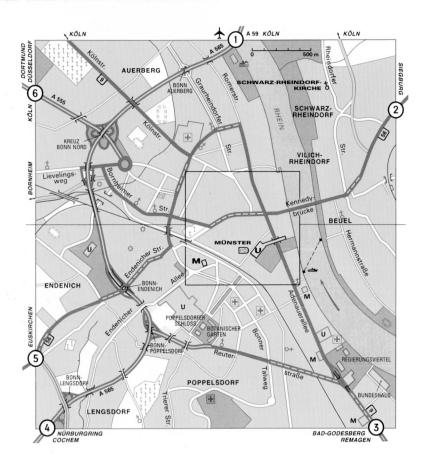

Bonn

Biella 31 F1
Bielsa 37 E2
Bielsa,
  Tunnel de . . . 37 E2
Bielsko-Biała . . . 112 B3
Bielsk Podlaski . . 112 C1
Bienne 27 D3
Bienne 27 E2
Bientina 60 C4
Bienvenida 43 D1
Bierné 23 E4
Bierre 26 B2
Biesbosch 16 C3
Biescas 37 D2
Biese 48 C4
Biesenthal 49 E3
Bietigheim-
  Bissingen 55 D2
Biferno 64 B2
Biga 115 E3
Biggar 5 D2
Biggleswade 9 F1
Bignasco 58 A3
Bihać 70 C3
Bihorului, M . . . 112 C4
Bijele Poljane . . . 76 B2
Bijeljani 75 F2
Bijeljina 72 B3
Bijelo Brdo 71 F2
Bijelolasica 70 B3
Bijelo Polje 76 B2
Bila Cerkva 113 E2
Bilbao 36 B1
Bileća 76 A2
Bilecik 115 F3
Bilećko jez 76 A2
Biłgoraj 112 C2
Bilhorod-
  Dnistrovs'kyj . . . 113 E4
Bilina 53 E3
Biljača 77 E2
Bilje 71 F2
Billerbeck 17 E3
Billericay 11 D2
Billingham 5 E4
Billingshurst 10 C3

Billom 29 F1
Billund 108 A3
Bilo 77 E1
Bilogora 71 D2
Bilopillja 113 F1
Bilto 94 C2
Bilzen 50 C3
Binaced 37 E3
Binačka Morava . . 77 D2
Binasco 60 A1
Binéfar 37 E3
Bingen 51 F4
Bingham 7 D3
Bingley 6 C2
Bingsjö 101 E4
Binic 22 C2
Binz 49 D1
Bioča 76 C2
Bioče 76 B2
Biograd 74 C1
Biogradsko,
  nac park 76 B2
Biokovo 75 E2
Bionaz 27 E4
Biot, le 27 E3
Birchington 11 D2
Birgi 68 A3
Biri 105 D2
Birkebeiner
  veien 104 C1
Birkeland 104 B4
Birkenfeld 54 B1
Birkenhead 6 B2
Birkenwerden . . . 49 D4
Birkerd 108 C3
Birkfeld 57 E4
Bîrlad 113 E4
Birmingham 9 E1
Birnau 55 D4
Birr 12 C4
Biržai 110 C3
Birżebugga 68 B4
Bisaccia 64 C3
Biscarrosse 28 A3
Biscarrosse-Plage . . 28 A3
Bisceglie 65 D3

Bischofsgrün 53 D4
Bischofsheim 52 B4
Bischofshofen . . . 59 E1
Bischofswerde . . . 53 F2
Bischofswiesen . . 56 C4
Bischofszell 58 A1
Bischwiller 21 F4
Bisenti 63 F1
Biševo 75 D2
Bishop Auckland . . 5 E4
Bishop's Castle . . . 9 D1
Bishop's Stortford . . 10 C2
Bisignano 67 E2
Bisko 75 D1
Bismark 48 C4
Bismo 100 B3
Bispgården 101 F2
Bispingen 48 A3
Bistar 77 E2
Bistra pl 77 D3
Bistrica
  (Crna Gora) 76 B2
Bistrica (Srbija) . . 76 B1
Bistrica do S. . . . 70 C2
Bistričak 71 E4
Bistrița 113 D4
Bistrița R. 113 D4
Bitburg 54 A1
Bitche 21 E3
Bitetto 65 D3
Bitonto 65 D3
Bitovnja 71 E2
Bitterfeld 53 D2
Bitti 66 B2
Bizákos 82 C3
Bizovac 71 F2
Bjala 115 D2
Bjarky 94 B3
Bjästa 102 A2
Bjelašnica 75 F1
Bjelašnica 76 A2
Bjelovar 71 D2
Bjerkreim 104 A4
Bjerkvik 94 B3
Bjerringbro 108 B2

Bjrkelangen . . . 105 D3
Björketorp 109 E3
Bjorkfjället 97 F3
Björkliden 94 B3
Björklinge 106 B3
Björköby 102 B2
Björksele 98 A4
Bjorli 100 B3
Björna 102 A2
Bjørnafjorden . . 104 A2
Björneborg 107 D1
Bjørnevatn 95 F2
Bjørntoppen 97 F1
Björsäter 109 E1
Bjurholm 102 A2
Bjursås 101 E4
Bjuv 108 C3
Blace 77 D1
Blackburn 6 C2
Black Head 12 B4
Black Isle 2 C3
Black Mt. 8 C2
Black Mts 9 D2
Blackpool 6 B2
Black Sea 115 F2
Blacksod B 12 A2
Blackstairs Mts . . 15 D3
Blackwater 15 D3
Blackwaterfoot . . . 4 B2
Blackwater, R. . . 14 C4
Blackwater Res . . . 2 C4
Blaenau Ffestiniog . . 6 A3
Blaenavon 9 D2
Blåfjellhatten . . . 101 E1
Blagaj 75 F2
Blagnac 29 D4
Blagoevgrad . . . 115 D3
Blåhammaren . . . 101 D2
Blåhø 100 C2
Blain 23 D4
Blainville 21 D4
Blair Atholl 3 D4
Blairgowrie 5 D1
Blå Jungfrun . . . 109 E2
Blakeney 7 F3
Blakstad 104 B4
Blåmannsisen . . . 97 F2

Blåmont 21 E4
Blanca 45 D2
Blanc, C 45 E3
Blanc, le 25 D3
Blanc, Mont 27 E4
Blanco, R 43 E3
Blandford Forum . . 9 D3
Blanes 32 B4
Blangy 19 E2
Blangy-le-Château . 19 D3
Blankenberge . . . 50 A3
Blankenburg 52 C2
Blankenheim 51 D4
Blankernhain 52 C3
Blanquefort 28 B2
Blanquilla 44 B2
Blanzac 28 C1
Blanzy 26 B3
Blåøret 100 C2
Blarney 14 B4
Blatná 56 C1
Blatnica 71 E4
Blato 75 E1
Blattniksele 98 A3
Blaubeuren 55 D3
Blauen 54 C4
Blaufelden 55 E2
Blaustein 55 E3
Blavet 22 C3
Blaye 28 B2
Blaževo 77 D1
Bleckede 48 B3
Bled 70 A2
Blefjell 104 C3
Bleiburg 70 B1
Bleicherode 52 B2
Bleik 94 A3
Bleiloch-Talsperre . 53 D3
Blekinge Län . . . 109 D3
Blendija 73 E4
Bléneau 26 A2
Blenheim Palace . . 9 E2
Blénod 21 D3
Bléone 31 D3
Blérancourt 19 F3
Bléré 25 D2
Blesle 29 F1
Bletchley 9 F2
Bletterans 26 C3
Blexen 47 F3
Bleymard, le 29 F3
Blidinje jez 75 E1
Blieskastel 54 B2
Bligny 26 C2
Blinisht 76 C3
Blinja 71 D3
Bloemendaal 16 B2
Blois 25 E2
Blokhus 108 B2
Blomberg 52 A1
Blönduós 96 B1
Blonville 19 D3
Bloody Foreland
  Head 12 C1
Blosenberg 53 D3
Bloška Polica 70 B2
Blovice 56 C1
Bludenz 58 B2
Blue Stack Mts . . 12 C2
Blumberg (Baden-
  Württemberg) . . . 54 C4
Blumberg
  (Brandenburg) . . 49 E4
Blyth 5 E3
Bø (Telemark) . . 104 C3
Bø (Vesterålen) . . 94 A3
Boadella, Emb de . 32 B3
Boal 34 C1
Boan 76 B2
Boara Pisani 61 D1
Bobbio 60 A2
Bobigny 19 E4
Bobingen 55 F3
Böblingen 55 D2
Boblitz 53 E1
Boborás 34 B2
Bobova 72 C4
Bóbr 53 F1
Bobrovycja 113 E2
Bobrujsk 111 E4
Bobrynec' 113 F3
Bočac 71 E4
Bocairent 45 E1

Bocca Trabaria . . . 61 E4
Bocche di
  Bonifacio 33 F4
Bocco, Pso del . . . 60 B3
Boceguillas 36 A4
Bocholt 17 D3
Bochov 53 E4
Bochum 17 E3
Bockel 48 A3
Bockenem 52 B1
Böckstein 59 E2
Bockum-Hövel . . 17 E3
Bocognano 33 F3
Boda 101 E4
Böda 109 F2
Bodafors 109 D2
Bodđani 72 B2
Bode 52 C1
Bodegraven 16 C3
Boden 98 B3
Bodenmais 56 B1
Bodensee 58 B1
Bodenteich 48 B4
Bodenwerder . . . 52 A1
Bodenwöhr 56 B1
Bodman-
  Radolfzell 55 D4
Bodmin 8 B4
Bodø 97 E1
Boecillo 35 E4
Boëge 27 D4
Boën 26 B4
Boeza 35 D2
Boffalora 60 A1
Bogarra 44 C1
Bogatič 72 C3
Bogdanci 77 F3
Bogdaniec 49 F3
Bogë 76 C2
Bogen (D) 56 B2
Bogen (N) 94 B3
Bogense 108 B3
Bogetići 76 B2
Boglárlelle 112 B4
Bognanco 27 F4
Bognes 94 A4
Bognor Regis 9 F3
Bogodol 75 F1
Bogojevo 72 B2
Bogomila 77 E3
Bogomolje 75 E2
Bogorodika 77 E3
Bogovina 73 E4
Bogøy 97 E1
Bogutovac 73 D4
Bohain-en-Verman-
  dois 20 A2
Boherboy 14 B3
Bohinjska Bistrica . 70 A2
Bohinjsko jez 70 A2
Böhlen 53 D2
Böhme 48 A4
Böhmenkirch 55 E2
Böhmer Wald . . . 56 B1
Bohmte 17 F2
Böhönye 114 A1
Bohuslav 113 E2
Boiano 64 B3
Boiro 34 A2
Bois-d'Amont . . . 27 D3
Boitzenburg 49 E3
Bóixols 37 F3
Boizenburg 48 B3
Bojana 76 B3
Bøjden 108 B4
Bojnik 77 D1
Boka Kotorska . . . 76 A3
Bokn 104 A3
Boknafjorden . . . 104 A3
Bol 75 E2
Bøla 101 D1
Bolbec 19 D3
Bolera,
  Emb de la 44 B2
Bolesławiec 112 A2
Boleszkowice . . . 49 E3
Bolhrad 113 E4
Boliden 98 B4
Boliqueime 42 B2
Boljanići 76 B1
Boljevac 73 E4
Boljevci 72 C3

Boljkovci 73 D4
Boljuni 75 F2
Bolkesjø 104 C3
Bollebygd 108 C1
Bollène 30 B3
Bollnäs 101 F4
Bollstabruk 101 F2
Bollullos de
  la Mitación 43 D2
Bollullos par
  del Condado . . . 42 C2
Bolmen 109 D3
Bolnâos
  de Calatrava . . . 40 A4
Bologna 60 C2
Bologne 26 C1
Bologoje 111 E1
Bolos 40 B4
Bolotana 66 B2
Bolsena 63 D1
Bolsena, L di 63 D2
Bolsward 16 C1
Boltaña 37 E2
Boltenhagen 48 B2
Bolton 6 C2
Bolungarvik 96 A1
Bolus Head 14 A4
Bolzano 59 D3
Bombarral 38 A3
Bomenzien 48 C3
Bom Jesus 34 A4
Bømlo 104 A3
Bonaigua,
  Pto de la 37 F2
Boñar 35 E2
Bonar Bridge 2 C3
Bonares 42 C2
Bonassola 60 B3
Bondeno 60 C2
Bondone, Mte . . . 58 C3
Bonefro 64 B2
Bo'-Ness 5 D2
Bonete 45 D1
Bonette,
  Col de la 31 D3
Bonhomme,
  Col du 27 E1
Bonifacio 33 F4
Bonn 51 E3
Bonnåsjøen 97 F1
Bonnat 25 E4
Bonndorf 54 C4
Bonnétable 23 F3
Bonneuil-
  Matours 25 D3
Bonneval
  (Eure-et-Loir) . . 25 E1
Bonneval (Savoie) . 31 E1
Bonneville 27 D4
Bonneville, la . . . 19 E4
Bonnières 19 E3
Bonnieux 30 C3
Bono 66 B2
Bonorva 66 B2
Bønsnes 104 C3
Boo 106 B4
Boom 50 B3
Boos 19 E3
Bootle 6 B2
Bopfingen 55 E2
Boppard 51 E4
Bor (CS) 53 E4
Bor (Srbija) 73 E3
Boračko jez 75 F1
Borås 108 C1
Borba 38 C4
Borbollón, Emb de . 39 D2
Borbona 63 F1
Borča 72 C3
Borci 75 F1
Bordeaux 28 B2
Bordeira 42 A2
Bordères-Louron . 37 E2
Border Forest Park,
  The 5 D3
Borders Region . . 5 D3
Bordesholm 48 A2
Bordighera 31 E3
Borðoy 96 A3
Bore 60 B2
Borello 61 D3
Borensberg 105 F4
Borêon, le 31 E3
Borga 107 F2

Borgafjäll 97 E4
Borga-fjällen 97 E4
Borgarnes 96 A2
Børgefjell 97 E3
Børgefjellet 97 E3
Borger 17 D1
Börger 17 E1
Borghetto 63 E2
Borghetto S.S. 31 F3
Borgholm 109 E2
Borgholzhausen 17 E2
Borghorst 17 E2
Borgia 67 F3
Borgomanero 58 A4
Borgone 31 E1
Borgonovo Val
  Tidone 60 B2
Borgorose 63 F2
Borgo San
  Dalmazzo 31 E2
Borgo
  San Lorenzo 61 D3
Borgosesia 58 A4
Borgo Tufico 61 E4
Borgo Val di Taro .. 60 B3
Borgo Valsugana ... 59 D3
Borgsjö 101 F3
Borgund 104 B1
Borgvattnet 101 F2
Boričje 76 B2
Borisov 111 D4
Borja (E) 36 C3
Borja (BH) 71 E4
Borken 17 E3
Borkenes 94 A3
Børkop 108 B3
Borkum 47 D3
Borlänge 105 F2
Bormes-les-
  Mimosas 31 D4
Bormida 60 A2
Bormio 58 C3
Born 48 C1
Borna 53 D2
Bornes 34 C4
Bornes, Sa de 34 C4
Bornholm 109 D4
Bornhöved 48 B2
Börnicke 49 D4
Bornos 43 D3
Bornos, Emb de ... 43 D3
Boroughbridge 7 D1
Borovec 115 D3
Boroviči 111 E1
Borovnica 70 B2
Borovo 72 B2
Borovsk 111 F2
Borre 104 C3
Borriol 41 E3
Borris 15 D3
Borrisokane 12 C4
Borşa 113 D3
Børselv 95 E1
Børselva 95 E2
Børselvfjellet 95 E2
Bórsio 86 B1
Bort-les-Orgues 29 E1
Börtnan 101 E2
Boryspil' 113 E2
Borzna 113 F1
Borzonasca 60 A3
Bosa 66 A2
Bosanci 70 C3
Bosanska Dubica ... 71 D3
Bosanska Gradiška .. 71 E3
Bosanska
  Kostajnica 71 D3
Bosanska Krupa ... 71 D3
Bosanska Rača 72 B3
Bosanski Brod 71 E3
Bosanski Kobaš ... 71 E3
Bosanski Novi 71 D3
Bosanski
  Petrovac 71 D4
Bosanski Šamac 71 D4
Bosansko
  Grahovo 71 D4
Bosansko Petrovo
  Selo 71 F3
Bosco 61 E4
Bosco
  Chiesanuova ... 59 D4
Bosilegrad 77 E2
Bosiljevo 70 C3

Bosjökloster 109 D3
Boskoop 16 C3
Bosna 71 F4
Bosna
  i Hercegovina ... 71 E4
Bošnjace 77 E1
Bošnjaci 72 B3
Bossóst 37 F2
Bostan 75 E2
Boštanj 70 B2
Boston 7 E3
Bosut 72 B2
Botev 115 D2
Botevgrad 115 D2
Bothel 5 D4
Boticas 34 B4
Botley 9 E3
Botngård 100 C1
Botnie, G de 102 A3
Botoš 72 C2
Botoşani 113 D3
Botrange 51 D4
Botsmark 102 A1
Botte Donato,
  Mte 67 F2
Bottenhavet 102 A3
Bottniska Viken
  Pohjanlahti 102 A3
Bottrop 17 E3
Botun 77 D4
Bouaye 24 B2
Boucau 28 A4
Bouchain 20 A2
Bouches-
  du-Rhône 30 B4
Boudry 27 C2
Bouillon 20 C2
Bouilly 26 B1
Boúka 86 C3
Boulay-Moselle ... 21 D3
Boulogne
  (Haute-Garonne) .. 37 F1
Boulogne
  (Pas-de-Calais) .. 19 E1
Boulogne R 24 B3
Bouloire 23 F3
Boulou, le 32 B2
Boumort 37 F3
Bourbon-
  Lancy 26 B3
Bourbon-
  l'Archambault 26 A3
Bourbonne-
  les-Bains 27 D1
Bourboule, la 29 E1
Bourbourg 19 F1
Bourbriac 22 C2
Bourdeaux 30 C2
Bourdeilles 28 C1
Bourg 28 B2
Bourg-Achard 19 D3
Bourganeuf 25 E4
Bourg-Argental ... 30 B1
Bourg-de-Péage ... 30 C2
Bourg-de-Visa 28 C3
Bourg-d'Oisans, le .. 31 D2
Bourg-en-Bresse ... 26 C3
Bourges 25 F3
Bourget, le 30 C1
Bourg-Lastic 29 E1
Bourg-Madame 32 A3
Bourgneuf
  -en-Retz 24 B3
Bourgogne 26 C2
Bourgoin-Jallieu .. 30 C1
Bourg-St-Andéol .. 30 B3
Bourg-St-Maurice .. 31 D1
Bourgtheroulde ... 19 D3
Bourgueil 25 D2
Bourmont 26 C1
Bourne 7 D3
Bourne,
  Gges de la 30 C2
Bournemouth 9 E3
Bourniá, Akr 87 E3
Bousquet-d'Orb,
  le 30 A4
Boussac 25 E4
Boussens 37 F1
Boutonne 24 C4
Bouxwiller 21 E3
Bouzonville 21 D3
Bovalino Marina .. 67 F4
Bova Marina 67 E4

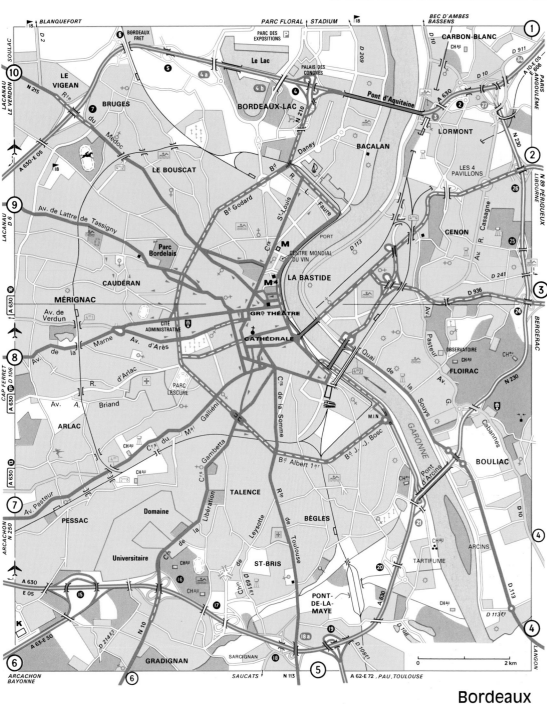

Bordeaux

Bovan 73 E4
Bovec 70 A2
Bóveda 34 B2
Bøverdal 100 B3
Boves 19 F2
Boves 31 E3
Bovey Tracy 8 C3
Bovolone 60 C1
Bowes 5 E4
Bowness 6 B1
Bowness-
  on-Solway 5 D3
Boxholm 109 E1
Boxmeer 17 D3
Boxtel 16 C3
Boyle 12 C2
Boyne 13 D3
Božaj 76 B3
Božava 74 C1
Bozdoğan 115 F4
Bozel 31 D1
Bozen 59 D3
Božica 77 E2
Boži Dar 53 E3
Bozouls 29 E3

Bozüyük 115 F3
Bozzolo 60 C2
Bra 31 F2
Brabant 50 B3
Brač 75 E2
Bracadale 2 B3
Bracadale, L 2 B3
Bracciano 63 E2
Bracciano, L di 63 E2
Bračevci 71 F2
Bracieux 25 E2
Bracco, Pso del ... 60 B3
Bračko-Hoby 109 D3
Bräcke 101 E2
Brackenheim 55 D2
Brackley 9 E2
Bracknell 9 F2
Brackwede 17 F3
Brad 112 C4
Bradano 65 D4
Bradashesh 76 C4
Bradford 6 C2
Bradford-on-Avon .. 9 D2
Bradina 75 F1
Brading 9 E3
Bradwell-on-Sea ... 11 D2

Braemar 3 D4
Braga 34 A4
Bragança 34 C3
Braguia, Pto de ... 35 F2
Braies, L di 59 D2
Brăila 113 E4
Braine 20 A3
Braine-le-Comte .. 50 B4
Braintree 11 D2
Brake 47 F3
Brakel 52 A2
Brálos 83 E3
Bramming 108 A3
Brampton 5 D3
Bramsche 17 E3
Brancaleone
  Marina 67 E4
Brancion 26 C3
Brand 58 B2
Brandbu 105 D2
Brande 108 A3
Brandenburg 49 D4

Brandenburg
  (Land) 49 D3
Brand-Erbisdorf .. 53 E3
Brander, Pass of ... 4 B1
Brandis 53 D2
Brändö 107 D2
Brandon 11 D1
Brandon Head ... 14 A3
Brandon Mt 14 A3
Brandýs Stará
  Boleslav 53 F3
Braničevo 73 E3
Braniewo 110 B4
Brallo
  di Pregola 60 A2
Braño Caballo ... 35 D2
Braňosera 35 F2
Br'ansk 111 E4
Brantôme 28 C1
Braskereidfoss ... 105 D2
Braslav 111 D3
Brašov 113 D3
Brassac-les-Mines .. 29 F1
Brasschaat 50 B3
Bratislava 112 A3
Brattvåg 100 A2

Bratunac 72 B4
Braubach 51 E4
Braunau 56 C3
Braunfels 51 F4
Braunlage 52 B2
Braunsbedra 53 D2
Braunschweig ... 52 B1
Braunton 8 C3
Braus, Col de 31 E3
Bravães 34 A3
Bravuogn 58 B3
Bray (IRL) 13 E4
Bray
  (Seine-et-Marne) .. 20 A4
Bray (Somme) ... 19 F2
Bray-Dunes 19 F1
Brazatortas 43 F1
Brbinj 74 C1
Brčko 72 B3
Brda 110 A4
Brddani 73 D4
Brea 36 C4
Brécey 18 B4
Brechin 3 E4
Brecht 50 C3

Břeclav 57 F1
Brecon 8 C1
Brecon Beacons
  Nat Pk 8 C2
Breda (E) 32 B4
Breda (NL) 16 C3
Bredbyn 102 A2
Bredelar 17 F3
Bredstedt 47 F1
Bree 50 C3
Bregalnica 77 F3
Breganze 59 D4
Bregenz 58 B1
Bréhal 18 B4
Bréhat, I de 22 C2
Breiðafjörður 96 A2
Breil-sur-Roya 31 E3
Breisach 54 B4
Breitengüßbach 52 C4
Breitungen 52 B3
Breivikbotn 95 D1
Breivikeidet 94 C2
Brekke 104 A1
Brekken 101 D2
Brekkvasselv 97 D4
Brekstad 100 C1
Bremanger
  Landet 100 A3
Bremen 47 F3
Bremerhaven 47 F3
Bremervörde 47 F3
Bremsnes 100 B2
Breña, Emb de la ... 43 E2
Brenes 43 D2
Brenna 53 D2
Brenner 59 D2
Brennilis 22 B3
Breno 58 C4
Brénod 26 C4
Brentwood 10 C2
Brescia 60 B1
Breskens 16 B4
Bresle 19 E2
Bresles 19 F3
Bressanone 59 D2
Bressay 3 F2
Bresse, la 27 E1
Bressuire 24 C3
Brest (F) 22 A2
Brest (UKR) 112 C1
Brest R. 23 D4
Brestanica 70 C2
Brestova 70 B3
Brestovac (HR) 71 E2
Brestovac (Srbija) . 73 E3
Brestovac (Srbija) . 77 D1
Brestovac (Srbija) . 77 E1
Brestovačka
  Banja 73 E3
Bretenoux 29 D2
Breteuil (Eure) 19 D4
Breteuil (Oise) 19 F3
Bretten 54 C2
Breuil-Cervinia 27 E4
Brevik 104 C4
Breza 71 F4
Brežđđe 72 C4
Brežice 70 C2
Breznica 70 C2
Breznica
  Đakovačka 71 F2
Březnice 56 C1
Brezno 112 B3
Brezolles 19 E4
Brezovica 77 D2
Brezovo Polje (BH) . 72 B3
Brezovo Polje (HR) . 71 E2
Briançon 31 D2
Briare 26 A2
Bribirske Mostine .. 75 D1
Bricquebec 18 B3
Brides 31 D1
Bridgend
  (Scotland) 4 A2
Bridgend (Wales) 8 C2
Bridge of Allan 4 C2
Bridgnorth 9 D1
Bridgwater 9 D3
Bridlington 7 E1
Bridport 9 D3
Briec 22 B3
Brie-Comte-
  Robert 19 F4
Brielle 16 B3

Brienne-
  le-Château 20 B4
Brienon 26 A1
Brienz 27 F3
Brienza 64 C4
Briey 21 D3
Brig 27 F3
Brigg 7 D2
Brighouse 6 C2
Brightlingsea 11 D2
Brighton 10 C3
Brignogan 22 A2
Brignoles 31 D4
Brihuega 40 B2
Briksdal 100 A3
Brilon 17 F3
Brimnes 104 B2
Brinches 42 B1
Brindisi 65 F3
Brinon 26 A2
Brione 19 D3
Brioude 29 F1
Brioux 24 C4
Briouze 18 C4
Brisighella 61 D3
Brissac-Quincé 24 C2
Brissago 58 A3
Bristol 9 D2
Bristol Chan. 8 C2
Brive-la-Gaillarde . 29 D2
Briviesca 36 A2
Brixen 59 D2
Brixham 8 C4
Brixlegg 59 D1
Brjánslækur 96 A1
Brka 72 B3
Brna 75 E2
Brnaze 75 D1
Brno 57 F1
Bro (Gotlands
  Län) 109 F4
Bro (Stockholms
  Län) 106 B3
Broad B 2 B2
Broadford (GB) 2 B3
Broadford (IRL) 12 B4
Broad Haven 12 B2
Broad Law 5 D3
Broadstairs 11 D3
Broadway 9 E1
Broager 108 A4
Broby 109 D3
Brocken 52 B2
Brod (BH) 76 A1
Brod (Makedonija) .. 77 D3
Brodarevo 76 B1
Brodica 73 E3
Brodick 4 B2
Brod na Kupi 70 B3
Brodnica 112 B1
Brody (PL) 53 F1
Brody (UKR) 113 D2
Broglie 19 D3
Brohl-Lützing 51 E4
Brolo 69 D2
Bromarv 107 D3
Brombachsee 55 E2
Brome 48 B4
Bromölla 109 D3
Bromsgrove 9 E1
Bromyard 9 D1
Bronchales 41 D2
Brønderslev 108 B2
Broni 60 A2
Brønnøysund 97 D3
Brøns 108 A3
Bronte 69 D3
Bronzani Majdan ... 71 D3
Broom, L 2 C2
Broons 22 C3
Brora 3 D3
Brösarp 109 D3
Brossac 28 B1
Brøstadbotn 94 B3
Brotas 38 B4
Broto 37 E2
Brotton 5 F4
Brøttum 105 D2
Brou (Ain) 26 C4
Brou
  (Eure-et-Loir) ... 25 E1
Brouage 24 B4
Brough 5 E3

Brough Head 3 D1
Broughshane 13 E1
Broughton-
  in-Furness 6 B1
Brouis, Col de 31 E3
Brovst 108 B2
Brownhills 9 E1
Brozas 39 D3
Bruay-en-Artois 19 F1
Bruay-sur-l'Escaut . 20 A1
Bruchsal 54 C2
Brück 53 D1
Bruck (D) 56 B1
Bruck
  (Niederösterreich) 57 F2
Bruck (Salzburg) ... 59 E1
Bruck an der Mur ... 57 E4
Brückl 70 B1
Bruckmühl 56 B3
Brüel 48 C2
Brués 34 B2
Bruges 50 A3
Brugg 27 F2
Brügge 17 E4
Brugge 50 A3
Brühl 17 E4
Brújula, Pto de la . 36 A2
Bruksvallarna 101 D3
Brûlon 23 E3
Brumath 21 E4
Brummen 17 D3
Brumunddal 105 D2
Bruneck 59 D2
Brunete 40 A2
Brunflo 101 E2
Brunico 59 D2
Brünigpass 27 F3
Bruniquel 29 D3
Brunkeberg 104 B3
Brunnen 58 A2
Brunsbüttel 47 F2
Brunssum 17 D4
Bruntál 112 A3
Bruravik 104 B2
Brus 77 D1
Brusand 104 A4
Brušane 70 C4
Brusasco 31 F1
Brusnik 73 F3
Brusson 27 F4
Brüssow 49 E2
Bruton 9 D3
Bruvno 70 C4
Bruxelles 50 B3
Bruyères 27 D1
Brvenik 76 C1
Bryne 104 A4
Brynmawr 9 D2
Brzan 73 D3
Brza Palanka 73 F3
Brzeće 77 D1
Brzeg 112 A2
Buarcos 38 B2
Buavåg 104 A3
Bubry 22 C3
Bučač 113 D3
Buçaco 38 B2
Buccheri 69 D4
Bucchianico 64 C2
Bucelas 38 A4
Buchan Ness 3 E3
Büchen 48 B3
Buchen 55 D1
Buchenwald 52 C3
Buchholz 48 A3
Buchloe 55 E3
Buchs 58 B2
Buchy 19 E3
Bucine 61 D4
Bučje 73 F4
Bückeburg 52 A1
Buckfastleigh 8 C4
Buckhaven 5 D2
Buckie 3 E3
Buckingham 9 F2
Buckinghamshire 9 F2
Buckovička
  Banja 73 D3
Buckow 49 E4
Bückwitz 49 D3
Bučovice 57 F1
Bucovina 113 D3
Bucureşti 115 D1

Bud 100 B2
Budapest 112 B4
Búðardalur 96 A2
Buddon Ness 5 D1
Buddusò 66 B2
Bude 8 B3
Büdelsdorf 48 A2
Budimlić Japra 71 D3
Büdingen 52 A4
Budinščina 70 C2
Budleigh
  Salterton 8 C3
Budrio 61 D2
Budva 76 B3
Budyně nad
  Ohře 53 F3
Buenache
  de Alarcón 40 C3
Buen Amor 39 E1
Buenavista
  de Valdavia 35 E3
Buendía 40 C2
Buendía, Emb de 40 C2
Buet, Mt. 27 E4
Bueu 34 A2
Bug 112 C1
Bugeat 29 D1
Bugojno 71 E4
Bugøynes 95 F2
Bugue, le 28 C2
Bühl 54 C3
Builth Wells 9 D1
Buin, Piz 58 B2
Buis-les-Baronnies . 30 C3
Buitrago
  del Lozoya 40 B1
Bujalance 43 F2
Bujanovac 77 E2
Bujaraloz 37 E4
Buje 70 A3

Brugge

Budapest

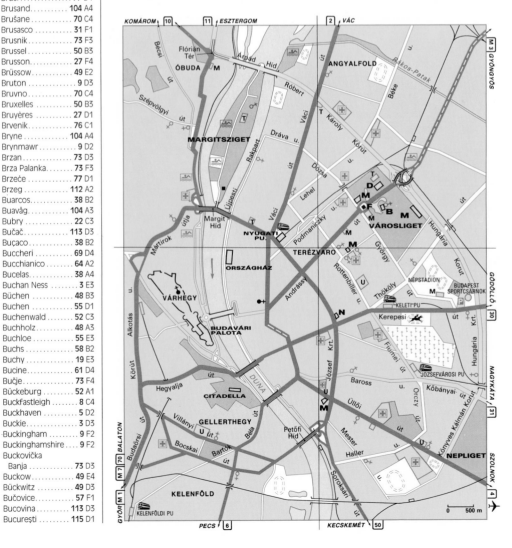

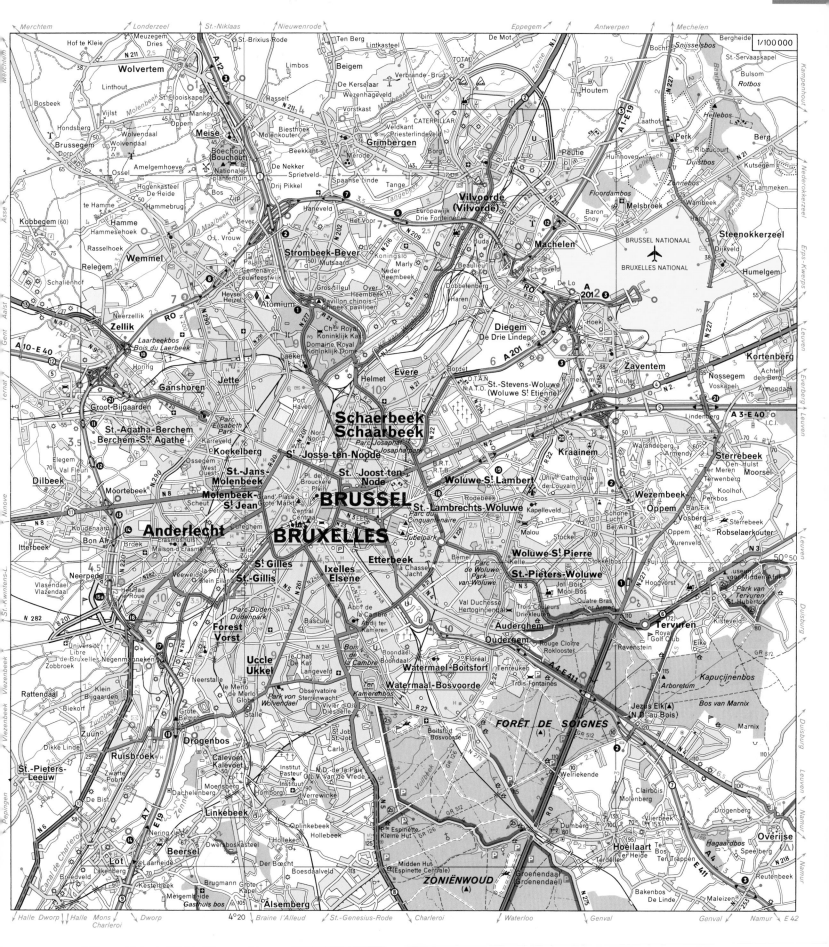

Bujeo, Pto del **43** D4
Bukinje **71** F3
Bukova Gora **75** E1
Bukovi **72** C4
Bukovo **77** D4
Bülach **58** A1
Buldan **115** F4
Bulgnéville **27** D1
Bullas **44** C2
Bulle **27** E3
Büllingen **51** E4
Bully **19** F1
Bultei **66** B2
Buna **75** F2
Bunclody **15** D3
Buncrana **13** D1
Bünde **17** F2
Bunde **47** E3
Bun Dobhráin **12** C2
Bundoran **12** C2
Bunë **76** B3
Bunessan **4** B1
Bungay **11** D1

Bunič **70** C4
Bunmahon **14** C4
Buñol **41** E4
Bunratty
  Castle **12** B4
Buntingford **9** F2
Buñuel **36** C3
Buonabitacolo . . . **67** D1
Buonalbergo **64** B3
Buonconvento . . . **61** D4
Buonfornello **68** C3
Bürgel **52** C3
Burbach **51** F3
Búrbaguena **41** D1
Bure **7** F3
Bureå **98** B4
Burela **34** C1
Büren **17** F3
Buren **47** D3
Burfjord **95** D2
Burford **9** E2
Burg (Sachsen-
  Anhalt) **48** C4

Burg (Schleswig-
  Holstein) **48** B1
Burgas **115** E2
Burgau **55** E3
Burgbernheim **55** E1
Burgdorf (CH) **27** E2
Burgdorf (D) **48** B4
Burgenland **57** F4
Burgess Hill **10** C3
Burggrub **52** C4
Burghasungen **52** A2
Burghausen **56** B3
Burgjoß **52** B4
Burgkunstadt **52** C4
Burglengenfeld . . . **55** F1
Burgohondo **39** F2
Burgos **35** F3
Burgsinn **52** B4
Burgstädt **53** E3
Burg Stargard **49** D2
Burgsvik **109** F4
Burgsviken **109** F4

Burguete **36** C1
Burgui **37** D2
Burguillo,
  Emb de **39** F2
Burguillos
  del Cerro **43** D1
Burhaniye **115** E4
Burhave **47** F3
Burie **28** B1
Burjassot **41** E4
Burk **53** F2
Burkau **53** F2
Burnham **9** D3
Burnham-
  on-Crouch **11** D2
Burnley **6** C2
Burntisland **5** D2
Buronzo **31** F1
Burrel **76** C3
Burriana **41** E3
Burrow Head **4** C4
Burry Port **8** C2
Bursa **115** F3

Burscheid **17** E4
Bürstadt **54** C1
Burton-upon-Trent . . **6** C3
Burträsk **98** B4
Burwick **3** E1
Bury **6** C2
Buryn' **113** F1
Bury St Edmunds . . **11** D1
Busalla **60** A3
Busambra, Rca **68** B3
Busca **31** E2
Buševa pl **77** D3
Buševec **70** C2
Bushat **76** C3
Bushmills **13** E1
Buskerud **104** C2
Buško Blato **75** E1
Busko-Zdrój **112** B2
Busovača **71** F4
Bussang **27** E1
Busseto **60** B2
Bussière-Badil **28** C1
Bussolengo **60** C1

Bussum **16** C2
Busto Arsizio **60** A1
Busto de Bureba . . **36** A2
Büsum **47** F2
Butera **68** C4
Buthrotum **114** C4
Bute **4** B2
Buttermere **5** D4
Buttevant **14** B3
Butt of Lewis **2** B2
Buttstädt **52** C2
Butzbach **51** F4
Bützow **48** C2
Buxtehude **48** A3
Buxton **6** C3
Buxy **26** C3
Buzancais **25** E3
Buzancy **20** C3
Buzău **113** E4
Buzău R. **113** E4
Buzet **70** A3
Bužim **70** C3
Bychov **111** E4

Bydgoszcz **112** A1
Bygdeå **102** B1
Bygdin **100** B3
Bygdin L **100** B3
Bygdsiljum **102** B1
Bygland **104** B3
Byglandsfjord **104** B4
Byglandsfjord L . . . **104** B3
Bykle **104** B3
Bykleheiene **104** B3
Bylderup-Bov **108** A4
Byrkjelo **100** B3
Byske **98** B4
Byskeälven **98** B3
Bytom **112** B2
Bytów **110** A4
Byxelkrok **109** E2

C

Cabañaquinta **35** D2
Cabañas **44** B2
Cabanes **41** F3
Cabannes, les **32** A2
Čabar **70** B3
Cabeceiras **34** B4
Cabeço de Vide . . . **38** C3
Cabella Ligure **60** A2
Cabeza del Buey . . **39** E4
Cabezas Rubias . . . **42** C2
Cabezo Gordo **42** C2
Cabezón **35** E4
Cabezón de la Sal . **35** F2
Cabezuela del
  Valle **39** E2
Cabo de Gata **44** C4
Cabourg **18** C3
Cabra **43** F2
Cabra del
  Santo Cristo **44** A2
Cabras **66** A3
Cabre, Col de **30** C2
Cabreira, Sa da . . . **34** B4
Cabreiros **34** B1
Cabrejas, Pto de . . **40** C3
Cabrejas, Sa de . . . **36** A3
Cabréra **36** C4
Cabrera, I de **45** F3
Cabrera, Sa de la . . **34** C3
Cabrerets **29** D3
Cabriel, R **41** D3
Cabril, Bgem do . . **38** B2
Cabrillas **39** E1
Cabrito, Pto del . . . **43** D4
Cabuérniga **35** F2
Čabulja **75** E1
Cacabelos **34** C2
Čačak **73** D4
Caccamo **68** B3
Cacela **42** B3
Cáceres **39** D3
Cachafeiro **34** A2
Cachopo **42** B2
Čačinci **71** E2
Cadabo **34** C2
Cadalso de
  los Vidrios **40** A2
Cadaqués **32** C3
Cadarache **30** C3
Cadaval **38** A3
Čaddavica **71** E4
Čadca **112** B3
Cadelbosco di
  Sopra **60** C2
Cadenabbia **58** B4
Cadena, Pto de la . **45** D2

Cadenberge **47** F2
Cadenet **30** C3
Cader Idris **6** A3
Cádiar **44** A3
Cadillac **28** B2
Cadipietra **59** D2
Cadi, Serra del . . . **32** A3
Cádiz **43** D4
Cádiz, B de **43** D4
Cádiz, G de **42** C3
Cadouin **28** C2
Caen **18** C3
Caerdydd **9** D2
Caerfyrddin **8** C2
Caergybi **6** A2
Caernarfon **6** A3
Caernarfon B **6** A3
Caerphilly **9** D2
Caersws **9** D1
Cafasan **77** D4
Cagli **61** E4
Cagliari **66** B4
Cagliari, G di **66** B4
Čaglin **71** E2
Cagnano Varano . . **64** C2
Cagnes **31** E3
Caha Mts **14** A4
Caher **14** C3
Cahersiveen **14** A4
Cahore Pt **15** E3
Cahors **29** D3
Cahul **113** E4
Caia, Bgem do . . . **38** C4
Caianello **64** A3
Caión **34** A1
Cairn Gorm **3** D4
Cairngorm Mts **3** D4
Cairnryan **4** B3
Cairo Montenotte . **31** F2
Caiseal **14** C3
Caisleán an
  Bharraigh **12** B3
Caistor **7** D2
Caivano **64** B4
Cajarc **29** D3
Čajetina **72** C4
Čajniče **76** B1
Čakor **76** C2
Čakovec **70** C1
Cakovice **53** F3
Çal **115** F4
Calabor **34** C3
Calabria **67** E2
Calaceite **41** F1
Calacuccia **33** F3
Cala d'Or **45** F3
Cala, Emb de la . . **43** D2
Calaf **37** F3
Calafat **114** C2

Calafell **37** F4
Calafort Ros Láir . . **15** D4
Cala Gonone **66** C2
Calahonda **44** A4
Calahorra **8** C4
Calais **19** E1
Calamocha **41** D1
Calañas **42** C2
Calanche, les **33** E3
Calanda **41** E1
Calanda, Emb de . . **41** E2
Calangianus **66** B1
Cala'n Porter **45** F2
Calar Alto **44** B3
Calasetta **66** A4
Calasparra **44** C2
Calatafimi **68** B3
Calatañazor **36** B3
Calatayud **36** C4
Calatorao **36** C4
Calau **53** E1
Calazzo **64** B3
Calbe **52** C1
Calcena **36** C3
Caldaro **59** D3
Caldarola **61** F4
Caldas da Rainha . . **38** A3
Caldas das Taipas . **34** A4
Caldas de Reis . . . **34** A2
Caldas de Vizela . . **34** A4
Caldeirão, Sa do . . **42** B2
Caldelas **34** A3
Caldera de Taburiente,
  Pque Nac de la . . **42** A4
Calderina **40** A4
Caldes de Boi **37** F2
Caldes de
  Malavella **32** B3
Caldes de
  Montbui **32** A4
Caldirola **60** A2
Caledonian Canal . . **2** C4
Calella
  (Palamós) **32** C3
Calella
  (Pineda de Mar) . **32** B4
Calenzana **33** F3
Calera de León . . . **43** D1
Calera y Chozas . . **39** F3
Caleruega **36** A3
Caletta, la **66** C2
Càlig **41** F2
Călimănești **115** D1
Călimani, M. **113** D4
Calitri **64** C3
Calizzano **31** F2

Callac **22** B3
Callan **15** D3
Callander **4** C1
Calla, Pso della . . . **61** D3
Callington **8** C4
Callosa d'En
  Sarrià **45** E1
Callosa de
  Segura **45** D2
Calmazzo **61** E3
Calmbach **54** C2
Calne **9** E2
Calolziocorte **58** B4
Calonge **32** B3
Calp **45** E1
Caltabellotta **68** B3
Caltagirone **69** D4
Caltanissetta **68** C3
Caltavuturo **68** C3
Caluso **31** E1
Calvados **18** C3
Calvi **33** E3
Calvitero **39** E2
Calvörde **48** C4
Calw **54** C2
Calzada de
  Calatrava **44** A1
Calzada de
  Valdunciel **39** E1
Cam **9** F1
Camacho, Pto **44** A3
Camaiore **60** C3
Camaldoli **61** D3
Camarasa **37** F3
Camarasa,
  Emb de **37** F3
Camarat, Cap **31** D4
Camarena **40** A2
Camarès **32** B1
Camaret **22** A3
Camarillas **41** E2
Camarillas,
  Emb de **44** C1
Camariñas **34** A1
Camarzana **35** D3
Camas **43** D2
Cambados **34** A2
Cambas **38** C2
Camberley **9** F2
Cambil **44** A2
Cambo-les-Bains . . **28** A4
Camborne **8** B4
Cambrai **20** A2
Cambre **34** B1
Cambremer **19** D3
Cambrian Mts **8** C1
Cambridge **10** C1
Cambridgeshire . . . **10** C1

Cambrils de Mar . . **37** F4
Camburg **52** C3
Camelford **8** B3
Camerino **61** E4
Camigliatello
  Silano **67** E2
Caminha **34** A3
Caminomorisco . . . **39** D2
Caminreal **41** D2
Camogli **60** A3
Campagna **64** C4
Campagne-lès-
  Hesdin **19** E2
Campan **37** E1
Campana **67** F2
Campanario **39** E4
Campania **64** B4
Campaspero **35** F4
Campbeltown **4** B3
Campi Bisenzio . . . **60** C3
Campiglia
  Marittima **62** C1
Campilhas,
  Bgem de **42** A1
Campillo de
  Altobuey **41** D3
Campillo de
  Aragón **36** C4
Campillo de
  Arenas **44** A2
Campillo de
  Llerena **43** D1
Campillos **43** E3
Campione **58** A4
Campi Salentina . . **65** F4
Campli **63** F1
Campo **37** E2
Campobasso **64** B3
Campobello di
  Licata **68** C4
Campobello di
  Mazara **68** A3
Campo Carlo
  Magno **58** C3
Campo de
  Beisteros **38** B1
Campo de Caso . . . **35** E2
Campo de
  Criptana **40** B4
Campo di Fiori . . . **58** A4
Campo di Giove . . **64** A2
Campoformido . . . **59** F3
Campogalliano . . . **60** C2
Campo
  Imperatore **63** F1
Campo Ligure **60** A3
Campo Maior **38** C4

Campomanes **35** D2
Campomarino **64** B2
Campora
  San Giovanni . . . **67** E3
Camporredondo,
  Emb de **35** E2
Camporrobles **41** D3
Campos **45** F3
Camposampiero . . **59** D4
Campos, Canal de . **35** E4
Campotosto, L di . . **63** F1
Campo Tures **59** D2
Camprodon **32** B3
Camucia **61** D4
Camuñas **40** B3
Canada de
  Benatanduz **41** E2
Cañadas, Pto **43** D1
Çanakkale **115** E3
Çanakkale Boğazı . **115** E3
Canal du Nord . . . **19** F2
Canal du Rhône au
  Rhin **27** E2
Canales de la
  Sierra **36** A3
Canals **41** E4
Canal San Bovo . . **59** D3
Cañamero **39** E3
Canarias, Is **42** B4
Canas de
  Senhorim **38** C1
Cañaveral **39** D3
Cañaveral de León . **43** D2
Cañaveras **40** C2
Canazei **59** D3
Cancale **18** B4
Cancárix **45** D1
Canche **19** E1
Cancon **28** C2
Candanchu **37** D2
Candas **35** D1
Candasnos **37** E4
Candé **23** E4
Candeeiros,
  Sa dos **38** A3
Candela **64** C3
Candelaria, Sa . . . **39** E2
Candelario **39** E2
Candelaro **64** C2
Candeleda **39** F2
Candes **25** D2
Canelles, Emb de . . **37** F3
Canelli **31** F2
Canero **35** D1
Canet de Mar **32** B4
Cañete **41** D3
Cañete de las
  Torres **43** F2
Cañete la Real . . . **43** E3

Canet-Plage **32** B2
Canfranc-
  Estación **37** D2
Cangas **34** A3
Cangas de Narcea . **34** C2
Cangas de Onís . . **35** E1
Canha **38** B4
Canicattì **68** C4
Canicattini Bagni . . **69** D4
Canigou, Pic du . . **32** B2
Canigral **41** D3
Caniles **44** B3
Canin, M **59** F3
Canino **63** D2
Canis **18** B3
Cañizal **39** E1
Canjáyar **44** B3
Canna **2** B4
Cannero Riviera . . **58** A4
Cannes **31** E4
Canneto **60** C4
Cannich **2** C3
Cannobio **58** A4
Cannock **9** E1
Canonbie **5** D3
Canosa di Puglia . . **64** C3
Canourgue, la **29** F3
Cansano **64** A2
Cansiglio **59** E3
Cantabria **35** F2
Cantal (Dépt) **29** E2
Cantal, Mts du . . . **29** E2
Cantalapiedra **39** F1
Cantalejo **40** A1
Cantalpino **39** E1
Cantanhede **38** B2
Cantavieja **41** E2
Čantavir **72** B1
Canterbury **11** D3
Cantillana **43** D2
Cantoira **31** E1
Cantoral **35** E2
Cantoria **44** C3
Cantù **60** A1
Canvey I **11** D2
Cany-Barville **19** D2
Caorle **59** E4
Caorso **60** B2
Capaccio **64** C4
Capaci **68** B3
Capalbio **63** D2
Capannelle,
  Pso delle **63** F1
Caparde **72** B3
Caparroso **36** C2
Capbreton **28** A4
Cap Corse **33** F2
Cap-d'Agde, le . . . **30** A4
Cap d'Antibes **31** E4

Terminal de Calais

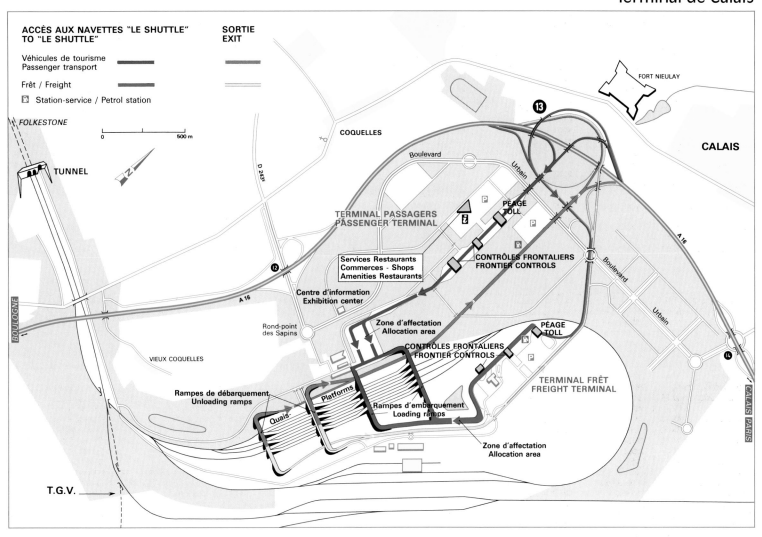

ACCÈS AUX NAVETTES "LE SHUTTLE"
TO "LE SHUTTLE"

SORTIE
EXIT

Véhicules de tourisme
Passenger transport

Frêt / Freight

Ⓢ Station-service / Petrol station

FOLKESTONE

0   500 m

N

TUNNEL

COQUELLES

FORT NIEULAY

CALAIS

Boulevard

Urbain

A 16

TERMINAL PASSAGERS
PASSENGER TERMINAL

PÉAGE
TOLL

CONTRÔLES FRONTALIERS
FRONTIER CONTROLS

Services Restaurants
Commerces - Shops
Amenities Restaurants

Boulevard

Urbain

Centre d'information
Exhibition center

BOULOGNE

A 16

Rond-point
des Sapins

VIEUX COQUELLES

Zone d'affectation
Allocation area

PÉAGE
TOLL

CONTRÔLES FRONTALIERS
FRONTIER CONTROLS

Rampes de débarquement,
Unloading ramps

Platforms

TERMINAL FRÊT
FREIGHT TERMINAL

Quais

Rampes d'embarquement
Loading ramps

Zone d'affectation
Allocation area

CALAIS PARIS

T.G.V.

Capdenac-Gare **29** E2	Carbonara, Pzo **68** C3	Carignan........... **20** C2	Carnsore Pt........ **15** D4	Carrickmacross **13** D3	Casale Monferrato . **31** F1	Cas-gwent........... **9** D2
Capel Curig **6** A3	Carbon-Blanc **28** B2	Carignano.......... **31** E2	Carnwath **5** D2	Carrick-on-	Casale sul Sile **59** E4	Cashel **14** C3
Capelle, la **20** B2	Carboneras **44** C3	Carina............. **77** D4	Caroch **41** D4	Shannon **12** C3	Casalmaggiore..... **60** B2	Casicas del Rio
Capendu........... **32** B2	Carboneras de	Cariñena.......... **36** C4	Carolles **18** B4	Carrick-on-Suir ... **14** C3	Casalpusterlengo .. **60** B2	Segura **44** B2
Capestang........ **30** A4	Guadazaón...... **41** D3	Carini............. **68** B3	Carovigno **65** E3	Carrigart........... **12** C1	Casamassima **65** D3	Casillas **39** D2
Capestrano **64** A2	Carbonero	Cariño............ **34** B1	Carrio.............. **34** B1	Casamicciola	Casina **60** C2
Capileira **44** A3	el Mayor........ **40** A1	Carinola **64** A3	Carovigno	Carrión de	Terme........... **64** A4	Casinos........... **41** E3
Capistrello **63** F2	Carbonia.......... **66** B4	Carisio **31** F1	Piacentino **60** B2	Calatrava **40** A4	Casa Nuevas **44** C2	Casnewydd **9** D2
Čapljina **75** F2	Carbonin **59** E2	Carlet............. **41** E4	Carpaţii	Carrión de	Casarabonela **43** E3	Casoio............ **34** C3
Capmany **32** B3	Carbonne.......... **37** F1	Carling **21** D3	Meridionali...... **114** C1	los Condes **35** E3	Casarano **65** F4	Casola in Lunigiana . **60** B3
Cappelle sul Tavo . **64** A1	Carcaboso **39** D2	Carlingford........ **13** E3	Carpenedolo **60** B1	Carrión, R. **35** E3	Casar de Cáceres . **39** D3	Casoli............ **64** A2
Cappoquin **14** C4	Carcabuey **43** F3	Carlingford L. **13** E3	Carpentras **30** C3	Carrizo de la	Casares **43** E4	Casoria **64** B4
Capracotta **64** A2	Carcaixent **41** E4	Carlisle **5** D3	Carpi.............. **60** C2	Ribera........... **35** D2	Casares de las	Caspe............. **37** E4
Capraia, I di **62** B1	Carcans **28** A2	Carlit, Pic **32** A2	Carpignano Sesia . **58** A4	Carro **30** C4	Hurdes **39** D2	Cassà de la Selva . **32** B3
Caprera, I **66** B1	Carcans-Plage **28** A2	Carloforte **66** A4	Carpineti **60** C3	Carrouges **18** C4	Casariche **43** E3	Cassagnes-
Capri **64** B4	Carcare **31** F2	Carlow **13** D4	Carpineto	Carrù **31** F2	Casarsa **59** E3	Begonhès **29** E3
Capriati a	Carcassonne...... **32** B1	Carlow (Co) **13** D4	Romano **63** F3	Carry-le-Rouet.... **30** C4	Casas de	Cassano allo Ionio . **67** E2
Volturno **64** A3	Carcastillo **36** C2	Carloway **2** B2	Carpinone **64** A3	Carsoli **63** F2	Don Pedro **39** E4	Cassano delle
Capri,I di **64** B4	Carcès **31** D4	Carluke **4** C2	Carquefou **24** B2	Cartagena **45** D3	Casas de Fernando	Murge **65** D3
Captieux **28** B3	Carche **45** D1	Carmagnola **31** E2	Carqueiranne **31** D4	Cártama **43** F4	Alonso **40** C4	Cassel............ **19** F1
Capua **64** B3	Čardak **71** F4	Carmarthen........ **8** C2	Carracedelo **34** C2	Casas de Juan	Cassino **64** A3
Capurso **65** D3	Çardak **115** F4	Carmarthen B. **8** B2	Carradale **4** B2	Cartaxo **38** A3	Núñez **41** D4	Cassis **30** C4
Capvern **37** E1	Cardedeu **32** B4	Carmaux **29** E3	Carraig na Siúire . **14** C3	Cartaya **42** C2	Casas del Puerto . **45** D1	Castalla **45** D1
Caracal **115** D2	Cardeña **43** F1	Carmona **43** E2	Carral **34** B1	Carter Bar **5** D3	Casas de Luján ... **40** B3	Castanet-Tolosan . **29** D4
Caracuel.......... **40** A4	Cardener, R. **32** A4	Carna **12** A3	Carrantuohill. **14** A4	Carteret **18** B3	Casas de Miravete . **39** E3	Castanheira de
Caragh, L **14** A4	Cardenete **41** D3	Carnac **22** C4	Carranza.......... **36** A1	Carvajal **43** F4	Casas Ibáñez **41** D4	Pêra **38** B2
Caraman **29** D4	Cardiff **9** D2	Carnaio, Pso del . **61** D3	Carrara **60** B3	Carvicais.......... **39** D1	Casas de Luján	Castaños,
Caramanico Terme . **64** A2	Cardigan **8** B1	Carn Ban.......... **2** C4	Carrascal **41** E2	Carvin **19** F1	Casasimarro **40** C4	Pto de los...... **39** D3
Caramulo **38** B1	Cardigan B **8** B1	Carndonagh **13** D1	Carrascosa del	Carvoeira **42** A3	Casatejada **39** E3	Castasegna **58** B3
Caramulo, Sa do . **38** B1	Cardona **32** A3	Carnedd Llewelyn . **6** A3	Campo **40** C3	Carvoeiro, C **38** A3	Casavieja **39** F2	Casteggio **60** A2
Caransebeş....... **114** C1	Carei **112** C3	Carnew **15** D3	Carrascoy **45** D2	Casabermeja **43** F3	Cascais **38** A4	Castejón **36** C3
Carantec **22** B2	Carentan **18** B3	Carnforth **6** B1	Carrasqueta,	Casa Branca	Cascante **36** C3	Castejón de
Caravaca de la	Cares, R. **35** E2	Carnia **59** F3	Port de la **45** E1	(Alentejo) **42** A1	Cascia **63** E1	Monègros **37** E4
Cruz............ **44** C2	Carevdar **71** D2	Carnia (Reg) **59** E3	Carrazeda de	Casa Branca	Casciana Terme .. **60** C4	Castejón de Sos... **37** E2
Caravai, Pso di ... **66** B3	Carev Dvor **77** D4	Carnlough **13** E1	Ansiães......... **34** B4	(Ribatejo)....... **38** B4	Cascina **60** C4	Castejón de
Caravius, M. is ... **66** B4	Carevo **115** E2	Carnon **30** B4	Carrazedo de	Casalarreina **36** B2	Casei Gerola **60** A2	Valdejasa **37** D3
Carbajales de Alba . **35** D4	Cargèse **33** E3	Carnota **34** A2	Montenegro **34** B4	Casalbordino **64** B1	Caselle in Pittari . **67** D1	Castelbuono **68** C3
Carballiño......... **34** B2	Carhaix-Plouguer . **22** B3	Carnoustie **5** D1	Carrbridge **3** D4	Casalbuttano **60** B1	Caselle Torinese . **31** E1	Casteldaccia **68** B3
Carballo **34** A1	Caria **38** C2		Carregado **38** A3	Casal di Principe . **64** A4	Caserio	Casteldelfino **31** E2
Carbayo **35** D2	Cariati **67** F2		Carregal do Sal.. **38** B2	Carreña de Cabrales **35** E1	del Puente **35** D3	Caserta **64** B3	Castel del Monte
Carbonara, C **66** C4	Cariçin Grad...... **77** D1		Carnoustie **5** D1	Carrickfergus **13** E2	Casalecchio	Casetas **37** D3	(Abruzzo) **63** F2

Castel del Monte
  (Puglia)........... 65 D3
Castel del Rio...... 61 D3
Castel di Sangro.... 64 A2
Castelfidardo...... 61 F4
Castelfiorentino ... 60 C4
Castelfranco
  Emilia........... 60 C2
Castelfranco in
  Miscano......... 64 B3
Castelfranco
  Veneto........... 59 D4
Castel Gandolfo.... 63 E3
Casteljaloux....... 28 B3
Castellabate....... 67 D1
Castellamare di
  Stabbia........... 64 B4
Castellammare
  d. Golfo........... 48 B3
Castellammare,
  G di............. 68 B3
Castellamonte..... 31 E1
Castellana Grotte ... 65 E3
Castellane........ 31 D3
Castellaneta...... 65 E4
Castellar de
  la Muela......... 41 D2
Castellar del
  Vallès........... 32 A4
Castellar de
  Santiago........ 44 B1
Castellar de
  Santisteban..... 44 B2
Castell' Arquato.... 60 B2
Castelldans....... 37 F4
Castelldefels..... 32 A4
Castell de Ferro.... 44 A4
Castelleone...... 60 B1
Castellfollit de
  la Roca......... 32 B3
Castellina in Chianti. 61 D4
Castell-nedd....... 8 C2
Castelló de
  la Plana........ 41 F3
Castello del Lago... 64 B3
Castelló
  d'Empúries....... 32 B3
Castellolí....... 32 A4
Castellón de
  la Plana........ 41 F3
Castellón de
  Rugat........... 45 E1
Castellote....... 41 E2
Castello Tesino... 59 D3
Castellterçol..... 32 A4
Castelluccia..... 63 F1
Castel Madama.... 63 F2
Castelmassa...... 60 C2
Castelmauro...... 64 B2
Castelmoron..... 28 C3
Castelnaudary.... 32 A1
Castelnau-de-
  Médoc.......... 28 B2
Castelnau-de-
  Montmiral....... 29 D3
Castelnau-
  Magnoac........ 37 E1
Castelnau-
  Montratier....... 29 D3
Castelnau-Rivière-
  Basse.......... 28 B4
Castelnovo ne'
  Monti.......... 60 B3
Castelnuovo
  Berardenga...... 61 D4
Castelnuovo Bocca
  d'Adda.......... 60 B2
Castelnuovo della
  Daunia.......... 64 B3
Castelnuovo di
  Garfagnana...... 60 C3
Castelnuovo di
  Porto.......... 63 E2
Castelnuovo
  Scrivia........ 60 A2
Castelo Branco.... 38 C2
Castelo de Bode,
  Bgem do........ 38 B3
Castelo de Paiva.. 34 A4
Castelo de Vide... 38 C3
Castelraimondo... 61 E4
Castelrotto..... 59 D3
Castel
  San Giovanni 60 A2

Castel
  San Lorenzo..... 64 C4
Castel San Pietro
  Terme.......... 61 D3
Castelsardo...... 66 B1
Castelsarrasin.... 29 D3
Castelserás...... 41 E1
Casteltermini.... 68 B3
Castelvecchio
  Subequo........ 63 F2
Castelvetrano.... 68 A3
Castel Volturno... 64 A4
Castets......... 28 A3
Castiadas....... 66 C4
Castiglioncello... 60 C4
Castiglione d'Adda. 60 B2
Castiglione dei
  Pepoli.......... 60 C3
Castiglione del
  Lago........... 61 D4
Castiglione della
  Pescaia........ 62 C1
Castiglione delle
  Stiviere........ 60 C1
Castiglione in
  Teverina........ 63 E1
Castiglione Messer
  Marino......... 64 B2
Castiglione Olona .. 60 A1
Castiglion
  Fiorentino...... 61 D4
Castilblanco..... 39 F4
Castilblanco de los
  Arroyos........ 43 D2
Castilla, Canal de .. 35 E4
Castilla-La Mancha . 40 A4
Castilla-León.... 35 D4
Castilla, Mar de .. 40 C2
Castilleja del
  Campo......... 43 D2
Castilléjar...... 44 B2
Castillejo...... 39 E1
Castillejo de Martin
  Viejo.......... 39 D1
Castillo de Loarre .. 37 D2
Castillo de Locubín . 43 F2
Castillon, Bge de .. 31 D3
Castillon-en-
  Couserans...... 37 F2
Castillon-la-
  Bataille........ 28 B2
Castillonnès..... 28 C2
Castillo, Pto del .. 44 A3
Castillo y
  Elejabeitia..... 36 B1
Castilruiz...... 36 C3
Castions di Strada. 59 F3
Castlebar...... 12 B3
Castlebay...... 2 A4
Castlebellingham .. 13 D3
Castleblayney.... 13 D3
Castlecomer..... 13 D4
Castledawson.... 13 D2
Castlederg...... 13 D2
Castledermot.... 13 D4
Castle Douglas .. 4 C3
Castleford...... 7 D2
Castleisland..... 14 B3
Castlemaine..... 14 A3
Castlepollard.... 13 D3
Castlerea...... 12 C3
Castlerock..... 13 D1
Castleton...... 6 C2
Castletownbere... 14 A4
Castletown
  (I of Man)........ 6 A1
Castletown
  (Scotland)........ 3 D2
Castlewellan.... 13 E2
Castocalbón.... 35 D3
Castrejón...... 39 F1
Castrejón, Emb de. 40 A3
Castres........ 32 B1
Castries....... 30 B4
Castril........ 44 B2
Castrillo de
  la Reina....... 36 A3
Castrillo de
  Villavega...... 35 F3
Castro......... 34 B2
Castro Caldelas .. 34 B3
Castrocaro Terme . 61 D3
Castrocontrigo.. 35 D3
Castro Daire..... 38 C1

Castro del Rio...... 43 F2
Castrogeriz...... 35 F3
Castro Laboreiro... 34 B3
Castro Marim..... 42 B2
Castromonte..... 35 E4
Castronuevo..... 35 D4
Castronuño...... 35 D4
Castropol...... 34 C1
Castrop-Rauxel... 17 E3
Castroreale..... 69 D2
Castroreale
  Terme.......... 69 D2
Castrotierra..... 35 E3
Castro Urdiales .. 36 A1
Castroverde..... 34 C2
Castro Verde..... 42 B2
Castroverde de
  Campos........ 35 E3
Castrovillari.... 67 E2
Castuera...... 39 E4
Cataluña....... 32 A3
Catalunya...... 37 F3
Catania....... 69 D3
Catania, G di 69 D3
Catanzaro...... 67 F3
Catanzaro Lido... 67 F3
Catarroja...... 41 E4
Cateau, le...... 20 A2
Catelet, le...... 20 A2
Catenanuova..... 69 D3
Cateż......... 70 C2
Cathair na Mart .. 12 B3
Čatići........ 71 F4
Catignano..... 64 A2
Catoira....... 34 A2
Catoute....... 35 D2
Catral........ 45 D2
Catria, Mte..... 61 E4
Cattenom...... 21 D3
Cattolica...... 61 E3
Catus......... 29 D2
Caudebec...... 19 D3
Caudete....... 45 D1
Caudiel....... 41 E3
Caudry....... 20 A2
Caulnes...... 23 D3
Caulonia..... 67 F4
Caumont-l'Eventé .. 18 C3
Caunes....... 32 B1
Căuşani...... 113 E4
Caussade..... 29 D3
Čausy........ 111 E4
Cauterets..... 37 D2
Cava de' Tirreni .. 64 B4
Cávado, R..... 34 A4
Cavaglià..... 31 F1
Cavaillon..... 30 C3
Cavalaire..... 31 D4
Cavalerie, la 29 F3
Cavalese..... 59 D3
Cavalière..... 31 D4
Cavan........ 13 D3
Cavan (Co).... 13 D3
Cavarzere..... 61 D1
Cavazzo...... 59 E3
Cavero, Pto de .. 36 C4
Cavezzo...... 60 C2
Cavo......... 62 C1
Cavo, Mte..... 63 E3
Cavour....... 31 E2
Cavtat........ 76 A3
Caya......... 38 C4
Cayeux....... 19 E2
Caylar, le...... 29 F3
Caylus....... 29 D3
Cayolle, Col de la. . 31 E3
Cayres....... 29 F2
Cazalla de la Sierra. 43 D2
Cazals....... 29 D2
Cazaubon..... 28 B3
Cazaux....... 28 A2
Cazères....... 37 F1
Cazin........ 70 C3
Cazma....... 71 D2
Cazorla....... 44 B2
Cazorla, Sa de .. 44 B2
Cea......... 34 B2
Ceadît-Lunga 113 E4
Ceanannus Mor... 13 D3
Cea, R........ 35 D3
Ceatharlach..... 13 D4
Cebolla....... 39 F3
Cebollera...... 36 B3

Cebreros 40 A2
Ceccano 63 F3
Cece 112 B4
Cechy......... 53 F4
Cecina......... 60 C4
Cecina R......... 60 C4
Cecita, L di 67 F2
Ceclavín......... 39 D3
Cedeira......... 34 B1
Cedillo, Bgem de . 38 C3
Cedrillas......... 41 E2
Cedrino......... 66 C2
Cedynia......... 49 E3
Cefalù......... 68 C3
Cega, R......... 40 A1
Cegléd......... 112 B4
Ceglie Messapico . 65 E3
Čegrane......... 77 D3
Čegelj......... 44 C2
Čehotina......... 76 A1
Ceira, R......... 38 C2
Čejč......... 57 F1
Celákovice..... 53 F3
Celano......... 63 F2
Celanova......... 34 B3
Celavevo......... 72 B2
Čelebić......... 75 D1
Čelebići......... 76 B1
Celemín, Emb de . 43 D4
Čelić......... 72 B3
Čelinac Donji 71 E3
Celje......... 70 B2
Cella......... 41 D2
Celle......... 48 B4
Celle Ligure..... 60 A3
Celles......... 24 C4
Čelopeci......... 77 D3
Celorico......... 34 B4
Celorico da Beira. . 38 C1
Čemerna pl...... 73 D4
Čemernica...... 71 E4
Čemerno......... 76 A2
Cenajo, Emb del .. 44 C1
Cencenighe..... 59 D3
Cenicero......... 36 B2
Čenta......... 72 C2
Centelles......... 32 B4
Cento......... 60 C2
Cento Croci, Pso. . 60 B3
Central Region ... 4 C1
Centre, Canal du .. 26 B3
Centuripe......... 69 D3
Cepagatti......... 64 A2
Čepin......... 71 F2
Ceppo......... 63 F1
Ceprano......... 63 F3
Cer......... 72 C3
Čeralije......... 71 E2
Cerbère......... 32 C3
Cercal (Alentejo) .. 42 A1
Cercal
  (Estremadura)... 38 A3
Cercedilla......... 40 A2
Cerchiara di
  Calabria....... 67 E2
Cerchov......... 56 B1
Cerdedo......... 34 A2
Cerdeira......... 39 D2
Cère......... 29 E2
Cerea......... 60 C1
Cereda, Pso di ... 59 D3
Čerepovec....... 111 F1
Ceres......... 31 E1
Ceresole Reale ... 31 E1
Céret......... 32 B3
Cerezo de Abajo . 36 A4
Cerezo de Riotirón. 36 A3
Cerignola......... 64 C3
Cérilly......... 26 A3
Cerisiers......... 26 A1
Cerisy-la-Salle ... 18 B3
Cerizay......... 24 C3
Čerkassy......... 113 F2
Cerknica......... 70 B2
Cerkniško jez.... 70 B2
Cerkno......... 70 A2
Cerler......... 37 E2
Černá......... 56 C2
Cerna......... 71 F2
Cernache de
  Bonjardim..... 38 B2
Čern'achovsk..... 110 B4
Cernadilla......... 34 C3

Cernavodă........ 115 E1
Cernay......... 27 E1
Černihiv......... 113 E1
Cernik......... 71 E3
Černivci......... 113 D3
Cernobbio......... 58 B4
Cerreto, Pso del . 60 B3
Cerreto Sannita .. 64 B3
Cerrigydrudion 6 B3
Čërrik......... 76 C4
Certaldo......... 60 C4
Certosa di Pavia .. 60 A2
Cervales......... 39 E3
Cervaro......... 64 C3
Cervati, Mte..... 67 D1
Cervatos......... 35 F2
Cervatos de la
  Cueza......... 35 E3
Červen'......... 111 D4
Cervera......... 37 F3
Cervera de la
  Cañada......... 36 C4
Cervera del Rio
  Alhama......... 36 C3
Cervera de
  Pisuerga....... 35 F2
Cerveteri......... 63 E2
Cervia......... 61 E3
Cervialto, Mte.... 64 C4
Cervignano del
  Friuli......... 59 F3
Cervinara......... 64 B3
Cervino......... 27 E4
Cervione......... 33 F3
Cervo......... 34 C1
Cèrvol, R......... 41 F2
Červonohrad..... 112 C2
Cesana Torinese ... 31 D2
Cesaró......... 69 D3
Cesena......... 61 D3
Cesenatico..... 61 E3
Cēsis......... 110 C2
Česká Kamenice . 53 F2
Česka Lípa....... 53 F3
České Budějovice.. 57 D1
České Velenice.... 57 D1
Český Krumlov... 57 D2
Česma......... 71 D2
Çeşme......... 115 E4
Cespedosa..... 39 E2
Cessalto......... 59 E4
Cetina (E)....... 36 C4
Cetina R
  (Hrvatska)...... 75 D1
Cetinje......... 76 B3
Cetraro......... 67 E2
Ceuti......... 45 D2
Ceva......... 31 F2
Cevedale, Mte ... 58 C3
Cévennes,
  Parc Nat des 29 F3
Cevico de la Torre . 35 F4
Čevo......... 76 B2
Ceyrat......... 29 F1
Ceyzériat......... 26 C4
Cèze......... 30 B3
Chabanais......... 25 D4
Chablis......... 26 B1
Chabreuil......... 30 C2
Chabris......... 25 E2
Chagny......... 26 C3
Chailland......... 23 E3
Chaillé......... 24 B3
Chaise-Dieu, la ... 29 F1
Chalabre......... 32 A2
Chalais......... 28 C1
Chalamont..... 26 C4
Chalampé......... 27 E1
Chalindrey..... 26 C2
Challans......... 24 B3
Challes......... 31 D1
Chalon......... 24 C2
Châlons-
  sur-Marne..... 20 B3
Chalon-sur-Saône . 26 C3
Châlus......... 28 C1
Cham......... 56 B1
Chambéry......... 31 D1
Chambley......... 21 D3
Chambly......... 19 F3
Chambon, Bge du . 31 D2
Chambon-Feugerolles,
  le.............. 30 B1

Chambon-sur-Lac.. 29 E1
Chambon-sur-
  Lignon, le....... 30 B2
Chambon-sur-
  Voueize....... 25 F4
Chambord......... 25 E2
Chambre, la..... 31 D1
Chamonix......... 27 E4
Champagnac-de-
  Belair.......... 28 C1
Champagne-
  Mouton......... 25 D4
Champagnole..... 27 D3
Champdeniers..... 24 C3
Champeaux..... 23 D3
Champéry......... 27 E4
Champex......... 27 E4
Champlitte......... 26 C2
Champlon, Bre.de . 50 C4
Champoluc..... 27 F4
Champorcher..... 31 E1
Champs-sur-
  Tarentaine..... 29 E1
Champtoceaux..... 24 B2
Chamrousse..... 31 D1
Chamusca......... 38 B3
Chanac......... 29 F3
Chanas......... 30 B1
Chantada......... 34 B2
Chantelle......... 26 A4
Chantemerle..... 31 D2
Chantilly......... 19 F3
Chantonnay..... 24 B3
Chanza, Emb del . 42 B2
Chança, R......... 42 C2
Chaource......... 26 B1
Chapel-en-le-Frith . 6 C2
Chapelle-d'Angillon,
  la............. 25 F2
Chapelle-de-
  Guinchay, la ... 26 C4
Chapelle-en-
  Valgaudemar, la.. 31 D2
Chapelle-en-Vercors,
  la............. 30 C2
Chapineria......... 40 A2
Charbonnières..... 26 C4
Charco Redondo,
  Emb de........ 43 D4
Chard......... 9 D3
Charente......... 28 B1
Charente (Dépt) .. 28 C1
Charente-
  Maritime...... 24 B4
Charenton-du-
  Cher.......... 25 F3
Charité, la....... 26 A2
Charleroi......... 50 B4
Charlestown..... 12 B3
Charleville....... 14 B3
Charleville-
  Mézières..... 20 C2
Charlieu......... 26 B4
Charlottenberg..... 105 D3
Charly......... 20 A3
Charmes......... 21 D4
Charny (Meuse)... 20 C3
Charny (Yonne)... 26 A1
Charolles......... 26 B3
Chârost......... 25 E3
Charquemont..... 27 E2
Charroux......... 25 D4
Chartre, la....... 23 F4
Chartres......... 19 E4
Châs......... 38 B1
Chasseneuil..... 28 C1
Chasseral la
  Neuveville..... 27 E2
Chasseron, le ... 27 D3
Châtaigneraie, la .. 24 C3
Château-Arnoux .. 31 D3
Châteaubourg..... 23 D3
Châteaubriant..... 23 E4
Château-Chinon .. 26 B2
Château-de-
  Bonaguil....... 29 D2
Château de
  Ventadour..... 29 E1
Château d'Oex ... 27 E3
Château-du-Loir .. 23 F4
Châteaudun..... 25 E1
Châteaugiron..... 23 D3
Château-Gontier .. 23 E4
Château-Landon . 25 F1

Château-la-
  Vallière.......... 25 D2
Château, le...... 24 B4
Châteaulin......... 22 B3
Châteaumeillant .. 25 F3
Châteauneuf
  (Charente)..... 28 B1
Châteauneuf
  (Ille-et-Vilaine).. 18 B4
Châteauneuf-de-
  Randon......... 29 F2
Châteauneuf-du-
  Faou.......... 22 B3
Châteauneuf-du-
  Pape.......... 30 B3
Châteauneuf-en-
  Thymerais 19 E4
Châteauneuf-la-
  Forêt.......... 29 D1
Châteauneuf-les-
  Bains.......... 26 A4
Châteauneuf-sur-
  Cher.......... 25 F3
Châteauneuf-sur-
  Loire.......... 25 F1
Châteauneuf-sur-
  Sarthe......... 23 E4
Châteauponsac .. 25 E4
Château-Porcien .. 20 B3
Château-Queyras . 31 D2
Château-Regnault . 20 C2
Châteaurenard
  (Loiret)........ 25 F1
Châteaurenard
  (Vaucluse)..... 30 B3
Château-Renault .. 25 D2
Châteauroux..... 25 E3
Château-Salins .. 21 D4
Château-Thierry .. 20 A3
Châteauvillain..... 26 C1
Châtel......... 27 E3
Châtelaillon-Plage . 24 B4
Châtelard, le...... 27 D4
Châtelaudren..... 22 C2
Châteldon......... 26 A4
Châtelet......... 50 C4
Châtelet, le (Cher) . 25 F3
Châtelet, le
  (Seine-et-Marne). 19 E4
Châtelguyon..... 26 A4
Châtellerault..... 25 D3
Châtel-Montagne.. 26 B4
Châtel-St-Denis .. 27 E3
Châtel-sur-
  Moselle........ 21 D4
Châtelus-
  Malvaleix..... 25 E4
Châtenois......... 27 D1
Chatham......... 11 D2
Châtillon......... 27 F4
Châtillon-Coligny . 26 A1
Châtillon-en-
  Bazois.......... 26 B2
Châtillon-en-Diois. . 30 C2
Châtillon-sur-
  Chalaronne..... 26 C4
Châtillon-sur-
  Indre.......... 25 E3
Châtillon-sur-
  Loire.......... 26 A2
Châtillon-sur-
  Marne........ 20 B3
Châtillon-sur-
  Seine.......... 26 B1
Châtre, la....... 25 E3
Chatsworth House. 6 C3
Chatteris......... 9 F1
Chaudes-Aigues .. 29 F2
Chauffailles..... 26 B4
Chaufour......... 19 E4
Chaulnes......... 19 F2
Chaumergy..... 26 C3
Chaumont-en-
  Vexin.......... 19 E3
Chaumont
  (Haute-Marne).... 26 C1
Chaumont (Loir-et-
  Cher).......... 25 E2
Chauny......... 20 A2
Chausey, I....... 18 B4
Chaussin......... 26 C3
Chauvigny......... 25 D3
Chaux-de-Fonds,
  la............. 27 E2

Chaves 34 B3
Chazelles 30 B1
Cheb 53 D4
Cheddar Gorge 9 D3
Chef-Boutonne 24 C4
Cheles 42 C1
Chełm 112 C2
Chełmno 112 A1
Chelmsford 11 D2
Cheltenham 9 E2
Chelva 41 D3
Chemillé 24 C2
Chemin 26 C3
Chemnitz 53 E3
Chénérailles 25 F4
Chenonceaux 25 E2
Chepstow 9 D2
Cher 25 F3
Cher (Dépt) 25 F2
Chera 41 D3
Cherbourg 18 B2
Chéroy 26 A1
Cherson 113 F3
Chert 41 F2
Cheshire 6 C2
Cheshunt 9 F2
Chesne, le 20 C3
Cheste 41 E4
Chester 6 B3
Chesterfield 7 D3
Chester-le-Street 5 E4
Chevagnes 26 A3
Chevillon 20 C4
Cheviot Hills, The 5 E3
Cheviot, The 5 E3
Chèvre, Cap de la 22 A3
Chevreuse 19 E4
Cheylard, le 30 B2
Chèze, la 22 C3
Chiampo 59 D4
Chianciano Terme 63 D1
Chianti 61 D4
Chiaramonte Gulfi 69 D4
Chiaravalle 61 F3
Chiaravalle Centrale 67 F3
Chiari 60 B1
Chiasso 58 A4
Chiavari 60 A3
Chiavenna 58 B3
Chichester 9 F3
Chiclana de la Frontera 43 D4
Chieming 56 B3
Chiemsee 56 B3
Chieri 31 E1
Chiers 20 C3
Chiesa in Valmalenco 58 B3
Chiesina Uzz. 60 C3
Chieti 64 A2
Chiltern Hills 9 F2
Chimay 50 B4
Chimorra 43 E1
Chinchilla de Monte Aragón 41 D4
Chinchón 40 B2
Chinon 25 D2
Chioggia 61 D1
Chioula, Col de 32 A2
Chipiona 42 C3
Chippenham 9 E2
Chipping Campden 9 E1
Chipping Norton 9 E2
Chipping Sodbury 9 D2
Chirivel 44 C2
Chisinau 113 E3
Chișineu-Criș 112 C4
Chisone 31 E2
Chiusa 59 D2
Chiusa di Pesio 31 E2
Chiusa Sclafani 68 B3
Chiusaforte 59 F3
Chiusi 63 D1
Chiva 41 E4
Chivasso 31 F1
Chlum u Třeboně 57 D1
Chmel'nyc'kyj 113 D2
Chmel'nyk 113 E2
Chociwel 49 F2
Chodov 53 E4
Chojna 49 E3
Chojnice 110 A4
Chojniki 113 E1

Cholet 24 C3
Chollerford 5 E3
Cholm 111 E2
Chomutov 53 E3
Chorges 31 D2
Chorley 6 C2
Chorol 113 F2
Choszczno 49 F3
Chotyn 113 D3
Chouto 38 B3
Chrastava 53 F2
Christchurch 9 E3
Christiansfeld 108 A3
Christiansø 109 D4
Chur 58 B2
Church Stretton 9 D1
Chust 112 C3
Ciamarella 31 E1
Cians, Gorges du 31 E3
Čičarija 70 A3
Čičavica 77 D2
Cicciano 64 B4
Čičevac 73 E4
Čičevo 76 A2
Cidacos, R 36 B3
Cidade Nova de Santo André 42 A1
Cidones 36 B3
Ciechanów 112 B1
Ciechocinek 112 B1
Ciempozuelos 40 B2
Cies, Is 34 A3
Cieszyn 112 B3
Cieza 45 D2
Cifuentes 40 C2
Cigliano 31 F1
Cigüela R 40 B3
Cijara, Emb de 39 F4
Cijevna 76 B3
Cilavegna 60 A1
Čilipi 76 A3
Cill Airne 14 B4
Cillas 36 C4
Cill Chainnigh 15 D3
Cilleros 39 D2
Cilleruela de Bezana 35 F2
Cill Mhantáin 13 E4
Cima Brenta 58 C3
Cima d'Asta 59 D3
Cimadolmo 59 E4
Cima Presanella 58 C3
Čimišlia 113 E4
Cimone, Mte. 60 C3
Cîmpeni 112 C4
Cîmpina 115 D1
Cîmpulung 115 D1
Cîmpulung Moldovenesc 113 D3
Cinca, R. 37 E3
Cincar 75 E1
Cinctorres 41 E2
Ciney 50 C4
Cinfães 34 A4
Cingoli 61 F4
Cinigiano 63 D1
Cinisi 68 B3
Cinovec 53 E3
Cinque Terre 60 B3
Cintegabelle 32 A1
Cinto, M 33 F3
Cintruénigo 36 C3
Ciórraga 36 B1
Ciotat, la 30 C4
Čiovo 75 D2
Cirencester 9 E2
Cirey 21 E4
Ciria 36 C3
Ciriè 31 E1
Cirò 67 F2
Cirò Marina 67 F2
Cîrpan 115 D2
Cisa, Pso della 60 B3
Cisneros 35 E3
Čista 74 C1
Cista Provo 75 E1
Cisterna di Latina 63 F3
Cisternino 65 E3
Cistierna 35 E2
Čitluk (Mostar) 75 F2
Čitluk (Posušje) 75 E1
Cittadella 59 D4
Città del Pieve 63 D1
Città di Castello 61 E4

Cittaducale 63 F2
Cittanova 67 E4
Cittareale 63 F1
Città Sant' Angelo 64 A1
Ciudad Encantada 40 C3
Ciudad Real 40 A4
Ciudad Rodrigo 39 D1
Ciutadella de Menorca 45 F1
Cividale del Friuli 59 F3
Civita Castellana 63 E2
Civitanova Marche 61 F4
Civitavecchia 63 D2
Civitella del Tronto 63 F1
Civitella Roveto 63 F2
Civray 25 D4
Çivril 115 F4
Cjurupynsk 113 F3
Clacton-on-Sea 11 D2
Clain 25 D4
Clairvaux-les-Lacs 27 D3
Clamecy 26 A2
Claonaig 4 B2
Clapham 6 C1
Clara 12 C4
Clare 11 D1
Clare 12 B3
Clare (Co) 12 B4
Clare I 12 A3
Claremorris 12 B3
Claudy 13 D1
Clausthal-Zellerfeld 52 B2
Claut 59 E3
Claviere 31 D2
Clavin, Pto de 39 D3
Clay Cross 6 C3
Claye-Souilly 19 F4
Clayette, la 26 B4
Clear I 14 A4
Clécy 18 C4
Clefmont 26 C1
Cléguérec 22 C3
Clelles 30 C2
Clères 19 E3
Clermont 19 F3
Clermont-en-Argonne 20 C3
Clermont-Ferrand 29 F1
Clermont-l'Hérault 30 A4
Clervaux 21 D2
Cléry 25 E2
Cles 58 C3
Clevedon 9 D2
Cleveland Hills 7 D1
Cleveleys 6 B2
Clew B. 12 B3
Clifden 12 A3
Clisham 2 B2
Clisson 24 B2
Clitheroe 6 C2
Cloghan 12 C4
Clogheen 14 C3
Clogherhead 13 E3
Clogher Head 14 A3
Clogh Mills 13 E1
Clonakilty 14 B4
Clonbur 12 B3
Clondalkin 13 D4
Clones 13 D2
Clonfert 12 C4
Clonmacnoise 12 C4
Clonmel 14 C3
Cloppenburg 17 E1
Clovelly 8 B3
Cloyes 25 E1
Cluain Meala 14 C3
Cluj-Napoca 112 C4
Clun 9 D1
Cluny 26 C3
Clusaz, la 27 D4
Cluse de Pontarlier 27 D3
Cluses 27 E4
Clusone 58 B4
Clwyd 6 B3
Clyde 4 C2
Clydebank 4 C2
Clyde, Firth of 4 B2
Coachford 14 B4
Coalisland 13 D2
Coalville 9 E1
Coaña 34 C1

Côa, R. 39 D2
Coatbridge 4 C2
Cobeña 40 B2
Cobh 14 C4
Coburg 52 C4
Coca 40 A1
Coca, Pso di 58 B3
Cocentaina 45 E1
Cochem 51 E4
Cockburnspath 5 E2
Cockermouth 5 D4
Codevigo 61 D1
Codigoro 61 D2
Codogno 60 B2
Codos 36 C4
Codroipo 59 E3
Coesfeld 17 E3
Coevorden 17 D2
Cofrentes 41 D4
Coghinas, L del 66 B2
Cognac 28 B1
Cogne 31 E1
Cogolin 31 D4
Cogolludo 40 B1
Coigach 2 C2
Coimbra 38 B2
Coin 43 E4
Coina 38 A4
Čoka 72 C1
Col 70 A2
Colares 38 A4
Cölbe 17 F4
Colchester 11 D2
Coldbackie 2 C2
Colditz 53 D2
Coldstream 5 E2
Coleford 9 D2
Coleraine 13 E1
Colfiorito 63 E1
Colico 58 B3
Coligny 26 C3
Colindres 36 A1
Colintraive 4 B2
Coll 2 A4
Collado Bajo 41 D2
Collado Villalba 40 A2
Coll de Nargó 37 F3
Collecchio 60 B2
Colle di Val d'Elsa 60 C4
Colleferro 63 F3
Colle Isarco 59 D2
Collesalvetti 60 C4
Colle Sannita 64 B3
Collesano 68 C3
Colli a Volturno 64 A3
Collina, Pso della 60 C3
Collinée 22 C3
Colline Metallifere 60 C4
Collio 58 C4
Collioure 32 B2
Collobrières 31 D4
Collodi 60 C3
Collonges 27 D4
Collonges-la-Rouge 29 D2
Colmar 27 E1
Colmars 31 D3
Colmenar 43 F3
Colmenar de Oreja 40 B3
Colmenar Viejo 40 A2
Colnabaichin 3 D4
Colne 6 C2
Colobraro 65 D4
Cologna Veneta 60 C1
Cologne 28 C4
Colombey-les-Belles 21 D4
Colombey-les-Deux-Eglises 26 C1
Colombière, Col de la 27 D4
Colombres 35 F1
Colomera 44 A3
Colonsay 4 A2
Colorno 60 B2
Colosimi 67 F3
Columbretes, I. 41 F3
Colunga 35 E1
Colwyn Bay 6 B2
Comacchio 61 D2
Comănești 113 D4
Coma-ruga 37 F4
Combarro 34 A2
Combeaufontaine 27 D1

Combe Laval 30 C2
Combe Martin 8 C3
Comber 13 E2
Combloux 27 E4
Combourg 18 B4
Combronde 26 A4
Comeglians 59 E2
Comeragh Mts. 14 C3
Comillas 35 F1
Comines 19 F1
Comino 68 B4
Comiso 69 D4
Commentry 26 A4
Commercy 20 C4
Como 58 B4
Como, L di 58 B3
Cómpeta 43 F3
Compiègne 19 F3
Comporta 38 A4
Comps-sur-Artuby 31 D3
Comrat 113 E4
Comunanza 63 F1
Concarneau 22 B3
Conches 19 D4
Concordia sulla Secchia 60 C2
Condat 29 E1
Condé 20 A1
Conde, Emb del 43 E3
Condé-en-Brie 20 A3
Condeixa-a-Nova 38 B2
Condé-sur-Noireau 18 C4
Condom 28 C3
Condrieu 30 B1
Conegliano 59 E3
Conejeros, Pto de los 38 C4
Conflans 21 D3
Confolens 25 D4
Cong 12 B3
Congleton 6 C3
Congost de Tresponts 32 A3
Congosto de Valdavia 35 E2
Congresbury 9 D2
Conil de la Frontera 43 D4
Conisbrough 7 D2
Coniston 5 D4
Conlie 23 F3
Conliège 26 C3
Connel 4 B1
Connaught 12 B3
Connemara 12 A3
Connerré 23 F3
Conn, L 12 B2
Čonoplja 72 B1
Conques 29 E2
Conquest, le 22 A2
Conquista 43 F1
Conselice 61 D2
Conselve 61 D1
Consett 5 E4
Constância 38 B3
Constanța 115 E1
Constantina 43 E2
Consuegra 40 A3
Consuma 61 D3
Contamines, les 27 E4
Contarina 61 D2
Conthey 27 E3
Contigliano 63 E2
Contin 2 C3
Contrasto, C del 68 C3
Contraviesa, Sa de la 44 B4
Contreras, Emb de 41 D3
Contres 25 E2
Contrexéville 27 D1
Conty 19 F2
Convento de Calatrava 44 A1
Conversano 65 E3
Conwy 6 A2
Cookstown 13 D2
Cootehill 13 D3
Cope 45 D3
Cope, C. 45 D3

Copertino 65 F4
Copparo 61 D2
Corabia 115 D2
Corato 65 D3
Coray 22 B3
Corbeil-Essonnes 19 F4
Corbie 19 F2
Corbigny 26 B2
Corbola 61 D2
Corbones, R 43 E2
Corbridge 5 E3
Corby 9 F1
Corcaigh 14 B4
Corcieux 27 E1
Córcoles, R 40 C4
Corconte 35 F2
Corcubión 34 A1
Cordes 29 D3
Córdoba 43 F2
Cordobilla de Lácara 39 D4
Cordobilla, Emb de 43 F3
Corduente 40 C2
Corella 36 C3
Coreses 35 D3
Corfe Castle 9 E3
Corgo 34 B2
Cori 63 F3
Coria 39 D2
Coria del Río 43 D3
Corias 34 C2
Corigliano Calabro 67 F2
Corinaldo 61 E3
Coripe 43 E3
Cork 14 B4
Cork (Co) 14 B4
Corlay 22 C3
Corleone 68 B3
Corleto Perticara 65 D4
Çorlu 115 E3
Cormatin 26 C3
Cormeilles 19 D3
Cormery 25 D2
Cormons 59 F3
Cornago 36 C3
Cornellana 35 D1
Corniche des Cévennes 29 F3
Corniglio 60 B3
Cornimont 27 E1
Čornobyl' 113 E1
Čornomors'ke 113 F4
Cornuda 59 D4
Cornus 29 F3
Cornwall 8 B4
Corps 31 D2
Corraes 34 C3
Corral de Almaguer 40 B3
Corral de Cantos 39 F3
Corralejo 42 C4
Corrales 35 D4
Corran 2 C4
Corraun 12 B2
Corredoiras 34 B2
Correggio 60 C2
Corrèze 29 D1
Corrèze (Dépt) 29 D1
Corrèze, R 29 D2
Corrib, L 12 B3
Corridonia 61 F4
Corrofin 12 B4
Corse 33 E2
Corse-du-Sud 33 F3
Corsham 9 D2
Čortanovci 72 C2
Corte 33 F3
Corte de Peleas 39 D4
Cortegada 34 B3
Cortegana 42 C2
Cortemaggiore 60 B2
Cortemilia 31 F2
Cortes de Aragón 41 E1
Cortes de Baza 44 B2
Cortes de la Frontera 43 E4
Cortijos Nuevos 44 B2
Cortina d'Ampezzo 59 E3
Čortkiv 113 D3
Cortona 61 D4

Coruche 38 B4
Corvara in Badia 59 D3
Corvera 45 D2
Corvera Toranzo 35 F2
Corwen 6 B3
Cosenza 67 E2
Cosham 9 E3
Cosne 26 A2
Cosne-d'Allier 26 A3
Cossato 31 F1
Cossé-le-Vivien 23 D3
Cosson 25 E2
Cossonay 27 D3
Costa Blanca 45 E2
Costa Brava 32 C3
Costa da Caparica 38 A4
Costa del Sol 44 A4
Costa de Santo André 42 A1
Costalunga, Pso di. 59 D3
Costa Smeralda 66 B1
Costa Vasca 36 B1
Costa Verde 35 D1
Costigliole d'Asti 31 F2
Coswig (Sachsen) 53 E2
Coswig (Sachsen-Anhalt) 53 D1
Côte-d'Or (Dépt) 26 C2
Côtes-d'Armor 22 C3
Côte-St-André, la 30 C1
Cotignac 31 D4
Cottbus 53 F1
Coubet, Collado de 32 B3
Coubre, Pointe de la 28 A1
Couches 26 B3
Couço 38 B4
Coucy-le-Château-Auffrique 20 A3
Couesnon 23 D3
Couhé 25 D3
Couilly 19 F4
Couiza 32 B2
Coulanges 26 A2
Coulanges-la-Vineuse 26 A2
Coulommiers 19 F4
Coulon 24 C4
Coulonges 24 C3
Coupar Angus 5 D1
Couptrain 18 C4
Courchevel 31 D1
Cour-Cheverny 25 E2
Courçon 24 C4
Courmayeur 27 E4
Couronne, la 28 C1
Courpière 29 F1
Cours 26 B4
Coursan 32 B1
Coursegoules 31 E3
Courseulles 18 C3
Courson-les-Carrières 26 A2
Courtenay 26 A1
Courthézon 30 C3
Courtine, la 29 E1
Courtomer 19 D4
Courtown 15 E3
Courtrai 50 A3
Courville 19 E4
Cousin 26 B2
Coussey 20 C4
Coutances 18 B3
Coutras 28 B2
Couvertoirade, la 29 F3
Couvin 50 C4
Couze 25 E4
Cova da Iria 38 B3
Covadonga 35 E1
Covadonga, Pque Nac de la Sa de 35 E2
Covarrubias 36 A3
Coventry 9 E1
Covilhã 38 C2
Cowbridge 8 C2
Cowdenbeath 5 D2
Cowes 9 E3
Cowfold 10 C3
Cozes 28 B1
Craco 65 D4
Craigavon 13 E2
Craighouse 4 B2

Craigievar Castle 3 E4
Craignure 4 B1
Crail 5 D2
Crailsheim. 55 E2
Craiova 115 D2
Cranborne 9 E3
Crans 27 E3
Craon 23 E3
Craonne 20 B3
Craponne 29 F1
Crathes Castle ... 3 E4
Crati 67 E2
Crato 38 C3
Craughwell. 12 B4
Crau, la 31 D4
Craven Arms...... 9 D1
Crawinkel........ 52 C3
Crawley 10 C3
Creag Meagaidh... 2 C4
Creagorry 2 A3
Crécy 20 A2
Crécy-en-
  Ponthieu 19 E2
Crécy-la-Chapelle .. 19 F4
Crediton 8 C3
Creegh 12 B4
Creeslough 12 C1
Creglingen 55 E1
Creil 19 F3
Crema 60 B1
Crémieu 26 C4
Cremona 60 B2
Créon 28 B2
Crepaja 73 D2
Crépy-en-Valois.. 19 F3
Cres 70 B4

Cres / 70 B4
Crescentino 31 F1
Crespino 61 D2
Crest 30 C2
Cresta 58 B3
Cresta del Gallo .. 45 D2
Créteil 19 F4
Crêtes, Route des.. 27 E1
Creully 18 C3
Creuse 25 E4
Creuse (Dépt) ... 25 E4
Creusot, le 26 B3
Creußen 53 D4
Creutzwald 21 D3
Creuzburg 52 B3
Crevacuore 58 A4
Crevalcore 60 C2
Crèvecœur-
  le-Grand.. 19 E3
Crevillente 45 D2
Crewe 6 C3
Crewkerne 9 D3
Crianlarich 4 C1
Criccieth 6 A3
Crickhowell 9 D2
Cricklade 9 E2
Crieff 4 C1
Criel 19 E2
Crikvenica 70 B3
Crimmitschau ... 53 D3
Crinan 4 B2
Criquetot-l'Esneval 19 D3
Crissolo 31 E2
Crişul Alb 112 C4
Crişul Negru .. 112 C4
Crişul Repede .. 112 C4

Crivitz 48 C2
Crkvice 76 A2
Crmljan 76 C2
Črmošnjice 70 B2
Črna 70 B1
Crna Bara (Srbija) .. 72 B3
Crna Bara
  (Vojvodina)........ 72 C1
Crnac (Hrvatska) .. 71 E2
Crnac (Srbija) .. 76 C1
Crna Gora 76 B2
Crna gora 77 E2
Crna reka 77 E4
Crna Trava 77 E1
Crnča 72 B4
Crni Drim 77 D4
Crni Guber 72 C4
Crni Lug (BH) .. 75 D1
Crni Lug (HR) .. 70 B3
Crni Timok 73 E4
Crni vrh *Mt* (BH) .. 71 D4
Črni vrh *Mt* (SLO) .. 70 B1
Črni vrh *Mt* (Srbija).. 76 C1
Črni vrh (SLO) .. 70 A2
Crnivec 70 B2
Crnjelovo Donje .. 72 B3
Črnkovci 71 F2
Crno jez 76 B2
Črnomelj 70 B3
Croagh Patrick.. 12 B3
Croce dello Scrivano,
  Pso .. 64 C4
Croce Domini,
  Pso di .. 58 C4
Crocello, Pso di .. 64 C4
Crocq.. 25 F4

Croisic, le 24 A2
Croisière, la .. 25 E4
Croix de Fer,
  Col de la .. 31 D1
Croix Haute,
  Col de la .. 30 C2
Croix-Valmer, la .. 31 D4
Crolly 12 C1
Cromarty 3 D3
Cromer 7 F3
Crook 5 E4
Croom 14 B3
Cross Fell 5 D4
Cross Hands 8 C2
Crosshaven 14 C4
Crossmaglen 13 D3
Crossmolina 12 B2
Crotone 67 F3
Crotoy, le 19 E2
Crowborough 10 C3
Crowland 9 F1
Crowle 7 D2
Croyde 8 C3
Croydon 9 F2
Crozant 25 E4
Crozon 22 A3
Cruden Bay 3 E3
Crudgington 6 C3
Crumlin 13 E2
Cruseilles 27 D4
Crussol 30 C3
Cruz 40 B3
Cruzamento de
  Pegões.. 38 A4
Cruz da Légua .. 38 A3
Cruz de Tejeda.. 42 B4

Crven Grm 75 E2
Crvenka 72 B2
Crymmych 8 B1
Csongrád....... 112 B4
Csorna 112 A4
Cuacos 39 E2
Cualedro 34 B3
Cuba 42 B1
Cubel 36 C4
Cucalón, Sa de .. 41 D1
Cuckfield 10 C3
Cudillero 35 D1
Čudovo 111 D1
Čudskoje Ozero .. 110 C1
Cuéllar 35 F4
Cuenca 40 C3
Cuenca, Serr de .. 40 C2
Cuerda 41 D3
Cuerda del Pozo,
  Emb de la .. 36 B3
Cuers 31 D4
Cuerva 40 A3
Cueva de la Pileta.. 43 E4
Cueva de la Vieja .. 41 D4
Cueva de Nerja .. 44 A4
Cueva Foradada,
  Emb de .. 41 E1
Cueva, Sa do .. 35 E1
Cuevas de
  Altamira .. 35 F1
Cuevas de Artà .. 45 F3
Cuevas de
  Canalobre .. 45 E1
Cuevas del
  Amanzora........ 44 C3

Cuevas del
  Becerro .. 43 E3
Cuevas del Campo. 44 B2
Cuevas del Drac. 45 F3
Cuevas del Valle .. 39 F2
Cuevas de
  San Clemente .. 35 F3
Cuevas de
  San Marcos.. 43 F3
Cuevas de
  Valporquero 35 D2
Cuevas de
  Vinromá. .. 41 F2
Cuglieri 66 A3
Cuijk 17 D3
Cuillin Sd. 2 B4
Cuillins, The .. 2 B3
Cuiseaux....... 26 C3
Cuisery 26 C3
Culan 25 F3
Culdaff 13 D1
Culebra, Sa de la .. 34 C3
Culemborg 16 C3
Cúllar Baza 44 B2
Cullen 3 E3
Cullera 41 E3
Cullompton 8 C3
Culoz 27 D4
Culross 5 D2
Cumbernauld 4 C2
Cumbre Alta 39 F3
Cumbres Mayores .. 42 C1
Cumbria 5 D4
Cumbrian Mts ... 5 D4
Cumiana 31 E2
Cumić 73 D3

Cumnock 4 C3
Cunault 24 C2
Cuneo 31 E2
Čunski 70 B4
Cuorgnè 31 E1
Cupar 5 D1
Cupello 64 B2
Cupramontana .. 61 E4
Cuprija 73 E4
Cure 26 B2
Cure, la 27 D3
Curia 38 B1
Currane, L 14 A4
Curtea de Argeş.. 115 D1
Curtis 34 B1
Čurug 72 C2
Cusano Mutri .. 64 B3
Cushendall. 13 E1
Cushendun 13 E1
Cusna, Mte 60 C3
Cusset 26 A4
Cutro 67 F3
Cuxhaven 47 F2
Cvikov 53 E3
Čvrsnica 75 E1
Čvrstec 71 D2
Cwmbrân 9 D2
Cybinka 49 F4
Cysoing 20 A1
Czarnków 112 A1
Czersk 110 A4
Częstochowa ... 112 B2
Człuchów 112 A1

D

Dabar 70 C3
Dąbie 49 E2
Dabie, Jez 49 E2
Dabilje 77 F3
Dabo 21 E4
Dachau 55 F3
Dachsteingruppe .. 59 F1
Dačice 57 E1
Dadià 81 F2
Dáfnes 86 C1

Dáfni (Límnos) 85 D1
Dáfni (Makedonía) .. 80 C4
Dáfni
  (Pelopónnissos) .. 86 C1
Dáfni (Stereá
  Eláda) .. 83 D4
Dafni (Stereá
  Eláda) .. 87 F1
Dáfnio 87 D3
Dafnónas
  (Stereá Eláda) .. 83 D3
Dafnónas (Thráki) .. 80 C2
Dafnotí 82 C2

Dafnoúdi, Akr 82 B4
Dagali 104 C2
Dagebüll 47 F1
Dagenham 10 C2
Dahlen 53 E2
Dahlenburg 48 B3
Dahme
  (Brandenburg) .. 53 E1
Dahme (Schleswig-
  Holstein) .. 48 B2
Dahme *R* 53 E1
Dahn 54 B2
Daimiel 40 A4

Daimuz.......... 41 E4
Dajt, Mal i 76 C4
Đakovica 76 C2
Đakovo 71 F2
Đala 72 C1
Dalälven 106 A3
Dalane 104 A4
Dalbeattie 4 C3
Dalbosjön 105 E4
Dalby 109 D3
Dale (Hordaland) .. 104 A2
Dale (Sogn og
  Fjordane) .. 104 A1
Dalen 104 B3
Dalhem 109 F4
Dalías 44 B3
Daliburgh 2 A3
Dalj 72 B2
Dalkeith 5 D2
Dalkey 13 E4
Dalmally 4 C1
Dalmellington .. 4 C3
Dalmine 60 B1
Dalry 4 C2
Dalsbruk 107 D3
Dalsfjorden 104 A1
Dalsjöfors 109 D1
Dals Långed 105 D4
Dalton 6 C1
Daluis, Gorges de .. 31 E3
Dalvík 96 B1
Dalwhinnie 2 C4
Damaskiniá 79 D3
Damássi 83 E1
Damazan 28 C3
Damelevières ... 21 D4
Damgan 22 C4
Damianó 79 F2
Dammartin-en-
  Goële.. 19 F3
Damme 17 F2
Damnjane 76 C2
Dampierre 27 D2
Dampierre-sur-
  Salon .. 27 D2
Damville 19 E4
Damvillers 20 C3
Dangé 25 D3
Danilovgrad 76 B2
Dannemarie 27 E2

Dannenberg 48 B3
Dâo, R. 38 C1
Daoulas 22 B3
Darda 71 F2
Dardesheim 52 C1
Darfo Boario
  Terme .. 58 C4
Dargilan,
  Grotte de .. 29 F3
Dargun 49 D2
Darlington 5 E4
Darłowo 110 A4
Darmstadt 54 C1
Darney 27 D1
Daroca 36 C4
Darque 34 A3
Darß 48 C1
Dartford 10 C2
Dartmoor Nat Pk .. 8 C3
Dartmouth 8 C4
Daruvar 71 E2
Darwen 6 C2
Dasburg 51 D4
Dasing 55 F3
Dassel 52 B2
Dassohóri 81 D2
Dassow 48 B2
Daugava 110 C3
Daugavpils 110 C3
Daun 51 E4
Dava 3 D3
Davat 77 D4
Daventry 9 E1
Davia 87 D2
Davidovac 73 F2
Dávlia 83 F4
Davor 71 E3
Davos 58 B2
Dawlish 8 C3
Dax 28 A4
Deàdnu 95 E2
Deal 11 D3
Deauville 19 D3
Deba 36 B1
Debar 77 D3
Debarska Banja
  Banjišta .. 77 D3
Debeli Lug 73 E3

Debeli vrh 70 B2
Debeljača 72 C2
Dębica 112 C4
De Bilt 16 C3
Dęblin 112 C2
Dębno 49 F3
Debrc 72 C3
Debrecen 112 C4
Dečani 76 C2
Decazeville 29 E2
Děčín 53 E3
Decize 26 A3
Dedemsvaart 17 D2
Degaña 34 C2
Degebe, R 38 B4
Degerfjärden ... 102 A2
Degerfors 105 E4
Degerndorf 56 B4
Deggendorf 56 B2
Dego 31 E2
Degracias 38 B2
De Haan 50 A3
Dehesa de
  Montejo .. 35 F2
Deià 45 E2
Deidesheim 54 C1
Deinze 50 B3
Deiva Marina ... 60 B3
Dej 112 C4
Deje 105 E4
Dejë, Mal 76 C3
De Koog 16 C1
Delčevo 77 F2
Delden 17 D2
Deleitosa 39 E3
Delémont 27 E2
Deléria 83 E1
Delet Teili 106 C3
Delfi 83 E4
Delft 16 B3
Delfzijl 47 D3
Delia 68 C4
Delianuova 67 E4
Deliblato 73 D2
Deliblatska
  Peščara .. 73 D2
Deliceto 64 C3
Delimedde 76 C1

Delitzsch 53 D2
Delle 27 E2
Dellen, N 101 F3
Dellen, S 101 F3
Delme 21 D3
Delmenhorst 47 F3
Delnice 70 B3
Delsbo 101 F3
Delta Dunării .. 113 D3
Delvin 13 D3
Delvináki 82 B1
Demanda, Sa de la. 36 B2
Demer 50 C3
Demidov 111 E3
Demirci 115 F4
Demir Kapija. .. 77 E3
Demmin 49 D2
Demoiselles,
  Grotte des .. 29 F3
Demonia 87 E4
Denain 20 A1
Denbigh 6 B3
Den Burg 16 C1
Dendermonde 50 B3
Dendre 50 B4
Dendrohóri 79 D3
Denekamp 17 E2
Den Haag 16 B3
Den Helder 16 C1
Denia 45 E1
Denizli 115 F4
Denkendorf 55 F2
Dennington 11 D1
Denny 4 C2
Den Oever 16 C1
Dent de Vaulion .. 27 D3
De Panne 50 A3
Đeravica 76 C2
Derby 6 C3
Derbyshire 6 C3
Der Chantecoq,
  L du .. 20 C4
Đerdap, H.E. .. 73 F2
Đerdap, Klisura .. 73 E3
Derekoy 115 E2
Derenburg 52 C1
Derg, L (Clare) .. 12 C4
Derg, L (Donegal) .. 12 C2
Der Grabow 49 D1
Dermatás, Akr .. 83 F1

Dijon

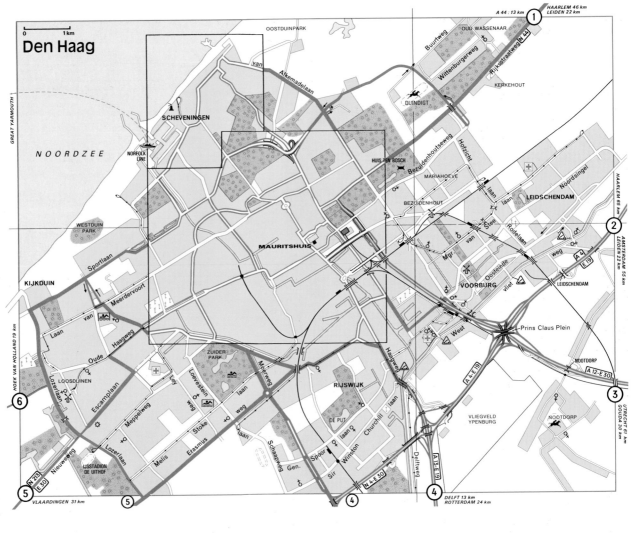

Den Haag

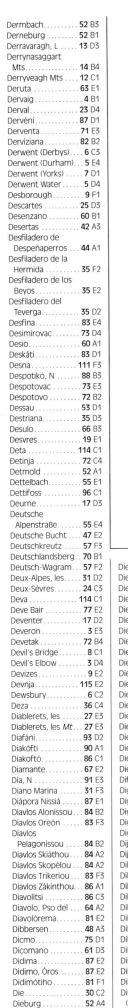

Dermbach..........52 B3
Derneburg.........52 B1
Derravaragh, L....13 D3
Derrynasaggart Mts...14 B4
Derryveagh Mts....12 C1
Deruta............63 E1
Dervaig...........4 B1
Derval............23 D4
Dervéni...........87 D1
Derventa..........71 E3
Derviziana........82 B2
Derwent (Derbys)...6 C3
Derwent (Durham)...5 E4
Derwent (Yorks)...7 D1
Derwent Water.....5 D4
Desborough........9 F1
Descartes.........25 D3
Desenzano.........60 B1
Desertas..........42 A3
Desfiladero de Despeñaperros...44 A1
Desfiladero de la Hermida...35 F2
Desfiladero de los Beyos...35 E2
Desfiladero del Teverga...35 D2
Desfina...........83 E4
Desimirovac.......73 D4
Desio.............60 A1
Deskáti...........83 D1
Desna.............111 F3
Despotikó, N......88 B3
Despotovac........73 E3
Despotovo.........72 B2
Dessau............53 D1
Destriana.........35 D3
Desulo............66 B3
Desvres...........19 E1
Deta..............114 C1
Đetinja...........72 C4
Detmold...........52 A1
Dettelbach........55 E1
Dettifoss.........96 C1
Deurne............17 D3
Deutsche Alpenstraße...55 E4
Deutsche Bucht....47 E2
Deutschkreutz.....57 F3
Deutschlandsberg...70 B1
Deutsch-Wagram....57 F2
Deux-Alpes, les...31 D2
Deux-Sèvres.......24 C3
Deva..............114 C1
Deve Bair.........77 E2
Deventer..........17 D2
Deveron...........3 E3
Devetak...........72 B4
Devil's Bridge....8 C1
Devil's Elbow.....3 D4
Devizes...........9 E2
Devnja............115 E2
Dewsbury..........6 C2
Deza..............36 C4
Diablerets, les...27 E3
Diablerets, les Mt...27 E3
Diafáni...........93 D2
Diakófti..........90 A1
Diakoftó..........86 C1
Diamante..........67 E2
Día, N............91 E3
Diano Marina......31 E3
Diápora Nissiá....87 E1
Díavlos Alonissou...84 B2
Díavlos Oreón.....83 F3
Díavlos Pelagonissou...84 B2
Díavlos Skiáthou...84 A2
Díavlos Skopélou...84 A2
Díavlos Trikeriou...84 B2
Díavlos Zákinthou...86 A1
Diavolitsi........86 C3
Diavolo, Pso del...64 A2
Diavolórema.......81 E2
Dibbersen.........48 A3
Dicmo.............75 D1
Dicomano..........61 D3
Didima............87 E2
Didimo, Óros......87 E2
Didimótiho........81 F1
Die...............30 C2
Dieburg...........52 A4
Diedorf...........52 B2

Diego Alvaro......39 E2
Diekirch..........21 D2
Diemel............52 A2
Diemelstadt.......52 A2
Diepholz..........17 F2
Dieppe............19 E2
Dierdorf..........51 E4
Dieren............17 D3
Diesdorf..........48 B4
Dießen............56 A3
Diest.............50 C3
Dietenheim........55 E3
Dietfurt..........55 F2
Dietikon..........27 F2
Dietmannsried.....55 E4
Dieulefit.........30 C2
Dieulouard........21 D4
Dieuze............21 D4
Diez..............51 F4
Diezma............44 A3
Differdange.......21 D3
Digerkampen.......100 B3
Digermulen........94 A4
Dignano...........59 E3
Digne-les-Bains...31 D3
Digoin............26 B3
Dijle.............50 C3
Dijon.............26 C2
Dikanäs...........97 F3
Dikea.............81 F1
Dikela............81 E2
Diksmuide.........50 A3
Diktéo Ándro......91 E4
Diktinéon.........90 B3
Dikti, Óros.......91 E4
Dilessi...........84 B4
Dilináta..........82 B4
Dilj..............71 E2
Dillenburg........51 F3
Dillingen (Bayern)...55 E2
Dillingen (Saarland)...54 A2
Dilofos...........81 F1

Dilos.............88 C2
Dilos, N..........88 C2
Dimena............87 E2
Dimitra...........83 E1
Dimitritsi........80 B2
Dimitrovgrad (BG)...115 D3
Dimitrovgrad (Srbija)...77 F1
Dimitsána.........86 C2
Dinami............67 E2
Dinan.............18 B4
Dinant............50 C4
Dinar.............115 F4
Dinara Mt.........75 D1
Dinara (Reg)......75 D1
Dinard............18 B4
Dinbych...........6 B3
Dinbych-y-pysgod...8 B2
Dingelstädt.......52 B2
Dingle............14 A3
Dingle............105 D4
Dingle (Reg)......14 A3
Dingle B..........14 A3
Dingli............68 B4
Dinglingen........54 C2
Dingolfing........56 B2
Dingwall..........2 C3
Dinjiška..........70 C4
Dinkelsbühl.......55 E2
Dinklage..........17 F2
Dinslaken.........17 D3
Dío...............79 F4
Diónissos.........87 E1
Dióriga Korinthou...87 D4
Dipótama..........80 C1
Dippoldiswalde....53 E2
Diráhio...........86 C3
Dirfis, Óros......84 B3
Disentis..........58 A3
Disgrazia, Mte....58 B3
Díspilio..........79 D3
Diss..............11 D1
Dissen............17 F2

Distomo...........83 E4
Distos............84 B4
Ditiki Rodópi.....80 C1
Dittaino..........69 D3
Ditzingen.........55 D2
Divača............70 A3
Divaráta..........82 B4
Divčibare.........72 C4
Dives.............18 C3
Dives R...........18 C3
Divič.............72 B4
Divjakë...........76 C4
Divljana..........77 E1
Divonne...........27 D3
Divor, Bgem do....38 B4
Divor, Rib de.....38 B4
Divoúnia, Ni......92 C2
Divri.............83 E3
Divuša............71 D3
Djupini...........96 A3
Djupvik...........94 C2
Djurås............105 F2
Djursland.........108 B2
Dmitrov...........111 F2
Dnipro............111 E3
Dniprodzeržins'ke Vodoschovyšče...113 F2
Dniprovs'kyj Lyman...113 F3
Dnister...........112 C3
Dnistrovs'kyj Lyman...113 F4
Dno...............111 D2
Dobbiaco..........59 E2
Dobel.............54 C2
Dobele............110 C3
Döbeln............53 E2
Doberlug-Kirchhain...53 E1
Döbern............53 F1
Dobersberg........57 E1
Dobieszczyn.......49 E2

Doboj.............71 F3
Dobošnica.........71 F3
Dobra (PL)........49 F2
Dobra (Srbija)....73 E3
Dobra R...........70 C3
Dobra Voda........73 D4
Dobra Voda Mt.....77 D3
Dobrašinci........77 F2
Dobratsch.........59 F2
Dobrčane..........77 D2
Dobriach..........59 F2
Dobrič............115 E2
Dobrica...........73 D2
Dobričevo.........73 D2
Dobri Do..........77 D1
Dobrinj...........70 B3
Dobřiš............53 F4
Dobrljin..........71 D3
Dobrna............70 B1
Dobromani.........75 D2
Dobro Polje.......76 A1
Dobrovnik.........70 C1
Dobrun............72 C4
Dobruš............111 E4
Dobruševo.........77 E4
Dobrzany..........49 F2
Döbšiná...........112 B3
Docksta...........102 A2
Doc Penfro........8 B2
Dodekánissa.......89 E3
Dodóni............82 B1
Doesburg..........17 D3
Doetinchem........17 D3
Doganović.........77 D2
Dogliani..........31 E2
Doïráni...........79 F2
Doïránis, L.......79 F2
Doiras, Emb de....34 C1
Dojransko Ez......77 F3
Dokanj............72 B3
Dokka.............104 D2
Dokkum............47 D3
Dokós, N..........87 E3

Doksy.............53 F3
Dolac.............76 C2
Dol-de-Bretagne...18 B4
Dole..............26 C2
Dôle, la..........27 D3
Dølemo............104 B4
Dolenci...........77 D4
Dolenja Vas.......70 B2
Dolenjske Toplice...70 B2
Dolga Vas.........71 D1
Dolgellau.........6 A3
Doliana...........78 C2
Dolianova.........66 B4
Dolíhi............79 E4
Doljani...........71 D4
Doljevac..........77 D1
Dolla.............12 C4
Döllach...........59 E2
Dollar............5 D2
Dolle.............48 C4
Dolni Dvořiště....57 D2
Dolno Kosovrasti...77 D3
Dolo..............61 D1
Dolomiti..........59 D3
Dolomiti Bellunesi, Parco Naz dello...59 D3
Dolores...........45 D2
Dolovo............73 D2
Dol Poustevna.....53 F2
Dolyna............112 C3
Domaševo..........75 D2
Domažlice.........56 B1
Dombås............100 B3
Dombasle..........21 D4
Dombóvár..........114 B1
Domburg...........16 B3
Domène............30 C1
Doméniko..........83 E1
Domèvre-en-Haye...21 D4
Domfront..........18 C4
Dömitz............48 C3
Domme.............29 D2

Dommitzsch........53 D2
Domnista..........83 D3
Domodossola.......58 A4
Domokós...........83 E2
Dompaire..........27 D1
Dompierre.........26 B3
Domrémy...........20 C4
Domusnovas........66 B4
Domžale...........70 B2
Don (England).....7 D2
Don (Scotland)....3 E4
Donaghadee........13 E2
Donau.............56 C2
Donaueschingen....54 C4
Donauwörth........55 E2
Donawitz..........57 E4
Don Benito........39 E4
Doncaster.........7 D2
Donegal...........12 C2
Donegal B.........12 C2
Donegal (Co)......12 C1
Dongen............16 C3
Donges............23 D4
Donington.........7 E3
Donja Bebrina.....71 F3
Donja Brela.......75 E2
Donja Brezna......76 B2
Donja Bukovica....76 B2
Donja Kamenica....73 E3
Donja Šatornja....73 D3
Donje Crniljevo...72 C3
Donje Dragovlje...77 E1
Donje Ljupče......77 D2
Donji Andrijevci...71 F3
Donji Barbeš......77 E1
Donji Kanzanci....75 D1
Donji Lapac.......71 D4
Donji Malovan.....75 E1
Donji Miholjac....71 E2

Donji Milanovac...... 73 E3	Dorfen............. 56 B3	Douai............. 19 F2
Donji Ruzani 75 D1	Dorfmark......... 48 A4	Douarnenez........ 22 A3
Donji Seget 75 D2	Dorgali.......... 66 C2	Doubs............ 26 C3
Donji Vakuf 71 E4	Dório............ 86 C3	Doubs (Dépt)...... 27 D3
Donji Vijačani 71 E3	Dorkáda.......... 80 A2	Doucier.......... 27 D3
Donji Zemunik 74 C1	Dorking.......... 10 C3	Doudeville........ 19 D2
Donjon, le 26 B3	Dormagen........ 17 E4	Doué............ 24 C2
Dønna 97 D3	Dormans......... 20 A3	Douglas (I of Man) .. 6 A1
Donnemarie-	Dornbirn......... 58 B2	Douglas (Scotland) ... 4 C2
Dontilly 20 A4	Dornburg........ 52 C3	Doukáto, Akr 82 B3
Donnersbachwald.. 57 D4	Dorndorf........ 52 B3	Doulaincourt 20 C4
Dønnes 97 D2	Dornes.......... 26 A3	Doulevant-le-
Donon........... 21 E4	Dornie........... 2 B3	Château 20 C4
Donon, Col du..... 21 E4	Dornoch.......... 3 D3	Doullens.......... 19 F2
Donostia-San	Dornoch Firth 3 D3	Doulus Head 14 A4
Sebastián 36 C1	Dornstetten 54 C3	Doune 4 C2
Donoússa, N 89 D3	Dornum.......... 47 E3	Doupov........... 53 E3
Donzenac 29 D2	Dorog........... 112 B4	Dourdan.......... 19 E4
Donzère.......... 30 B2	Dorogobuž 111 E3	Dourgne.......... 32 A1
Donzy........... 26 A2	Dorohoi......... 113 D3	Douro........... 34 A4
Doorn........... 16 C3	Dorotea......... 101 F1	Douro, R......... 34 A4
Doornik.......... 50 A4	Dörpstedt........ 48 A1	Douvaine......... 27 D3
Dora Baltéa 27 E4	Dorset............ 9 D3	Douve........... 18 B3
Dora Riparia 31 E1	Dorsten......... 17 E3	Douvres.......... 18 C3
Dorat, le 25 D4	Dortan........... 27 D3	Dover........... 11 D3
Đorče Petrov..... 77 D3	Dortmund........ 17 E3	Dover, Str of 11 D3
Dorchester........ 9 D3	Dortmund-Ems-	Dovre........... 100 D3
Dordives 25 F1	Kanal.......... 17 E2	Dovrefjell........ 100 C3
Dordogne 29 E1	Dorum.......... 47 F3	Dovsk........... 111 E4
Dordogne (Dépt) .. 28 C2	Dörzbach........ 55 D1	Down............ 13 E2
Dordogne R....... 28 B2	Dosbarrios....... 40 B3	Downham Market .. 10 C1
Dordrecht........ 16 C3	Dos Hermanas 43 D3	Downpatrick 13 E2
Dore............ 29 F1	Dosse........... 49 D3	Dowra........... 12 C2

Doxarás 83 E2
Doxáto 80 C2
Dozulé 19 D3
Drac 30 C2
Dračevo 77 E3
Drachten 17 D1
Drag 94 A4
Dragalovci 71 E3
Dragaš 77 D3
Drăgăşani 115 D1
Dragaši 76 B1
Draginac 72 C3
Draginje 72 C3
Dragočaj 71 E3
Dragocvet 73 D4
Dragoevo 77 E3
Dragoman 114 C2
Dragonera, I. 45 E3
Dragoni 64 B3
Dragør 108 C3
Dragoš 77 E4
Dragotiná 82 A2
Dragovic 71 E2
Dragovića Polje 76 B2
Dragozetići 70 B3
Dragsfjärd 107 D3
Dragsvik 100 A3
Draguignan 31 D4
Dráma 80 C2
Dráma (Nomos) 80 C1
Drammen 104 C3
Drammen selva 104 C3
Drangajökull 96 A1
Drangedal 104 C3
Dranske 49 D1
Drápano, Akr 90 C3
Drasenhofen 57 F1
Drau 59 F2
Dráva 71 E2
Dravograd 70 B1
Drawno 49 F2

Drawsko
  Pomorskie 112 A1
Draženov 56 B1
Draževac 72 C3
Drebkau 53 F1
Dreki 96 C2
Drenewydd 9 D1
Drenovac 77 E2
Drenovci 72 B3
Drenovo 77 E3
Drenthe 17 D1
Drépano
  (Makedonía) 79 E3
Drépano
  (Pelopónnissos) . . . 87 E2
Drépano, Akr
  (Anáfi) 91 E1
Drépano, Akr
  (Makedonía) 80 B4
Dresden 53 E2
Dreux 19 E4
Drežnik-Grad 70 C3
Driebergen 16 C3
Driebes 40 B2
Driméa 83 E3
Drimós 79 F3
Drin 76 C3
Drina 76 A1
Drini i Zi 77 D3
Drinit, Gjiri i 76 B3
Drinjača 72 B4
Drinjača R 72 B4
Drinovci 75 E2
Driopída 88 A2
Driós 88 C3
Drisht 76 C3
Driva 100 B2
Drlače 72 C4
Drnholec 57 F1
Drniš 75 D1
Drnje 71 D1

Drnovo 70 C2
Drøbak 105 D3
Drobeta-Turnu
  Severin 114 C1
Drochtersen 48 A2
Drogheda 13 D3
Drohobyč 112 C1
Droichead Átha 13 D3
Droichead Nua 13 D4
Droitwich 9 E1
Drokija 113 E3
Dromcolliher 14 B3
Drôme (Dépt) 30 C2
Drôme R 30 C2
Dromore (Down) 13 E2
Dromore (Tyrone) . . . 13 D2
Dronero 31 E2
Dronfield 7 D2
Drongaráti 82 B4
Dronne 28 C1
Dronninglund 108 B2
Dronten 16 C2
Drosendorf Stadt 57 E1
Drossáto 79 F2
Drosseró 79 E2
Drossiá 84 A4
Drossohóri 83 E4
Drossopigi (Árta) 82 C2
Drossopigi
  (Ioánina) 78 C4
Drossopigi
  (Makedonia) 79 D3
Drottningholm 106 B4
Droué 25 E1
Drulingen 21 E3
Drumkeeran 12 C2
Drummore 4 B4
Drumnadrochit 2 C3
Drumochter,
  Pass of 2 C4
Drumshanbo 12 C2

Drusenheim 21 F4
Druskininkai 110 C4
Druten 16 C3
Drvenik (HR) 75 D2
Drvenik (HR) 75 E2
Dryburgh 5 D3
Drymen 4 C2
Dubăsari 113 E3
Duben 53 E1
Dubi 53 E3
Dubica 71 D3
Dublin 13 E4
Dublin (Co) 13 D4
Dubna 111 F2
Dubňany 57 F1
Dubno 113 D2
Dubona 73 D3
Duboštica 71 F4
Dubovac 73 D2
Dubovsko 71 D4
Dubrava (HR) 71 D2
Dubrava (Pelješac) . . 75 F2
Dubrava Stara 71 E3
Dubrave 71 F3
Dubrave Donje 72 B3
Dubravica 73 D3
Dubrovnik 76 A2
Ducey 18 B4
Ducherow 49 E2
Duchkov 53 E3
Duchovščina 111 E3
Duclair 19 D3
Dudelange 21 D3
Duderstadt 52 B2
Dudley 9 E1
Dudweiler 54 B2
Dueñas 35 E4
Duero, R 35 D4
Duesund 104 A1
Dufftown 3 D3
Duga Poljana 76 C1

Duga Resa 70 C3
Dugi Otok 74 C1
Dugi Rat 75 D2
Dugo Selo 70 C2
Duingt 27 D4
Duino 59 F3
Duisburg 17 D3
Dukagjin 76 C2
Duken 53 E1
Dukat 77 E2
Duleek 13 D3
Dulje 77 D2
Dülken 17 D4
Dülmen 17 E3
Dulnain Bridge 3 D4
Dulovo 115 E2
Dumbarton 4 C2
Dumbria 34 A1
Dumfries 4 C3
Dumfries and
  Galloway 4 C3
Dun 20 C3
Dunaföldvár 112 B4
Dunajvci 113 D3
Dunărea 113 E4
Dunaújváros 112 B4
Dunav 72 B2
Dunav 114 D2
Dunbar 5 D2
Dunblane 4 C2
Duncansby Head 3 D2
Dundalk 13 D3
Dundalk B 13 E3
Dun Dealgan 13 D3
Dundee 5 D1
Dundonnell 2 C3
Dundrum B 13 E2
Dunfanaghy 12 C1
Dunfermline 5 D2
Dungannon 13 D2
Dún Garbhán 14 C4
Dungarvan 14 C4

Dungarvan
  Harbour 14 C4
Dungeness 11 D3
Dungiven 13 D1
Dunglow 12 C1
Dunje 77 E4
Dunkeld 5 D1
Dunkerque 19 F1
Dún Laoghaire 13 E4
Dun-le-Palestel 25 E4
Dunmanus B 14 A4
Dunmanway 14 B4
Dunmore 12 B3
Dunmore East 15 D4
Dunnamanagh 13 D1
Dún na nGall 12 C2
Dunnet 3 D2
Dunnet Head 3 D2
Dunoon 4 C2
Duns 5 D2
Dunshaughlin 13 D3
Dunstable 9 F2
Dunster 8 C3
Dun-sur-Auron 25 F3
Dunvegan 2 B3
Dunvegan Head 2 B3
Duolbbadasgai'sa . . . 95 E1
Đurakovac 76 C2
Durance 30 C3
Durango 36 B1
Duran, Pso 59 D3
Duras 28 C2
Duratón, R 40 A1
Durban-Corbières . . . 32 B2
Durbuy 50 C4
Dúrcal 44 A3
Đurđevac 71 D2
Đurđevića Tara 76 B1
Durdevik 72 B4
Düren 51 D3
Durham 5 E4

Durham (Co) 5 E4
Durlach 54 C2
Durlas 14 C3
Durmanec 70 C2
Durmitor 76 B2
Durness 2 C2
Dürnkrut 57 F2
Dürnstein 57 E2
Durrës 76 C4
Durrësi, Gjiri i 76 C4
Durrow 12 C4
Dursey I 14 A4
Dursley 9 D2
Durtal 23 E4
Duruelo de la
  Sierra 36 B3
Dusina 75 F1
Düsseldorf 17 E4
Duved 101 D2
Duvno 75 E1
Duži (BH) 75 F2
Duži (BH) 76 A2
Dverberg 94 A3
Dvor 71 D3
Dyfed 8 C1
Dyje 57 F1
Dyrnes 100 B1
Dyrøya 94 B3
Džami tepe 77 F3
Džaniči 75 F1
Džep 77 E1
Dzermiádo 91 E4
Dzeržinsk 111 D4
Dzierżoniów 112 A2
Džumajlija 77 E3
Dźwirzyno 49 F1

E

Eaglescliffe 5 E4
Eaní 79 D4
Earith 10 C1
Earlston 5 D2
Earn 5 D1
Easingwold 7 D1
Easky 12 B2
Eastbourne 10 C3
East Dereham 7 F3
Easter Ross 2 C3
East Grinstead 10 C3
East Kilbride 4 C2
Eastleigh 9 E3
East Linton 5 D2
East Retford 7 D2
East Sussex 10 C3
Eaux-Bonnes 37 D2
Eauze 28 B3
Ebbw Vale 9 D2
Ebeleben 52 C2
Ebeltoft 108 B3
Eben 59 F1
Ebenfurth 57 F3
Ebensee 56 C3
Eberbach 55 D1
Ebermannstadt 52 C4
Ebern 52 C4
Eberndorf 70 B1
Ebersbach 53 F2
Ebersberg 56 B3
Eberstein 70 B1
Eberswalde 49 E3
Ebmath 53 D3
Eboli 64 C4
Ebrach 52 C4
Ebreichsdorf 57 F3
Ebreuil 26 A4
Ebro, Emb del 35 F2
Ebro, R 37 D2
Ebstorf 48 B3
Eccleshall 6 C3
Eceabat 115 E3
Echallens 27 D3
Echarmeaux, les 26 B4

Echarri-Aranaz 36 C2
Echegárate,
  Pto de 36 B1
Echelles, les 30 C1
Echt 17 D4
Echte 52 B2
Echternach 21 D2
Écija 43 E2
Ečka 72 C2
Eckartsberga 52 C2
Eckernförde 48 A1
Eckerö 106 C3
Ecommoy 23 F4
Ecos 19 E3
Écouché 18 C4
Ecrins, les 31 D2
Ecrins, Massif des . . 31 D2
Ecrins,
  Parc Nat des 31 D2
Ecueillé 25 E3
Ed 105 D4
Eda glasbruk 105 D3
Edam 16 C2
Edane 105 E3
Eday 3 E1
Eddrachillis B 2 C2
Ede 16 C3
Edelény 112 B3
Edelweißspitze 59 E2
Eden 5 D4
Edenderry 13 D3
Edenkoben 54 C2
Eder 52 A3
Eder-Stausee 52 A3
Édessa 79 E3
Edewecht 47 E3
Edgeworthstown 12 C3
Edinburgh 5 D2
Edineţi 113 D3
Edipsós 83 F3
Edirne 115 E3
Edland 104 B3
Edolo 58 C3
Edremit 115 E4
Edsåsdalen 101 D2
Edsbro 106 B3
Edsbyn 101 E4

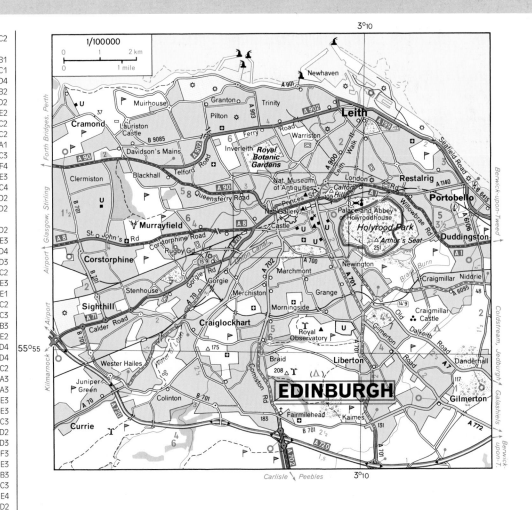

EDINBURGH

1/100000

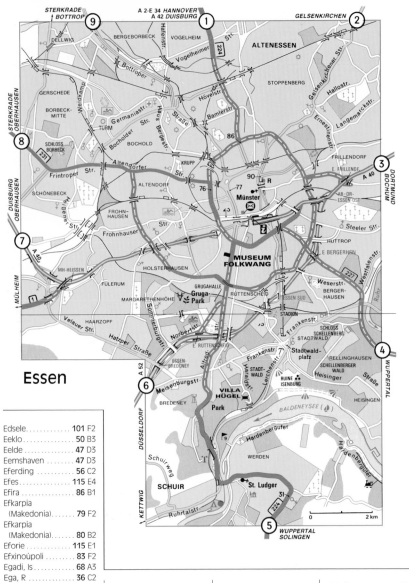

Essen

Edsele............ 101 F2
Eeklo............ 50 B3
Eelde............ 47 D3
Eemshaven....... 47 D3
Eferding......... 56 C2
Efes............ 115 E4
Efira............ 86 B1
Efkarpía
  (Makedonía).... 79 F2
Efkarpía
  (Makedonía).... 80 B2
Eforie........... 115 E1
Efxinoúpoli....... 83 F2
Egádi, Is........ 68 A3
Ega, R.......... 36 C2
Egeln........... 52 C1
Egéo Pélagos..... 84 A1
Eger........... 112 B3
Egersund........ 104 A4
Egeskov......... 108 B4
Egestorf......... 48 A3
Egg............ 58 B1
Eggenburg....... 57 E2
Eggenfelden...... 56 B2
Eggesin......... 49 E2
Eggum.......... 94 A3
Eghezée........ 50 C4
Egiáli.......... 89 D3
Egie........... 87 D4
Egilsstaðir....... 96 C2
Égina.......... 87 E2
Égina, N........ 87 F2
Eginio.......... 79 F3
Égio........... 83 E4
Égira.......... 87 D1
Egletons........ 29 D1
Eglinton......... 13 D1
Egloffstein....... 55 F1
Egmond aan Zee... 16 C2
Egósthena....... 87 E1
Egremont........ 5 D4
Egtved.......... 108 A3
Egüés.......... 36 C2
Eguzon......... 25 E3
Ehinádes Nissiá... 82 C4
Ehingen......... 55 D3
Ehinos.......... 81 D2
Ehra-Lessien...... 48 B4
Ehrang-Pfalzel.... 54 A1
Ehrenberg....... 52 B3
Ehrenhausen..... 70 C1
Ehrwald......... 58 C1
Eibar........... 36 B1
Eibenstock....... 53 D3
Eibiswald........ 70 B1
Eichstätt........ 55 F2

Eide........... 100 B2
Eider.......... 48 A2
Eidfjord........ 104 B2
Eidfjorden....... 104 B2
Eiði........... 96 A3
Eidkjosen....... 94 B2
Eidsborg........ 104 B3
Eidsbugarden.... 100 B3
Eidsdal......... 100 B2
Eidsfjorden...... 94 A3
Eidsfoss........ 104 C3
Eidsvåg........ 100 B2
Eidsvoll........ 105 D2
Eigg........... 2 B4
Eikelandsosen.... 104 A2
Eiken.......... 104 B4
Eikeren......... 104 C3
Eikesdal........ 100 B2
Eilean Donan Castle.. 2 B3
Eilenburg....... 53 D2
Eilsleben........ 52 C1
Einbeck........ 52 B2
Eindhoven....... 16 C4
Einsiedeln....... 58 A2
Eisenach........ 52 B3
Eisenberg....... 53 D3
Eisenerz........ 57 D3
Eisenerzer Alpen.. 57 D4
Eisenhüttenstadt.. 49 F4
Eisenkappel..... 70 A1
Eisenstadt....... 57 F3
Eisfeld......... 52 C3
Eišiškės........ 110 C4
Eisleben........ 52 C2
Eislingen........ 55 D2
Eisriesenwelt-
  Höhle......... 59 E1
Eitorf.......... 51 E3
Eivissa......... 45 D4
Ejea de los
  Caballeros..... 37 D3

Ejulve.......... 41 E2
Ekára.......... 83 E2
Ekenäs........ 107 E3
Ekshärad....... 105 E3
Eksjö.......... 109 D1
Elafohóri........ 81 F1
Elafoníssi....... 87 E4
Élafos.......... 82 B2
El Algar........ 45 D2
El Almendro..... 42 C2
El Aquián....... 44 B4
El Arahal....... 43 E3
El Arenal....... 45 E3
El Atazar, Emb de.. 40 B1
Eláti (Makedonía).. 79 E4
Eláti (Thessalía)... 83 D2
Eláti Mt........ 82 B3
Elátia......... 83 E3
Elatohóri....... 79 E3
Elatoú........ 83 D4
Elatóvrissi...... 83 D3
Elba, Isola d'.... 62 C2
El Barco de Ávila.. 39 E2
Elbasan........ 76 C4
Elbe.......... 48 B3
Elbe-Lübeck-Kanal.. 48 B2
El Berrón....... 35 D1
Elbe-Seitenkanal.. 48 B4
Elbeuf......... 19 D3
Elbigenalp...... 58 C2
Elbingerode..... 52 C2
Elbląg......... 110 B4
Elburg......... 17 D2
El Bodón....... 39 D2
El Bonillo...... 40 C4
El Bosque...... 43 E3
El Burgo....... 43 E3
El Burgo de Osma.. 36 A3
El Burgo Ranero.. 35 E3
El Cabaco...... 39 E2

El Caló........ 45 D4
El Campello..... 45 E1
El Campo de
  Peñaranda.... 39 F1
El Carpio...... 43 F2
El Carpio de Tajo.. 39 F3
El Casar de
  Talamanca.... 40 B2
El Castillo de las
  Guardas...... 43 D2
El Centenillo.... 44 A1
El Cerro de
  Andévalo..... 42 C2
Elche de la Sierra.. 44 C1
El Coronil...... 43 D3
El Cubillo...... 41 D3
El Cubo de
  Don Sancho... 39 D1
El Cubo de Tierra del
  Vino........ 39 E1
El Cuervo...... 43 D3
Elda.......... 45 D1
Elde.......... 48 C3
Eldena........ 48 C3
Elefsína....... 87 F1
Eleftherés
  (Makedonía)... 80 C2
Eleftherés
  (Stereá Eláda).. 87 E1
Eleftherés
  (Thessalía)... 83 E1
Eléft-hero..... 78 C4
Eleftherohóri... 79 D4
Eleftheroúpoli... 80 C2
El Ejido....... 44 B4
Elemir........ 72 C2
Eléna........ 115 D2
Eleófito....... 82 C3
Eleohóri...... 80 C3
Eleohória..... 80 A3

Eleónas....... 83 E4
Eleoússa...... 93 F1
El Escorial..... 40 A2
El Espinar..... 40 A2
El Figueró..... 32 B4
El Formigal.... 37 D2
Elgå......... 100 D3
Elgin......... 3 D3
Elgóibar...... 36 B1
Elgol........ 2 B4
El Grado...... 37 E3
El Grado, Emb de.. 37 E3
El Grao (Castelló de la
  Plana....... 41 F3
El Grao (Valencia).. 41 E4
Elhovo....... 115 E2
El Hoyo de Pinares.. 40 A2
Eliá......... 87 D4
Elie......... 5 D2
Elikónas, Óros... 83 F4
Elimäki....... 107 F2
Elinikó....... 86 C2
Elinohóri..... 81 F1
Elizondo...... 36 C1
Ełk......... 110 C4
Ellesmere..... 6 B3
Ellesmere Port.. 6 B2
Ellingen...... 55 E2
Ellon........ 3 E4
Ellös....... 108 C1
Ellrich....... 52 B2
Ellwangen.... 55 E2
El Madroño.... 42 C2
El Maestrazgo.. 41 E2
Elmas........ 66 B4
El Masnou..... 32 B4
El Molar...... 40 B2
El Molinillo.... 40 A3
El Moral...... 44 C2
Elmshorn..... 48 A2
Elne........ 32 B2
Elnesvågen.... 100 B2
Elóna....... 87 D3
Elopía...... 83 F4
Elorn....... 22 C3
Élos (Kríti)... 90 B3
Élos
  (Pelopónissos).. 87 D4
Eloúnda..... 91 E3
Eloyes...... 27 D1
El Pardo..... 40 A2
El Paular..... 40 A1
El Pedernoso.. 40 B3
El Pedroso.... 43 D2
El Perelló
  (Catalunya)... 41 F2
El Perelló
  (Valencia)... 41 E4
Elphin....... 12 C3
El Picazo..... 40 C4
El Pinell de Brai.. 41 F1
El Pobo de
  Dueñas..... 41 D2
El Pont
  d'Armentera... 37 F4
El Portal..... 43 D4
El Port de la Selva.. 32 C3
El Port de Llança.. 32 B3
El Portet de Morella.. 45 E1
El Prat de
  Llobregat.... 32 A4
El Puente.... 36 A1
El Puente del
  Arzobispo.... 39 F3
El Puerto de
  Sagunto.... 41 E3
El Puerto de Santa
  María....... 43 D4
El Real de la Jara.. 43 D2
El Real de
  San Vicente... 39 F2
El Remolcador,
  Pto........ 41 E3
El Robledo.... 39 F4
El Rocío..... 42 C3
El Romeral... 40 B3
El Rompido... 42 C3
El Ronquillo... 43 D2
El Royo...... 36 B3
El Rubio..... 43 E3
Elsa........ 60 C4
El Saler..... 41 E4
El Salobral... 40 C4
El Saucejo... 43 E3

Elsdorf....... 17 D4
Elserdorf..... 55 F2
El Serrat..... 32 A2
Elsfleth...... 47 F3
Elsterberg.... 53 D3
Elsterwerda... 53 E2
El Tiemblo.... 40 A2
Eltisley..... 9 F1
Eltmann..... 52 C4
El Toboso.... 40 B3
El Torcal..... 43 F3
Eltz........ 51 E4
El Vado, Emb de.. 40 B1
Elvanfoot.... 4 C3
Elvas....... 38 C4
Elvekrok..... 100 B3
El Vellón, Emb de.. 40 A2
Elven....... 22 C4
El Vendrell... 37 F4
Elverum..... 105 D2
El Vicario, Emb de.. 40 A4
El Villar de Arnedo.. 36 C2
El Viso...... 43 E1
El Viso del Alcor.. 43 D2
Elx........ 45 D2
Ely........ 10 C1
Elygsfors.... 109 E3
Elzach...... 54 C3
Elze....... 52 B1
Emån...... 109 E2
Embessós.... 82 C3
Embid...... 41 D1
Embid de Ariza.. 36 C4
Émbonas..... 93 E1
Emboriós (Hios).. 89 D1
Emboriós (Simi).. 93 E1
Embrun..... 31 D2
Emden..... 47 E3
Emet....... 115 F4
Emilia-Romagna.. 60 C3
Emlichheim... 17 E2
Emmaboda... 109 E2
Emmeloord... 16 C2
Emmen..... 17 E1
Emmendingen.. 54 C3
Emmerich.... 17 D3
Emocriós.... 89 F3
Em. Papás... 80 B2
Empoli..... 60 C4
Ems....... 17 E1
Emsdetten... 17 E2
Ems-Jade-Kanal.. 47 E3
Emskirchen.. 55 E1
Enáfors..... 101 D2
Enäjärvi.... 103 E4
Enånger.... 101 F4
Encamp.... 32 A2
Encausse... 37 E1
Encinas de Abajo.. 39 E1
Encinasola... 42 C1
Encinedo... 34 C3
Endelave... 108 B3
Endrinal.... 39 E2
Enego..... 59 D3
Enfesta.... 34 A2
Eng....... 59 D1
Engadin.... 58 B3
Engarés.... 88 C3
Engelberg... 27 F3
Engelhartszell.. 56 C2
Engeløya.... 97 E1
Engelsdorf... 53 D2
Engelskirchen.. 17 E4
Engen..... 58 A1
Enger..... 17 F2
Engerdal... 101 D3
Enghien.... 50 B3
England.... 9 F1
English Channel.. 10 A4
Engstingen.. 55 D3
Enguera.... 41 E4
Enguidanos.. 41 D3
Enhammarsfjärden
  .... 101 F4
Enipéas.... 83 D2
Enkhuizen.. 16 C2
Enköping.. 106 B3
Enna..... 68 C3
Enneberg.. 59 D3
Ennell, L.... 12 C3
Ennepetal.. 17 E4
Ennezat.... 26 A4
Ennis..... 12 B4
Enniscorthy.. 15 D3

Enniskerry.... 13 D4
Enniskillen.... 13 D2
Ennistimon.... 12 B4
Enns....... 57 D3
Enns R...... 57 D3
Eno........ 103 F3
Enol, L...... 35 E2
Enonkoski... 103 F3
Enontekiö... 95 D3
Énos, Óros... 86 A1
Enschede... 17 E2
Ensisheim.. 27 E1
Entlebuch.. 27 F2
Entraygues-sur-
  Truyère.... 29 E2
Entredichos.. 40 C3
Entre-os-Rios.. 34 A4
Entrepeñas,
  Emb de.... 40 C2
Entrevaux.. 31 E3
Entrèves... 27 E4
Entroncamento.. 38 B3
Envalira, Pto de.. 32 A2
Envermeu.. 19 E2
Enviken... 101 E4
Enz....... 54 C2
Enza...... 60 B2
Enzklösterle.. 54 C2
Eochaill.... 14 C4
Eolie o Lípari, Is... 69 D2
Eo, R...... 34 C1
Epanomí.. 79 F3
Epe...... 17 D2
Epernay.. 20 B3
Epernon.. 19 E4
Epidávrou, Kólpos.. 87 E2
Epidávrou Limirás,
  Kólpos.... 87 E4
Épila.... 36 C3
Epinac... 26 B3
Epinal... 27 D1
Epine, l'.. 20 B3
Episkopí (Kríti).. 90 C3
Episkopí (Kríti).. 91 E3
Episkopí
  (Makedonía).. 79 E3
Episkopí
  (Pelopónissos).. 87 E3
Epitálio.. 86 B2
Eppan.. 59 D3
Epping.. 10 C2
Eppingen.. 55 D2
Epsom.. 10 C3
Eptahóri.. 78 C4
Eptálofos.. 83 E3
Epte.... 19 E3
Epworth.. 7 D2
Eraclea.. 59 E4
Eraclea-Mare.. 59 E4
Eräjärvi.. 103 D3
Erásmio, N... 81 D2
Eratiní.. 83 E4
Eratinó.. 80 C2
Erátira.. 79 D3
Erba.... 58 B4
Erbach.. 55 D1
Erbalunga.. 33 F2
Erbendorf.. 53 D4
Ercina, L de la.. 35 E2
Ercolano.. 64 B4
Érd.... 112 B4
Erdek.. 115 E3
Erdevik.. 72 B2
Erding.. 56 A3
Erdre.. 23 D4
Erdut.. 72 B2
Eresma, R.. 40 A1
Eressós.. 85 E2
Erétria.. 84 B4
Erezée.. 50 C4
Erfde.. 48 A2
Erft.... 17 D4
Erftstadt.. 51 E3
Erfurt.. 52 C3
Erges, R.. 39 D2
Ergoldsbach.. 56 B2
Eriboll, L... 2 C2
Erice.. 68 A3
Ericeira.. 38 A3
Ericht, L... 2 C4
Erikoússa, N.. 78 A4
Eriksberg.. 106 A4
Eriksmåle.. 109 E2
Erillas.. 43 E1

Erimanthos. 86 C2	Escabas, R. 40 C2	Eskifjörður 96 C2	Esquivias 40 A2	Estremadura 38 A3	Europoort. 16 B3	Evrótas. 87 D3
Erimanthos, Óros. . 86 C1	Escairón 34 B2	Eskilstuna 106 A4	Essarts, les 24 B3	Estremoz 38 C4	Euskadi. 36 B2	Evry 19 F4
Eripol, Pto del . . . 37 E3	Escalada 35 F2	Eskisehir 115 F3	Esse. 102 C1	Estret de	Euskirchen 51 E3	Évzoni 79 F2
Erithrès 87 E1	Escalante 36 A1	Eskoriatza 36 B1	Essen	Collegats 37 F3	Eußenhausen 52 B3	Exaplátanos 79 E2
Erkelenz 17 D4	Escaldes, les 32 A2	Esla, R 35 D4	(Niedersachsen) . . 17 E2	Estrées-St-Denis . . 19 F3	Eutin 48 B2	Éxarhos 83 F4
Erkner 49 E4	Escalona 40 A2	Eslarn 56 B1	Essen (Nordrhein-	Esztergom 112 B4	Evangelismós 83 E1	Excideuil 29 D1
Erla 37 D3	Escalonilla 40 A3	Eslohe. 17 F4	Westfalen) 17 E3	Etables 22 C2	Evangelistria 83 F4	Exe 8 C3
Erlangen 55 F1	Escalos de Cima . . 38 C2	Eslöv 109 D3	Essenbach 56 B2	Etain 20 C3	Evaux-les-Bains. . . 25 F4	Exeter 8 C3
Erlsbach 59 E2	Escandón,	Espa 105 D2	Essex. 11 D2	Etampes 19 F4	Évdilos. 89 D2	Exmes 19 D4
Ermenonville 19 F3	Pto de 41 D2	Espadañedo 34 C3	Essimi 81 E2	Etaples 19 E1	Evendorf 48 B3	Exmoor Nat Pk 8 C3
Ermidas-Aldeia . . . 42 A1	Esca, R 37 D2	Espadán, Sa de . . . 41 E3	Esslingen. 55 D2	Etel 22 B4	Evenes 94 B3	Exmouth 8 C3
Ermióni 87 E2	Escárène, l' 31 E3	Espalion 29 E3	Essonne 25 F1	Etelhem. 109 F4	Evenskjær 94 B3	Exohi (Ípiros) 78 C4
Ermoúpoli 88 B2	Escároz 37 D2	Esparreguera 32 A4	Essoyes 26 B1	Etive, L 4 B1	Evergem 50 B3	Exohi (Makedonia) . 79 E3
Ermsleben 52 C2	Escatrón 37 D4	Espedal 100 C3	Est, Canal de l' . . . 27 D1	Etna, M 69 D3	Everöd 109 D3	Exohi (Makedonia) . 80 B1
Erndtebrück 17 F4	Escaut (B) 50 B3	Espejo 43 F2	Estaca, Pto de la . . 42 A4	Etne 104 A3	Evertsberg 101 E4	Exómvourgo 88 C2
Erne 13 D3	Escaut (F) 20 A2	Espelette 28 A4	Estacas de Trueba,	Etolia-Akarnanía . . 82 C3	Evesham 9 E1	Exter 17 F2
Ernée 23 E3	Esch (D) 51 F4	Espelkamp 17 F2	Pto de las 35 F2	Etolikó 82 C4	Evian 27 D3	Extremadura 39 E4
Erne, R 12 C2	Esch (L) 21 D2	Espenschied. 51 F4	Estadilla 37 E3	Etrépagny 19 E3	Évijärvi. 102 C2	Eydehavn 104 C4
Ernestinovo 71 F2	Eschede. 48 B4	Espera 43 D3	Estagel 32 B2	Etretat 19 D2	Evinohóri 83 D4	Eye 9 F1
Ernstbrunn 57 F2	Eschenbach 53 D4	Esperó, Pta. 45 F2	Estaires 19 F1	Ettelbruck 21 D2	Évinos. 83 D3	Eyemouth 5 E2
Erquy 22 C2	Eschershausen . . . 52 B1	Espichel, C. 38 A4	Estarreja 38 B1	Etten 16 C3	Evisa 33 F3	Eye Pen 2 B2
Errazu 36 C1	Eschwege 52 B2	Espiel 43 E1	Estats, Pic d' 37 F2	Ettenheim 54 C3	Evje 104 B4	Eygues 30 C2
Errigal Mt 12 C1	Eschweiler 51 D3	Espigüete. 35 E2	Estavayer 27 E3	Ettington 9 E1	Évlalo 81 D2	Eyguières 30 C2
Erris Head 12 A2	Escombreras 45 D3	Espinama 35 E2	Este 61 D1	Ettington 9 E1	Évlalo 81 D2	Eygurande 29 E1
Erskine Bridge 4 C2	Escorihuela 41 E2	Espinho 34 A4	Estepa 43 E3	Ettlingen 54 C2	Evolène 27 E4	Eyjafjörður 96 A1
Erstein 21 E4	Escudo, Pto del . . . 35 F2	Espinilla 35 F2	Estepona 43 E4	Eugénie-les-Bains . 28 B4	Évora 38 B4	Eymet 28 C2
Ervenik 75 D1	Escúllar 44 B3	Espinosa de	Esteras de	Eume, Emb del . . . 34 B1	Évoramonte 38 B4	Eymoutiers 29 D1
Ervidel 42 B1	Escurial 39 E4	Cerrato 35 F4	Medina 36 B4	Eume, R 34 B1	Evran 18 B4	Eyre 28 B3
Ervy 26 B1	Esens 47 E3	Espinosa de los	Esterel 31 E4	Eupen 51 D4	Evrecy 18 C3	Eyrieux 30 B2
Erwitte 17 F3	Esera, R 37 E2	Monteros 36 A1	Esternay 20 A4	Eura 107 D2	Evreux 19 E3	Eysturoy 96 A3
Erzberg 57 D3	Esguevillas de	Espoo 107 E3	Esterri d'Àneu 37 F2	Eurajoki 107 D2	Evritania 83 D2	Eyzies, les 29 D2
Erzen 76 C4	Esgueva 35 F4	Esporles 45 E3	Estissac 26 B1	Euratsfeld 57 D3	Evron 23 E3	Ezcaray. 36 B2
Erzgebirge. 53 E3	Esguevillas de	Esposende 34 A4	Estói 42 B3	Eure 19 E4	Evropós 79 F2	Eze 31 E3
Esbjerg 108 A3	Esgueva 35 F4	Espot 37 F2	Estoril 38 A4	Eure (Dépt) 19 E3	Évros 81 F2	Ezine 115 E4
Esblada. 37 F4	Esino 61 E1	Espuña, Sa de 44 C2	Estrela, Sa da 38 C2	Eure-et-Loir. 25 E1	Évros R 81 F2	
Esbo 107 E3	Esk 5 D3	Esquedas 37 D3	Estrella 44 A1	Europabrücke. 59 D2	Évrostina 87 D1	

F

Faak 59 F2	Fällfors. 98 B4	Farra d'Alpago 59 E3
Fabara 37 E4	Fallingbostel 48 A4	Fársala 83 E2
Fåberg. 105 D2	Falmouth. 8 B4	Farsø 108 A2
Fabero 34 C2	Falset 37 F4	Farsund 104 A4
Fåborg 108 B4	Falster 108 C4	Farum 108 C3
Fabriano 61 E4	Falterona Mte 61 D3	Fasano 65 E3
Fábricas de Riópar. 44 C1	Fălticeni 113 D3	Fašku Vaskojoki . . 95 E3
Fabro 63 D1	Falun. 105 F2	Fastiv 113 E2
Facinas 43 D4	Falzarego, Pso . . . 59 D3	Fátima 38 B3
Facture 28 A2	Fámjin 96 A4	Fatmomakke 97 E4
Faenza 61 D3	Fanad Head 13 D1	Faucille, Col de la . . 27 D3
Færøerne 96 A3	Fanári	Faucogney 27 D1
Faeto 64 B3	(Pelopónnissos) . . 87 E2	Faulquemont 21 D3
Fafe 34 A4	Fanári	Fauquembergues . 19 E1
Făgăraş 113 D4	(Pelopónnissos) . . 86 C2	Fauske 97 F2
Făgăraşului, M . . . 113 D4	Fanári (Thessalia) . 83 D2	Fauville. 19 D3
Fågelfors. 109 E2	Fanári (Thráki) 81 D2	Fåvang 100 C3
Fagernes	Fanári, Akr 89 D3	Favara (E) 41 E4
(Oppland) 104 C2	Fanefjord 108 C4	Favara (I) 68 C4
Fagernes (Troms) . . 94 C2	Fani i Madh 76 C3	Faverges 27 D4
Fagersta 105 F3	Fani i Vogël 76 C3	Faverney 27 D1
Fairford 9 E2	Fanjeaux 32 A1	Faversham 11 D3
Fair Head 13 E1	Fannich, L 2 C3	Favignana, I 68 A3
Fair I 3 F3	Fano 61 E3	Fawley. 9 E3
Fakenham 7 E3	Fanø 108 A3	Faxaflói 96 A2
Fakoviči 72 C4	Fanø Bugt 108 A3	Fayence 31 D4
Fakse 108 C4	Fanós 79 F2	Fayl-Billot 26 C1
Fakse Ladeplads. . 108 C4	Faouët, le 22 B3	Fayón 37 E4
Falaise 18 C4	Faou, le 22 B3	Fay-sur-Lignon . . . 30 B2
Falakró, Óros 80 C1	Farángi Samariás . 90 B4	Fažana 70 A4
Falássarna 90 B4	Farángi Víkou 78 C4	Feale 14 B3
Falcade 59 D3	Fara Novarese 58 A4	Fécamp 19 D2
Falces 36 C2	Fårbo 109 E2	Féclaz, la 31 D1
Falconara	Fardes, R 44 A3	Feda 104 B4
Marittima 61 F3	Fareham 9 E3	Feggesund 108 A2
Falcone 69 D2	Fårevejle 108 B3	Fehmarn 48 B1
Falcone, C del 66 A1	Färgelanda 105 D4	Fehmarnbelt 48 B1
Falerna 67 E3	Färila 101 F3	Fehmarnsund 48 B1
Faliráki 93 F1	Farindola 63 F1	Fehrbellin 49 D3
Falkefjellet 95 F1	Faringdon 9 E2	Fehring 57 F4
Falkenberg (D) 53 E2	Farini d'Olmo 60 B2	Fejø 108 B4
Falkenberg (S). . . . 108 C2	Färjestaden 109 E2	Feketić 72 B2
Falkensee 49 D4	Farkadóna 83 E1	Felanitx 45 F3
Falkenstein 53 D3	Farkaždin 72 C2	Felbertauern-
Falkirk 4 C2	Farlete 37 D3	tunnel 59 E2
Falkland 5 D2	Farmakoníssi 89 F2	Feld 59 F2
Falkonéra, N 87 E3	Farnborough 9 F3	Feldafing 56 A3
Falköping 109 D1	Farnese 63 D2	Feldbach 57 F4
Fallersleben 48 B4	Farnham 9 F3	Feldberg (Baden-
	Faro 42 B3	Württemberg) . . . 54 C4
	Fårö 109 F3	Feldberg (Mecklenburg-
	Fårösund 109 F3	Vorpommern) . . . 49 D3

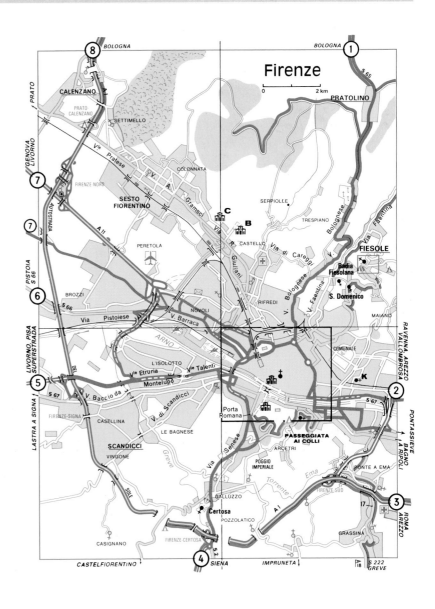

Folkestone Terminal

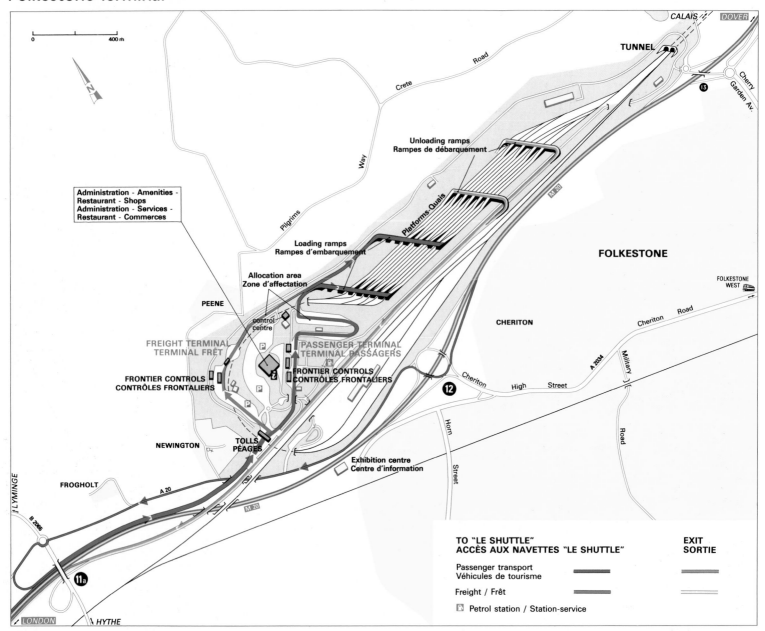

Feldkirch 58 B2	Ferlach 70 A1	Ferté-Milon, la . . . 20 A3	Fife Ness 5 D1
Feldkirchen 59 F2	Fermanagh 12 C2	Ferté-St-Aubin, la . . 25 E2	Figália 86 C2
Felgueiras 34 A4	Fermo 61 F4	Ferté-sous-	Figeac 29 E2
Felixstowe 11 D2	Fermoselle 34 C4	Jouarre, la 20 A3	Figline Valdarno . . 61 D4
Fellbach 55 D2	Fermoy 14 C4	Ferté-Vidame, la . . 19 D4	Figueira da Foz . . . 38 B2
Felletin 25 F4	Fernancaballero . . . 40 A4	Fertilia 66 A2	Figueira de Castelo
Fellingsbro 105 F3	Fernán Núñez 43 F2	Fervenza, Emb de . . 34 A1	Rodrigo 39 D1
Felton 5 E3	Ferney-Voltaire . . . 27 D4	Festós 91 B1	Figueiró dos
Feltre 59 D3	Fernpaß 58 C1	Festre, Col du 30 C2	Vinhos 38 B2
Femer Bælt 108 B4	Ferrandina 65 D4	Festvåg 97 E1	Figueras 32 B3
Femundsmarka . . . 101 D3	Ferrara 61 D2	Fethard 14 C3	Figueres 32 B3
Fene 34 B1	Ferreira 34 C1	Fetlar 3 F1	Figueruela de
Fener 59 D3	Ferreira do	Fetsund 105 D3	Arriba 34 C3
Fenestrelle 31 E1	Alentejo 42 B1	Feucht 55 F1	Fihtio 87 D2
Fénétrange 21 E3	Ferreira do Zêzere . 38 B3	Feuchtwangen 55 E2	Filabres, Sa de los . 44 B3
Feolin Ferry 4 B2	Ferreiras 42 A3	Feunte Dé 35 E2	Filadélfi 80 B3
Fer à Cheval,	Ferreras de Abajo . 35 D3	Feurs 26 B4	Filadelfia 67 F3
Cirque du 27 E4	Ferreries 45 F2	Feyzin 30 B1	Filáki 83 E2
Feraklós 93 F2	Ferreruela de	Ffestiniog 6 A3	Filákio 81 F1
Ferbane 12 C4	Huerva 41 D1	Fflint 6 B2	Filakopi 88 A4
Ferdinandovac 71 D1	Ferret, Cap 28 A2	Fiano R. 63 E2	Filérimos 93 F1
Ferdinandshof 49 E2	Ferrette 27 E2	Fiastra 61 F4	Filey 7 E1
Fère-	Ferriere 60 B2	Ficarolo 60 C2	Filfola 68 B4
Champenoise . . . 20 B4	Ferrières 25 F1	Fichtel-gebirge . . . 53 D4	Fili 87 F1
Fère-en-	Ferrol 34 B1	Fidenza 60 B2	Filia (Lésvos) 85 F2
Tardenois 20 A3	Ferru, M. 66 B3	Fieberbrunn 59 E1	Filia
Fère, la 20 A2	Ferté-Alais, la 19 F4	Fier 114 B3	(Pelopónissos) . 86 C1
Ferentino 63 F3	Ferté-Bernard, la . . 23 F3	Fiera di Primiero . . 59 D3	Filiátes 82 B1
Féres 81 F2	Ferté-Frênel, la . . . 19 D4	Fierzës, Liq i 76 C3	Filiatrá 86 B3
Feria 43 D1	Ferté-Gaucher, la . 20 A4	Fiesole 61 D3	Filicudi, I 68 C2
Feričanci 71 E2	Ferté-Macé, la . . . 18 C4	Fife 5 D2	Filiourí 81 E2

Filipi 80 C2	Finowfurt 49 E3	Fiumicino 63 E3
Filipiáda 82 C2	Finspång 105 F4	Fivemiletown 13 D2
Filipjakov 74 C1	Finsteraarhorn 27 F3	Fivizzano 60 B3
Filipos, Akr. 88 B3	Finsterau 56 C2	Fjällåsen 94 C4
Filipstad 105 E3	Finsterwalde 53 E1	Fjällbacka 105 D4
Filira 81 E2	Finström 106 C3	Fjällnäs 101 D4
Figueira de Castelo	Fillan 100 C1	Fjärdhundra 106 B3
Fille-fjell 104 B1	Fintona 13 D2	Fjærland 100 A3
Filo 83 E2	Fintown 12 C1	Fjätervålen 101 D3
Filótas 79 D3	Fionnphort 4 A1	Fjelie 108 C3
Filottrano 61 F4	Fiorenzuola	Fjellerup 108 B2
Finale Emilia 60 C2	d'Arda 60 B2	Fjerritslev 108 A2
Finale Ligure 31 F3	Firenze 60 C3	Fjerze 76 C2
Fiñana 44 B3	Firenzuola 61 D3	Flå 104 C2
Finca de la	Firminy 30 B1	Fladså 108 A3
Concepción . . . 43 F3	Firmo 67 E2	Fladungen 52 B3
Finchingfield 11 D2	Fischamend Markt . 57 F2	Flaine 27 E4
Findhorn 3 D3	Fischbach 55 F1	Flakk 100 C1
Finikas 88 B2	Fischbeck 48 C4	Flåm 104 B1
Finikoúndas 86 C4	Fischen 55 E4	Flamborough Head . 7 F1
Finistère 22 B3	Fishbourne 9 E3	Flambourári 82 C1
Finisterre, Emb de . 40 A3	Fishguard 8 B1	Flámbouro
Finja 109 D3	Fiskárdo 82 B4	(Makedonía) . . . 79 D3
Finn 13 D1	Fiskari 107 E3	Flámbouro
Finneidfjord 97 E3	Fiskebøl 94 A3	(Makedonía) . . . 80 B2
Finnentrop 17 F4	Fismes 20 A3	Flamignano 63 F2
Finnmark 95 D2	Fissíni 85 D1	Flamouriá 79 E3
Finnmarksvidda . . . 95 D3	Fitero 36 C3	Flannan I 2 A2
Finnøy 104 A3	Fíties 82 C3	Flåsjön 101 F1
Finnsnes 94 B3	Fitjar 104 A2	Flåten 94 C2
Finow 49 E3	Fiuggi 63 F3	Flatey 96 A1

Flatråker ... 104 A2
Flattnitz ... 59 F2
Flatval ... 100 C1
Flèche, la ... 23 E4
Fleetwood ... 6 B1
Flekkefjord ... 104 A4
Flen ... 106 A4
Flensborg Fjord ... 108 A4
Flensburg ... 48 A1
Flers ... 18 C4
Flesberg ... 104 C3
Flesnes ... 94 A3
Fleurance ... 28 C4
Fleurier ... 27 D3
Fleurus ... 50 C4
Fleury ... 19 F4
Fleury-sur-Andelle ... 19 E3
Fléves, N ... 87 F2
Flevoland ... 16 C2
Flexenpaß ... 58 B2
Flims Waldhaus ... 58 B2
Flint ... 6 B2
Flisa ... 105 D2
Flix ... 37 E4
Flixecourt ... 19 F2
Flize ... 20 C2
Floda ... 105 F2
Flogny ... 26 B1
Flöha ... 53 E3
Flomohóri ... 87 D4
Flora ... 77 F3
Florac ... 29 F3
Flor da Rosa ... 38 C3
Florennes ... 50 C4
Florensac ... 30 A4
Florenville ... 20 C2
Florešti ... 113 E3
Floriáda ... 82 C2
Floridia ... 69 D4
Flórina ... 79 D2
Flórina (Nomos) ... 79 D3
Florø ... 104 A1
Flörsheim-Dalsheim ... 54 C1
Flötningen ... 101 D3
Floúda, Akr ... 92 C1
Floúnda ... 91 E3
Flüelapass ... 58 B2
Flüelen ... 58 A2
Flühli ... 27 F3
Flumendosa ... 66 C3
Flumen, R. ... 37 D3
Flumet ... 27 D4
Fluminimaggiore ... 66 A4
Flums ... 58 B2
Fluvià, R. ... 32 B3
Foča ... 76 A1
Foça ... 115 E4
Foce Verde ... 63 F3
Fochabers ... 3 D3
Fockbek ... 48 A2
Focșani ... 113 E4
Fódele ... 91 D3
Foggia ... 64 C3
Föglö ... 106 C3
Fohnsdorf ... 57 D4
Föhr ... 47 F1
Foiano della Chiana ... 61 D4
Foinaven ... 2 C2
Foix ... 32 A2
Fojnica (BH) ... 75 F1
Fojnica (BH) ... 75 F2
Fokí ... 83 E4
Fokstuhø ... 100 C3
Folda ... 97 E1
Foldereid ... 97 D4
Foldfjorden ... 97 D4
Foleá ... 80 C2
Folégandros ... 91 D1
Folégandros, N. ... 91 D1
Følen ... 104 A3
Folgaria ... 59 D1
Folgefonna ... 104 B2
Folgoët, le ... 22 A2
Folgoso de la Ribera ... 35 D2
Foligno ... 63 E1
Folkestad ... 100 A3
Folkestone ... 11 D3
Follafoss ... 101 D1
Folldal ... 100 C3
Follebu ... 104 C1

Follina ... 59 E3
Föllinge ... 101 E1
Follonica ... 62 C1
Folmava ... 56 B1
Folói ... 86 C2
Fombellida ... 35 F4
Fond-de-France, le ... 31 D1
Fondevila ... 34 B3
Fondi ... 63 F3
Fondo ... 59 D3
Fonfría (Aragón) ... 37 D4
Fonfría (Castilla-León) ... 35 D4
Fongen ... 101 D2
Fonn ... 100 A3
Fonni ... 66 B3
Fonollosa ... 32 A4
Fonsagrada ... 34 C2
Fontaine ... 27 E1
Fontainebleau ... 19 F4
Fontaine-de-Vaucluse ... 30 C3
Fontaine-Française ... 26 C2
Fontaine-Henry ... 18 C3
Fontaine-le-Dun ... 19 D2
Fontanigorda ... 60 A3
Fonte Longa ... 34 B4
Fontenay ... 26 B2
Fontenay-le-Comte ... 24 C3
Fontenay-Trésigny ... 19 F4
Fontevraud-l'Abbaye ... 25 D2
Fontfroide, Abbaye de ... 32 B2
Fontgombault ... 25 D3
Fontibre ... 35 F2
Fontiveros ... 39 F1
Fontoy ... 21 D3
Font-Romeu ... 32 A2
Fontvieille ... 30 B4
Fonz ... 37 E3
Fonzaso ... 59 D3
Foppolo ... 58 B3
Forata, Emb de ... 41 E4
Forbach ... 21 E3
Forca Canapine ... 63 F1
Forca Caruso ... 64 A2
Forca d'Acero ... 64 A2
Forcall ... 41 E2
Forcalquier ... 30 C3
Forcarei ... 34 A2
Forchheim ... 55 F1
Forclaz, Col de la ... 27 E4
Forcola di Mte Rest. ... 59 E3
Førde ... 100 A3
Førdefjorden ... 104 A1
Förderstedt ... 52 C1
Fordingbridge ... 9 E3
Fordongianus ... 66 B3
Foreland ... 9 F3
Forenza ... 64 C3
Foresta di Burgos ... 66 B2
Føresvik ... 104 A3
Forêt d'Orient, Lac de la ... 26 B1
Forez, Monts du ... 29 F1
Forfar ... 5 D1
Forges-les-Eaux ... 19 E3
Forggensee ... 55 F4
Forio ... 64 A4
Forlì ... 61 D3
Forlì del Sannio ... 64 A2
Forlimpopoli ... 61 D3
Formazza ... 58 A3
Formby ... 6 B2
Formentera ... 45 D4
Formentor, C ... 45 F2
Formerie ... 19 E3
Formia ... 64 A3
Formigine ... 60 C2
Fornaci di Barga ... 60 C3
Fornells ... 45 F1
Forni Avoltri ... 59 E2
Forni di Sopra ... 59 E3
Forno di Zoldo ... 59 E3
Fornos de Algodres ... 38 C1
Fornovo di Taro ... 60 B2
Forøy ... 97 E2

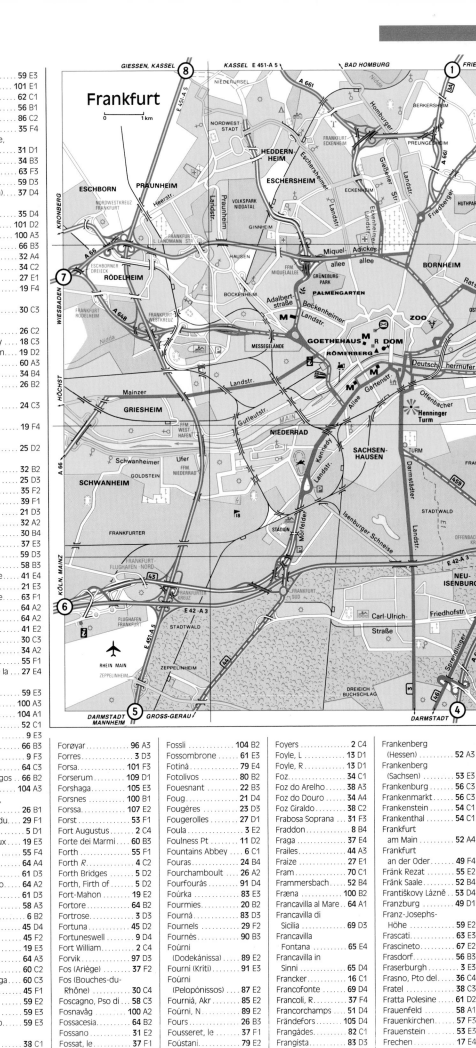

Frankfurt

Forøyar ... 96 A3
Forres ... 3 D3
Forsa ... 101 F3
Forserum ... 109 D1
Forshaga ... 105 E3
Forsnes ... 100 B1
Forssa ... 107 E2
Forst ... 53 F1
Fort Augustus ... 2 C4
Forte dei Marmi ... 60 B3
Forth ... 55 F1
Forth R. ... 4 C2
Forth Bridges ... 5 D2
Forth, Firth of ... 5 D2
Fort-Mahon ... 19 E2
Fortore ... 64 B2
Fortrose ... 3 D3
Fortuna ... 45 D2
Fortuneswell ... 9 D4
Fort William ... 2 C4
Forvik ... 97 D3
Fos (Ariège) ... 37 F2
Fos (Bouches-du-Rhône) ... 30 C4
Foscagno, Pso di ... 58 C3
Fosnavåg ... 100 A2
Fossacesia ... 64 B2
Fossano ... 31 E2
Fossat, le ... 37 F1
Fossbakken ... 94 B3
Fosses ... 50 C4

Fossli ... 104 B2
Fossombrone ... 61 E3
Fotiná ... 79 E4
Fotolívos ... 80 B2
Fouesnant ... 22 B3
Foug ... 21 D4
Fougères ... 23 D3
Fougerolles ... 27 D1
Foula ... 3 E2
Foulness Pt ... 11 D2
Fouras ... 24 B4
Fourchamboult ... 26 A2
Fourfourás ... 91 D4
Foúrka ... 83 E3
Fourmies ... 20 B2
Fourná ... 83 D3
Fournels ... 29 F2
Fournés ... 90 B3
Fourni (Dodekánissa) ... 89 E2
Fourni (Kríti) ... 91 E3
Foúrni (Pelopónnissos) ... 87 E2
Fourniá, Akr ... 85 E2
Foúrni, N ... 89 E2
Fours ... 26 B3
Foússeret, le ... 37 F1
Foústani ... 79 E2
Fowey ... 8 B4
Foxford ... 12 B2

Foyers ... 2 C4
Foyle, L ... 13 D1
Foyle, R ... 13 D1
Foz ... 34 C1
Foz do Arelho ... 38 A3
Foz do Douro ... 34 A4
Foz Giraldo ... 38 C2
Frabosa Soprana ... 31 F3
Fraddon ... 8 B4
Fraga ... 37 E4
Frailes ... 44 A3
Fraize ... 27 E1
Fram ... 70 C1
Frammersbach ... 52 B4
Fræna ... 100 A2
Francavilla al Mare ... 64 A1
Francavilla di Sicilia ... 69 D3
Francavilla Fontana ... 65 E4
Francavilla in Sinni ... 65 D4
Francker ... 16 C1
Francofonte ... 69 D4
Francolí, R. ... 37 F4
Francorchamps ... 51 D4
Frändefors ... 105 D4
Frangádes ... 82 C1
Frangísta ... 83 D3
Frangokástelo ... 90 C4
Frangy ... 27 D4

Frankenberg (Hessen) ... 52 A3
Frankenberg (Sachsen) ... 53 E3
Frankenburg ... 56 C3
Frankenmarkt ... 56 C3
Frankenstein ... 54 C1
Frankenthal ... 54 C1
Frankfurt am Main ... 52 A4
Frankfurt an der Oder ... 49 F4
Fränk Rezat ... 55 E2
Fränk Saale ... 52 B4
Františkovy Lázně ... 53 D2
Franzburg ... 49 D1
Franz-Josephs-Höhe ... 59 E2
Frascati ... 63 E3
Frascineto ... 67 E2
Frasdorf ... 56 B3
Fraserburgh ... 3 E3
Frasno, Pto del ... 36 C4
Fratel ... 38 C3
Fratta Polesine ... 61 D2
Frauenfeld ... 58 A1
Frauenkirchen ... 57 F3
Frauenstein ... 53 E3
Frechen ... 17 E4
Frechilla ... 35 E3
Freckenhorst ... 17 F3

Fredensborg ... 108 C3
Fredericia ... 108 B3
Frederikshavn ... 108 B1
Frederikssund ... 108 C3
Frederiksværk ... 108 C3
Fredrika ... 102 A1
Fredriksberg ... 105 E3
Fredrikstad ... 105 D3
Fregenal de la Sierra ... 42 C1
Fregene ... 63 E3
Fréhel, Cap. ... 22 C2
Frei ... 100 B2
Freiberg ... 53 E3
Freiberger Mulde ... 53 D2
Freiburg (Baden-Württemberg) ... 54 C4
Freiburg (Niedersachsen) ... 48 A2
Freienhufen ... 53 E1
Freilassing ... 56 C3
Freilingen ... 51 F4
Freising ... 55 F3
Freistadt ... 57 D2
Freital ... 53 E2
Freiwalde ... 53 E1
Freixedas ... 38 C1
Freixido ... 34 C3
Freixo de Espada à Cinta ... 39 D1
Fréjus ... 31 D4

Fréjus, Tunnel du . . . 31 D1
Frenchpark . . . 12 C3
Frêne, Col du . . . 31 D1
Freren . . . 17 E2
Freshford . . . 12 C4
Freshwater . . . 9 E3
Fresnay-sur-Sarthe . . . 23 F3
Fresne-St-Mamès . . 27 D2
Fresnes-en-Woëvre . . . 20 C3
Fresno Alhándiga . . . 39 E1
Fresvikbreen . . . 104 B1
Freudenberg (Baden-Württemberg) . . . 55 D1
Freudenberg (Nord-rhein-Westfalen) . . 17 F4
Freudenstadt . . . 54 C3
Frévent . . . 19 F2
Freyburg . . . 52 C2
Freyenstein . . . 48 C3
Freyung . . . 56 C2
Fri . . . 93 D3
Frias . . . 36 A2
Frias de Albarracin . 41 D2
Fribourg . . . 27 E3
Fridingen . . . 55 D3
Friedberg (A) . . . 57 F3
Friedberg (Bayern) . 55 F3
Friedberg (Hessen) . 52 A4
Friedeburg . . . 47 E3
Friedersdorf . . . 49 E4
Friedland (Mecklenburg-Vorpommern) . . . 49 D2
Friedland (Niedersachsen) . . 52 B2
Friedrichroda . . . 52 B3
Friedrichshafen . . . 55 D4
Friedrichskoog . . . 47 F2
Friedrichsort . . . 48 A1
Friedrichstadt . . . 47 F1
Friedrichsthal . . . 54 B2
Friesach . . . 57 D4
Friesack . . . 49 D4
Friesland . . . 16 C1
Friesoythe . . . 17 E1
Frigiliana . . . 44 A4
Frihetsli . . . 94 C3
Friis veien . . . 100 C3
Frikes . . . 82 B4
Frilingiánika . . . 90 A1
Frinton-on-Sea . . . 11 D2
Friol . . . 34 B2
Fristad . . . 109 D1
Fritsla . . . 108 C1
Fritzlar . . . 52 A3
Friuli-Venezia Giulia . 59 E3
Frizington . . . 5 D4
Frodsham . . . 6 B2
Frogner . . . 105 D3
Frohavet . . . 100 C1
Frohburg . . . 53 D2
Frohnleiten . . . 57 E4
Froissy . . . 19 F3
Froitzheim . . . 51 D3
Frome . . . 9 D3
Fromentine . . . 24 A3
Frómista . . . 35 F3
Fronteira . . . 38 C4
Frontenay-Rohan-Rohan . . . 24 C4
Frontenhausen . . . 56 B2
Frontera . . . 42 A4
Frontignan . . . 30 A4
Fronton . . . 29 D3
Frosinone . . . 63 F3
Frosolone . . . 64 B3
Frösön . . . 101 E2
Frosta . . . 100 C1
Frostavallen . . . 109 D3
Frøstrup . . . 108 A2
Frouard . . . 21 D4
Froússa . . . 82 C2
Frövi . . . 105 F3
Frøya . . . 100 B1
Frøyfjorden . . . 100 B1
Frøysjøen . . . 100 A3
Fruges . . . 19 F1
Fruška . . . 72 B2
Frutigen . . . 27 E3
Frýdek-Místek . . . 112 B3
Fteliá . . . 80 C2
Ftéri (Makedonía) . . . 79 E4
Ftéri (Pelopónissos) . . . 86 C1
Fthiótida . . . 83 E3
Fucecchio . . . 60 C4
Fuencaliente (Castilla-la-Mancha) . . . 43 F1
Fuencaliente (Is Canarias) . . . 42 A4
Fuendejalón . . . 36 C3
Fuendetodos . . . 37 D4
Fuengirola . . . 43 F4
Fuenlabrada . . . 40 A2
Fuenlabrada de los Montes . . . 39 F4
Fuenmayor . . . 36 B2
Fuensalida . . . 40 A3
Fuensanta de Martos . . . 43 F2
Fuensanta, Emb de la . . . 44 C1
Fuente-Alamo . . . 45 D1
Fuente Alamo . . . 45 D2
Fuentecén . . . 35 F4
Fuente de Cantos . . 43 D1
Fuente del Maestre . . . 43 D1
Fuente de Pedro Naharro . . . 40 B3
Fuente de Piedra . . . 43 E3
Fuente el Fresno . . . 40 A4
Fuenteguinaldo . . . 39 D2
Fuentelapeña . . . 39 E1
Fuente Obéjuna . . . 43 E1
Fuente Palmera . . . 43 E2
Fuentepinilla . . . 36 B3
Fuentesauco . . . 39 E1
Fuentes de Andalucía . . . 43 E2
Fuentes de Ayódar . . . 41 E3
Fuentes de Ebro . . . 37 D4
Fuentes de León . . . 43 D1
Fuentes de Nava . . . 35 E3
Fuentes de Oñoro . . 39 D1
Fuentes de Ropel . . 35 D3
Fuentes de Valdepero . . . 35 F3
Fuentidueña . . . 35 F4
Fuentidueña de Tajo . . . 40 B3
Fuerte del Rey . . . 44 A2
Fuerteventura . . . 42 C4
Fügen . . . 59 D1
Fuglebjerg . . . 108 B4
Fugløysundet . . . 94 C2
Fulda . . . 52 B3
Fulda R . . . 52 B3
Fulgatore . . . 68 A3
Fulpmes . . . 59 D2
Fulufjället . . . 101 D4
Fumay . . . 20 B2
Fumel . . . 28 C3
Funäsdalen . . . 101 D2
Funchal . . . 42 A3
Fundão . . . 38 C2
Funes . . . 59 D2
Fuorn, Pso dal . . . 58 C3
Furadouro . . . 38 B1
Furci . . . 64 B2
Furkapass . . . 58 A3
Furnace . . . 4 B2
Furnás . . . 45 D3
Fürstenau . . . 17 E2
Fürstenberg . . . 49 D3
Fürstenfeld . . . 57 F4
Fürstenfeldbruck . . . 55 F3
Fürstenlager . . . 54 C1
Fürstenwalde . . . 49 E4
Fürstenwerder . . . 49 E3
Fürstenzell . . . 56 C2
Furtei . . . 66 B3
Fürth . . . 55 E1
Furth . . . 56 B1
Furtwangen . . . 54 C3
Furudal . . . 101 E4
Furuflaten . . . 94 C2
Fuscaldo . . . 67 E2
Fusch . . . 59 E1
Fuschl . . . 56 C3
Fuseta . . . 42 B3
Fushë Arrez . . . 76 C3
Fushë Muhur . . . 76 C3
Fusignano . . . 61 D2
Füssen . . . 55 E4
Fustiñana . . . 36 C3
Futa, Pso della . . . 60 C3
Futog . . . 72 C2
Futrikelv . . . 94 B2
Fuzine . . . 70 B3
Fyn . . . 108 B4
Fyne, L . . . 4 B2
Fynshav . . . 108 B4
Fyresdal . . . 104 B3
Fyresvatn . . . 104 B3
Fyrkat . . . 108 B2

G

Gaaldorf . . . 57 D4
Gabarret . . . 28 B3
Gabela . . . 75 F2
Gaberl-Sattel . . . 57 E4
Gabia la Grande . . . 44 A3
Gabicce Mare . . . 61 E3
Gabriel y Galán, Emb de . . . 39 E2
Gabrovka . . . 70 B2
Gabrovo . . . 115 D2
Gacé . . . 19 D4
Gacilly, la . . . 23 D4
Gacko . . . 76 A2
Gäddede . . . 97 E4
Gadebusch . . . 48 B2
Gádor . . . 44 B3
Gádor, Sa de . . . 44 B3
Gadžin Han . . . 77 E1
Găeşti . . . 115 D1
Gaeta . . . 64 A3
Gaeta, Golfo di . . . 64 A3
Gagarin . . . 111 F2
Gaggenau . . . 54 C2
Gagnef . . . 105 F2
Gail . . . 59 E2
Gailbergsattel . . . 59 E2
Gaildorf . . . 55 D2
Gailey . . . 9 E1
Gaillac . . . 29 D3
Gaillimh . . . 12 B3
Gaillon . . . 19 E3
Gainsborough . . . 7 D2
Gairloch . . . 2 B3
Gaj . . . 73 D2
Gajdobra . . . 72 B2
Gakovo . . . 72 B1
Galan . . . 37 E1
Galanádo . . . 88 C3
Galanianá . . . 90 A2
Galanta . . . 112 A3
Galapagar . . . 40 A2
Galarinós . . . 80 A3
Galaroza . . . 42 C2
Galashiels . . . 5 D2
Galatádes . . . 79 E3
Galatáki . . . 84 A3
Galatás (Argolída) . . . 87 E2
Galatás (Korinthía) . . . 87 D1
Galaţi . . . 113 E4
Galatina . . . 65 F4
Galatini . . . 79 D3
Galátista . . . 80 A3
Galatone . . . 65 F4
Galaxídi . . . 83 E4
Galdakao . . . 36 B1
Galdhøpiggen . . . 100 B3
Galeata . . . 61 D3
Galegos . . . 38 C3
Galende . . . 34 C3
Galera . . . 44 B2
Gagliano del Capo . . . 65 F4
Galibier, Col du . . . 31 D1
Galicia . . . 34 B2
Galičica . . . 77 D4
Galičnik . . . 77 D3
Galikós . . . 79 F3
Galipsós . . . 80 B2
Galisteo . . . 39 D2
Galiz, Pto de . . . 43 D4
Gallarate . . . 60 A1
Gallardon . . . 19 E4
Gallargues . . . 30 B3
Gállego, R . . . 37 D3
Galley Head . . . 14 B4
Galliate . . . 60 A1
Gallipoli . . . 65 F4
Gällivare . . . 98 B2
Gallneukirchen . . . 57 D2
Gällö . . . 101 E2
Gallo, C . . . 68 B2
Gallocanta, L de . . . 41 D1
Gallo, R . . . 41 D2
Galloway Forest Park . . . 4 C3
Gallspach . . . 56 C3
Gallur . . . 36 C3
Gälöfjärden . . . 106 B4
Galston . . . 4 C2
Galten . . . 108 B3
Galtür . . . 58 C3
Galty Mts . . . 14 C3
Galveias . . . 38 B3
Gálvez . . . 40 A3
Galway . . . 12 B3
Galway (Co) . . . 12 B3
Galway B . . . 12 B4
Gamaches . . . 19 E2
Gambarie . . . 67 E4
Gaming . . . 57 D3
Gamleby . . . 109 E1
Gammelstaden . . . 98 C3
Gammertingen . . . 55 D3
Gampenjoch . . . 58 C3
Gams . . . 58 B2
Gamvik . . . 95 E1
Gamzigrad . . . 73 E4
Ganacker . . . 56 B2
Gand . . . 50 B3
Gándara . . . 34 B1
Ganderkesee . . . 17 F1
Gandesa . . . 41 F1
Gandia . . . 41 E4
Gandino . . . 58 B4
Gandria . . . 58 A4
Gangáles . . . 91 D4
Ganges . . . 29 F3
Gangi . . . 68 C3
Gangkofen . . . 56 B2
Gannat . . . 26 A4
Gänserndorf . . . 57 F2
Gañuelas . . . 45 D2
Gap . . . 31 D2
Garabit, Viaduc de . . 29 F2
Garajonay . . . 42 A4
Garajonay (Parque Nac) . . . 42 A4
Gara, L . . . 12 C3
Garching . . . 56 B3
Garcia . . . 37 E4
Garcia de Sola, Emb de . . . 39 F4
Garciaz . . . 39 E3
Gard (Dépt) . . . 30 B3
Gard R . . . 30 B3
Garda . . . 60 C1
Garda, L di . . . 58 C4
Gardanne . . . 30 C4
Gårdby . . . 109 E2
Garde . . . 109 F4
Garde-Freinet, la . . . 31 D4
Gardelegen . . . 48 C4
Gardermoen . . . 105 D3
Gardiken . . . 97 F3
Gardíki . . . 83 D3
Garding . . . 47 F2
Gardjönäs . . . 97 F3
Gärdnäs . . . 101 E1
Gardone Riviera . . . 60 C1
Gardone Val Trompia . . . 60 B1
Gärdslösa . . . 109 E2
Gardunha, Sa da . . . 38 C2
Garður . . . 96 A2
Garešnica . . . 71 D2
Garessio . . . 31 F3
Garforth . . . 7 D2
Gargaliáni . . . 86 B3
Gargano, Promontorio del . . 64 C2
Garganta . . . 44 B2
Garganta del Chorro . . . 43 E3
Garganta del Escalar . . . 37 E2
Garganta la Olla . . . 39 E2
Gargantas . . . 40 C2
Gargantas del Sil . . . 34 B2
Gargellen . . . 58 B2
Gargilesse . . . 25 E3
Gargnano . . . 58 C4
Gargnäs . . . 98 A3
Garigliano . . . 64 A3
Gariglione, Mte . . . 67 F3
Garipa . . . 91 E4
Garlasco . . . 60 A2
Garlin . . . 28 B4
Garlstorf . . . 48 B3
Garmisch-Partenkirchen . . . 55 F4
Garona, R . . . 37 F2
Garonne . . . 28 B2
Garpenberg . . . 105 F3
Garphyttan . . . 105 F4
Garraf . . . 32 A4
Garrafe de Torio . . . 35 D2
Garray . . . 36 B3
Garrel . . . 17 E1
Garrovillas . . . 39 D3
Garrucha . . . 44 C3
Gars . . . 57 E2
Gartempe . . . 25 E4
Gartow . . . 48 C3

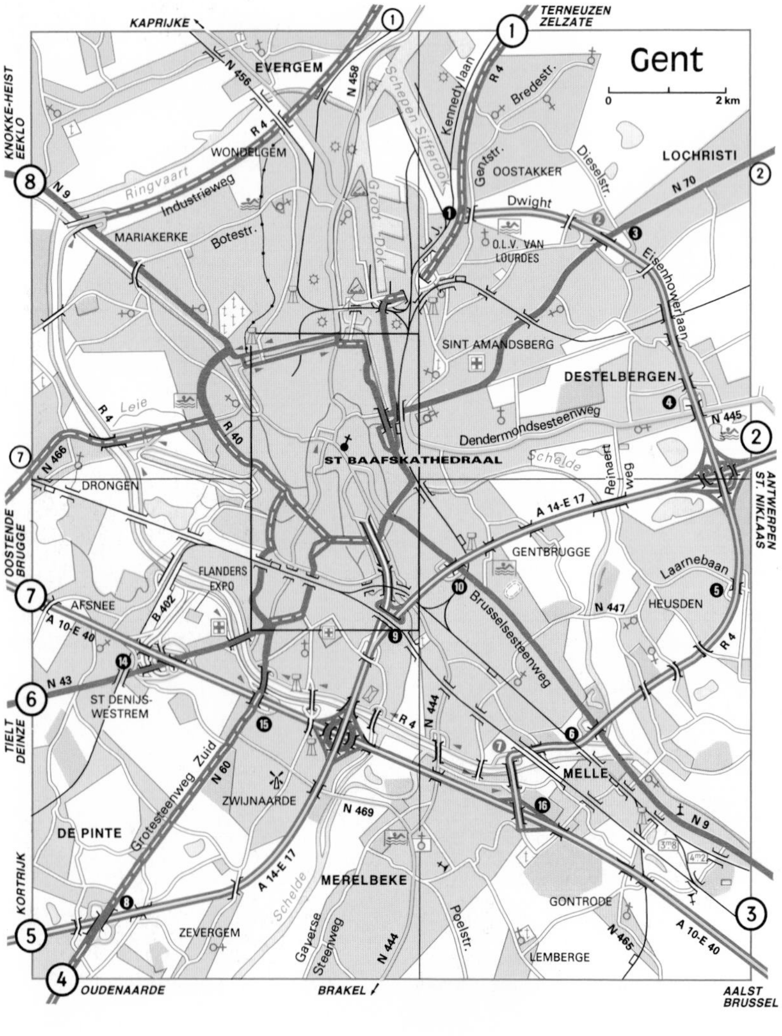

Gent
0
2 km
KAPRIJKE
TERNEUZEN ZELZATE
EVERGEM
LOCHRISTI
KNOKKE-HEIST EEKLO
WONDELGEM
MARIAKERKE
OOSTAKKER
Kennedylaan
Bredestr.
Industrieweg
Ringvaart
Botestr.
Dwight
O.L.V. VAN LOURDES
Eisenhowerlaan
SINT AMANDSBERG
DESTELBERGEN
Dendermondsesteenweg
ST BAAFSKATHEDRAAL
Leie
DRONGEN
ANTWERPEN ST NIKLAAS
OOSTENDE BRUGGE
FLANDERS EXPO
AFSNEE
GENTBRUGGE
Laarnebaan
HEUSDEN
Brusselsesteenweg
ST DENIJS-WESTREM
TIELT DEINZE
ZWIJNAARDE
MELLE
DE PINTE
Grotesteenweg Zuid
MERELBEKE
GONTRODE
LEMBERGE
ZEVERGEM
KORTRIJK
OUDENAARDE
BRAKEL
AALST BRUSSEL
Poelstr.

Gartz 49 E3
Garvagh 13 D1
Garvão 42 A2
Garve 2 C3
Garynahine 2 B2
Garz 49 D1
Gaschurn 58 B2
Gassino Torinese . . . 31 E1
Gastoúni 86 B1
Gata
  (Extremadura) 39 D2
Gata (Valencia) 45 E1
Gata, C de 44 C4
Gata, Sa de 39 D2
Gatčina 111 D1
Gatehouse of Fleet . . 4 C3
Gateshead 5 E3
Cattinara 31 F1
Cattorna 60 A3
Gatwick Airport 10 C3
Gaucín 43 E4
Gauja 110 C2
Gaula 100 C2
Gauldalen 100 C2
Gaulstad 101 D1
Gausta 104 C3
Gauting 56 A3
Gavà 32 A4
Gavardo 60 B1
Gavarnie 37 E2
Gavarnie, Cirque de . 37 E2
Gavdopoúla, N 90 B4
Gávdos, N 90 C4
Gave d'Oloron 28 A4
Gavi 60 A2
Gavião 38 B3
Gavia, Pso di 58 C3
Gavirate 58 A4
Gävle 106 B2
Gävleborgs Län 101 E3
Gävlebukten 106 B2
Gavoi 66 B2
Gavray 18 B4
Cávrio 88 B1
Gåvsta 106 B3
Gåxsjö 101 E1
Gazzuolo 60 C2
Gdańsk 110 A4
Gdov 111 D1
Gdynia 110 A4
Geaune 28 B4
Gebesee 52 C2

Gebze 115 F3
Gedern 52 A4
Gediz 115 F4
Gediz R 115 E4
Gedser 108 C4
Geel 50 C3
Geertruidenberg . . . 16 C3
Geesthacht 48 B3
Gefell 53 D3
Géfira
  (Makedonía) 79 F3
Géfira
  (Pelopónissos) . . . 87 E4
Gefíria 83 E2
Gefrees 53 D4
Gehren 52 C3
Geilenkirchen 17 D4
Geilo 104 C2
Geiranger 100 B3
Geirangerfjorden . . . 100 B3
Geisa 52 B3
Geiselhöring 56 B2
Geisenfeld 55 F2
Geisenhausen 56 B2
Geising 53 E3
Geisingen 54 C4
Geislingen 55 E2
Geismar 52 B2
Geisnes 97 D4
Geithain 53 D2
Gela 68 C4
Gelderland 17 D2
Geldern 17 D3
Geldrop 16 C3
Geleen 17 D4
Gelibolu 115 E3
Gelnhausen 52 A4
Gelsa 37 D4
Gelsdorf 51 E4
Gelsenkirchen 17 E3
Gelting 48 A1
Gembloux 50 C4
Gemeaux 26 C2
Gémenos 30 C4
Gemert 17 D3
Gemlik 115 F3
Gemona del Friuli . . . 59 F3
Gémozac 28 B1
Gemünd 51 D4
Gemünden (Bayern) . 52 B4
Gemünden
  (Hessen) 52 A3

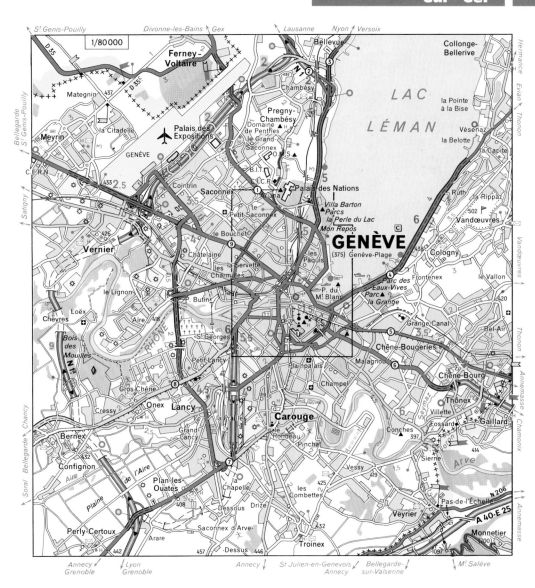

Gemünden
  (Rheinland-Pfalz) . . 54 B1
Genádio 93 E2
Gençay 25 D4
Generalísimo
  Emb del 41 D3
Generalski Stol 70 C3
General-Toševo 115 E2
Generoso, Mte 58 A4
Genève 27 D4
Genil, R 43 E2
Genissèa 81 D2

Génissiat,
  Barrage de 27 D4
Genk 50 C3
Genlis 26 C2
Genna Cruxi 66 C3
Gennargentu,
  Mti del 66 B3
Gennep 17 D3
Gennes 24 C2
Génolhac 29 F3
Genova 60 A3
Genova, Golfo di . . . 60 A4

Genova, Val di 58 C3
Gent 50 B3
Genthin 49 D4
Gentioux 29 D1
Genzano di
  Lucania 64 C3
Genzano di Roma . . 63 E3
Georgiani 79 E3
Georgioúpoli 90 C3
Georgítsi 87 D3
Gera 53 D3
Geraardsbergen 50 B3

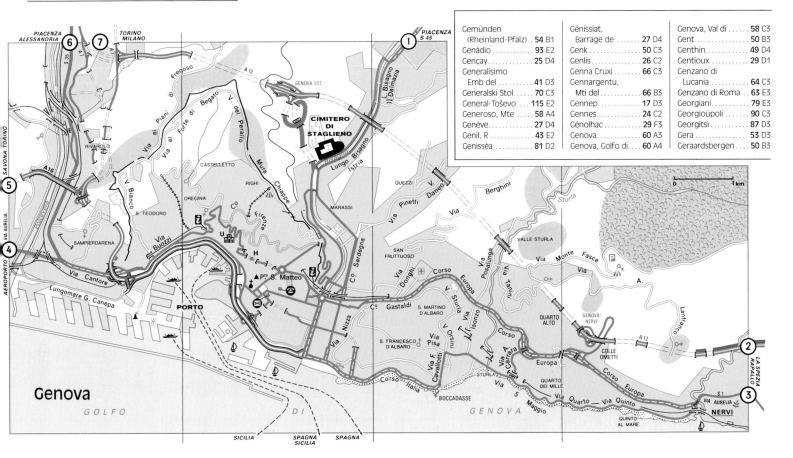

Genova

GOLFO   DI   GENOVA

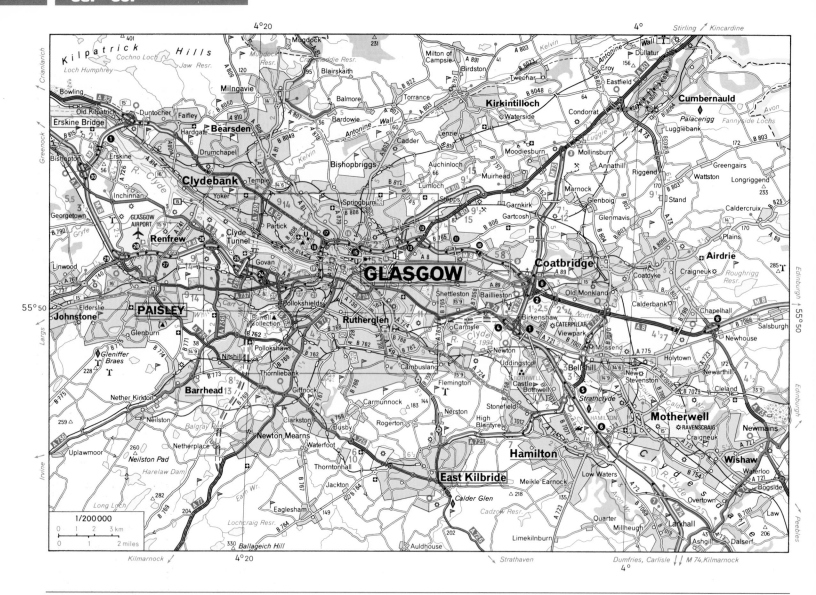

Gerabronn 55 E2	Geroplátanos 80 B3	Giardini 69 D3	Giogo di Scarperia . . 61 D3
Gerace 67 F4	Gerovo 70 B3	Giáros, N 88 B2	Gioia del Colle 65 E3
Gerakári (Kríti) 90 C4	Gerri de la Sal 37 F3	Giarratana 69 D4	Gioia Tauro 67 E4
Gerakári	Gers 28 C3	Giarre 69 D3	Gióna, Óros 83 E3
(Makedonía) 79 F2	Gers (Dépt) 28 C4	Giat 29 E1	Gioúhtas 91 D4
Gerakaroú 80 A3	Gersau 58 A2	Giaveno 31 E1	Gioúra, N 84 B2
Gerakás 87 E4	Gersfeld 52 B4	Giba 66 B4	Giovinazzo 65 D3
Gérakas, Akr 84 B2	Gerstetten 55 E2	Gibostad 94 B2	Giovi, Pso dei 60 A3
Geráki 87 D3	Gersthofen 55 E2	Gibraleón 42 C2	Girifalco 67 F3
Gerakini 80 B4	Gerswalde 49 E3	Gibraltar 43 E4	Giromagny 27 E1
Gerakovoúni 83 F3	Gesäuse 57 D3	Gideå 102 A2	Girona 32 B3
Gerània 87 E1	Gescher 17 E3	Gideälven 102 A2	Gironde 28 B1
Gérardmer 27 E1	Geseke 17 F3	Gieboldehausen 52 B2	Gironde (Dépt) 28 B2
Geras 57 E2	Gesualdo 64 B3	Gien 26 A2	Gironella 32 A3
Gerbeviller 21 D4	Geta 106 C2	Giengen 55 E2	Girvan 4 C3
Gerbier de Jonc 30 B2	Getafe 40 A2	Giens 31 D4	Gisburn 6 C2
Gerbini 69 D3	Gets, les 27 E4	Gießen 51 F3	Gislaved 109 D2
Gerbstedt 52 C2	Gettorf 48 A1	Giethoorn 17 D2	Gisors 19 E3
Gerena 43 D2	Gevelsberg 17 E4	Gifhorn 48 B4	Gissi 64 B2
Gerês 34 B3	Gevgelija 77 F4	Gigha I 4 B2	Gistel 50 A3
Gerês, Sa do 34 B3	Gévora, R 38 C4	Giglio, I del 62 C2	Githio 87 D4
Geretsried 56 A3	Gevrey-	Giglio Porto 62 C2	Gittun 98 A2
Gérgal 44 B3	Chambertin 26 C2	Gignac 30 A4	Giugliano in
Géfira 87 E4	Gex 27 D3	Gijón 35 D1	Campo 64 B4
Geringswalde 53 E2	Geysir 96 B2	Gilching 56 A3	Giuliana 68 B3
Gerlitzen 59 F2	Geyve 115 F3	Gilford 13 E2	Giulianova 64 A1
Gerlos 59 D2	Gföhl 57 E2	Giljevo 76 C1	Giurgiu 115 D2
Gerlospaß 59 D1	Ghedi 60 B1	Gilleleje 108 C3	Give 108 A3
Gérmas 79 D3	Gheorgheni 113 D4	Gillhov 101 E2	Givors 30 B1
Germering 55 F3	Ghilarza 66 B3	Gillingham (Dorset) . . 9 D3	Givry 26 C3
Germersheim 54 C2	Ghisonaccia 33 F3	Gillingham (Kent) . . . 11 D2	Givry-en-Argonne . . . 20 C3
Gernika-Lumo 36 B1	Ghisoni 33 F3	Gill, L 12 C2	Gizéla 81 D2
Gernrode 52 C2	Giali, N 89 F4	Gilze 16 C3	Giżycko 110 B4
Gernsbach 54 C2	Giáltra 83 F3	Gimenells 37 E3	Gjalicë, M 77 D3
Gernsheim 54 C1	Gianitsá 79 E3	Gimnó 84 B4	Gjendesheim 100 B3
Gerola Alta 58 B3	Gianitsi 84 C4	Gimo 106 B3	Gjendsmundshavn . . 104 A2
Geroliménas 87 D4	Giannádes 82 A1	Gimont 28 C4	Gjesvær 95 D1
Gerolstein 51 D4	Giannutri, I di 63 D2	Gingst 49 D1	Gjirokastër 114 C4
Gerolzhofen 52 B4	Gianoúli 81 F2	Ginosa 65 D4	Gjøra 100 C2
Gerona 32 B3	Giant's Causeway . . . 13 E1	Ginzling 59 D2	Gjøv 96 A3
			Gjøvik 105 D2

Gjuhezës, Kepi i . . . 114 B4	Glendalough 13 D4	Gmünd (Kärnten) . . . 59 F2
Gla 83 F4	Glenelg 2 B4	Gmünd (Nieder-
Gladbeck 17 E3	Glenfinnan 2 B4	österreich) 57 D2
Gladenbach 17 F4	Glengarriff 14 A4	Gmunden 56 C3
Gladstad 97 D3	Glenluce 4 C3	Gnarp 101 F3
Glafsfjorden 105 E3	Glen More 2 C4	Gnesta 106 B4
Gláma 96 A1	Glen More Forest	Gniezno 112 A1
Glamis 5 D1	Park 3 D4	Gnjilane 77 D2
Glamis Castle 5 D1	Glennamaddy 12 C3	Gnoien 49 D2
Glamoč 71 E4	Glenrothes 5 D2	Gnosjö 109 D2
Glamorgan 8 C2	Glenties 12 C1	Goat Fell 4 B2
Glamsbjerg 108 B3	Glifa 83 F3	Goce Delčev 115 D3
Glan 54 B1	Glifáda	Goch 17 D3
Glandon, Col du 31 D1	(Atiki-Pireás) 87 F1	Goðafoss 96 B1
Glandorf 17 F2	Glifáda (Fokida) 83 D4	Godalming 9 F3
Glan-	Gliki 82 B2	Godby 106 C3
Münchweiler 54 B1	Glikóvrissi 87 D4	Godelheim 52 A2
Glanshammar 105 F4	Glina 70 C3	Goderville 19 D3
Glarus 58 A2	Glittertind 100 B3	Godmanchester 9 F1
Glasgow 4 C2	Gliwice 112 B2	Gödöllő 112 B4
Glas Maol 3 D4	Globočica 77 D2	Godovič 70 A2
Glastonbury 9 D3	Gloggnitz 57 E3	Goduš 72 B3
Glauchau 53 D3	Głogów 112 A2	Goeree 16 B3
Glava 105 D3	Glomfjord 97 E2	Goes 16 B3
Glavatičevo 75 F1	Glomma 105 D3	Göggingen 55 F3
Glavičice 72 B3	Glommersträsk 98 B3	Göhren 49 D1
Glavnik 77 D1	Gloppet 102 B2	Goirle 16 C3
Give 108 A3	Glossop 6 C2	Góis 38 C2
Gledić 73 D4	Gloucester 9 D2	Goito 60 C1
Gledićske pl 73 D4	Gloucestershire 9 D2	Gokčanica 73 D4
Givry-en-Argonne . . . 20 C3	Gložan 72 B2	Gökçe 115 E3
Gleinalmtunnel 57 E4	Głubczyce 112 A2	Gol 104 C2
Gleisdorf 57 E4	Glubokoje 111 D3	Gola 71 D2
Glen Albyn 2 C4	Głuchołazy 112 A2	Golada 34 B2
Glenamoy 12 B2	Glücksburg 48 A1	Golczewo 49 F2
Glénan, I de 22 B4	Glückstadt 48 A2	Goldbach 52 A4
Glenariff 13 E1	Glumsø 108 C4	Goldberg 48 C2
Glenarm 13 E1	Glušci 72 C3	Goldenstedt 17 F1
Glenbeigh 14 A4	Glyn Ebwy 9 D2	Golega 38 B3
Glencolumbkille 12 C1	Gmund (D) 56 A4	Golema reka 77 D3

Golemo Selo	77 E2	Gornji Stepoš	73 E4
Goleniów	49 F2	Gornji Vakuf	75 E1
Goleš	77 E2	Gornji Zabar	71 F3
Golfe-Juan	31 E4	Gorno Orizari	77 E3
Golfo Aranci	66 C1	Goro	61 D2
Goli	70 B4	Gorodok	111 D3
Golija (Crna Gora)	76 A2	Gorredijk	17 D1
Golija (Srbija)	76 C1	Gorron	23 E3
Goljak	77 D2	Gort	12 B4
Goljaki, M.	70 A2	Gorteen	12 C3
Goljam Perelik	115 D3	Gortin	13 D2
Göllersdorf	57 E2	Górtis	91 D4
Golling	59 E1	Gortmore	12 B3
Golo	33 F3	Gorumna I.	12 B3
Golpejas	39 E1	Góry Świętokrzyskie	112 B2
Golspie	3 D3	Görzke	53 D1
Golßen	53 E1	Gorzów Wielkopolski	49 F3
Golubac	73 E3	Gosaldo	59 D3
Golubovci	76 B3	Gosau	59 F1
Golubovec	70 C2	Gosausee	59 F1
Golzow	49 D4	Göschenen	58 A3
Gómara	36 B3	Gościno	49 F1
Gomáti	80 B3	Gosforth	5 D4
Gombrèn	32 A3	Goslar	52 B1
Gomecello	39 E1	Gospić	70 C4
Gomel'	111 E4	Gospođinci	72 C2
Gomera	42 A4	Gosport	9 E3
Gómfi	83 D2	Gossau	58 B2
Gommern	52 C1	Gosselies	50 B4
Goncelin	31 D1	Gossensass	59 D2
Gondomar (E)	34 A3	Gößl	56 C3
Gondomar (P)	34 A4	Gößnitz	53 D3
Gondrecourt	20 C4	Gössweinstein	52 C4
Gönen	115 E3	Gostivar	77 D3
Góni	83 E1	Göstling	57 D3
Goniá	90 B3	Gostyń	112 A2
Goniès	91 D3	Götaälv	108 C1
Gonnesa	66 B4	Göta Kanal	105 E4
Gonnosfanadiga	66 B4	Göteborg	108 C1
Goole	7 D2	Göteborgs och Bohus Län	108 C1
Goor	17 D2	Götene	105 E4
Goppenstein	27 F3	Gotha	52 C3
Göppingen	55 D2	Gothem	109 F4
Gora	70 C3	Gotland	109 F4
Goražde	76 A1	Gotlands Län	109 F4
Gördalen	101 D3	Gotska Sandön	106 C4
Gordes	30 C3	Göttingen	52 B2
Gorenja Vas	70 A2	Götzis	58 B2
Gorey (GB)	18 B3	Gouarec	22 C3
Gorey (IRL)	15 D3	Gouda	16 C3
Gorgona, I di	60 B4	Gouménissa	79 F2
Gorgonzola	60 A1	Goumois	27 E2
Gorgopótamos	78 C4	Goúra	87 D1
Gorica (BH)	75 E2	Gourdon	29 D2
Gorica (Makedonija)	77 D4	Gourin	22 B3
Goričan	71 D1	Gournay-en-Bray	19 E3
Gorice	70 B3	Gournès	91 E3
Gorinchem	16 C3	Gourniá	91 E4
Goritsà	87 D3	Gourock	4 C2
Gorizia	59 F3	Gouveia	38 C2
Gorjanci	70 C2	Goúves	91 E3
Gorki	111 E3	Gouvià	82 A1
Gorleston-on-Sea	7 F4	Gouzon	25 F4
Gorlice	112 B3	Goveddari	75 E2
Görlitz	53 F2	Gowienica	49 F2
Gorna Orjahovica	115 D2	Göynük	115 F3
Gornja Dobrinja	72 C4	Gozd	70 A1
Gornja Grabovica	75 F1	Gozo	68 B4
Gornja Kamenica	73 F4	Gozzano	58 A4
Gornja Klina	77 D2	Graal-Müritz	48 C1
Gornja Ljubovidđa	72 C4	Graben-Neudorf	54 C2
Gornja Ljuta	75 F1	Grabenstätt	56 B3
Gornja Ploča	70 C4	Grabovac	75 E2
Gornja Radgona	70 C1	Grabovci	72 C3
Gornja Sabanta	73 D4	Grabow	48 C3
Gornja Sanica	71 D4	Gračac	70 C4
Gornja Slatina	71 F3	Gračanica (BH)	71 F3
Gornja Toplica	72 C4	Gračanica (Crna Gora)	76 B2
Gornja Toponica	73 E4	Gračanica (Kosovo)	77 D2
Gornja Tuzla	72 B3	Gračanica (Srbija)	72 C4
Gornje Dubočke	76 A2	Graçay	25 E2
Gornje Ratkovo	71 E4	Grächen	27 F4
Gornje Selo	75 D2	Gradac (Crna Gora)	76 B1
Gornji Grad	70 B2	Gradac (HR)	75 E2
Gornji Kokoti	76 B3	Gradac (Srbija)	76 C1
Gornji Kosinj	70 C4	Gradačac	71 F3
Gornji Lapac	71 D4	Gradara	61 E3
Gornji Lukavac	76 A2	Gradče, Ez	77 F2
Gornji Milanovac	73 D4	Gradec	71 D2
Gornji Petrovci	70 C1		
Gornji Podgradci	71 D3		
Gornji Rajić	71 E3		

Gradefes	35 E2	Granier, Col du	30 C1
Gradeška pl.	77 F3	Granitis	80 B1
Gradina	77 F1	Granitsa	83 D2
Gradisca d'Isonzo	59 F3	Granja (Alentejo)	42 C1
Gradište (HR)	71 E2	Granja (Douro)	34 A4
Gradište (Makedonija)	77 E2	Granja de Torrehermosa	43 E1
Grado (E)	35 D1	Granja, Pto de la	43 D1
Grado (I)	59 F4	Granollers	32 A4
Gradsko	77 E3	Granön	102 A1
Gradskovo	73 F3	Gran Paradiso	31 E1
Grafelfing	56 A3	Gran San Bernardo, Colle del	27 E4
Grafenau	56 C2	Gran San Bernardo, Traforo del	27 E4
Gräfenberg	55 F1	Gran Sasso d'Italia	63 F1
Gräfenhainichen	53 D1	Gransee	49 D3
Grafenwöhr	55 F1	Gran Tarajal	42 C4
Grafing	56 B3	Grantham	7 D3
Gragnano	64 B4	Grantown-on-Spey	3 D3
Grahovo (BH)	76 A2	Granville	18 B4
Grahovo (SLO)	70 A2	Granvin	104 B2
Graiguenamanagh	15 D3	Grappa, Mte.	59 D3
Grain	11 D2	Grasleben	52 C1
Grainau	55 F4	Grasmere	5 D4
Grajewo	110 C2	Grassano	65 D4
Gram	108 A3	Grasse	31 E3
Gramat	29 D2	Gråsten	108 A4
Gramatikó	83 E2	Grästorp	108 C1
Gramatikoú	83 D1	Gratangen	94 B3
Graméni	80 C2	Gratini	81 E2
Graméno	82 B1	Gratkorn	57 E4
Grametten	57 D1	Graubünden	58 B2
Grammichele	69 D4	Grau-du-Roi, le	30 B4
Grámos, Óros	78 C4	Graulhet	29 D4
Grampian	3 E4	Graus	37 E3
Grampian Mts	4 C1	Gravalos	36 C3
Gramsh	77 D4	Grave	17 D3
Gramzow	49 E3	Grave, la	31 D1
Gran	105 D2	Gravedona	58 B3
Granada	44 A3	Gravelines	19 F1
Granadella	37 E4	Gravellona-Toce	58 A4
Granadilla de Abona	42 B4	Grave, Pointe de	28 A1
Granard	12 C3	Gravesend	11 D2
Gran Canaria	42 B4	Gravià	83 E3
Grancey-le-Château	26 C2	Gravina in Puglia	65 D3
Grandas	34 C1	Gravona	33 F3
Grand Ballon	27 E1	Gravoúna	80 C2
Grand Bois, Col du	30 B1	Gray	26 C2
Grand-Bornand, le	27 D4	Grays Thurrock	10 C2
Grand-Bourg	25 E4	Graz	57 E4
Grandcamp-Maisy	18 C3	Grazalema	43 E3
Grand Canal d'Alsace	27 E1	Grazzanise	64 A3
Grand Canyon du Verdon	31 D3	Grdelica	77 E1
Grand-Champ	22 C4	Great Blasket I.	14 A3
Grand-Colombier	27 D4		
Grand-Combe, la	30 B3		
Grand-Combin	27 E4		
Grand-Couronne	19 D3		
Grand-Croix	30 B1		
Grande Casse	31 D1		
Grande de Europa, Punta	43 E4		
Grande Dixence, Bge de la	27 E4		
Grande-Motte, la	30 B4		
Grande Sassière	31 E1		
Grandes Rousses	31 D1		
Grand-Fougeray	23 D4		
Grand-Lemps, le	30 C1		
Grand Lieu, L de	24 B3		
Grand-Lucé, le	23 F4		
Grand Morin	20 A4		
Grândola	42 A1		
Grandpré	20 C3		
Grand-Pressigny, le	25 D3		
Grand Rhône	30 B4		
Grandrieu	29 F2		
Grand-Serre, le	30 C1		
Grands Goulets	30 C2		
Grandval, Bge de	29 F2		
Grandvilliers	19 E3		
Grañén	37 D3		
Grängärde	105 F3		
Grangemouth	5 D2		
Grange-Over-Sands	6 B1		
Grängesberg	105 F3		
Granges-sur-Vologne	27 E1		

Great Driffield	7 D1	Griá, Akr	88 B1
Great Dunmow	11 D2	Grianan of Aileach	13 D1
Great Grimsby	7 E2	Griebenow	49 D2
Great Malvern	9 D1	Gries	59 D2
Great Ormes Head	6 A2	Gries im Sellrain	58 C2
Great Ouse	7 E3	Grieskirchen	56 C3
Great Torrington	8 C3	Griffen	70 B1
Great Yarmouth	7 F4	Grignan	30 C2
Grebbestad	105 D4	Grigno	59 D3
Greccio	63 E2	Grignols	28 B3
Greding	55 F2	Grimaldi	67 E3
Gredos	39 F2	Grimaud	31 D4
Gredos, Sa de	39 F2	Grimma	53 D2
Greenhead	5 D3	Grimmen	49 D2
Greenlaw	5 D2	Grimone, Col de	30 C2
Greenock	4 C2	Grimsbu	100 C3
Greenodd	6 B1	Grimselpass	27 F3
Greggio	31 F1	Grimsey	96 B1
Gregolimano	83 F3	Grimstad	104 B4
Greifenburg	59 E2	Grindaheim	104 C2
Greiffenberg	49 E3	Grindavik	96 A2
Greifswald	49 D1	Grindelwald	27 F3
Greifswalder Bodden	49 D1	Grindsted	108 A3
Grein	57 D2	Griñón	40 A2
Greiz	53 D3	Grintavec	70 B2
Grená	108 B2	Gripsholm	106 B4
Grenade (Haute-Garonne)	29 D4	Grisignano	61 D1
Grenade (Landes)	28 B3	Gris Nez, Cap	19 E1
Grenchen	27 E2	Grisolles	29 D4
Grenoble	30 C1	Grisslehamn	106 B3
Grense Jakobselv	95 F2	Griva	79 E2
Créoux-les-Bains	31 D3	Grizáno	83 D1
Cressåmoen	101 E1	Grk	71 F3
Gresse	30 C2	Grljan	73 F3
Gressoney-la-Trinite	27 F4	Grmec	71 D4
Gressoney-St-Jean	27 F4	Grøa	100 C2
Gresten	57 D3	Gröbming	59 F1
Grêsy	31 D1	Grocka	73 D3
Greußen	52 C2	Gröditz	53 E2
Greve	61 D4	Grodno	110 C4
Greven	17 E2	Groenlo	17 D3
Grevená	79 D4	Grøtsundet	94 C2
Grevená (Nomos)	79 D4	Gröer Arber	56 B1
Grevenbroich	17 D4	Groitzsch	53 D2
Grevenbrück	17 F4	Croix	22 B4
Grevenítio	82 C1	Groix, I de	22 B4
Grevesmühlen	48 B2	Gronau	17 E2
Greve Strand	108 C3	Grönenbach	55 E4
Greyabbey	13 E2	Grong	97 D3
Greystones	13 E4	Gröningen	52 C1
Grez-en-Bouère	23 E4	Grönskåra	109 E2
Grezzana	60 C1		
Grgur	70 B4		

Grosio	58 C3
Grosne	26 C3
Gross Beerberg	52 C3
Gross Bösenstein	57 D4
Großbreitenbach	52 C3
Großburgwedel	48 A4
Großenbrode	48 B1
Großenhain	53 E2
Großenkneten	47 E4
Großenzersdorf	57 F2
Grosse Pierre	27 E1
Grosse Röder	53 E2
Grosser Plöner See	48 B2
Grosseto	62 C1
Gross Feldberg	51 F4
Gross-Gerau	54 C1
Groß Gerungs	57 D2
Großglockner	59 E2
Großglockner Hochalpenstraße	59 E2
Großhabersdorf	55 E1
Groß Otscher	57 E3
Großpetersdorf	57 F4
Gross Priel	57 D3
Gross Rachel	56 C2
Großraming	57 D3
Großraschen	53 E1
Groß Reken	17 E3
Großröhrsdorf	53 F2
Groß Rosennock	59 F2
Grossschönau	53 F2
Groß-Schönebeck	49 E3
Groß Siegharts	57 E2
Gross-Umstadt	55 D1
Großvenediger	59 E2
Großweil	56 A4
Grostenquin	21 D3
Grosuplje	70 B2
Grötlingbo	109 F4
Grotta di Nettuno	66 A2
Grottaglie	65 E4
Grottaminarda	64 B3
Grottammare	61 F4
Grotte di Pertosa	64 C4
Grotteria	67 F4
Grouin, Pte du	18 B4
Grove	34 A2
Grövelsjön	101 D3
Grovfjord	94 B3
Grubišno Polje	71 D2
Gruda	76 A3
Grude	75 E2
Grudziądz	112 B1
Gruinard B.	2 C3

Gruissan ... 32 B2
Grums ... 105 E3
Grünau ... 56 C3
Grünberg ... 52 A3
Grünburg ... 57 D3
Grundarfjörður ... 96 A2
Grundforsen ... 101 D4
Grundlsee ... 56 C3
Grundlsee L ... 56 C3
Grundsund ... 108 C1
Grundtjärn ... 101 F2
Grünstadt ... 54 C1
Grünwald ... 56 A3
Grupčin ... 77 D3
Gruyères ... 27 E3
Gruža ... 73 D4
Gruža R ... 73 D4
Grycksbo ... 105 F2
Gryfice ... 49 F2
Gryfino ... 49 E3
Gryllefjord ... 94 B2
Grythyttan ... 105 E3
Grytøya ... 94 B3
Grza ... 73 E4
Gschütt, Paß ... 59 F1
Gstaad ... 27 E3
Gstadt ... 56 B3
Guadahortuna ... 44 A2

Guadaira, R ... 43 E3
Guadajira, R ... 39 D4
Guadajoz, R ... 43 F2
Guadalajara ... 40 B2
Guadalaviar ... 41 D2
Guadalaviar, R ... 41 D2
Guadalcacín, Emb de ... 43 D3
Guadalcanal ... 43 D1
Guadalén, Emb de ... 44 A1
Guadalén, R ... 44 B1
Guadalest ... 45 E1
Guadalete, R ... 43 D4
Guadalfeo, R ... 44 A4
Guadalhorce, R ... 43 E4
Guadalimar, R (Andalucia) ... 43 D3
Guadalimar, R (Andalucia) ... 44 B2
Guadalmellato, Emb de ... 43 F2
Guadalmena, Emb de ... 44 B1
Guadalmena, R ... 44 B1
Guadalmez, R ... 43 F1
Guadalope, R ... 41 E2
Guadalquivir, R ... 43 D3
Guadal, R ... 44 B2

Guadalteba-Guadalhorce, Emb del ... 43 E3
Guadalupe ... 39 E3
Guadalupe, Sa de ... 39 E3
Guadarrama ... 40 A2
Guadarrama, Pto de ... 40 A2
Guadarrama, R ... 40 A2
Guadarrama, Sa de ... 40 A1
Guadarranque, Emb del ... 43 E4
Guadassuar ... 41 E4
Guadazaón, R ... 40 C3
Guadiamar, R ... 43 D3
Guadiana Menor, R ... 44 B2
Guadiana, R ... 39 F4
Guadiaro ... 43 E4
Guadiaro, R ... 43 E4
Guadiato, R ... 43 E2
Guadiela, R ... 40 C2
Guadix ... 44 B3
Guajaraz, Emb de ... 40 A3
Gualdo Tadino ... 61 E4
Guara, Sa de ... 37 E3
Guarda ... 38 C1
Guardamar del Segura ... 45 D2

Guardiagrele ... 64 A2
Guardia Sanframondi ... 64 B3
Guardias Viejas ... 44 B4
Guardo ... 35 E2
Guareña ... 39 D4
Guarrizas, R ... 44 A1
Guarromán ... 44 A2
Guastalla ... 60 C2
Gubbio ... 61 E4
Guben ... 53 F1
Guberevac ... 73 D4
Gubin ... 53 F1
Guča ... 73 D4
Guca Gora ... 71 E4
Gúdar, Sa de ... 41 E2
Gudavac ... 71 D3
Gudbrandsdalen ... 100 C3
Guderup ... 108 A4
Gudhjem ... 109 D4
Gudingen ... 109 E1
Gudow ... 48 B3
Gudvangen ... 104 B2
Guebwiller ... 27 E1
Guémené ... 22 B3
Guémené-Penfao ... 23 D4
Güeñes ... 36 B1
Guer ... 23 D3

Guérande ... 22 C4
Guerche-de-Bretagne, la ... 23 D3
Guerche, la ... 26 A3
Guéret ... 25 E4
Guérigny ... 26 A2
Guerlédan, L de ... 22 C3
Guernsey ... 18 A3
Guéthary ... 28 A4
Gueugnon ... 26 B3
Güglingen ... 55 D2
Guglionesi ... 64 B2
Guía ... 42 B4
Guía de Isora ... 42 A4
Guichen ... 23 D3
Guidonia ... 63 E2
Guignes ... 19 F4
Guijo de Granadilla ... 39 D2
Guijuelo ... 39 E2
Guildford ... 9 F3
Guillaumes ... 31 E3
Guillena ... 43 D2
Guillestre ... 31 D2
Guillon ... 26 B2
Guilvinec ... 22 A3
Guimarães ... 34 A4
Guimiliau ... 22 B2

Guînes ... 19 E1
Guingamp ... 22 C2
Guipavas ... 22 A2
Guisborough ... 5 F4
Guiscard ... 19 F3
Guise ... 20 A2
Guíssona ... 37 F3
Guist ... 7 F3
Guitiriz ... 34 B1
Guîtres ... 28 B2
Gujan-Mestras ... 28 A2
Gulbene ... 110 C2
Guldborg Sund ... 108 C4
Gullesfjorden ... 94 A3
Gullfoss ... 96 B2
Gullkrona fjärd ... 107 D3
Gullspång ... 105 E4
Gumiel de Hizán ... 36 A3
Gummersbach ... 17 E4
Gundelfingen ... 55 E3
Gundelsheim ... 55 D2
Gunnarn ... 97 F4
Gunnarsbyn ... 98 B3
Gunnärsfjärden ... 98 C3
Gunnarskog ... 105 E3
Gunten ... 27 F3
Günterode ... 52 B2
Guntín de Pallares ... 34 B2

Günzburg ... 55 E3
Gunzenhausen ... 55 E2
Gurk ... 70 A1
Gurk R ... 59 F2
Gurrea de Gállego ... 37 D3
Gusev ... 110 B4
Gusinje ... 76 C2
Guspini ... 66 B3
Güssing ... 57 F4
Güsten ... 52 C1
Güstrow ... 48 C2
Gutcher ... 3 F1
Gutenstein ... 57 E3
Gütersloh ... 17 F3
Gutulia ... 100 D3
Gützkow ... 49 D2
Guyhirn ... 10 C1
Gvardejsk ... 110 B4
Gvarv ... 104 C3
Gvozd ... 76 B2
Gweebarra B ... 12 C1
Gwent ... 9 D2
Gwynedd ... 8 A3
Gy ... 27 D2
Gyöngyös ... 112 B4
Győr ... 112 A4
Gysinge ... 106 A3
Gyula ... 112 C4

H

Haag (A) ... 57 D3
Haag (D) ... 56 B3
Haag am Hausruck ... 56 C3
Haaksbergen ... 17 D2
Haamstede ... 16 B3
Haapajärvi ... 103 D1
Haapajärvi L ... 103 D1
Haapakoski ... 103 E2
Haapamäki (Keski-Suomen Lääni) ... 102 C3
Haapamäki (Oulun Lääni) ... 103 D1
Haapavesi ... 103 D1
Haapsalu ... 110 B2
Haar ... 56 A3
Haaren ... 17 F3
Haarlem ... 16 B2
Habay ... 20 C2
Habo ... 109 D1
Habsheim ... 27 E1
Hachenburg ... 51 F3
Hachmühlen ... 52 A1
Hackås ... 101 E2
Hadamar ... 51 F4
Haddington ... 5 D2
Hadersdorf ... 57 E2
Haderslev ... 108 A4
Hadjač ... 113 F1
Hadleigh ... 11 D2
Hadmersleben ... 52 C1
Hadrian's Wall ... 5 E3
Hadselfjorden ... 94 A3
Hadsten ... 108 B2
Hadsund ... 108 B2
Hadžići ... 75 F1
Haganj ... 71 D2
Hægebostad ... 104 B4
Hagen (Niedersachsen) ... 47 F3
Hagen (Nordrhein-Westfalen) ... 17 E4
Hagenow ... 48 B3
Hagetmau ... 28 B4
Hagfors ... 105 E3
Häggdånger ... 101 F3
Haggenås ... 101 E2
Hagondange ... 21 D3
Hague, Cap de la ... 18 B2
Haguenau ... 21 E3
Hahn ... 47 F3
Hahnbach ... 55 F1
Haigerloch ... 55 D3
Hailsham ... 10 C3
Hailuoto ... 99 D4

Hainaut ... 50 B4
Hainburg ... 57 F2
Hainfeld ... 57 E3
Hainichen ... 53 E2
Hajdúböszörmény ... 112 C4
Hajdučica ... 73 D2
Hajdúszoboszló ... 112 C4
Hajla ... 76 C2
Hajnówka ... 112 C1
Hajsyn ... 113 E3
Hajvoron ... 113 E3
Hakarp ... 109 D1
Hakkas ... 98 B2
Häkkilä ... 103 D2
Halámky ... 57 D2
Halandritsa ... 86 C1
Halbe ... 53 E1
Halberstadt ... 52 C1
Halden ... 105 D4
Haldensleben ... 48 C4
Halesowen ... 9 E1
Halesworth ... 11 E1
Halhjem ... 104 A2
Halifax ... 6 C2
Halikko ... 107 E2
Halju ... 95 D4
Halkeró ... 80 C2
Hálki (Dodekánissa) ... 93 E1
Halki (Kikládes) ... 88 C3
Hálki (Thessalia) ... 83 E1
Halkiádes ... 83 E2
Halkida ... 84 B4
Halkidikí ... 80 B3
Hálki, N ... 93 E1
Halkidóna ... 79 F3
Halkió ... 85 F4
Halkío ... 87 D1
Hallands Län ... 108 C2
Halle (B) ... 50 B3
Halle (Nordrhein-Westfalen) ... 17 F2
Halle (Sachsen-Anhalt) ... 53 D2
Hällefors ... 105 E3
Hälleforsnäs ... 105 F4
Hallein ... 56 C3
Hällekis ... 105 E4
Hallenberg ... 17 F4
Hallencourt ... 19 E2
Halle-Neustadt ... 53 D2
Hällesjö ... 101 F2
Hällevadsholm ... 105 D4
Halligen ... 47 F1
Hallingdal ... 104 C2
Hallingskarvet ... 104 B2

Hall in Tirol ... 59 D1
Hällnäs ... 102 A1
Hallsberg ... 105 F4
Hallstadt ... 52 C4
Hallstahammar ... 105 F3
Hallstatt ... 59 F1
Hallstavik ... 106 B3
Halluin ... 19 F1
Halmstad ... 108 C2
Hals ... 108 B2
Halsa ... 100 B2
Halsafjorden ... 100 B2
Hälsingtuna ... 101 F3
Halsskov ... 108 B3
Halstead ... 11 D2
Halsteren ... 16 B3
Halsua ... 102 C2
Haltdålen ... 101 D2
Haltern ... 17 E3
Halti-Haldi ... 94 C3
Halver ... 17 E4
Ham ... 19 F2
Hamar ... 105 D2
Hamarøy ... 94 A4
Hamburg ... 48 A3
Hambye ... 18 B4
Hamdorf ... 48 A2
Hämeenkyrö ... 102 C3
Hämeen Lääni ... 102 C3
Hämeenlinna ... 107 E2
Hämelerwald ... 52 B1
Hameln ... 52 A1
Hamersleben ... 52 C1
Hamilí, N ... 92 C2
Hamilton ... 4 C2
Hamina ... 103 F4
Hamm ... 17 F4
Hammarland ... 106 C3
Hammarstrand ... 101 F2
Hammaslahti ... 103 F2
Hammel ... 108 B2
Hammelburg ... 52 B4
Hammerdal ... 101 E2
Hammerfest ... 95 D1
Hammershus ... 109 D4
Hamneidet ... 94 C2
Hamningberg ... 95 F1
Hamoir ... 50 C4
Hampshire ... 9 E3
Hamra ... 101 E3
Hamra (Reg) ... 101 E3
Hamre ... 104 B4
Hamzali ... 77 E3
Hamzići ... 75 F2
Hanákia ... 86 B2
Hanau ... 52 A4
Hânceşti ... 113 E4

Handrás ... 91 F4
Hanerau-Hademarschen ... 48 A2
Hangö ... 107 E3
Hangon läntinenselkä ... 107 D3
Hangö västra fjärd ... 107 D3
Haniá (Haniá) ... 90 B3
Haniá (Lakonía) ... 87 D3
Haniá (Nomos) ... 90 B3
Hánia (Thessalía) ... 83 F2
Hani i Hotit ... 76 B3
Haníon, Kólpos ... 90 B3
Haniótis ... 80 B4
Hankamäki ... 103 E1
Hankasalmen as ... 103 D3
Hankasalmi ... 103 D3
Hankensbüttel ... 48 B4
Hanko ... 107 E3
Hannover ... 48 A4
Hannut ... 50 C4
Hanöbukten ... 109 D3
Han Pijesak ... 72 B4
Hansnes ... 94 C2
Han-sur-Lesse ... 50 C4
Hanstedt ... 48 A3
Hanstholm ... 108 A2
Haparanda ... 98 C3
Harads ... 98 B3
Harafjärden ... 98 C3
Haraldshaugen ... 104 A3
Haranes ... 97 D4
Haravgí ... 79 E3
Harburg (Bayern) ... 55 E2
Harburg (Hamburg) ... 48 A3
Hårby ... 108 B4
Hardangerfjorden ... 104 A2
Hardangerjøkulen ... 104 B2
Hardangervidda ... 104 B2
Hardbakke ... 104 A1
Hardegg ... 57 E1
Hardelot ... 19 E1
Hardenberg ... 17 D2
Hardheim ... 55 D1
Hardwick Hall ... 7 D3
Hareid ... 100 A2
Harelbeke ... 50 A3
Haren (D) ... 17 E1
Haren (NL) ... 47 D3
Harewood ... 6 C2
Haria ... 42 C3
Haringvlietdam ... 16 B3
Haritoméni ... 80 B2

Härjångsfjällen ... 101 D2
Harjavalta ... 107 D2
Harjunpää ... 107 D1
Hårkan ... 101 E2
Härkmeri ... 102 B3
Harlech ... 6 A3
Harlesiel ... 47 E3
Harleston ... 11 D1
Harlingen ... 16 C1
Harlow ... 10 C2
Harmånger ... 101 F3
Harmanli ... 115 E3
Härnösand ... 101 F3
Haro ... 36 B2
Harokopió ... 86 C4
Haroldswick ... 3 F1
Haroué ... 21 D4
Harøyfjorden ... 100 A2
Harpenden ... 9 F2
Harplinge ... 108 C2
Harpstedt ... 17 F1
Harris ... 2 A2
Harrislee ... 47 F1
Harris, Sd of ... 2 A3
Harrogate ... 6 C1
Härryda ... 108 C1
Harsefeld ... 48 A3
Harsprånget ... 98 B2
Harstad ... 94 B3
Harsvik ... 96 C4
Hartberg ... 57 F4
Hårteigen ... 104 B2
Hartha ... 53 E2
Hartkjølen ... 101 E1
Hartland Pt ... 8 B3
Hartlepool ... 5 F4
Hartmannsdorf ... 53 E2
Hartola ... 103 D3
Harwich ... 11 D2
Harz ... 52 B2
Harzgerode ... 52 C2
Hase ... 17 E2
Haselünne ... 17 E2
Haskovo ... 115 D3
Haslach (A) ... 56 C2
Haslach (D) ... 54 C3
Hasle ... 109 D4
Haslemere ... 9 F3
Haslev ... 108 C4
Hasparren ... 28 A4
Hassela ... 101 F3
Hasselfelde ... 52 C2
Hasselt ... 50 C3
Haßfurt ... 52 B4
Hássia, Óri ... 83 D1
Hässleholm ... 109 D3
Hastière ... 50 C4

Hastings ... 11 D3
Hasvik ... 95 D1
Hatě ... 57 E1
Hateg ... 114 C1
Hatfield ... 9 F2
Hatherleigh ... 8 C3
Hattem ... 17 D2
Hattfjelldal ... 97 E3
Hattingen ... 17 E3
Hattula ... 107 E2
Hattuvaara (Lieksa) ... 103 F1
Hattuvaara (Ilomantsi) ... 103 F2
Hatvan ... 112 B4
Hatvik ... 104 A2
Hatzí ... 82 C2
Haubourdin ... 19 F1
Hauge ... 104 A4
Haugesund ... 104 A3
Hauho ... 107 E2
Haukelifjell ... 104 B2
Haukeligrend ... 104 B3
Haukipudas ... 99 D3
Haukivesi ... 103 E3
Haukivuori ... 103 E3
Haunstetten ... 55 F3
Haus ... 59 F1
Hausach ... 54 C3
Hausham ... 56 A4
Hausjärvi ... 107 E2
Hautajärvi ... 99 E2
Hautecombe ... 27 D4
Haute-Corse ... 33 F3
Hautefort ... 29 D1
Haute-Garonne ... 29 D4
Haute-Loire ... 29 D2
Haute-Marne ... 26 C1
Hautes-Alpes ... 31 D2
Haute-Saône ... 27 D1
Haute-Savoie ... 27 D4
Haute-Vienne (Dépt) ... 29 D1
Hauteville-Lompnes ... 27 D4
Hautmont ... 20 B2
Haut-Rhin (Dept) ... 27 E1
Havant ... 9 F3
Havári ... 86 B1
Havdalsfjellet ... 97 E4
Havdáta ... 82 B4
Havel ... 49 D4
Havelange ... 50 C4
Havelberg ... 48 C3
Haverfordwest ... 8 B2
Haverhill ... 11 D1
Haverö ... 101 E3

Havneby ... 108 A4
Havøysund ... 95 D1
Havraň ... 53 E3
Havre, Le ... 19 D3
Hawes ... 6 C1
Hawick ... 5 D3
Hawkhurst ... 11 D3
Hayange ... 21 D3
Haye-du-Puits, la ... 18 B3
Haye-Pesnel, la ... 18 B4
Hayle ... 8 A4
Hay-on-Wye ... 9 D1
Haywards Heath ... 10 C3
Hazebrouck ... 19 F1
Headford ... 12 B3
Heanor ... 7 D3
Héas ... 37 E2
Heathfield ... 10 C3
Heathrow Airport ... 9 F2
Hebrides, Outer ... 2 A2
Hebrides, Sea of the ... 2 A3
Heby ... 106 B3
Hechingen ... 55 D3
Hecho ... 37 D2
Hechtel ... 50 C3
Hecklingen ... 52 C1
Hedal ... 104 C2
Heddal ... 104 C3
Hédé ... 23 D3
Hede ... 101 E3
Hedemora ... 105 F3
Hedenäset ... 98 C2
Hedensted ... 108 B3
Hedesundafjärdarna ... 106 B3
Hedeviken ... 101 E3
Hedmark ... 104 C1
Hedon ... 7 E2
Heemstede ... 16 C2
Heerde ... 17 D2
Heerenveen ... 17 D1
Heerlen ... 51 D3
Heeze ... 16 C4
Hegge ... 104 C1
Hegra ... 101 D2
Heia ... 94 C3
Heide ... 47 F2
Heidelberg ... 54 C1
Heidenau ... 53 E2
Heidenheim ... 55 E2
Heidenreichstein ... 57 E1
Heikendorf ... 48 A1
Heikkila ... 99 F2
Heilbronn ... 55 D2
Heiligenberg ... 55 D4
Heiligenblut ... 59 E2

Heiligenhafen 48 B1
Heiligenkirchen 17 F3
Heiligenkreuz 57 F4
Heiligenstadt 52 B2
Heilsbronn 55 E1
Heimari 103 E3
Heimdal 100 C2
Heimertingen 55 E3
Heinävaara 103 F2
Heinävesi 103 E2
Heinola 107 F1
Heinolan mlk 107 F1
Heinsberg 17 D4
Heist 50 A3
Heist-op-den-
  Berg 50 C3
Hejde 109 F4
Hekla 96 B2
Hekuravë, Maj'e . . . 76 C2
Helagsfjället 101 D2
Hélatros, Akr 93 D3
Heldeburg 52 C4
Heldrungen 52 C2
Helechal 43 E1
Helensburgh 4 C2
Helgåa (N) 101 D1
Helgaå (S) 109 D3
Helgasjön 109 D2
Helgoland 47 E2
Hella Is 96 B2
Hella N 104 B1
Hellemofjorden 97 F1
Hellendoorn 17 D2
Hellesylt 100 A3
Hellevoetsluis 16 B3
Hellin 44 C1
Hellvik 104 A4
Helmbrechts 53 D4
Helme 52 C2
Helmond 17 D3
Helmsdale 3 D2
Helmsley 7 D1
Helmstadt 55 D1
Helmstedt 52 C1
Helpter Berge 49 E2
Helsa 52 B2
Helsingborg 108 C3
Helsinge 108 C3
Helsingfors 107 F3
Helsingør 108 C3
Helsinki 107 F3
Helston 8 B4
Helvetinjärvi 102 C3
Helvick Head 14 C4
Hemau 55 F2
Hemavan 97 E3
Hemel Hempstead . . . 9 F2
Hemer 17 E3
Hemme 100 C2
Hemmoor 48 A2
Hemnefjorden 100 C1
Hemnes 105 D3
Hemnesberget 97 E2
Hemsedal 104 C2
Hemsedal V 104 C2
Henares, R 40 B2
Hendaye 28 A4
Hengelo 17 D2
Hengersberg 56 B2
Hengstpaß 57 D3
Hénin-Beaumont . . . 19 F1
Henley 9 E1
Henley-on-Thames . . 9 F2
Henneberg 52 B3
Hennebont 22 B3
Hennef 51 E3
Hennigsdorf 49 D4
Henrichemont 25 F2
Henstedt-Ulzburg . . . 48 A2
Henstridge 9 D3
Hepoköngäs 99 E4
Heppenheim 54 C1
Heraclea 77 E4
Hérault 29 F4
Hérault (Dépt) . . . 30 A4
Herbault 25 E2
Herbertingen 55 D3
Herbiers, les 24 B3
Herbignac 22 C4
Herbolzheim 54 C3
Herborn 51 F3
Herbrechtingen 55 E2
Herbstein 52 A3
Herceg Novi 76 A3

Hercegovac 71 D2
Hercegov Goleša . . . 76 B1
Hereford 9 D1
Hereford and
  Worcester 9 D1
Herencia 40 B4
Herentals 50 C3
Herford 17 F2
Héricourt 27 E2
Heringsdorf 49 E2
Herisau 58 B2
Hérisson 26 A3
Hérisson,
  Cascades du 27 D3
Herk 50 C3
Herleshausen 52 B3
Hermagor 59 F2
Herma Ness 3 F1
Hermannsburg 48 B4
Hermansverk 104 B1
Hermenault, l' 24 C3
Herment 29 E1
Hermeskeil 54 B1
Hermigua 42 A4
Hermsdorf 53 D3
Hernani 36 C1
Hernansancho 39 F1
Herne 17 E3
Herne Bay 11 D3
Herning 108 A3
Heroldsberg 55 F1
Herónia 83 F4
Herøy 100 A2
Herrala 107 F2
Herre 104 C3
Herrenberg 55 D3
Herrenchiemsee 56 B3
Herrera
  (Andalucia) 43 E3
Herrera (Aragón) . . . 37 D4
Herrera Mt 37 D4
Herrera de
  Alcántara 38 C3
Herrera del Duque . . 39 F4
Herrera de
  Pisuerga 35 F3
Herrera, Pto de . . . 36 B2
Herreruela 39 D3
Herrestad 108 C1
Herrieden 55 E2
Herrljunga 109 D1
Herrnburg 48 B2
Herrnhut 53 F2
Herrsching 56 A3
Herrskog 102 A2
Hersbruck 55 F1
Herselt 50 C3
Hérso 79 F2
Hersónissos
  Akrotíri 90 C3
Hersónissos
  Methánon 87 E2
Hersónissos
  Spinalónga 91 E3
Herstal 51 D3
Herten 17 E3
Hertford 9 F2
Hertfordshire 9 F2
Hervás 39 E2
Herzberg
  (Brandenburg) . . . 53 E1
Herzberg
  (Niedersachsen) . . 52 B2
Herzogenaurach . . . 55 E1
Herzogenburg 57 E2
Herzsprung 49 D3
Hesdin 19 E2
Hesel 47 E3
Hessen 52 A3
Hesseng 95 F2
Hessisch-
  Lichtenau 52 B2
Hessisch
  Oldendorf 52 A1
Hestfjørður 96 A4
Hetekylä 99 E3
Hetin 72 C1
Hettange 21 D3
Hettstedt 52 C2
Heubach 55 E2
Heuchin 19 F1
Heukuppe 57 E3
Hevlin 57 F1
Hexham 5 E3

Heyrieux 30 C1
Heysham 6 B1
Hiddensee 49 D1
Hieflau 57 D3
Hiekkasarkät 102 C1
Hierbas 41 E3
Hierro 42 A4
Hiersac 28 C1
Hietaniemi 95 F4
Higham Ferrers 9 F1
Highland 2 C3
High Peak 6 C2
High Willhays 8 C3
High Wycombe 9 F2
Higuera de Arjona . . 44 A2
Higuera de la
  Serena 43 E1
Higuera de la
  Sierra 43 D2
Higuera de Vargas . . 42 C1
Higuera la Real . . . 42 C1
Higueruela 41 D4
Hiidenportti 103 E1
Hiiumaa 110 B1
Hijar 37 D4
Hilchenbach 17 F4
Hildburghausen 52 C3
Hilden 17 E4
Hilders 52 B3
Hildesheim 52 B1
Hiliomódi 87 E1
Hillegom 16 B2
Hillerød 108 C3
Hillesøy 94 B2
Hillswick 3 F1
Hiloús, Akr 92 C1
Hilpoltstein 55 F2
Hiltula 103 E3
Hilvarenbeek 16 C4
Hilversum 16 C2
Himanka 102 C1
Himaros 80 A2
Himmerland 108 B2
Hinckley 9 E1
Hindelang 55 E4
Hindhead 9 F3

Hindsholm 108 B3
Hinnøya 94 A3
Hinodejo 36 B3
Hinojares 44 B2
Hinojosa de Duero . . 39 D1
Hinojosa del
  Duque 43 E1
Hinterrhein 58 B3
Hintersee (Bayern) . . 56 B4
Hintersee (Mecklenburg-
  Vorpommern) 49 E2
Hinterstoder 57 D3
Hintertux 59 D2
Hinterweidenthal . . . 54 B2
Hios 85 F4
Hios, N 85 E4
Hirschau 55 F1
Hirschberg 53 D3
Hirschegg 58 B2
Hirsingue 27 E2
Hirson 20 B2
Hirşova 115 E1
Hirtshals 108 B1
Hirvasvaara 99 E2
Hirvensalmi 103 E3
Hirvilahti 103 E2
Hirwaun 8 C2
Hisarja 115 D2
Histria 115 E1
Hitchin 9 F2
Hitra 100 C1
Hitzacker 48 B3
Hjälmaren 105 E3
Hjartdal 104 C3
Hjellestad 104 A2
Hjelmeland 104 B3
Hjelmsøya 95 D1
Hjo 109 D1
Hjørring 108 B1
Hjørundfjorden 100 A3
Hlebine 71 D1
Hlemoútsi 86 B1
Hlobyne 113 F2
Hlomó, Óros 83 F3
Hluboká 57 D1
Hluchiv 113 F1

Hobro 108 B2
Höchberg 55 D1
Hochdorf 27 F2
Hochfeiler 59 D2
Hochfelden 21 E4
Hochgolling 59 F1
Hochgrabe 59 E2
Hochosterwitz 70 B1
Hochreichart 57 D4
Hochschober 59 E2
Hochschwab 57 D3
Hochspeyer 54 C1
Höchst 55 D1
Höchstadt 55 E1
Hochtannbergpaß . . . 58 B2
Hochtor (Osttirol) . . . 59 E2
Hochtor
  (Steiermark) . . . 57 D3
Hockenheim 54 C2
Hoddesdon 9 F2
Hodenhagen 48 A4
Hœdic 22 C4
Hódmezővásárhely 114 B1
Hodnet 6 B3
Hodonín 57 F1
Hodoš 70 C1
Hodovo 75 F2
Hoedekenskerke . . . 16 B4
Hoek van Holland . . 16 B3
Hoemsbu 100 B2
Hof 53 D4
Hofgeismar 52 A2
Hofheim 52 B4
Hofles 97 D4
Höfn 96 C2
Hofors 105 F2
Hofsjökull 96 B2
Höganäs 108 C3
Høgebru 100 A3
Höglekardalen 101 E2
Högsäter 105 D4
Högsby 109 E2
Høgset 100 B2
Hohe Acht 51 E4

Hohenau 57 F2
Hohenberg 57 E3
Hohenems 58 B2
Hohengandern 52 B2
Hohenlimburg 17 E4
Hohenlinden 56 B3
Hohenlockstedt 48 A2
Hohenmölsen 53 D2
Hohenpeißenberg . . . 56 A4
Hohenseeden 48 C4
Hohenstein 53 D3
Hohentauern 57 D4
Hohenwestedt 48 A2
Hohenzollern 55 D3
Hoher Zinken 56 C3
Hohe Tauern 59 E2
Hohe Tauern,
  Nat Pk 59 E2
Hóhlakas 93 E2
Hohneck 27 E1
Hohwachter
  Bucht 48 B1
Hohwald, le 21 E4
Højer 108 A4
Hokksund 104 C3
Hol 104 C2
Hola Pristan' 113 F3
Holbæk 108 C3
Holbeach 7 E3
Holdorf 17 F2
Holič 57 F1
Höljäkkä 103 E1
Höljes 101 D4
Hollabrunn 57 E2
Hollen 104 B4
Hollenstedt 48 A3
Höllental 57 E3
Holles 97 D4
Hollfeld 52 C4
Hollingsholm 100 B2
Hollola 107 F2
Hollum 16 C1
Hollywood 13 D4
Holm (N) 97 D3
Holm (S) 101 F2
Hólmavik 96 A1

Holmec 70 B1
Holmen 105 D2
Holmestrand 104 C3
Holmfirth 6 C2
Holmön 102 B1
Holmsjön 101 E3
Holmslands Klit. . . . 108 A3
Holmsund 102 B1
Holomóndas,
  Óros 80 B3
Holstebro 108 A2
Holsted 108 A3
Holsworthy 8 C3
Holt 7 F3
Holwerd 47 D3
Holy Cross Abbey . . . 14 C3
Holyhead 6 A2
Holy I (Anglesey) . . . 6 A2
Holy I
  (Northumberland) . . 5 E2
Holywell 6 B2
Holywood 13 E2
Holzappel 51 F4
Holzgau 58 C2
Holzkirchen 56 A3
Holzleitner Sattel . . . 58 C2
Holzminden 52 A2
Homberg
  (Hessen) 52 A3
Homberg (Nordrhein-
  Westfalen) 17 D3
Homburg 54 B2
Hommelstø 97 D3
Hommelvik 100 C2
Hommersåk 104 A3
Homoljske
  planine 73 E3
Hondarribia
  Fuenterrabia 36 C1
Hondón de las
  Nieves 45 D2
Hönebach 52 B3
Hønefoss 104 C3
Honfleur 19 D3
Høng 108 B3
Hónikas 87 D2

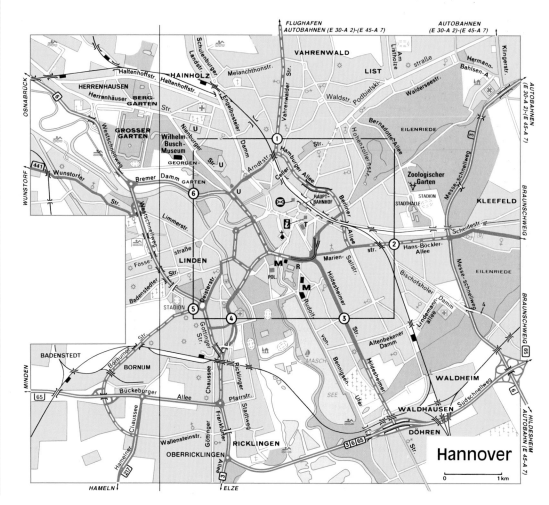

Hannover

0   1 km

Honiton ... 9 D3
Honkajoki ... 102 B3
Honningsvåg ... 95 E1
Honrubia ... 40 C3
Honrubia de la Cuesta ... 36 A3
Hontalbilla ... 40 A1
Hontoria del Pinar ... 36 A3
Hooge ... 47 F1
Hoogeveen ... 17 D2
Hoogezand ... 47 D3
Hoogstraten ... 50 C2
Hook Head ... 15 D4
Höör ... 109 D3
Hoorn ... 16 C2
Hopetoun House ... 5 D2
Hopfgarten ... 59 D1
Hopperstad ... 104 B1
Hóra (Dodekánissa) ... 89 E2
Hóra (Pelopónissos) ... 86 C3
Hora Svatého Šebestiána ... 53 E3
Horažd'ovice ... 56 C1
Horb ... 54 C3
Hörby ... 109 D3
Horcajo de los Montes ... 39 F4
Horcajo de Santiago ... 40 B3
Horcajo de Trevélez ... 44 A3
Horcajo-Medianero ... 39 E2
Horche ... 40 B2
Hordaland ... 104 B2
Horden ... 5 E4
Horeftó ... 83 F2

Horezu ... 115 D1
Horgen ... 58 A2
Horgoš ... 72 C1
Horley ... 10 C3
Horn (A) ... 57 E2
Horn (Baden-Württemberg) ... 55 D4
Horn (N) ... 97 D3
Horn (Nordrhein-Westfalen) ... 52 A2
Hornachos ... 43 D1
Hornachuelos ... 43 E2
Hornavan ... 98 A2
Hornberg ... 54 C3
Hornbjarg ... 96 A1
Hornburg ... 52 B1
Horncastle ... 7 E3
Horndal ... 106 A3
Horneburg ... 48 A3
Hörnefors ... 102 A2
Hörnerkirchen ... 48 A2
Hornet ... 100 C2
Hornindal ... 100 A3
Hornindalsvatn ... 100 A3
Hørning ... 108 B3
Hornisgrinde ... 54 C3
Horni Počernice ... 53 F3
Horni Slavkov ... 53 E4
Hornos ... 44 B2
Hornoy ... 19 E2
Hornsea ... 7 E2
Hörnum ... 47 F1
Horodnya ... 111 E4
Horodok (UKR) ... 112 C2
Horodyšče ... 113 F2
Hořovice ... 53 E4
Horsens ... 108 B3
Horsham ... 10 C3
Hørsholm ... 108 C3

Horšovský Týn ... 56 B1
Horst ... 48 B3
Horstmar ... 17 E2
Hortafjorden ... 97 D3
Horten ... 104 C3
Hortezuela ... 36 B4
Hortiátis ... 80 A3
Horyn' ... 113 D2
Hospental ... 58 A3
Hospital ... 14 C3
Hospital de Orbigo ... 35 D3
Hossa ... 99 F3
Hossegor ... 28 A4
Hostalric ... 32 B4
Hotagen ... 101 E1
Hotagen L ... 101 E1
Hotagsfjällen ... 101 E1
Hoting ... 101 F1
Hotton ... 50 C4
Houat ... 22 C4
Houches, les ... 27 E4
Houdain ... 19 F1
Houdan ... 19 E4
Houeillès ... 28 B3
Houffalize ... 51 D4
Houghton-le-Spring ... 5 E4
Houlgate ... 18 C3
Houmnikó ... 80 B2
Hoúni ... 83 D3
Hourtin ... 28 A2
Houtskår ... 107 D3
Hov ... 108 B3
Hovärken ... 101 D3
Hovden ... 104 B3
Hove ... 10 C3
Hoverlja ... 113 D3
Hovet ... 104 B2

Hovmantorp ... 109 E2
Høvringen ... 100 C3
Howden ... 7 D2
Howth ... 13 E4
Höxter ... 52 A2
Hoy ... 3 D1
Hoya ... 17 F1
Høyanger ... 100 A3
Hoyerswerda ... 53 F2
Hoylake ... 6 B2
Høylandet ... 97 D4
Hoym ... 52 C1
Hoyos ... 39 D2
Höytiäinen ... 103 F2
Hoz de Beteta ... 40 C2
Hozoviótissa ... 89 D3
Hracholuská přehr nádrž ... 53 E4
Hradec-Králove ... 112 A2
Hrádek ... 57 E1
Hrádek nad Nisou ... 53 F2
Hranice (Severomoravský) ... 112 A3
Hranice (Západočeský) ... 53 D4
Hrasnica ... 75 F1
Hrastnik ... 70 B2
Hrastovlje ... 70 A3
Hřensko ... 53 F2
Hrísey ... 96 B1
Hríssafa ... 87 D3
Hrissi, N ... 91 E4
Hrissó ... 80 B2
Hrissoskalitissa ... 90 B3
Hrissoúpoli ... 80 C2
Hrissovítsi ... 86 C2
Hristiani, N ... 91 D1
Hristianó ... 86 C3
Hristós ... 89 D2

Hrómio ... 79 D4
Hrtkovci ... 72 C3
Hrušovany ... 57 F1
Hrvace ... 75 D1
Hrvatska ... 70 C2
Hückeswagen ... 17 E4
Hucknall ... 7 D3
Hucqueliers ... 19 E1
Hude ... 47 F3
Hudiksvall ... 101 F3
Huebra, R ... 39 E1
Huedin ... 112 C4
Huélago ... 44 A3
Huélamo ... 40 C2
Huelgoat ... 22 B3
Huelma ... 44 A2
Huelva ... 42 C2
Huelva, Riv. de ... 43 D2
Huércal-Overa ... 44 C3
Huérguina ... 41 D3
Huerta del Rey ... 36 A3
Huerta de Valdecarábanos ... 40 A3
Huertahernando ... 40 C2
Huerto ... 37 E3
Huerva, R ... 37 D4
Huesa ... 44 B2
Huesca ... 37 D3
Huéscar ... 44 B2
Huesna, Emb de ... 43 D2
Huete ... 40 B3
Huétor-Santillán ... 44 A3
Huétor-Tájar ... 43 F3
Hüfingen ... 54 C4
Huftarøy ... 104 A2
Huisne ... 23 F3
Huittinen ... 107 D2
Huizen ... 16 C2

Hulst ... 16 B4
Hultsfred ... 109 E2
Humada ... 35 F3
Humanes ... 40 B1
Humber Bridge ... 7 D2
Humber, R. ... 7 E2
Humberside ... 7 D2
Humberside (Airport) ... 7 D2
Humenné ... 112 C3
Humppila ... 107 E2
Hundested ... 108 C3
Hundorp ... 100 C3
Hunedoara ... 114 C1
Hünfeld ... 52 B3
Hungerford ... 9 E2
Hunnebostrand ... 105 D4
Húnsflói ... 96 A1
Hunspach ... 21 F3
Hunsrück ... 54 B1
Hunstanton ... 7 E3
Hunte ... 17 F1
Huntingdon ... 9 F1
Huntly ... 3 E3
Hurdal ... 105 D2
Huriel ... 25 F4
Hurones, Emb de los ... 43 D3
Hurskaala ... 103 E3
Hurum ... 104 C1
Hurup ... 108 A2
Husafell ... 96 B2
Húsavík Is ... 96 B1
Husavik N ... 104 A2
Husbands Bosworth ... 9 F1
Hushinish ... 2 A2
Huşi ... 113 E4

Huskvarna ... 109 D1
Husnes ... 104 A2
Hustadvika ... 100 B2
Hustopeče ... 57 F1
Husum (D) ... 47 F1
Husum (S) ... 102 A2
Hutovo ... 75 F2
Hutovo Blato ... 75 D2
Hüttenberg ... 57 D4
Hüttschlag ... 59 E1
Huttula ... 103 D3
Huttwil ... 27 F2
Huy ... 50 C4
Hvalba ... 96 A4
Hvalfjörður ... 96 A2
Hvalpsund ... 108 A2
Hvalvík ... 96 A3
Hvar ... 75 D2
Hvar I. ... 75 E2
Hvarski kan. ... 75 D2
Hveragerði ... 96 A2
Hveravellir ... 96 B2
Hvidbjerg ... 108 A2
Hvide Sande ... 108 A3
Hvitá ... 96 B2
Hvittingfoss ... 104 C3
Hvitträsk ... 107 E3
Hvolsvöllur ... 96 B3
Hwlffordd ... 8 B3
Hyde ... 6 C2
Hyen ... 100 A3
Hyères ... 31 D4
Hyères, Iles d' ... 31 D4
Hylsfjorden ... 104 A3
Hyltebruk ... 108 C2
Hyrynsalmi ... 99 E4
Hythe ... 11 D3
Hyvinkää ... 107 E2
Hyypiö ... 99 D2

I

Ía ... 91 E1
Ialomiţa ... 115 E1
Iaşi ... 113 E3
Iasmos ... 81 D2
Ibañeta, Pto ... 36 C1
Ibar ... 73 D4
Ibbenbüren ... 17 E2
Ibestad ... 94 B3
Ibi ... 45 E1
Ibias, R ... 34 C2
Ibiza ... 45 D4
Ibiza I ... 45 D3
Iblei, Mti ... 69 D4
Ičnja ... 113 F1
Icod de los Vinos ... 42 A4
Idanha a Nova ... 38 C2
Idar-Oberstein ... 54 B1
Idéo Ándro ... 91 D4
Ídi, Óros ... 91 D4
Idre ... 101 D3
Idrija ... 70 A2
Idrijca ... 70 A2
Idro ... 58 C4
Idstein ... 51 F4
Ieper ... 50 A3
Ierápetra ... 91 E4
Ierissós ... 80 B3
Ieropigi ... 78 C3
If, Château d' ... 30 C4
Ifestía ... 85 D1
Ifjord ... 95 E1
Ifjordfjellet ... 95 E1
Igalo ... 76 A3
Iga Vas ... 70 B2
Iggesund ... 101 F3
Iglesias ... 66 B4
Igls ... 59 D2
Igoumenitsa ... 82 B2
Igrane ... 75 E2
Igualada ... 37 F4

Ihtiman ... 115 D2
Ii ... 99 D3
Iijarvi ... 95 E2
Iijoki ... 99 D3
Iisalmi ... 103 E1
Iisvesi ... 103 E2
IJmuiden ... 16 B2
IJssel ... 17 D3
IJsselmeer ... 16 C2
IJsselmuiden ... 17 D2
IJzendijke ... 16 B4
IJzer ... 50 A3
Ikaalinen ... 102 C3
Ikaría, N ... 89 D2
Ikast ... 108 A3
Ilandža ... 73 D2
Ilanz ... 58 B3
Ilche ... 37 E3
Ilchester ... 9 D3
Ile-Bouchard, l' ... 25 D3
Ile-Rousse, l' ... 33 F2
Ilfracombe ... 8 C3
Ílhavo ... 38 B1
Ilia ... 83 F1
Ilía ... 86 B1
Ilida ... 86 B1
Ilidza ... 75 F1
Ilijas ... 71 F4
Iliki ... 84 A4
Iliki, L ... 84 A4
Iliókastro ... 87 E2
Ilirska Bistrica ... 70 B3
Ilkeston ... 7 D3
Ilkley ... 6 C2
Illana ... 40 B2
Illano ... 34 C1
Illar ... 44 B3
Ille ... 23 D3
Ille et Rance, Canal d' ... 23 D3
Ille-et-Vilaine ... 23 D3
Iller ... 55 E4
Illertissen ... 55 E3
Illescas ... 40 A2
Ille-sur-Têt ... 32 B2
Illhæusern ... 27 E1
Illičivs'k ... 113 F4
Illiers-Combray ... 25 E1
Illingen ... 55 D2

Illmitz ... 57 F3
Illora ... 44 A3
Illueca ... 36 C4
Ilm ... 52 C3
Ilmajoki ... 102 C2
Ilmenau R ... 48 B3
Ilmenau ... 52 C3
Il'men, Ozero ... 111 D1
Ilminster ... 9 D3
Ilok ... 72 B2
Ilomantsi ... 103 F2
Ilova ... 71 D2
Ilovik ... 70 B4
Ilsenburg ... 52 B1
Ilsfeld ... 55 D2
Imathia ... 79 E3
Imatra ... 103 F4
Ímeros ... 81 E2
Imitós ... 87 F1
Imitós ... 87 F1
Immenstaad ... 55 D4
Immenstadt ... 55 E4
Immingham ... 7 E2
Immingham Dock ... 7 E2
Imola ... 61 D3
Imotski ... 75 E1
Imperia ... 31 F3
Imphy ... 26 A3
Impruneta ... 61 D4
Imst ... 58 C2
Ina ... 49 F3
Inari ... 95 E3
Inarijärvi ... 95 E3
Inarijoki ... 95 E3
Inca ... 45 F2
Inchnadamph ... 2 C2
Inchtree ... 2 C4
Incisa in Val d'Arno ... 61 D4
Incudine, M ... 33 F4
Indal ... 101 F3
Indalsälven ... 101 E2
Indija ... 72 C2
Indre ... 25 D2
Indre (Dépt) ... 25 D3
Indre-et-Loire ... 25 D2
Infiesto ... 35 E1
Ingå ... 107 E3
Ingelmunster ... 50 A3
Ingleton ... 6 C1

Ingolstadt ... 55 F2
Ingrandes ... 23 E4
Ingwiller ... 21 E3
Inhul ... 113 F3
Inhulec' ... 113 F3
Inhulec' R ... 113 F3
Iniesta ... 41 D4
Inió ... 107 D2
Inión aukko ... 107 D2
Inis ... 12 B4
Inis Córthaidh ... 15 D3
Inishbofin ... 12 A3
Inishcrone ... 12 B2
Inisheer ... 12 B4
Inishkea ... 12 A2
Inishmaan ... 12 B4
Inishmore ... 12 B4
Inishmurray ... 12 C2
Inishowen ... 13 D1
Inishowen Head ... 13 D1
Inishshark ... 12 A3
Inishtrahull ... 13 D1
Inishturk ... 12 A3
Inkee ... 99 E3
Inkoo ... 107 E3
Inn (CH) ... 58 B3
Inn (D) ... 56 B3
Innbygda ... 104 C1
Inndyr ... 97 E1
Innellan ... 4 B2
Innerleithen ... 5 D2
Inner Sd ... 2 B3
Innfield ... 13 D3
Innhavet ... 97 F1
Innichen ... 59 E2
Inning ... 56 A3
Innsbruck ... 59 D2
Innset ... 94 B3
Innvik ... 100 A3
Inói (Pelopónissos) ... 86 B1
Inói (Stereá Eláda) ... 84 A4
Inoússes ... 85 F4
Inoússes, N ... 85 F4
Inowrocław ... 112 A1
Ins ... 27 E2
Ińsko ... 49 F2
Interlaken ... 27 F3
Întorsura Buzǎului ... 113 D4
Inveraray ... 4 B1

Inverbervie ... 3 E4
Invergarry ... 2 C4
Invergordon ... 3 D3
Inverkeithing ... 5 D2
Invermoriston ... 2 C4
Inverness ... 2 C3
Inverurie ... 3 E4
Inzell ... 56 B3
Ioánina ... 82 C1
Ioánina (Nomos) ... 82 B1
Ioaninon, L ... 82 C1
Iona ... 4 A1
Ionia ... 79 F3
Iónia Nissiá ... 82 A2
Íos ... 88 C4
Íos, N ... 88 C4
Ipáti ... 83 E3
Ipéria ... 83 E3
Iphofen ... 55 E1
Ípiros ... 82 B2
Ipsili Ráhi ... 80 C2
Ípsos ... 82 A1
Ipsoúnda ... 86 C2
Ipswich ... 11 D2
Iput' ... 111 E4
Iráklia (Makedonía) ... 80 A2
Iráklia (Stereá Eláda) ... 83 E3
Iráklia, N ... 88 C3
Iráklio ... 91 D3
Iráklio (Nomos) ... 91 D4
Irati, R ... 36 C2
Irbes Šaurums ... 110 B2
Irdning ... 57 D4
Iregua, R ... 36 B2
Iréo (Argolida) ... 87 D2
Iréo (Dodekánissa) ... 89 E2
Iréo (Korinthía) ... 87 E1
Iréo, Akr ... 87 E1
Íria ... 87 E2
Irig ... 72 C2
Irish Sea ... 13 F3
Iriški venac ... 72 C2
Irixoa ... 34 B1
Irnijärvi ... 99 E3
Iron-Bridge ... 9 D1
Irschenberg ... 56 B3
Irsina ... 65 D3
Irún ... 36 C1

Irurzun ... 36 C2
Irvine ... 4 C2
Irvinestow ... 12 C2
Irxleben ... 52 C1
Isaba ... 37 D2
Isaccea ... 113 E4
Isafjarðardjúp ... 96 A1
Ísafjörður ... 96 A1
Isane ... 100 A3
Isar ... 56 B2
Isarco ... 59 D2
Isbister ... 3 F1
Iscar ... 35 E4
Ischgl ... 58 C2
Ischia ... 64 A4
Ischia, I d' ... 64 A4
Ise ... 105 D3
Isefjord ... 108 C3
Iselle ... 58 A3
Iselsberg ... 59 E2
Iseo ... 60 B1
Iseo, L d' ... 58 B4
Iseran, Col de l' ... 31 E1
Isère (Dépt) ... 30 C2
Isère (R) ... 30 C1
Iserlohn ... 17 E3
Isernia ... 64 A3
Isfjellet ... 94 B3
Isfjorden ... 100 B2
Ishavsleden ... 94 C3
Ishëm ... 76 C4
Ishëm R ... 76 C4
Isigny ... 18 C3
Isili ... 66 B3
Iskår ... 115 D2
Is'kuras ... 95 E2
Isla ... 3 D3
Isla ... 36 A1
Isla Cristina ... 42 C3
Isla Mayor ... 43 D3
Island Magee ... 13 E2
Islay ... 4 A2
Isle ... 28 C2
Isle-Adam, l' ... 19 F3
Isle-de-Noé, l' ... 28 C4

Isle-Jourdain, l' (Vienne) ... 25 D4
Isle of Man ... 6 A1
Isle of Portland ... 9 D4
Isle of Whithorn ... 4 C4
Isle of Wight ... 9 E4
Isleornsay ... 2 B4
Isles of Scilly ... 8 A4
Ísala ... 115 E3
Isle-sur-la-Sorgue,l' ... 30 C3
Isle-sur-le-Doubs, l' ... 27 D2
Isle-sur-Serein, l' ... 26 B2
Ismaning ... 55 F3
Isnäs ... 107 F2
Isny ... 55 E4
Iso-Evo ... 107 E2
Isojärvi ... 103 D3
Isojoki ... 102 B3
Isokylä ... 99 E2
Isokyrö ... 102 B2
Isola ... 31 E3
Isola del Gran Sasso d'Italia ... 63 F1
Isola della Scala ... 60 C1
Isola del Liri ... 64 A3
Isola di Capo Rizzuto ... 67 F3
Isona ... 37 F3
Isonzo ... 59 F3
Isorella ... 60 B1
Iso-Syöte ... 99 E3
Ispica ... 69 D4
Issambres, les ... 31 D4
Issel ... 17 D3
Issigeac ... 28 C2
Issoire ... 29 F1
Issóva, M. ... 86 C2
Íssoma ... 86 C1
Issoudun ... 25 E3
Is-sur-Tille ... 26 C2
Issy-l'Evêque ... 26 B3
Ist ... 74 B1
Istán ... 43 E4
İstanbul ... 115 F3
Istarske Toplice ... 70 A3
Istérnia ... 88 B2
Istha ... 52 A2
Isthmía ... 87 E1

Istibanja 77 F2
Istiéa 83 F3
Istindan 94 B3
Istok 76 C2
Istres 30 C4
Ístrios 93 E2
Isturits et d'Oxocelhaya, Grottes d' 28 A4
Itä-Aure 102 C3
Itäinen Suomenlahti 107 F2
Itanós 91 F3
Itéa (Flórina) 79 D2
Itéa (Grevená) 79 D4
Itéa (Stereá Eláda) 83 E4
Itéa (Thessalía) 83 E2
Itéas, Kólpos 83 E4
Itháki 82 B4
Itháki, N 82 B4
Ithómi 86 C3
Iti 83 E3
Ítilo 87 D4
Íti, Óros 83 E3
Iton 19 E3
Itri 64 A3
Itta 52 B3
Ittiri 66 A2
Itz 52 C4
Itzehoe 48 A2
Ivaceviči 112 C1
Ivajlovgrad 115 E3
Ivalo 95 E3
Ivalojoki Ävvil 95 E3
Ivančice 57 F1
Ivančići 71 F4
Ivančna Gorica 70 B2
Ivanec 70 C1
Ivangrad 76 C2
Ivanić Grad 71 D2
Ivanjica 73 D4
Ivanjska 71 E3
Ivankovo 71 F2
Ivano-Frankivs'k 113 D3
Ivanščica 70 C2
Ivan Sedlo 75 F1
Ivanska 71 D2
Iveland 104 B4
Iveragh 14 A4
Ivira 80 B2
Iviron 80 C4
Ivrea 31 F1
Ivry-la-Bataille 19 E4
Ixiá 93 F1
Ixworth 11 D1
Iž 74 C1
Izeda 34 C4
Izegem 50 A3
Izernore 26 C4
Izlake 70 B2
Izmaïl 113 E4
İzmir 115 E4
İzmit 115 F3
Iznájar 43 F3
Iznájar, Emb de 43 F3
Iznallos 44 A3
İznik 115 F3
İznik Gölü 115 F3
Izoard, Col d' 31 D2
Izola 70 A3
Iz Veli 74 C1
Izvor (Makedonija) 77 D4
Izvor (Makedonija) 77 E3
Izvor (Srbija) 73 E4

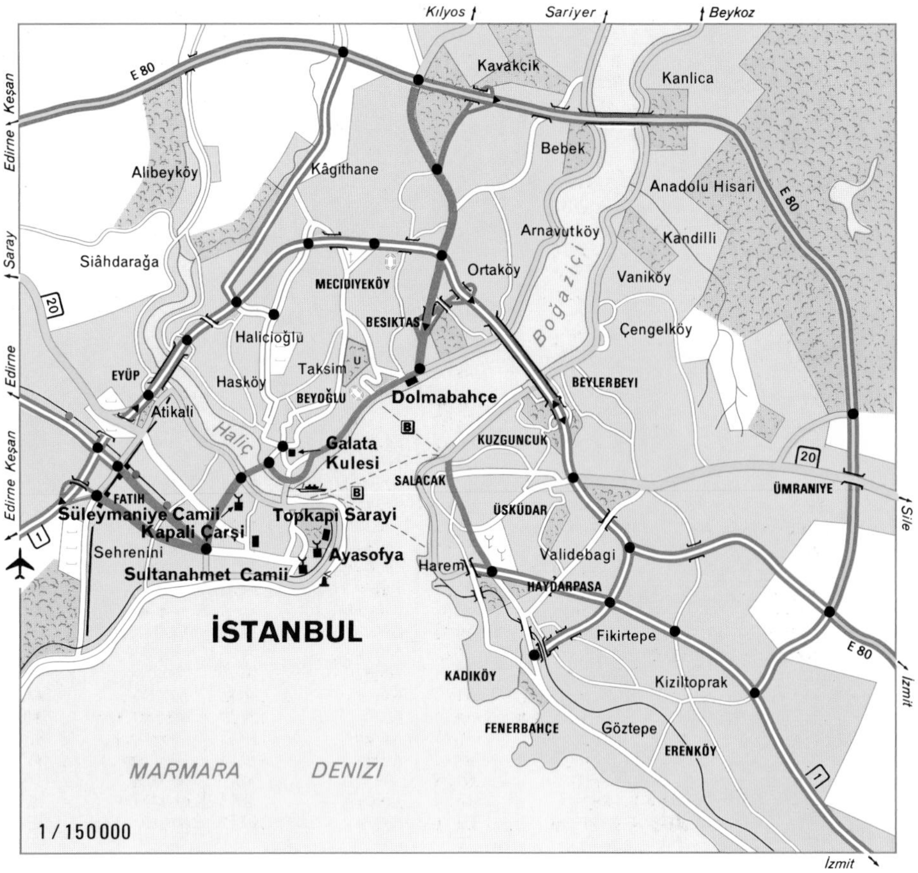
Kılyos
Sarıyer
Beykoz
E 80
Edirne
Keşan
Saray
Kavakcik
Kanlica
Bebek
Alibeyköy
Kâğithane
Anadolu Hisari
Arnavutköy
Kandilli
Siâhdarağa
Ortaköy
Vaniköy
MECIDIYEKÖY
Boğaziçi
BESIKTAS
Halicioğlu
Çengelköy
EYÜP
Taksim
Hasköy
BEYOĞLU
Dolmabahçe
BEYLERBEYI
Atikali
Haliç
KUZGUNCUK
Galata Kulesi
SALACAK
ÜMRANIYE
FATIH
Süleymaniye Camii
Kapali Çarşi
Topkapi Sarayi
ÜSKÜDAR
Şile
Sehrenini
Ayasofya
Validebagi
Sultanahmet Camii
Harem
HAYDARPASA
İSTANBUL
Fikirtepe
KADIKÖY
Kiziltoprak
İzmit
FENERBAHÇE
Göztepe
ERENKÖY
MARMARA DENIZI
1 / 150000

J

Jaala 107 F2
Jaäsjärvi 103 D3
Jabalón, R 44 A1
Jabbeke 50 A3
Jablanac 70 B4
Jablan Do 76 A2
Jablanica 75 F1
Jablanica (Reg) 77 D4
Jablanica *R* 77 D1
Jablaničko jez 75 F1
Jablonec nad Nisou 112 A2
Jablonné v Podještědí 53 F3
Jablons'kyj Pereval 113 D3
Jabugo 42 C2
Jabuka (BH) 76 A1
Jabuka (Srbija) 76 B1
Jabuka (Vojvodina) 73 D2
Jabuka, I 74 C2
Jabukovac (HR) 71 D3
Jabukovac (Srbija) 73 F3
Jabukovik 77 E1
Jaca 37 D2
Jáchymov 53 E3
Jadar (BH) 72 C4
Jadar (Srbija) 72 B3
Jäder 106 A3
Jaderberg 47 F3
Jadovik 76 B1
Jadovnik 71 D4
Jadranska Lešnica 72 B3
Jadransko More 74 B2
Jadraque 40 B1
Jaén 44 A2
Jagodnjac 71 F2
Jagst 55 E2
Jagsthausen 55 D2
Jahorina 76 A1
Jahorina (Reg) 76 A1
Jahotin 113 F2
Jajce 71 E4
Jäkkvik 97 F2
Jakobselv 95 F2
Jakobstad 102 C1
Jakšić 71 E2
Jakupica 77 E3
Jalasjärvi 102 C3
Jaligny 26 A3
Jalón, R 36 C3
Jalovik Izvor 73 F4
Jambol 115 E2
Jamena 72 B3
Jämijärvi 102 C3
Jäminkipohja 102 C3
Jämjö 109 E3
Jammerbugten 108 A2
Jamnička Kiselica 70 C2
Jämsä 103 D3
Jämsänkoski 103 D3
Jämtlands Län 101 E2
Janakkala 107 E2
Janče 77 D3
Jandia, Pta de 42 C4
Jándula, Emb del 44 A1
Jandula, R 44 A1
Jänisselkä 103 F2
Janja 72 B3
Janjevo 77 D2
Janjina 75 E2
Jankov kamen 76 C1
Jañona 39 D2
Jantra 115 D2
Janville 25 E1
Janzé 23 D3
Japetić 70 C2
Jäppilä 103 E2
Jaraba 36 C4
Jarafuel 41 D4
Jaraicejo 39 E3
Jaraíz 39 E2
Jarak 72 C3
Jarama, R 40 B2
Jarandilla de la Vera 39 E2
Järbo 106 A2
Jarcevo 111 E3
Jard 24 B3
Jæren 104 A4
Jaren 105 D2
Jargeau 25 E1
Jarkovac 73 D2
Jarmen 49 D2
Jarmenovci 73 D3
Jarnac 28 B1
Jarnages 25 E4
Järna (Kopparbergs Län) 105 E2
Järna (Stockholms Län) 106 B4
Jarny 21 D3
Jarocin 112 A2
Jaroměřice 57 E1
Jarosław 112 C2
Järpen 101 E2
Jarrow 5 E3
Järvelä 107 F2
Järvenpää 107 E2
Järvsö 101 F3
Jaša Tomić 73 D2
Jasenak 70 B3
Jasenica (BH) 71 D3
Jasenica (Srbija) 73 D3
Jasenovac 71 D3
Jasenovo (Crna Gora) 76 B2
Jasenovo (Srbija) 76 B1
Jasenovo (Vojvodina) 73 D2
Jasień 53 F1
Jasika 73 E4
Jasikovo 73 E3
Jasło 112 C3
Jasmund 49 D1
Jastrebarsko 70 C2
Jastrowie 112 A1
Jászberény 112 B4
Jau, Col de 32 B2
Jaufenpass 59 D2
Jaunay-Clan 25 D3
Jaunpass 27 E3
Jausiers 31 D2
Javalambre 41 D3
Javalambre, Sa de 41 E3
Javalón 41 D2
Javea 45 E1
Jävenitz 48 C4
Javie, la 31 D3
Javor 76 C1
Javořice 57 D1
Javoriv 112 C2
Javornjača 71 D4
Jävre 98 B4
Javron 23 E3
Jedburgh 5 D3
Jędrzejów 112 B2
Jeesiö 95 E4
Jeetze 48 B3
Jegun 28 C4
Jegunovce 77 D3
Jēkabpils 110 C3
Jektevik 104 A2
Jelah 71 E3
Jelašca 76 A1
Jelenia Góra 112 A2
Jelenje 70 B3
Jelgava 110 C3
Jelling 108 A3
Jel'n'a 111 E3
Jelsa (HR) 75 E2
Jelsa (N) 104 A3
Jelsi 64 B3
Jemnice 57 E1
Jena 52 C3
Jenbach 59 D1
Jengejetneme 97 E4
Jennersdorf 57 F4
Jeppo 102 C2
Jerez de la Frontera 43 D3
Jerez de los Caballeros 42 C1
Jérica 41 E3
Jerichow 49 D4
Jerisjärvi 95 D4
Jerpoint Abbey 15 D3
Jersey 18 A3
Jerte 39 E2
Jerte, R 39 E2
Jerxheim 52 B1
Jerzu 66 C3
Jesenice (CS) 53 E4
Jesenice (SLO) 70 A1
Jeseník 112 A2
Jesi 61 F4
Jesolo 59 E4
Jessen 53 D1
Jessheim 105 D3
Jeßnitz 53 D2
Jetzelsdorf 57 E2
Jeumont 20 B1
Jevenstedt 48 A2
Jever 47 E3
Jevišovice 57 E1
Jevnaker 105 D2
Jezerane 70 C3
Jezerce 77 D2
Jezercë, M 76 C2
Jezero 71 E4
Jezero Šćit 75 E1
Jezersko 70 B1
Ježevica 72 C4
Jičín 112 A2
Jiekkevarre 94 C2
Jihlava 57 E1
Jihlava *R* 57 E1
Jiloca, R 41 D2
Jílové u Prahy 53 F4
Jimbolia 114 C1
Jimena 44 A2
Jimena de la Frontera 43 E4
Jindřichovice 53 D3
Jindřichuv Hradec 57 D1
Jirkov 53 E3
Jiu 115 D2
Jizera 53 F3
Joachimsthal 49 E3
Jockfall 98 C2
Jódar 44 A2
Jodoigne 50 C3
Joensuu 103 F2
Jõgeva 110 C1
Johanngeorgenstadt 53 D3
John o'Groats 3 D2
Johnstone 4 C2
Johovac 71 F3
Joigny 26 A1
Joinville 20 C4
Jokela 107 E2
Jokijärvi 99 E3
Jokikylä 99 E4
Jokioinen 107 E2
Jokkmokk 98 B2
Jökulsá-á Fjöllum 96 C1
Joloskylä 99 D3
Jølstravatnet 100 A3
Jomala 106 C3
Jönåker 106 A4
Jondal 104 B2
Jongunjärvi 99 E3
Joniškis 110 C3
Jönköping 109 D1
Jönköpings Län 109 D2
Jonzac 28 B1
Jordbro 106 B4
Jordbruksveien 95 D2
Jormlien 97 E4
Jörn 98 B4
Joroinen 103 E3
Jørpeland 104 A3
Jørstadmoen 105 D2
Jošanica 73 E4
Jošanička Banja 76 C1
Jošavka 71 E3
Josenfjorden 104 A3
Jose Toran, Emb de 43 E2
Josipdol 70 C3
Josipovac 71 F2
Josselin 22 C3
Jostedalsbreen 100 A3
Jotunheimen 100 B3
Jou, Coll de 32 A3
Joué 25 D2
Jougne 27 D3
Joutjärvi 107 F2
Joutsa 103 D3
Joutseno 103 E4
Joutsijärvi 99 E2
Joyeuse 30 B2
Juankoski 103 E2
Juan-les-Pins 31 E4
Jüchen 17 D4
Juchnov 111 F3
Judaberg 104 A3
Judenau 57 E2
Judenburg 57 D4
Judio 43 F1
Juelsminde 108 B3
Jugenheim 54 C1
Jugon 22 C3
Jugorje 70 B2
Juillac 29 D1
Juist 47 E3
Jukkasjärvi 94 C4
Jülich 17 D4
Julierpass 58 B3
Jullouville 18 B4
Jumaliskylä 99 F4
Jumeaux 29 F1
Jumièges 19 D3
Jumilhac-le-Grand 29 D1
Jumilla 45 D1
Jumilla, Pto de 45 D1
Juminen 103 E1
Jumisko 99 E2
Juneda 37 F4
Jungfrau 27 F3
Junik 76 C2
Juniville 20 B3
Junkeren 97 E2
Junosuando 95 D4
Junsele 101 F2
Juntusranta 99 F3
Juojärvi 103 E2
Juoksenki 98 C2
Juorkuna 99 E4
Jura 4 B2
Jura (Canton) 27 E2
Jura (Dépt) 27 D3
Jura, Sd of 4 B2
Jurbarkas 110 C3
Jurjevo 70 B4
Jūrmala 110 C2
Jurmofjärden 107 D3
Jurmu 99 E3
Juromenha 38 C4
Jurva 102 B2
Jussey 27 D1
Justel 34 D3
Jüterbog 53 E1
Juuka 103 E2
Juupajoki 103 D3
Juurusvesi 103 E2
Juva (Mikkelin Lääni) 103 E3
Juva (Turun ja Porin Lääni) 107 D2
Juvigny-le-Tertre 18 C4
Juvigny-sous-Andaine 18 C4
Juvola 103 E3
Juzennecourt 26 C1
Južna Morava 73 E4
Jyderup 108 B3
Jylland 108 A3
Jyrkkä 103 E1
Jyväskylä 103 D3

K

Kaakamo . . . 99 D3
Kaamanen . . . 95 E3
Kaamaskoki . . . 95 E2
Kaaresuvanto . . . 95 D3
Kaarina . . . 107 D2
Kaatsheuvel . . . 16 C3
Kaavi . . . 103 E2
Kaavinjärvi . . . 103 E2
Kåbdalis . . . 98 B3
Kablart . . . 72 C4
Kač . . . 72 C2
Kačanik . . . 77 D2
Kačarevo . . . 73 D2
Kačikol . . . 77 D2
Kadaň . . . 53 E3
Kadi Bogaz . . . 73 F4
Kadrifakovo . . . 77 E3
Kafiréas, Akr. . . . 84 C4
Kafiréa, Stenó . . . 88 B1
Kåfjord . . . 95 E1
Kåfjorden . . . 94 C2
Kaga . . . 106 A4
Kaharlyk . . . 113 E2
Kahla . . . 52 C3
Kaiáfas . . . 86 B2
Kailbach . . . 55 D1
Kaïmaktsalán . . . 79 E2
Kainasto . . . 102 B3
Kaindorf . . . 57 E4
Kaipola . . . 103 D3
Kairala . . . 95 F4
Kaisergebirge . . . 59 D1
Kaiserslautern . . . 54 B1
Kaisheim . . . 55 E2
Kaitumälven . . . 94 C4
Kaiuđđerovo . . . 73 E2
Kajaani . . . 99 E4
Kakan . . . 74 C1
Kakanj . . . 71 F4
Kaki Thálassa . . . 88 A1
Kaki Vigla . . . 87 F1
Kakslauttanen . . . 95 E3
Kalajoki . . . 102 C1
Kalajoki R. . . . 102 C1
Kalak . . . 95 E1
Kalamáki (Lárissa) . . . 83 F2
Kalamáki (Magnissia) . . . 84 A2
Kalamáki, Akr. . . . 85 D2
Kalamáta . . . 86 C3
Kalambáka . . . 83 D1
Kalambáki . . . 80 C2
Kalámi . . . 89 E1
Kalamiótissa . . . 91 F1
Kalamitsi (Makedonía) . . . 80 B4
Kalamitsi (Stereá Eláda) . . . 82 B3
Kálamos, N . . . 82 C3
Kalamoti . . . 85 F4
Kalamotó . . . 80 A3
Kalándra . . . 80 A4
Kalá Nerá . . . 83 F2
Kalá Nissiá . . . 87 E1
Kalanti . . . 107 D2
Kalapódi . . . 83 F3
Kälarne . . . 101 F2
Kalavárda . . . 93 E1
Kalávrita . . . 86 C1
Kal'azin . . . 111 F1
Kalbe . . . 48 C4
Kalce . . . 70 A2
Kaldakvisl . . . 96 B2
Kaléndzi (Ípiros) . . . 82 C2
Kaléndzi (Pelopónissos) . . . 86 C1
Kalenić . . . 73 D4
Kalérgo . . . 84 C4
Kalesija . . . 72 B3
Kali . . . 74 C1
Kaliakoúda . . . 83 D3
Kaliáni . . . 87 D1
Kalidromo, Óros . . . 83 E3
Kalífitos . . . 80 C2
Kali Liménes . . . 91 E4
Kalí Limni . . . 93 D3
Kalimassiá . . . 85 F4
Kalimenci, Ez . . . 77 F2
Kálimnos . . . 89 F3
Kálimnos, N . . . 89 E3

Kaliningrad . . . 110 B4
Kalinkoviči . . . 113 E1
Kalinovik . . . 75 F1
Kalipéfki . . . 79 E4
Kaliráhi . . . 79 D4
Kalithéa (Dodekánissa) . . . 93 F1
Kalithéa (Ilía) . . . 86 C2
Kalithéa (Makedonía) . . . 80 B2
Kalithéa (Messinia) . . . 86 C3
Kalithéa (Stereá Eláda) . . . 83 D3
Kalithéa (Thessalia) . . . 80 B4
Kalithiés . . . 93 F1
Kalithiro . . . 83 D2
Kalivári . . . 88 B1
Kalives (Kriti) . . . 90 C3
Kalives (Thássos) . . . 80 C3
Kalivia (Ahaïa) . . . 86 C1
Kalivia (Atiki-Piréas) . . . 87 F1
Kalivia (Etolia-Akarnania) . . . 82 C3
Kalivia (Korinthia) . . . 87 D1
Kalivia Varikoú . . . 79 F4
Kalix . . . 98 C3
Kalixälven . . . 98 C2
Kaljord . . . 94 A3
Kalkar . . . 17 D3
Kalkkinen . . . 107 F1
Kall . . . 101 D2
Kallaktjåkkå . . . 94 B4
Kallavesi . . . 103 E2
Kållby . . . 102 C1
Källby . . . 105 E4
Kallinge . . . 109 E3
Kallio . . . 102 C3
Kalliojoki . . . 99 F4
Kallislahti . . . 103 E3
Kallmünz . . . 55 F2
Kallsjön . . . 101 D1
Kalmar . . . 109 E2
Kalmar Län . . . 109 E2
Kalmar sund . . . 109 E2
Kalmit . . . 54 C2
Kalna . . . 73 F4
Kalnik . . . 71 D2
Kalnik Mt . . . 71 D2
Kalocsa . . . 112 B4
Kalogerikoú . . . 87 D2
Kalogriá . . . 86 B1
Kalohóri . . . 83 D1
Kaló Horió . . . 91 E4
Kalókastro . . . 80 A2
Kaló Neró . . . 86 C3
Kaloní (Lésvos) . . . 85 F2
Kaloni (Pelopónissos) . . . 87 E2
Kalonis, Kólpos . . . 85 F2
Kaloskopi . . . 83 E3
Kalotássi, Akr . . . 89 D4
Kaló Vig . . . 108 B3
Kalpáki . . . 78 C4
Kals . . . 59 E2
Kalsdorf . . . 57 E4
Kaltbrunn . . . 58 A2
Kaltenkirchen . . . 48 A2
Kaltennordheim . . . 52 B3
Kaltern . . . 59 D3
Kaltezés . . . 87 D2
Kaluga . . . 111 F3
Kalundborg . . . 108 B3
Kaluš . . . 112 C3
Kalvåg . . . 104 A1
Kalvehave . . . 108 C4
Kälviä . . . 102 C1
Kalvola . . . 107 E2
Kalvträsk . . . 98 B4
Kamáres (Kriti) . . . 91 D4
Kamáres (Páros) . . . 88 C3
Kamáres (Pelopónissos) . . . 83 D4
Kamáres (Sifnos) . . . 88 B3
Kamári . . . 91 E1
Kamariótissa . . . 81 E3
Kambanós, Akr . . . 88 B1
Kambiá . . . 85 E4
Kámbos (Kriti) . . . 90 B3
Kámbos (Pelopónissos) . . . 86 C3
Kámbos (Stereá Eláda) . . . 83 D4

Kamčija . . . 115 E2
Kamen . . . 17 E3
Kamenari . . . 76 A3
Kaména Voúria . . . 83 F3
Kamenica . . . 77 F2
Kamenice . . . 57 E1
Kaméni, N . . . 91 E1
Kamenjak, Rt . . . 70 A4
Kamensko (HR) . . . 71 E2
Kamensko (HR) . . . 75 E1
Kamenz . . . 53 F2
Kamień Pomorski . . . 49 E2
Kamieński, Zalew . . . 49 E2
Kamilári . . . 91 D4
Kaminia . . . 86 B1
Kámiros . . . 93 E1
Kámiros Kastélo . . . 93 E1
Kam'janec'-Podil'skyj . . . 113 D3
Kam'janka . . . 113 F2
Kamnik . . . 70 B2
Kamp . . . 57 E2
Kamp-Bornhofen . . . 51 E4
Kampen (D) . . . 47 F1
Kampen (NL) . . . 17 D2
Kamp-Lintfort . . . 17 D3
Kanal . . . 70 A2
Kanála . . . 88 A4
Kanal Dunav-Tisa-Dunav . . . 73 D2
Kanália . . . 55 D4
Kanatádika . . . 83 F3
Kánava . . . 88 A4
Kándanos . . . 90 B3
Kandel . . . 54 C2
Kandel Mt . . . 54 C3
Kandern . . . 54 C4
Kandersteg . . . 27 F3
Kándia . . . 87 E2
Kandila (Pelopónissos) . . . 87 D2
Ķándila (Stereá Eláda) . . . 82 C3
Kandili . . . 84 A3
Kandíra . . . 115 F3
Kandrše . . . 70 B2
Kanestraum . . . 100 B2
Kanfanar . . . 70 A3
Kangádio . . . 86 B1
Kangasala . . . 107 E1
Kangaslampi . . . 103 E2
Kangasniemi . . . 103 D3
Kangosjärvi . . . 95 D4
Kaniv . . . 113 F2
Kanjiža . . . 72 C1
Kankaanpää . . . 102 C3
Kannonkoski . . . 103 D2
Kannus . . . 102 C1
Kannusjärvi . . . 103 E4
Kanturk . . . 14 B3
Kaona . . . 73 D4
Kaonik (BH) . . . 71 F4
Kaonik (Srbija) . . . 73 E4
Kapandriti . . . 87 F1
Kaparéli . . . 83 F4
Kapariá . . . 88 B2
Kapele, Vrh . . . 70 C3
Kapellskär . . . 106 C3
Kapélo, Akr . . . 90 A2
Kapfenberg . . . 57 E3
Kaplice . . . 57 D2
Kaposvár . . . 114 B1
Kapp . . . 105 D2
Kappel . . . 51 E4
Kappeln . . . 48 A1
Kappelshamnsviken . . . 109 F3
Kaprije . . . 74 C1
Kaprun . . . 59 E1
Kapsáli . . . 90 A2
Kapsas . . . 87 D2
Kapsoúri . . . 88 B1
Kapuvár . . . 112 A4
Karabiga . . . 115 E3
Karaburun . . . 115 E4
Karačev . . . 111 F4
Karan . . . 72 C4
Karasjåkka . . . 95 E2
Karasjok . . . 95 E2
Karasu . . . 115 F3
Karats . . . 98 A2
Karavás . . . 90 A1
Karavómilos . . . 83 F3

Karavónissia . . . 92 C2
Karavostássis . . . 91 D1
Kårböle . . . 101 E3
Karcag . . . 112 B4
Kardámena . . . 89 F3
Kardamíli . . . 85 E4
Kardámili . . . 86 C3
Kardeljevo . . . 75 E2
Kárdla . . . 110 B1
Karditsa . . . 55 D4
Karditsa (Nomos) . . . 55 D4
Karerpass . . . 59 D3
Karesuando . . . 95 D3
Karfás . . . 85 F4
Karhukangas . . . 99 D4
Karhula . . . 103 F4
Karhunkierros . . . 99 F2
Karhutunturi . . . 95 F4
Kariá (Pelopónissos) . . . 87 D2
Kariá (Stereá Eláda) . . . 83 F3
Kariés (Makedonía) . . . 80 C4
Kariés (Pelopónissos) . . . 87 D3
Karigasniemi . . . 95 E2
Karijoki . . . 102 B3
Karinainen . . . 107 D2
Kariótisa . . . 79 E3
Karis . . . 107 E3
Káristos . . . 88 A1
Karitena . . . 86 C2
Karjaa . . . 107 E3
Karjalohja . . . 107 E3
Karkaloú . . . 86 C2
Karkinágri . . . 89 D2
Karkku . . . 107 D1
Kärkölä . . . 107 E2
Karleby . . . 102 C1
Karlevi . . . 109 E3
Karlino . . . 49 F1
Karlobag . . . 70 C4
Karlovac . . . 70 C3
Karlováßi . . . 89 E1
Karlovo . . . 115 D2
Karlovy Vary . . . 53 E4
Karlsborg . . . 105 E4
Karlsburg . . . 49 D2
Karlsfeld . . . 55 F3
Karlshamn . . . 109 D3
Karlshuld . . . 55 F2
Karlskoga . . . 105 E4
Karlskrona . . . 109 E3
Karlsruhe . . . 54 C2
Karlstad . . . 105 E3
Karlstadt . . . 52 B4
Karlstift . . . 57 D2
Karløy . . . 104 A3
Karnezéika . . . 87 E2
Karnobat . . . 115 E2
Kärnten . . . 59 F2
Karolinerleden . . . 101 E2
Karow . . . 48 C2
Kárpankylä . . . 99 F2
Kárpathos . . . 93 D3
Kárpathos, N . . . 93 D3
Karpeníssi . . . 83 D3
Karperi . . . 80 A2
Karperó . . . 79 D4
Kärsämäki . . . 103 D1
Karsatjåkka . . . 94 B4
Kärsava . . . 111 D2
Karstädt . . . 48 C3
Karstula . . . 103 D2
Kartal . . . 115 F3
Kartéri (Ípiros) . . . 82 B2
Kartéri (Pelopónissos) . . . 87 D1
Karterós . . . 91 D3
Kártsino, Akr . . . 84 C3
Kartuzy . . . 110 A4
Karungi . . . 98 C3
Karunki . . . 98 C3
Karup . . . 108 A2
Kárvala . . . 102 C2
Kärväskylä . . . 103 D2
Karvia . . . 102 C3
Karviná . . . 112 B3
Karvoskylä . . . 103 D1

Karvounári . . . 82 B2
Karwendelgebirge . . . 59 D1
Kašalj . . . 76 C1
Kašin . . . 111 F1
Kašina . . . 70 C2
Kaskinen . . . 102 B3
Kasko . . . 102 B3
Káspakas . . . 85 D1
Kašperské Hory . . . 56 C1
Kassándra . . . 80 B4
Kassándras, Kólpos . . . 80 B4
Kassándria . . . 80 A4
Kassel . . . 52 A2
Kassiópi . . . 82 A1
Kassópi . . . 82 B2
Kássos, N . . . 93 D3
Kastaniá (Makedonía) . . . 79 E3
Kastaniá (Pelopónissos) . . . 87 D1
Kastaniá (Thessalia) . . . 82 C1
Kastaniá (Thessalia) . . . 83 D2
Kastaniés . . . 81 F1
Kastaniótissa . . . 83 F3
Kastéla . . . 84 B4
Kastélhoms . . . 106 C3
Kastéli (Kriti) . . . 90 B3
Kastéli (Kriti) . . . 91 E4
Kastellaun . . . 51 E4
Kastelórizo . . . 93 F2
Kastélou, Akr . . . 93 D3
Kastelruth . . . 59 D3
Kaštel Stari . . . 75 D1
Kaštel Žegarski . . . 75 D1
Kasterlee . . . 50 C3
Kastl . . . 55 F1
Kastóri . . . 87 D3
Kastoriá . . . 79 D3
Kastoriá (Nomos) . . . 78 C3
Kastoriás, L . . . 79 D3
Kastós, N . . . 82 C4
Kastráki (Kikládes) . . . 88 C3
Kastráki (Stereá Eláda) . . . 82 C3
Kastráki (Thessalia) . . . 83 D1
Kastrakíou, Teh L . . . 82 C3
Kastri (Pelopónissos) . . . 87 D2
Kastri (Stereá Eláda) . . . 83 E3
Kastri (Thessalia) . . . 83 F1
Kástro (Pelopónissos) . . . 86 B1
Kástro (Skiathos) . . . 84 A2
Kástro (Stereá Eláda) . . . 83 F4
Kastrossikiá . . . 82 B2
Katafígio . . . 79 E4
Katáfito . . . 80 B1
Katáfourko . . . 82 C3
Katahás . . . 79 F3
Katákolo . . . 86 B2
Katálako . . . 85 D1
Katáno, Akr . . . 88 A3
Katápola . . . 89 D3
Katára . . . 82 C1
Katastári . . . 86 A1
Katavia . . . 93 E2
Katelimátsa . . . 91 F1
Kateliós . . . 86 A1
Katerini . . . 79 F4
Katerloch . . . 57 E4
Katharó . . . 91 E4
Katheni . . . 84 B4
Katići . . . 76 C1
Kätkäsuvanto . . . 95 D4
Katlanovo . . . 77 D3
Katlanovska Banja . . . 77 E3
Katlenburg-Duhm . . . 52 B2
Káto Ahaïa . . . 86 B1
Káto Alissós . . . 86 B1
Káto Asséa . . . 87 D2
Káto Dolianá . . . 87 D2
Káto Figália . . . 86 C2
Káto Gadzéa . . . 83 F2
Katohí . . . 82 C4
Káto Kamíla . . . 80 B2
Káto Klinés . . . 79 D3
Káto Makrinoú . . . 83 D4
Katoméri, Akr . . . 88 C3

Káto Moussounitsa . . . 83 E3
Káto Nevrokópi . . . 80 B1
Káto Ólimbos . . . 83 E1
Káto Tithoréa . . . 83 E4
Katoúna (Lefkáda) . . . 82 B3
Katoúna (Stereá Eláda) . . . 82 C3
Káto Vassiliki . . . 83 D4
Káto Vérga . . . 86 C3
Káto Vérmio . . . 79 E3
Káto Vlassia . . . 86 C1
Katowice . . . 112 B2
Káto Zahlaroú . . . 86 C1
Káto Zákros . . . 91 F4
Katrineholm . . . 106 A4
Katschberg . . . 59 F2
Katschberg-Tunnel . . . 59 F2
Kattegat . . . 108 C2
Katwijk aan Zee . . . 16 B2
Kaub . . . 51 F4
Kaufbeuren . . . 55 E3
Kauhajärvi . . . 102 C2
Kauhajoki . . . 102 B3
Kauhaneva-Pohjankangas . . . 102 C3
Kauhava . . . 102 C2
Kaukonen . . . 95 E4
Kaunas . . . 110 C3
Kaupanger . . . 104 B1
Kaustinen . . . 102 C2
Kautokeino . . . 95 D3
Kautokeinoelva . . . 95 D3
Kauttua . . . 107 D2
Kavadarci . . . 77 E3
Kavajë . . . 76 C4
Kavála . . . 80 C2
Kavála (Nomos) . . . 80 C2
Kaválas, Kólpos . . . 80 C2
Kavarna . . . 115 E2
Kavili . . . 81 F1
Kavirio-Hlói . . . 81 E4
Kävlinge . . . 108 C3
Kávos . . . 82 A2
Kavoússi . . . 91 F4
Käylä . . . 99 E2
Kaysersberg . . . 27 E1
Kazan . . . 73 E2
Kažani . . . 77 E4
Kazanlâk . . . 115 D2
Kazárma . . . 86 C3
Kazimierz Dolny . . . 112 C2
Kazincbarcika . . . 112 B3
Kdyně . . . 56 B1
Kéa . . . 88 A2
Keadew . . . 12 C2
Keady . . . 13 D2
Keähkkiljohka . . . 95 D3
Keal, L na . . . 4 B1
Kéa Meriá . . . 88 A2
Kéa, N . . . 88 A2
Kebnekaise . . . 94 B4
Kebnekaise Mt . . . 94 B4
Kebock Head . . . 2 B2
Kecskemét . . . 112 B4
Kédainiai . . . 110 C3
Kédros . . . 83 D2
Kędzierzyn-Koźle . . . 112 B2
Keel . . . 12 A2
Keerbergen . . . 50 C3
Kefalári . . . 87 D2
Kefálas, Akr . . . 80 C3
Kefáli, Akr . . . 90 A2
Kefaloniá, N . . . 82 B4
Kefálos . . . 89 F4
Kéfalos, Akr . . . 88 C3
Kefalóvrisso (Ípiros) . . . 78 C4
Kefalóvrisso (Pelopónissos) . . . 86 C2
Kefalóvrisso (Stereá Eláda) . . . 82 C3
Kefalóvrisso (Thessalia) . . . 83 D1
Keflavík . . . 96 A2
Kehl . . . 54 C3
Kehlstein . . . 56 C4
Kehrókambos . . . 80 C2
Kéhros . . . 81 D2
Keighlëy . . . 6 C2
Keimaneigh, Pass of . . . 14 B4

Keitele . . . 103 D2
Keitele L . . . 103 D2
Keith . . . 3 D3
Kéla . . . 79 D2
Kelankylä . . . 99 E3
Kelberg . . . 51 E4
Kelbra . . . 52 C2
Këlcyrë . . . 114 C4
Kelebija . . . 72 B1
Kelefá . . . 87 D4
Kelheim . . . 55 F2
Kellinghusen . . . 48 A2
Kellojärvi . . . 99 F4
Kellokoski . . . 107 E2
Kells . . . 13 D3
Kelso . . . 5 E1
Kelujärvi . . . 95 E4
Kemberg . . . 53 D1
Kembs . . . 27 E1
Kemi . . . 99 D3
Kemihaara . . . 95 F4
Kemijärvi . . . 99 E2
Kemijärvi L . . . 99 E2
Kemijoki . . . 99 D3
Keminmaa . . . 99 D3
Kemiö . . . 107 D3
Kemnath . . . 53 D4
Kempele . . . 99 D4
Kempen . . . 17 D4
Kempenich . . . 51 E4
Kempten . . . 55 E4
Kendal . . . 6 B1
Kéndras, Akr . . . 88 B3
Kendrikó . . . 79 F2
Kenilworth . . . 9 E1
Kenmare . . . 14 A4
Kenmare River . . . 14 A4
Kennacraig . . . 4 B2
Kenoúrgio . . . 83 D3
Kent . . . 11 D3
Kentallen . . . 4 B1
Kenzingen . . . 54 C3
Keramía . . . 85 F2
Keramidi . . . 83 F2
Keramítsa . . . 82 B1
Kéramos . . . 85 E4
Keramoti . . . 81 D2
Kerassiá (Évia) . . . 84 A3
Kerassiá (Thessalia) . . . 83 F2
Kerassiés . . . 79 E2
Kerassohóri . . . 83 D3
Kerassóna . . . 82 C2
Kérata, Akr . . . 83 F3
Keratéa . . . 87 F2
Kerava . . . 107 E2
Kerdília, N . . . 80 B3
Kérës . . . 72 C1
Keri . . . 86 A2
Kerimäki . . . 103 F3
Kerken . . . 17 D3
Kerketéas, Óros . . . 89 E1
Kerkétio, Óri . . . 83 D2
Kerkini, Óros . . . 80 A1
Kerkíni, L . . . 80 A2
Kérkira . . . 82 A1
Kérkira, N . . . 82 A1
Kerkonkoski . . . 103 D2
Kerkrade . . . 51 D3
Kernascléden . . . 22 B3
Kéros, N . . . 88 C3
Kerpen . . . 17 D4
Kerrera . . . 4 B1
Kerry . . . 14 B3
Kerry Head . . . 14 A3
Kerteminde . . . 108 B3
Kértezi . . . 86 C1
Kerzers . . . 27 E2
Kesälahti . . . 103 F3
Keşan . . . 115 E3
Kesch, Piz . . . 58 B3
Kesh . . . 12 C2
Keski-Suomen Lääni . . . 103 D2
Kessariani . . . 87 F1
Kestilä . . . 99 D4
Keswick . . . 5 D4
Keszthely . . . 112 A4
Kętrzyn . . . 110 B4
Kettering . . . 9 F1
Kettletoft . . . 3 E1
Kettwig . . . 17 E4
Ketzin . . . 49 D4
Keukenhof . . . 16 B2
Keurusselkä . . . 103 D3

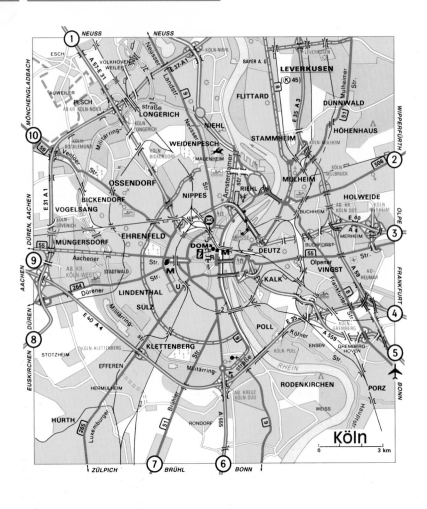

Köln

Kikinda 72 C1
Kikládes.......... 88 B2
Kil 105 E3
Kila 79 D3
Kiláda (Makedonia) 79 E3
Kiláda
  (Pelopónissos) .. 87 E2
Kilafors 101 F4
Kilbaha 12 A4
Kilbeggan 12 C4
Kilbirnie 4 C2
Kilboghamn 97 E2
Kilbotn 94 B3
Kilbrannan Sd. 4 B2
Kilchoan 2 B4
Kilcock 13 D4
Kilcormac 12 C4
Kilcreggan 4 C2
Kilcullen 13 D4
Kildare 13 D4
Kildare (Co) 13 D4
Kildorrery 14 C3
Kilfenora 12 B4
Kilgarvan 14 B4
Kilija 113 E4
Kilingi-Nõmme 110 C2
Kilíni 86 B1
Kilíni, Óros. 87 D1
Kilkee 12 A4
Kilkeel 13 E3
Kilkenny 15 D3
Kilkenny (Co) 15 D3
Kilkhampton 8 B3
Kilkieran B. 12 A3
Kilkis 79 F2
Kilkís (Nomos) 79 F2
Killadysert 12 B4
Killala B. 12 B4
Killaloe 12 B4
Killarney 14 B4
Killashandra 12 C3
Killenaule 14 C3
Killimer 12 B4

Killin 4 C1
Killinkoski 102 C3
Killorglin 14 A3
Killybegs 12 C2
Killyleagh 13 E2
Kilmaine 12 B3
Kilmallock 14 B3
Kilmarnock 4 C2
Kilmartin 4 B2
Kilmore Quay. 15 D4
Kilmurry 12 B4
Kilninver 4 B1
Kilnsea 7 E2
Kilpisjärvi 94 C3
Kilpisjärvi L 94 C3
Kilrea 13 D1
Kilronan 12 B4
Kilrush 12 B4
Kilsyth 4 C2
Kiltamagh 12 B3
Kiltealy 15 D3
Kilwinning 4 C2
Kílyos 115 F3
Kimássi 84 A3
Kiméria 81 D2
Kimi 84 B3
Kimina 79 F3
Kimis, Órmos 84 B4
Kimísseos
  Theotókou 87 D2
Kimito 107 D3
Kimolos 88 B4
Kimolos, N. 88 B4
Kimólou Sifnou,
  Stenó 88 B3
Kimry 111 F2
Kimstad 105 F4
Kinaros, N. 89 D3
Kinbrace 3 D2
Kindberg 57 E3
Kindelbrück 52 C2
Kinéta 87 E1
Kingisepp 111 D1

Kingissepp 110 B2
Kingsbridge 8 C4
Kingscourt 13 D3
King's Lynn 7 E3
Kingston 9 F2
Kingston-upon-
  Hull 7 E2
Kingswear 8 C4
Kington 9 D1
Kingussie 3 D4
Kinira. 81 D3
Kinlochbervie 2 C2
Kinlochewe 2 C3
Kinloch Rannoch ... 4 C1
Kinna 108 C1
Kinnairds Head 3 E3
Kinnasniemi 103 F2
Kinnegad 13 D3
Kinnitty 12 C4
Kinnula 103 D2
Kinross 5 D2
Kinsale 14 B4
Kinsarvik 104 B2
Kintaus 103 D3
Kintore 3 E4
Kintyre 4 B2
Kinvarra 12 B4
Kióni 82 B4
Kiparissí 87 E3
Kiparissía 86 C3
Kiparissiakós
  Kólpos 86 B3
Kiparissías, Óri .. 86 C3
Kipárissos 83 E2
Kipi (Ípiros) 78 C4
Kipi (Thráki) 81 F2
Kipina 99 D3
Kipos, Akr. 81 E3
Kippure 13 D4
Kipséli 83 E2
Kir. 76 C2
Kirá Panagiá, N .. 84 B2

Kirchbach 57 E4
Kirchberg (Nieder-
  österreich) 57 E2
Kirchberg
  (Rheinland-Pfalz). 54 B1
Kirchberg
  (Sachsen) 53 D3
Kirchberg (Tirol) .. 59 E1
Kirchberg an der
  Pielach 57 E3
Kirchdorf. 57 D3
Kirchenlamitz 53 D4
Kirchenthumbach .. 53 D4
Kirchhain 52 A3
Kirchheim (Baden-
  Württemberg) ... 55 D2
Kirchheim
  (Hessen) 52 B3
Kirchheimbolanden 54 C1
Kirchheim unter
  Teck 55 D2
Kirchhundem 17 F4
Kirchlengern 17 F2
Kirchmöser 49 D4
Kirchschlag 57 E3
Kiriaki 81 F1
Kiriáki 83 F4
Kiriš 111 E1
Kırkağaç 115 E4
Kirkby Lonsdale 6 C1
Kirkby Stephen 5 E4
Kirkcaldy 5 D2
Kirkcolm 4 B3
Kirkcudbright....... 4 C3
Kirkenær 105 D2
Kirkenes 95 F2
Kirkeøy 105 D4
Kirkestinden 94 B3
Kirkham 6 B2
Kirki 81 E2
Kirkintilloch 4 C2
Kirkjubøur 96 A4
Kirkkonummi...... 107 E2
Kırklareli 115 E3

Kirkonmaanselkä .. 103 F4
Kirkwall 3 E1
Kirn 54 B1
Kirov 111 F3
Kirovohrad 113 F2
Kirovsk 111 D1
Kirriemuir 5 D1
Kirtorf 52 A3
Kiruna 94 C4
Kisa 109 E1
Kisac 72 C2
Kiseljak (Loznica) .. 72 B3
Kiseljak (Sarajevo) .. 75 F2
Kiseljak (Tuzla). .. 71 F3
Kisko 107 E3
Kiskőrös........... 112 B4
Kiskunfélegyháza .. 112 B4
Kiskunhalas....... 114 B1
Kissámou, Kólpos .. 90 B3
Kißlegg 55 E4
Kissoú Kámbos .. 90 C4
Kistanje 75 D1
Kisúujszállás 112 B4
Kisvárda 112 C3
Kita 87 D4
Kitee 103 F3
Kithira 90 A2
Kithira, N. 90 A2
Kithnos............ 88 A2
Kithnos, N. 88 A2
Kithnou, Stenó 88 A2
Kitinen 95 E4
Kitka 99 E2
Kitriés, Akr. 86 C3
Kittilä 95 E4
Kittsee 57 F2
Kitzbühel 59 E1
Kitzingen 55 E1
Kiukainen 107 D2
Kiuruvesi 103 D1
Kiutaköngäs 99 E2
Kivalo 99 D3
Kivéri 87 D2
Kivi 88 B2
Kivijärvi 103 D2
Kivijärvi L (Keski-Suomen
  Lääni) 103 D2
Kivijärvi L
  (Kymen-Lääni) .. 103 E4
Kivilahti 103 F2
Kivitaipale 99 D3
Kivotós 79 D4
Kizário 81 E2

Klimpfjäll 97 E4
Klin 111 F2
Klina 76 C2
Klinča Selo......... 70 C2
Klincy 111 E4
Klingenbach 57 F3
Klingenthal 53 D3
Klinovec 53 E3
Klintehamn 109 E4
Klippan 108 C3
Klippen 97 E3
Klippitztörl 57 D4
Klis 75 D1
Klissoúra 79 D3
Klisura
  (Makedonija) 77 F3
Klisura (Srbija) ... 77 E1
Klitoria 86 C1
Klitten 53 F2
Klixbüll 47 F1
Kljajićevo 72 B2
Ključ 71 E3
Kłodzko 112 A2
Kløfta 105 D3
Klokkarvik 104 A2
Klokočevac 73 F3
Klos 76 C4
Kloštar 71 D2
Kloštar Ivanić 71 D2
Klösterle 58 B2
Klosterneuburg 57 F2
Klosters 58 B2
Kloten 58 A4
Klötze 48 C4
Klöverträsk 98 B3
Klövsjö 101 E3
Kluczbork 112 A2
Klupe 71 E3
Klütz 48 B2
Knapdale 4 B2
Knappogue Castle . 12 B4
Knäred 109 D2
Knaresborough 6 C1
Knarvik 104 A2
Kneginec 71 D1
Kneža 115 D2
Knežak 70 B3
Kneževi Vinogradi . 71 F2
Kneževo 71 F2
Knežica 71 D3
Knežina 72 B4
Knić 73 D4
Knídi 79 D4
Knighton 9 D1
Knight's Town 14 A4
Knin 75 D1
Knittelfeld 57 D4
Knivskjellodden ... 95 D1
Knivsta 106 B3
Knjaževac 73 F4
Knockmealdown
  Mts. 14 C3
Knokke-Heist 50 A3
Knole House 10 C3
Knossós 91 D3
Knutsford 6 C2
Koarvikodds 95 E3
Kobarid 70 A2
Kobbfjorden 95 D1
Kobel'aki 113 F2
Kobern-Gondorf ... 51 E4
Kobišnica 73 F3
Koblenz 51 E4
Kobrin 112 C1
Koca D 115 F3
Kočani 77 E2
Koceljevo 72 C3
Kočerin 75 E2
Kočevje 70 B2
Kočevski rog 70 B2
Kochel 56 A4
Kocher 55 E2
Kodiksami 107 D2
Kodisjoki 107 D2
Köflach 57 E4
Køge 108 C3
Køge Bugt. 108 C3
Kohtla-Järve 110 C1
Koikkala 103 E3
Koirakoski 103 E1
Koitajoki 103 F2
Koitelainen 95 E4
Koitere 103 F2

Koivujärvi 103 D1
Koivusuo 103 F2
Kokála 87 D4
Kökar 106 C3
Kokári 89 E1
Kökarsfjärden 106 C3
Kokemäenjoki 107 D1
Kokemäki 107 D2
Kokin Brod 76 B3
Kökino Neró........ 83 F1
Kokkola 102 C2
Kokoti 83 D2
Koksijde-Bad 50 A3
Kola 71 E3
Koláka 83 F4
Kolari (SF) 98 C1
Kolari (Srbija) 73 D3
Kolåsen 101 D1
Kolašin 76 B2
Kolbäck 105 F3
Kołbacz. 49 F2
Kołbaskowo 49 E2
Kolbermoor 56 B3
Kolby Kås 108 B3
Kolding 108 A3
Kolho 103 D3
Koli 103 F2
Kolima 103 D2
Kolimvári 90 B3
Kolín 112 A3
Kolindrós 79 E3
Kolines 87 D3
Kolka 110 B2
Kolkanlahti 103 D2
Kolkasrags 110 B2
Kölleda 52 C2
Kolmården 106 A4
Köln 17 E4
Koło 112 B1
Kołobrzeg 49 F1
Koločep 75 F2
Kolomyja 113 D3
Koloveč 56 B1
Kolovrat 76 B1
Kolpino 111 D1
Kolsva 105 F3
Kolubara 72 C3
Kolvereid 97 D4
Komagfjord 95 D2
Kómanos 79 D3
Komar 71 E4
Kómara 81 F1
Komarnica 76 B2
Komárno 112 B4
Kómbóti 82 C2
Koméno 82 C3
Kómi (Kikládes) ... 88 B2
Kómi (Híos) 89 D1
Komílio 82 B3
Komin 70 C2
Kómito 88 B1
Komiža 75 D2
Komló 114 B1
Komninádes 78 C3
Komniná
  (Makedonia) 79 D3
Komniná (Thráki) .. 81 D2
Komorane 77 D2
Komotiní 81 E2
Komovi. 76 B2
Komulanköngäs ... 99 E2
Konak 73 D2
Konakovo 111 F2
Končanica 71 D2
Kondiás 85 D1
Kondopoúli 85 D1
Kondós, Akr. 88 B3
Kondovázena 86 C1
Kondrić 71 F2
Konecka pl 77 E3
Køng 108 C4
Köngernheim 54 C1
Konginkangas 103 D2
Kongsberg 104 C3
Kongselva 94 A3
Kongsfjord 95 F1
Kongsvinger 105 D3
Kœnigsbourg 27 E1
Königsbrück 53 E2
Königsbrunn 55 F3
Königsfeld 54 C3
Königslutter 52 B1
Königsschlösser ... 55 F4

Königssee 56 C4
Königssee L 56 C4
Königstein (Hessen) . 51 F4
Königstein (Sachsen) ... 53 F2
Königswiesen 57 D2
Königswinter 51 E3
Königs-Wusterhausen 49 E4
Konin 112 A1
Koniskós 83 D1
Konístres 84 B4
Kónitsa 78 C4
Konj 75 E1
Konjevrate 75 D1
Konjic 75 F1
Konjsko 76 A2
Konjuh 71 F4
Konkämäälven 94 C3
Könnern 52 C2
Konnevesi 103 D2
Konnevesi L 103 D2
Könönpelto 103 E3
Konopište 77 E3
Konotop 113 F1
Konsko 77 F4
Konsmo 104 B4
Konstantinovy Lázně . 53 E4
Konstanz 55 D4
Kontich 50 B3
Kontiolahti 103 F2
Kontiomäki 99 E4
Konttajärvi 98 C2
Konz 54 A1
Kopaída 83 F4
Kopáni 82 C2
Kopanós 79 E3
Kopaonik 77 D1
Koparnes 100 A2
Kópasker 96 C1
Köpenick 49 E4
Koper 70 A3
Kopervik 104 A3
Köping 105 F3
Köpingsvik 109 E2
Koplik 76 B3
Köpmanholmen... 102 A2
Koporiče 77 D1
Koppang 100 C3
Kopparberg 105 F3
Kopparbergs Län . 105 E2
Kopparleden 101 E2
Kopperby 48 A1
Kopperveien ... 100 D3
Koprivna 71 F3
Koprivnica (BH) ... 71 D1
Koprivnica (Srbija) . 73 F3
Korab 77 D3
Kórakas, Akr. 88 C3
Koralpe 70 B1
Korana 70 C3
Korbach 52 A2
Korbevac 77 E2
Korbovo 73 F2
Korçë 114 C3
Korčula 75 E2
Korčula I 75 E2
Korčulanski kan. .. 75 E2
Korensko sedlo .. 70 A1
Kórfos 87 E2
Korgåsen 95 F2
Korgen 97 E3
Koria 107 F2
Korifássi 86 C3
Korikio Ándro ... 83 E4
Kórimvos 81 F1
Korini 83 F4
Korinós 79 F4
Korinthia 87 D1
Korinthiakós Kólpos .. 87 D1
Kórinthos 87 E1

Korissía 88 A2
Korissós 79 D3
Korita (BH) 76 A2
Korita (Crna Gora) .. 76 B2
Korita (Mljet) 75 F2
Korithi 86 A1
Koritnik 76 C1
Koritnik, M. 77 D3
Korkeakangas ... 103 F3
Korkeakoski 103 D2
Körmend 112 A4
Kornat 74 C1
Kornati 74 C1
Korneuburg 57 F2
Kornofoléa 81 F2
Kornwestheim 55 D2
Koróna 79 F2
Koróni 86 C4
Korónia 83 F4
Korónia, L 80 A3
Koronída 88 C3
Koronissia 82 C3
Kóronos 88 C3
Koronoúda 80 A2
Koropí 87 F1
Körös 112 B4
Korosten' 113 E2
Korostyšiv 113 E2
Korouoma 99 E2
Korpilahti 103 D3
Korpilombolo ... 98 C2
Korpo 107 D3
Korppoo 107 D3
Korsberga 109 E2
Korsfjorden 104 A2
Korsholm 102 B2
Korsnäs 102 B2
Korsør 108 B4
Korsun'-Ševčenkivs'kyj . 113 F2
Korsvoll 100 B2
Kortesjärvi 102 C2
Kórthio 88 B2
Kortrijk 50 A3
Kortteenperä ... 99 D2
Korvala 99 D2
Korvaluoma ... 102 C3
Korvatunturi ... 95 F3
Kos 89 F3
Kosančić 77 D1
Kosanica 76 B1
Kościan 112 A2
Kościerzyna ... 110 A4
Kosel 77 D4
Koserow 49 E1
Košice 112 C3
Kosjerić 72 C4
Koška 71 F2
Koskenkorva ... 102 B2
Koskenpää 103 D3
Koski (Hameen Lääni) 107 E2
Koski (Turun ja Porin Lääni) 107 D2
Kóskina 84 B4
Koskue 102 C3
Kosmaj 73 D3
Kosmás 87 D3
Kósmio 81 E2
Kos, N 89 F3
Kosovo 77 D2
Kosovo Polje ... 77 D2
Kosovska Kamenica 77 D2
Kössen 59 E1
Kósta 87 E3
Kostajnica 71 D3
Kostanjevac ... 70 C2
Kostanjevica .. 70 C2
Kostenec 115 D3
Koster 105 D4
Kostolac. 73 D3
Kostonjärvi ... 99 E3

Kostopil' 113 D2
Kóstos 88 C3
Kostrzyn 49 F4
Kosturino 77 F3
Kosula 103 E2
Koszalin 110 A4
Kőszeg 112 A4
Kotala (Keski-Suomen Lääni) 102 C3
Kotala (Lapin Lääni) . 99 E1
Kótas 79 D3
Kotel 115 E2
Köthen 53 D1
Kotka 103 F4
Kotor 76 B3
Kotoriba 71 D1
Kotorsko 71 F3
Kotor Varoš ... 71 E4
Kotovs'k 113 E3
Kotraža 73 D4
Kótronas 87 D4
Kotroniá 81 F2
Kötschach-Mauthen . 59 E2
Kőttsjön 101 F2
Kötzting 56 B1
Koufália 79 F3
Koufonísi (Kikládes) .. 88 C3
Koufonísi (Kriti) ... 91 F4
Koufós 80 B4
Kouklií 82 B1
Koukounariés ... 84 A2
Koúla 81 D1
Kouméika 89 E2
Koúndouros ... 88 A2
Kounoupéli 86 B1
Koura 102 C2
Koúrenda 82 B1
Kourkouli 84 A3
Kournás 90 C3
Kouroúta 86 B2
Koutselió 82 C1
Koutsó 81 D2
Koutsóhero ... 83 E1
Kouvola 107 F2
Kovačica 72 C2
Kovel' 112 C2
Kovero 73 D3
Kovin 73 D3
Köyliö 107 D2
Kozáni 79 D3
Kozáni 79 D3
Kozara 71 D3
Kozarac (BH) ... 71 D3
Kozarac (HR) ... 71 F2
Kožel'sk 111 F3
Kozica 75 E2
Kozina 70 A3
Kozjak 77 E4
Kozjatyn ... 113 E2
Kozluk 72 B3
Kožuf 77 F4
Kragenæs 108 B4
Kragerø 104 C4
Kragujevac ... 73 D4
Krajišnik 73 D2
Krajkovac 77 D1
Krakhella 104 A1
Krajn 76 C3
Krajnik Dln. ... 49 E3
Krakow 48 C2
Kraków 112 B2
Kraljaca Sutjeska. 71 F4
Kraljevica 70 B3
Kraljevo 73 D4
Kralovice 53 E4
Kralupy 53 F3
Kramfors 101 F2
Kranenburg ... 17 D3
Krani 77 E4
Kraniá Elassónas ... 79 E4

Kraniá (Makedonía) ... 79 D4
Kraniá (Thessalía) ... 82 C1
Kranichfeld 52 C3
Kranidi 87 E2
Kranj 70 A2
Kranjska Gora ... 70 A1
Krapina 70 C2
Krapinske Toplice .. 70 C2
Krašić 70 C2
Kráslava 111 D3
Kraslice 53 D3
Krasná Lipa 53 F2
Kraśnik 112 C2
Krasno Polje ... 70 C4
Krasnyj Cholm ... 111 F1
Krasnystaw ... 112 C2
Kráthio 87 D1
Krátigos 85 F3
Kratovo 77 E2
Kratovska-Stena .. 72 C4
Krauchenwies ... 55 D3
Krautheim 55 D1
Kravarsko 70 C2
Krefeld 17 D4
Kremasti (Pelopónissos) . 87 E3
Kremasti (Ródos) .. 93 F1
Kremastón, Teh L. . 83 D3
Kremenčuc'ke Vodoschovyšče . 113 F2
Kremenčuk 113 F2
Kremenec' ... 113 D2
Kremidi, Akr. 87 E4
Kremmen 49 D3
Kremna 72 C4
Kremnica 112 B3
Krems 57 E2
Kremsmünster ... 57 D3
Krepoljin 73 E3
Kreševo 75 F1
Krestcy 111 E1
Kréstena 86 B2
Kreuth 56 A4
Kreuzbergpass ... 59 E2
Kreuzlingen 58 A1
Kreuztal 17 F4
Kría Vríssi (Évia) .. 84 A3
Kría Vríssi (Makedonía) . 79 E3
Krikelo 83 D3
Krikelos 82 C3
Krikelos, Akr. ... 89 F4
Kriós, Akr. 90 B4
Krionéri (Makedonía) ... 80 A2
Krionéri (Pelopónissos) . 86 C3
Krionéri (Pelopónissos) . 87 D1
Kriopigi 80 B4
Kristalopigí ... 78 C3
Kristdala 109 E2
Kristiansand ... 104 B4
Kristianstad ... 109 D3
Kristianstads Län . 109 D3
Kristiansund ... 100 B2
Kristiinankaupunki . 102 B3
Kristineberg . 98 A4
Kristinehamn ... 105 E4
Kristinestad ... 102 B3
Krithéa 79 F2
Krithina, Óros ... 87 E4
Kritikó Pélagos ... 90 B2

Kriti, N. 91 E3
Kritinía 93 E1
Kritsá 91 E4
Kriva Feja 77 E2
Krivaja (BH) 71 F4
Krivaja (Vojvodina) .. 72 B1
Kriva Palanka ... 77 E2
Kriva reka 77 E2
Krivogaštani ... 77 E4
Krivolak 77 E3
Križanov 57 E1
Križevci 71 D2
Križište 75 E2
Krk 70 B3
Krk I 70 B3
Krka 70 B2
Krka R 75 D1
Krkonoše 112 A2
Krmčine 74 C1
Krn 70 A2
Krnjača 72 C3
Krnjak 70 C3
Krnjeuša 71 D4
Krnjevo 73 D3
Krnov 112 A3
Krnovo 76 B2
Krøderen 104 C2
Krokeés 87 D3
Krokeide 104 A2
Krokek 106 A4
Krokilio. 83 D4
Krokom 101 E2
Krókos 79 E4
Kroksjö 98 A4
Krolevec 113 F1
Kröller Müller ... 17 D3
Kromeříž ... 112 A3
Kronach 52 C4
Kronobergs Län . 109 D2
Kronoby 102 C1
Kronshagen ... 48 A1
Kronštadt ... 111 D1
Kröpelin 48 C2
Kropp 48 A1
Kroppenstedt ... 52 C1
Krosno 112 C3
Krosno Odrzańskie . 53 F1
Krotoszyn ... 112 A2
Kroussónas ... 91 D4
Kroviíj, Pal. ... 81 E2
Krrabe, M. 76 C3
Krško 70 C2
Krstac 76 A2
Krstača 76 C2
Krstinja 70 C3
Kruë i Fushës ... 76 C3
Kruiningen 16 B4
Krujë 76 C4
Krumbach 55 E3
Krumpendorf ... 70 A1
Krün 55 F4
Krupà 53 E4
Krupac (BH) ... 75 F1
Krupac (Crna Gora) 76 B2
Krupac (Srbija) ... 77 E1
Krupaja 73 E3
Krupa na Vrbasu . 71 E4
Krupanj 72 C3
Krupište 77 E3
Krupka 53 E3
Kruså 108 A4
Kruščica 71 E4
Kruščica, Jezero . 70 C4
Kruševac 73 E4
Kruševica 73 D3
Kruševo 77 E4
Krute 76 B3
Kruunupyy ... 102 C1
Krvavec 70 B2
Krynica 112 B3
Kryvyj Rih ... 113 F3
Krzeszyce 49 F4

Kteniás, Óros ... 87 D2
Ktísmata 82 B1
Kubitzer Bodden . 49 D1
Küblis 58 B2
Kučaj 73 E4
Kučevište 77 D2
Kučevo 73 E3
Kuchl 59 E1
Kučina Kosa ... 71 D4
Kućište 76 C2
Kudowa-Zdrój ... 112 A2
Kufstein 59 D1
Kühlungsborn ... 48 C2
Kuhmalahti ... 103 D3
Kuhmo 99 F4
Kuhmoinen ... 103 D3
Kuivajoki 99 D3
Kuivajärvi 99 F4
Kuivalahti 107 D2
Kuivaniemi ... 99 D3
Kuivasjärvi ... 102 C3
Kuivi 95 E2
Kuk. 70 C4
Kukavica 77 E1
Kukës 76 C3
Kukkia 107 E1
Kukko 102 C2
Kukujevci ... 72 B2
Kukulje 71 E3
Kula (BG) ... 114 C2
Kula (TR) ... 115 F4
Kula (Vojvodina) ... 72 B2
Kuldiga 110 B3
Kulen Vakuf ... 71 D4
Kulina 73 E4
Kulju 107 E1
Kulkjica 74 C1
Kullaa 107 D1
Kulm 27 F2
Kulmbach ... 52 C4
Kuloharju 99 E2
Külsheim 55 D1
Kultakero 99 E1
Kultsjön 97 E4
Kum 70 B2
Kumane 72 C2
Kumanovo ... 77 E2
Kumla 105 F4
Kumlinge 106 C2
Kummavuopio . 94 C3
Kummerower See . 49 D2
Kumputunturi . 95 E4
Kumrovec ... 70 C2
Kungälv ... 108 C1
Kungsbacka ... 108 C1
Kungshamn ... 105 D4
Kungsör ... 105 F3
Kunoy 96 A3
Kunrau 48 B4
Kunszentmárton . 112 B4
Künzelsau 55 D2
Kuolimo 103 E2
Kuolio 99 E3
Kuopio ... 103 E2
Kuopion Lääni . 103 E2
Kuorboaivi ... 95 E2
Kuorevesi ... 103 D3
Kuortane 102 C2
Kuortti 103 D3
Kupa 70 B3
Kupa 70 C3
Kupferzell 55 D2
Kupinova Glava . 73 E3
Kupinovo ... 72 C3
Kupres 75 E1
Kupreška vrata . 75 E1
Kurfar 59 D3
Kurikka 102 B2
Kuřim 57 F1
Kuršėnai ... 110 C3

Kuršskij Zaliv. 110 B3
Kursu 99 E2
Kuršumlija 77 D1
Kuršumlijska Banja . 77 D1
Kurtakko 95 D4
Kuru 102 C3
Kusadak 73 D3
Kuşadasi 115 E4
Kusel 54 B1
Küsnacht 58 A2
Küssnacht 58 A2
Kustavi 107 D2
Küstenkanal ... 17 E1
Kütahya 115 F3
Kutina 71 D2
Kutjevo 71 E2
Kutná-Hora ... 112 A3
Kutno 112 B1
Kuttanen 95 D3
Kuttura 95 E3
Kúty 57 F2
Kuumu 99 F4
Kuusamo 99 E3
Kuusamojärvi ... 99 F2
Kuusankoski ... 107 F2
Kuusjärvi ... 103 E2
Kuusjoki ... 107 E2
Kuvšinovo ... 111 E2
Kuzma 70 C1
Kuzmin 72 B3
Kvæfjord 94 A3
Kvaløy 94 B2
Kvaløya 95 D1
Kvalsund 95 D1
Kvalvåg 100 B2
Kvam 100 C3
Kvænangen ... 94 C2
Kvænangsbotn... 95 D2
Kvanndal ... 104 B2
Kvanne 100 B2
Kvarner 70 B4
Kvarnerič ... 70 B4
Kvernes 100 B2
Kvevlax. 102 B2
Kvikkjokk ... 98 A2
Kvikne 100 C2
Kvina 104 B4
Kvinesdal. ... 104 B4
Kvinesdal V. ... 104 B4
Kvisvik 100 B2
Kviteseid ... 104 B3
Kvitnes 100 B2
Kvitsøy 104 A3
Kwidzyn 110 B4
Kyïv 113 E2
Kyïvs'ke Vodoschovyšče . 113 E2
Kyjov 57 F1
Kyläinpää ... 102 B2
Kylänlahti ... 103 F1
Kyleakin 2 B3
Kyle of Lochalsh ... 2 B3
Kyle of Tongue ... 2 C2
Kylerhea 2 B3
Kylestrome ... 2 C2
Kyll 51 D4
Kyllburg 51 D4
Kylmäkoski ... 107 E2
Kylmälä 99 D4
Kymen Lääni . 103 F4
Kynsivesi ... 103 D3
Kyritz 49 D3
Kyrksæterøra ... 100 C2
Kyrkslätt ... 107 E3
Kyrönjoki ... 102 C2
Kyrösjärvi ... 102 C3
Kyselka 53 E3
Kyšice 53 F4
Kyyjärvi ... 102 C2
Kyyvesi ... 103 E3

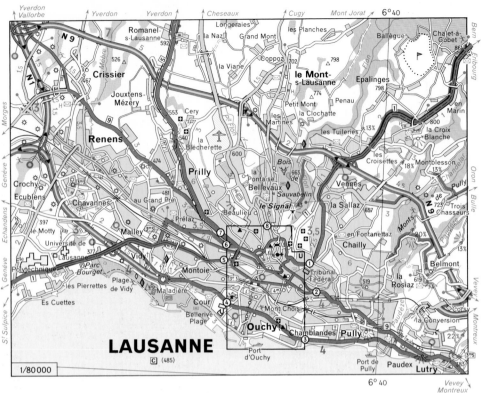

L

Laa an der Thaya 57 F2
La Adrada 39 F2
Laage 48 C2
Laakajärvi 103 E1
La Alberca 39 E2
La Alberca de
  Záncara 40 C3
La Albergueria de
  Argañán 39 D2
La Albuera 38 C4
La Alcarria 40 C2
La Algaba 43 D2
La Almarcha 40 C3
La Almunia de Doña
  Godina 36 C4
La Antillas 42 C3
La Azohía 45 D3
Labacolla 34 A2
La Baells, Emb de . . . 32 A3
Labajos 40 A1
La Bañeza 35 D3
La Barca de la
  Florida 43 D3
Labasheeda 12 B4
Labastida 36 B2
Labastide-
  Clairence 28 A4
Labastide-Murat 29 D2
Labastide-
  Rouairoux 32 B1
Labe 53 F3
Labin 70 A3
Labinot Fushë 76 C4
La Bisbal de Falset . . 37 E4
La Bisbal
  d'Empordà 32 B3
Laboe 48 A1
Labouheyre 28 A3
Labouret, Col du 31 D3
La Bóveda de Toro . . 35 D4
La Brède 28 B2
Labrit 28 B3
Labruguière 32 B1
Labudnjača 72 B2
Laç 76 C4
La Cabrera 40 B1
Lacalahorra 44 B3
La Campana 43 E2
Lacanau 28 A2
Lacanau-Océan 28 A2
Lacapelle-Marival . . . 29 D2

Laćarak 72 B3
La Carlota 43 E2
La Carolina 44 A1
Lacaune 32 B1
Lacaune, Mts de 32 B1
La Cava 41 F2
La Cazada de
  Oropesa 39 E3
Lacedonia 64 C3
Läckö 105 E4
Lac Lêman 27 E3
La Codosera 38 C3
Laconi 66 B3
La Coronada 39 E4
La Coruña 34 B1
Lacq 28 B4
La Cumbre 39 E3
La Espina 35 D1
Ladbergen 17 E2
Ládi 81 F1
Ladispoli 63 E2
Ladoeiro 38 C3
Ladožskoje
  Ozero 111 D1
Láerma 93 E2
La Felguera 35 D1
Laferté 27 D1
Laffrey 30 C2
Láfka 87 D1
Láfkos 83 F2
Lafnitz 57 F4
La Font de la
  Figuera 45 D1
La Franca 35 E1
Lafrançaise 29 D3
La Fregeneda 39 D1
La Frontera 40 C2
La Fuente de San
  Esteban 39 D1
Lagan 109 D2
Lagan R 109 D2
Laganá, Kólpos 86 A2
Laganás 86 A2
Lagarfljót 96 C2
La Garganta 34 C1
La Garriga 32 B4
Lagartera 39 E3
Lagastrello, Pso di . . . 60 B3
Lagen 100 C3
Lågen
  (Buskerud) 104 C3
Lågen
  (Oppland) 100 C3

Laggan 2 C4
Laggan, L 2 C4
Laginá
  (Makedonía) 79 F3
Laginá (Thráki) 81 F2
La Jonquera 32 B3
La Gineta 40 C4
Lagnieu 26 C4
Lagny 19 F4
Lago 67 E3
Lagoa 42 A2
Lagoaça 34 C4
Lagonegro 65 D4
Lagonissi 87 F2
Lagos 42 A2
Lágos 81 D2
Łagów 49 F4
La Granjuela 43 E1
Lagrasse 32 B2
Laguardia 36 B2
La Guardia 40 B3
La Guardia de Jaén . . 44 A2
Laguarres 37 E3
Laguarta 37 E2
Laguiole 29 E2
Laguna de Duero 35 E4
Lahanás 80 A2
La Hermida 35 E2
La Herradura 44 A4
Lahinch 12 B4
Lahn 17 F4
Lahnstein 51 E4
Laholm 108 C2
Laholmsbukten 108 C2
La Horcajada 39 E2
La Horra 35 F4
Lahr 54 C3
Lahti 107 F2
Laichingen 55 D3
Laide 2 B3
La Iglesuela del Cid . . 41 E2
Laignes 26 B1
Laigueglia 31 F3
Laihia 102 B2
Laïliás 80 B2
Laimbach 57 D2
Laimoluokta 94 C3
Lainate 60 A1
Lainioälven 95 D4
Laïrg 2 C2
Laissac 29 E3
Laïsta 78 C4
Laisvall 97 F3
Laitikkala 107 E2
Laitila 107 D2

La Jana 41 F2
Lajkovac 72 C3
Laká 82 A2
Lakavica 77 E3
Lake District
  Nat Pk 5 D4
Lakí 89 E3
Láki 90 B3
Lákmos, Óri 82 C1
Lákoma 81 E3
Lákones 82 A1
Lakonía 87 D3
Lakonikós Kólpos . . . 87 D4
Lakópetra 86 B1
Laksefjorden 95 E1
Lakselv 95 D2
Laktaši 71 E3
L'Ampolla 41 F2
Lamstedt 47 F3
La Mudarra 35 E4
La Muela 37 D4
Lamure 26 B4
Lana 58 C3
Lanaja 37 D3
Lanaken 51 D3
Lanark 4 C2
La Nava de
  Ricomalillo 39 F3
La Nava de
  Santiago 39 D4
Lancashire 6 B2
Lancaster 6 B1
Lanchester 5 E4
Lanciano 64 A2
Landau (Bayern) 56 B2
Landau (Rheinland-
  Pfalz) 54 C2
Landeck 58 C2
Landerneau 22 B2
Landes 28 B3
Landes de
  Lanvaux 22 C3
Landete 41 D3
Landévennec 22 A3
Landivisiau 22 B2
Landivy 18 C4
Landmannalaugar . . . 96 B2
Landquart 58 B2
Landrecies 20 A2
Landriano 60 A1
Landsberg (Bayern) . . 56 A3
Landsberg (Sachsen-
  Anhalt) 53 D2
Land's End 8 A4

Landshut 56 B2
Landskapet
  Åland 106 C2
Landskrona 108 C3
Landstuhl 54 C2
Landverk 101 D2
Lanersbach 59 D2
Lanesborough 12 C3
Langáda (Híos) 85 F4
Langáda
  (Pelopónissos) 87 D4
Langadás 79 F3
Langádas 87 D3
Langa de Duero 36 A3
Langádia 86 C2
Langadíkia 80 A3
Langangen 104 C4
Langeac 29 F2
Langeais 25 D2
Langeland 108 B4
Langelandsbælt 108 B4
Langelmäki 103 D3
Langelmävesi 103 D3
Langelsheim 52 B1
Langenargen 55 D4
Langenau 55 E3
Langenberg 53 D3
Langenbruck 55 F2
Langenburg 55 D2
Langeneß 47 F1
Langenfeld 17 E4
Längenfeld 58 C2
Langenhagen 48 A4
Langenhahn 51 F3
Langen (Hessen) 52 A4
Langen
  (Niedersachsen) . . . 47 F3
Langenlois 57 E2
Langenthal 27 F2
Langenwang 57 E3
Langenzenn 55 E1
Langeoog 47 E3
Långeserud 105 E3
Langeskov 108 B3
Langesund 104 C4
Langevåg 100 A2
Langevåg 104 A3
Långfjället 101 D3
Langfjord 95 D2
Langfjorden 95 E1
Langfjordjøkelen 94 C2
Langforden 100 B2
Langhirano 60 B2
Langholm 5 D3
Langjökull 96 B2
Langnau 27 F2
Langogne 29 F2
Langon 28 B2
Langøya 94 A3
Langport 9 D3
Langres 26 C1
Langrune 18 C3
Långsele 101 F2
Långshyttan 105 F2
Långträsk 98 B3
Lanjarón 44 A3
Lanke 49 E3
Lanmeur 22 B2
Lannemezan 37 E1
Lannilis 22 A2
Lannion 22 B2
Lanouaille 29 D1
Lans-en-Vercors 30 C1
Lanslebourg 31 E1
Lanta 29 D4
Lantosque 31 E3
La Nuez de Arriba . . . 35 F3
Lanusei 66 C3
Lanvollon 22 C2
Lanzahita 39 F2
Lanzarote 42 C3
Lanzo Torinese 31 E1
Laois 12 C4
La Oliva
  (Is Canarias) 42 C4
La Oliva (Navarra) . . 36 C2
Laon 20 A3
La Orotava 42 B4
La Paca 44 C2
La Palma 42 A4
La Palma del
  Condado 42 C2

Lambiri 83 D4
Lámbou Míli 85 F2
Lambrecht 54 C2
Lamego 34 B4
La Mesa Roldán 44 C3
Lamía 83 E3
Lamlash 4 B2
Lammermuir Hills 5 D2
Lammhult 109 D2
Lammi 107 E2
La Molina 32 A3
Lamotte-Beuvron . . . 25 E2
Lampaul 22 A2
Lampedusa 68 A4
Lampedusa, I di 68 A4
Lampertheim 54 C1
Lampeter 8 C1
L'Ampolla 41 F2
La Laguna 42 B4
La Lantejuela 43 E3
Lálas 86 C2
Lalbenque 29 D3
L'Albufera 41 E4
L'Alcúdia 41 E4
L'Alcúdia de
  Crespins 41 E4
L'Aldea 41 F2
Lalín 34 B2
Lalinac 73 F4
Lalinde 28 C2
La Línea de la
  Concepción 43 E4
Laliótis 87 D1
Lalm 100 C3
La Losa 44 B2
Lalouvesc 30 B1
Lalueza 37 E3
La Luisiana 43 E2
Lama dei Peligni 64 A2
La Magdalena 35 D2
Lamalou 30 A4
La Manche 10 A4
La Manga del
  Mar Menor 45 D2
Lamarche 27 D1
La Marmora, P 66 B3
Lamarque 28 B2
Lamastre 30 B2
Lambach 56 C3
Lamballe 22 C3
Lambesc 30 C4
Lámbia 86 C1

La Panadella 37 F4
Lápas 86 B1
Lapa, Sa da 38 C1
Laperdiguera 37 E3
La Pinilla 36 A4
Lapinjärvi 107 F2
Lapin Lääni 95 E4
Lapinlahti 103 E2
La Platja d'Aro 32 B4
La Plaza 35 D2
Lapleau 29 E1
Laplume 28 C3
La Pobla 41 E4
La Pobla de Lillet . . . 32 A3
La Pobla de
  Massaluca 37 E4
La Pobla de Segur . . 37 F3
La Pobla de
  Vallbona 41 E3
La Pobla Tornesa . . . 41 F3
Lapoutroie 27 E1
Lapovo 73 D3
Lappajärvi 102 C2
Lappajärvi L 102 C2
Lappalaisten-
  Kesätuvat 95 D3
Lappea 98 C4
Lappeenranta 103 F4
Lappfjärd 102 B3
Lappfors 102 C2
Lappi 107 D2
Lappoå 102 C2
Lappohja 107 E3
Lappträsk 98 C3
Lappträsk 107 F2
Lappvesi 106 C2
Lapua 102 C2
Lapuanjoki 102 C2
La Puebla de
  Almoradiel 40 B3
La Puebla de
  Cazalla 43 E3
La Puebla de Híjar . . 37 D4
La Puebla de
  los Infantes 43 E2
La Puebla del Río . . . 43 D3
La Puebla de
  Montalbán 39 F3
La Puebla de
  Valverde 41 D2
La Pueblanueva 39 F3
La Puerta de
  Segura 44 B1
Lapväärtti 102 B3
L'Aquila 63 F2
La Rábida 42 C3
La Rábita 44 B4
Laracha 34 A1
Laragh 13 D4
Laragne-
  Montéglin 30 C3
La Rambla 43 F2
Lärbro 109 F3
Larche (Alpes-de-
  Haute-Provence) . . 31 D3
Larche (Corrèze) 29 D2
Larche, Col de 31 E2
Lærdalsøyri 104 C2
Lardarello 60 C4
Lárdos 93 F2
Lárdos, Akr 93 F2
Laredo 36 A1
Laren 16 C2
Largentière 30 B2
Largs 4 C2
Lárimna 84 A4
La Rinconada 43 D2
Larino 64 B2
La Rioja 36 B2
Lárissa 83 E1
Lárissa (Nomos) 83 E1
Larmor 22 B4
Larne 13 E2
La Robla 35 D2
La Roca 32 B4
La Roca de la
  Sierra 39 D4
Larochette 21 D2
La Roda
  (Andalucía) 43 E3
La Roda (Castilla-la-
  Mancha) 40 C4
Laroles 44 B3
Laroquebrou 29 E2

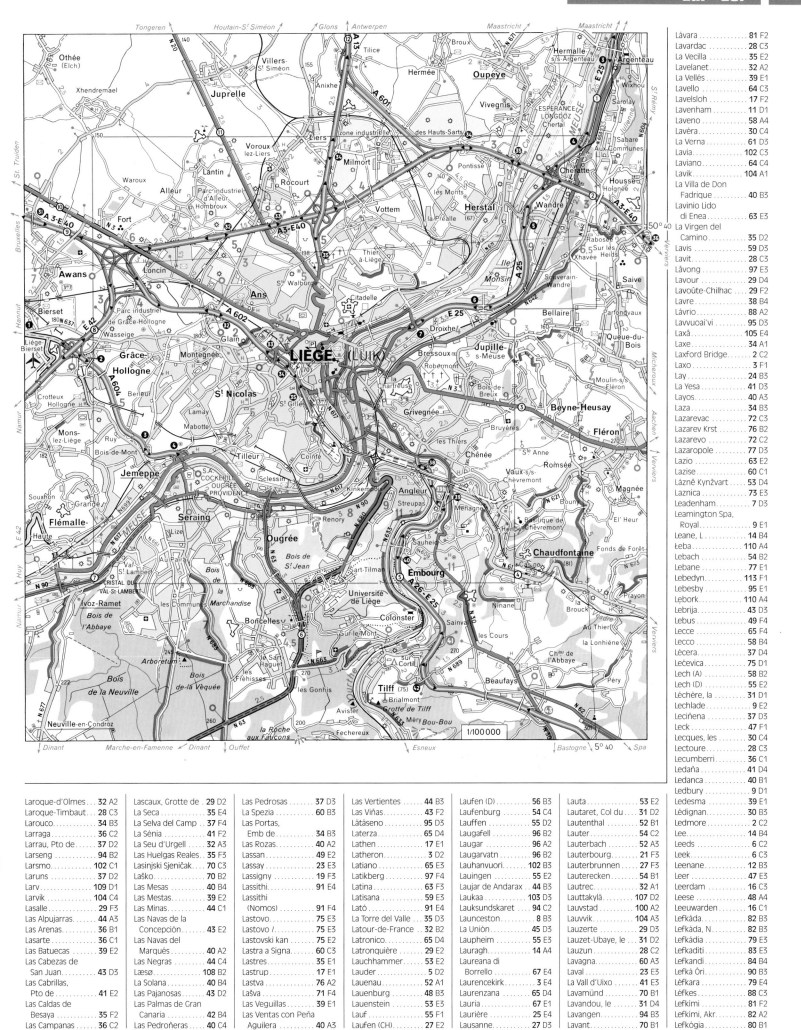

Lávara	81	F2
Lavardac	28	C3
La Vecilla	35	E2
Lavelanet	32	A2
La Vellès	39	E1
Lavello	64	C3
Lavelsloh	17	D1
Lavenham	11	D1
Laveno	58	A4
Lavèra	30	C4
La Verna	61	D3
Lavia	102	C3
Laviano	64	C4
Lavik	104	A1
La Villa de Don Fadrique	40	B3
Lavinio Lido di Enea	63	E3
La Virgen del Camino	35	D2
Lavis	59	D3
Lavit	28	C3
Lävong	97	E3
Lavour	29	D4
Lavoûte-Chilhac	29	F2
Lavre	38	B4
Lávrio	88	A2
Lavvuoai'vi	95	D3
Laxå	105	E4
Laxe	34	A1
Laxford Bridge	2	C2
Laxo	3	F1
Lay	24	B3
La Yesa	41	E3
Layos	40	A3
Laza	34	B3
Lazarevac	72	C3
Lazarev Krst	76	B2
Lazarevo	72	C2
Lazaropole	77	D3
Lazio	63	E2
Lazise	60	C1
Lázně Kynžvart	53	D4
Laznica	73	E3
Leadenham	7	D3
Leamington Spa, Royal	9	E1
Leane, L	14	B4
Łeba	110	A4
Lebach	54	B2
Lebane	77	E1
Lebedyn	113	F1
Lebesby	95	E1
Lębork	110	A4
Lebrija	43	D3
Lebus	49	F4
Lecce	65	F4
Lecco	58	B4
Lécera	37	D4
Lečevica	75	D1
Lech (A)	58	B2
Lech (D)	55	E2
Léchère, la	31	D1
Lechlade	9	E2
Leciñena	37	D3
Leck	47	F1
Lecques, les	30	C4
Lectoure	28	C3
Lecumberri	36	C1
Ledaña	41	D4
Ledanca	40	B1
Ledbury	9	E1
Ledesma	39	D1
Lédignan	30	B3
Ledmore	2	C2
Lee	14	B4
Leeds	6	C2
Leek	6	C3
Leenane	12	B3
Leer	47	E3
Leerdam	16	C3
Leese	48	A4
Leeuwarden	16	C1
Lefkáda	82	B3
Lefkáda, N	82	B3
Lefkádia	79	E3
Lefkadíti	83	E3
Lefkandi	84	A3
Lefká Óri	90	B3
Léfkara	79	E4
Léfkes	88	C3
Lefkími	81	F2
Lefkími, Akr	82	A2
Lefkógia	80	B1

Laroque-d'Olmes	32	A2	Lascaux, Grotte de	29	D2	Las Pedrosas	37	D3	Las Vertientes	44	B3	Laufen (D)	56	B3	Lauta	53	E2
Laroque-Timbaut	28	C3	La Seca	35	E4	La Spezia	60	B3	Las Viñas	43	F2	Laufenburg	54	C4	Lautaret, Col du	31	D2
Larouco	34	B3	La Selva del Camp	37	F4	Las Portas, Emb de	34	B3	Lätäseno	95	D3	Lauffen	55	D2	Lautenthal	52	B1
Larraga	36	C2	La Sénia	41	F2				Laterza	65	D4	Laugafell	96	B2	Lauter	54	C2
Larrau, Pto de	37	D2	La Seu d'Urgell	32	A3	Las Rozas	40	A2	Lathen	17	E1	Laugar	96	B1	Lauterbach	52	A3
Larseng	94	B2	Las Huelgas Reales	35	F3	Lassan	49	E2	Latheron	3	D2	Laugarvatn	96	B2	Lauterbourg	21	F3
Larsmo	102	C1	Lasinjski Sjeničak	70	C3	Lassay	23	E3	Latiano	65	E3	Lauhanvuori	102	B3	Lauterbrunnen	27	F3
Laruns	37	D2	Laško	70	B2	Lassigny	19	F3	Latikberg	97	F3	Lauingen	55	E2	Lauterecken	54	B1
Larv	109	D1	Las Mesas	40	B4	Lassithi	91	E4	Latina	63	F3	Laujar de Andarax	44	B3	Lautrec	32	A1
Larvik	104	C4	Las Mestas	39	E2	Lassithi (Nomos)	91	F4	Latisana	59	E3	Laukaa	103	D3	Lauttakylä	107	D2
Lasalle	29	F3	Las Minas	44	C1	Lastovo	75	E3	Lató	91	E4	Lauksundskaret	94	C2	Lauvstad	100	A2
Las Alpujarras	44	A3	Las Navas de la Concepción	43	E3	Lastovo I	75	E3	La Torre del Valle	35	D3	Launceston	8	B3	Lauvvik	104	A3
Las Arenas	36	B1				Lastovski kan	75	E2	Latour-de-France	32	B2	La Unión	45	D3	Lauzerte	29	D3
Lasarte	36	C1	Las Navas del Marqués	40	A2	Lastra a Signa	60	C3	Latronico	65	D4	Laupheim	55	D3	Lauzet-Ubaye, le	31	D2
Las Batuecas	39	E2	Las Negras	44	C4	Lastres	35	E1	Latronquière	29	E2	Lauragh	14	A4	Lauzun	28	C2
Las Cabezas de San Juan	43	D3	Læsø	108	B2	Lastrup	17	E1	Lauchhammer	53	E2	Laureana di Borrello	67	E4	Lavagna	60	A3
Las Cabrillas, Pto de	41	E2	La Solana	40	B4	Lastva	76	A2	Lauder	5	D2	Laurencekirk	3	E4	Laval	23	E3
Las Caldas de Besaya	35	F2	Las Pajanosas	43	D2	Lašva	71	F4	Lauenau	52	A1	Laurenzana	65	D4	La Vall d'Uixo	41	E3
Las Campanas	36	C2	Las Palmas de Gran Canaria	42	B4	Las Ventas con Peña Aguilera	40	A3	Lauenburg	48	B3	Lauria	67	E1	Lavamünd	70	B1
			Las Pedroñeras	40	C4				Laufen (CH)	27	D3	Laurière	25	E4	Lavandou, le	31	D4
									Lausanne	27	D3	Lavangen	94	B3	Lavant	70	B1

Lille

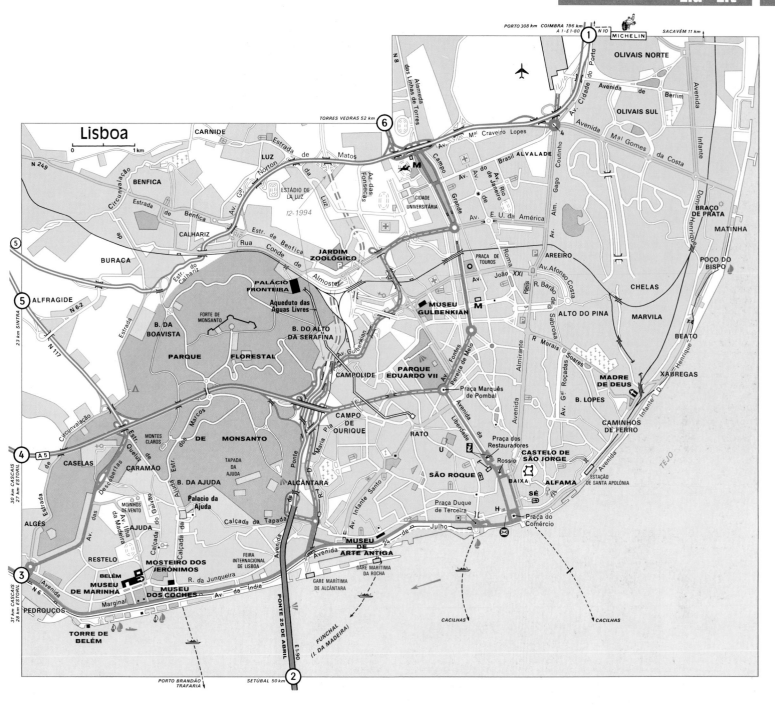

Lisboa

Lido di Savio **61** E3	Lifford **13** D1	Lilienfeld **57** E3	Limenária **80** C3	Lincoln........... **7** D3	Linyola **37** F3	Lirkia **87** D2
Lido di Spina **61** D2	Liffré **23** D3	Liljendal **107** F2	Limerick **14** B3	Lincolnshire **7** D3	Linz (A) **57** D2	Lis **76** C3
Lido di Venezia ... **61** D1	Lifjell **104** C3	Lilla Edet **108** C1	Limerick (Co) **14** B3	Lindås........... **104** A2	Linz (D) **51** E4	Lisac **71** E4
Lidoriki **83** E4	Ligià **86** B1	Lillby **102** C2	Limfjorden **108** A2	Lindau **55** D4	Lion **18** C3	Lisboa **38** A4
Lido Silvana **65** E4	Lignano	Lille **19** F1	Limia, R **34** B3	Linden **52** C4	Lion-d'Angers, le . **23** E4	Lisburn **13** E2
Lidzbark	Sabbiadoro ... **59** F4	Lille Bælt **108** A3	Limingen **97** E4	Lindenberg **55** E4	Lioni **64** C4	Liscia **66** B1
Warmiński ... **110** B4	Ligné **23** D4	Lillebonne **19** D3	Liminka **99** D4	Linderhof **55** F4	Lióprasso **83** D1	Lisdoonvarna **12** B4
Liebenwalde **49** D3	Lignières **25** F3	Lillehammer **105** D2	Liminpuro **99** E4	Lindesberg **105** F3	Lioran, le **29** E2	Lisieux **19** D3
Lieberose......... **53** F1	Ligny-en-Barrois . **20** C4	Lillerød **108** C3	Limljani **76** B3	Lindesnes **104** B4	Lipar **72** B2	Lisina **71** E4
Liège **51** D4	Ligny-le-Châtel .. **26** B1	Lillers **19** F1	Límnes **87** E2	Lindhem **106** A4	Lipari **69** D2	Liskeard **8** B4
Liège (Prov)...... **51** D4	Ligouriò **87** E2	Lillesand **104** B4	Limni **84** A3	Lindö **106** A4	Lipari, I **69** D2	Lisková **56** B1
Lieksa **103** F1	Ligueil **25** D3	Lillestrøm **105** D3	Limnià **80** C2	Lindos **93** F2	Lipenská přehr	Lisle **29** D3
Lienz **59** E2	Liguria **60** A3	Lillhärdal **101** E3	Limnítsa **83** D4	Lindoso **34** B3	nádrž **56** C2	Lismore (GB) **4** B1
Liepāja **110** B3	Liháda **83** F3	Lillo **40** B3	Límnos, N **85** D1	Lindow **49** D3	Liperi **103** F2	Lismore (IRL) **14** C4
Lier **50** C3	Liikasenvaara **99** E2	Lillögda **102** A1	Limoges **29** D1	Lindsdal **109** E2	Lipiany **49** F3	Lisnaskea **13** D2
Liérganes **35** F2	Lijeva Rijeka **76** B2	Lillsholmsjön ... **101** E1	Limogne **29** D3	Lingbo **106** A4	Lipica **70** C3	Lišnja **71** E3
Liernais **26** B2	Lijevi Dubravčak . **71** D2	Lim **76** B1	Limone Piemonte .. **31** E3	Linge **100** D2	Lipik **71** D2	Lison, Source du .. **27** D3
Lieser **59** F2	Lika **70** C4	Lima **101** D4	Limonest **26** C4	Lingen **17** E2	Lipkovo **77** E2	Lisoviči **71** F3
Liesjärvi **107** D2	Likenäs **105** E2	Limáni	Limours **19** E4	Linguaglossa **69** D3	Lipljan **77** D2	Lisse **16** C2
Liestal **27** E2	Likeo, Óri **86** C3	Hersoníssou ... **91** E3	Limoux **32** B2	Linken **49** E2	Lipno **57** D2	List **47** F1
Lieto **107** D2	Likódimo, Óros ... **86** C3	Limáni Litohórou . **79** F4	Lin **77** D4	Linköping **106** A4	Lipova **112** C4	Listafjorden **104** A4
Liétor **44** C1	Likófos **81** F2	Lima, R **34** A3	Linares **44** A2	Linlithgow **5** D2	Lipovac **72** B3	Lištica **75** E2
Lieurey **19** D3	Likoporiá **87** D1	Limavady **13** D1	Linares del Arroyo,	Linnansaari **103** E3	Lippe **17** E3	Listowel **14** B3
Lievestuore **103** D3	Likórahi **78** C4	Limbach **53** D2	Emb de **36** A3	Linnhe, L **4** B1	Lippstadt **17** F3	Lit **101** E2
Liévin **19** F1	Likóstomo **80** C2	Limbara, M **66** B2	Linares de Mora .. **41** E2	Linosa, I di **68** A4	Lipsí **89** E2	Lit-et-Mixe **28** A3
Liezen **57** D3	Likouría **86** C1	Limburg (B) **50** C3	Linares de Riofrio **39** E2	Linsell **101** E3	Lipsí, N **89** E2	Lithakiá **86** A2
Liffey **13** D4	Liland **94** B3	Limburg (D) **51** F4	Linariá **84** C3	Linslade **9** F2	Liptovský Mikuláš **112** B3	Lithári, Akr **84** C3
Liffol-le-Grand .. **20** C4	Lilea **83** E3	Limburg (NL) **17** D4	Linas, M **66** B4	Linthal **58** A2	Liqenas **77** D4	Lithines **91** F4

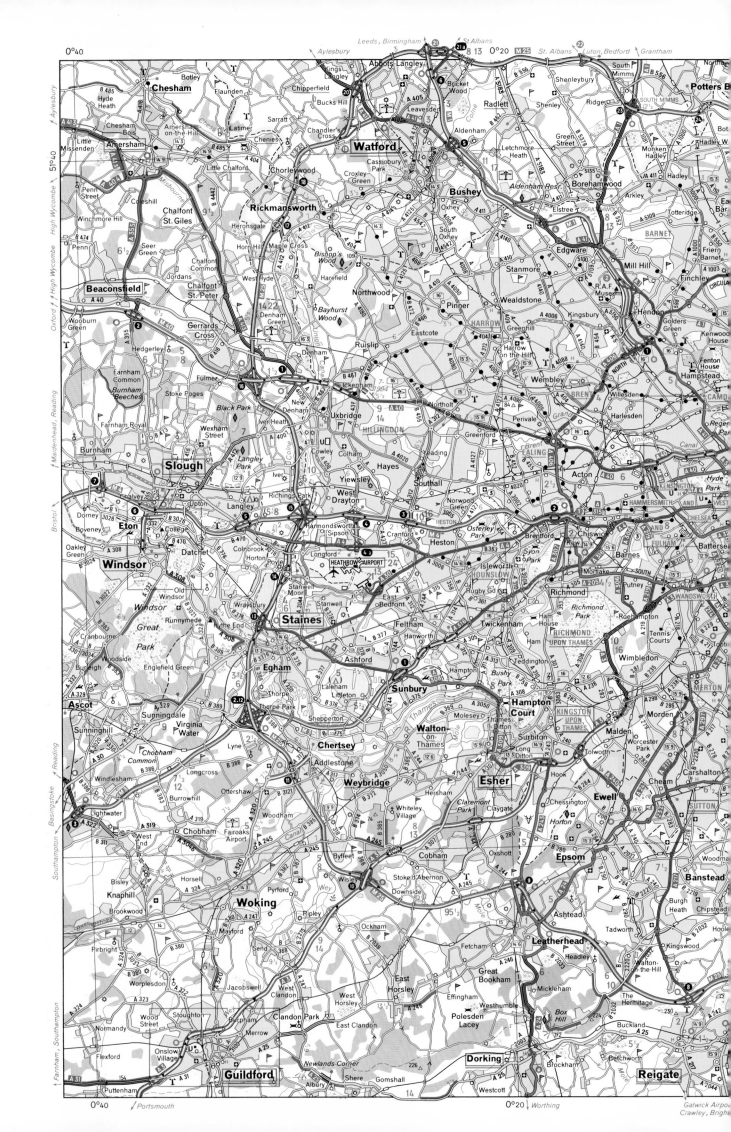

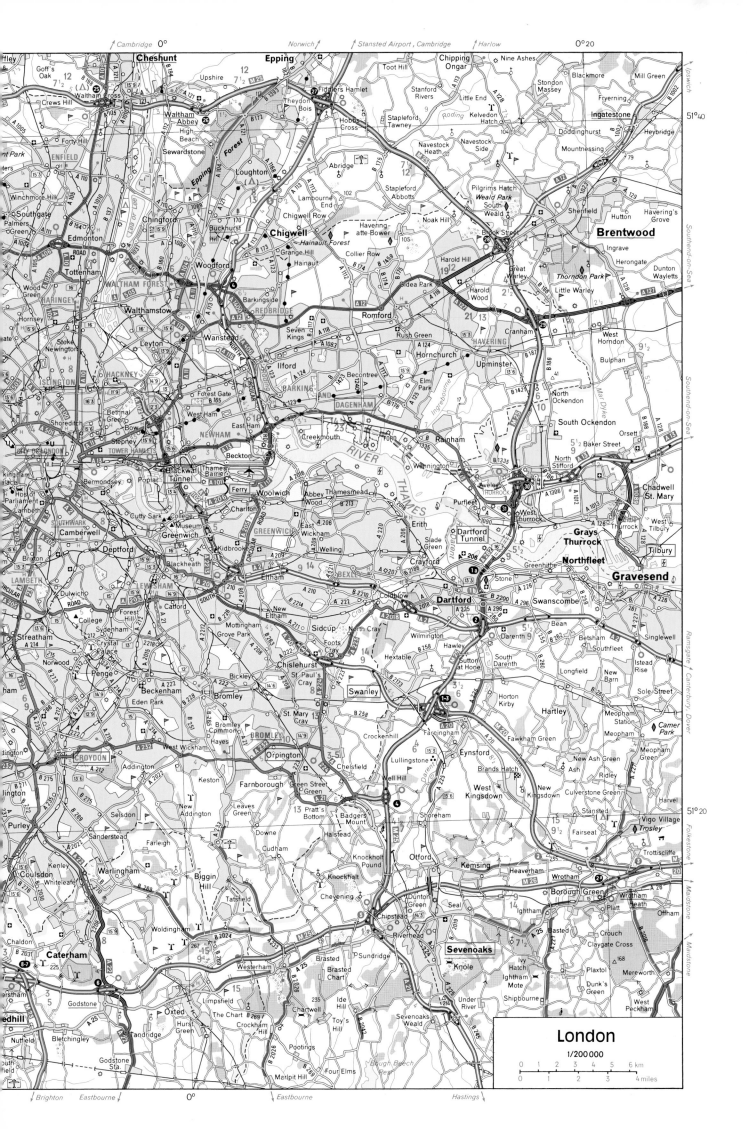

London

1/200 000

0 1 2 3 4 5 6 km
0 1 2 3 4 miles

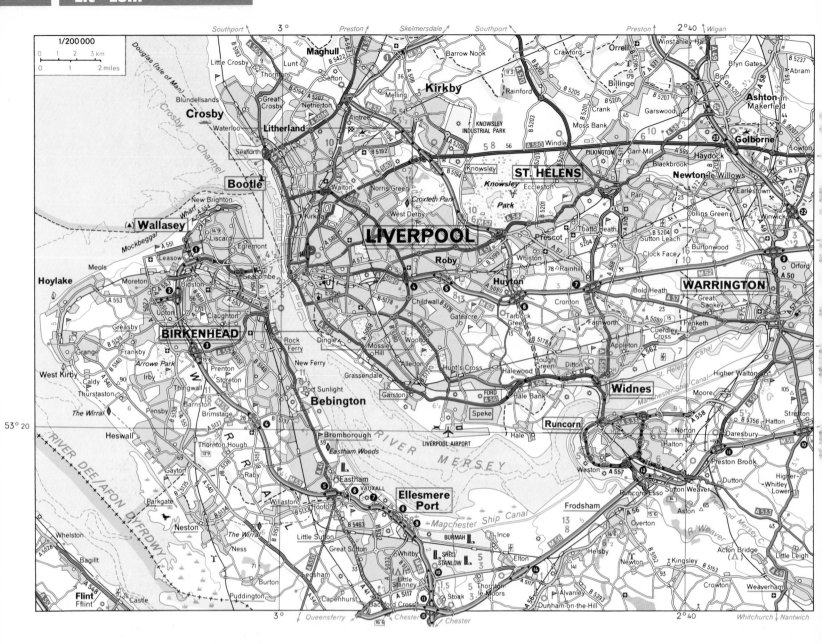

Lithino, Akr. 91 D4	Liverdun 21 D4	Ljuboml' 112 C2	Llangefni 6 A2	Loburg 53 D1	Lødingen 94 A3	Loimaa 107 E2
Lithio 85 E4	Livernon 29 D2	Ljubostinja 73 D4	Llangollen 6 B3	Locana 31 E1	Lodosa 36 C2	Loimaan kunta 107 E2
Lití 79 F3	Liverpool 6 B2	Ljuboten 77 D2	Llangurig 8 C1	Locarno 58 A3	Łódź 112 B2	Loimijoki 107 D2
Litija 70 B2	Liverpool B 6 B2	Ljubovija 72 C4	Llanidloes 8 C1	Lochaline 4 B1	Loeches 40 B2	Loing 26 A2
Litóhoro 79 F4	Livigno 58 C3	Ljubuša 75 E1	Llano, Pto 39 E3	Lochboisdale 2 A3	Loen 100 A3	Loire 25 E1
Litoměřice 53 F3	Livingston 5 D2	Ljubuški 75 E2	Llanrhystud 8 C1	Lochcarron 2 B3	Løfallstrand 104 A2	Loire 23 E4
Litomyšl 112 A3	Livno 75 E1	Ljugarn 109 F4	Llanrwst 6 A3	Lochearnhead 4 C1	Lofário 81 E2	Loire (Dépt) 29 F1
Litschau 57 D1	Livo 99 E3	Ljungan 101 F3	Llanwrtyd-Wells .. 8 C1	Lochem 17 D2	Lofer 59 E1	Loire-Atlantique .. 23 E4
Littlehampton 10 C3	Livojärvi 99 E2	Ljungby 109 D2	Llanymyddfri 8 C1	Loches 25 D3	Löffingen 54 C4	Loir-et-Cher 25 E2
Little Minch, The .. 2 A3	Livojoki 99 E3	Ljungbyhed 109 D3	Llarga 41 E4	Loch Garman 15 D3	Lofoten 97 E1	Loiret 25 E2
Little Moreton Hall .. 6 C3	Livold 70 B3	Ljungdalen 101 D3	Llavorsi 37 F2	Lochgelly 5 D2	Lofsdalen 101 D3	Loiri 66 B1
Littleport 10 C1	Livorno 60 C4	Ljungsbro 105 F4	Lleida 37 E4	Lochgilphead 4 B2	Lofthus 104 B3	Loiron 23 E3
Litvinov. 53 E3	Livorno Ferraris... 31 F1	Ljungskile 108 C1	Llera 43 D1	Lochinver 2 C2	Loftus 5 F4	Loitz 49 D2
Livaara 99 F3	Livron 30 B2	Ljusdal 101 F3	Llerena 43 D1	Lochmaben 5 D3	Log 70 A2	Loja 43 F3
Liváda, Akr 88 C2	Lixoúri 82 B4	Ljusnan 101 E3	Lles 32 A3	Lochmaddy 2 A3	Logarska dolina .. 70 B1	Lojsta 109 F4
Livade 70 A3	Lizard 8 B4	Ljusne 101 F4	Llessui 37 F2	Loch Ness 2 C3	Logatec, D. 70 A2	Lokalahti 107 D2
Livaderó (Dráma) .. 80 C2	Lizard Pt 8 B4	Ljutiči 76 B1	Lleyn Pen 6 A3	Lochranza 4 B2	Logroño 36 C2	Lokan Tekojärvi .. 95 F4
Livaderó (Kozáni) .. 79 E4	Lizarra 36 C2	Ljutoglav 77 D2	Llíria 41 E3	Lochvycja 113 F2	Logrosán. 39 E3	Løken 105 D3
Livádi (Kíthira) 90 A2	Lizy 19 F3	Ljutomer 70 C1	Llívia 32 A2	Lochy, L 2 C4	Løgstør 108 A2	Lokeren 50 B3
Livádi (Makedonía) .. 80 A3	Lizzano in	Llagostera 32 B3	Llobregat, R 32 A3	Lockenhaus 57 F3	Løgten 108 B3	Loket 53 E4
Livádi (Sérifos) 88 A3	Belvedere. 60 C3	Llanberis 6 A3	Llodio 36 B1	Lockerbie. 5 D3	Løgumkloster 108 A4	Lokka 95 F4
Livádi (Thessalía) .. 79 E4	Ljeskove Vode 71 E3	Llanca 32 C3	Lloret de Mar 32 B4	Löcknitz 49 E2	Lohals 108 B4	Løkken (N) 100 C2
Livadiá	Ljig 72 C3	Llandeilo 8 C2	Llucmajor 45 F2	Locle, le 27 E2	Lohberg 56 B1	Løkken (S) 108 B1
(Makedonía) .. 80 A2	Ljubaništa 77 D4	Llandovery 8 C1	Llynclys 6 B3	Locmariaquer 22 C4	Lohilahti 103 E3	Lokn'a 111 D2
Livadiá	Ljubašivka 113 E3	Llandrindod Wells .. 9 D1	Lnáre 56 C1	Locminé 22 C3	Lohiniva 99 D1	Lokrum 76 A2
(Stereá Eláda) .. 83 F4	Ljubata, D. 77 E2	Llandudno 6 A2	Loanhead 5 D2	Locorotondo 65 E3	Lohja 107 E3	Lokve (HR) 70 B3
Livádia (Tílos) 89 F4	Ljubelj 70 A1	Llandysul 8 C1	Loano 31 F3	Locquirec 22 B2	Lohjanjärvi 107 E2	Lokve (SLO) 70 A2
Livaditis 80 C1	Ljubija 71 D3	Llanelli 8 C2	Löbau 53 F2	Locri 67 F4	Lohne 17 E2	Lokve (Vojvodina) .. 73 D2
Livadohóri 85 D1	Ljubinje 75 F2	Llanerchymedd ...6 A2	Löbejün 53 D2	Locronan 22 B3	Löhne 17 F2	Lolland 108 B4
Livanátes 83 F3	Ljubiš 72 C4	Llanes 35 E1	Lobenstein 52 C3	Loctudy 22 B3	Lohr 52 B4	L'Olleria 45 E1
Livari 76 B3	Ljubišnja 76 B1	Llanfairfechan 6 A2	Łobez 49 F2	Lodè 66 C2	Lohtaja 102 C1	Lom (BG) 115 D2
Livarot 19 D4	Ljubljana 70 B2	Llanfair-ym-Muallt .. 9 D1	Löbnitz 49 D1	Lodève 30 A4	Loiano 60 C3	Lom (CS) 53 E3
Livenza 59 E4	Ljubno 70 B1	Llanfyllin 6 B3	Lobo 36 A4	Lodi 60 B1	Rioveggio. 60 C3	Lom (N) 100 B3
Liverá 79 D3	Ljubojno. 77 E4	Llangadog 8 C2	Lobón 39 D4	Løding 97 E1	Loibltunnel 70 A1	Loma Negra 36 C3

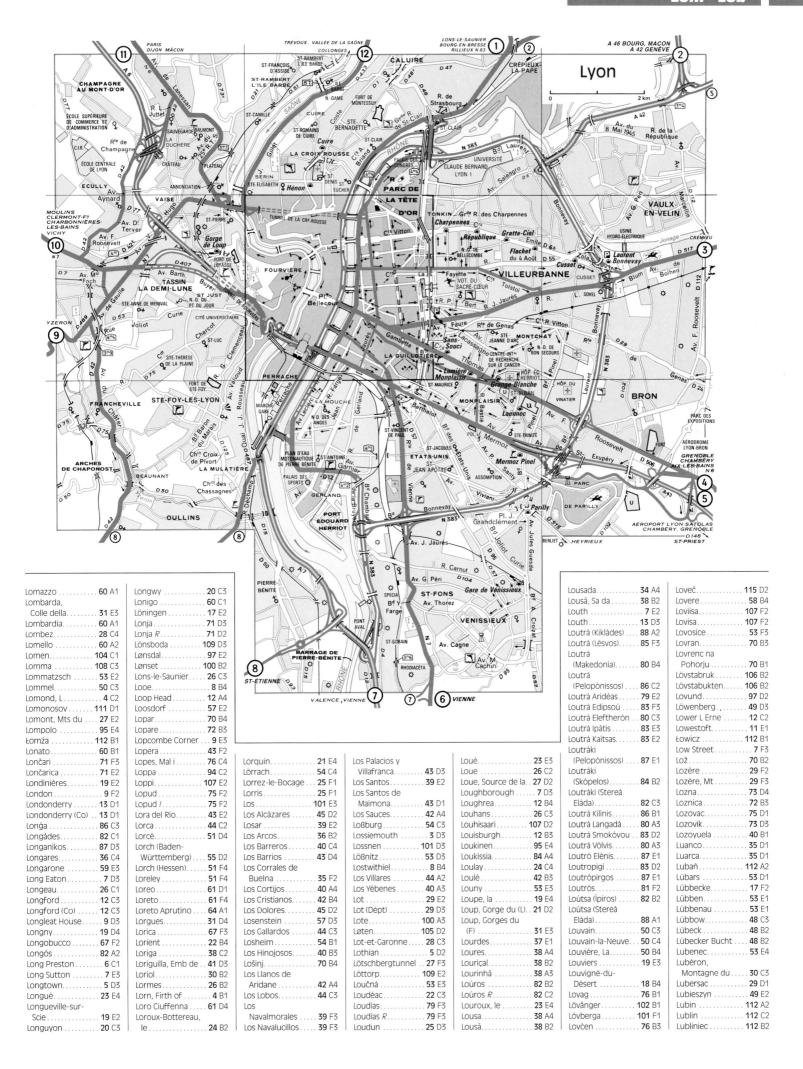

Lyon

Lomazzo	60 A1	Longwy	20 C3
Lombarda,		Lonigo	60 C1
Colle della	31 E3	Löningen	17 E2
Lombardia	60 A1	Lonja	71 D2
Lombez	28 C4	Lonja *R*.	71 D2
Lomello	60 A2	Lönsboda	109 D3
Lomen	104 C1	Lønsdal	97 E2
Lomma	108 C3	Lønset	100 B2
Lommatzsch	53 E2	Lons-le-Saunier	26 C3
Lommel	50 C3	Looe	8 B4
Lomond, L	4 C2	Loop Head	12 A4
Lomonosov	111 D1	Loosdorf	57 E2
Lomont, Mts du	27 E2	Lopar	70 B4
Lompolo	95 E4	Lopare	72 B3
Łomża	112 B1	Lopcombe Corner	9 E3
Lonato	60 B1	Lopera	43 F2
Lončari	71 F3	Lopes, Mal i	76 C4
Lončarica	71 E2	Loppa	94 C2
Londinières	19 E2	Loppi	107 E2
London	9 F2	Lopud	75 F2
Londonderry	13 D1	Lopud *I*.	75 F2
Londonderry (Co)	13 D1	Lora del Río	43 D2
Longá	86 C3	Lorca	44 C2
Longádes	82 C1	Lorcé	51 D4
Longanikos	87 D3	Lorch (Baden-	
Longares	36 C4	Württemberg)	55 D2
Longarone	59 E3	Lorch (Hessen)	51 F4
Long Eaton	7 D3	Loreley	51 F4
Longeau	26 C1	Loreo	61 D1
Longford	12 C3	Loreto	61 F4
Longford (Co)	12 C3	Loreto Aprutino	64 A1
Longleat House	9 D3	Lorgues	31 D4
Longny	19 D4	Lorica	67 F3
Longobucco	67 F2	Lorient	22 B4
Longós	82 A2	Loriga	38 C2
Long Preston	6 C1	Loriguilla, Emb de	41 D3
Long Sutton	7 E3	Losinj	70 B4
Longtown	5 D3	Los Llanos de	
Longué	23 E4	Aridane	42 A4
Longueville-sur-		Loriol	30 B2
Scie	19 E2	Lormes	26 B2
Longuyon	20 C3	Lorn, Firth of	4 B1
		Loro Ciuffenna	61 D4
		Loroux-Botterau,	
		le	24 B2

Lorquin	21 E4	Los Palacios y	
Lörrach	54 C4	Villafranca	43 D3
Lorrez-le-Bocage	25 F1	Los Santos	39 E2
Lorris	25 F1	Los Santos de	
Los	101 E3	Maimona	43 D1
Los Alcázares	45 D2	Los Sauces	42 A4
Losar	39 E2	Loßburg	54 C3
Los Arcos	36 B2	Lossiemouth	3 D3
Los Barreros	40 C4	Lossnen	101 D3
Los Barrios	43 D4	Lößnitz	53 D3
Los Corrales de		Lostwithiel	8 B4
Buelna	35 F2	Los Villares	44 A2
Los Cortijos	40 A4	Los Yébenes	40 A3
Los Cristianos	42 B4	Lot	29 E2
Los Dolores	45 D2	Lot (Dépt)	29 D3
Losenstein	57 D3	Lote	100 A3
Los Gallardos	44 C3	Lot-et-Garonne	28 C3
Losheim	54 B1	Lothian	5 D2
Los Hinojosos	40 B3	Lötschbergtunnel	27 F3
Los Llanos de		Loučná	53 E3
Aridane	42 A4	Loudéac	22 C3
Los Lobos	44 C3	Loudías	79 F3
Los		Loudías *R*.	79 F3
Navalmorales	39 F3	Loudun	25 D3
Los Navalucillos	39 F3		

Loué	23 E3	Lousada	34 A4
Loue	26 C2	Lousã, Sa da	38 B2
Loue, Source de la	27 D2	Louth	7 E2
Loughborough	7 D3	Louth	13 D3
Loughrea	12 B4	Loutrá (Kikládes)	88 B4
Louhans	26 C3	Loutrá (Lésvos)	85 F3
Louhisaari	107 D2	Loutrá	
Louisburgh	12 B3	(Makedonía)	80 B4
Loukinen	95 E4	Loutrá	
Loukíssia	84 A4	(Pelopónissos)	86 C2
Loulay	24 C4	Loutrá Arídeas	79 E2
Loulé	42 B3	Loutrá Edipsoú	83 F3
Louny	53 E3	Loutrá Eleftherón	80 C2
Loupe, la	19 E4	Loutrá Ipátis	83 E3
Loup, Gorge du (L)	21 D2	Loutrá Kaïtsas	83 E2
Loup, Gorges du		Loutráki	
(F)	31 E3	(Pelopónissos)	87 E1
Lourdes	37 E1	Loutráki	
Loures	38 A4	(Skópelos)	84 B2
Louriçal	38 B2	Loutráki (Stereá	
Lourinhã	38 A3	Eláda)	82 C3
Loúros	82 B2	Loutrá Kilínis	86 B1
Loúros *R*.	82 C2	Loutrá Langadá	80 A3
Louroux, le	23 E4	Loutrá Smokóvou	83 D2
Lousa	38 A4	Loutrá Vólvis	80 A3
Lousã	38 B2	Loutró Elénis	87 E1
		Loutropigí	83 D2
		Loutrópirgos	87 E1
		Loutró	81 F2
		Loútsa (Ípiros)	82 B2
		Loútsa (Stereá	
		Eláda)	88 A1
		Louvain	50 C3
		Louvain-la-Neuve	50 C4
		Louvière, La	50 B4
		Louviers	19 E3
		Louvigné-du-	
		Désert	18 B4
		Lovag	76 B1
		Lövånger	102 B1
		Lövberga	101 F1
		Lovćen	76 B3

Loveč	115 D2	
Lovere	58 B4	
Loviisa	107 F2	
Lovisa	107 F2	
Lovosice	53 E3	
Lovran	70 B3	
Lovrenc na		
Pohorju	70 B1	
Lövstabruk	106 B2	
Lövstabukten	106 B2	
Lovund	97 D2	
Löwenberg	49 D3	
Lower L Erne	12 C2	
Lowestoft	11 E1	
Łowicz	112 B1	
Low Street	7 F3	
Lož	70 B2	
Lozère	29 F3	
Lozère, Mt	29 F3	
Lozna	73 D4	
Loznica	72 B3	
Lozovac	75 D1	
Lozovik	73 D3	
Lozoyuela	40 B1	
Luanco	35 D1	
Luarca	35 D1	
Lubań	112 A2	
Lübars	53 D1	
Lübbecke	17 F2	
Lübben	53 E1	
Lübbenau	53 E1	
Lübbow	48 C3	
Lübecker Bucht	48 B2	
Lubenec	53 E4	
Lubéron,		
Montagne du	30 C3	
Lubersac	29 D1	
Lubieszyn	49 E2	
Lubin	112 A2	
Lublin	112 C2	
Lubliniec	112 B2	

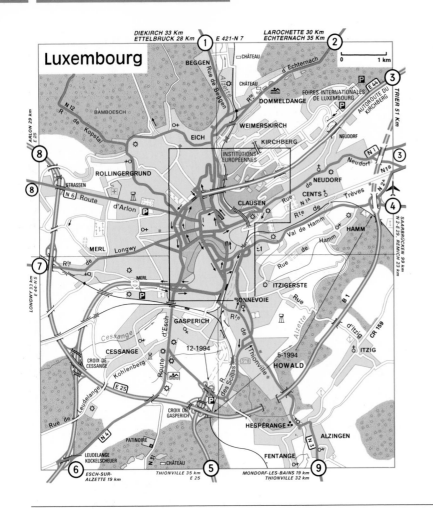

Luxembourg

Ludwigshafen (Rheinland-		Lun	70 B4
Pfalz)	54 C1	Luna	37 D3
Ludwigslust	48 C3	Luna, Emb	
Ludwigstadt	52 C3	Barrios de	35 D2
Luère, Col de la	26 C4	Luna, R	35 D2
Lug	75 E1	Lunas	30 A4
Lug R	73 D3	Lund	108 C3
Luga	111 D1	Lunde (Sogn og	
Luga R	111 D1	Fjordane)	100 A3
Lugagnano Val		Lunde (Telemark)	104 C3
d'Arda	60 B2	Lunden	47 F2
Lugano	58 A4	Lundy	8 B3
Lugau	53 D3	Lune	6 B1
Lügde	52 A1	Lüneburg	48 B3
Lugnano in		Lunel	30 B4
Teverina	63 E2	Lünen	17 E3
Lugo (E)	34 B2	Lünersee	58 B2
Lugo (I)	61 D2	Lunéville	21 D4
Lugoj	114 C1	Lungern	27 F3
Lugones	35 D1	Lungro	67 E2
Luhačovice	112 A3	Luninec	113 D1
Luhalahti	102 C3	Lunz	57 D3
Luhanka	103 D3	Luodonselkä	99 D4
Luhtapohja	103 F2	Luogosanto	66 B1
Luik	51 D4	Luonteri	103 E3
Luimneach	14 B3	Luopioinen	107 E1
Luiña	35 D1	Luosto	99 D1
Luing	4 B1	Luoto	102 C1
Luino	58 A4	Lupoglav	71 D2
Luiro	95 F4	Luque	43 F2
Luisenburg	53 D4	Lurbe-St-Christau	37 D1
Luka (BH)	75 F1	Lurcy-Lévis	26 A3
Luka (HR)	74 C1	Lure	27 D1
Luka (Srbija)	73 E3	Lure, Mgne de	30 C3
Lukavac	71 F3	Lurgan	13 E2
Lukavica	71 F3	Luri	33 F2
Lukovica	70 B2	Lurisia	31 E3
Lukovit	115 D2	Lurøy	97 D2
Lukovo		Lury	25 E3
(Makedonija)	77 D4	Lušci Palanka	71 D4
Lukovo (Srbija)	73 E4	Lushnjë	76 C4
Lukovo (Srbija)	77 D1	Lusi	107 F1
Lukovo Šugarje	70 C4	Lusignan	24 C3
Luleå	98 C3	Lusigny	26 B1
Luleälven	98 B3	Lusk	13 E3
Lüleburgaz	115 E3	Luso	38 B2
Lumbarda	75 E2	Lussac	28 B2
Lumbier	36 C2	Lussac-les-	
Lumbrales	31 D1	Châteaux	25 D4
Lumbres	19 F1	Lussan	30 B3
Lumezzane	60 B1	Lustenau	58 B2
L'udinovo	111 F3	Luster	100 B3
Ludlow	9 D1	Lustrafjorden	100 B3
Ludvika	105 F3	Lütjenburg	48 B2
Ludwigsburg	55 D2	Luton	9 F2
Ludwigsfelde	49 D4	Lutterberg	52 A2
Ludwigshafen (Baden-		Lutterworth	9 E1
Württemberg)	55 D4	Lutto	95 F3

Lutzelbourg	21 E4		
Lützen	53 D2		
Lutzerath	51 E4		
Lutzmannsburg	57 F3		
Lützow	48 B2		
Luumäki	103 F4		
Luupuvesi	103 D1		
Luvia	107 D2		
Luxembourg (Grand-			
Duché)	21 D2		
Luxembourg			
(Prov)	20 C2		
Luxeuil	27 D1		
Luynes	25 D2		
Lužani	71 E3		
Luzarches	19 F3		
Luzech	29 D3		
Luzern	27 F2		
Lužnica	77 E1		
Lužnice	57 D1		
Luz-St-Sauveur	37 E2		
Luzy	26 B3		
Luzzara	60 C2		
Luzzi	67 E2		
L'viv	112 C2		
Lychen	49 D3		
Lyckebyån	109 E3		
Lycksele	98 A4		
Lydd	11 D3		
Lydney	9 D2		
Lye	109 F4		
Lygna	104 B4		
Lyme B	9 D3		
Lyme Regis	9 D3		
Lymington	9 E3		
Łyna	110 B4		
Lyndhurst	9 E3		
Lyness	3 D1		
Lyngdal	104 B4		
Lyngen	94 C2		
Lyngseidet	94 C2		
Lyngsnes	97 D4		
Lynmouth	8 C3		
Lynton	8 C3		
Lyon	26 C4		
Lyons-la-Forêt	19 E3		
Lys	19 F1		
Lysá	53 F3		
Lysefjorden	104 A3		
Lyseheiene	104 B3		
Lysekil	108 C1		
Lyss	27 E2		
Lysvik	105 E3		
Lytham St Anne's	6 B2		

Lubmin	49 D1	Lucan	13 D4	Lucera	64 C3	Ludbreg	71 D1
Lubniewice	49 F4	Lučani	73 D4	Lüchow	48 C3	Lude, le	23 F4
Lubniewsko, Jez	49 F4	Lúcar	44 B3	Luciana	39 F4	Lüdenscheid	17 E4
Lubny	113 F2	Lucca	60 C3	Lucito	64 B2	Ludiente	41 E3
Lubrin	44 C3	Luče	70 B2	Luc'k	113 D2	Lüdinghausen	17 E3
Lubsko	53 F1	Luce B	4 B3	Lucka	53 D2	L'udinovo	111 F3
Lubsza	53 F1	Lucena	43 F3	Luckau	53 E1	Ludlow	9 D1
Lübtheen	48 B3	Lucena del Cid	41 E3	Luckenwalde	53 E1	Ludvika	105 F3
Lübz	48 C3	Lucenay-l'Evêque	26 B2	Luc, le	31 D4	Ludwigsburg	55 D2
Luc	18 C3	Luc-en-Diois	30 C2	Lucomagno,		Ludwigsfelde	49 D4
Lucainena de las		Lučenec	112 B3	Pso del	58 A3	Ludwigshafen (Baden-	
Torres	44 C3	Luceni	36 C3	Luçon	24 B3	Württemberg)	55 D4

M

Maakalla	102 C1	Macgillycuddy's		Maddalena La	66 B1	Maesteg	8 C2	Magoúla	86 B2	Mainz	51 F4	Makrihóri
Maalanti	102 B2	Reeks	14 A4	Maddaloni	64 B3	Mafra	38 A3	Magre, R	41 D4	Maira	31 E2	(Thessalia)	83 E1
Maam Cross	12 B3	Machault	20 B3	Madeira,		Magacela	39 E4	Magura	77 D2	Mairena del Alcor	43 D2	Makrinitsa	83 F2
Maaninka	103 E2	Machecoul	24 B3	Arquipélago da	42 A3	Magallón	36 C3	Maherádo	86 A1	Maisach	55 F3	Makrinóros	82 C3
Maaninkavaara	99 E2	Machero	39 F4	Madeira, I da	42 A3	Magaña	36 B3	Mahlu	103 D2	Maison-Neuve	26 B1	Makriplágio	80 C2
Maanselkä	103 E1	Machichaco, C	36 B1	M'adel'	111 D3	Magaz	35 F3	Mahón	45 F2	Maisons-Blanches,		Makriráhi	83 E3
Maarestatunturit	95 E3	Machine, la	26 A3	Madeleine,		Magdalena,		Mahora	41 D4	les	25 D4	Makrívrahos, Akr.	81 E3
Maarianhamina	106 C3	Machovo jez	53 F3	Col de la	31 D1	Pto de la	35 D2	Mahovo	71 D2	Maisons-Blanches		Makrohóri	79 E3
Maarianvaara	103 E2	Machrihanish	4 B3	Madero, Pto del	36 C3	Magdeburg	52 C1	Mähring	53 D4	Maissau	57 E2	Makroníssi	88 A2
Maas	16 C3	Machynlleth	6 A3	Maderuelo	36 A3	Magenta	60 A1	Maia	34 A4	Maizières	21 D3	Maksniemi	99 D3
Maaseik	51 D3	Mackendorf	52 C1	Madesimo	58 B3	Magerøya	95 E1	Maials	37 E4	Maja	70 C3	Mala	14 B4
Maasmechelen	51 D3	Mackenrode	52 B2	Madine, Lac de	20 C3	Maggia	58 A3	Maîche	27 E2	Majales, Pto de los	40 A4	Malå	98 A4
Maassluis	16 B3	Mačkovci	70 C1	Madon	21 D4	Maggiore, L	58 A4	Maida	67 F3	Majdanpek	73 E3	Mala Bosna	72 B1
Maastricht	51 D3	Macocha	57 F1	Madona	110 C2	Maghera	13 D1	Maidenhead	9 F2	Majevica	72 B3	Malacky	57 F2
Määttälänvaara	99 F2	Macomer	66 B2	Madonie Nebrodi	68 C3	Magherafelt	13 D2	Maidstone	11 D3	Majšperk	70 C1	Maladeta	37 E2
Mablethorpe	7 E2	Mâcon	26 C4	Madonna di		Mágina	44 A2	Maiella, la	64 A2	Makarska	75 E2	Malaga	43 F3
Macael	44 C3	Macotera	39 F1	Campiglio	58 B3	Magione	61 E2	Maienfeld	58 B2	Makce	73 E3	Malagón	40 A4
Mação	38 B3	Macroom	14 B4	Madrid	40 A2	Maglaj	71 F3	Maignelay	19 F3	Makedonia	79 F2	Malahide	13 D3
Macclesfield	6 C2	Macugnaga	27 F4	Madrid (Prov)	40 A2	Maglič	73 D4	Maigue	14 B3	Makedonija	77 E3	Malaja Višera	111 E1
Macdonald	44 C3	Mačvanska		Madridejos	40 B3	Maglič Mt	76 A1	Maillezais	24 C3	Makedonski Brod	77 D3	Mala Kapela	70 C3
Macdonald	38 B3	Mitrovica	72 C3	Madrigal de las Altas		Magliano di Marsi	63 F2	Mailly-le-Camp	20 B4	Makljen	75 E1	Mala Krsna	73 D3
Macduff	3 E3	Mačvanski		Torres	39 F1	Magliano in		Main	55 D1	Makó	114 B1	Malalbergo	61 D2
Maceda	34 B3	Pričinović	72 C3	Madrigal de la Vera	39 E2	Toscana	63 D2	Mainar	36 C4	Makovo	77 E4	Malámata	83 D4
Macedo de		Madara	115 E2	Madrigalejo	39 E4	Magliano Sabina	63 E2	Mainburg	55 F2	Makrakómi	83 E3	Malandrino	83 E4
Cavaleiros	34 C4	Maddalena, Arc		Madrona	40 A1	Maglić	73 D4	Maine-et-Loire	23 E4	Makri	81 E2	Malangen	94 B2
Macelj	70 C1	della	66 B1	Madrona, Sa	44 A1	Magnac-Laval	25 E4	Mainistir na Búille	12 C3	Makríamos	80 C3	Mälaren	106 B3
Macerata	61 F4	Maddalena, Colle		Madroñera	39 E3	Magnissia	83 E2	Mainland (Orkney)	3 D1	Makrigialos	79 F3	Mala Subotica	71 D1
Macerata Feltria	61 E3	della	31 E2	Maël-Carhaix	22 B3	Magnor	105 D3	Mainland (Shetland)	3 F2	Makrigialós	91 F4	Malaucène	30 C3
		Maddalena, I	66 B1	Maella	37 E4	Magny-en-Vexin	19 E3	Maintenon	19 E4	Makrihóri		Mala Vyska	113 F2
										(Makedonia)	80 C2	

Madrid

0 2 km

Malax 102 B2
Malbork 110 B4
Malbuisson 27 D3
Malcata, Sa de . . . 39 D2
Malcesine 58 C4
Malchin 49 D2
Malchiner See 49 D2
Malchow 49 D2
Maldegem 50 B3
Maldon 11 D2
Malé 58 C3
Maléas, Akr 87 E4
Máleme 90 B3
Malène, la 29 F3
Malente
  Gremsmühlen 48 B2
Male Pijace 72 C1
Máles 91 E4
Malesherbes 25 F1
Malessina 83 F3
Malestroit 22 C3
Malgomaj 97 F4
Malgrat de Mar . . . 32 B4
Mália 91 E3
Malicorne 23 E4
Mali Haian 70 C4
Mali Iddos 72 B2
Mali kanal 72 B2
Mali Lošinj 70 B4
Malines 50 B3
Malin Head 13 D1
Malinska 70 B3
Mali Požerevac . . . 73 D3
Mališevo 77 D2
Maliskylä 103 D1
Malit, Maj'e 76 C3
Mali Zvornik 72 B4
Maljen 72 C4
Malko Tårnovo . . . 115 E2
Mallaig 2 B4
Mållejus 95 D2
Mallén 36 C3
Mallersdorf-
  Pfaffenberg 56 B2
Malles Venosta . . . 58 C2
Mallnitz 59 E2
Mallorca 45 E2
Mallow 14 B4
Mallwyd 6 A3
Malm 101 D1
Malmberget 98 B2
Malmédy 51 E4
Malmesbury 9 E2
Malmköping 106 A4
Malmö 108 C3
Malmöhus Län . . . 109 D3
Malmslätt 106 A4
Malo 59 D4
Maloja 58 B3
Malojaroslavec . . . 111 F3
Malo Konjari 77 E4
Malo-les-Bains . . . 19 F1
Malónas 93 F1
Malori 64 B4
Måløy 100 A3
Malpartida de
  Cáceres 39 D3
Malpartida de
  Plasencia 39 E2
Malpica (E) 34 A1
Malpica (P) 38 C3
Mals 58 C2
Målselv 94 B3
Målselva 94 B3
Målsnes 94 B3
Malsta 101 F3
Malta 59 F2
Malta/. 68 B4
Maltby 7 D2
Maltiotunturi 95 F4
Malton 7 D1
Maluenda 36 C4
Malung 105 E2
Malungsfors 101 D4
Malveira 38 A4
Malvik 100 C2
Malyn 113 E2
Malzieu-Ville, le . . 29 F2
Mamaia 115 E1
Mamarrosa 38 B1
Mamers 23 F3
Mammola 67 F4
Mamonovo 110 B4
Mampodre 35 E2

Mamry, Jez 110 B4
Manacor 45 F3
Manacore 64 C2
Manamansalo 99 E4
Manasija 73 E3
Mancha Real 44 A2
Manche 18 B3
Manchester 6 C2
Manching 55 F2
Manciano 63 D2
Mandal 104 B4
Mandal selva 104 B4
Mandamádos 85 F2
Mandas 66 B3
Mandela 63 E2
Mandelieu 31 E4
Manderscheid 51 E4
Mandínia 87 D2
Mandoúdi 84 A3
Mandráki 89 F4
Mándra (Stereá
  Eláda) 87 F1
Mándra (Thráki) . . . 81 F2
Mandre 70 B4
Mandrikó 93 E1
Mandrioli, Pso dei . 61 D3
Manduria 65 E4
Måne 104 C3
Manerbio 60 B1
Manětín 53 E4
Manfredonia 64 C2
Manfredonia, G di . 64 C2
Mangalia 115 E2
Mángana 81 D2
Manganári 88 C4
Manger 104 A2
Mangerton Mt. . . . 14 B4

Mangrt, Planica . . . 59 F2
Mangualde 38 C1
Maniago 59 E3
Manilva 43 E4
Man, I of 6 A1
Máni
  (Pelopónissos) . . 87 D4
Máni (Thráki) 81 F1
Manisa 115 E4
Mánises 41 E4
Manjača 71 E4
Mank 57 E2
Mânkarbo 106 B3
Manlleu 32 B3
Mannersdorf 57 F2
Mannheim 54 C1
Mannu 66 B4
Manojlovac slap . . 75 D1
Manojlovce 77 E1
Manoppello 64 A2
Manorhamilton . . . 12 C2
Manosque 30 C3
Manresa 32 A4
Manschnow 49 F4
Mansfeld 52 C2
Mansfield 7 D3
Mansilla de las
  Mulas 35 E3

Mansilla, Emb de . . 36 B3
Mansle 25 D4
Manteigas 38 C2
Mantes 19 E4
Mantiel 40 C2
Mantova 60 C2
Mäntlahti 103 F4
Mantorp 109 E1
Mäntsälä 107 F2
Mänttä 103 D3
Mäntyharju 103 E3
Mäntyjärvi 99 E2
Mäntyluoto 102 B3
Manzal, Pto del . . . 35 D2
Manzanares 40 B4
Manzanares el
  Real 40 A2
Manzaneda 34 C3
Manzanera 41 E3
Manzat 26 A4
Manziana 63 D2
Maó 45 F2
Maqellarë 77 D3
Maqueda 40 A2
Maramures 112 C3
Maranchón 40 C1
Maranchón,
  Pto de 40 C1

Maranello 60 C2
Maranhâo,
  Bgem do 38 B4
Marano 59 F3
Marano di Napoli . 64 B4
Marano, L di 59 F4
Marans 24 B4
Marão, Sa do 34 B4
Marássia 81 F1
Maratea 67 E2
Marateca 38 A4
Marathéa 83 D2
Marathiá, Akr 86 A2
Marathiás 83 D3
Marathókambos . . 89 E1
Marathónas 87 F1
Marathópoli 86 B3
Márathos 83 F2
Marbach 55 D2
Mårbacka 105 E3
Marbella 43 E4
Marburg 17 F4
Marby 101 E2
Marčana 70 A4
March (A) 57 F2
March (GB) 10 C1
Marchamalo 40 B2
Marchaux 27 D2

Marche 61 E4
Marche-en-
  Famenne 50 C4
Marchegg 57 F2
Marchena 43 E3
Marchenoir 25 E1
Marchiennes 20 A1
Marciac 28 C4
Marciana Marina . . 62 C1
Marcianise 64 B3
Marcigny 26 B4
Marcilla 36 C2
Marcillac-Vallon . . 29 E3
Marcillat-en-
  Combraille 25 F4
Marcilly-le-Hayer . . 20 B4
Marckolsheim 27 E1
Marco de
  Canaveses 34 A4
Marcoule 30 B3
Mære 101 D1
Maree, L 2 C3
Mare Ligure 60 A4
Marene 31 E2
Marennes 28 A1
Marentes 34 C2
Maréttimo, I- 68 A3
Mareuil (Dordogne) . 28 C1

Mareuil (Vendée) . . 24 B3
Margarites 91 D3
Margariti 82 B2
Margate 11 D2
Margherita di
  Savoia 65 D3
Marguerittes 30 B3
María 44 C2
Maria Cristina,
  Emb de 41 E3
Mariannelund 109 E1
Mariánské Lázně . . 53 E4
Maria Saal 70 A1
Maria Taferl 57 E2
Mariazell 57 E3
Maribo 108 C4
Maribor 70 C1
Mariborsko
  Pohorje 70 C1
Marica 115 D3
Mariefred 106 B4
Mariehamn 106 C3
Marienberg 53 E3
Marienborn 52 C1
Marienburg 51 E4
Marienstedt 48 B3
Mariestad 105 E4
Marignane 30 C4

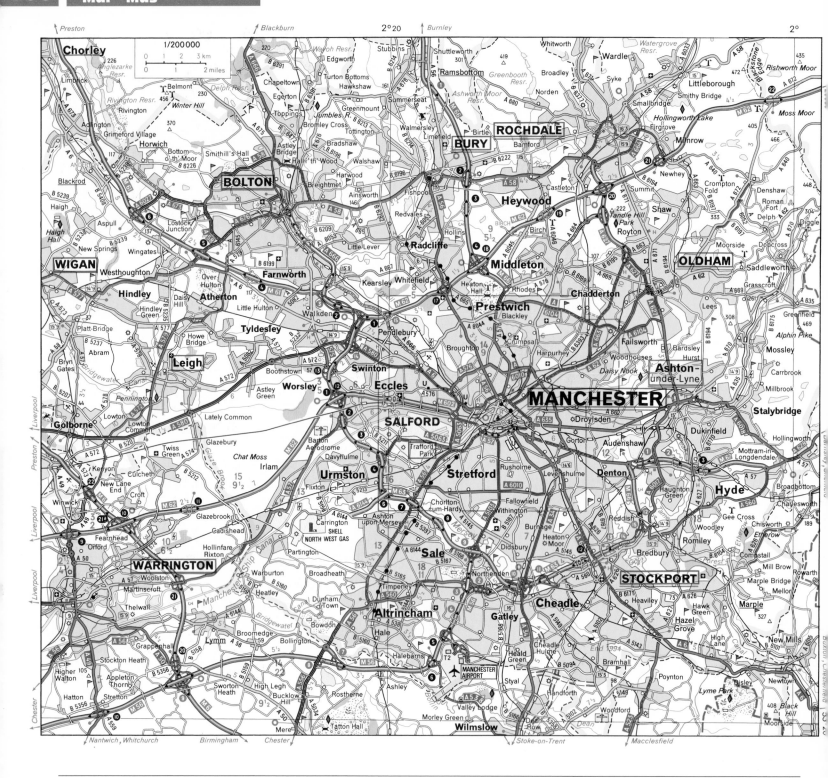

Marigny	18 B3	Marineo	68 B3	Markkleeberg	53 D2	Marl	17 E3	Maronias, Akr	81 E2
Marigny-le-Châtel	20 B4	Marines	19 E3	Markneukirchen	53 D4	Marlborough	9 E2	Maronne	29 E2
Marija Bistrica	70 C2	Maringues	26 A4	Markópoulo (Atiki-		Marle	20 B2	Maros	114 B1
Marijampolė	110 C4	Marinha Grande	38 A2	Piréas)	84 B4	Marlow (D)	48 C2	Marostica	59 D4
Marikirk	3 E4	Marinkainen	102 C1	Markópoulo (Atikii-		Marlow (GB)	9 F2	Marotta	61 E3
Marín	34 A2	Marino	63 E3	Piréas)	87 F1	Marmande	28 C3	Márpissa	88 C3
Marina	75 D2	Marismas,		Markópoulo		Marmara Denizi	115 E3	Marquartstein	56 B3
Marina di		Pto de las	43 D2	(Kefaloniá)	86 A1	Marmári	88 A1	Marquion	19 F2
Camerota	67 D2	Marjaniemi	99 D4	Markovac (Srbija)	73 D3	Mármaro	85 F4	Marquise	19 E1
Marina di Campo	62 C2	Marjina Gorka	111 D4	Markovac		Marmolada, Mte	59 D3	Marradi	61 D3
Marina di Carrara	60 B3	Markaryd	109 D3	(Vojvodina)	73 D3	Marmolejo	43 F2	Marraskoski	99 D2
Marina di Castagneto-		Markdorf	55 D4	Markov manastir	77 E3	Marmoutier	21 E4	Marsaglia	60 A2
Donoratico	62 C1	Marken	16 C2	Markranstädt	53 D2	Marnay	27 D2	Marsala	68 A3
Marina di		Markermeer	16 C2	Markstein, le	27 E1	Marne	47 F2	Marsberg	17 F3
Gioiosa Jonica	67 F4	Market Drayton	6 C3	Marktbreit	55 E1	Marne (Dépt)	20 B4	Marsciano	63 E1
Marina di Grosseto	62 C1	Market Harborough	9 F1	Markt Erlbach	55 E1	Marne R	19 F4	Marseillan	30 A4
Marina di Massa	60 B3	Markethill	13 D2	Marktheidenfeld	55 D1	Marne au Rhin, Canal		Marseille	30 C4
Marina di		Market Rasen	7 D2	Markt Indersdorf	55 F3	de la	20 C4	Marseille-en-	
Pietrasanta	60 B3	Market Weighton	7 D2	Marktl	56 B3	Marnitz	48 C3	Beauvaisis	19 E3
Marina di Pisa	60 C4	Markgröningen	55 D2	Marktoberdorf	55 E4	Marofa	39 D1	Marsfjällen	97 E4
Marina di Ragusa	69 D4	Markina	36 B1	Marktredwitz	53 D4	Marolles-les-		Marsico Nuovo	64 C4
Marina di Ravenna	61 D2	Märkisch		Markt St Florian	57 D3	Braults	23 F3	Marske-by-the-Sea	5 F4
Marinella	68 B3	Buchholz	53 E1	Markušica	71 F2	Marónia	81 E2	Mars-la-Tour	21 D3
Märsta	106 B3	Martinengo	60 B1
Marstal	108 B4	Martinet	32 A3
Marstrand	108 C1	Martingança	38 A2
Marta	63 D2	Martinniemi	99 D3
Martano	65 F4	Martino	83 F4
Martel	29 D2	Martín, R	41 E1
Martelange	21 D2	Martinščica	70 B4
Martes, Sa de	44 A2	Martis	66 B2
Marthon	28 C2	Martjanci	70 C1
Martignacco	59 F3	Martofte	108 B3
Martigné-		Martonvaara	103 F2
Ferchaud	23 D4	Martorell	32 A4
Martigny	27 E4	Martos	44 A2
Martigny-les-Bains	27 D1	Martti	95 F4
Martigues	30 C4	Marttila	107 D2
Martim Longo	42 B2	Marvão	38 C3
Martin	112 B3	Marvejols	29 F2
Martina	58 C2	Maryport	5 D4
Martina Franca	65 E3	Mary, Puy	29 E2
Martin Brod	71 D4	Marzagran	20 B3
Martinci Čepinski	71 F2	Mas-Cabardès	32 B1
Martin de la Jara	43 E3	Mas-d'Agenais, le	28 C3
Martin de Yeltes	39 D1	Mas-d'Azil, le	37 F1

Mas de Barberans .. 41 F2
Mas de las Matas... 41 E2
Masegoso 40 C2
Masevaux 27 E1
Masi............. 95 D2
Maside 34 B2
Mask, L 12 B3
Masku 107 D2
Maslenica 74 C1
Maslinica 75 D2
Maslovare 71 E4
Måsøy 95 D1
Maspalomas....... 42 B4
Massa 60 B3
Massa Fiscaglia ... 61 D2
Massafra 65 E4
Massamagrell..... 41 E3
Massa Marittima .. 62 C1
Massa Martana ... 63 E1
Massarosa 60 C3
Massat 37 F2
Massegros, le 29 F3
Masseube 28 C4
Massiac 29 F1
Mastihári 89 F3
Mástiho, Akr 89 D1
Masueco 34 C4
Maszewo 49 F2
Mat 76 C3
Matachel, R 43 D1
Mátala 91 D4
Matalascañas 42 C3
Matalavilla, Emb de . 35 D2
Matalebreras 36 C3
Matallana 35 D2
Mataránga........ 83 E2
Mataró 32 B4
Matarraña, R 41 F2
Mataruška Banja .. 73 D4
Matejče 77 E2
Matelica 61 E4
Matelles, les 30 A4
Matera 65 D4
Matese, Mti del ... 64 B3
Mateševo 76 B2
Mátészalka 112 C3
Mateus 34 B4
Matfors 101 F3
Matha 24 C4
Mathráki, N 78 A4
Máti 88 A1
Matignon 18 A4
Matka 77 D3
Matku 107 E2
Matlock 6 C3
Matosinhos....... 34 A4
Matour 26 B4
Mátra 112 B3
Matrei (Osttirol) .. 59 E2
Matrei (Tirol) 59 D2
Matterhorn 27 E4
Mattersburg...... 57 F3
Mattighofen...... 56 C3
Mattinata......... 64 C2
Mattsee 56 C3
Mattsmyra 101 E4
Matulji........... 70 B3
Matute 36 B3
Maubeuge 20 B1
Maubourguet 28 B4
Maubuisson 28 A2
Mauchline........ 4 C2
Mauerkirchen ... 56 C3
Mauguio 30 B4
Maula 99 D3
Maulbronn 54 C2
Maulde 29 D1
Mauléon 24 C3
Mauléon-Licharre .. 28 A4
Maumturk Mts. ... 12 B3
Maun............ 70 B4
Maure........... 23 D3
Maure, Col de 31 D3
Maures, Massif
  des............ 31 D4
Mauriac 29 E2
Mauria, Pso...... 59 E3
Mauron 22 C3
Maurs 29 E2
Mautern 57 D4
Mauterndorf 59 F1
Mauthausen 57 D2
Mauvezin 28 C4
Mauvoisin, Bge de . 27 E4

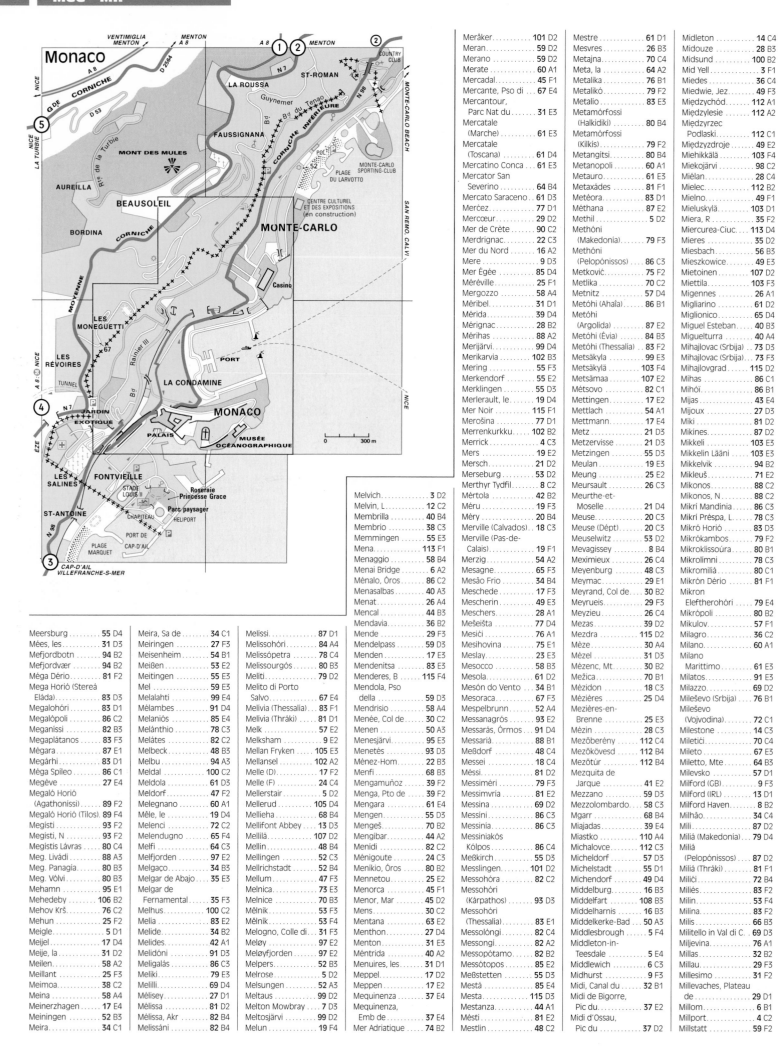

Meersburg 55 D4
Mées, les 31 D3
Mefjordbotn 94 B2
Mefjordvær 94 B2
Mèga Dério 81 F2
Mega Horió (Stereá Eláda) 83 D3
Megalohóri 83 D1
Megalópoli 86 C2
Meganíssi 82 B3
Megaplátanos 83 F3
Mégara 87 E1
Mégarhi 83 D1
Méga Spíleo 86 C1
Megève 27 E4
Megaló Horió (Agathoníssi) 89 F2
Megaló Horió (Tílos) 89 F4
Megísti 93 F2
Megísti, N 93 F2
Megístis Lávras 80 C4
Meg. Livádi 88 A3
Meg. Panagía 80 B3
Meg. Vólvi 80 B3
Mehamn 95 E1
Mehedeby 106 B2
Mehov Krš 76 C2
Mehun 25 F2
Meigle 5 D1
Meijel 17 D4
Meije, la 31 D2
Meilen 58 A2
Meillant 25 F3
Meimoa 38 C2
Meina 58 A4
Meinerzhagen 17 E4
Meiningen 52 B3
Meira 34 C1

Meira, Sa de 34 C1
Meiringen 27 F3
Meisenheim 54 B1
Meißen 53 E2
Meitingen 55 E3
Mel 59 E3
Melalahti 99 E4
Mélambes 91 D4
Melaniós 85 E4
Melánthio 78 C3
Melátes 82 C2
Melbeck 48 B3
Melbu 94 A3
Meldal 100 C2
Meldola 61 D3
Meldorf 47 F2
Mêle, le 19 D4
Melenci 72 C2
Melendugno 65 F4
Melfi 64 C3
Melfjorden 97 E2
Melgaço 34 B3
Melgar de Abajo 35 E3
Melgar de Fernamental 35 F3
Melhus 100 C2
Melía 83 E2
Melide 34 B2
Melides 42 A1
Melidóni 91 D3
Meligalás 86 C3
Melíki 79 E3
Melilli 69 D4
Mélisey 27 D1
Mélissa 81 D2
Mélissa, Akr 82 B4
Melissáni 82 B4

Melissi 87 D1
Melissohóri 84 A4
Melissópetra 78 C4
Melissourgós 80 B3
Melíti 79 D2
Melito di Porto Salvo 67 E4
Melívia (Thessalía) 83 F1
Melívia (Thráki) 81 D1
Melk 57 E2
Melksham 9 E2
Mellan Fryken 105 E3
Mellansel 102 A3
Melle (D) 17 F2
Melle (F) 24 C4
Mellerstair 5 D2
Mellerud 105 D4
Mellieha 68 B4
Mellin 48 B4
Mellingen 52 C3
Mellrichstadt 52 B4
Mellum 47 F3
Melnica 73 E3
Melnice 70 B3
Mělník 53 F3
Melón 34 B3
Melogno, Colle di 31 F2
Meløy 97 E2
Meløyfjorden 97 E2
Melpers 52 B3
Melrose 5 D2
Melsungen 52 A3
Meltaus 99 D2
Melton Mowbray 7 D3
Meltosjärvi 99 D2
Melun 19 F4

Melvich 3 D2
Melvin, L. 12 C2
Membrilla 40 B4
Membrio 38 C3
Memmingen 55 E3
Mena 113 F1
Menaggio 58 B4
Menai Bridge 6 A2
Ménalo, Óros 86 C2
Menasalbas 40 A3
Menat 26 A4
Mencal 44 B3
Mendavia 36 B2
Mende 29 F3
Mendelpass 59 D3
Menden 17 E3
Mendenitsa 83 E3
Menderes, B 115 F4
Mendola, Pso della 59 D3
Mendrisio 58 A4
Menée, Col de 30 C2
Menen 50 A3
Menesjärvi 95 E3
Menetés 93 D3
Ménez-Hom 22 B3
Menfi 68 B3
Mengamuñoz 39 F2
Menga, Pto de 39 F2
Mengara 61 E4
Mengen 55 D3
Mengeš 70 B2
Mengibar 44 A2
Menidi 82 C2
Ménigoute 24 C3
Menikio, Óros 80 B2
Mennetou 82 C2
Menorca 45 F1
Menor, Mar 45 D3
Mens 30 C2
Mentana 63 E2
Menthon 27 D4
Menton 31 E3
Méntrida 40 A2
Menuires, les 31 D1
Meppel 17 D2
Meppen 17 E2
Mequinenza 37 E4
Mequinenza, Emb de 37 E4
Mer Adriatique 74 B2

Meråker 101 D2
Meran 59 D2
Merano 59 D2
Merate 60 A1
Mercadal 45 F1
Mercante, Pso di 67 E4
Mercantour, Parc Nat du 31 E3
Mercatale (Marche) 61 E3
Mercatale (Toscana) 61 D4
Mercatino Conca 61 E3
Mercato San Severino 64 B4
Mercato Saraceno 61 D3
Merčez 77 D1
Mercoeur 29 D2
Mer de Crète 90 C2
Merdrignac 22 C3
Mer du Nord 16 A2
Mere 9 D3
Mer Égée 85 D4
Méréville 25 F1
Mergozzo 58 A4
Méribel 31 D1
Mérida 39 D4
Mérignac 28 B2
Mérihas 88 A2
Merijärvi 99 D4
Merikarvia 102 A3
Mering 55 F3
Merkendorf 55 E2
Merklingen 55 D3
Merlerault, le 19 D4
Mer Noir 115 F1
Merošina 77 D1
Merrenkurkku 102 B2
Merrick 4 C3
Mers 19 E2
Mersch 21 D2
Merseburg 53 D2
Merthyr Tydfil 8 C2
Mértola 42 B2
Méru 19 F3
Méry 20 B4
Merville (Calvados) 18 C3
Merville (Pas-de-Calais) 19 F1
Merzig 54 A2
Mesagne 65 F3
Mesão Frio 34 B4
Meschede 17 F3
Mescherin 49 E3
Meschers 28 A1
Mešeišta 77 D4
Mesiči 76 A1
Mesihovina 75 E1
Meslay 23 E3
Mesocco 58 B3
Mesola 61 D2
Mesón do Vento 34 B1
Mesoraca 67 F3
Mespelbrunn 52 A4
Messanagrós 93 E2
Messarás, Órmos 91 D4
Messariá 88 B1
Meßdorf 48 C4
Messei 18 C4
Méssi 81 D2
Messiméri 79 D2
Messímvria 81 E2
Messina 69 D2
Messíni 86 C3
Messinía 86 C3
Messiniakós Kólpos 86 C4
Meßkirch 55 D3
Messlingen 101 D2
Messohóri 82 C2
Messohóri (Kárpathos) 93 D3
Messohóri (Thessalía) 83 E1
Messolóngi 82 C4
Messongí 82 A2
Messopótamo 82 B2
Messótopos 85 E2
Meßstetten 55 D3
Mestá 85 E4
Mestanza 44 A1
Mésti 81 E2
Mestlin 48 C2

Mestre 61 D1
Mesvres 26 B3
Metajna 70 C4
Meta, la 64 A2
Metalika 76 B1
Metalikó 79 F2
Metalio 83 E3
Metamórfossi (Halkidiki) 80 B4
Metamórfossi (Kilkis) 79 F2
Metangítsi 80 B4
Metanopoli 60 A1
Metauro 61 E3
Metaxádes 81 F1
Metéora 83 D1
Méthana 87 E2
Methil 5 D2
Methóni (Makedonía) 79 F3
Methóni (Pelopónnissos) 86 C3
Metković 75 F2
Metlika 70 C2
Metnitz 57 D4
Metóhi (Ahaía) 86 B1
Metóhi (Argolída) 87 E2
Metóhi (Évia) 84 B3
Metóhi (Thessalía) 83 F2
Metsäkyla 99 E3
Metsäkylä 103 F4
Metsämaa 107 E2
Métsovo 82 C1
Mettingen 17 E2
Mettlach 54 A1
Mettmann 17 E4
Metz 21 D3
Metzervisse 21 D3
Metzingen 55 D3
Meulan 19 E3
Meung 25 E2
Meursault 26 C3
Meurthe-et-Moselle 21 D4
Meuse 20 C3
Meuse (Dépt) 20 C3
Meuselwitz 53 D2
Mevagissey 8 B4
Meximieux 26 C4
Meyenburg 48 C3
Meymac 29 E1
Meyrand, Col de 30 B2
Meyrueis 29 F3
Meyzieu 26 C4
Mezas 39 D2
Mezdra 115 D2
Mèze 30 A4
Mézel 31 D3
Mézenc, Mt 30 B2
Mežica 70 B1
Mézidon 18 C3
Mézières 25 D4
Mézières-en-Brenne 25 E3
Mézin 28 C3
Mezöberény 112 C4
Mezökövesd 112 B4
Mezötúr 112 C4
Mezquita de Jarque 41 E2
Mezzano 59 D3
Mezzolombardo 58 C3
Mgarr 68 B4
Miajadas 39 E4
Miastko 110 A4
Michalovce 112 C3
Micheldorf 57 D3
Michelstadt 55 D1
Michendorf 49 D4
Middelburg 16 B3
Middelfart 108 B3
Middelharnis 16 B3
Middelkerke-Bad 50 A3
Middlesbrough 5 E4
Middleton-in-Teesdale 5 E4
Middlewich 6 C3
Midhurst 9 F3
Midi, Canal du 32 B1
Midi de Bigorre, Pic du 37 E2
Midi d'Ossau, Pic du 37 D2

Midleton 14 C4
Midouze 28 B3
Midsund 100 B2
Mid Yell 3 F1
Miedes 36 C4
Miedwie, Jez 49 F3
Międzychód 112 A1
Międzylesie 112 A2
Międzyrzec Podlaski 112 C1
Międzyzdroje 49 E1
Miehikkälä 103 D1
Miekojärvi 98 C2
Miélan 28 C4
Mielec 112 B2
Mielno 49 F1
Mieluskylä 103 D1
Miera, R 35 F2
Miercurea-Ciuc. 113 D1
Mieres 35 D2
Miesbach 56 B3
Mieszkowice 49 E3
Mietoinen 107 D2
Miettila 103 F3
Migennes 26 A1
Migliarino 61 D2
Miglionico 65 D4
Miguel Esteban 40 B3
Miguelturra 40 A4
Mihajlovac (Srbija) 73 F3
Mihajlovac (Srbija) 73 F3
Mihajlovgrad 115 D2
Mihas 86 C1
Mihói 86 B1
Mijas 43 E4
Mijoux 27 D3
Miki 81 D2
Mikines 87 D2
Mikkeli 103 E3
Mikkelin Lääni 103 E3
Mikkelvik 94 B2
Mikleuš 71 E2
Mikonos 88 C2
Mikonos, N 88 C2
Mikrí Mandínia 86 C3
Mikrí Préspa, L. 78 C3
Mikró Horió 83 D3
Mikrókambos 79 F2
Mikroklissoúra 80 B1
Mikrolimni 78 C3
Mikromiliá 80 C1
Mikrón Dério 81 F1
Mikron Eleftherohóri 79 E4
Mikrópoli 80 B2
Mikulov 57 F1
Milagro 36 C2
Milano 60 A1
Milano Marittimo 61 E3
Milatos 91 E3
Milazzo 69 D2
Mileševo (Srbija) 76 B1
Mileševo (Vojvodina) 72 C1
Milestone 14 C3
Miletići 70 C4
Mileto 67 E3
Miletto, Mte 64 B3
Milevsko 57 D1
Milford (GB) 9 F3
Milford (IRL) 13 D1
Milford Haven 8 B2
Milhão 34 C4
Mili 87 D2
Miliá (Makedonía) 79 D4
Miliá (Pelopónnissos) 87 D2
Miliá (Thráki) 81 F1
Milići 72 B4
Miliés 83 F2
Milín 53 F4
Milina 83 F2
Milis 66 B3
Militello in Val di C. 69 D3
Miljevina 76 A1
Millas 32 B2
Millau 29 F3
Millesimo 31 F2
Millevaches, Plateau de 29 D1
Millom 6 B1
Millport 4 C2
Millstatt 59 F2

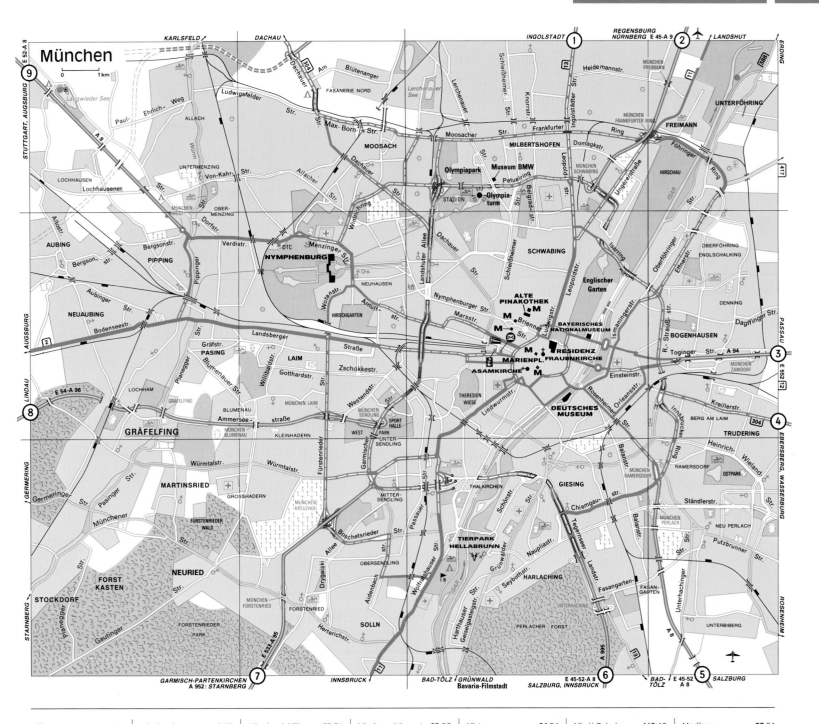

München

Millstreet ... 14 B4	Minehead ... 8 C3	Mirador del Fito ... 35 E1	Mirebeau (Vienne) ... 25 D3	Místros ... 84 B4	Mladá Boleslav ... 112 A2	Modřany ... 53 F4
Milltown Malbay ... 12 B4	Minerbe ... 60 C1	Miraflores ... 35 F3	Mirecourt ... 27 D1	Misurina ... 59 E2	Mladá Vožice ... 57 D1	Modrava ... 56 C1
Milly ... 19 F4	Minerbio ... 61 D2	Miraflores de la	Mirepoix ... 32 A2	Mitchelstown ... 14 C3	Mladenovac ... 73 D3	Modriča ... 71 F3
Milmarcos ... 36 C4	Minervino Murge ... 65 D3	Sierra ... 40 A1	Mires ... 91 D4	Mittelland-Kanal ... 17 F2	Mlado Nagoričane ... 77 E2	Modrište ... 77 D3
Milmersdorf ... 49 E3	Minglanilla ... 41 D3	Miramar (F) ... 31 E4	Miribel ... 26 C4	Mithimna ... 85 F2	Mladost, Ez. ... 77 E3	Modugno ... 65 D3
Milna ... 75 D2	Mingorria ... 39 F1	Miramar (P) ... 34 A4	Mirina ... 85 D1	Mitikas ... 82 C3	Mlava ... 73 E3	Moëlan ... 22 B3
Miločer ... 76 B3	Minguez, Pto ... 41 D2	Miramare ... 61 E3	Mirna ... 70 B2	Mitikas Mt ... 79 E4	Mława ... 112 B1	Moelv ... 105 D2
Milohnić ... 70 B3	Mingulay ... 2 A4	Miramas ... 30 C4	Mirna R ... 70 A3	Mitilini ... 85 F2	Mlini ... 76 A2	Moen ... 94 B3
Milopótamos ... 90 A1	Minho ... 34 A3	Mirambeau ... 28 B1	Miroč ... 73 E3	Mitilinii ... 89 E1	Mlinište ... 71 D4	Moena ... 59 D3
Milos ... 88 A4	Miničevo ... 73 F4	Mirambélou, Kólpos 91 F3	Miroševce ... 77 E1	Mitrašinci ... 77 F3	Mljet ... 75 E2	Moers ... 17 D3
Miloševa Kula ... 73 E3	Minilla, Emb de la ... 43 D2	Miramont-de-	Mirotice ... 56 C1	Mitrópoli ... 83 D2	Mljetski Kanal ... 75 F2	Moesa ... 58 B3
Milos, N ... 88 A4	Ministra, Sierra ... 36 B4	Guyenne ... 28 C2	Mirovice ... 56 C1	Mitrovica ... 77 D1	Mnichovo	Moffat ... 5 D3
Miltach ... 56 B1	Minkiö ... 107 E2	Miranda de Ebro ... 36 B2	Mirow ... 49 D3	Mitsikéli, Óros ... 82 B1	Hradiště ... 53 F3	Mogadouro ... 34 C4
Miltenberg ... 55 D1	Miño, R ... 34 B2	Miranda del	Mirsíni ... 91 E4	Mittelberg (Tirol) ... 58 C2	Moälven ... 102 A2	Mogadouro,
Milton Keynes ... 9 D1	Minsk ... 111 D4	Castañar ... 39 E2	Mirtiés ... 89 E1	Mittelberg	Moaña ... 34 A3	Sa do ... 34 C4
Milutinovac ... 73 F2	Mińsk Mazowiecki ... 112 B1	Miranda do Corvo ... 38 B2	Mirtóo Pélagos ... 87 E3	(Vorarlberg) ... 58 B2	Moate ... 12 C3	Mogente ... 45 D1
Mimizan ... 28 A3	Minsterley ... 9 D1	Miranda do Douro ... 34 C4	Mírtos ... 91 E4	Mittenwald ... 55 F4	Mocejón ... 40 A3	Mogila ... 77 E4
Mimizan-Plage ... 28 A3	Minthi, Óros ... 86 C2	Mirande ... 28 C4	Mírtos, Akr ... 93 E2	Mittenwalde ... 49 E4	Möckern ... 52 C1	Mogil'ov ... 111 E4
Mimoň ... 53 F3	Mintlaw ... 3 E3	Mirandela ... 34 C4	Mírtou, Kólpos ... 82 B4	Mittersill ... 59 E1	Möckmühl ... 55 D2	Moglia ... 60 C2
Mina ... 87 D4	Miokovićevo ... 71 E2	Mirandola ... 60 C2	Mirueña ... 39 F1	Mitterteich ... 53 D4	Moclin ... 44 A3	Mogliano Veneto ... 59 E4
Mina de São	Mionica ... 72 C3	Mirano ... 61 D1	Mišar ... 72 C3	Mittweida ... 53 E2	Modane ... 31 D1	Mogón ... 44 B2
Domingos ... 42 B2	Mionnay ... 26 C4	Mira, R ... 42 A2	Misi ... 99 D2	Mizen Head ... 14 A4	Modbury ... 8 C4	Mogorrit ... 41 D2
Minas de Riotinto ... 42 C2	Mira (E) ... 41 D3	Mirador de Llesba ... 35 E2	Misilmeri ... 68 B3	Miżhir'ja ... 112 B3	Modena ... 60 C2	Moguer ... 42 C2
Minaya ... 40 C4	Mira (I) ... 61 D1	Miravalles ... 34 C2	Miskolc ... 112 B3	Mjällån ... 101 F2	Módi ... 83 E3	Mohács ... 114 B1
Minch, The ... 2 B2	Mira (P) ... 38 B1	Miravci ... 77 F3	Mislinja ... 70 B1	Mjällom ... 102 A2	Modica ... 69 D4	Moher, Cliffs of ... 12 B4
Mincio ... 60 C1	Mirabella Imbaccari 68 C4	Miravete, Pto de ... 39 E3	Mistelbach ... 57 F2	Mjöbäck ... 108 C2	Modigliana ... 61 D3	Mohill ... 12 C3
Mindelheim ... 55 E3	Mira de Aire ... 38 B3	Mirditë ... 76 C3	Misterbianco ... 69 D3	Mjölby ... 109 E1	Mödling ... 57 F2	Möhkö ... 103 F2
Minden ... 17 F2	Mirador de Coto	Mirebeau	Mistrás ... 87 D3	Mjøndalen ... 104 C3	Modračko jez ... 71 F3	Móhlos ... 91 F4
Mindin ... 24 A2	Rondo ... 34 A2	(Côte-d'Or) ... 26 C2	Mistretta ... 68 C3	Mjøsa ... 105 D2	Modran ... 71 F3	Möhne ... 17 F3

Moholm 105 E4
Mohyliv-
  Podils'kyj 113 E3
Moi 104 A4
Moià 32 A4
Moie 61 E4
Moimenta 34 C3
Moimenta da Beira .. 38 C1
Mo i Rana 97 E2
Moirans 30 C1
Moirans-en-
  Montagne 27 D3
Moisdon 23 D4
Moisiovaara 99 F4
Moisling 48 B2
Moissac 29 D3
Moita 38 A4
Moixent 45 D1
Mojácar 44 C3
Mojados 35 E4
Mojkovac 76 B2
Mojón Pardo, Pto
  de 36 B3
Mojstrana 70 A1
Mokra Gora 72 C4
Mokra Gora Mts 76 C2
Mokrin 72 C1
Mokronog 70 B2
Mokro Polje 75 D1
Mol (B) 50 C3
Mol (Vojvodina) 72 C1
Mola di Bari 65 E3
Molài 87 D4
Molat 74 B1
Molat / 74 B1
Molatón 41 D4
Mold 6 B3
Molde 100 B2
Moldefjorden 100 B2
Moldova 113 E3
Moldova Nouă 114 C1
Moldoveanu 113 D4
Møldrup 108 B2
Moledo do Minho .. 34 A3
Molène 22 A2
Molfetta 65 D3
Molières 29 D3
Molina de Aragón .. 40 C2
Molina de Segura .. 45 D2
Molinella 61 D2
Molinicos 44 C1
Molins de Rei 32 A4
Molise 64 B2
Moliterno 65 D4
Molitg-les-Bains 32 B2
Mólivos, Akr 85 F2
Molkom 105 E3
Möllbrücke 59 F2
Mollerussa 37 F3
Molliens-Vidame ... 19 E2
Mollina 43 F3
Mölln 48 B2
Mollösund 108 C1
Mölnlycke 108 C1
Molodečno 111 D4
Mologa 111 F1
Mólos 83 E3
Molpe 102 B2
Mols 108 B3
Molsheim 21 E4
Molve 71 D1
Molveno 58 C3
Mombeltrán 39 F2
Mombuey 35 D3
Mommark 108 B4
Momo 60 A1
Møn 108 C4
Monach, Sd of 2 A3
Monadhliath Mts ... 2 C4
Monå fjärd 102 B2
Monaghan 13 D2
Monaghan (Co) 13 D2
Monasterace
  Marina 67 F4
Monasterboice 13 D3
Monasterevin 13 D4
Monasterio de
  Rodilla 36 A2
Monastier, le 30 B2
Monastir 66 B4
Monastiráki (Stereá
  Eláda) 82 C3
Monastiráki
  (Thráki) 81 F2

Monastíri Doukáto .. 81 E2
Monastíri, N 83 E2
Monbazillac 28 C2
Moncalieri 31 E2
Moncalvo 31 F1
Monção 34 A3
Moncarapacho 42 B3
Moncayo, Sa
  de 36 C3
Mönchdorf 57 D2
Mönchengladbach . 17 D4
Monchique 42 A2
Monchique,
  Sa de 42 A2
Monclar-de-
  Quercy 29 D3
Moncófar 41 E3
Moncontour (Côtes-
  d'Amor) 22 C3
Moncontour
  (Vienne) 24 C3
Moncoutant 24 C3
Monda 43 E4
Mondariz 34 A3
Mondavio 61 E3
Mondego, Cabo .. 38 A2
Mondego, R 38 B2
Mondéjar 40 B2
Mondello 68 B2
Mondim 34 B4
Mondolfo 61 E3
Mondoñedo 34 C1
Mondorf 21 D3
Mondoubleau 23 F3
Mondovì 31 F2
Mondragon 30 B3
Mondragone 64 A3
Mondsee 56 C3
Monein 28 B4
Monemvassia 87 E4
Monesi 31 E3
Monesterio 43 D1
Monestier-de-
  Clermont 30 C2
Monestiés 29 E3
Monêtier, le 31 D2
Moneygall 12 C4
Moneymore 13 D2
Monfalcone 59 F3
Monflanquin 28 C2
Monforte 38 C4
Monforte de
  Lemos 34 B2
Mongie, la 37 E2
Mongó 45 E1
Monguelfo 59 D2
Monheim 55 E2
Mönichkirchen 57 F3
Mon-Idée 20 B2
Monifieth 5 D1
Moni, N 87 E4
Monistrol 32 A4
Monistrol-d'Allier .. 29 F2
Monistrol-sur-
  Loire 30 B1
Mönkebude 49 E2
Monmouth 9 D2
Monnickendam ... 16 C2
Monodéndri 78 C4
Monódrio 84 B4
Monólithos 93 E4
Monopoli 65 E3
Monor 112 B4
Monóvar 45 D1
Monpazier 28 C2
Monreal 51 E4
Monreal del
  Campo 41 D2
Monreale 68 B3
Monrepôs, Pto de . 37 D2
Monroy 39 D3
Monroyo 41 E2
Mons 50 B4
Monsanto 38 C2
Monsaraz 42 C1
Monschau 51 D4
Monségur 28 C2
Monselice 61 D1
Monserrat 41 E4
Møns Klint 108 C4
Monsols 26 B4
Mönsterås 109 E3
Monsummano
  Terme 60 C3

Montabaur 51 F4
Montagnac 30 A4
Montagnana 61 D1
Montagne Noire ... 32 B1
Montagnes
  Noires 22 B3
Montagrier 28 C1
Montaigu 24 B3
Montaigu-de-
  Quercy 29 D3
Montaigut 26 A4
Montaione 60 C4
Montalbán 41 E2
Montalbo 40 C3
Montalcino 63 D1
Montalegre 34 B3
Montalieu 26 C4
Montalivet 28 A1
Montalto delle
  Marche 61 F4
Montalto di Castro . 63 D2
Montalto Uffugo .. 67 E2
Montalvão 38 C3
Montamarta 35 D4
Montana 27 E3
Montañana 37 D3
Montánchez 39 D3
Montanejos 41 E3
Montargil 38 B3
Montargil, Bgem
  de 38 B4
Montargis 25 F1
Montastruc-la-
  Conseillère 29 D4
Montauban (Ille-et-
  Vilaine) 23 D3
Montauban (Tarn-et-
  Garonne) 29 D3
Montbard 26 B2
Montbazens 29 E3
Montbazon 25 D2
Montbéliard 27 E2
Montbenoît 27 D2
Mont Blanc 27 E4
Montblanc 37 F4
Mont Blanc,
  Tunnel du 27 E4
Montbozon 27 D2
Montbrió del
  Camp 37 F4
Montbrison 30 B1
Montbron 28 C1
Montceau-les-
  Mines 26 B3
Montcenis 26 B3
Mont Cenis, Col du . 31 E1
Montchanin 26 B3
Montcornet 20 B2
Montcuq 29 D3
Mont-de-Marsan .. 28 B3
Montdidier 19 F3
Mont-Dore, le 29 E1
Monteagudo de las
  Vicarias 36 B4
Montealegre 35 E4
Montealegre del
  Castillo 45 D1
Montebello Ionico . 67 E4
Montebello
  Vicentino 60 C1
Montebelluna 59 E4
Monte Bianco,
  Traforo di 27 E4
Montebourg 18 B3
Monte-Carlo-
  Monaco 31 E3
Montecarotto 61 E4
Montecatini-
  Terme 60 C3
Montecchio 61 E3
Montecchio
  Maggiore 60 C1
Montech 29 D3
Monte Citerna,
  Pso del 60 C3
Montecorvino
  Rovella 64 B4
Montecristo, I di .. 62 C2
Monte Croce Carnico,
  Pso di 59 E2
Monte Croce di
  Comelico, Pso .. 59 E2
Monte da
  Pedra 38 C3

Monte da Rocha,
  Bgem de 42 B2
Montedoro 68 C3
Montefalco 63 E1
Montefalcone di Val
  Fortore 64 B3
Montefalcone nel
  Sannio 64 B2
Montefeltro 61 D3
Montefiascone 63 E2
Montefiore dell'
  Aso 61 F4
Montefiorino 60 C3
Montefrío 43 F3
Montegallo 63 F1
Montegiorgio 61 F4
Monte Giovo, Pso
  di 59 D2
Montegranaro 61 F4
Montegrotto
  Terme 61 D1
Montehermoso 39 D2
Montejicar 44 A2
Montejo de
  Tiermes 36 A4
Montejunto,
  Sa de 38 A4
Monteleone di
  Spoleto 63 E1
Montélimar 30 B2
Montella 64 B4
Montellano 43 D3
Monteluco 63 E1
Montelupo
  Fiorentino 60 C4
Montemaggiore
  Belsito 68 C3
Montemagno 31 F1
Montemayor 43 F2
Montemayor de
  Pililla 35 E4
Montemor-o-Novo . 38 B4
Montemor-o-
  Velho 38 B2
Montemuro,
  Sa do 38 C1
Montendre 28 B1
Montenegro de
  Cameros 36 B3
Montenero di
  Bisaccia 64 B2
Montenero
  Sabino 63 E2
Montepulciano 61 D4
Monte Real 38 B2
Montereale
  (Abruzzo) 63 F1
Montereale
  (Friuli-Venezia) . 59 E3
Montereau 19 F4
Monte Redondo .. 38 B2
Monterenzio 61 D3
Monteriggioni 61 D4
Monteroni di
  Lecce 65 F4
Monte Rosa 27 F4
Monterosso al
  Mare 60 B3
Monterotondo 63 E2
Monterotondo
  Marittimo 62 C1
Monterosso 34 B2
Monterrubio de la
  Serena 43 E1
Monterubbiano ... 61 F4
Montesano sulla
  Marcellana 64 C4
Monte San Savino . 61 D4
Monte Sant'
  Angelo 64 C2
Montesarchio 64 B3
Montescaglioso .. 65 D4
Montesilvano
  Marina 64 A1
Montesquieu-
  Volvestre 37 F1
Montesquiou 28 C4
Montet, le 26 A3
Montets, Col des .. 27 E4
Montevarchi 61 D4
Monteviejo, Pto
  de 35 E2
Montfaucon (Maine-
  et-Loire) 24 B2

Montfaucon-
  d'Argonne 20 C3
Montfaucon-en-
  Velay 30 B1
Montfort 23 D3
Montfort-en-
  Chalosse 28 B4
Montfort-
  l'Amaury 19 E4
Montfort-sur-
  Risle 19 D3
Montgaillard 32 A2
Montgenèvre 31 D2
Montgenèvre, Col
  de 31 D2
Montgiscard 29 D4
Montgomery 9 D1
Montguyon 28 B1
Monthermé 20 C2
Monthey 27 E4
Monthois 20 C3
Monthureux 27 D1
Monti 66 B2
Montichiari 60 B1
Monticiano 61 D4
Montiel 44 B1
Montier-en-Der ... 20 C4
Montignac 29 D2
Montigny-le-Roi .. 26 C1
Montigny-sur-
  Aube 26 C1
Montijo (E) 39 D4
Montijo (P) 38 A4
Montilla 43 F2
Montioni 62 C1
Montivilliers 19 D3
Montjean 23 E4
Montlhéry 19 F4
Montlieu 28 B1
Montlouis 25 D2
Mont-Louis 32 A3
Montluçon 25 F4
Montluel 26 C4
Montmarault 26 A4
Montmartin 18 B3
Montmédy 20 C3
Montmélian 31 D1
Montmirail
  (Marne) 20 A4
Montmirail
  (Sarthe) 23 F3
Montmirey-le-
  Château 26 C2
Montmoreau 28 C1
Montmorency 19 F4
Montmorillon 25 D4
Montmort 20 B3
Montoggio 60 A3
Montoire 23 F4
Montoito 38 C4
Montone 61 D3
Montorio al
  Vomano 63 F1
Montório 63 E2
Montoro, Emb de . 43 F1
Montpellier 30 A4
Montpellier-le-Vieux,
  Chaos de 29 F3
Montpezat-de-
  Quercy 29 D3
Montpezat-sous-
  Bauzon 30 B2
Montpon-
  Ménestérol 28 C2
Montpont 26 C3
Montréal (Aude) .. 32 A2
Montréal (Gers) ... 28 C3
Montréal-la-Cluse . 26 C4
Montredon-
  Labessonnie ... 32 B1
Montréjeau 37 E1
Montrésor 25 E2
Montresta 66 A2
Montreuil 19 E1
Montreuil-Bellay .. 24 C2
Montreux 27 E3
Montrevault 24 B2
Montrevel 26 C3
Montrichard 25 E2
Mont-roig del
  Camp 37 F4
Montrond-les-
  Bains 30 B1
Montrose 5 E1

Mont-St-Michel, le . 18 B4
Mont-St-Vincent .. 26 B3
Montsalvy 29 E2
Montsant, Sa del .. 37 F4
Montsauche 26 B2
Montsec, Serra de . 37 F3
Montseny 32 B4
Montseny, Sa de .. 32 B4
Montserrat 32 A4
Mont-sous-
  Vaudrey 26 C3
Monts-sur-
  Guesnes 25 D3
Montsûrs 23 E3
Montuenga 39 F1
Montuïri 45 F3
Monviso 31 E2
Monza 60 A1
Monzón 37 E3
Monzón de
  Campos 35 F3
Moordorf 47 E3
Moorfoot Hills 5 D2
Moosburg 56 B2
Mór 112 B4
Mora (E) 40 A3
Mora (P) 38 B4
Mora (S) 101 E4
Morača 76 B2
Morača R 76 B2
Morača klisura 76 B2
Móra d'Ebre 37 E4
Mora de Rubielos .. 41 E2
Moraira, Cap de .. 45 E1
Moraítika 82 A2
Morakovo, G 76 B2
Mora la Nova 41 F1
Moral de Calatrava . 40 A4
Moraleda de
  Zafayona 44 A3
Moraleja 39 D2
Moraleja de
  Sayago 39 E1
Morales de Rey 35 D3
Morales de Toro .. 35 E4
Morano Calabro ... 67 E2
Mora, Pto de la .. 44 A3
Morar, L 2 B4
Mörarp 108 C3
Morasverdes 39 D2
Morata de Jalón .. 36 C4
Morata de Tajuña . 40 B2
Moratalla 44 C2
Morata, Pto de ... 36 C4
Morava 57 E1
Morava R 112 A3
Moravče 70 B2
Moravci 70 C1
Moravica 73 D4
Moravské
  Budějovice 57 E1
Moravske Toplice .. 70 C1
Moravský Krumlov . 57 E1
Moray Firth 3 D3
Morbach 54 B1
Morbegno 58 B3
Morbihan 22 C3
Mörbisch 57 F3
Mörbylånga 109 E3
Morcenx 28 A3
Morciano di
  Romagna 61 E3
Morcone 64 B3
Morcote 58 A4
Morcuera, Pto de
  la 40 A1
Mordelles 23 D3
Morecambe 6 B1
Morecambe Bay .. 6 B1
Moreda 44 A3
Morée 25 E1
Moreleja del Vino .. 35 D4
Morella 41 E2
Møre og Romsdal . 100 B2
Mores 66 B2
Morestel 30 C1
Moret 19 F4
Moreton 7 E3
Moretonhampstead . 8 C3
Moreuil 19 F2
Morez 27 D3
Morfasso 60 B2
Mórfio 82 B2

Morgat 22 A3
Morges 27 D3
Morgex 27 E4
Morgins, Pas de .. 27 E4
Morhange 21 D3
Mori 58 C4
Morina 76 C3
Moritzurg 53 E2
Morjärv 98 C3
Morlaas 37 E1
Morlaix 22 B2
Mormanno 67 E2
Mormant 19 F4
Mormoiron 30 C3
Mornant 30 B1
Mórnou, Teh L 83 E4
Morón de
  Almazán 36 B4
Morón de la
  Frontera 43 E3
Morosaglia 33 F3
Morović 72 B3
Morpeth 5 E3
Morrón 44 B3
Mörrum 109 D3
Mors 108 A2
Morsbach 17 E4
Mörsil 101 E2
Morsleben 52 C1
Mortagne 28 B1
Mortagne-au-
  Perche 19 D4
Mortagne-sur-
  Sèvre 24 C3
Mortágua 38 B2
Mortain 18 C4
Mortara 60 A2
Morteau 27 D2
Mortrée 19 D4
Morven 3 D2
Moryń 49 E3
Morzine 27 E4
Morzyczyn 49 F2
Mosbach 55 D2
Mosby 104 B4
Mošćenice 70 B3
Mošćenička Draga . 70 B3
Moschendorf 57 F4
Mosel 51 E4
Moselle (Dépt) ... 21 D3
Moselle R 27 D4
Moshokariá 83 E3
Moshopótamos ... 79 E3
Mosjøen 97 E3
Moskenesøya 97 E1
Moskenstraumen .. 97 E1
Mosko 76 A2
Moskosel 98 B3
Moskva 111 F2
Moskva R 111 F2
Moslavačka gora .. 71 D2
Mosonmagyaróvár 112 A4
Mosor 75 E2
Mosqueruela 41 E2
Moss 105 D3
Mossala 107 D3
Mossat 3 D4
Mosses, Col des .. 27 E3
Mössingen 55 D3
Most (CS) 53 E3
Most (SLO) 70 A2
Mosta 68 B4
Mostar 75 F2
Mosteiro 34 A2
Mosterhamn 104 A3
Móstoles 40 A2
Mostonga 72 B2
Mostrim 12 C3
Mosty 110 C4
Mostys'ka 112 C2
Møsvatn 104 B3
Mosvik 101 D1
Mota del Cuervo .. 40 B3
Mota del Marqués . 35 E4
Motajica 71 E3
Motala 105 F4
Motala S 106 A4
Mothe-Achard, la . 24 B3
Motherwell 4 C2
Mothe-St-Héray, la . 24 C4
Motilla del Palancar 40 C3
Motovun 70 A3
Motril 44 A4
Motta di Livenza .. 59 E4

Motta S.A. 69 D3
Motta Visconti 60 A1
Motte-Chalancon, la 30 C2
Motte, la 31 D3
Mottola 65 E4
Mouchard 27 D3
Moudon 27 E3
Moúdros 85 D1
Mougins 31 E4
Mouhijärvi 107 D1
Mouilleron-en-Pareds 24 C3
Moulins 26 A3
Moulins-Engilbert 26 B3
Moulins-la-Marche 19 D4
Moult 18 C3
Moúnda, Akr 86 A1
Mountain Ash 8 C2
Mount Bellew 12 C3
Mountmellick 13 D4
Mountrath 12 C4
Mount's B 8 B4
Mountsoúna 88 C3
Moura 42 B1
Mourão 42 C1
Moúrdzeflos, Akr 85 D1
Mourenx 28 B4
Mouríki 84 A4
Mourmelon-le-Grand 20 B3
Mourne 13 D2
Mourne Mts 13 E3
Mourniés 90 B3
Mourujärvi 99 E2
Mouscron 50 A3
Moustiers-Ste-Marie 31 D3
Mouthe 27 D3
Mouthier 27 D2
Mouthoumet 32 B2
Moutier 27 E2
Moûtiers 31 D1
Moutiers-les-Mauxfaits 24 B3
Mouy 19 F3
Mouzakéi 82 C1
Mouzáki 83 D2
Mouzon 20 C2
Moville 13 D1
Moy 12 B2
Moyenneville 19 E2
Moyeuvre 21 D3
Moyuela 37 D4
Možajsk 111 F2
Mozirje 70 B1
Mozyr' 113 E1
Mrągowo 110 B4
Mrakovica 71 D3
Mramorak 73 D2
Mratinje 76 A1
Mrazovac 70 C3
Mrčajevci 73 D4
Mrežičko 77 E4
Mrkonjić Grad 71 E4
Mrkopalj 70 B3
Mrzeżyno 49 F1
Mšeno 53 F3
Msta 111 E1
Mstislavl' 111 E3
Mú 42 B2
Muć 75 D1
Muccia 61 E4
Much 17 E4
Mücheln 52 C2
Much Wenlock 9 D1
Mucientes 35 E4
Muck 2 B4
Muckle Roe 3 F1
Muckross House 14 B4
Mudanya 115 F3
Mudau 55 D1
Muddus 98 B2
Muel 37 D4
Muelas del Pan 35 D4
Muff 13 D1
Muge 38 B3
Mügeln 53 E2
Muggia 59 F4
Mugron 28 B4
Mugueimes 34 B3
Mühlbach 59 E1
Mühlberg 53 E2
Mühldorf 56 B3
Mühlen-Eichsen 48 B2
Mühlhausen 52 B2
Mühltroff 53 D3
Muhniemi 107 F2
Muhos 99 D4
Muhu 110 B2
Muineachán 13 D2
Muine Bheag 15 D3
Muirkirk 4 C3
Muir of Ord 2 C3
Mukačeve 112 C3
Mukos 77 E3
Mula 45 D2
Mülacker 54 C2
Mula, R 45 D2
Mulargia, L 66 B3
Mulhacén 44 A3
Mülheim 17 E3
Mulhouse 27 E1
Mull 4 B1
Müllheim 54 C4
Mullingar 13 D3
Mull of Galloway 4 B4
Mull of Kintyre 4 B3
Mull of Oa 4 A2
Müllrose 49 F4
Mull, Sd of 4 B1
Mullsjö 109 D1
Mulrany 12 B2
Multia 103 D3
Mumbles, The 8 C2
Muñana 39 F2
Münchberg 53 D4
Müncheberg 49 E4
München 56 A3
Münchhausen 17 F4
Münden 52 B2
Mundesley 7 F3
Mundford 11 D1
Mundo, R 44 C1
Munera 40 C4
Mungia 36 B1
Muñico 39 F2
Muniesa 37 D4
Munkebo 108 B3
Munkedal 105 D4
Munkfors 105 E3
Münnerstadt 52 B4
Muñogalindo 39 F2
Munsala 102 B2
Munsfjället 101 E1
Münsingen (CH) 27 E3
Münsingen (D) 55 D3
Munster (F) 27 E1
Münster (CH) 27 F3
Münster (Niedersachsen) 48 B3
Münster (Nordrhein-Westfalen) 17 E3
Münstertal 54 C4
Münzenberg 52 A4
Münzkirchen 56 C2
Muodoslompolo 95 D4
Muojärvi 99 F2
Muonio 95 D4
Muonioälven 95 D4
Muotkatonturit 95 E2
Mur 57 E4
Mura 70 C1
Muraglione, Pso del 61 D3
Murano 61 D1
Murat 29 E2
Murato 33 F3
Murat-sur-Vèbre 32 B1
Murau 57 D4
Muravera 66 C4
Murça 34 B4
Murchante 36 C3
Murcia 45 D2
Murcia (Reg) 44 C2
Mur-de-Barrez 29 E2
Mur-de-Bretagne 22 C3
Mureck 57 E4
Mure, la 30 C2
Mureş 112 C4
Muret 29 D4
Murg 54 C2
Murguia 36 B1
Muri 27 F2
Murias de Paredes 35 D2
Murino 76 C2
Muriqan 76 B3
Müritz See 49 D3
Murjek 98 B2
Murlough Bay 13 E1
Murnau 56 A4
Muro 33 F3
Muro de Alcoy 45 E1
Murol 29 E1
Murole 102 C3
Muro Lucano 64 C4
Muros 34 A2
Mürren 27 F3
Murrhardt 55 D2
Murska Sobota 70 C1
Mursko Središče 70 C1
Murten 27 E3
Murter 74 C1
Murter I 74 C1
Murtosa 38 B1
Murtovaara 99 F3
Murvica 74 C1
Murviel 30 A4
Mürz 57 E3
Mürzsteg 57 E3
Mürzzuschlag 57 E3
Musala 115 D3
Mussalo 103 F4
Musselburgh 5 D2
Musselkanaal 17 E1
Mussidan 28 C2
Mussomeli 68 C3
Mussy 26 B1
Mustair 58 C3
Mustasaari 102 B2
Mustèr 58 A3
Mustion as 107 E3
Mustvee 110 C1
Muta 70 B1
Mutala 102 C3
Mutterstadt 54 C1
Mutzschen 53 E2
Muurame 103 D3
Muurasjärvi 103 D1
Muuratjärvi 103 D3
Muurla 107 E2
Muurola 99 D2
Muuruvesi 103 E2
Muxía 34 A1
Muy, le 31 D4
Muzillac 22 C4
Muzzana del Turgnano 59 F3
Mweelrea Mts 12 B3
Myckegensjö 101 F2
Mykines 96 A3
Mykolaïv (L'vyv) 112 C3
Mykolaïv (Odesa) 113 F3
Myllykoski 107 F2
Myllykylä 102 C3
Myllymäki 102 C2
Mynämäki 107 D2
Mýrdalsjökull 96 B3
Myre 94 A3
Myrhorod 113 F2
Myrlandshaugen 94 B3
Myronivka 113 E2
Myrskylä 107 F2
Myrviken 101 E2
Mysen 105 D3
Mysingen 106 B4
Myśla 49 F3
Myślibórskie, Jez 49 F3
Myślibórz 49 F3
Mývatn 96 B1
Mže 53 E4

N

Naab 55 F1
Naamijoki 98 C2
Naantali 107 D2
Naarajärvi 103 E3
Naarva 103 F2
Naas 13 D4
Näätämöjoki 95 F2
Nabburg 56 B1
Načeradec 57 D1
Náchod 112 A2
Naddvik 104 B1
Nadela 34 B2
Nădlac 114 C1
Nadur 68 B4
Nadvirna 113 D3
Näfels 58 A2
Nafpaktías, Óri 83 D4
Náfpaktos 83 D4
Náfplio 87 D2
Naggen 101 F3
Nagold 54 C3
Nagu 107 D3
Nagyatád 114 A1
Nagykálló 112 C3
Nagykanizsa 114 A1
Nagykőrös 112 B4
Nahe 48 A2
Nahe *R* 54 B1
Naila 53 D4
Nailloux 32 A1
Nailsworth 9 D2
Nairn 3 D3
Najac 29 D3
Nájera 36 B2
Najerilla, R 36 B2
Nakkila 107 D1
Nakło 112 A1
Nakovo 72 C1
Nakskov 108 B4
Näljänkä 99 E3
Na Logu 70 A2
Nalón, R 35 E2
Naltijärvi 95 D3
Namdalseid 97 D4
Nämdöfjärden 106 B4
Náměšt 57 E1
Namsen 97 D4
Namsos 97 D4
Namsskogan 97 D4
Namur 50 C4
Namur (Prov) 50 C4
Nancy 21 D4
Nangis 19 F4
Nannestad 105 D2
Nant 29 F3
Nanterre 19 F4
Nantes 24 B2
Nantes, Canal de 22 C3
Nanteuil-le-Haudouin 19 F3
Nantiat 25 E4
Nantua 26 C4
Nantwich 6 C3
Nao, C de la 45 F1
Náoussa (Kiklades) 88 C3
Náoussa (Makedonía) 79 E3
Napapiiri 99 D2
Napoli 64 B4
Napoli, G di 64 A4
Napoule, la 31 E4
Narberth 8 B2
Nærbø 104 A4
Narbolia 66 B3
Narbonne 32 B1
Narbonne-Plage 30 A4
Narcao 66 B4
Narcea, R 35 D1
Nardò 65 F4
Narew 112 C1
Narila 103 E3
Narkaus 99 D2
Narni 63 E2
Naro 68 C4
Naro-Fominsk 111 F2
Nærøy 97 D4
Närpes 102 B3
Närpio 102 B3
Narta 71 D2
Nartháki 83 E2
Nartháki, Óros 83 E2
Narva 111 D1
Narvik 94 B3
Nås 105 E2
Näsåker 101 F2
Năsăud 113 D4
Nasbinals 29 F2
Našice 71 E2
Näsijärvi 102 C3
Naso 69 D2
Nassau 51 F4
Nassereith 58 C2
Naßfeld-Paß 59 F2
Nässjö 109 D1
Nastola 107 F2
Næstved 108 C4
Natalinci 73 D3
Nattaset 95 F3
Nattavaara 98 B2
Nättraby 109 E3
Naucelle 29 E3
Nauders 58 C2
Nauen 49 D4
Naul 13 D3
Naumburg 52 C2
Naunhof 53 D2
Naussac, Bge de 29 F2
Naustdal 100 A3
Nauvo 107 D3
Nava 35 E1
Nava, Colle di 31 F3
Navacelles, Cirque de 29 F3
Navacepeda 39 E2
Navacerrada 40 A2
Navacerrada, Pto de 40 A1
Navachica 44 A3
Navaconcejo 39 E2
Nava de la Asunción 40 A1
Nava del Rey 35 E4
Navafria, Pto de 40 A1
Navahermosa 39 F3
Navalcán 39 F2
Navalcarnero 40 A2
Navaleno 36 B3
Navalmanzano 40 A1
Navalmoral de la Mata 39 E3
Navalperal de Pinares 40 A2
Navaluenga 39 F2
Navalvillar de Pela 39 E4
Navamorcuende 39 F2
Navan 13 D3
Navarra 36 C2
Navarredonda de la Sierra 39 F2
Navarrenx 28 B4
Navarrés 41 E4
Navarrete 36 B2
Navascués 37 D2
Navas del Madroño 39 D3
Navas de Oro 40 A1
Navas de San Juan 44 B2
Navasfrías 39 D2
Navatalgordo 39 F2
Nave 60 B1
Nävekvarn 106 A4
Navelli 63 F2
Naver, L 2 C2
Naveros 43 D4
Navia 34 C1
Navia de Suarna 34 C2
Navia, R 34 C1
Navl'a 111 F4
Náxos 88 C3
Náxos Días 88 C3
Náxos, N 88 C3
Nay 37 E1
Nazaré 38 A3
Naze, The 11 D2
Nazilli 115 F4
Ndrejaj 76 C2
Ndroq 76 C4
Nea 101 D2
Néa Agathoúpoli 79 F3
Néa Alikarnassés 91 D3
Néa Anhíalos 83 F2
Néa Artáki 84 B4
Néa Éfessos 79 F4
Néa Epídavros 87 E2
Néa Fókeada 80 A4
Neagh, L 13 E2
Néa Hilí 81 E2
Néa Iraklitsa 80 C2
Néa Kalikrátia 79 F4
Néa Kariá 81 D2
Néa Karváli 80 C2
Néa Kerassoús 82 C2
Néa Kíos 87 D2
Néa Koróni 86 C3
Néa Mákri 88 A1
Néa Messángala 83 F1
Néa Mihanióna 79 F3
Néa Moní 85 E4
Néa Moudaniá 80 A4
Néa Péla 79 F3
Néa Péramos (Stereá-Eláda) 87 E1
Néa Péramos (Makedonía) 80 C2
Neápoli (Kríti) 91 E4
Neápoli (Makedonía) 79 D3
Neápoli (Pelopónissos) 87 E4
Néa Róda 80 B3
Néa Sánda (Makedonía) 79 F2
Néa Sánda (Thráki) 81 E2
Néa Sílata 80 A3
Néa Skióni 80 B4
Néa Stíra 84 B4
Néa Triglia 80 A4
Neath 8 C2
Néa Víssa 81 F1
Néa Zoí 79 E2
Néa Zíhni 80 B2
Nebel 47 F1
Nebelhorn 55 E4
Nebljusi 70 C4
Nebra 52 C2
Nechranická přehr nádrž 53 E3
Neckar 55 D1
Neckarelz 55 D2
Neckargemünd 54 C1
Neckarsteinach 54 C1
Neckarsulm 55 D2
Nečujam 75 D2
Neda 34 B1
Nédas 86 C2
Nedelišće 70 C1
Nedervetil 102 C1
Nedstrand 104 A3
Neede 17 D2
Needles, The 9 E3
Neermoor 47 E3
Nefyn 6 A3
Negoiu 113 D4
Negorci 77 F3
Negotin 73 F3
Negotino 77 E3
Negra de Urbión, L 36 B3
Negrar 60 C1
Negratin, Emb del 44 B2
Negreira 34 A2
Nègrepelisse 29 D3
Negru Vodă 115 E2
Neheim-Hüsten 17 F3
Neiden 95 F2
Neige, Crêt de la 27 D3
Neila 36 B3
Neiße 53 F1
Nejdek 53 E3
Nekromandío Efíras 82 B2
Neksø 109 D4
Nela, R 36 A1
Nelas 38 C1
Nelidovo 111 E2
Nellim 95 F3
Nelson 6 C2
Neman 110 B3
Neméa 87 D1
Nemours 25 F1
Nemunas 110 C3
Nemyriv 113 E3
Nenagh 12 C4
Nene 10 C1
Nénita 85 F4
Nenzing 58 B2
Neohoráki 84 A4
Neohóri (Etolía-Akarnanía) 82 C4
Neohóri (Évia) 84 B4
Neohóri (Fthiótida) 83 E3
Neohóri (Ípiros) 82 C2
Neohóri (Kardítsa) 83 D2
Neohóri (Magnissía) 84 A2
Neohóri (Pelopónissos) 86 C2
Neohóri (Thráki) 81 F1
Neohóri (Tríkala) 83 D1
Néo Monastíri 83 E2
Néon Petrítsi 80 A2
Néos Marmarás 80 B4
Néos Skopós 80 B2
Néouvielle, Pic de 37 E2
Nephin 12 B2
Nephin Range 12 B2
Nepomuk 56 C1
Nera 63 E1
Nérac 28 C3
Neráida (Amárandóos) 83 D2
Neráida (Neohóri) 83 D2
Neratovice 53 F3
Nerdvika 100 B1
Neresheim 55 E2
Nereto 63 F1
Neretva 76 A1
Neretva klisura 75 F1
Neretvanski kan 75 E2
Nerezi 77 D3
Nerezine 70 B4
Nerežišća 75 D2
Neris 110 C3
Néris-les-Bains 25 F4
Nerja 44 A4
Néronde 26 B4
Nérondes 26 A3
Nerotrivia 84 A3
Nerpio 44 C2
Nerva 42 C2
Nervesa della Battaglia 59 E4
Nervi 60 A3
Nervión, R 36 B1
Nes (Akershus) 105 D3
Nes (Buskerud) 104 C2

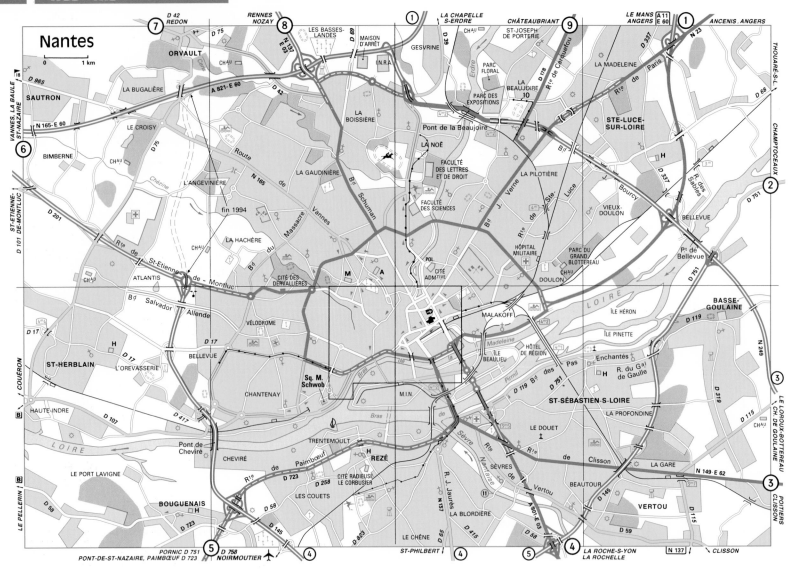

Nantes

Nes (NL) **16** C1	Neufchâtel-en-	Neunkirchen (A) ... **57** F3	Neuvy-St-
Nesbyen **104** C2	Bray **19** E2	Neunkirchen (D) ... **54** B2	Sépulchre **25** E3
Nesebâr **115** E2	Neufelden **56** C2	Neuötting **56** B3	Neuvy-sur-
Nesjøen **101** D2	Neuffen **55** D3	Neupölla **57** E2	Barangeon **25** F2
Neskaupstaður .. **96** C2	Neugersdorf **53** F2	Neuruppin **49** D3	Neuwied **51** E4
Nesle **19** F2	Neuhardenberg ... **49** E4	Neusiedl. **57** F3	Névache **31** D2
Nesoddtangen.... **105** D3	Neuhaus (Mecklenburg-	Neusiedler See ... **57** F3	Nevea, Pso di ... **59** F3
Nesseby **95** F1	Vorpommern) .. **48** B3	Neuss **17** D4	Nevel' **111** D3
Nesselwang **55** E4	Neuhaus	Neustadt (Baden-	Nevers **26** A3
Ness, L **2** C3	(Niedersachsen) ... **47** F2	Württemberg) ... **54** C4	Nevesinje **75** F2
Nestáni **87** D2	Neuhaus	Neustadt	Nevlunghavn ... **104** C4
Nestório **78** C2	(Thüringen) ... **52** C3	(Brandenburg) .. **49** D3	Nevŝa **81** D2
Néstos **81** D2	Neuhausen **58** A1	Neustadt (Coburg) . **52** C4	New Abbey **4** C3
Nesvik **104** A3	Neuhaus-im-	Neustadt (Hessen) . **52** A3	New Alresford **9** E3
Nesviž **111** D4	Solling **52** A2	Neustadt	Newark-on-Trent ... **7** D3
Neto **67** F3	Neuhofen an	(Ingolstadt) **55** F2	Newbiggin-by-the-
Netolice **56** C1	der Krems **57** D3	Neustadt (Sachsen) . **53** F2	Sea **5** E3
Netretić **70** C3	Neuillé-Pont-Pierre . **25** D2	Neustadt (Schleswig-	Newborough **6** A2
Nettetal **17** D4	Neuilly-en-Thelle ... **19** F3	Holstein) **48** B2	Newbridge **13** D4
Nettuno **63** E3	Neuilly-l'Rêal **26** A3	Neustadt	Newburgh (Fife) ... **5** D1
Neuastenberg **17** F4	Neuilly-l'Evêque ... **26** C1	(Thüringen) ... **53** D3	Newburgh
Neubeckum **17** F3	Neuilly-St-Front ... **20** A3	Neustadt am	(Grampian) **3** E4
Neubourg, le..... **19** D3	Neu-Isenburg **52** A4	Rübenberge **48** A4	Newbury **9** E2
Neubrandenburg .. **49** D2	Neukalen **49** D2	Neustadt an der	Newcastle **13** E2
Neubukow **48** C2	Neukirch **53** F2	Aisch **55** E1	Newcastle Emlyn .. **8** C1
Neuburg **55** F2	Neukirchen (A) ... **59** D1	Neustadt an der	Newcastle-under-
Neuchâtel **27** E2	Neukirchen (D) ... **47** F1	Waldnaab **53** D4	Lyme. **6** C3
Neu Darchau **48** B3	Neukloster **48** C2	Neustadt an der	Newcastle-upon-
Neuenburg **47** E3	Neulengbach **57** E2	Weinstraße **54** C2	Tyne **5** E3
Neuenbürg **54** C2	Neu Lübbenau ... **53** E1	Neustadt Glewe ... **48** C3	Newcastle West ... **14** B3
Neuendorf **49** D1	Neum **75** F2	Neustift **59** D2	New Cumnock **4** C3
Neuenhaus **17** E2	Neumarkt (D) ... **55** F1	Neustrelitz **49** D3	New Deer **3** E3
Neuenkirchen **48** A3	Neumarkt	Neu-Ulm **55** E3	New Forest **9** E3
Neuenstadt **55** D2	(Salzburg) **56** C3	Neuve-Lyre, la ... **19** D4	New Galloway **4** C3
Neuenstein **52** B3	Neumarkt	Neuves-Maisons... **21** D4	Newgrange **13** D3
Neuerburg **54** A1	(Steiermark) **57** D4	Neuvic (Corrèze) .. **29** E1	Newhaven **10** C3
Neufahrn **56** B2	Neumarkt-St Veit.. **56** B3	Neuvic (Dordogne) . **28** C2	Newmarket (GB) ... **11** D1
Neuf-Brisach **27** E1	Neumünster **48** A2	Neuville **26** C4	Newmarket (IRL) .. **14** B3
Neufchâteau (B) .. **20** C2	Neunagelberg **57** D2	Neuville-aux-Bois .. **25** E1	Newmarket on
Neufchâteau (F) .. **20** C4	Neunburg **56** B1	Neuville-de-Poitou . **25** D3	Fergus **12** B4
Neufchâtel **20** B3	Neung **25** E2	Neuvy-le-Roi **25** D2	
Newnham **9** D2	Nicotera **67** E4	Nijar **44** C3	
Newport (Dyfed) .. **8** B1	Nidda **52** A4	Nijemci **72** B2	
Newport (Gwent) .. **9** D2	Nidderau **52** A4	Nijkerk **16** C2	
Newport (I of Wight) . **9** E3	Niddegen **51** D3	Nijmegen **17** D3	
Newport (Mayo) .. **12** B3	Nidelva **104** B4	Nijverdal **17** D2	
Newport	Nidrí **82** B3	Níkea **83** E2	
(Shropshire)...... **6** C3	Niebla **42** C2	Níki **79** D2	
Newport	Niebüll **47** F1	Nikiá **89** F4	
(Tipperary) **12** C4	Niechorze **49** F1	Nikifóros **80** C2	
Newport-on-Tay .. **5** D1	Nied **21** D3	Nikissiani **80** C2	
Nevers **26** A3	Nieddu, M. **66** C2	Nikitas **80** B4	
Newport Pagnell... **9** F1	Niederalteich **56** B2	Nikkaluokta **94** C4	
Newquay **8** B4	Niederaula **52** B3	Nikoléika **86** C4	
New Quay **8** C1	Niederbronn **21** E3	Nikopol **115** D2	
New Romney **11** D3	Niederelsungen ... **52** A2	Nikópoli **82** B3	
New Ross **15** D4	Niedere Tauern... **57** D4	Nikópolis, Órmos .. **82** B2	
Newry **13** E2	Niederjossa **52** B3	Nikšić **76** B2	
Newton Abbot ... **8** C4	Niederkrüchten ... **17** D4	Nilakka **103** D2	
Newton-Aycliffe ... **5** E4	Niederösterreich ... **57** E3	Nilivaara **98** B2	
Newton Ferrers .. **8** C4	Niedersachsen ... **48** A4	Nilsiä **103** E2	
Newtonmore **2** C4	Niederstetten **55** D1	Nîmes **30** B3	
Newton Stewart .. **4** C3	Niederstotzingen ... **55** E3	Nimféa **81** E2	
Newtownabbey ... **13** E2	Niederzerf **54** A1	Nimféo **79** D3	
Newtownards ... **13** E2	Nienburg	Nímos, N. **93** E1	
Newtownbutler ... **13** D2	(Niedersachsen)... **48** A4	Nin **74** C1	
Newtown (England) . **9** D1	Niemegk **53** D1	Ninove **50** B3	
Newtown (Wales) .. **9** D1	Niemisel **98** C3	Niort **24** C4	
Newtownhamilton . **13** D2	Nienburg	Nipfjället **101** D3	
Newtown St	(Sachsen-Anhalt). **52** C1	Nípsa **81** F2	
Boswells **5** D3	Nieras **94** B4	Niš **77** E1	
Newtown-upon-	Nierstein **54** C1	Nisa **38** C3	
Tyne **5** E3	Niesky **53** F2	Nisa, Rib de ... **38** C3	
Newtownstewart... **13** D2	Niesłysz, Jez. ... **49** F4	Nišava **77** E1	
Nexon **29** D1	Nieuweschans ... **47** E3	Niscemi **68** C4	
Neyland **8** B2	Nieuwpoort **50** A3	Niška Banja **77** E1	
Nez de Jobourg .. **18** B2	Nièvre **26** B2	Nissáki **82** A1	
Niáta **87** D3	Niforéka **86** B1	Nissan **109** D2	
Niaux, Grotte de .. **32** A2	Nigríta **80** B2	Nisser **104** B3	
Nibe **108** B2	Niforéka ...	Nissilä **103** D1	
Nicastro **67** E3	Nicolosi **69** D3	Nissíros, N. **89** F4	
Nice **31** E4	Nickelsdorf **57** F3	Nissum Bredning .. **108** A2	
Nicosia **68** C3	Niinivesi **103** D2		

Nissum Fjord...... 108 A2
Nith.............. 4 C3
Niton............. 9 E4
Nitra............ 112 B3
Nitry............ 26 B2
Nittedal........ 105 D3
Nittenau......... 56 B1
Nittendorf....... 55 F2
Nivala.......... 102 C1
Nive............ 28 A4
Nivelles......... 50 B4
Nivernais........ 26 B3
Nivolet, Colle del ... 31 E1
Niwica.......... 53 F1
Nizke Beskydy.... 112 C3
Nižyn........... 113 F1
Nizza Monferrato... 31 F2
Njegoš.......... 76 A2
Njivice......... 70 B3
Njunis.......... 94 C3
Njupeskär...... 101 D3
Noailles......... 19 F3
Noáin.......... 36 C2
Noarvaš........ 95 D3
Noblejas........ 40 B3
Nocera.......... 64 B4
Nocera Tirinese... 67 E3
Nocera Umbra... 61 E4
Noceto.......... 60 B2
Noci............ 65 E3
Nodeland....... 104 B4
Nogara.......... 60 C1

None............. 31 E2
Nonio........... 58 A4
Nontron........ 28 C1
Nónza.......... 33 F2
Noord-Brabant... 16 C3
Noord-Holland... 16 C2
Noord-Oost-
  Polder....... 16 C2
Noordwijk aan Zee . 16 B2
Noordzee....... 46 B3
Noormarkku.... 102 B3
Nora........... 105 F3
Norberg........ 105 F3
Norcia.......... 63 F1
Nord........... 20 A1
Nord Beveland... 16 B3
Nordborg....... 108 A4
Nordby (Fanø)... 108 A3
Nordby (Samsø).. 108 B3
Norddeich...... 47 E3
Nordeide....... 100 A3
Norden......... 47 E3
Nordenau...... 17 F4
Nordenham.... 47 E3
Norderney..... 47 E3
Norderstedt.... 48 A2
Nordfjord...... 100 A3
Nordfjordeid.... 100 A3
Nordfold....... 97 E1
Nordfolda...... 97 E1
Nordfriesische
  Inseln........ 47 E1

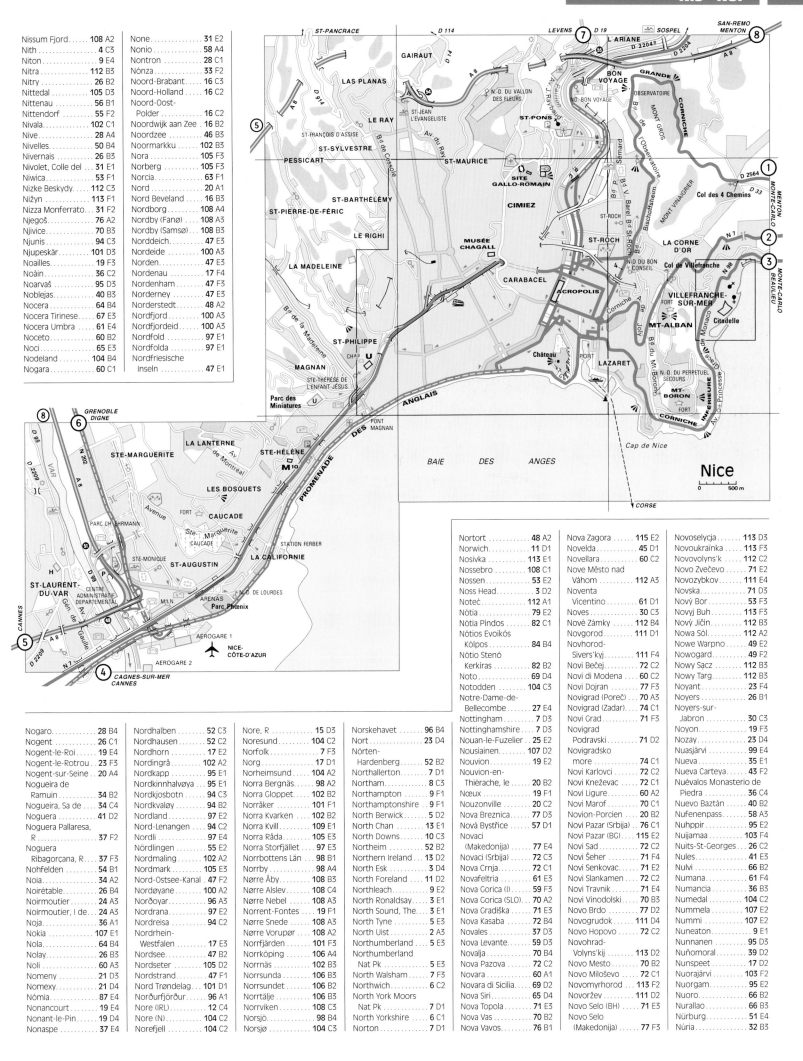

Nogaro.......... 28 B4
Nogent.......... 26 C1
Nogent-le-Roi... 19 E4
Nogent-le-Rotrou.. 23 F3
Nogent-sur-Seine.. 20 A4
Nogueira de
  Ramuín..... 34 B2
Nogueira, Sa de... 34 C4
Noguera........ 41 D2
Noguera Pallaresa,
  R............ 37 F2
Noguera
  Ribagorçana, R.. 37 F3
Nohfelden..... 54 B1
Noia........... 34 A2
Noirétable..... 26 B4
Noirmoutier.... 24 A3
Noirmoutier, I de.. 24 A3
Noja........... 36 A1
Nokia......... 107 E1
Nola........... 64 B4
Nolay.......... 26 B3
Noli........... 60 A3
Nomeny........ 21 D3
Nomexy........ 21 D4
Nómia......... 87 E4
Nonancourt.... 19 E4
Nonant-le-Pin... 19 D4
Nonaspe....... 37 E4

Nordhalben...... 52 C3
Nordhausen...... 52 C2
Nordhorn....... 17 E2
Nordingrå...... 102 A2
Nordkapp....... 95 E1
Nordkinnhalvøya.. 95 E1
Nordkjosbotn... 94 C3
Nordkvaløy.... 94 B2
Nordland....... 97 E2
Nord-Lenangen... 94 C2
Nordli......... 97 E4
Nördlingen..... 55 E2
Nordmaling.... 102 A2
Nordmark...... 105 E3
Nord-Ostsee-Kanal. 47 F2
Nordøyane..... 100 A2
Norðoyar...... 96 A3
Nordrana...... 97 E2
Nordreisa..... 94 C2
Nordrhein-
  Westfalen.... 17 E3
Nordsee....... 47 B2
Nordseter..... 105 D2
Nordstrand.... 47 F1
Nord Trøndelag.. 101 D1
Norðurfjörður... 96 A1
Nore (IRL).... 12 C4
Nore (N).... 104 C2
Norefjell.... 104 C2

Nore, R 15 D3
Noresund........ 104 C2
Norfolk......... 7 F3
Norg............ 17 D1
Norheimsund.... 104 A2
Norra Bergnäs.... 98 A2
Norra Gloppet... 102 B2
Norråker....... 101 F1
Norra Kvarken... 102 B2
Norra Kvill.... 109 E1
Norra Råda.... 105 E3
Norra Storfjället.. 97 E3
Norrbottens Län.. 98 B1
Norrby......... 98 A4
Nørre Åby.... 108 B3
Nørre Alslev.... 108 C4
Nørre Nebel.... 108 A3
Norrent-Fontes... 19 F1
Nørre Snede.... 108 A3
Nørre Vorupør... 108 A2
Norrfjärden.... 101 F3
Norrköping.... 106 A4
Norrnäs....... 102 B3
Norrsunda.... 106 B2
Norrsundet.... 106 B2
Norrtälje.... 106 B3
Norrviken.... 108 C3
Norsjö......... 98 B4
Norsjø........ 104 C3

Norskehavet.... 96 B4
Nort............ 23 D4
Nörten-
  Hardenberg... 52 B2
Northallerton.... 7 D1
Northam....... 8 C3
Northampton... 9 F1
Northamptonshire. 9 F1
North Berwick... 5 D2
North Chan.... 13 E1
North Downs... 10 C3
Northeim...... 52 B2
Northern Ireland.. 13 D2
North Esk.... 3 D4
North Foreland... 11 D2
Northleach.... 9 E2
North Ronaldsay.. 3 E1
North Sound, The.. 3 E1
North Tyne.... 5 E3
North Uist.... 2 A3
Northumberland.. 5 E3
Northumberland
  Nat Pk.... 5 E3
North Walsham... 7 F3
Northwich.... 6 C2
North York Moors
  Nat Pk.... 7 D1
North Yorkshire.. 6 C1
Norton..... 7 D1

Nortort 48 A2
Norwich........... 11 D1
Nosivka........... 113 E1
Nossebro.......... 108 C1
Nossen............ 53 E2
Noss Head......... 3 D2
Noteć............ 112 A1
Nótia............. 79 E2
Nótia Píndos....... 82 C1
Nótios Evoïkós
  Kólpos.......... 84 B4
Nótio Stenó
  Kerkíras......... 82 B2
Noto.............. 69 D4
Notodden 104 C3
Notre-Dame-de-
  Bellecombe...... 27 E4
Nottingham........ 7 D3
Nottinghamshire ... 7 D3
Nouan-le-Fuzelier .. 25 E2
Nousiainen....... 107 D2
Nouvion.......... 19 E2
Nouvion-en-
  Thiérache, le...... 20 B2
Nœux............ 19 F1
Nouzonville....... 20 C2
Nova Breznica..... 77 D3
Nová Bystřice..... 57 D1

Nova Zagora....... 115 E2
Novelda........... 45 D1
Novellara......... 60 C2
Nove Město nad
  Váhom.......... 112 A3
Noventa
  Vicentino........ 61 D1
Noves............ 30 C3
Nové Zámky...... 112 B4
Novgorod........ 111 D1
Novhorod-
  Sivers'kyj....... 111 F4
Novi Bečej........ 72 C2
Novi di Modena.... 60 C2
Novi Dojran....... 77 F3
Novigrad (Poreč).. 70 A3
Novigrad (Zadar).. 74 C1
Novi Grad........ 71 F3
Novigrad
  Podravski....... 71 D2
Novigradsko
  more........... 74 C1
Novi Karlovci..... 72 C2
Novi Kneževac.... 72 C1
Novi Ligure....... 60 A2
Novi Marof....... 70 C1
Novion-Porcien.... 20 B2
Novi Pazar (Srbija).. 76 C1
Novi Pazar (BG).. 115 E2
Novi Sad........ 72 C2
Novi Šeher....... 71 F4
Novi Senkovac.... 71 E2
Novi Slankamen.. 72 C2
Novi Travnik...... 71 E4
Novi Vinodolski.. 70 B3
Novo Brdo....... 77 D2
Novogrudok...... 111 D4
Novo Hopovo... 72 C2
Novohrad-
  Volyns'kij....... 113 D2
Novo Mesto....... 70 B2
Novo Miloševo.... 72 C1
Novomyrhorod... 113 F2
Novoržev........ 111 D2
Novo Selo (BH).. 71 E3
Novo Selo
  (Makedonija)... 77 F3

Novoselycja....... 113 D3
Novoukrainka..... 113 F3
Novovolyns'k..... 112 C2
Novo Zvečevo... 71 E2
Novozybkov...... 111 E4
Novska........... 71 D3
Nový Bor......... 53 F3
Novyj Buh........ 113 F3
Nový Jičín........ 112 B3
Nowa Sól........ 112 A2
Nowe Warpno... 49 E2
Nowogard........ 49 F2
Nowy Sącz....... 112 B3
Nowy Targ....... 112 B3
Noyant.......... 23 F4
Noyers.......... 26 B1
Noyers-sur-
  Jabron......... 30 C3
Noyon........... 19 F3
Nozay........... 23 D4
Nuasjärvi........ 99 E4
Nueva........... 35 E1
Nueva Carteya... 43 F2
Nuévalos Monasterio de
  Piedra.......... 36 C4
Nuevo Baztán... 40 E4
Nufenenpass..... 58 A3
Nuhppir......... 95 E2
Nuijamaa....... 103 E4
Nuits-St-Georges... 26 C2
Nules........... 41 E3
Nulvi........... 66 B2
Numana......... 61 F3
Numancia....... 36 B3
Numedal........ 104 C2
Nummela....... 107 E2
Nummi......... 107 E2
Nuneaton....... 9 E1
Nunnanen....... 95 D3
Nuñomoral...... 39 D2
Nunspeet....... 17 D2
Nuorajärvi...... 103 F2
Nuorgam....... 95 E2
Nuoro.......... 66 B2
Nurallao........ 66 B3
Nürburg........ 51 E4
Núria.......... 32 B3

Nurmes 103 E1
Nurmijärvi (Pohjois-Karjalan Lääni).... 103 F1
Nurmijärvi (Uudenmaan Lääni) ... 107 E2
Nurmo........... 102 C2

Nürnberg 55 F1
Nürtingen 55 D3
Nus 27 E4
Nusse 48 B2
Nuštar 71 F2
Nuthe 49 D4
Nuttlar 17 F3

Nuttupera 103 D1
Nuutajärvi 107 E2
Nuvvos-Ailigas..... 95 E2
Nyåker 102 A1
Nybergsund 105 E2
Nyborg 108 B4
Nybro 109 E2

Nyirbátor 112 C3
Nyíregyháza........ 112 C3
Nykarleby 102 B2
Nykøbing F (Storstrøm) ... 108 C4
Nykøbing M (Viborg) ... 108 A2

Nykøbing S (Vestsjælland) ... 108 C3
Nyköping 106 B4
Nykvarn 106 B4
Nynäshamn 106 B4
Nyon............. 27 D3
Nyons............ 30 C3

Nýřany 53 E4
Nýrdalur 96 B2
Nýrsko........... 56 B1
Nyrud 95 F2
Nysa............. 112 A2
Nysa Łużycka 53 F1
Nysäter 105 E3

Nyseter 100 B3
Nysted 108 C4
Nyvoll 95 D2

O

Oadby 9 F1
Oakham 9 F1
Oanes............ 104 A3
Óassi 87 D1
Oban 4 B1
O Barco 34 C3
Obbola 102 B1
Obdach 57 D4
Obdacher Sattel . 57 D4
Obedska bara 72 C3
Obejo 43 F2
Oberalppass 58 A3
Oberammergau 55 F4
Oberau 56 A4
Oberaudorf 56 B4
Oberdrauburg 59 E2
Oberessfeld 52 C4
Obergrafendorf .. 57 D4
Obergrünzburg ... 55 E4
Obergurgl 58 C2
Oberhaslach 21 E4
Oberhausen 17 E3
Oberhof 52 C3
Oberjoch-Paß 58 C1
Oberkirch 54 C1
Oberkirchen 17 F4
Oberkochen 55 E2
Obermarchtal 55 D3
Obernai 21 E4
Obernberg 56 C3
Obernburg 55 D1
Oberndorf (A) ... 56 C3
Oberndorf (D) ... 54 C4
Obernzell 56 C2
Oberölsbach...... 55 F1
Oberösterreich .. 56 C2
Oberprechtal 54 C3
Oberpullendorf .. 57 F3
Oberseebach 21 F3
Obersontheim ... 55 E2
Oberstaufen 55 E4
Oberstdorf 55 E4
Oberstein 54 B1
Obertauern...... 59 F1
Obertraun....... 59 F1
Oberursel 51 F4
Obervellach 59 E2
Oberviechtach... 56 B1
Oberwart 57 F4
Oberwesel 51 F4
Oberwiesenthal.. 53 E3
Oberwölz 57 D4
Oberzeiring 57 D4
Óbidos 38 A3
Obilić.......... 77 D2
Obing 56 B3
Obiou, l' 30 C2
Objat 29 D1
Obninsk 111 F3
O Bolo 34 C3
Obón 41 E1
Oborniki 112 A1
Obornjača 72 C3
Oborovo 70 C2
Obrenovac 72 C3
Obrež 72 C3
Obrov 70 A3
Obrovac (Split) . 75 D1
Obrovac (Zadar) . 74 C1
Obršani........ 77 E4
Obsteig 58 C2
Obudovac 71 F3
Obzor 115 E2
Obzova 70 B3
Očakiv 113 F3

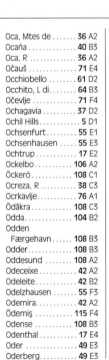

Map of Nürnberg / Fürth area.

Oca, Mtes de 36 A2
Ocaña 40 B3
Oca, R 36 A2
Očauš 71 E4
Occhiobello 61 D2
Occhito, L di..... 64 B3
Očevlje 71 F4
Ochagavia 37 D2
Ochil Hills 5 D1
Ochsenfurt 55 E1
Ochsenhausen 55 E3
Ochtrup 17 E2
Ockelbo 106 A2
Öckerö 108 C1
Ocreza, R 38 C3
Ocrkavlje 76 A1
Ödåkra 108 C3
Odda 104 B2
Odden
  Færgehavn 108 B3
Odder 108 B3
Oddesund 108 A2
Odeceixe 42 A2
Odeleite 42 B2
Odelzhausen 55 F3
Odemira 42 A2
Ödemiş 115 F4
Odense 108 B3
Odenthal 17 E4
Oder 49 E3
Oderberg 49 E3

Oderbruch 49 E3
Oderbucht 49 E1
Oderhaff 49 E2
Oderzo 59 E4
Odesa 113 E4
Ödeshög 109 D1
Odet 22 B3
Odiel, R......... 42 C2
Odivelas 42 A4
Odivelas, Bgem de 42 B1
Odolo 60 B1
Odorheiu
  Secuiesc..... 113 D4
Odra 112 A2
Odžaci 72 B2
Odžak (BH) 71 F3
Odžak (Crna Gora) 76 B1
Oebisfelde 48 B4
Öebro 105 F4
Oederan 53 E3
Oeiras 38 A4
Oelde 17 F3
Oelsnitz (Plauen) 53 D3
Oelsnitz (Zwickau) 53 D3
Oettingen 55 E2
Oetz 58 C2
Ofanto 64 C3
Ofenpass 58 C2
Offaly 12 C4
Offenbach 52 A4
Offenburg 54 C3

Offida 63 F1
Oise (Dépt) 19 F3
Offranville 19 E2
Ofir 34 A4
Ofotfjorden 94 B3
Oggiono 60 A1
Ogliastro Cilento 67 D1
Oglio 58 C4
Ognon 27 D2
Ogošte 77 E2
Ogražden 77 F3
Ogre 110 C2
Ogulin 70 C3
Ohi, Óros 88 A1
Ohiró 80 B1
Ohlstadt 56 A4
Ohorn 53 F2
Ohrdruf 52 C3
Ohre 48 B4
Ohře 53 E3
Ohrid 77 D4
Ohridsko Ez 77 D4
Öhringen 55 D2
Ohrit, Liq i 77 D4
Óhthia 82 C3
Ohthoniá 84 B4
Oijärvi 99 D3
Oijärvi L........ 99 D3
Oikarainen 99 D2
Oirschot 16 C3
Oise 20 B2

Olazagutía 36 B2
Olbernhau 53 E3
Olbia 66 B1
Oldcastle 13 D3
Oldebroek........ 17 D2
Oldeide 100 A3
Olden 100 A3
Oldenburg (Niedersachsen)... 47 F3
Oldenburg (Schleswig Holstein) 48 B1
Oldenzaal........ 17 E2
Olderdalen 94 C2
Oldervik 94 C2
Oldfjällen 101 E1
Oldham........... 6 C2
Old Head of Kinsale 14 B4
Oldmeldrum 3 E4
Oldsum.......... 47 F1
Oleggio 60 A1
Oleiros 38 C2
Oleksandrija 113 F2
Ólen 104 A3
Oléron, Ile d' .. 24 B4
Olesa 32 A4
Oleśnica 112 A2
Oletta 33 F2
Olette 32 C2
Olevs'k 113 D1

Ølgod 108 A3
Olhão 42 B3
Olhava 99 D3
Oliana 32 A3
Oliana, Emb d' .. 32 A3
Olib 70 B4
Olib / 70 B4
Oliena 66 B2
Oliete 37 E4
Olimbía 86 C2
Olímbia (Makedonia).... 80 B3
Olimbiáda (Thessalia)... 79 E4
Ólimbos 93 D2
Ólimbos, Óros (Évia).... 84 B4
Ólimbos, Óros (Pieriá)... 79 E4
Ólinthos 80 A4
Olite 36 C2
Oliva 45 E1
Oliva de la Frontera 42 C1
Oliva de Mérida . 39 D4
Olivares 40 C3
Oliveira de Azeméis 38 B1
Oliveira de Frades 38 B1
Oliveira do Bairro 38 B1
Oliveira do Douro 34 B4

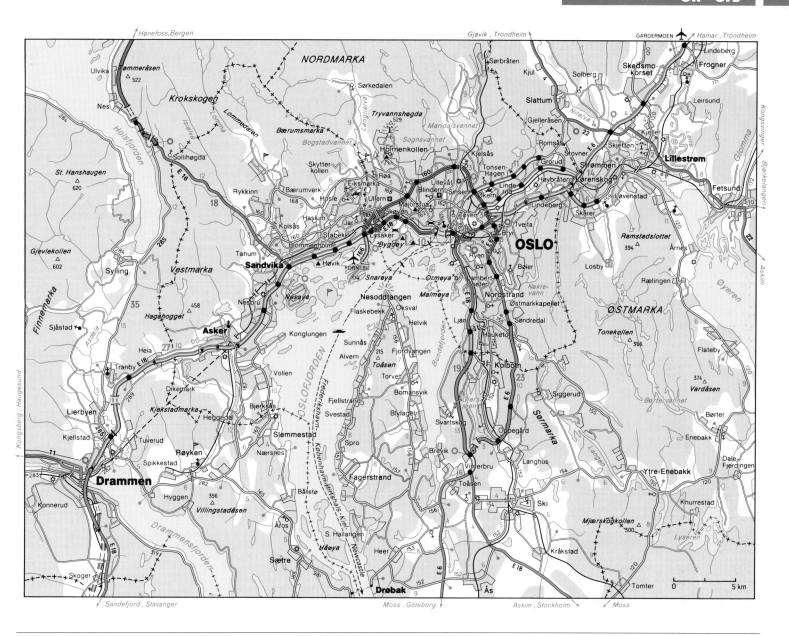

Oliveira do Hospital	38 C2	Oltenia	115 D1	Ontiñena	37 E3	Oradea	112 C4
Olivenza	38 C4	Oltenița	115 E1	Ontinyent	45 E1	Oradour-sur-Glane	25 D4
Olivenza, R de	38 C4	Olula del Río	44 C3	Ontojärvi	99 F4	Oradour-sur-Vayres	28 C1
Olivet	25 E1	Olvega	36 C3	Ontur	45 D1	Orahova	71 D3
Olivone	58 A3	Olvera	43 E3	Onzain	25 E1	Orahovac	77 D2
Olleria, Pto de l'	41 E4	Omagh	13 D2	Oostburg	16 B4	Orahovica	71 E2
Ollerton	7 D3	Omali	79 D4	Oostelijk-Flevoland	16 C2	Oraison	31 D3
Ollières, les	30 B2	Omalós	90 B3	Oostende	50 A3	Orajärvi	98 C2
Olliergues	29 F1	Omarska	71 D3	Oosterbeek	17 D3	Orange	30 B3
Ollioules	31 D4	Ombrone	63 D1	Oosterend	16 C1	Orani	66 B2
Ollöla	103 F2	Omegna	58 A4	Oosterhout	16 C3	Oranienbaum	53 D1
Olmedillo de Roa	35 F4	Omiš	75 E2	Oostkamp	50 A3	Oranienburg	49 D3
Olmedo (E)	35 E4	Omišalj	70 B3	Oostmalle	50 C3	Oranmore	12 B3
Olmedo (I)	66 A2	Omme Å	108 A3	Oost-Vlaanderen	50 B3	Orašac (HR)	75 F2
Olmeto	33 F4	Ommen	17 D2	Oost-Vlieland	16 C1	Orašac (Srbija)	73 D3
Olocau del Rey	41 E2	Omodeo, L	66 B3	Ootmarsum	17 E2	Orašje	71 F3
Olofström	109 D3	Omoljica	73 D3	Opatija	70 B3	Orăștie	114 C1
Olombrada	35 F4	Omorfohóri	83 E1	Opatovac	72 B2	Oravainen	102 B2
Olomouc	112 A3	Ömossa	102 B3	Opava	112 A3	Oravais	102 B2
Olonzac	32 B1	Oña	36 A2	Opladen	17 E4	Oravikoski	103 E2
Oloron Ste Marie	37 D1	Oñati	36 B1	Oplenac	73 D3	Oravița	114 C1
Olost	32 A3	Oncala, Pto de	36 C3	Opočka	111 D2	Orb	30 A4
Olot	32 B3	Onda	41 E3	Opole	112 A2	Orba	45 E1
Olovo	71 F4	Ondara	45 E1	Opovo	72 C2	Ørbæk	108 B4
Olpe	17 F4	Ondárroa	36 B1	Oppach	53 F2	Orbassano	31 E2
Olsberg	17 F3	Oneglia	31 F3	Oppdal	100 C2	Orbe	27 D3
Olshammar	105 F4	Onesse-et-Laharie	28 A3	Oppenau	54 C3	Orbec	19 D3
Olst	17 D2	Oneşti	113 D4	Oppenheim	54 C1	Orbetello	63 D2
Ølstykke	108 C3	Onich	2 C4	Opphaug	100 C1	Orbey	27 E1
Olsztyn	110 B4	Onkamo (Lapin Lääni)	99 E2	Oppido Lucano	64 C4	Orbigo, R	35 D2
Olszyna	53 F1	Onkamo (Pohjois Karjalan Lääni)	103 F2	Oppido Mamertina	67 E4	Orce	44 B2
Olt	115 D2	Onkivesi	103 E2	Oppland	104 C1	Orce, R	44 B2
Oltedal	104 A3	Ons, I de	34 A2	Oputten	16 C2	Orcera	44 B1
Olten	27 F2	Ontaneda	35 F2	Ora	59 D3	Orchies	20 A1
						Orcières	31 D2
Orcival	29 E1	Orhi, Pic d'	37 D1	Orly	19 F4
Orco	31 E1	Orhomenós	83 F4	Orménio	81 F1
Ordes	34 A1	Oria	44 C3	Ormília	80 B4
Ordesa, Parque Nac. de	37 E2	Oria	65 E4	Órmos	79 F3
Ordino	32 A2	Oria, R	36 C1	Órmos Korthíou	88 B1
Ordizia	36 C1	Origny Sainte-Benoîte	20 A2	Órmos Panagías	80 B4
Orduña	36 B1	Orihuela	45 D2	Órmos Prínou	80 C3
Orduña, Pto de	36 B1	Orihuela del Tremedal	41 D2	Ormož	70 C1
Ore	101 E4	Orimattila	107 F2	Ormsjö	97 F4
Orea	41 D2	Orini	80 B2	Ormsjön	101 F1
Öreälven	102 A1	Oriolo	65 D4	Ormskirk	6 B2
Orebić	75 E2	Oripää	187 E3	Ormtjernkampen	104 C1
Örebro Län	105 F3	Orissaare	110 B2	Ornain	20 C4
Öregrund	106 B3	Oristano	66 B3	Ornans	27 D2
Öregrundsgrepen	106 B2	Oristano, G di	66 A3	Orne (Calvados)	18 C4
Orei	83 F3	Orivesi	102 C3	Orne (Dépt)	20 B3
Orellana de la Sierra	39 E4	Orivesi L	103 F2	Orne (Meuse)	21 D3
Orellana, Emb de	39 E4	Orjahovo	115 D2	Ørnes	97 E2
Orellana la Vieja	39 E4	Orjaivik	100 B2	Ornós	88 C2
Orense	34 B3	Ørje	105 D3	Örnsköldsvik	102 A2
Oréo	81 D2	Orjen	76 B2	Or'ol	111 F4
Oreókastro	79 F3	Orjiva	44 A3	Orolik	72 B2
Orestiáda	81 F1	Orkanger	100 C2	Orom	72 B1
Oresund	108 C3	Örkelljunga	109 D3	Oron-la-Ville	27 E3
Orfós, Akr	89 F4	Orkla	100 C2	Oropesa	39 F3
Orgáni	81 E2	Orkney Is	3 E1	Orosei	66 C2
Organyà	32 A3	Ørlandet	100 C1	Orosei, G di	66 C2
Organyà	37 F3	Orlando, C d'	69 D2	Orosháza	112 B4
Orgaz	40 A3	Orlane	77 D1	Orpesa	41 F3
Orgelet	26 C3	Orlate	77 D2	Orpierre	30 C3
Orgères-en-Beauce	25 E1	Orléans	25 E1	Orpington	10 C2
Orgon	30 C3	Orlická přehr nádrž	56 C1	Orra	100 C3
Orgosolo	66 B2	Orlovat	72 C2	Orsa	101 E4
Orhei	113 E3			Orša	111 E3
				Orsajön	101 E4
				Orsay	19 F4

Orsières 27 E4
Orsogna 64 A2
Orşova 114 C1
Ørsta 100 A2
Örsundsbro 106 B3
Orta Nova 64 C3
Orta San Giulio 58 A4
Orte 63 E2
Ortegal, C 34 B1
Orth 57 F2
Orthez 28 B4
Ortigueira 34 B1
Ortisei 59 D3
Ortles 58 C3
Ortnevik 104 B1
Orton 5 D4
Ortona 64 A2
Ortrand 53 E2
Örträsk 102 A1
Orubica 71 E3
Orune 66 B2
Orusco 40 B2
Orvalho 38 C2
Orvieto 63 E1
Órvilos, Óros 80 B1
Orvinio 63 E2
Orzinuovi 60 B1
Os 100 D3
Osa de la Vega 40 B3
Osâm 115 D2
Osby 109 D2
Oschatz 53 E2
Oschersleben 52 C1
Oschiri 66 B2
Osečina 72 C3
Oseja de Sajambre 35 E2
Osen 96 C4
Osera de Ebro 37 D4
Osijek 71 F2

Osilo 66 B2
Osimo 61 F4
Osinja 71 E3
Osipaonica 73 D3
Osipoviči 111 D4
Osječenica 71 D4
Oskarshamn 109 E2
Oskarström 108 C2
Oslava 57 E1
Oslo 105 D3
Oslo (Fylke) 105 D3
Oslofjorden 104 C3
Ösmo 106 B4
Osnabrück 17 F2
Ośno Lubuskie 49 F4
Osogovija 77 F2
Osogovske planine 77 E2
Osoppo 59 E3
Osor 70 B4
Osorno 35 F3
Osøyri 104 A2
Ospedaletti 31 E3
Ospitaletto 60 B1
Oss 16 C3
Óssa 80 A2
Ossa de Montiel 40 B4
Óssa, Óros 83 F1
Ossa, Sa de 38 C4
Ossiach 59 F2
Ossiacher See 59 F2
Óssios Loukás 83 F4
Ossun 37 E1
Ostaškov 111 E2
Østbirk 108 B3
Østby 105 E2
Oste 47 F3
Osted 108 C3
Oster 113 E1

Osterburg 48 C4
Osterburken 55 D1
Österbybruk 106 B3
Østerby Havn 108 B2
Österbymo 109 E1
Österdalälven 101 D3
Østerdalen 100 C3
Österfärnebo 106 A3
Osterfeld 53 D2
Östergötlands Län 109 E1
Osterhofen 56 B2
Osterholz Scharmbeck 47 F3
Osteria del Gatto 61 E4
Osterode 52 B2
Osterøya 104 A2
Östersund 101 E2
Östersundom 107 F2
Österväla 106 B3
Øster Vrå 108 B2
Osterwieck 52 B1
Østfold 105 D3
Ostfriesische Inseln 47 D3
Östhammar 106 B3
Ostheim 52 B4
Ostia Antica 63 E3
Ostiglia 60 C2
Östmark 105 E3
Ostra 61 E3
Ostrach 55 D4
Óstra Gloppet 102 B2
Östra Silen 105 D4
Ostrava 112 B3
Oštrelj 71 D4
Ostritz 53 F2
Ostróda 110 B4
Ostroh 113 D2
Ostrołęka 112 B1

Ostrov (CS) 53 E3
Ostrov (RO) 115 E1
Ostrov (ROS) 111 D2
Ostrowiec Świętokrzyski 112 B2
Ostrów Mazowiecki 112 B1
Ostrów Wielkopolski 112 A2
Ostrožac (BH) 70 C3
Ostrožac (BH) 75 D3
Ostsee 48 C1
Osttirol 59 E2
Ostuni 65 E3
Osuna 43 E3
Oswestry 6 B3
Oświęcim 112 B2
Otanmäki 103 D1
Otava (CS) 56 C1
Otava (SF) 103 E3
Oteren 94 C3
Oteševo 77 D4
Othem 109 F4
Othery 9 D3
Othoní, N 78 A4
Óthris, Óros 83 E3
Otívar 44 A3
Otley 6 C2
Otnes 100 C3
Otočac 70 C4
Otočec 70 B2
Otok 72 B2
Otoka 71 D3
Otra 104 B4
Otranto 65 F4
Otsamo 95 E3
Otta 100 C3
Ottana 66 B2
Ottaviano 64 B4

Ottenschlag 57 E2
Ottensheim 57 D2
Otterburn 5 E3
Otter Ferry 4 B2
Otterlo 17 D3
Otterndorf 47 F2
Otterøy 97 D4
Ottersberg 47 F3
Otterup 108 B3
Ottery St Mary 9 D3
Ottmarsheim 27 E1
Ottnang 56 C3
Ottobeuren 55 E3
Ottobrunn 56 A3
Ottsjö 101 D2
Ottweiler 54 B2
Otwock 112 B1
Otziás 88 A2
Ötztal 58 C2
Ötztaleralpen 58 C2
Ouchy 27 D3
Oucques 25 E1
Oud Beijerland 16 B3
Ouddorp 16 B3
Oude Maas 16 B3
Oudenaarde 50 B3
Oudenbosch 16 C3
Oude-Pekela 47 E3
Ouessant, Ile d' 22 A2
Oughterard 12 B3
Ouistreham 18 C3
Oul 51 D4
Oulainen 99 D4
Oulanka 99 E2
Oulankajoki 99 E2
Oulchy-le-Château 20 A3
Oulu 99 D3
Oulujärvi 99 E4
Oulujoki 99 D4

Oulun Lääni 99 E4
Oulunsalo 99 D4
Oulx 31 D2
Ounasjoki 99 D2
Oundle 9 F1
Our 54 A1
Ouranópoli 80 B4
Ource 26 C1
Ourcq 20 A3
Ourense 34 B3
Ourique 42 B2
Ourol 34 B1
Ourthe 20 C1
Ourville 19 D2
Ouse, R. 7 D2
Oust 37 F2
Outes, Sa de 34 A2
Outokumpu 103 E2
Outomuro 34 B3
Outwell 10 C1
Ouvèze 30 C3
Ouzouer 25 E1
Ouzouer-le-Marché 25 E1
Ovada 60 A2
Ovanåker 101 F4
Ovar 38 B1
Ovčar Banja 73 D4
Ovedskloster 109 D3
Overath 17 E4
Øverbygd 94 C3
Overflakkee 16 B3
Overhalla 97 D4
Överhörnäs 102 A2
Overijssel 17 D2
Overijse 50 C3
Överkalix 98 C2
Övermark 102 B2
Översjuktan 97 F3
Övertorneå 98 C2

Överum 109 E1
Överuman 97 E3
Oviedo 35 D1
Ovindoli 63 F2
Øvre Anarjokka 95 D3
Øvre Årdal 100 B3
Øvre Dividalen 94 C3
Övre Fryken 105 E3
Øvre Pasvik 95 F2
Øvre Soppero 95 D4
Ovruč 113 C1
Owel, L. 13 D3
Oxelösund 106 B4
Oxford 9 E2
Oxfordshire 9 E2
Oxiá, N 82 C4
Oxiá (Stereá Eláda) 83 D3
Oxiá (Thessalia) 83 D2
Oxie 108 C3
Oxilithos 84 B4
Ox Mts, The 12 C2
Oyarzun 36 C1
Oybin 53 F2
Øye 104 C1
Øyer 104 C1
Øyeren 105 D3
Oy-Mittelberg 55 E4
Oyntdartfjørður 96 A3
Oyón 36 B2
Oyonnax 27 D4
Øystese 104 B2
Oyten 47 F3
Ozalj 70 C2
Ožbalt 70 B1
Ózd 112 B3
Ozeblin 70 C4
Ozieri 66 B2
Ozren 71 F3
Ozren Devica 73 E4

P

Paakkila 103 E2
Paalasmaa 103 E1
Páamo de Masa, Pto de 35 F3
Paar 55 F1
Paasselkä 103 F3
Paavola 99 D4
Pabianice 112 B2
Pacaudière, la 26 B4
Paceco 68 A3
Pachino 69 D4
Packsattel 57 E4
Paço de Sousa 34 A4
Paços de Ferreira 34 A4
Pacov 57 D1
Pacy 19 E4
Padasjoki 107 E1
Padej 72 C1
Paddene 75 D1
Paderborn 17 F3
Paderne 42 B2
Padiham 6 C2
Padina 72 C2
Padinska Skela 72 C2
Padirac, Gouffre de 29 D2
Padjelanta 97 F1
Padornelo 34 C3
Padova 61 D1
Padrela, Sa da 34 B4
Padrón 34 A2
Padru 66 B2
Padstow 8 B3
Padul 44 A3
Paesana 31 E2
Paestum 64 B4
Pag 70 C4
Pag / 70 B4
Paganico 63 D1
Pagassés, N 83 F2
Pagassitikós Kólpos 83 F2
Paglia 63 D1
Pagny 21 D3

Pagóndas (Évia) 84 A3
Pagóndas (Sámos) 89 E2
Pagoúria 81 D2
Paguera 45 E3
Páhi 87 E1
Pahiá Ámos 91 F4
Pahis, Akr. 80 C3
Paide 110 C1
Paignton 8 C4
Päijänne 103 D3
Páiko, Óros 79 E2
Paimbœuf 23 D4
Paimio 107 D2
Paimpol 22 C2
Painswick 9 E2
Paisley 4 C2
Paistunturit 95 E2
País Vasco 36 B1
Paittasjärvi 94 C4
Paiva, R 38 B1
Pajala 98 C1
Pajara 42 C4
Pajares, Pto de 35 D2
Paklenica Nac Park 70 C4
Pakoštane 74 C1
Pakrac 71 E2
Pakračka Poljana 71 D2
Paks 112 B4
Palacios de la Sierra 36 A3
Palacios del Sil 34 C2
Palacios de Sanabria 34 C3
Palade, Pso del 58 C3
Paládio 81 D2
Palafrugell 32 C3
Palagía 81 E2
Palagiano 65 E4
Palagonia 69 D3
Palagruža 75 D3
Palaia 60 C4
Palaiseau 19 F4
Palais, le 22 C4
Palamás 83 E2
Palamós 32 C3

Palancia, R. 41 E3
Palanga 110 B3
Pala, Pto del 34 C1
Palas de Rei 34 B2
Palata 64 B2
Palatitsia 79 E3
Palatna 77 D1
Palau 66 B1
Palavas 30 B2
Palazzo del Pero 61 D4
Palazzolo Acreide 69 D4
Palazzolo sull' Oglio 60 B1
Palazzo San Gervasio 64 C3
Palazzuolo sul Senio 61 D3
Paldiski 110 C1
Pale 76 A1
Paléa Epidavros 87 E2
Palékastro 91 F4
Palena 64 A2
Palencia 35 E3
Paleohóra (Égina) 87 E2
Paleohóra (Kriti) 90 B4
Paleohóri (Árta) 82 C2
Paleohóri (Grevená) 79 D4
Paleohóri (Halkidiki) 80 B3
Paleohóri (Ioánina) 82 B2
Paleohóri (Lésvos) 85 F3
Paleohóri (Pelopónnisos) 87 D3
Paleohóri (Thessalia) 83 D1
Paleokastritsa 82 A1
Paleókastro (Halkidiki) 80 A3
Paleókastro (Kozáni) 79 D4
Paleókastro (Sámos) 89 F2
Paleókastro (Séres) 80 B2
Paleókastro (Stereá Eláda) 83 D3

Paleokómi 80 B2
Paleópirgos (Stereá Eláda) 83 D4
Paleópirgos (Thessalia) 83 F1
Paleópoli (Ándros) 88 B1
Paleópoli (Samothráki) 81 E2
Paleós Kavála 80 C2
Paleós Xánthis 81 D2
Palermo 68 B3
Páleros 82 C3
Palérou, Órm 82 B3
Palestrina 63 F2
Palež 72 B4
Páli 89 F4
Palić 72 B1
Palidoro 63 E2
Palinges 26 B3
Palinuro 67 D2
Palioúri 80 B4
Paliouriá 79 D4
Paliseul 20 C2
Pälkäne 107 E1
Pálkem 98 B2
Pallas Ounastunturi 95 D3
Pallastunturi 95 D3
Pallice, la 24 B4
Palluau 24 B3
Palma 45 E3
Palmaces, Emb de 36 B4
Palma del Rio 43 E2
Palma di Montechiaro 68 C4
Palmadula 66 A2
Palmanova 59 F3
Palmela 38 A4
Palmi 67 E4
Palo del Colle 65 D3
Palojoensuu 95 D3
Palojoki 95 D3
Palokki 103 E2
Palomäki 103 E2

Palomares del Campo 40 C3
Palomas 39 D4
Palomas, Pto de las 44 B2
Palombara Sabina 63 E2
Palombera, Pto de 35 F2
Palomera 41 D2
Pálos, Akr. 88 B2
Palos, C de 45 D3
Palos de la Frontera 42 C3
Pals 32 C3
Pålsboda 105 F4
Paltamo 99 E4
Paltaselkä 99 E4
Paluzza 59 E2
Pàmfila 85 F2
Pamhagen 57 F3
Pamiers 32 A2
Pampilhosa 38 B2
Pampilhosa da Serra 38 C2
Pampliega 35 F3
Pamplona 36 C2
Pamporovo 115 D3
Pamukkale 115 F4
Panagia (Ípiros) 82 C2
Panagía (Limnos) 85 D1
Panagía (Makedonía) 79 D4
Panagía (Thássos) 81 D3
Panagía (Thessalia) 83 E2
Panagjurište 115 D2
Panahaïkó, Óros 83 D4
Panaro 60 C3
Pancalieri 31 E2
Pančevo 73 D2
Pančićev vrh 77 D1
Pancorbo 36 A2
Pandánassa 87 E4
Pandeleimónas 79 F4
Pandino 60 B1
Pandokrátor 82 A1
Pandrup 108 B2
Panes 35 F2

Panetolikó, Óros 83 D3
Panetólio 82 C4
Panevėžys 110 C3
Pangbourne 9 E2
Pangéo, Óros 80 B2
Paniza, Pto de 36 C4
Pankajärvi 103 F1
Pankakoski 103 F1
Pankow 49 E4
Panórama (Dráma) 80 B2
Panórama (Thessaloniki) 80 A3
Panormítis 93 E1
Pánormos (Kikládes) 88 B2
Pánormos (Kriti) 91 D3
Päntäne 102 B3
Pantelleria 68 A4
Pantelleria, I di 68 A4
Paola 67 E2
Pápa 112 A4
Papádes 84 A3
Papádos 85 F3
Páparis 86 C2
Pápas, Akr. 89 D2
Papasidero 67 E2
Papa Stour 3 F1
Papenburg 47 E3
Papíkio 81 D2
Pápingo 78 C4
Pappenheim 55 F2
Papuk Mt. 71 E2
Papuk (Reg) 71 E2
Parabita 65 F4
Paracin 73 E4
Paracuellos de Jiloca 36 C4
Parada de Cunhos 34 B4
Paradas 43 E3
Paradela 34 B3
Paradissia 86 C2
Parádissos 81 D2
Parainen 107 D3
Parajes 34 C1
Parakálamos 78 C4
Parákila 85 F2

Paralia (Aháïa) 86 C1
Paralia (Lakonia) 87 E3
Paralia (Makedonía) 79 E4
Paralia (Stereá Eláda) 83 D3
Paralia Akrátas 87 D1
Paralia Ástros 87 D2
Paralia Kimis 84 B3
Paralia Kotsikiás 84 A3
Paralia Skotinas 79 E4
Paralia Tiroú 87 E3
Paralimni 84 A4
Paralovo 77 D2
Paramé 18 B4
Paramera, Pto de 39 F2
Paramithiá 82 B2
Páramo del Sil 34 C2
Paranésti 80 C2
Parapanda 43 F3
Parapótamos 82 B1
Paraspóri, Akr 93 D2
Paray-le-Monial 26 C3
Parchim 48 C3
Pardubice 112 A3
Paredes 34 A4
Paredes de Coura 34 A3
Paredes de Nava 35 E3
Pareja 40 C2
Pareloup, Lac de 29 E3
Parentis-en-Born 28 A3
Párga 82 B2
Pargas 107 D3
Parikkala 103 F3
Paríngului, M 114 C1
Paris 19 F4
Parkalompolo 95 D4
Parkano 102 B3
Parla 40 A2
Parlavà 32 B3
Parma 60 B2
Parnassós, Óros 83 E4
Parndorf 57 F3
Párnitha, Óros 87 F1
Párnonas, Óros 87 D3
Pärnu 110 C2
Parola 107 E2

Páros 88 C3
Páros, N. 88 B3
Parrett 9 D3
Parsberg 55 F2
Parsdorf 56 A3
Parseierspitze 58 C2
Parsęta 49 F1
Parsteiner See 49 E3
Partakko 95 F2
Partanna 68 B3
Partenen 58 B2
Partenkirchen 55 F4
Parthenay 24 C3
Parthéni 89 E3
Partille 108 C1
Partinico 68 B3
Partizani 73 D3
Partizanske Vode . . 72 C4
Partney 7 E3
Partry Mountains . . 12 B3
Pasaia-Pasajes 36 C1
Pas de Calais 11 E3
Pas-de-Calais
  (Dépt.) 19 E1
Pas-en-Artois 19 F2
Pasewalk 49 E2
Pashalitsa 83 E2
Pasikovci 71 E2
Pašman 74 C1
Pašman I 74 C1
Passais 18 C4
Passá-Limáni 85 E4
Passás, N 85 E4
Passau 56 C2
Passavás 87 D4
Passero, C 69 D4
Passignano sul
  Trasimeno 61 D4
Passwang 27 E2
Pastrana 40 E2
Paštrik 76 C3
Pásztó 112 B4
Patay 25 E1
Pateley Bridge 6 C1
Patéras, Óros 87 E1
Paterna del Campo . 43 D2
Paterna de Rivera . 43 D4
Paternion 59 F2
Paternò 69 D3
Paternopoli 64 B3
Patersdorf 56 B2
Patiópoulo 82 C2
Patitíri 84 B2
Pátmos 89 E2
Pátmos, N 89 E2
Pátra 83 D4
Patraïkós Kólpos . . 82 C4
Patreksfjörður 96 A1
Patrington 7 E2
Pattada 66 B2
Patterdale 5 D4
Patti 69 D2
Pattijoki 99 D4
Patvinsuo 103 F2
Pau 37 D1
Pauillac 28 B2
Paúl 38 C2
Paularo 59 E2
Paulhaguet 29 F2
Paullo 60 A1
Pavia (I) 60 A2
Pavia (P) 38 B4
Pavilly 19 D3
Pavino Polje 76 B1
Pávliani 83 E3
Pávlos 83 F4
Pavullo nel
  Frignano 60 C3
Paxí 82 A2
Paxí, N 82 A2
Payerne 27 E3
Paymogo 42 C2
Payrac 29 D2
Pazardžik 115 D3
Pazin 70 A3
Pčinja 77 E2
Péage-de-
  Roussillon, le . . . 30 B1
Peak District Nat Pk . 6 C2
Peal de Becerro . . . 44 B2
Peanía 87 F1
Peares, Emb de
  los 34 B2

Peč 76 C2
Peča 70 B1
Peccioli 60 C4
Pečenjevce 77 E1
Pech-Merle,
  Grotte du 29 D3
Pećigrad 70 C3
Pečinci 72 C3
Pecka 72 C4
Peckelsheim 52 A2
Pécs 114 B1
Pečsa Banja 76 C2
Pečurice 76 B3
Pedaso 61 F4
Pedersker 109 D4
Pedersöre 102 C2
Pédi 93 E1
Pedrafita do
  Cebreiro 34 C2
Pedrafita do Cebreiro,
  Pto de 34 C2
Pedrajas de San
  Esteban 35 E4
Pedralba
  (Castilla-León) . . 34 C3
Pedralba
  (Valencia) 41 E3
Pedras Salgadas . . . 34 B4
Pedraza de la
  Sierra 40 A1
Pedrera 43 E3
Pedrizas, Pto de
  las 43 F3
Pedro Abad 43 F2
Pedro Bernardo 39 F2
Pedrógão
  (Alentejo) 42 B1
Pedrógão
  (Estremadura) . . . 38 A2
Pedrógão Grande . . . 38 B2
Pedrola 36 C3
Pedro Muñoz 40 B4
Peebles 5 D2
Peel 6 A1
Peene 49 D2
Peenemünde 49 E1
Peer Gynt veien . . . 100 C3
Pefkári 80 C3
Pefkí 83 F3
Péfkos 78 C3
Pega 38 C2
Pegalajar 44 A2
Pegau 53 D2
Pegli 60 A3
Pegnitz 55 F1
Pego 45 E1
Pego do Altar,
  Bgem de 38 B4
Pegognaga 60 C2
Pegolotte 61 D1
Pehčevo 77 F3
Peine 52 B1
Peio Terme 58 C3
Peira-Cava 31 E3
Peißenberg 56 A4
Peiting 56 A4
Peitz 53 F1
Pek 73 D3
Péla 79 E2
Péla (Nomos) 79 F3
Pelado 41 D3
Pelagie, Is 68 A4
Pelasgía 83 F3
Pelat, Mt 31 D2
Pełczyce 49 F3
Pelekános 79 D3
Pélekas 82 A1
Peletá 87 E3
Pelhřimov 57 D1
Pelinéo 85 E4
Pelister 77 E4
Pelješac 75 E2
Pelkosenniemi 99 E1
Pellegrino, M 68 B2
Pellegrino
  Parmense 60 B2
Pellegrue 28 C2
Pellerin, le 24 B2
Pellesmäki 103 E2
Pello 98 C3
Pellworm 47 F1
Pelopónnisos 86 C2
Peloritani, M 69 D2
Peltosalmi 103 E1

Peltovuoma 95 D3
Pélussin 30 B1
Pelvoux, Mt 31 D2
Pembroke 8 B2
Pembroke Dock 8 B2
Pembrokeshire Coast
  Nat Pk 8 B1
Penacova 38 B2
Peña de Francia . . . 39 D2
Peña de Francia,
  Sa de 39 D2
Peña de Oroel 37 D2
Penafiel 34 A4
Peñafiel 35 F4
Peñaflor 43 E2
Peña Gorbea 36 B1
Peñalara 40 A1
Penalva do
  Castelo 38 C1
Penamacor 38 C2
Peña Mira 34 C3
Peña Nofre 34 B3
Peña Prieta 35 E2
Peñaranda de
  Bracamonte 39 F1
Peñaranda de
  Duero 36 A3
Peñarroya 41 E2
Peñarroya, Emb de . 40 B4
Peñarroya-
  Pueblonuevo 43 E1
Penarth 9 D2
Peña, Sa de la 37 D2
Peña Sagra 35 F2
Peñas, C de 35 D1
Peñascosa 44 C1
Peñas de Cervera . . 36 A3
Peñas de San
  Pedro 44 C1
Peña Trevinca 34 C3
Peña Ubiña 35 D2
Peñausende 35 D4
Pendagii 83 D4
Pendálofo 82 C4
Pendálofos 78 C4
Pendéli 87 F1
Pendéli Mt 87 F1
Pendeória 83 E4
Pénde Vrísses 80 A2
Pendine 8 B2
Peneda-Gerês,
  Pque Nac da 34 A3
Peneda, Sa da 34 A3
Penedono 38 C1
Peneira, Sa da 34 A3
Perjasica 70 C3
Penela 38 B2
Pénestin 22 C4
Penha 34 A4
Penhas da Saúde . . . 38 C2
Penhas Juntas 34 C4
Penhir, Pte de 22 A3
Penice, Pso del . . . 60 A2
Peniche 38 A3
Penicuik 5 D2
Penig 53 D2
Peñíscola 41 F2
Penkun 49 E3
Penmaenmawr 6 A2
Penmarch, Pte de . . 22 A3
Pennabilli 61 E3
Penne 63 F1
Penne-d'Agenais . . . 28 C3
Pennes, Pso di 59 D2
Pennines, The 6 C1
Penrhyndeudraeth . . 6 A3
Penrith 5 D4
Penryn 8 B4
Penserjoch 59 D2
Pentland Firth 3 D2
Pentland Hills 5 D2
Pentrefoelas 6 B3
Penyagolosa 41 E3
Penyal d'Ifach 45 E1
Pen-y-bont 8 C2
Penzance 8 A4
Penzberg 56 A4
Penzlin 49 D2
Peqin 76 C4
Perahóra 87 E1
Peraleda de
  Zaucejo 43 E1
Peralejos de
  las Truchas 40 C2
Perales del
  Alfambra 41 D2

Perales del Puerto . 39 D2
Perales de Tajuña . . 40 B2
Perales, Pto de . . . 39 D2
Peralta 36 C2
Peralta de Alcofea . 37 E3
Peralva 42 B2
Pérama (Ípiros) . . . 82 C1
Pérama (Kérkira) . . 82 A1
Pérama (Kríti) 91 D3
Pérama (Lésvos) . . . 85 F3
Pérama (Stereá
  Eláda) 87 F1
Peraméri 98 C3
Peräseinäjoki 102 C2
Perast 76 B3
Peratáta 86 A1
Percy 18 B4
Perdido, M 37 E2
Pérdika (Égina) . . . 87 F2
Pérdika
  (Ioánina) 82 C2
Pérdika
  (Thesprotía) 82 B2
Perdikáki 82 C3
Perdikas 79 D3
Peréa (Péla) 79 E3
Peréa
  (Thessaloníki) . . . 79 F3
Perejaslav-
  Chmel'nyc'kyj . . . 113 F2
Pereruela 35 D4
Perg 57 D2
Pergine
  Valsugana 59 D3
Pérgola 61 E4
Perho 102 C2
Perhonjoki 102 C1
Periana 43 F3
Périers 18 B3
Perigueux 28 C2
Periklia 79 E3
Perino 60 B2
Perissa 91 E1
Perista 83 D3
Peristerá 80 A3
Peristéra, N 84 B2
Perithório 80 B1
Perívlepto 83 F2
Perivóli 78 C4
Perivóli, N 83 E2
Perivólio 83 D3
Perković 75 D1
Perleberg 48 C3
Perlez 72 C2
Përmet 114 C4
Pernå 107 F2
Pernaja 107 F2
Pernarec 53 E4
Pernes 30 C3
Pernik 114 C2
Perniö 107 E3
Pernitz 57 E3
Pernštejn 57 E1
Péronne 19 F2
Perosa Argentina . . 31 E2
Pérouges 26 C4
Perpignan 32 B2
Perranporth 8 B4
Perrero 31 E2
Perreux 26 B4
Perros-Guirec 22 B2
Persenbeug 57 D2
Pershore 9 E1
Perstorp 109 D3
Perth 5 D1
Perthus, le 32 B3
Pertisau 59 D1
Pertoča 70 C1
Pertoúli 83 D1
Pertteli 107 E2
Pertuis 30 C3
Pertunmaa 103 D3
Pertusa 37 E3
Peručac Vrelo 72 C4
Peručko jez 75 D1
Perugia 61 E4
Perušić 70 C4
Péruwelz 50 B4
Pervenchères 23 F3
Pervomajs'k 113 F3
Pesaro 61 E3
Pescara 64 A1
Pescasseroli 64 A2

Peschici 64 C2
Peschiera del
  Garda 60 C1
Pescia 60 C3
Pescina 63 F2
Pescocostanzo 64 A2
Pescolanciano 64 A2
Pescopagano 64 C4
Pescorocchiano 63 F2
Peshkopi 77 D3
Pesiökylä 99 E3
Pesmes 26 C2
Pesočani 77 D4
Pêso da Régua 34 B4
Pesoz 34 C1
Pessáni 81 F2
Peštani 77 D4
Pešter 76 C2
Pestovo 111 F1
Pešurići 72 B4
Petačinci 77 E1
Petäjäskoski 99 D2
Petäjävesi 103 D3
Petalax 102 B2
Petalida, Akr 88 B3
Petalidi 86 C3
Petalii, Nissi 88 A1
Petalión, Kólpos . . 88 A1
Pétange 21 D3
Pétas 82 C2
Petehovac 70 B3
Peterborough 9 F1
Peterhead 3 E3
Peterlee 5 E4
Petersfield 9 F3
Petershagen 17 F2
Pethelinós 80 B2
Petilia Policastro . 67 F3
Petina 64 C4
Petkula 95 E4
Petlovača 72 C3
Petra (E) 45 E2
Pétra (Lésvos) 85 F3
Pétra (Makedonía) . 79 E4
Petralia 68 C3
Petralona 80 A3
Petraná 79 E4
Petrčane 74 C1
Petrella, Mte 64 A3
Petrer 45 D1
Pétres 79 D3
Petreto-
  Bicchisano 33 F4
Petrič 115 D3
Petrijevki 71 F2
Petrina 86 C3
Petrinja 71 D2
Petrodvorec 111 D1
Petrohóri 83 D1
Pétrola 45 D1
Petróna 82 C3
Petroşani 114 C1
Petrotá 81 F1
Petrothálassa 87 E2
Petrotó 83 D2
Petroússa 80 B2
Petrovac (BH) 70 C3
Petrovac (Crna
  Gora) 76 B3
Petrovac (Srbija) . . 73 E3
Petrovaradin 72 C2
Petrovčić 72 C2
Petrovec 77 E3
Petrovice 53 F4
Petrovići 72 B4
Pettenbach 56 C3
Pettigoe 12 C2
Petworth 9 F3
Peuerbach 56 C3
Peura 99 E2
Pewsey 9 E2
Peyrat-le-
  Château 29 D1
Peyrehorade 28 A4
Peyresourde, C de . 37 D2
Peyriac-Minervois . 32 B1
Peyrolles 30 C4
Peyrol, Pas de 29 E2

Peyruis 31 D3
Pézenas 30 A4
Pezinok 112 A3
Pezoúla 81 D2
Pfaffenhofen 55 F2
Pfäffikon 58 A2
Pfalzgrafenweiler . 54 C3
Pfarrkirchen 56 B2
Pfeffenhausen 56 B2
Pforzheim 54 C2
Pfreimd 56 B1
Pfronten 55 E4
Pfullendorf 55 D4
Pfullingen 55 D3
Pfunds 58 C2
Pfungstadt 54 C1
Phalsbourg 21 E4
Philippeville 50 C4
Philippsreut 56 C2
Piacenza 60 B2
Piadena 60 B2
Piana 33 F3
Piana d. Albanesi . . 68 B3
Piancastagnaio 63 D1
Piancavallo 59 E3
Piandelagotti 60 C3
Pian delle
  Fugazze, Pso 59 D4
Pian del Voglio . . . 60 C3
Pianella 64 A1
Pianello 61 E4
Pianoro 61 D3
Pianosa, I (Mare
  Adriatico) 64 C1
Pianosa, I (Mare
  Tirreno) 62 B2
Piansano 63 D2
Piapaxaro, P 34 C2
Pias 42 B1
Piatra-Neamţ 113 D4
Piave 59 E4
Piazza al Serchio . . 60 B3
Piazza Armerina . . . 68 C3
Piazza Brembana . . . 58 B4
Piazzola sul
  Brenta 59 D4
Piber 57 E4
Pibeste, P de 37 E1
Pićan 70 A3
Picassent 41 E4
Piccolo San Bernardo,
  Colle del 27 E4
Picerno 64 C4
Pickering 7 D1
Pico 64 A3
Pico, Pto del 39 F2
Pico Ruivo 42 A3
Picos de Europa . . . 35 E2
Picote, Bgem de . . . 34 C4
Picquigny 19 F2
Pidna 79 F3
Piedicavallo 27 F4
Piedicroce 33 F3
Piediluco 63 E2
Piedimonte Matese . 64 B3
Piedrabuena 40 A4
Piedrafita 35 D2
Piedrahita 39 E2
Piedralaves 39 F2
Piedra, R 36 C4
Piedras Albas 39 D3
Piedra San Martín,
  Collado de la . . . 37 D2
Piedras, Emb de . . . 42 C2
Piedrasluengas,
  Pto de 35 F2
Piedratajada 37 D3
Pieksämäki 103 E3
Pielavesi 103 D2
Pielavesi L 103 D2
Pielinen 103 F1
Pieljekaise 97 F2
Piemonte 31 E2
Piennes 20 C3
Pienza 61 D4
Pieriá 79 E4
Piéria, Óri 79 E4
Pierowall 3 E1
Pierre-Buffière . . . 29 D1
Pierre-de-Bresse . . 26 C3
Pierrefitte 20 C3
Pierrefitte-
  Nestaias 37 E2
Pierrefonds 19 F3

Pierrefontaine-les-
  Varans 27 D2
Pierrefort 29 E2
Pierrelatte 30 B3
Pieskehaure 97 F2
Piešťany 112 A3
Pietarsaaren mlk . . 102 C2
Pietarsaari 102 C1
Pietra Ligure 31 F3
Pietralunga 61 E4
Pietraperzia 68 C3
Pietrasanta 60 B3
Pietra Spada, Pso
  di 67 F4
Pietrosu 113 D3
Pieux, les 18 B3
Pieve de' Burgondi
  del Cairo 60 A2
Pieve di Bono 58 C4
Pieve di Cadore . . . 59 E3
Pieve di Soligo . . . 59 E3
Pieve di Teco 31 F3
Pievepelago 60 C3
Pieve Santo
  Stefano 61 D4
Pigádi 83 E3
Pigés 82 C2
Pigi 83 D4
Pigna 31 E3
Pigón, L 82 C1
Pihlajaveden as . . . 102 C3
Pihlajavesi 102 C3
Pihlajavesi L 103 F3
Pihlava 102 B3
Pihtipudas 103 D2
Piikkiö 107 D2
Piippola 103 D1
Piispajärvi 99 F3
Pikal'ovo 111 E1
Pikérmi 87 F1
Piła 112 A1
Pilat-Plage 28 A2
Pilas 43 D3
Pila, Sa de la 45 D2
Pilat, Mt 30 B1
Pilatus 27 F2
Piléa 81 F2
Piles 41 E4
Pilés 93 D3
Pili (Makedonía) . . 78 C2
Pili (Stereá Eláda) . 87 F1
Pili (Thessalía) . . . 83 D2
Pilica 112 B2
Pílio 84 A3
Pílio 89 F3
Pílio, Óros 83 F2
Pillon, Col du 27 E3
Pilorí 79 D4
Pílos 86 C3
Pilštanj 70 C2
Pina 37 D4
Piña de Campos 35 E3
Pinar 43 E3
Pineda de la Sierra . 36 A2
Pineda de Mar 32 B4
Pinerolo 31 E2
Pineto 64 A3
Piney 20 B4
Pinhal de Leiria . . 38 A2
Pinhal Novo 38 A4
Pinhão 34 B4
Pinheiro 34 A4
Pinhel 39 D1
Piniós
  (Pelopónnisos) . . . 86 C1
Piniós (Thessalía) . 83 E1
Pinkafeld 57 F3
Pinneberg 48 A3
Pino 33 F2
Pinofranqueado 39 D2
Pinols 29 F2
Pinoso 45 D1
Pinos Puente 44 A3
Pinsk 113 D1
Pintado, Emb de . . . 43 D2
Pintamo 99 E3
Pinto 40 A2
Pinzano al
  Tagliamento 59 E3
Pinzolo 58 C3
Piobbico 61 E4
Piombino 62 C1
Pione 60 B2
Pionsat 26 A4

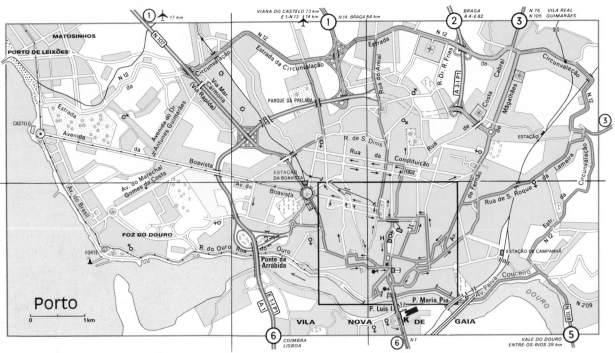

Porto

Piotrków Trybunalski 112 B2	Pivdennyj Buh. 113 E2	Platanítis 83 D4	Plitvička jezera 70 C3	Pódareš 77 F3	Poix-Terron 20 B2
Piove di Sacco. . . . 61 D1	Pivka 70 A3	Plátanos (Kríti) 90 B3	Plitvički Ljeskovac. . 70 C4	Podbořany 53 E3	Pojate 73 E4
Piovene Rocchette 59 D4	Pivnica 71 E2	Plátanos (Pelopónnissos) . . . 87 D3	Plješevica 70 C4	Podčetrtek 70 C2	Pojo 107 E3
Pipéri, N 84 C2	Pivnice 72 B2		Pljevlja 76 B1	Podensac 28 B2	Pokka 95 E3
Pipriac 23 D3	Pivsko jezero 76 A2	Plátanos (Thessalía) 83 F2	Ploaghe 66 B2	Podersdorf 57 F3	Poklečani 75 E1
Piqueras, Pto de . . 36 B3	Pizarra 43 F3	Plataría 82 B2	Ploče 75 E2	Podgajci Posavski . . 72 B3	Pokljuka 70 A2
Piran 70 A3	Piz Buin 58 B2	Plateau-d'Assy 27 E4	Plochingen 55 D2	Podgarič 71 D2	Pokupsko 70 C3
Pireás 87 F1	Pizzighettone 60 B2	Plateés 87 E1	Płock 112 B1	Podgora 75 E2	Polače 75 E2
Pirgadíkia 80 B3	Pizzo 67 E3	Pláti 81 F1	Plöckenpaß 59 E2	Podgorac(HR) 71 F2	Polacra, Pta de la . . 44 C4
Pirgetós 83 E1	Pizzoli 63 F2	Platiána 86 C2	Plöckenstein 56 C2	Podgorac (Srbija) . . 73 E3	Pola de Allande . . . 34 C1
Pirgi (Dráma) 80 B2	P'jatychatky 113 E2	Platičevo 72 C3	Pločno 75 E1	Podgorica 76 B3	Pola de Gordón, la . 35 D2
Pirgi (Híos) 85 E4	Pjörsá 96 B2	Platikambos 83 E1	Ploërmel 22 C3	Podgrad 70 A3	Pola de Laviana . . . 35 E2
Pirgi (Kérkira) 82 A1	Plabennec 22 A2	Platis Gialós (Kefaloniá) 86 A1	Ploiești 115 D1	Podhum 75 E1	Pola de Lena 35 D1
Pirgi (Kozáni) 79 E3	Plačenska pl. 77 D4		Plomári. 85 F3	Podíl's'ka Vyso579na 113 D3	Pola de Siero 35 D1
Pirgos (Íos) 88 C4	Plačkovica 77 F3	Platis Gialós (Mikonos) 88 C2	Plomb du Cantal . . 29 E2	Podjuchy 49 E2	Polán 40 A3
Pirgos (Kríti) 91 D4	Plagiá (Makedonía) 79 F2		Plombières 27 D1	Podkoren 70 A1	Polcenigo 59 E3
Pirgos (Makedonía) . 79 F3	Plagiá (Thráki) 81 E2	Platis Gialós (Sífnos) 88 B3	Plomin 70 B3	Podlugovi 71 F4	Połczyn-Zdrój 110 A4
Pirgos (Pelo/pónnissos) . . . 86 B2	Plagne, la 31 D1	Platistomo 83 E3	Plön 48 B2	Podnovlje 71 F3	Polegate 10 C3
Pirgos (Sámos) 89 E2	Plaisance 28 B4	Plattling 56 B2	Plonéour- Lanvern 22 A3	Podogorá 82 C3	Poles 113 D1
Pirgos (Stereá Eláda) 83 F4	Pláka (Límnos) 85 D1	Platja de Gandia . . . 41 E4	Płoń, Jez. 49 F3	Podohóri 80 B2	Polesella 61 D2
Pírgos Diroú 87 D4	Pláka (Pelo/pónnissos) . . . 87 E3	Platja de San Juan . 45 E1	Płońsk 112 B1	Podol'sk 111 F2	Polessk 110 B4
Piriac 22 C4	Pláka (Thráki) 81 E2	Plau 48 C3	Płoty 49 F2	Podpec 70 B2	Polhov Gradec 70 A2
Pirin 115 D3	Pláka, Akr. 85 D1	Plaue 49 D4	Plouagat 22 C2	Podrašnica 71 E4	Policastro 67 D1
Pirkkala 107 E1	Pláka Litohórou . . . 79 F4	Plauen 53 D3	Plouaret. 22 B2	Podravska Slatina . . 71 E2	Policastro, Golfo di. 67 D2
Pirmasens 54 B2	Plakiás 90 C4	Plauer See (Brandenburg) . . 49 D4	Plouay 22 B3	Podromanija 72 B4	
Pirna 53 F2	Planá 53 E4		Ploubalay 18 A4	Podsreda 70 C2	Police 49 E2
Pirok 77 D3	Plana 76 A2	Plauer See (Mecklenburg- Vorpommern) . . 48 C3	Plœuc 22 C3	Podsused 70 C2	Poličnik 74 C1
Pirot 77 E1	Planches-en- Montagne, les . . 27 D3		Ploudalmézeau. . . . 22 A2	Podturen 71 D1	Policoro 65 D4
Pirovac. 74 C1	Plancoët 22 C3	Plav 76 C2	Plouescat 22 B2	Poduri 71 D1	Polidéndri 84 B4
Pirsógiani 78 C4	Plandište 73 D2	Plavča 70 C3	Plougasnou 22 B2	Podujevo 77 D1	Polidrossos 83 E3
Pirttikoski 99 E2	Plánice 56 C1	Plavna 73 E3	Plougastel- Daoulas 22 A3	Podunavci 73 D4	Poliegos 88 B4
Pisa 60 C4	Planina (Celje) 70 C2	Plavnica. 76 B3		Poel 48 C2	Poligiros 80 A3
Pisciotta 67 D1	Planina (Jesenice) . . 70 A1	Plavnik I 70 B4	Plougonven 22 B2	Poganovo 77 E1	Polignano a Mare. . . 65 E3
Pisek 56 C1	Planina (Postojna) . 70 A2	Plavnik Mt. 70 B3	Plouguenast 22 C3	Poggibonsi 60 C4	Poligny 27 D3
Piškorevci 71 F2	Planinica 73 E4	Playa Blanca 42 C4	Plouha 22 C2	Poggio Imperiale . . 64 C2	Polihnítos 85 F3
Pisogne 58 C4	Planitz 53 D3	Pleaux. 29 E2	Plouigneau 22 B2	Poggio Mirteto 63 E2	Polikárpi 79 E2
Pisses 88 A2	Plános 86 A1	Pleine-Fougères. . . . 18 B4	Ploumanac'h 22 B2	Poggio Renatico . . . 61 D2	Polikástano 78 C3
Pissódéri 79 D3	Plansee 58 C1	Pleinfeld 55 F2	Plouzévédé 22 B2	Poggio Rusco 60 C2	Polikastro 79 F2
Pissónas. 84 B4	Plasencia 39 D2	Pleiße 53 D2	Plovdiv 115 D3	Pogoniani 78 B4	Polimilos 79 E3
Pissos 28 B3	Plaški 70 C3	Plélan-le-Grand. . . . 23 D3	Plumbridge 13 D2	Pogradec 77 D4	Polinéri (Makedonía) 79 D4
Pisticci 65 D4	Plasy 53 E4	Plélan-le-Petit 22 C3	Plungė 110 B3	Pohja 107 E3	
Pistoia 60 C3	Platamona Lido 66 A2	Pléneuf 22 C2	Pl'ussa 111 D1	Pohja-Lankila 103 E2	Polinéri (Thessalía) . 82 C2
Pisuerga, R 35 E4	Platamónas (Kavalá) 80 C2	Plentzia 36 B1	Pluvigner. 22 C3	Pohjaslahti (Keski- Suomen Lääni) . . 102 C3	Políhni 85 D1
Piteå 98 B3		Plépi 87 E2	Plužine 76 A1		Polipótamo 79 D3
Piteälven 98 B3	Platamónas (Piería) 79 F4	Plešin 73 D4	Plympton 8 C4	Pohjaslahti (Lapin Lääni) . . . 99 D2	Polipótamos 84 C4
Pitești 115 D1	Platanákia 79 F2	Plestin 22 B2	Plymstock 8 C4		Poliraho 79 E4
Pithagório 89 E2	Platanés 90 C3	Pleternica 71 E2	Plzeň 53 E4	Pohjois-Karjalan Lääni 103 F2	Polirinía 90 B3
Pithio (Thessalía). . . 79 E4	Platáni 68 B3	Plettenberg 17 F4	Po. 60 C2		Polis, M. 77 D4
Pithio (Thráki) 81 F1	Plataniá (Makedonía). . . 80 C2	Pletvar 77 E3	Poarta de Fier. 114 C1	Pohořelice 57 F1	Polissito 81 D2
Pithiviers 25 F1		Pleumartin 25 D3	Pobierowo 49 F1	Pohorje 70 B1	Polistena 67 E4
Pitigliano 63 D2	Platánia (Pelo/pónnissos) . 86 C2	Pleumeur-Bodou . . . 22 B2	Poblet 37 F4	Poiana Brașov 113 D4	Polithéa 82 C1
Pitlochry 3 D1	Plataniá (Thessalía) . 84 A2	Pleven 115 D2	Pobrđde 76 C1	Poio. 34 A2	Politiká 84 A4
Pitomača 71 D2	Platanistós 88 A1	Pleyben 22 B2	Počep 111 F4	Poiré, le 24 B3	Poljana (SLO) 70 B1
Pittenweem 5 D2		Pliego 44 C2	Počinok 111 E3	Poirino 31 E2	Poljana (Srbija) 73 D3
		Plitra 87 D4	Počitelj 75 F2	Poissons 20 C4	Poljčane 70 C1
		Plitvice 70 C3	Pocking 56 B2	Pôitsamaa 110 C2	Polje 71 E2
			Poćuta 72 C4	Poix 19 E2	Poljica 75 E2

Poljice 71 F4	
Polla 64 C4	
Põlläkkä 103 E2	
Pöllau 57 E4	
Polle 52 A1	
Pollença 45 F2	
Pollfoss 100 B3	
Pollino, Mte. 67 E2	
Pollos 35 E4	
Polmak 95 E2	
Polock 111 D3	
Polonne 113 D2	
Polperro 8 B4	
Poltava. 113 F2	
Polvijärvi 103 F2	
Polzela 70 B2	
Pomar. 37 E3	
Pomarance 60 C4	
Pomarkku 102 B3	
Pombal 38 B2	
Pómbia 91 D4	
Pomellen 49 E2	
Pomezi 53 D4	
Pomezia. 63 E3	
Pomigliano d'Arco 64 B4	
Pommersfelden 55 E1	
Pomokaira 95 E4	
Pomorie 115 E2	
Pomorze 110 A4	
Pomovaara 95 E4	
Pompei 64 B4	
Pomposa 61 D2	
Poncin. 26 C4	
Pondoiráklia 79 F2	
Pondokómi 79 D3	
Ponferrada 34 C2	
Ponikovica 72 C4	
Pons 28 B1	
Ponsacco 60 C4	
Pontacq 37 E1	
Pontailler. 26 C2	
Pont-à-Marcq 20 A1	
Pont-à-Mousson . . . 21 D3	
Pontão 38 B2	
Pontardawe 8 C2	
Pontarddulais 8 C2	
Pontarion 25 E4	
Pontarlier 27 D3	
Pontassieve 61 D3	
Pontaubault 18 B4	
Pont-Audemer 19 D3	
Pontaumur. 26 A4	
Pont-Aven 22 B3	
Pont Canavese 31 E1	
Pontcharra 31 D1	
Pontchartrain 19 E4	
Pontchâteau 23 D4	
Pont-Croix 22 A3	
Pont-d'Ain 26 C4	
Pont-de-Beauvoisin, le 30 C1	
Pont-de-Chéruy 30 C1	
Pont-de-Claix, le . . . 30 C2	
Pont-de-Dore 26 A4	
Pont-de-l'Arche 19 E3	
Pont-de-Montvert, le 29 F3	
Pont-de-Roide 27 E2	
Pont-de-Salars 29 E3	
Pont-d'Espagne 37 E2	
Pont de Suert 37 F2	
Pont-de-Vaux 26 C3	
Pont-de-Veyle. 26 C4	
Pont-d'Oléron 28 A1	
Pont-d'Ouilly 18 C4	
Pont-du- Château 26 A4	
Pont-du-Gard 30 B3	
Ponte Arche 58 C3	
Ponteareas 34 A3	
Pontebba 59 F2	
Pontecagnano 64 B4	
Ponte Caldelas 34 A2	
Ponteceno 60 B2	
Ponte Ceso 34 A1	
Pontecorvo 64 A3	
Ponte da Barca 34 A3	
Pontedecimo 60 A3	
Ponte de Lima. 34 A3	
Pontedera 60 C4	
Ponte de Sor 38 B3	
Pontedeume 34 B1	
Ponte di Legno. 58 C3	

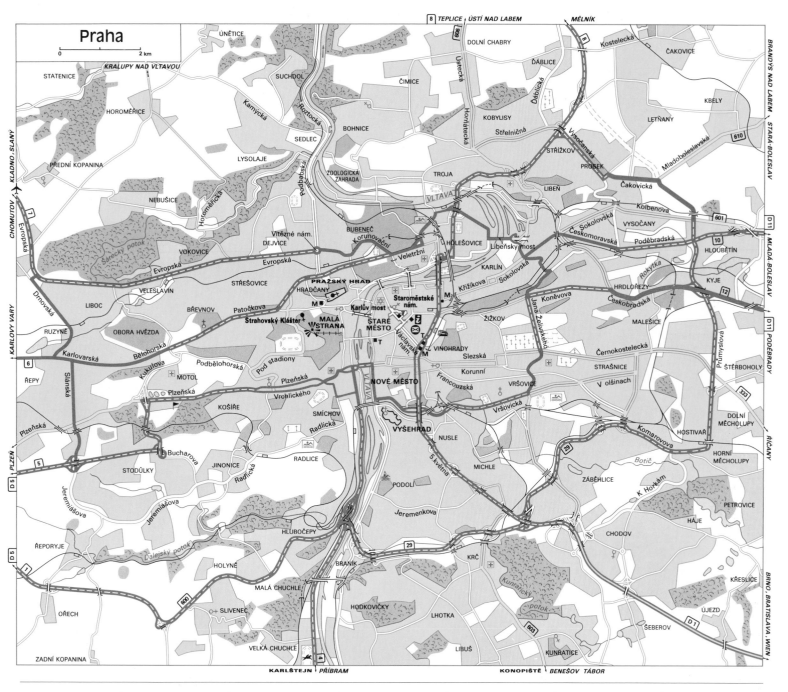

Praha

0   2 km

Ponte di Piave......59 E4	Ponts...........37 F3	Porcuna..........43 F2	Porta, la...........33 F3	Portglenone.......13 E1	Portnaguran.........2 B2	Pórto Kágio........87 D4
Pontefract..........7 D2	Pont-Ste-	Pordenone........59 E3	Portalegre........38 C3	Porthcawl..........8 C2	Portnahaven........4 A2	Pörtom.........102 B2
Pontelandolfo....64 B3	Maxence......19 F3	Poreč............70 A3	Portalė, Pto del...37 D2	Porthmadog.........6 A3	Port-Navalo.......22 C4	Portomaggiore....61 D2
Ponte-Leccia.....33 F3	Pont-St-Esprit...30 B3	Pori............107 D1	Portalrubio.......41 D2	Porthmós	Porto (F).........33 E3	Portomarin.......34 B2
Pontenelle Alpi...59 E3	Pont St-Martin...31 E1	Porjus...........98 B2	Portariá..........83 F2	Elafonissou....90 A1	Porto (P).........34 A4	Porto-Maurizio...31 F3
Pont-en-Royans...30 C1	Pont-St-Vincent...21 D4	Porkkalanselkä..107 E3	Portarlington.....13 D4	Portici...........64 B4	Porto Azzuro......62 C1	Porto Moniz......42 A3
Ponte San Pietro...60 B1	Pont-Scorff......22 B3	Porma, Emb del..35 E2	Port Askaig........4 B2	Pórtile de Fier...114 C1	Pórto Carrás.....80 B4	Portomouro.......34 A2
Pontet, le........30 C3	Ponts-de-Cê, les..23 E4	Porma, R.........35 E2	Portavogie........13 E2	Portilla de la Reina..35 E2	Porto Ceresio.....58 A4	Portonovo........34 A2
Ponte Tresa......58 A4	Pontsenni.........8 C1	Pornainen.......107 F2	Porta-Westfalica...51 F1	Portillo..........35 E4	Porto Cervo......66 B1	Porto Petro......45 F3
Pontevico........60 B1	Pont-sur-Yonne...26 A1	Pörnbach.........55 F2	Port-Bacarès......32 B2	Portillo de la	Porto Cesareo....65 F4	Porto Pino.......66 B4
Pontfaverger-	Pontvallain......23 F-4	Pornic...........24 A2	Portbail.........18 B3	Canda..........34 C3	Porto Cristo......45 F3	Pórto Ráfti.......88 A1
Moronvilliers...20 B3	Pontypool.........9 D2	Pornichet........24 A2	Portbou..........32 C3	Portillo de	Porto de Envalira..32 A2	Porto Recanati...61 F4
Pontgibaud.......29 E1	Pontypridd........8 C2	Póros (Kefaloniá)..86 A1	Port Charlotte.....4 A2	Padornelo.....34 C3	Porto de Lagos....42 A2	Porto Rotondo....66 C1
Pontigny.........26 B1	Ponza, I.........63 F4	Póros (Lefkáda)...82 B3	Port, Col de......37 F2	Portillo, Pto del...39 E2	Porto de Mós.....38 A3	Portorož.........70 A3
Pontinia.........63 F3	Ponziane, I......63 F4	Póros (Póros).....87 E2	Port-Cros........31 D4	Portimão.........42 A2	Portodemouros,	Porto San Giorgio..61 F4
Pontinvrea.......31 F2	Poole............9 E3	Póros, N.........87 E2	Port-de-Bouc.....30 C4	Portimo..........99 D2	Emb de.......34 B2	Porto Sant' Elpidio..61 F4
Pontivy.........22 C3	Poperinge........50 A3	Porozina.........70 B3	Porte, Col de.....30 C1	Portinatx, Cala de..45 D3	Porto do	Porto Santo......42 A3
Pont-l'Abbé.......22 A3	Popinci..........72 C3	Pórpi............81 D2	Port-Einon........8 C2	Portishead.........9 D3	Barqueiro.....34 B1	Porto Santo, I de..42 A3
Pont-l'Evêque....19 D3	Popoli...........64 A2	Porquerolles......31 D4	Portella	Port-Joinville.....24 A3	Porto do Son.....34 A2	Porto Santo
Pontlevoy........25 E2	Popovac..........73 E4	Porrentruy........27 E2	Femmina Morta..69 D3	Port Láirge......15 D4	Porto Empedocle..68 B4	Stefano.......63 D2
Pontoise.........19 E3	Popovača.........71 D2	Porretta Terme...60 C3	Port Ellen........4 A2	Portland, Bill of..9 D4	Porto Ercole.....63 D2	Portoscuso......66 A4
Pontones........44 B2	Popova Šapka.....77 D3	Porriño..........34 A3	Portelo..........34 C3	Port-la-Nouvelle...32 B2	Portoferraio.....62 C1	Porto Tolle......61 D2
Pontón, Pto del...35 E2	Popov Most......76 A1	Porsangen........95 E1	Port-en-Bessin...18 C3	Portlaoise........13 D4	Portofino........60 A3	Porto Torres.....66 A2
Pontoon.........12 B2	Popovo..........115 E2	Porsangerhalvøya..95 D1	Port Erin.........6 A1	Portelen.........34 C3	Port of Ness......2 B2	Porto-Vecchio....33 F4
Pontorson.......18 B4	Poppenhausen....52 B4	Porsgrunn.......104 C3	Pórtes...........87 F2	Porto do	Porto Garibaldi...61 D2	Portovenere.....60 B3
Pontremoli.......60 B3	Poppi............61 D3	Pórshöfn.........96 C1	Portet-d'Aspet,	Barqueiro.....34 B1	Porto, G de......33 E3	Portpatrick.......4 B3
Pontresina.......58 B3	Poprad..........112 B3	Portadown........13 D2	Col de.......37 F2	Port-Manech......22 B3	Pórto Germenó....87 E1	Portree..........2 B3
Pontrieux........22 C2	Porcari..........60 C3	Portaferry........13 E2	Portezuelo.......39 D3	Portmarnock......13 E4	Portogruaro.....59 E4	Portrush.........13 D1
Pontrilas.........9 D2	Porchov.........111 D2	Portaje, Emb de...39 D3	Port Glasgow......4 C2	Portnacroish......4 B1	Portoheli........87 E2	Port-Ste-Marie...28 C3

Port-St-Louis 30 B4
Port St Mary 6 A1
Portsalon 13 D1
Pörtschach 70 A1
Portsmouth 9 F3
Portstewart 13 D1
Port-sur-Saône 27 D1
Port Talbot 8 C2
Porttipahdan
tekojärvi 95 E4
Portugalete 36 B1
Portumna 12 C4
Port-Vendres 32 B2
Port William 4 C4
Porvoo 107 F2
Porvoonjoki 107 F2
Porzuna 40 A4
Posada 66 C2
Posadas 43 E2
Pöschenhöhe 56 C3
Pošechonje-
Volodarsk 111 F1
Posedarje 74 C1
Posets, Pico 37 E2
Posio 99 E2
Positano 64 B4
Poßneck 52 C3
Possidi 80 A4
Possidonia 88 B2
Posta 63 F1
Postavy 111 D3
Postira 75 D2
Postojna 70 B2
Postojnska jama . . . 70 A2
Poštorná 57 F1
Posušje 75 E1
Potami 80 C1
Potamiá 87 D3
Potamiés 91 E4
Potamós
(Andikithira) 90 A2
Potamós (Kíthira) . . 90 A1
Potamoúla 82 C3
Potenza 64 C4
Potenza R. 61 E4
Potenza Picenza . . 61 F4
Potes 35 E2
Potidea, N. 80 A4
Potigny 18 C3
Potoci 75 F1
Potok 71 D2
Potós 80 C3
Potpećko jez. 76 B1
Potsdam 49 D4
Pottenstein 57 E3
Potters Bar 9 F2
Pöttmes 55 F2
Potton 9 F1
Pouancé 23 D4
Pougues-les-
Eaux 26 A2
Pouilly (Nièvre) . . . 26 A2
Pouilly (Rhône) . . . 26 B4
Pouilly-en-Auxois . . 26 C2
Poulaphouca
Reservoir 13 D4
Poúlari, Akr. 92 C1
Pouldu, le 22 B3
Pouliguen, le 24 A2
Poúlithra 87 E3
Poúnda 88 C3
Poúnda, Akr. 84 B4
Pournári 83 E2
Pournári, Teh L . . . 82 C2
Pourniás, Kólpos . . 85 D1
Pourri, Mt 31 D1

Poussu 99 F3
Pouyastruc 37 E1
Pouzauges 24 C3
Pouzin, le 30 B2
Považská
Bystrica 112 B3
Poveda 40 C2
Povlja 75 E2
Povljana 70 C4
Povljen 72 C4
Póvoa de Lanhoso . 34 A4
Póvoa de Varzim . . 34 A4
Powerscourt 13 D4
Powys 9 D1
Poysdorf 57 F1
Pöytyä 107 D2
Poza de la Sal 36 A2
Požarevac 73 D3
Požega 72 C4
Požeranje 77 D2
Poznań 112 A1
Pozo Alcón 44 B2
Pozoblanco 43 F1
Pozo Cañada 44 C1
Pozo de
Guadalajara 40 B2
Pozo Higuera 44 C1
Pozohondo 44 C1
Pozondón 41 D2
Pozozal, Pto. 35 F2
Pozuelo (Castilla-la-
Mancha) 44 C1
Pozuelo
(Extremadura) . . . 39 D2
Pozuelo de
Calatrava 40 A4
Pozzallo 69 D4
Pozzomaggiore . . . 66 B2
Pozzuoli 64 A4
Pozzuolo 59 F3
Präbichl 57 D3
Prača 76 A1
Prachatice 56 C1
Prada, Emb de . . . 34 C3
Pradairo 34 C2
Pradarena, Pso di . 60 B3
Pradelles 29 F2
Prádena 36 A4
Prades (E) 37 F4
Prades (F) 32 B2
Prado del Rey 43 D3
Pradoluengo 36 A2
Prägraten 59 E2
Praha 53 F4
Prahecq 24 C4
Prahova 115 D1
Prahovo 73 F3
Praia a Mare 67 E2
Praia da Barra 38 B1
Praia da Rocha . . . 42 A2
Praia da Vieira 38 A2
Praia de Mira 38 B1
Praia de Santa
Cruz 38 A3
Praia de Tocha . . . 38 B2
Prali 31 E2
Pralognan 31 D1
Pra-Loup 31 D2
Prámanda 82 C2
Pramollo, Pso di . . 59 F2
Prangio 81 F1
Pranjani 72 C4
Prapatnica 75 D1
Prassiá 83 D2
Prassiés 90 C3
Præstø 108 C4

Prat de Compte . . . 41 F1
Pratella 64 A3
Prati di Tivo 63 F1
Prato (Toscana) . . . 60 C3
Prato (Umbria) 63 E1
Pratola Peligna . . . 64 A2
Pratomagno 61 D4
Prato-Sornico 58 A3
Prats-de-Mollo . . . 32 B3
Pravdinsk 110 B4
Pravia 35 D1
Praz 27 E4
Prebold 70 B2
Précy-sous-Thil . . . 26 B2
Predappio 61 D3
Predazzo 59 D3
Preddvor 70 B2
Predeal 113 D4
Predejane 77 E1
Predel 70 A2
Predela 115 D3
Predil, Pso di 59 F2
Predjama 70 A2
Predoi 59 D2
Predošćica 70 B3
Pré-en-Pail 23 E3
Preetz 48 B2
Pregarten 57 D2
Preiner Gscheid . . . 57 E3
Prekaja 71 D4
Prekestolen 104 A3
Preko 74 C1
Preljina 73 D4
Prelog 71 D2
Preločšica 71 D2
Premantura 70 A4
Prèmery 26 A2
Premià de Mar . . . 32 B4
Premilcuore 61 D3
Premnitz 49 D4
Premuda 74 B1
Premuda I. 74 B1
Prenj 75 F1
Prenjas 77 D4
Prenzlau 49 E3
Prepolac 77 D1
Přerov 112 A3
Prerow 48 C1
Pré-St-Didier 27 E4
Preševo 77 E2
Presjeka 76 B2
Preslav 115 D2
Presolana, Pso
della 58 B4
Prešov 112 B3
Prespansko Ez . . . 77 D4
Pressath 53 D4
Pressbaum 57 E2
Prestatyn 6 B2
Presteigne 9 D1
Preste, la 32 B3
Prestfoss 104 C3
Preston 6 B2
Prestonpans 5 D2
Prestwick 4 C2
Pretoro 64 A2
Prettau 59 D2
Prettin 53 D1
Pretzsch 53 D1
Preuilly 25 D3
Préveli 90 C4
Préveza 82 B3
Préveza (Nomos) . . 82 B2
Prevršac 71 D3
Prezid 70 B3

Pribini 71 E4
Priboj (BH) 72 B3
Priboj (Srbija) 76 B1
Přibram 53 F4
Priego 40 C2
Priego de
Córdoba 43 F3
Prien 56 B3
Prienai 110 C4
Prievidza 112 B3
Prigradica 75 E2
Prijeboj 70 C3
Prijedor 71 D3
Prijepolje 76 B1
Prilep 77 E3
Prilike 73 D4
Priluka 75 E1
Primaube, la 29 E3
Primel-Trégastel . . 22 B2
Primišlje 70 C3
Primolano 59 D3
Primorsk 111 D1
Primošten 75 D2
Primstal 54 B1
Princetown 8 C3
Prinés 90 C3
Prínos 80 C3
Prior, C 34 B1
Prisad 77 E3
Prisl op 113 D3
Prisoje 75 E1
Priština 77 D2
Pritzerbe 49 D4
Pritzier 48 B3
Pritzwalk 48 C3
Privas 30 B2
Priverno 63 F3
Privlaka (Vincovci) . 71 F2
Privlaka (Zadar) . . 70 C4
Prizren 77 D2
Prizzi 68 B3
Prnjavor (BH) 71 E3
Prnjavor (Srbija) . . 72 B3
Proaza 35 D1
Probištip 77 E2
Probstzella 52 C3
Procida 64 A4
Pródromos 83 F4
Proenca-a-Nova . . 38 B3
Proevska Banja . . . 77 E2
Profitis Ilias 93 E1
Profondeville 50 C4
Próhoma 79 F3
Prokletije 76 C2
Prokópi 84 A3
Prokuplje 77 D1
Prolom 77 D1
Prómahi 79 E2
Promahónas 80 A1
Promina, V. 75 D1
Promíri 84 A2
Pronsfeld 51 D4
Propriano 33 F4
Proskinás 83 F4
Prosna 112 A2
Prossedi 63 F3
Prossilio 81 D2
Prossotsáni 80 B2
Prostějov 112 A3
Próti 80 C1
Próti, N 86 B3
Protoklíssio 81 F1
Prötzel 49 E4
Proussós 83 D3
Provatónas 81 F2
Provence, Canal de . 30 C4

Provenchères 21 E4
Provins 20 A4
Prozor 75 E1
Prudhoe 5 E3
Prukljansko jezero . 75 D1
Prüm 51 D4
Pruna 43 E3
Prunetta 60 C3
Prut 113 D3
Prut 113 E4
Pružany 112 C1
Prvić 70 B4
Pryluky 113 F1
Pryp'at' 112 C1
Przasnysz 112 B1
Przełęcz Dukielska . 112 C3
Przemyśl 112 C2
Przybiernów 49 F2
Psača 77 E2
Psahná 84 B4
Psáka 82 B2
Psális, Akr. 88 A4
Psará 85 E4
Psarádes 78 C2
Psará, N 85 E4
Psári (Arkadia) . . . 86 C2
Psári (Korinthía) . . 87 D1
Psári (Mt) 80 C3
Psáthi 88 B4
Psathópirgos 83 D4
Psathotópi 82 C2
Psel 113 F2
Psérimos, N 89 F3
Psihikó 83 E2
Psihró 91 E4
Psínthos 93 F1
Pskov 111 D2
Pskovskoje
Ozero 111 D2
Pšov 53 E3
Psunj 71 E2
Pteléa 80 C2
Ptéri 83 D2
Ptolemaïda 79 D3
Ptóo 84 A4
Ptuj 70 C1
Puchberg 57 E3
Pučišća 75 E2
Puckeridge 9 F2
Puçol 41 E3
Pudasjärvi 99 E3
Puebla de Alcocer . 39 E4
Puebla de
Almenara 40 B3
Puebla de Beleña . 40 B1
Puebla de
Benifasar 41 F2
Puebla de Don
Fadrique 44 B2
Puebla de D.
Rodrigo 39 F4
Puebla de
Guzmán 42 C2
Puebla de la
Calzada 39 D4
Puebla de la Reina . 39 D4
Puebla de Lillo . . . 35 E2
Puebla de Obando . 39 D3
Puebla de
Sanabria 34 C3
Puebla de Trives . . 34 C3
Pueblica de V. 35 D3
Puente de Domingo
Flórez 34 C3

Puente de Génave . 44 B1
Puente de los
Fierros 35 D2
Puente Genil 43 F3
Puente la Reina . . . 36 C2
Puente la Reina
de Jaca 37 D2
Puentenansa 35 F2
Puente Nuevo,
Emb de 43 E1
Puentes, Emb de . . 44 C2
Puentes Viejas,
Emb de 40 B1
Puerto Castilla . . . 39 E2
Puerto de Alcudia . 45 F2
Puerto de Andratx . 45 E3
Puerto de la Cruz . 42 B4
Puerto de la
Encina 43 E3
Puerto del Rosario . 42 C4
Puerto de
Mazarrón 45 D3
Puerto de
Pollença 45 F2
Puerto de
San Vicente 39 F3
Puerto de Sóller . . 45 E2
Puerto Lápice 40 B4
Puertollano 44 A1
Puerto Lumbreras . 44 C3
Puerto Real 43 D3
Puerto Serrano . . . 43 E3
Pugets-Théniers . . 31 E3
Puglia 65 D3
Puhos (Oulun
Lääni) 99 E3
Puhos (Pohjois-
Karjalan Lääni) . . 103 F3
Puhosjärvi 99 E3
Puhovac 71 F4
Puigcerda 32 A3
Puig Major 45 E2
Puignal 32 A2
Puig-reig 32 A3
Puigsacalm 32 B3
Puiseaux 25 F1
Puisserguier 30 A4
Pujols 28 B2
Pukë 76 C3
Pukiš 72 B3
Pukkila 107 F2
Pula (HR) 70 A4
Pula (I) 66 B4
Pulaj 76 B3
Puławy 112 C2
Pulborough 10 C3
Pulkau 57 E2
Pulkkila 99 D4
Pulpi 44 C3
Pulsnitz 53 E2
Pułtusk 112 B1
Punat 70 B3
Punkaharju 103 F3
Punkalaidun 107 D2
Punta Ala 62 C1
Punta di Penna . . . 64 B2
Puntagorda 42 A4
Punta Križa 70 B4
Punta Raisi 68 B2
Punta Umbría 42 C3
Puokio 99 E4
Puolanka 99 E4

Purkersdorf 57 E2
Purmerend 16 C2
Purnu 103 D3
Purullena 44 B3
Puruvesi 103 F3
Puškin 111 D1
Püspökladány . . . 112 C4
Pustoška 111 D2
Pusula 107 E2
Puszcza 112 C1
Putanges 18 C4
Putbus 49 D1
Putgarten 49 D1
Putignano 65 E3
Putinci 72 C2
Putlitz 48 C3
Puttelange 21 E3
Puttgarden 48 B1
Putyvl' 113 F1
Puula 103 D3
Puumala 103 E3
Puy de Dôme 29 E1
Puy-de-Dôme
(Dépt) 29 E1
Puy de Sancy 29 E1
Puy-en-Velay, le . . 30 A2
Puy-Guillaume . . . 26 A4
Puylaurens 29 D4
Puy-l'Evêque 29 D3
Puymirol 28 C3
Puymorens, Col de . 32 A3
Pwllheli 6 A3
Pyhä-Häkki 103 D2
Pyhäjärvi
(Hämeen Lääni) . 107 E1
Pyäjärvi (Oulun
Lääni) 103 D1
Pyhäjärvi (Pohjois-
Karjalan Lääni) . . 103 E3
Pyhäjärvi (Turun ja
Porin Läani 107 D2
Pyhäjärvi L 103 D1
Pyhäjoki (Oulun
Lääni) 99 D4
Pyhäjoki (Turun ja
Porin Lääni) . . . 107 D2
Pyhäjoki R 99 D4
Pyhälto 103 F4
Pyhäntä
(Piipola) 103 D1
Pyhäntä (Ristijärvi) . 99 E4
Pyhäranta 107 D2
Pyhäsalmi 103 D1
Pyhäselkä 103 F2
Pyhäselkä L 103 F2
Pyhätunturi 99 D2
Pyhatunturi 99 E2
Pyhävuori 102 C2
Pyhitysvaara 99 E3
Pyhrnpaß 57 D3
Pyhtää 107 F2
Pyla 28 A2
Pylkönmäki 103 D2
Pyrénées 37 E2
Pyrénées-
Atlantiques 28 A4
Pyrénées-
Orientales 32 B2
Pyrénées, Parc
Nat des 37 E2
Pyrjatyn 113 F2
Pyrzyce 49 F3
Pyttis 107 F2

Q

Qaf'e Shllahut 76 C3
Qaf'e Shtamës . . . 76 C4
Quakenbrück 17 E2
Quarré-les-
Tombes 26 B2
Quarteira 42 B3
Quarto d'Altino . . . 61 D1

Quartu San Elena . 66 B4
Quatre Chemins . . 24 B3
Quatretonda 41 E4
Quedlinburg 52 C2
Queenborough . . . 11 D2
Queen Elizabeth
Forest Park 4 C2
Queensferry 6 B2
Quejigares, Pto de . 40 A4
Queluz 38 A4

Queralbs 32 B3
Querfurt 52 C2
Quérigut 32 A2
Quero 40 B3
Quesada 44 B2
Quesnoy, le 20 A2
Questembert 22 C4
Quettehou 18 B3
Quiberon 22 C4
Quickborn 48 A2

Quiévrain 50 B4
Quigley's Point . . . 13 D1
Quillan 32 B2
Quillane, Col de la . 32 A2
Quillebeuf 19 D3
Quimper 22 B3
Quimperlé 22 B3
Quincinetto 31 E1
Quincoces de Yuso . 36 A1
Quingey 27 D2

Quintana
(Andalucía) 43 E2
Quintana
(Extremadura) . . 39 E4
Quintana del
Puente 35 F3
Quintana Martin
Galindez 36 A2
Quintana de la
Orden 40 B3

Quintanar de la
Sierra 36 B3
Quintanar del Rey . 40 C4
Quintana
Redonda 36 B3
Quintanilha 34 C4
Quintanilla de
Onésimo 35 F4
Quintin 22 C3
Quinto 37 D4

Quinzano d'Oglio . . 60 B1
Quipar, R 44 C2
Quiroga 34 C2
Quissac 30 B3
Qukës 77 D4
Quoich, L 2 C4

R

Raab 56 C2
Raab R 57 E4
Raabs 57 E1
Raahe 99 D4
Raajärvi 99 D2
Rääkkylä 103 F2
Raalte 17 D2
Raanujärvi 99 D2
Raasay 2 B3
Raasay, Sd of 2 B3
Raattama 95 D4
Rab 70 B4
Rab I 70 B4
Råba 112 A4
Rabac 70 B3
Råbade 34 B1
Rabastens 29 D4
Rabastens-de-
    Bigorre 37 E1
Rabat 68 B4
Rabe 72 C1
Rabka 112 B3
Rabrovo
    (Makedonija) 77 F3
Rabrovo (Srbija) 73 E3
Rača (Kragujevac) . . 73 D3
Rača (Radan) 77 D1
Racconigi 31 E2
Rače 70 C1
Rachiv 112 C3
Racibórz 112 A2
Račinovci 72 B3
Račišće 75 E2
Radalj 72 B3
Radan 77 D1
Rădăuţi 113 D3
Radbuza 56 B1
Rade 48 A3
Råde 105 D3
Radeberg 53 E2
Radebeul 53 E2
Radeburg 53 E2
Radeče 70 B2
Radechiv 112 C2
Radenci 70 C1
Radenthein 59 F2
Radevowald 17 E4
Radici, Pso delle . . . 60 C3
Radicondoli 60 C4
Radika 77 D3
Radimlje 75 F2
Radiovce 77 D3
Radlje 70 B1
Radljevo 72 C3
Radnice 53 E4
Radohinës, Maj'e . . . 76 C2
Radojevo 73 D1
Radom 112 B2
Radomsko 112 B2
Radomyšľ 113 E2
Radotin 53 F4
Radovče 76 B2
Radovići 76 B3
Radoviš 77 F3
Radovljica 70 A2
Radovnica 77 E2
Radøy 104 A2
Radstadt 59 F1
Radstädter
    Tauernpaß 59 F1
Radstock 9 D2
Raduša 75 E1
Radusa 77 D3
Radviliškis 110 C3
Radzyń Podlaski . . . 112 C2
Raesfeld 17 E3
Raffadali 68 B4
Rafina 88 A1
Ragama 39 F1
Raglan 9 D2
Rago 97 F1
Ragua, Pto de la . . 44 B3
Raguhn 53 D1
Ragunda 101 F2
Ragusa 69 D4
Rahden 17 F2
Råhes 83 F3
Rahlstedt 48 B3
Raia, Rib de 38 B4
Rain 55 F2
Räisäla 99 E2

Raisduoddarhal'di . . 94 C2
Raisio 107 D2
Raittijärvi 94 C3
Rajac 73 F3
Raja-Jooseppi 95 F3
Rajamäki 107 E2
Rajince 77 E2
Raka 70 C2
Rakalj 70 A4
Rakitna 70 B2
Rakitnica 71 D2
Rakkestad 105 D3
Rakova Bara 73 E3
Rakovac 71 E3
Rakovica 70 C3
Rakovnik 53 E4
Rakvere 110 C1
Ralja 73 D3
Ram 73 D2
Ramacca 69 D3
Ramales de la
    Victoria 36 A1
Ramallosa 34 A2
Ramberg 97 E1
Rambervillers 21 D4
Rambouillet 19 E4
Rambucourt 20 C4
Ramno 77 D2
Ramnoús 84 B4
Ramor, L 13 D3
Ramsau 56 B4
Ramsau 59 F1
Ramsele 101 F2
Ramsey
    (Cambridge) 9 F1
Ramsey (I of Man) . . . 6 A1
Ramsgate 11 D3
Ramsjö 101 E3
Ramstein 54 B1
Ramsund 94 B3
Ramundberget . . . 101 D2
Ramvik 101 F2
Rana 97 D3
Ranalt 59 D2
Rance 22 C3
Randaberg 104 A3
Randak 104 B3
Randalstown 13 E2
Randan 26 A4
Randanne 29 E1
Randazzo 69 D3
Randers 108 B2
Randijaure 98 A2
Randow 49 E2
Randsfjorden 105 D2
Råneå 98 C3
Råneälven 98 B2
Rangsdorf 49 E4
Rankweil 58 B2
Rannoch, L 4 C1
Ranovac 73 E3
Rantasalmi 103 E3
Rantsila 99 D4
Ranua 99 D3
Raon-l'Etape 21 E4
Rapallo 60 A3
Rapolano Terme . . . 61 D4
Rapolla 64 C3
Rapperswil 58 A2
Rapsáni 83 E1
Raptópoulo 86 C3
Raša 70 A3
Räsälä 103 E2
Raša R 70 A3
Rasbo 106 B3
Rascafria 40 A1
Rasdorf 52 B3
Raseiniai 110 C3
Rasimbegov Most . . 77 E4
Reç 76 C3
Rasina 73 E4
Raška 76 C1
Rasno 75 E2
Raso, C 38 A4
Rasquera 41 F1
Rastatt 54 C2
Rastede 47 F3
Rastegai'sa 95 E2
Rastenberg 52 C2
Rastenfeld 57 E2
Rasueros 39 F1
Rätan 101 E3
Rateče 70 A1
Ratekau 48 B2
Rates 34 A4

Rathdowney 12 C4
Rathdrum 13 D4
Rathenow 49 D4
Rathfriland 13 E2
Rathkeale 14 B3
Rathlin I 13 E1
Rath Luirc 14 B3
Rathmelton 13 D1
Rathmore 14 B4
Rathmullan 13 D1
Raticosa, Pso della . 61 D3
Ratingen 17 E4
Ratkovac 76 C2
Ratkovo 72 B2
Ratten 57 E3
Rattenberg 59 D1
Rattersdorf 57 F3
Rattray 5 D1
Rattray Head 3 E3
Rättvik 101 E4
Ratzeburg 48 B2
Raubling 56 B3
Raucourt-et-Flaba . 20 C2
Raudanjoki 99 D2
Raudaskylä 102 C1
Raufarhöfn 96 C1
Raufoss 105 D2
Rauha 103 E4
Rauhamäki 103 D3
Rauland 104 B3
Rauma (N) 100 B3
Rauma (SF) 107 D2
Rauris 59 E1
Rautalampi 103 D2
Rautas 94 C4
Rautavaara 103 E1
Rautio 102 C1
Rautjärvi 103 F3
Ravan 71 F4
Ravanica 73 E4
Ravanjska 70 C4
Ravanusa 68 C4
Ravello 64 B4
Raven 71 D2
Ravenna 61 D2
Ravensbrück 49 D3
Ravensburg 55 D4
Ravna Dubrava 77 E1
Ravna Gora 70 B3
Ravna Reka 73 E3
Ravne na
    Koroškem 70 B1
Ravnište 77 D1
Ravnje 72 B3
Ravno 75 F2
Ravno Bučje 73 F4
Ravno, G 75 E1
Rawicz 112 A2
Rawtenstall 6 C2
Rayleigh 11 D2
Rayol 31 D4
Råyrinki 102 C2
Ražana 72 C4
Ražanac 70 C4
Razboj 71 E3
Razbojna 77 D1
Raždaginja 76 C1
Razelm 113 E4
Razgrad 115 E2
Razlog 115 D3
Razlovci 77 F2
Raz, Pte du 22 A3
Reading 9 F2
Reales 43 E4
Réalmont 32 B1
Rebais 20 A4
Rebbenesøy 94 B2
Rebordelo 34 C4
Recanati 61 F4
Recco 60 A3
Recey 26 C1
Rechnitz 57 F4
Rečica (HR) 70 C3
Rečica (RB) 111 E4
Recke 17 E2
Recklinghausen 17 E3
Recknitz 48 C2
Recoaro Terme 59 D4
Recuerda 36 A4
Recz 49 F2
Red B 13 E1
Redcar 5 F4

Redditch 9 E1
Redhill 10 C3
Redon 23 D4
Redondela 34 A3
Redondo 38 C4
Redruth 8 B4
Ree, L 12 C3
Rees 17 D3
Reeth 6 C1
Refsnes 94 A3
Reftele 109 D2
Rega 49 F2
Regalbuto 69 D3
Regen 56 B2
Regensburg 56 B2
Regenstauf 56 B2
Reggello 61 D4
Reggio di Calabria . 67 E4
Reggiolo 60 C2
Reggio nell' Emilia . 60 C2
Reghin 113 D4
Regnitz 55 E1
Reguengos de
    Monsaraz 42 B1
Rehau 53 D4
Rehburg-
    Loccum 48 A4
Rehden 17 F2
Rehna 48 B2
Reichenau (A) 57 E3
Reichenau (CH) . . . 58 B2
Reichenbach
    (Dresden) 53 F2
Reichenbach
    (Chemnitz) 53 D3
Reichertshofen 55 F2
Reichshoffen 21 E3
Reigate 10 C3
Reillanne 30 C3
Reims 20 B3
Reinach 27 F2
Reinbek 48 B3
Reinberg 49 D1
Reine 97 E1
Reinfeld 48 B2
Reinheim 54 C1
Reinli 104 C2
Reinosa 35 F2
Reinøy 94 C2
Reisaelva 94 C3
Reischenhart 56 B3
Reisjärvi 103 D1
Reiss 3 D2
Reit im Winkl 56 B4
Reitzenhain 53 E3
Reka 70 A3
Rekovac 73 E4
Reksmestad 104 B1
Remagen 51 E4
Rémalard 23 D3
Remeskylä 103 D1
Remich 21 D2
Remiremont 27 D1
Remolinos 36 C3
Remouchamps 51 D4
Remoulins 30 B3
Rempstone 7 D3
Remscheid 17 E4
Rémuzat 30 C2
Rena 105 D2
Renaix 50 B3
Renazé 23 E4
Renchen 54 C3
Rende 67 E2
Rendina
    (Makedonia) 80 B3
Rendina (Thessalia) 83 D3
Rendsburg 48 A2
Renginio 83 F3
Rengsdorf 51 E4
Reni 113 E4
Renish Pt 2 A3
Renko 107 E2
Renkum 17 D3
Rennebu 100 C2
Rennerod 51 F3
Rennes 23 D3
Rennes-les-Bains . . 32 B2
Rennesøy 104 A3
Rennweg 59 F2
Reno 61 D2
Rensjön 94 C4
Renwez 20 B2

Réole, la 28 B2
Replot 102 B2
Replotfjärden 102 B2
Repojoki 95 E3
Reposaari 102 B3
République, Col de
    la 30 B1
Repvåg 95 E1
Requena 41 D4
Réquista 29 E3
Rerik 48 C2
Resanovci 71 D4
Resavica 73 E3
Reschenpaß 58 C2
Resen
    (Makedonija) 77 D4
Resen (Srbija) 77 E2
Resende 34 B4
Resia, Pso di 58 C2
Reşiţa 114 C1
Resko 49 F2
Resmo 109 E3
Resna 76 B3
Resnik 73 D3
Ressons 19 F3
Restafjorden 94 C2
Restelica 77 D3
Resuttano 68 C3
Retezatului, M 114 C1
Rethel 20 B3
Rethem 48 A4
Rethen 52 B1
Réthimno 90 C3
Réthimno
    (Nomos) 90 C3
Retiers 23 D3
Retortillo, Emb de . 43 E2
Retuerta 41 D1
Retuerta del
    Bullaque 39 F3
Retuerta, Emb de . 36 A3
Retz 57 E2
Reuilly 25 E3
Reus 37 F4
Reusel 16 C4
Reuss 27 F2
Reuterstadt-
    Stavenhagen 49 D2
Reutlingen 55 D3
Reutte 58 C1
Revard, Mt 27 D4
Revel 29 D4
Revesbotn 95 D1
Revigny 20 C4
Revin 20 B2
Revolcadores 44 C2
Revonlahti 99 D4
Revsnes 104 B1
Rewal 49 F1
Reyðarfjörður 96 C2
Reykholt 96 A2
Reykjavik 96 A2
Rezekne 111 D2
Rezzato 60 B1
Rezzoaglio 60 A3
Rgotina 73 F3
Rhaeadr 8 C1
Rhayader 8 C1
Rheda-
    Wiedenbrück . . . 17 F3
Rhede 17 D3
Rhein 17 D3
Rheinbach 51 E4
Rheinberg 17 D3
Rheinböllen 54 B1
Rheine 17 E2
Rheinfelden (CH) . . 27 F2
Rheinfelden (D) . . . 54 C4
Rheinhausen 17 D3
Rheinland-Pfalz . . . 51 E4
Rheinsberg 49 D3
Rheinwaldhorn 58 B3
Rhêmes N.D. 31 E1
Rhenen 16 C3
Rheydt 17 D4
Rhinau 21 E4
Rhinow 49 D4
Rho 60 A1
Rhondda 8 C2
Rhône 26 C4
Rhône (Dépt) 26 B4
Rhône à Sète,
    Canal du 30 B3

Rhosneigr 6 A2
Rhossili 8 C2
Rhüden 52 B1
Rhum 2 B4
Rhum, Sd of 2 B4
Rhune, la 28 A4
Rhuthun 6 B3
Rhyl 6 B2
Rhynern 17 E3
Rhynie 3 E4
Riaillé 23 D4
Riákia 79 E3
Rial 34 A2
Riaño 35 E2
Riaño, Emb de 35 E2
Rians 30 C4
Riansares R 40 B3
Rianxo 34 A2
Riaza 36 A4
Ribadavia 34 B3
Ribadelago 34 C3
Ribadeo 34 C1
Riba de Saelices . . 40 C1
Riba de Santiuste . 36 B4
Ribadesella 35 E1
Ribarci 77 E2
Ribariče 76 C1
Ribarska Banja 73 E4
Ribas de Campos . . 35 E3
Ribas de Sil 34 B2
Ribatejo 38 B3
Ribble 6 C2
Ribe 108 A3
Ribeauvillé 27 E1
Ribécourt 19 F3
Ribeira de Pena . . . 34 B4
Ribeira, Emb de la . 34 B1
Ribemont 20 A2
Ribera 68 B3
Ribera de Cardós . . 32 A2
Ribera del Fresno . 43 D1
Ribes de Freser . . . 32 B3
Ribiers 30 C3
Ribnica (BH) 71 F4
Ribnica (Kočevje) . 70 B2
Ribnica (Postojna) . 70 A3
Ribnica na
    Pohorju 70 B1
Ribnik 70 C2
Ribnitz-Damgarten . 48 C1
Ribolla 62 C1
Říčany 53 F4
Riccia 64 B3
Riccione 61 E3
Riceys, les 26 B1
Richelieu 25 D3
Richmond
    (London) 9 F2
Richmond (Yorks) . . 6 C1
Richtenberg 49 D1
Rickling 48 A2
Ricla 36 C4
Ricobayo, Emb de . 35 D4
Riddica 72 B1
Riec 22 B3
Ried
    (Oberösterreich) . 56 C3
Ried (Tirol) 58 C2
Riedenburg 55 F2
Riedlingen 55 D3
Riegel 54 C3
Riegersburg 57 F4
Riego de la Vega . . 35 D3
Riesa 53 E2
Riesi 68 C4
Riestedt 52 C2
Rietberg 17 F3
Rieti 63 E2
Rieumes 29 D4
Rieupeyroux 29 E3
Rieux 37 F1
Riez 31 D3
Riezlern 58 B2
Rīga 110 C2
Rigáni 83 D4
Rīgas Jūras Līcis . . 110 B2
Rigeo 83 E2
Rigi 58 A2
Rignac 29 E3
Rignano Flaminio . . 63 E2
Rihéa 87 E3

Riihimäki 107 E2
Riisitunturi 99 E2
Riistavesi 103 E2
Riječa 72 B4
Rijeka 70 B3
Rijeka Crnojevića . . 76 B3
Rijssen 17 D2
Riksgränsen 94 B3
Rila 115 D3
Rila Mts 115 D3
Rillo 41 D2
Rillo de Gallo 40 C1
Rimavská-Sobota . 112 B3
Rimbo 106 B3
Rimini 61 E3
Rîmnicu Sărat 113 E4
Rîmnicu Vîlcea 115 D1
Rimnio 79 E4
Rimske Toplice 70 B2
Rincón de la
    Victoria 43 F4
Rincón de Soto . . . 36 C2
Rindal 100 C2
Ringaskiddy 14 C4
Ringe 108 B4
Ringebu 100 C3
Ringford 4 C3
Ringkøbing 108 A3
Ringkøbing
    Fjord 108 A3
Ring of Kerry 14 A4
Ringsaker 105 D2
Ringstad 104 A1
Ringsted 108 C3
Ringvassøy 94 B2
Ringwood 9 E3
Rinia, N 88 C2
Rinkaby 109 D3
Rinns Pt 4 A2
Rinteln 52 A1
Rinvyle Pt 12 A3
Río 83 D4
Riocavado de la
    Sierra 36 A3
Riogordo 43 F3
Riola Sardo 66 A3
Riolo Terme 61 D3
Riom 26 A4
Riomaggiore 60 B3
Rio Maior 38 A3
Rio Marina 62 C1
Riom-ès-
    Montagnes 29 E1
Rionero in Vulture . 64 C3
Rio, Punta del 44 B4
Rioseco de Tapia . . 35 D2
Rioz 27 D2
Ripač 70 C4
Ripanj 73 D3
Riparbella 60 C4
Ripatransone 61 F4
Ripley 7 D3
Ripoli 32 A3
Ripollet 32 A4
Ripon 6 C1
Riquewihr 27 E1
Risan 76 B2
Risbäck 97 E4
Risca 9 D2
Riscle 28 B4
Risle 19 D3
Risnes 104 B4
Risnjak 70 B3
Risør 104 C4
Risøyhamn 94 A3
Risøysundet 94 A3
Rissa 100 C1
Ristiina 103 E3
Ristijärvi 99 E4
Ristilampi 99 D2
Ristovac 77 E2
Risum-Lindholm . . . 47 F1
Ritíni 79 E4
Ritoniemi 103 E2
Ritsóna 84 A4
Rittmannshausen . . 52 B3
Riudoms 37 F4
Riva 58 C4
Rivarolo Canavese . 31 E1
Rive-de-Gier 30 B1
Rives 30 C1
Rivesaltes 32 B2
Rivière-Thibouville,
    la 19 D3

Rivio	**82** C3	Rizário	**79** E2	Rjukan	**104** C3	Robbio	**60** A1	Robledillo de Gata	**39** D2	Rocamadour	**29** D2	Roccamonfina	**64** A3
Rivisondoli	**64** A2	Rizia	**81** F1	Röbel	**49** D3	Robledo	**44** C1	Roccadaspide	**64** C4	Roccapalumba	**68** B3
Rivne	**113** D2	Rizoma	**83** D1	Roadside	**3** D2	Robertsfors	**102** B1	Robledo de		Rocca di Mezzo	**63** F2	Roccaraso	**64** A2
Rivoli	**31** E1	Rizómilos	**83** F2	Roan	**96** C4	Robertville	**51** D4	Chavela	**40** A2	Rocca di Papa	**63** E3	Rocca San
Rivolta d'Adda	**60** B1	Rizovoúni	**83** D2	Roanne	**26** B4	Robič	**70** A2	Robres	**37** D3	Roccalbegna	**63** D1	Casciano	**61** D3
Riza	**83** D4	Rjånes	**100** A2	Roaringwater B.	**14** A4	Roble	**44** C1	Roca, C da	**38** A4	Roccalumera	**69** D2	Rocca Sinibalda	**63** F2

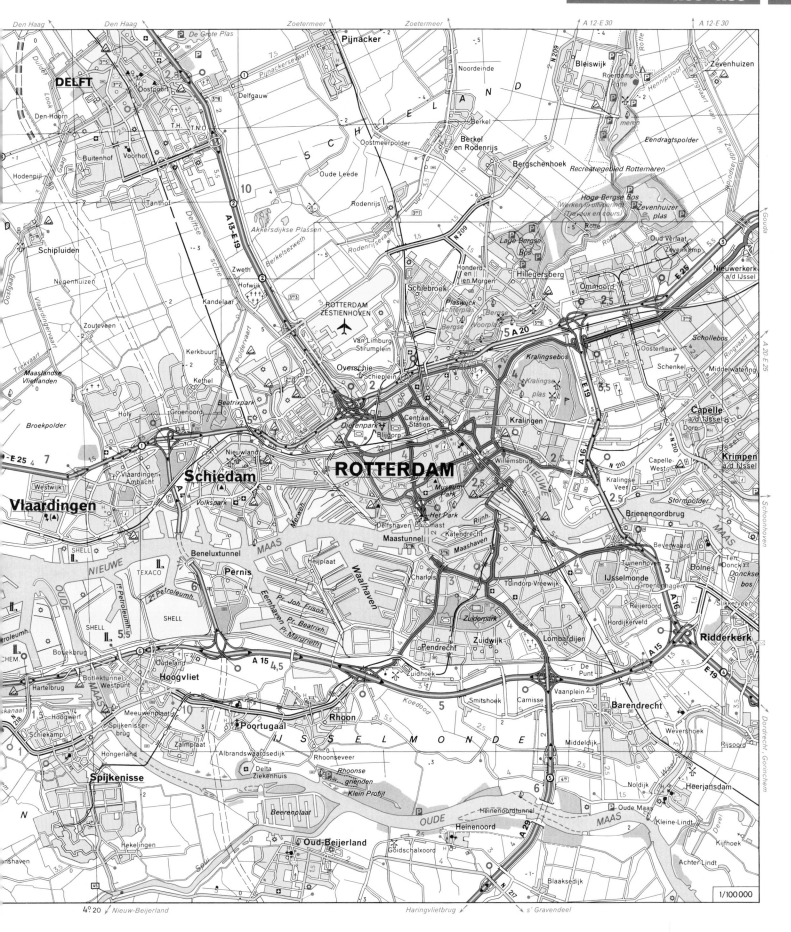

Roccastrada....... 63 D1	Rochdale 6 C2	Rochechouart....... 28 C1	Rochefort-en- Terre.............. 22 C4	Rochefoucauld, la.. 28 C1	Rochepot, le 26 C3	Roche-sur-Yon, la .. 24 B3
Roccella Jonica 67 F4	Roche-Bernard, la .. 22 C4	Roche-Derrien, la... 22 C2		Roche-Guyon, la.... 19 E3	Roches, Col des ... 27 E2	Rochette, la....... 31 D1
Rocchetta Sant' Antonio 64 C3	Rochebonne 30 B2	Roche-en- Ardenne, la 51 D4	Rochefort- Montagne 29 E1	Rochehaut 20 C2	Rocheservière 24 B3	Rochlitz 53 D2
Roc de Fraussa 32 B3	Roche-Canillac, la.. 29 D2	Rochefort (B)....... 50 D4	Rochefort-sur- Nenon 26 C2	Rochelle, La 24 B4	Rochester 11 D2	Rociana del Condado 42 C3
	Roche-Chalais, la 28 B2	Rochefort (F)....... 24 B4		Rochemaure 30 B2	Roche-sur-Foron, la 27 D4	Rockenhausen 54 B1
				Roche-Posay, la ... 25 D3		

Rock of Cashel 14 C3
Rocroi 20 B2
Róda 82 A1
Rodach 52 C4
Rodacherbrunn 52 C3
Roda de Isábena 37 E3
Rodavgi 82 C2
Rødberg 104 C2
Rødby 108 B4
Rødbyhavn 108 B4
Rødding (Ribe) 108 A3
Rødding (Viborg) 108 A2
Rödeby 109 E3
Rodeiro 34 B2
Rødekro 108 A4
Rodel 2 A3
Rodellar 37 E3
Roden 47 D3
Ródenas 41 D2
Rödermark 52 A4
Rodewisch 53 D3
Rodez 29 E3
Rodiezmo 35 D2
Rodi Garganico 64 C2
Roding 56 B1
Roditis 81 E2
Rodnei, M. 113 D3
Rododáfni 83 D4
Rodohóri 79 E3
Rodolívos 80 B2
Rödön 101 E2
Rodonit, Gjiri i 76 C4
Rodópi (Nomos) 81 E2
Rodopi Mts 115 D3
Rodópoli 79 F2
Rodópós 90 B3
Ródos 93 F1
Ródos, N 93 F2
Rodováni 90 B3
Rodvattnet 102 A1
Rødven 100 B2
Rødvig 108 C4
Roermond 17 D4
Roeselare 50 A3
Rogač 75 D2
Rogača 73 D3
Rogačica (Kosovo) 77 D3
Rogačica (Srbija) 72 C4
Rogačov 111 E4
Rogaland 104 A3
Rogaška Slatina 70 C1
Rogatec 70 C2
Rogatica 76 A1
Rogätz 48 C4
Rogen 101 D3
Rogen L. 101 D3
Roggendorf 48 B2
Roggiano Gravina 67 E2
Roggosen 53 F1
Rogliano (F) 33 F2
Rogliano (I) 67 E3
Rognan 97 E2
Rogozna 76 C1
Rogoznica 75 D2
Rohan 22 C3
Rohatin 113 D3

Rohr 52 B3
Rohrbach (A) 56 C2
Rohrbach (F) 21 E3
Rohrbrunn 52 A4
Rohrer Sattel 57 E3
Roignais 27 E4
Roine Mallasvesi 107 E1
Roisel 19 F2
Roissy 19 F4
Rojales 45 D2
Rök 109 D1
Røkland 97 F2
Rokovci 71 F2
Rokua 99 E4
Rokycany 53 E4
Røldal 104 B3
Rolfstorp 108 C2
Rolla 94 B3
Rollag 104 C3
Rolle 27 D3
Rolle, Pso di 59 D3
Rolvsøya 95 D1
Roma 63 E2
Romagnano Sesia 31 F1
Roman 113 D4
Romana 66 B2
Romanche 31 D1
Romangordo 39 E3
România 73 D1
Romanija 71 F4
Romans 30 C2
Romanshorn 58 B1
Romantische straße 55 E3
Rombas 21 D3
Rombo, Pso del 58 C2
Römhild 52 B4
Romilly 20 B4
Rømø 108 A3
Romont 27 E3
Romorantin 25 E2
Romny 113 F1
Romsdalen 100 B2
Romsdalsfjorden 100 B2
Romsey 9 E3
Rona 2 B3
Ronaldsway 6 A1
Roncade 59 E4
Roncal 37 D2
Ronce 28 A1
Roncegno 59 D3
Roncesvalles 36 C1
Ronchamp 27 D1
Ronchi 59 F3
Ronciglione 63 E2
Roncobilaccio 60 C3
Ronda 43 E3
Rondane 100 C3
Ronda, Serr de 43 E4
Rønde 108 B3
Rondeslottet 100 C3
Rondissone 31 F1
Rondvassbu 100 C3
Rönnäng 108 C1
Rønne 109 D4
Ronneburg 53 D3

Ronneby 109 E3
Ronnebyån 109 E3
Rønnede 108 C4
Rönnöfors 101 E1
Ronse 50 B3
Roosendaal 16 B3
Roperuelos del Páramo 35 D3
Ropi 94 C3
Ropinsalmi 94 C3
Ropotovo 77 E3
Roquebillière 31 E3
Roquebrun 30 A4
Roquebrune-Cap-Martin 31 E3
Roquebrussanne, la 31 D4
Roquecourbe 32 B1
Roquefort 28 B3
Roquefort-sur-Soulzon 29 F3
Roque-Gageac, la 29 D2
Roquemaure 30 B3
Roquesteron 31 E3
Roquetas de Mar 44 B4
Roquevaire 30 C4
Rora Head 3 D1
Rore 71 D4
Røros 101 D2
Rørøy 97 D3
Rorschach 58 B1
Rørvig 108 C3
Rørvik (Nord Trøndelag) 97 D4
Rørvik (Sør Trøndelag) 100 C1
Ros' 113 E2
Rosà 59 D4
Rosal de la Frontera 42 C1
Rosans 30 C2
Rosarito, Emb de 39 E2
Rosarno 67 E4
Roscoff 22 B2
Ros Comáin 12 C3
Roscommon 12 C3
Roscommon (Co) 12 C3
Roscrea 12 C4
Rose (Crna Gora) 76 A3
Rose (I) 67 E2
Rosegg 70 A1
Roselend, Cormet de 27 E4
Rosell 41 F2
Rosendal 104 A2
Rosenheim 56 B3
Rosenhof 56 B2
Rosenthal 53 F3
Roses 32 C3
Roses, Golfo de 32 C3
Roseto degli Abruzzi 64 A1
Rosheim 21 E4
Rosice 57 F1
Rosières 19 F2
Rosiers, les 24 C2
Rosignano Marittimo 60 C4

Roșiori de Vede 115 D2
Roskilde 108 C3
Roški slap 75 D1
Roslavl' 111 E3
Rosmaninhal 38 C3
Røsnæs 108 B3
Rosolina Mare 61 D1
Rosolini 69 D4
Rosoman 77 E3
Rosova dolina 115 D2
Rosporden 22 B3
Rossano 67 F2
Rossan Pt. 12 C1
Rosscarbery 14 B4
Roßdorf 54 C1
Rosses Point 12 C1
Roßhaupten 55 E4
Rossija 111 E2
Rossio 38 B3
Rosskreppfjorden 104 B3
Rosslare 15 D4
Rosslare Harbour 15 D4
Roßlau 53 D1
Rosslea 13 D2
Rossön 101 F1
Ross-on-Wye 9 D2
Røssvatnet 97 E3
Røssvik 97 E3
Roßwein 53 E2
Rosthwaite 5 D4
Røstlandet 97 D1
Rostock 48 C2
Rostrenen 22 B3
Rostrevor 13 E3
Rostujávri 94 C3
Røsvik 94 A4
Rosvik 98 C3
Rota 43 D3
Rotenburg (Hessen) 52 B3
Rotenburg (Niedersachsen) 48 A3
Roth 55 F1
Rötha 53 D2
Rothbury 5 E3
Röthenbach 55 F1
Rothenburg 53 F2
Rothenburg ob der Tauber 55 E1
Rothéneuf 18 B4
Rotherham 7 D2
Rothes 3 D3
Rothesay 4 B2
Rothwell 9 F1
Rotja, Pta 45 D4
Rotonda 67 E2
Rotondella 65 D4
Rotondo, M. 33 F3
Rott (Bayern) 56 A3
Rott (Bayern) 56 B3
Rott R 56 B2
Rottach-Egern 56 A4
Rotten 27 F3
Rottenbach 52 C4
Rottenburg (Baden-Württemberg) 55 D3
Rottenburg (Bayern) 56 B2

Rottenmann 57 D4
Rottenmanner Tauern 57 D4
Rotterdam 16 B3
Rottne 109 D2
Rottneros 105 E3
Rottweil 54 C3
Rötz 56 B1
Roubaix 20 A1
Roudnice 53 F3
Rouen 19 E3
Rouffach 27 E1
Rougé 23 D4
Rougemont 27 D2
Rougemont-le-Château 27 E1
Rouillac 28 B1
Roujan 30 A4
Roulans 27 D2
Roulers 50 A3
Roundstone 12 A3
Rousay 3 E1
Roússa 81 E1
Rousses, les 27 D3
Rousset, Col de 30 C2
Rovaniemi 99 D2
Rovato 60 B1
Rovereto 59 D4
Roverud 105 D3
Roviès 83 F3
Rovigo 61 D2
Rovinj 70 A3
Rovišče 71 D2
Roxen 106 A4
Roxo, Bgem do 42 B1
Royal Canal 12 C3
Royal Leamington Spa 9 E1
Royal Tunbridge Wells 10 C3
Royan 28 A1
Royat 29 E1
Roybon 30 C1
Roye 19 F3
Royère-de-Vassivière 25 E4
Røyrvik 97 E4
Royston 9 F2
Röyttä 98 C3
Rožaje 76 C2
Rožanstvo 72 C4
Rozay-en-Brie 19 F4
Rozier, le 29 F3
Rožmberk 57 D1
Rožmitál 53 F4
Rožňava 112 B3
Rozoy 20 B2
Roztocze 112 C2
Roztoky 53 F3
Rozvadov 56 B1
Rrasë 76 C3
Rrëshen 76 C3
Rrogozhinë 76 C4
Rtanj 73 E4
Rtanj (Reg) 73 E4
Ruabon 6 B3
Rubbestadneset 104 A2

Rubena 35 F3
Rubeži 76 B2
Rubha a'Mhail 4 B2
Rubha Còigeach 2 C2
Rubha Réidh 2 B3
Rubí 32 A4
Rubiães 34 A3
Rubi de Bracamonte 39 F1
Rubielos de Mora 41 E3
Rubiera 60 C2
Rubio 35 F4
Rudare 77 D1
Rüdersdorf 49 E4
Rüdesheim 51 F4
Rudkøbing 108 B4
Rudn'a 111 E3
Rudna Glava 73 E3
Rudnica (Crna Gora) 76 B1
Rudnica (Srbija) 76 C1
Rudnik (Kosovo) 76 C2
Rudnik (Reg) 73 D4
Rudnik (Srbija) 73 D4
Rudo 76 B1
Rudolstadt 52 C3
Rue 19 E2
Ruecas, R 39 E4
Rueda 35 E4
Rueda de Jalón 36 C3
Ruelle 28 C1
Ruffec 25 D4
Ruffieux 27 D4
Rugby 9 E1
Rugeley 6 C3
Rügen 49 D1
Rugles 19 D4
Rugova klisura 76 C2
Ruhla 52 B3
Ruhland 53 E2
Ruhner Berge 48 C3
Ruhpolding 56 B3
Ruhr 17 E3
Ruidera 40 B4
Rüjiena 110 C2
Ruka 99 E2
Rukatunturi 99 E2
Ruma 72 C2
Rumblar, Emb del 44 A2
Rumboci 75 E2
Rumburk 53 F2
Rumengol 22 B3
Rumenka 72 C2
Rumigny 20 B2
Rumilly 27 D4
Runcorn 6 B2
Runde 100 A2
Rundvik 102 A2
Runn 105 F2
Runni 103 D1
Runtuna 106 B4
Ruohtir 95 E2
Ruokojärvi 103 F3
Ruokolahti 103 F3
Ruokovesi 103 E2
Ruokto 98 B1

Ruoms 30 B2
Ruotsinpyhtää 107 F2
Ruovesi 102 C3
Rupa 70 B3
Rupea 113 D4
Ruppiner See 49 D3
Rupt 27 D1
Rur 17 D4
Ruše 70 C1
Ruse 115 D2
Ruševo 71 E2
Rush 13 E3
Rushden 9 F1
Ruski Krstur 72 B2
Rusko 107 D2
Rusko Selo 72 C1
Ruskele 98 A4
Russborough 13 D4
Rüsselsheim 51 F4
Russenes 95 D1
Russey, le 27 E2
Russi 61 D3
Rust 57 F3
Rustefjelbma 95 E1
Ruswil 27 F2
Rute 43 F3
Rüthen 17 F3
Ruthin 6 B3
Rüti 58 A2
Rutigliano 65 E3
Rutledal 104 A1
Ruuhitunturi 99 E2
Ruukki 99 D4
Ruuponsaari 103 D2
Ruurlo 17 D3
Ruvo di Puglia 65 D3
Ruwer 54 A1
Ruynes-en-Margeride 29 F2
Ružomberok 112 B3
Ry 108 B3
Rybinsk 111 F1
Rybinskoje Vodochranilišče 111 F1
Rybnik 112 B2
Rychnov nad Kněžnou 112 A3
Ryd 109 D3
Ryde 9 E3
Rye 11 D3
Ryfylke 104 A3
Rygge 105 D3
Rykene 104 B4
Ryl'sk 113 F1
Ryman 49 E4
Rymättylä 107 D2
Rypefjord 95 D1
Rysjedalsvika 104 A1
Ryttylä 107 E2
Rzepin 49 F4
Rzeszów 112 C2
Ržev 111 F2

S

Sääksjärvi 102 C2
Saal 55 F2
Saalach 59 E1
Saalbach 59 E1
Saale 52 C1
Saaler Bodden 48 C1
Saales 21 E4
Saalfeld 52 C3
Saalfelden 59 E1
Saane 27 E3
Saanen 27 E3
Saar 54 A2
Saarbrücken 54 B2
Saarburg 54 A1
Saaremaa 110 B2
Saarenkylä 99 D2
Saari 103 F3

Saariharju 99 E3
Saarijärvi 103 D2
Saarikoski 94 C3
Saariselkä 95 F3
Saariselkä (Reg) 95 F3
Saaristomeri 107 D3
Saarland 54 A2
Saarlouis 54 B2
Saas- Fee 27 F4
Šabac 72 C3
Sabadell 32 A4
Sabaudia 63 F3
Sabbioneta 60 C2
Sabero 35 E2
Sabiñánigo 37 D2
Sabiote 44 B2
Sabini, Mti 63 E2
Sablé 23 E4
Sables-d'Olonne, les 24 B3

Sables-d'Or 22 C2
Sæbo 100 A2
Sabóia 42 A2
Sabôr, R 34 C4
Sabres 28 B3
Sabrosa 34 B4
Sabugal 39 D2
Sæby 108 B2
Sa Calobra 45 E2
Sacavém 38 A4
Sacedon 40 C2
Saceruela 39 F4
Sachsen 53 F2
Sachsen-Anhalt 48 C4
Sacile 59 E3
Sacra di San Michele 31 E1
Sacramenia 35 F4
Sacratif, C 44 A4
Sada 34 B1

Sádaba 36 C2
Sado, R 38 A4
Sadurniño 34 B1
Saelices 40 B3
Safara 42 C1
Säffle 105 E4
Saffron Walden 10 C2
Safonovo 111 E3
Sagard 49 D1
S'Agaró 32 B4
Sagéika 86 B1
Sagfjorden 94 A4
Sagiáda 82 B1
Sagra, Sa de la 44 B2
Sagres 42 A3
Sagres, Pta de 42 A3
Sagunt 41 E3
Sagunto 41 E3
Sagvåg 104 A3
Sahagún 35 E3

Sahalahti 107 E1
Šahinovići 71 E3
Sahl 108 A2
Sahloinen 103 D3
Saignelégier 27 E2
Saija 95 F4
Saillagouse 32 A3
Saillans 30 C2
Saimaa 103 E3
Saimaanranta 103 E4
Sains-du-Nord 20 B2
Sains-Richaumont 20 B2
St Abb's Head 5 E2
St Aegyd 57 E3
St-Affrique 29 E3
St-Agnant 24 B4
St-Agrève 30 B2
St-Aignan 25 E2
St-Aignan-sur-Roë 23 E3
St-Amarin 27 E1

St Alban 29 F2
St Albans 9 F2
St Alban's Head 9 E4
St-Amand-en-Puisaye 26 A2
St-Amand-les-Eaux 20 A1
St-Amand-Longpré 25 D2
St-Amand-Montrond 25 F3
St-Amans-des-Cots 29 E2
St-Amans 29 F1
St-Amans-Soult 32 B1
St-Amant 29 F1
St-Amant-Roche-Savine 29 F1

St-Ambroix 30 B3
St-Amé 27 D1
St-Amour 26 C3
St Andrä 70 B1
St Andreasberg 52 B2
St-André-de-Cubzac 28 B2
St-André-de-l'Eure 19 E4
St-André-de-Vézines 29 F3
St-André-les-Alpes 31 D3
St Andrews 5 D1
St-Anthème 30 B1
St-Antonin-Noble-Val 29 D3
St Anton 58 C2
St-Arnoult 19 E4
St Asaph 6 B2

St-Astier. 28 C2
St-Auban. 31 D3
St-Aubin-
  d'Aubigné 23 D3
St-Aubin-du-
  Cormier 23 D3
St-Aubin. 18 C3
St-Aulaye. 28 C2
St-Avold. 21 D3
St-Aygulf. 31 D4
St-Beauzély 29 E3
St Bees Head 4 C4
St-Benoît-du-
  Sault. 25 E3
St-Benoît. 25 F2
St-Bertrand-de-
  Comminges. 37 E1
St-Béat 37 F2
St-Bénin-d'Azy 26 A3
St Blasien. 54 C4
St-Blin. 26 C1
St-Bonnet. 31 D2
St-Bonnet-de-
  Joux 26 B3
St-Bonnet-le-
  Château 30 B1
St-Brévin 24 A2
St-Briac 18 A4
St-Brice-en-Coglès . 18 B4
St Brides B. 8 B2
St-Brieuc 22 C2
St-Calais 23 F3
St-Cast 18 A4
St Catherine's Pt. . . . 9 E4
St-Cergue 27 D3
St-Cernin 29 E2
St-Céré. 29 D2
St-Chamas 30 C4
St-Chamond 30 B1
St-Chély-d'Apcher. . 29 F2
St-Chély-d'Aubrac . 29 E2
St-Chinian 32 B1
St Christophen 57 E2
St-Ciers 28 B1
St-Cirq-Lapopie 29 D3
St-Clair-sur-l'Elle . . 18 C3
St-Clar. 28 C3
St-Claud. 25 D4
St-Claude 27 D3
St Clears 8 C2
St-Cyprien 29 D2
St-Cyprien-Plage . . 32 B2
St David's 8 B1
St David's Head 8 B1
St-Denis (Charente-
  Maritime) 24 B4
St-Denis-d'Orques . 23 E3
St-Denis (Seine-
  St-Denis) 19 F4
St-Didier-en-
  Velay. 30 B1
St-Dié 21 E4
St-Dier-
  d'Auvergne 29 F1
St-Dizier 20 C4
St-Donat-sur-
  l'Herbasse 30 C1
St-Eloy-les-Mines . . 26 A4
St-Emilion 28 B2
St-Etienne (Alpes-de-
  Haute-Provence). . 30 C3
St-Etienne-
  Cantalès, Bge de . 29 E2
St-Etienne-de-
  Baïgorry 28 A4
St-Etienne-de-
  Lugdarès 29 F2
St-Etienne-de-
  Montluc 24 B2
St-Etienne-de-
  St-Geoirs 30 C1
St-Etienne-de-
  Tinée 31 E3
St-Etienne-en-
  Dévoluy 31 D2
St-Etienne (Loire) . . 30 B1
St-Fargeau 26 A2
St-Félicien 30 B1
St-Finan's B 14 A4
St-Firmin. 31 D2
St-Florent (Cher) . . 25 F3
St-Florent (Corse) . 33 F2
St-Florentin 26 B1

St-Flour 29 F2
St-François-
  Longchamp. 31 D1
St-Fulgent 24 B3
St Gallen (A) 57 D3
St Gallen (CH) 58 B2
St Gallenkirch 58 B2
St-Galmier 30 B1
St-Gaudens 37 F1
St-Gaultier 25 E3
St-Genest-
  Malifaux 30 B1
St-Gengoux-le-
  National 26 C3
St-Geniez-d'Olt 29 E3
St-Genis-de-
  Stonge 28 B1
St-Genis-Laval 30 B1
St-Genix 30 C1
St-Geoire 30 C1
St Georgen (A) 56 C3
St Georgen
  am Langsee 70 B1
St Georgen (D) 54 C3
St-Georges 23 E4
St Georges Channel. . 8 A4
St-Georges-de-
  Didonne 28 A1
St-Georges-en-
  Couzan 29 F1
St-Germain-de-
  Calberte 29 F3
St-Germain-des-
  Fossés 26 A4
St-Germain-du-
  Bois. 26 C3
St-Germain-du-
  Plain 26 C3
St-Germain-du-
  Teil. 29 F3
St-Germain 19 F4
St-Germain-Laval . . 26 B4
St-Germain-
  Lembron 29 F1
St-Germain-les-
  Belles 29 D1
St-Germain-
  l'Herm 29 F1
St-Gertraud 58 C3
St-Gervais-
  d'Auvergne 26 A4
St-Gervais 27 E4
St-Gervais-sur-
  Mare 30 A4
St-Géry 29 D3
St-Gildas-de-
  Rhuys. 22 C4
St-Gildas-des-Bois . 23 D4
St-Gildas, Pte de . . 24 A2
St Gilgen 56 C3
St-Gilles-Croix-de-
  Vie. 24 A3
St-Gilles 30 B4
St-Gingolph 27 E3
St-Girons 37 F2
St-Girons-Plage. . . . 28 A3
St Goar 51 E4
St Goarshausen . . . 51 E4
St-Gobain 20 A3
St Govan's Head . . . 8 B2
St-Guénolé 22 A3
St-Guilhem-le-
  Désert. 29 F3
St-Haon-le-Châtel . 26 B4
St Helens 6 B2
St-Hélier 18 B3
St-Hilaire-des-
  Loges 24 C3
St-Hilaire-de-
  Villefranche 28 B1
St-Hilaire-du-
  Harcouet 18 B4
St-Hilaire. 32 B2
St-Hippolyte-du-
  Fort. 29 F3
St-Hippolyte. 27 E2
St-Honoré. 26 B3
St-Hubert. 20 C2
St-Imier. 27 E2
St Ingbert. 54 B2
St Ives (Cambs) . . . 9 F1
St Ives (Cornwall). . 8 A4
St-Jacques 23 D3
St-Jacut. 18 A4

St Jakob. 59 D2
St Jakob im
  Rosental 70 A1
St James 18 B4
St-Jean-Brévelay . . 22 C3
St-Jean-Cap-
  Ferrat. 31 E3
St-Jean-d'Angély . . 24 C4
St-Jean-de-
  Bournay 30 C1
St-Jean-de-Daye . . 18 B3
St-Jean-de-Losne . 26 C2
St-Jean-de-Luz 28 A4
St-Jean-de-
  Maurienne 31 D1
St-Jean-de-Monts . 24 A3
St-Jean-du-Bruel . . 29 F3
St-Jean-du-Gard . . 30 A3
St-Jean-en-
  Royans 30 C2
St-Jean-Pied-de-
  Port 28 A4
St-Jeoire 27 D4
St Johann im
  Pongau 59 E1
St Johann in Tirol . . 59 E1
St John's Pt 13 E2
St-Jouin-de-
  Marnes 24 C3
St-Juéry 29 E3
St-Julien-Chapteuil . 30 B2
St-Julien-de-
  Vouvantes 23 D4
St-Julien-du-Sault . 26 A1
St-Julien-en-
  Genevois 27 D4
St-Julien 26 C3
St-Julien-l'Ars 25 D3
St-Junien 25 D4
St Just 8 A4
St-Just-en-
  Chaussée 19 F3
St-Just-en-
  Chevalet 26 B4
St-Justin 28 B3
St Keverne 8 B4
St Lambrecht 57 D4
St-Lary-Soulan 37 E2
St-Laurent
  (Calvados) 18 C3
St-Laurent-de-la-
  Salanque 32 B2
St-Laurent-du-
  Pont 30 C1
St-Laurent-en-
  Grandvaux 27 D3
St-Laurent-les-
  Bains. 29 F2
St-Laurent-Médoc . 28 B2
St-Laurent
  (Vendée) 24 C3
St-Laurent
  (Vienne) 28 C1
St-Léger 26 B3
St Leonhard (I) 59 D2
St Leonhard (Nieder-
  österreich) 57 E3
St Leonhard (Tirol) . 58 C2
St-Léonard-de-
  Noblat 25 E4
St Lorenzen 59 E2
St-Lô 18 C3
St-Louis 27 E2
St-Loup-Lamairé . . 24 C3
St-Loup-sur-
  Semouse 27 D1
St-Luc 27 F3
St-Lunaire 18 B4
St-Lys 29 D4
St-Macaire. 28 B2
St Magnus B 3 F1
St-Maixent-l'Ecole . 24 C3
St-Malo-de-la-
  Lande. 18 B3
St-Malo. 18 B4
St-Mamet-la-
  Salvetat 29 E2
St-Mandrier 31 D4
St-Marcellin 30 C1
St-Margarethen . . . 48 A2
St Margaret's Hope . 3 E1
St-Mars-la-Jaille . . 23 D4
St-Martin (Charente-
  Maritime) 24 B4

St-Martin-
  d'Auxigny 25 F2
St-Martin-de-
  Belleville 31 D1
St-Martin-de-Crau . 30 B4
St-Martin-de-
  Londres 29 F4
St-Martin-de-
  Seignan 28 A4
St-Martin-de-
  Valamas 30 B2
St-Martin-en-
  Bresse 26 C3
St-Martin (Pyrénées-
  Orientales) 32 B2
St Martin's 8 A4
St-Martin-Vésubie . 31 E3
St-Martory 37 F1
St Mary's 8 A4
St Märgen 54 C4
St-Mathieu 28 C1
St-Mathieu, Pte
  de 22 A3
St-Maurice 27 E4
St Mawes 8 B4
St-Maximin-la-Ste
  Baume 31 D4
St-Médard-en-
  Jalles 28 B2
St-Méen 22 C3
St Michaelisdonn . . 48 A2
St Michael
  (Salzburg) 59 F2
St Michael's Mount . 8 A4
St Michael
  (Steiermark) 57 E4
St-Michel-de-
  Maurienne 31 D1
St-Michel-en-
  Grève 22 B2
St-Michel-en-
  l'Herm 24 B4
St-Michel 20 B2
St-Michel-Mont-
  Mercure 24 C3
St-Mihiel 20 C3
St Monance 5 D2
St-Moritz 58 B3
St-Nazaire 24 A2
St-Nectaire 29 E1
St Neots 9 F1
St-Nicolas-
  d'Aliermont 19 E2
St-Nicolas-de-la-
  Grave. 28 C3
St-Nicolas-de-
  Port 21 D4
St-Nicolas-du-
  Pélem 22 C3
St-Niklaas 50 B3
St Niklaus 27 F4
St-Oedenrode 16 C3
St-Omer 19 F1
St Oswald 59 F2
St-Pair. 18 B4
St-Palais (Charente-
  Maritime) 28 A1
St-Palais (Pyrénées-
  Atlantiques) 28 A4
St-Pardoux-la-
  Rivière 28 C1
St Paul (A) 70 B1
St-Paul (Alpes-de-
  Haute-Provence) . 31 D2
St-Paul (Alpes-
  Maritimes) 31 E3
St-Paul-Cap-de-
  Joux 29 D4
St-Paul-de-
  Fenouillet 32 B2
St-Paulien 29 F2
St-Paul-Trois-
  Châteaux 30 B3
St-Pé-de-Bigorre . . 37 E1
St-Pée 28 A4
St-Péray 30 B2
St Peter in der Au . . 57 D3
St-Peter-Ording . . . 47 F2
St Peter Port 18 A3
St-Petersburg. 111 D1
St-Philbert 24 B3
St-Pierre (Charente-
  Maritime) 24 B4

St-Pierre-
  d'Albigny 31 D1
St-Pierre-de-
  Chartreuse 30 C1
St-Pierre-de-
  Chignac 28 C2
St-Pierre-Eglise . . . 18 B2
St-Pierre-le-
  Moûtier 26 A3
St-Pierre
  (Morbihan) 22 C4
St-Pierre-sur-
  Dives 18 C3
St-Pois. 18 C4
St-Pol-de-Léon 22 B2
St-Pol-sur-
  Ternoise 19 F2
St-Pons-de-
  Thomières 32 B1
St-Porchaire 28 B1
St Pölten 57 E2
St-Pourçain 26 A4
St-Privat. 29 E2
St-Quay-Portrieux . 22 C2
St-Quentin 20 A2
St-Rambert 30 B1
St-Rambert-
  d'Albon 30 B1
St-Rambert-en-
  Bugey 26 C4
St-Raphaël 31 E4
St-Renan 22 A2
St-Rémy-de-
  Provence 30 B3
St-Rémy-sur-
  Durolle 26 B4
St-Riquier 19 E2
St-Romain-de-
  Colbosc. 19 D3
St-Rome-de-Tarn . . 29 E3
St-Saëns 19 E3
St-Satur 26 A2
St-Saulge 26 A2
St-Sauveur-en-
  Puisaye 26 A2
St-Sauveur-
  Lendelin 18 B3
St-Sauveur-le-
  Vicomte 18 B3
St-Sauveur-sur-
  Tinée 31 E3
St-Savin (Gironde) . 28 B2
St-Savinien 24 C4
St-Savin (Vienne) . 25 D3
St-Seine-l'Abbaye . 26 C2
St-Sernin-sur-
  Rance 29 E3
St-Sever
  (Calvados) 18 C4
St-Sever (Landes) . 28 B4
St-Sulpice-les-
  Feuilles 25 E4
St-Symphorien-de-
  Lay. 26 B4
St-Symphorien-
  d'Ozon 30 B1
St-Symphorien 28 B3
St-Symphorien-sur-
  Coise 30 B1
St-Trivier-de-
  Courtes 26 C3
St-Trivier-sur-
  Moignans 26 C4
St-Trojan 28 A1
St-Tropez 31 D4
St-Truiden 50 C3
St Ulrich 59 D3
St-Vaast-la-
  Hougue. 18 B3
St Valentin an der
  Haide. 58 C2
St-Valentin 57 D3
St-Valery 19 E2
St-Valery-en-Caux . 19 D3
St-Valier 30 B1
St-Vallier-de-
  Thiey 31 D3
St-Varent 24 C3
St-Vaury 25 E4
St-Veit 70 A1
St-Véran 31 E2
St-Vincent 27 F4
St-Vincent-de-
  Tyrosse 28 A4

St Vith 51 D4
St-Vivien-de-
  Médoc 28 A1
St-Wandrille 19 D3
St Wendel 54 B1
St Wolfgang 56 C3
St-Yorre 26 A4
St-Yrieix-la-
  Perche 29 D1
Ste-Adresse 19 D3
Ste-Anne-d'Auray . 22 C4
Ste-Baume, la 31 D4
Ste-Croix-du-
  Mont 28 B2
Ste-Croix 27 D3
Ste-Croix, Lac de . . 31 D3
Ste-Croix-
  Volvestre 37 F1
Ste-Enimie 29 F3
Ste-Foy-la-Grande . 28 C2
Ste-Foy-
  l'Argentière 30 B1
Ste-Geneviève-sur-
  Argence 29 E2
Ste-Hélène 28 B2
Ste-Hermine 24 B3
Ste-Livrade 28 C3
Ste-Lucie-de-
  Tallano 33 F4
Ste-Marie-aux-
  Mines 21 E4
Ste-Maure-de-
  Touraine 25 D2
Ste-Maxime 31 D4
Ste-Menehould . . . 20 C3
Ste-Mère-Eglise . . 18 B3
Ste-Odile, Mt 21 E4
Ste-Sévère 25 F3
Ste-Suzanne 23 E3
Ste-Tulle 30 C3
Saintes 28 B1
Stes-Maries-de-la-
  Mer 30 B4
Saison R. 37 E1
Saissac 32 B1
Šajkaš 72 C2
Sakarya 115 F3
Sakskøbing 108 B4
Sakule 72 C2
Säkylä 107 D2
Sala 106 A3
Salacgrîva 110 C2
Sala Consilina 64 C4
Salada 41 E3
Salakovac 73 D3
Salamajärvi 102 C2
Salamajärvi L 103 D2
Salamanca 39 E1
Salamína 87 F1
Salamína, N. 87 E1
Salándi 87 E2
Salangen 94 B3
Salar 43 F3
Salardú 37 F2
Salas 35 D1
Salaš 73 F3
Salas de los
  Infantes 36 A3
Salazar, R. 37 D2
Salbohed 105 F3
Salbris 25 E2
Salcombe. 8 C4
Saldaña 35 E3
Saldus. 110 B3
Sale 60 A2
Sâlekinna 100 D3
Salem 55 D4
Salemi. 68 A3
Sälen 101 D4
Salen (Highland) . . 2 B4
Salen (Mull) 4 B1
Salernes 31 D4
Salerno. 64 B4
Salerno, Golfo di . . 64 B4
Salers 29 E2
Salève, Mt. 27 D4
Salgótarján 112 B3
Salgueiro do
  Campo 38 C2
Sali 74 C1
Salice Terme 60 A2
Salies-de-Béarn . . 28 A4
Salies-du-Salat . . . 37 F1
Salignac-Eyvigues . 29 D2

Salihli. 115 F4
Salime, Emb. de. . . . 34 C1
Salina, I. 69 D2
Salinas (Andalucía) . 43 F3
Salinas (Asturias) . . 35 D1
Salinas, C 45 F3
Salindres 30 B3
Salins 27 D3
Salisbury. 9 E3
Salla 99 E3
Sallanches 27 E4
Sallent 32 A4
Sallent-de-Gállego. . 37 D2
Salles. 32 A1
Salles-Curan 29 E3
Salling 108 A2
Salling Sund 108 A2
Salmerón 40 C2
Salmoral 39 F1
Saló 60 B1
Salo 107 E2
Salobreña 44 A4
Salona 75 D1
Salon-de-
  Provence 30 C4
Salonta 112 C1
Salorino 38 C3
Salor, R. 39 D3
Salou 37 F4
Salou, C de 37 F4
Salpausselkä 107 F2
Salsbruket. 97 D4
Salses-le-Château . 32 B2
Salso 68 C3
Salsomaggiore
  Terme 60 B2
Salsta 106 B3
Saltaş 8 C4
Saltburn-by-the-
  Sea 5 F4
Saltcoats 4 C2
Saltee Is 15 D4
Saltfjellet 97 E2
Saltfjorden 97 E2
Salto 34 B4
Saltoluokta 94 B4
Saltvik 106 C3
Saluggia 31 F1
Saluzzo 31 E2
Salvacañete 41 D3
Salvagnac 29 D3
Salvan 27 E4
Salvaterra de
  Magos 38 A3
Salvatierra-
  Agurain 36 B2
Salvatierra de los
  Barros 42 C1
Salvattera de Miño . 34 A3
Salvetat-Peyralès,
  la 29 E3
Salvetat-sur-Agout,
  la 32 B1
Salviac. 29 D2
Sælvig 108 B3
Sálvora, I de 34 A2
Salza 57 E3
Salzach 56 B3
Salzburg 56 C3
Salzburg (Prov) . . . 59 E1
Salzgitter-Bad 52 B1
Salzgitter-
  Lebenstedt 52 B1
Salzhausen 48 B3
Salzkammergut . . . 56 C3
Salzkotten 17 F3
Salzwedel 48 C4
Šamac Slavonski . . 71 F3
Sama de Langreo. . 35 D1
Samarina 78 C4
Samatan 28 C4
Sambatikí 87 E3
Sambiase 67 E3
Sambir 112 C3
Samboal 40 A1
Sambre 50 B4
Sambuca di Sicilia . 68 B3
Samedan 58 B3
Sameiro, Mte. 34 A4
Samer 19 E1
Sámi 82 B4
Samikó 86 B3
Sammatti 107 E2

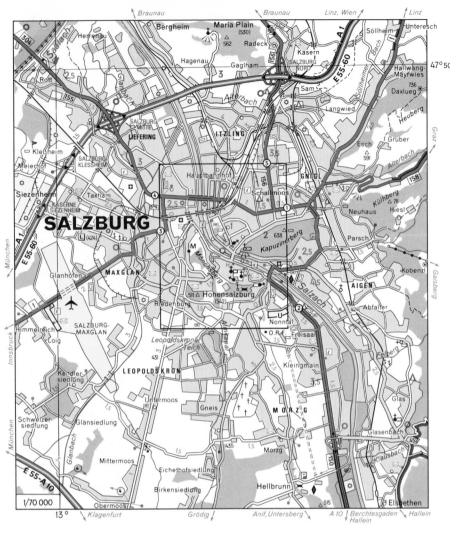

Sammichele 65 E3
Samnanger 104 A2
Samobor 70 C2
Samodreža 77 D2
Samoëns 27 E4
Samokov (BG) 115 D3
Samokov
  (Makedonija) 77 D3
Samora Correia 38 A4
Samos 34 C2
Samoš 73 D2
Sámos 89 F1
Sámos, N 89 E1
Samothráki 81 E3
Samothráki, N 81 E3
Samper de
  Calanda 37 D4
Sampeyre 31 E2
Samsø 108 B3
Samsø Bælt 108 B3
Samtens 49 D1
Samugheo 66 B3
San 112 C2
San Adrián 36 C2
San Adrián, C de 34 A1
San Agata de Goti . . 64 B3
San Agata di
  Militello 69 D2
San Agustín 40 B2
San Amaro 34 B2
San Andrea Frius . . . 66 B3
San Andrés del
  Rabanedo 35 D2
San Antioco, I di . . . 66 A4
San Antioco 66 B4
San Antonio 66 B1
San Bartolomé de
  las Abiertas 39 F3
San Bartolomé de la
  Torre 42 C2
San Bartolomeo in
  Galdo 64 B3

San Benedetto del
  Tronto 61 F4
San Benedetto in
  Alpe 61 D3
San Benedetto Po . . 60 C2
San Bernardino 58 B3
San Bernardino,
  Pso del 58 B3
San Biagio
  Platani 68 B3
San Bonifacio 60 C1
San Candido 59 E2
San Carlos de la
  Rápita 41 F2
San Carlos del
  Valle 40 B4
San Casciano in Val
  di Pesa 60 C4
San Cataldo
  (Puglia) 65 F4
San Cataldo
  (Sicilia) 68 C3
San Cipirello 68 B3
San Clemente,
  Emb de 44 B2
San Clemente 40 C4
San Colombano al
  Lambro 60 B2
San Cosme 34 C1
San Cristóbal 42 C1
San Cristóbal de
  Entreviñas 35 D3
San Cristóbal de la
  Polantera 35 D3
San Cristóbal de la
  Vega 39 F1
San Damiano d'Asti . 31 F2
San Daniele del
  Friuli 59 E3
San Daniele Po 60 B2
San Demetrio
  Corone 67 E2

San Donaci 65 F4
San Donà di Piave . . 59 E4
San Emiliano 35 D2
San Esteban de
  Gormaz 36 A3
San Esteban del
  Molar 35 D3
San Esteban del
  Valle 39 F2
San Esteban de
  Pravia 35 D1
San Fele 64 C4
San Felice a
  Cancello 64 B3
San Felice Circeo . . . 63 F3
San Felices de Los
  Gallegos 39 D1
San Felice sul
  Panaro 60 C2
San Felipe 40 C1
San Feliu de
  Guixols 32 B4
San Ferdinando di
  Puglia 64 C3
San Fernando 43 D4
San Francisco
  Javier 45 D4
San Fratello 69 D2
San Gavino
  Monreale 66 B3
San Gemini 63 E1
San Giacomo 59 D2
San Gimignano 60 C4
San Ginesio 61 F4
San Giorgio del
  Sannio 64 B3
San Giorgio di
  Nogaro 59 F3
San Giorgio Ionico . . 65 E4
San Giorgio 31 E4
San Giorgio
  Piacentino 60 B2

San Giovanni a
  Piro 67 D2
San Giovanni di
  Sinis 66 A3
San Giovanni in
  Fiore 67 F2
San Giovanni in
  Persiceto 60 C2
San Giovanni
  Lupatoto 60 C1
San Giovanni
  Rotondo 64 C2
San Giovanni
  Suergiu 66 B4
San Giovanni
  Valdarno 61 D4
San Giuliano
  Terme 60 C4
San Giustino 61 D4
San Glorio, Pto de . . 35 E2
San Gottardo, Pso
  del 58 A3
San Ildefonso o la
  Granja 40 A1
San Isidro 44 C3
San Isidro, Pto de . . 35 E2
San Javier 45 D2
San José
  (Andalucía) 44 C4
San José (Ibiza) 45 D4
San Juan Bautista . . 45 D3
San Juan de
  Alicante 45 E1
San Juan de
  Aznalfarache 43 D2
San Juan de la
  Peña 37 D2
San Juan del Olmo . 39 F2
San Juan de los
  Terreros 44 C3
San Juan del
  Puerto 42 C2

San Juan, Emb de . . 40 A2
San Just Desvern . . . 32 A4
San Just, Sa de 41 E2
San Lazzaro di
  Savena 61 D2
San Leo 61 E3
San Leonardo de
  Yagüe 36 A3
San Leonardo 59 D2
San Leonardo, Pso . 64 A2
San Lorenzo (E) 36 B2
San Lorenzo (I) 63 D1
San Lorenzo de
  Calatrava 44 A1
San Lorenzo de la
  Parrilla 40 C3
San Lucido 67 E3
San Luis de
  Sabanillas 43 E4
San Luis 45 F2
San Marcello 61 F4
San Marcello
  Pistoiese 60 C3
San Marco
  Argentano 67 E2
San Marco dei
  Cavoti 64 B3
San Marco in
  Lamis 64 C2
San Marino 61 E3
San Martino di
  Castrozza 59 D3
San Martín de
  Castañeda 34 C3
San Martín de la
  Vega 40 B2
San Martín de
  Mondoñedo 34 C1
San Martín de
  Montalbán 39 F3
San Martín de
  Valdeiglesias 40 A2
San Mateo de
  Gállego 37 D3
San Mauro Forte . . . 65 D4
San Michele all'
  Adige 59 D3
San Miguel 45 D3
San Miguel de
  Escalada 35 E3
San Miguel del
  Arroyo 35 E4
San Miguel de
  Salinas 45 D2
San Millán 36 A2
San Millán de la
  Cogolla 36 B2
San Millán de Lara . . 36 A3
San Ninato 60 C4
San Nicolás del
  Puerto 43 E2
San Nicolás de
  Tolentino 42 B4
San Nicoló
  Ferrarese 61 D2
San Nicoló Gerrei . . 66 B3
San Ninfa 68 B3
San Pancrazio
  Salentino 65 F4
San Pedro 44 C1
San Pedro de
  Alcántara 43 E4
San Pedro del
  Arroyo 39 F1
San Pedro de
  Latarce 35 E4
San Pedro del
  Pinatar 45 D2
San Pedro de
  Mérida 39 D4
San Pedro
  Manrique 36 B3
San Pedro, Sa de . . 39 D3
San Pellegrino,
  Pso 59 D2
San Pellegrino
  Terme 58 B4
San Piero a Sieve . . 61 D4
San Pietro, I di 66 A4
San Pietro in
  Casale 60 C2
San Pietro
  Vernotico 65 F4
San Polo d'Enza . . . 60 C2

San Quirico
  d'Orcia 63 D1
San Rafael de Navallana,
  Emb de 43 F2
San Rafael 40 A2
San Remo 31 F3
San Roque
  (Andalucía) 43 E4
San Roque
  (Galicia) 34 A1
San Rufo 64 C4
San Salvador de
  Cantamuda 35 F2
San Salvador 45 F3
San Salvo 64 B2
San Sebastiano
  Curone 60 A2
San Sebastián,
  Emb de 34 C3
San Sebastián 42 A4
San Severino
  Marche 61 F4
San Severo 64 C2
San Silvestre de
  Guzmán 42 C2
San Sperate 66 B4
San Stefano di
  Camastra 68 C3
San Stefano
  Quisquina 68 B3
San Telmo 42 C2
San Valentino alla
  Muta 58 C2
San Vicente de
  Alcántara 38 C3
San Vicente de la
  Barquera 35 F1
San Vicente de la
  Cabeza 35 D4
San Vicente del
  Raspeig 45 E1
San Vicenzo 62 C1
San Vigilio di
  Marebbe 59 D2
San Vigilio, Pso di . . 60 C1
San Vitero 34 C3
San Vito al
  Tagliamento 59 E3
San Vito Chietino . . 64 A2
San Vito dei
  Normanni 65 E3
San Vito di C. 59 E3
San Vito 66 C4
San Vito lo Capo . . . 68 B3
San Vito sullo
  Ionio 67 F3
San Víttore del
  Lazio 64 A3
Sana 71 D4
Saná 80 A3
Sanabria, L de 34 C3
Sanary 30 C4
Sancergues 26 A2
Sancerre 26 A2
Sanchidrián 39 F1
Sancho, Emb de . . . 42 C2
Sanclèr 8 C2
Sancoins 26 A3
Sancti Petri 43 D4
Sancti Spiritus 39 D1
Sand (Hedmark) . . . 105 D2
Sand (Rogaland) . . . 104 A3
Sandane 100 A3
Sandarne 101 F4
Sandau 48 C4
Sanday 3 E1
Sandbach 6 C3
Sanddøla 97 D4
Sande (D) 47 D2
Sande (Møre og
  Romsdal) 100 A2
Sande (P) 34 A4
Sande (Vestfold) . . . 104 C3
Sandefjord 104 C3
Sandeid 104 A3
Sandfjellet 95 E1
Sandgerði 96 A2
Sand in Taufers 59 D2
Sandnes 104 A3
Sandness 3 F1
Sandnessjøen 97 D3
Sando 39 D1
Sandoméri 86 B1

Sandomierz 112 C2
Sandown 9 E3
Sandoy 96 A4
Sandøy 100 A2
Sandrigo 59 D4
Sandringham
  House 7 E3
Sandstad 100 C1
Sandur 96 A4
Sandviken 106 B2
Sandvikvåg 104 A2
Sandwich 11 D3
Sandy 9 F1
Sånfjället 101 E3
Sangarcia 40 A1
Sangerhausen 52 C2
Sangis 98 C3
Sangonera, R. 45 D2
Sangro 64 A2
Sangüesa 36 C2
Sanguinaires, Iles . . 33 E4
Sanguinet 28 A3
Sani 80 A4
Sanitz 48 C2
Sankt Olof 109 D3
Sanlúcar de
  Barrameda 43 D3
Sanlúcar de
  Guadiana 42 B2
Sanlúcar la
  Mayor 43 D2
Sanluri 66 B3
Sannainen 107 F2
Sannazzaro 60 A2
Sannicandro di
  Bari 65 D3
Sannicandro
  Garganico 64 C2
Sanok 112 C3
Sanquhar 4 C3
Sansepolcro 61 D4
Sanski Most 71 D3
Sant' Agata di
  Puglia 64 C3
Sant Agusti de
  Lluçanès 32 A3
Sant Andreu de
  Llavaneres 32 B4
Sant' Angelo de'
  Lombardi 64 C3
Sant' Angelo in
  Vado 61 E4
Sant' Angelo
  Lodigiano 60 A2
Sant Antoni, C de . . 45 F1
Sant Antoni de C. . . 32 B3
Sant Antoni de
  Portmany 45 D3
Sant Antoni,
  Emb de 37 F3
Sant' Apollinare in
  Classe 61 D3
Sant' Arcangelo di
  Romagna 61 E3
Sant Boi de
  Lluçanès 32 A3
Sant Celoni 32 B4
Sant Cugat 32 A4
Sant' Elia a Pianisi . . 64 C3
Sant' Elpidio a
  Mare 61 F4
Sant Esteve d'en
  Bas 32 B3
Sant'Eufemia,
  Golfodi 67 E3
Sant'Eufemia
  Lamezia 67 E3
Sant Gervàs 37 F3
Sant Hilari Sacalm. . 32 B3
Sant Hipòlit de
  Voltregà 32 A3
Sant Joan de les
  Abadesses 32 B3
Sant Julià de Lòria . . 32 A3
Sant Llorenc de
  Morunys 32 A3
Sant Marti
  d'Empuries 32 B3
Sant Mateu 41 F2
Sant'Onofrio 67 E3
Sant Pau de
  Seguries 32 B3
Sant Pere de Roda . 32 C3
Sant Pol de Mar . . . 32 B4

Sant Ponç, Emb de . 32 A3
Sant Quirze de
  Besora 32 B3
Sant Quirze Safaja . 32 A4
Sant Ramon 37 F3
Sant Sadurni
  d'Anoia 32 A4
Santa Amalia .. 39 D4
Santa Ana 40 C4
Santa Anna, Emb
  de 37 E3
Santa Bàrbara
  (Catalunya)..... 41 F2
Santa Bàrbara
  (Andalucía)..... 42 C2
Santa Bàrbara Mt . 44 B3
Santa Catarina .. 42 B3
Santa Caterina
  Pittinuri 66 A3
Santa Caterina
  Valfurva...... 58 C3
Santa Caterina
  Villarmosa 68 C3
Santa Cesarea
  Terme 65 F4
Santa Clara-a-
  Velha 42 A2
Santa Clara, Bgem
  de 42 A2
Santa Coloma de
  Farners 32 B3
Santa Coloma de
  Queralt 37 F4
Santa Colombo de
  Somoza 35 D3
Santa Comba Dão . 38 B2
Santa Comba de
  Rossas 34 C4
Santa Comba .. 34 A1
Santa Cristina de
  Lena 35 D2
Santa Croce di
  Magliano....... 64 B2
Santa Cruz de
  Campezo 36 B2
Santa Cruz de la
  Palma 42 A4
Santa Cruz de la
  Sierra....... 39 E3
Santa Cruz de la
  Zarza 40 B3
Santa Cruz del
  Retamar 40 A2
Santa Cruz de
  Moya 41 D3
Santa Cruz de
  Mudela 44 A1
Santa Cruz de
  Tenerife ... 42 B4
Santa Cruz .. 36 C4
Santa Elena.... 44 A1
Santa Eufemia .. 43 E1
Santa Eugenia .. 34 A2
Santa Eulalia del
  Rio 45 D3
Santa Eulalia de
  Oscos 34 C1
Santa Eulalia .. 41 D2
Santa Eulália .. 38 C4
Santa Fe (Andalucía) 44 A3
Santa Fé
  (Catalunya)...... 32 B4
Santa Fiora .. 63 D1
Santa Galdana,
  Cala 45 F2
Santa Gertrude .. 58 C3
Santa Giusta .. 66 B3
Santa Inés,
  Pto de 36 B3
Santa Liestra y San
  Quilez 37 E3
Santa Lucia d. Mela. 69 D2
Santa Luz .. 34 C4
Santa Luzia .. 42 A2
Santa Magdalena de
  Pulpis 41 F2
Santa Margarida do
  Sádão....... 42 B1
Santa Margarida i Els
  Monjos 32 A4
Santa Margarita.. 45 F2
Santa Margherita .. 66 B4
Santa Margherita di
  Belice 68 B3

Santa Margherita
  Ligure 60 A3
Santa Maria Capua
  Vetere 64 B3
Santa Maria, C de .. 42 B3
Santa Maria da
  Feira 38 B1
Santa Maria
  d'Angeli........ 63 E1
Santa Maria del
  Campo Rus .. 40 C3
Santa Maria della
  Versa 60 A2
Santa Maria di
  Leuca,C 65 F4
Santa María la Real
  de Nieva 40 A1
Santa María la Real
  de Oseira 34 B2
Santa Maria
  Maggiore 58 A3
Santa Marina .. 35 E2
Santa Marina del
  Rey 35 D3
Santa Marinella .. 63 D2
Santa María de
  Huerta 36 B4
Santa María del
  Campo....... 35 F3
Santa María del
  Páramo 35 D3
Santa María de
  Nieva 44 C3
Santa María de
  Valverde 35 D3
Santa-María-Siché .. 33 F4
Santa Marta .. 39 D4
Santa Marta de
  Penaguião .. 34 B4
Santa Marta de
  Tormes 39 E1
Santa Olalla del
  Cala........ 43 D2
Santa Olalla .. 39 E4
Santa Pau .. 32 B3
Santa Pola .. 45 E2
Santa Ponsa .. 45 E3
Santa Sofia .. 61 D3
Santa Sofia
  d'Epiro........ 67 E2
Santa Susanna.. 32 B4
Santa Tecla .. 34 A3
Santa Teresa di
  Riva........ 69 D2
Santa Teresa, Emb
  de 39 E2
Santa Teresa
  Gallura 66 B1
Santaella .. 43 E2
Santana
  (Estremadura) .. 38 A4
Santana (Madeira) .. 42 A3
Santana de Serra .. 42 A2
Santander .. 35 F1
Santanyí .. 45 F2
Santarém .. 38 B3
Santas Martas .. 35 E3
Santeramo in
  Colle........ 65 D3
Santes Creus .. 37 F4
Santesteban.. 36 C1
Santhià .. 31 F1
Santiago de
  Alcántara 38 C3
Santiago de
  Compostela.. 34 A2
Santiago de la
  Espada 44 B2
Santiago de la
  Ribera 45 D2
Santiago do
  Cacém .. 42 A1
Santiago do
  Escoural .. 38 B4
Santibáñez de
  Béjar 39 E2
Santibáñez de la
  Peña 35 E2
Santibáñez de la
  Sierra 39 E2
Santibáñez de
  Vidriales .. 35 D3
Santillana del Mar.. 35 F1
Santiponce .. 43 D2

Säntis 58 B2
Santisteban del
  Puerto....... 44 B1
Santo Domingo de la
  Calzada 36 B2
Santo Domingo de
  Silos 36 A3
Santo Domingo,
  Ptode .. 43 D1
Santo Estêvão
  (Beira Baixa) .. 38 C2
Santo Estêvão
  (Estremadura) .. 38 A4
Santo Estêvão, Rib
  de 38 A4
Santo Pedro da
  Torre....... 34 A3
Santo Severa .. 63 D2
Santo Stefano di
  Cadore....... 59 E2
Santo
  Stefano d'Aveto.. 60 B2
Santo Stino di
  Livenza .. 59 E4
Santo Tirso .. 34 A4
Santo Tomé .. 44 B2
Santok .. 49 F3
Santolea, Emb de.. 41 E2
Santomera, Emb
  de 45 D2
Santoña .. 36 A1
Santo-Pietro-di-
  Tenda 33 F2
Santorini, N .. 91 E1
Santuario de San
  Ignacio de Loyola. 36 B1
Santuario d'Oropa .. 27 F4
Santu Lussurgiu .. 66 B3
Santurtzi .. 36 B1
Sanxenxo .. 34 A2
Sanza .. 67 D1
São Bartolomeu de
  Messines........ 42 A2
São Brás de
  Alportel 42 B3
São Cristóvão.... 38 B4
São Domingos.. 42 A1
São Gregório .. 34 B3
São Jacinto .. 38 B1
São João da
  Pesqueira.. 34 B4
São João de
  Madeira .. 38 B1
São João de
  Tarouca .. 38 C1
São João dos
  Caldeireiros .. 42 B2
São José da
  Lamarosa .. 38 B3
São Leonardo.. 42 C1
São Mamede, Sa
  de .. 38 C3
São Manços .. 42 B1
São Marcos da
  Serra .. 42 A2
São Marcos do
  Campo .. 42 B1
São Martinho das
  Amoreiras .. 42 A2
São Martinho do
  Porto .. 38 A3
São Matias .. 42 B1
São Miguel de
  Machede .. 38 B4
São Pedro de
  Açor .. 38 C2
São Pedro de
  Moel.. 38 A2
São Pedro do Sul.. 38 C1
São Romão .. 38 C2
São Teotónio .. 42 A2
São Vicente, C de .. 42 A2
São Vicente da
  Beira .. 38 C2
Saône .. 26 C3
Saône-et-Loire .. 26 B3
Saorge .. 31 E3
Sapanca .. 115 F3
Sapataria .. 38 A3
Sàpes .. 81 E2
Sapiéndza, N .. 86 C4
Sa Pobla .. 45 F2
Sappada .. 59 E2
Sappee.. 107 E2

Sapri 67 D1
Säräisniemi .. 99 E4
Sarajärvi .. 99 E3
Sarajevo .. 76 A1
Sarakini .. 79 E2
Sarakinko .. 84 B3
Saramon .. 28 C4
Sarandáporo .. 79 E4
Sarandáporos .. 78 C4
Sarandë .. 114 C4
Saraváli .. 86 C1
Saray .. 115 E3
Sarayköy .. 115 F4
Šarbanovac.. 73 E3
Sarbinowo (Gorzów
  Wlkp) .. 49 F3
Sarbinowo
  (Koszalin) .. 49 F1
Sárbogárd .. 112 B4
Sarca .. 58 C3
Sardara .. 66 B3
Sardegna .. 66 A2
Sardínia .. 82 C3
Sardoal .. 38 B3
Sardona, Piz.. 58 B2
Sarek .. 98 A1
Šarengrad .. 72 B2
Sarentino .. 59 D2
Šärfjället .. 101 D2
Sargans .. 58 B2
Sariá, N .. 93 D2
Sari-d'Orcino .. 33 F3
Sarine .. 27 E3
Sariñena .. 37 E3
Sark .. 18 A3
Särkisalmi .. 103 F3
Särkisalo .. 107 D3
Särna .. 101 D3
Sarnano .. 61 F4
Sarnen .. 27 F2
Sarnico .. 60 B1
Sarno .. 64 B4
Sarnthein .. 59 D2
Sarny .. 113 D2
Särö .. 108 C1
Saròn .. 35 F2
Sarone .. 59 E3
Saronída .. 87 F2
Saronikós Kólpos .. 87 E1
Saronno .. 60 A1
Sárospatak .. 112 C3
Sar Planina .. 77 D3
Sarpsborg .. 105 D3
Sarracín .. 35 F3
Sarral .. 37 F4
Sarralbe .. 21 E3
Sarrans, Bge de .. 29 E2
Sarre .. 21 E3
Sarrebourg .. 21 E4
Sarreguemines .. 21 E3
Sarre-Union .. 21 E4
Sarrià .. 34 B2
Sarrión .. 41 E3
Sarroch .. 66 B4
Sarsina .. 61 D3
Sars-Poteries .. 20 B2
Sarstedt .. 52 B1
Sarteano .. 63 D1
Sartène .. 33 F4
Sarthe .. 23 E4
Sarthe (Dépt) .. 23 F3
Sartilly .. 18 B4
Sarule .. 66 B2
Sárvár .. 112 A4
Sarvsjö .. 101 D2
Sarzana .. 60 B3
Sarzeau .. 22 C4
Sarzedas .. 38 C2
Sasa .. 77 F2
Sassari .. 66 A2
Sassello .. 60 A3
Sassenage .. 30 C1
Sassenberg .. 17 F3
Sassenheim .. 16 B2
Sassetta .. 62 C1
Saßnitz .. 49 D1
Sasso .. 63 E2
Sassoferrato .. 61 E4
Sassoleone .. 61 D3
Sasso Marconi .. 60 C3
Sassuolo .. 60 C2

Sástago .. 37 D4
Sasyk, Ozero .. 113 E4
Sátão .. 38 C1
Säter .. 105 F3
Satillieu .. 30 B1
Satolas .. 30 C1
Šator .. 75 D1
Sátoraljaújhely .. 112 C3
Šatorina .. 70 B4
Satov .. 57 E1
Satow .. 48 C2
Sátres .. 81 D2
Satrup .. 48 A1
Sattel .. 58 A2
Sattledt .. 57 D3
Satu Mare .. 112 C3
Saualpe .. 70 B1
Sauca .. 36 B4
Saucelle, Emb de .. 39 D1
Sauda .. 104 A3
Sauðárkrókur .. 96 B1
Sauerlach .. 56 A3
Sauerland .. 17 F4
Saugues .. 29 F2
Saujon .. 28 B1
Saukkovaara .. 99 E4
Sauland .. 104 C3
Sauldre .. 26 A2
Saulgau .. 55 D3
Saulieu .. 26 B2
Sault .. 30 C3
Saulx .. 27 D1
Saulxures .. 27 E1
Saumur .. 24 C2
Saundersfoot.. 8 B2
Sauris .. 59 E3
Saut du Doubs.. 27 E2
Sautet, Bge du .. 30 C2
Sautusjärvi .. 94 C4
Sauve .. 30 B3
Sauveterre-de-
  Béarn .. 28 A4
Sauveterre-de-
  Guyenne .. 28 B2
Sauveterre-de-
  Rouergue .. 29 E3
Sauvo .. 107 D2
Sauxillanges .. 29 F1
Sauze d'Oulx .. 31 E2
Sauze, le .. 31 D2
Sauze-Vaussais .. 24 C4
Sauzon .. 22 B4
Sava .. 65 E4
Sava R .. 71 E3
Sàvalia .. 86 B1
Sävar .. 102 B1
Savelli .. 67 F2
Savenay .. 23 D4
Saverdun .. 32 A1
Saverne .. 21 E4
Savigliano .. 31 E2
Savignac-les-Eglises. 28 C1
Savignano Irpino .. 64 C3
Savignano sul
  Rubicone .. 61 E3
Savigny-sur-Braye .. 23 F4
Saviñán .. 36 C4
Savine, Col de la .. 27 D3
Savines-le-Lac .. 31 D2
Savinja .. 70 B1
Savino Selo .. 72 B2
Savitaipale .. 103 E4
Sävja .. 106 B3
Šavnik .. 76 B2
Savognin .. 58 B3
Savona .. 60 A3
Savonlinna .. 103 E3
Savonranta .. 103 F3
Sævråsvåg .. 104 A2
Sävsjö .. 109 D2
Savudrija .. 70 A3
Savukoski .. 95 F4
Sawbridgeworth .. 10 C2
Sawel Mt .. 13 D1
Sax .. 45 D1
Saxmundham .. 11 E1
Saxnäs .. 97 E4
Sayatón .. 36 B4
Säynätsalo .. 103 D3
Säyneinen .. 103 E2
Sazadón,
  Pto de .. 35 D3
Sázava .. 112 A3

Scaër .. 22 B3
Scafa .. 64 A2
Scafati .. 64 B4
Scafell Pikes .. 5 D4
Scala di Santa
  Regina .. 33 F3
Scalasaig.. 4 B2
Scalby .. 7 D1
Scalea .. 67 E2
Scalloway .. 3 F2
Scalpay .. 2 B3
Scandiano .. 60 C2
Scanno .. 64 A2
Scansano .. 63 D1
Scanzano .. 65 D4
Scapa Flow .. 3 D1
Scarba .. 4 B1
Scarborough .. 7 D1
Scardovari .. 61 E2
Scarinish .. 2 A4
Scarpe .. 20 A1
Scarriff .. 12 B4
Ščedro .. 75 E2
Šćepan Polje .. 76 A1
Scey-sur-Saône .. 27 D2
Schaalsee .. 48 B2
Schachendorf .. 57 F4
Schafberg .. 56 C3
Schaffhausen .. 58 A1
Schafstädt .. 52 C2
Schagen .. 16 C2
Schaprode .. 49 D1
Scharbeutz .. 48 B2
Schärding .. 56 C2
Scharnhorn .. 47 F2
Scharmützelsee .. 49 E4
Scharnitz .. 59 D1
Schauinsland
  Feldberg .. 54 C4
Scheeßel .. 48 A3
Scheggia .. 61 E4
Scheibbs .. 57 E3
Scheifling .. 57 D4
Scheinfeld .. 55 E1
Schelde .. 50 B3
Schenefeld
  (Hamburg) .. 48 A3
Schenefeld
  (Itzehoe) .. 48 A2
Scherfede .. 52 A2
Schermbeck .. 17 E3
Scheßlitz .. 52 C4
Scheveningen .. 16 B3
Schia .. 60 B3
Schiedam .. 16 B3
Schieder-
  Schwalenberg .. 52 A1
Schiehallion. .. 4 C1
Schierling .. 56 B2
Schiermonnikoog .. 47 D3
Schiermonnikoog/. .. 47 D3
Schiers .. 58 B2
Schifferstadt .. 54 C2
Schildau .. 53 D2
Schilpario .. 58 C3
Schiltach .. 54 C3
Schio .. 59 D4
Schirmeck .. 21 E4
Schirnding .. 53 D4
Schkeuditz .. 53 D2
Schkölen .. 53 D3
Schladming .. 59 F1
Schlagsdorf .. 48 B2
Schlanders .. 58 C3
Schlangenbad .. 51 F4
Schleching .. 56 B3
Schlei .. 48 A1
Schleiden .. 51 D4
Schleiz .. 53 D3
Schleswig .. 48 A1
Schleswig-Holstein .. 48 A1
Schleusingen .. 52 C3
Schlieben .. 53 E1
Schliersee .. 56 B4
Schlitz .. 52 B3
Schlotheim .. 52 B2
Schluchsee .. 54 C4
Schlucht,
  Col de la .. 27 E1
Schlüchtern .. 52 B4
Schluderbach .. 59 E2
Schluderns .. 58 C3
Schlüsselfeld .. 55 E1
Schlutup .. 48 B2

Schmalkalden .. 52 B3
Schmallenberg .. 17 F4
Schmidmühlen .. 55 F1
Schmilka .. 53 F2
Schmölln
  (Mecklenburg-
  Vorpommern) .. 49 E3
Schmölln
  (Thüringen) .. 53 D3
Schnackenburg .. 48 C3
Schnaittenbach .. 55 F1
Schneeberg (A) .. 57 E3
Schneeberg
  (Bayern) .. 53 D4
Schneeberg
  (Sachsen) .. 53 D3
Schneverdingen .. 48 A3
Schoberpaß .. 57 D4
Schöckl. .. 57 E4
Schönau .. 54 C4
Schönberg (A) .. 59 D2
Schönberg (Bayern). 56 C2
Schönberg
  (Mecklenburg-
  Vorpommern) 48 B2
Schönberg
  (Sachsen) 53 D4
Schönberg (Schleswig-
  Holstein) 48 B1
Schönbrunn .. 57 F2
Schönebeck .. 52 C1
Schöneck .. 53 D3
Schönecken .. 51 D4
Schönefeld .. 49 E4
Schönewalde .. 53 E1
Schongau .. 55 F4
Schöningen .. 52 C1
Schönmünzach .. 54 C3
Schönsee .. 56 B1
Schönthal .. 56 B1
Schönwald .. 54 C3
Schönwalde .. 48 B2
Schoonhoven .. 16 C3
Schopfheim .. 54 C4
Schöppenstedt .. 52 B1
Schoppernau .. 58 B2
Schorndorf .. 55 D2
Schortens .. 47 E3
Schotten .. 52 A4
Schouwen
  Duiveland.. 16 B3
Schramberg .. 54 C3
Schrems .. 57 D2
Schrobenhausen .. 55 F2
Schröcken. .. 58 B2
Schrozberg. .. 55 E1
Schruns .. 58 B2
Schuls .. 58 C2
Schüttorf .. 17 E2
Schwaan .. 48 C2
Schwabach .. 55 E1
Schwäbisch
  Gmünd .. 55 D2
Schwäbisch Hall .. 55 D2
Schwabmünchen .. 55 E3
Schwaigern .. 55 D2
Schwalmstadt-
  Treysa .. 52 A3
Schwalmstadt-
  Ziegenhain .. 52 A3
Schwandorf .. 56 B1
Schwanebeck .. 52 C1
Schwanenstadt.. 56 C3
Schwanewede .. 47 F3
Schwarmstedt .. 48 A4
Schwarza (A). .. 57 E3
Schwarza (D). .. 52 C3
Schwarzach .. 59 E1
Schwarze Elster .. 53 E1
Schwarzenbach .. 53 D4
Schwarzenbek .. 48 B3
Schwarzenberg .. 53 E3
Schwarzenburg .. 27 E3
Schwarzenfeld .. 56 B1
Schwarzheide .. 53 E2
Schwarzsee .. 27 E3
Schwarzwald .. 54 C3
Schwaz .. 59 D1
Schwechat .. 57 F2
Schwedt .. 49 E3
Schweich .. 54 A1
Schweinfurt .. 52 B4
Schweinitz .. 53 E1
Schwelm .. 17 E4

Schwendi. 55 E3
Schwenningen 54 C3
Schwerin 48 C2
Schweriner See. 48 C2
Schwerte 17 E3
Schwetzingen 54 C1
Schwielochsee. 53 F1
Schwyz 58 A2
Sciacca 68 B3
Scicli 69 D4
Scilla 67 E4
Scilly, Is of 8 A4
Scole 11 D1
Sconser 2 B3
Scopello 58 A4
Scordia 69 D3
Scorff 22 B3
Ščors 113 E1
Scorzè 59 E4
Scotch Corner 6 C1
Scotland. 2 C4
Scourie 2 C2
Scrabster 3 D2
Scridain, L 4 B1
Scrivia 60 A2
Ščučin 110 C4
Scunthorpe 7 D2
Scuol. 58 C2
Seaford 10 C3
Seaham 5 E4
Seaton 9 D3
Seaton Delaval 5 E3
Sebečevo 76 C1
Sebeş 114 C1
Sebež 111 D3
Sebnitz 53 F2
Sečanj. 73 D2
Secchia 60 C2
Seckau 57 D4
Seclin 19 F1
Secondigny 24 C3
Sedan 20 C2
Sedano 35 F2
Seda, Rib de 38 C3
Sedbergh. 6 C1
Séderon 30 C3
Sedgefield 5 E4
Sedičany 53 F4
Sedico 59 E3
Sedilo 66 B2
Sedini 66 B2
Sedlare 77 D2
Sedlec-Prčice. 53 F4
Sée. 18 C4
Seebenau. 48 B4
Seebergsattel 70 B1
Seeboden 59 F2
Seebruck 56 B3
Seefeld. 58 C1
Seehaus 56 C3
Seehausen
  (Magdeburg). 52 C1
Seehausen
  (Stendal) 48 C3
Seeheim 54 C1
Seelisberg 58 A2
Seelow 49 E4
Sées 19 D4
Seesen 52 B1
Seevetal 48 A3
Seewalchen 56 C3
Seewiesen 57 E3
Sefkerin 72 C2
Segesta 68 A3
Segl 58 B3
Segni 63 F3
Segonzac 28 B1
Segorbe 41 E3
Segovia 40 A1
Segré. 23 E4
Segre. 37 E3
Segre, R 32 A3
Segura 38 C3
Segura de la
  Sierra 44 B1
Segura de León 43 D1
Segura de los
  Baños 41 D1
Segura, R. 45 D2
Segura, Sa de 44 B2
Sehnde. 52 B1
Seia 38 C2
Seiches 23 E4
Seifhennersdorf 53 F2

Seignelay. 26 B1
Seil 4 B1
Seiland 95 D1
Seilandsjøkelen 95 D1
Seilhac. 29 D1
Seille (Meurthe-et-
  Moselle) 21 D4
Seille (Saône-et-
  Loire) 26 C3
Seinäjoki 102 C2
Seine 19 E3
Seine-et-Marne 19 F4
Seine-Maritime 19 D3
Sein, I de 22 A3
Seitenstetten 57 D3
Seitsemisen 102 C3
Seixal 38 A4
Seixo 34 B3
Sejerø 108 B3
Sejerø Bugt 108 B3
Sejm 113 F1
Sékoulas 86 C2
Šekovići 72 B4
Selargius 66 B4
Selassia 87 D3
Selb 53 D4
Selbekken 100 C1
Selbu 101 D2
Selbusjøen 100 C2
Selby 7 D2
Selce 70 B3
Selçuk 115 E4
Sele 64 C4
Selečka pl 77 E4
Selenter See 48 B1
Sélero 81 D2
Sélestat 21 E4
Selevac 73 D3
Selfoss 96 A2
Séli 79 E3
Selia 90 C4
Selianitika 83 D4
Seligenstadt 52 A4
Selinia 87 F1
Selinunte 68 A3
Selishtë 76 C3
Selište 73 E3
Selje 100 A3
Seljord 104 C3
Selkämeri 102 B3
Selkirk 5 D3
Sellajoch 59 D3
Sella Nevea 59 F3
Sella, Pso di 59 D3
Selles 25 E2
Sellières 26 C3
Sellin 49 D1
Selm 17 E3
Selmsdorf 48 B2
Selna 71 F3
Selommes 25 E2
Selongey 26 C2
Seløy 97 D3
Selsey 9 F3
Selsey Bill 9 F3
Selters 52 A4
Seltz. 21 F3
Sélune 18 C4
Selva 59 D3
Selvino 58 B4
Seman. 114 B3
Semeljci 71 F2
Semič 70 B2
Seminara 67 E4
Semizovac. 71 F4
Semmering 57 E3
Semmering-Paß 57 E3
Semois 20 C2
Semproniano 63 D1
Semur-en-Auxois. . . 26 B2
Semur-en-
  Brionnais. 26 B4
Sena. 37 E3
Sénas 30 C3
Sendim. 34 C4
Senez 31 D3
Senftenberg 53 E2
Sengsengeb 57 D3
Senigallia 61 F3
Senise 65 D4
Senj 70 B3
Senja Ånderdalen . . 94 B3
Senje 73 E4
Senlis 19 F3

Sennecey-le-Grand . 26 C3
Sennen 8 A4
Sennestadt 17 F3
Sennori 66 A2
Senonches 19 E4
Senones 21 E4
Senorbi 66 B3
Senožeče 70 A2
Sens 26 A1
Senta 72 C1
Šentilj 70 C1
Šentjernej 70 C2
Šentjur 70 C2
Šentvid na
  Šlemenu 70 B1
Šépeaux 26 A1
Šepetivka 113 D2
Sepino 64 B3
Sepúlveda 36 A4
Sequeros 39 E2
Sequillo, R 35 E4
Seraing 50 C4
Seravezza 60 B3
Seregno 60 A1
Serein 26 B2
Serena, Emb de la . . 39 E4
Séres 80 B2
Séres (Nomos) 80 B2
Serfaus 58 C2
Serfopoúla, N 88 B3
Seriate 60 B1
Sérifos 88 A3
Sérifos, N 88 A3
Serifou, Stenó 88 A3
Sermaize-les-
  Bains 20 C4
Sermide 60 C2
Sermoneta 63 F3
Sernancelhe 38 C1
Serón 44 B3
Serón de Nágima . . 36 B4
Seròs 37 E4
Serpa 42 B1
Serpeddi, P. 66 B4
Serpis, R 45 E1
Serra 41 E3
Serracapriola 64 B2
Serrada 35 E4
Serradifalco 68 C3
Serradilla 39 D3
Serramanna 66 B4
Serrana, Pto de la . . 39 E3
Serra San Bruno . . . 67 F3
Serravalle Scrivia . . 60 A2
Serre Chevalier 31 D2
Serre-Ponçon, Bge
  de 31 D2
Serres 30 C2
Serrières 30 B1
Serrota 39 F2
Sersale 67 F3
Sertà 38 B2
Servan 18 B4
Sérvia 79 E4
Servian 30 A4
Servigliano 61 F4
Sesa 37 D3
Sesena 40 A2
Sesia 27 F4
Sesimbra 38 A4
Sesklio, N. 93 E1
Sesma 36 C2
Sessa Aurunca 64 A3
Sesta Godano 60 B3
Šestanovac 75 E2
Sestino 61 E3
Sesto 59 E2
Sesto Calende 60 A1
Sesto Fiorentino . . . 60 C3
Sesto San
  Giovanni 60 A1
Sestola 60 C3
Sestriere 31 E2
Sestri Levante 60 B3
Sestrunj 74 C1
Sestrunj I. 74 C1
Sestu 66 B4
Sesvete 70 C2
Séta 84 B4
Setcases 32 B3
Sète 30 A4
Setenil 43 E3
Setermoen 94 B3
Setesdalen 104 B3

Setesdalsheiene. . . 104 B3
Settebagni 63 E2
Settimo Torinese . . . 31 E1
Settle 6 C1
Settons, les 26 B2
Setúbal 38 A4
Seudre 28 B1
Seui 66 B3
Seulo 66 B3
Seurre 26 C2
Sevastianá 79 E3
Sevenoaks 10 C3
Sévérac-le-
  Château 29 F3
Sever do Vouga 38 B1
Severn Bridge 9 D2
Severn, Mouth of
  the 9 D2
Severn,R. 9 D2
Sever, R 38 C3
Seveso 60 A1
Sevettijärvi 95 F2
Sevilla 43 D2
Sevilleja de la Jara . . 39 F3
Sevlievo 115 D2
Sevnica 70 C2
Sevojno 72 C4
Sèvre Nantaise 24 C3
Sèvre Niortaise 24 C3
Sévrier 27 D4
Sevsk. 111 F4
Sexten 59 E2
Seyches 28 C2
Seyda 53 D1
Seyðisfjörður 96 C2
Seyne 31 D3
Seyne, la 31 D4
Seyssel 27 D4
Sežana 70 A2
Sézanne 20 B4
Sezimovo-Ústi 57 D1
Sezze 63 F3
Sfáka 91 F4
Sfakiá 90 C4
Sfaktiría, N. 86 C3
Sfikiá, L. 79 E3
Sfîntu Gheorghe . . 113 D4
Sforzacosta 61 F4
's Gravendeel 16 C3
's Gravenhage 16 B3
Sgùrr Mór 2 C3
Sgùrr na Ciche 2 B4
Shaftesbury 9 D3
Shanklin 9 E4
Shannon 12 B4
Shannon, Mouth
  of the 12 A4
Shannon, R. 12 B4
Shap 5 D4
Shapinsay 3 E1
Shebenik, Mal i 77 D4
Sheelin, L. 13 D3
Sheep Haven 12 C1
Sheep's Head 14 A4
Sheerness 11 D2
Sheffield 6 C2
Shefford 9 F2
Shëmri (Shkodër) . . 76 C3
Shëmri (Tiranë) 76 C4
Shëngjin 76 C3
Sheppey, I of 11 D2
Shepshed 7 D3
Shepton Mallet 9 D3
Sherborne. 9 D3
Shercock 13 D3
Sheringham 7 F3
Shetland Is 3 E2
Shiel Bridge 2 C4
Shieldaig 2 B3
Shiel, L. 2 B4
Shijak 76 C4
Shinás 79 E3
Shiniás 88 A1
Shin, L 2 C2
Shínos 83 D3
Shinoússa, N 88 C3
Shipston-on-Stour . . 9 E1
Shiza, N 86 C4
Shkodër 76 B3
Shkodrës, Liq i 76 B3
Shkumbin 76 C4

Sholári 80 A3
Shoreham. 10 C3
Shpat, Mal i 77 D4
Shrewsbury 6 B3
Shrewton 9 E3
Shropshire 9 D1
Shupenzë 77 D4
Sía, Pto de la 36 A1
Siátista 79 D4
Šiauliai 110 C3
Sibari 67 E2
Sibbhult 109 D3
Sibbo 107 F2
Sibbofjärden 107 F2
Šibenik 75 D1
Šibenik Mt. 75 E2
Sibinj 71 E3
Sibiu. 113 D4
Sićevo 73 F4
Siciè, Cap. 31 D4
Sicignano degli
  Alburni 64 C4
Sicilia 68 B2
Sicó 38 B2
Šid 72 B2
Sidári 82 A1
Sideby 102 B3
Sidensjö 102 A2
Siderno 67 F4
Sideros, Akr. 91 F3
Sidirò 81 E2
Sidirókastro 80 A2
Sidirónero 80 C1
Sidlaw Hills 5 D1
Sidmouth 9 D3
Siebenlehn 53 E2
Siedlce 112 C1
Sieg 51 E3
Siegburg. 51 E3
Siegen 17 F4
Siegsdorf 56 B3
Siekierki 49 E3
Siena 61 D4
Sieppijärvi 98 C1
Sieradz 112 B2
Sierck 21 D3
Sierentz 27 E1
Sierninghofen. 57 D3
Sierpc 112 B1
Sierra Boyera, Emb
  de 43 E1
Sierra de Fuentes . . 39 D3
Sierra de Yeguas . . . 43 E3
Sierre 27 E3
Sievi 102 C1
Sievin as 102 C1
Sifnos, N 88 B3
Sifnou, Stenó 88 B3
Sigean. 32 B2
Sigerfjord 94 A3
Siggjarvåg 104 A3
Sighetu
  Marmaţiei 112 C3
Sighişoara 113 D4
Siglufjörður 96 B1
Sigmaringen 55 D3
Signy-l'Abbaye 20 B2
Sigri 85 E2
Sigtuna 106 B3
Sigüenza 36 B4
Sigulda 110 C2
Siiddasjávri 94 B4
Siikainen 102 B3
Siikajoki 99 D4
Siikajoki R 99 D4
Siilinjärvi 103 E2
Sijarinska Banja . . . 77 D1
Sikaminiá 85 F2
Sikás 101 E2
Siki 84 A2
Sikiá (Makedonía) . . 80 A4
Sikiá
  (Pelopónissos) . . . 87 E4
Sikinos 88 C4
Sikinos, N 88 C4
Sikióna 87 D1
Sikoráhi 81 E2
Sikoúrio. 83 E1
Sikovuono 95 E3
Sila, La 67 F3
Silandro 58 C3
Silba 70 B4
Silba I. 70 B4
Silbaš 72 B2

Sildegapet 100 A2
Šile. 115 F3
Siles 44 B1
Sirevåg 104 A4
Siliqua 66 B4
Silistra. 115 E1
Silivri 115 E3
Siljan (N) 104 C3
Siljan (S) 101 E4
Siljansnäs 101 E4
Silkeborg 108 A3
Silla 41 E4
Silleda 34 B2
Silleiro, C 34 A3
Sillé-le-Guillaume . . 23 E3
Sillian 59 E2
Silloth 5 D4
Šilo 70 B3
Silo 81 E2
Sil, R. 34 C2
Sils 32 B4
Sils im Engadin . . . 58 B3
Siltakylä 107 F2
Silvalen 97 D3
Silvaplana 58 B3
Silvares 38 C2
Silves 42 A2
Silvi Marina 64 A1
Silvrettagruppe. . . . 58 B2
Silz 58 C2
Simancas 35 E4
Simandra 80 A3
Šimanovci 72 C3
Simav. 115 F4
Simaxis 66 B3
Simbach (Inn). 56 B3
Simbach (Isar) 56 B2
Simbruini, Mti 63 F2
Simeto 69 D3
Sími 93 E1
Šimići 71 E3
Sími, N 93 E1
Simlångsdalen 108 C2
Simmerath 51 D4
Simmern 54 B1
Simo 99 D3
Simojärvi 99 E2
Simojoki 99 D3
Simola 103 F4
Simonos Pétras . . . 80 C4
Simonsbath 8 C3
Simonswald 54 C3
Simópoulo 86 B1
Simplonpass 27 F3
Simrishamn 109 D3
Sinaia 113 D4
Sinalunga 61 D4
Sinarádes 82 A1
Sinarcas 41 D3
Sindelfingen 55 D2
Sındırgı. 115 F4
Sindos 79 F3
Sines 42 A1
Sines, C de 42 A1
Sinettä 99 D2
Sineu 45 F3
Singen 55 D3
Singöfjärden 106 B3
Singra, Pto de 41 D2
Siniscola 66 C2
Sinj. 75 D1
Sinjajevina 76 B2
Sinni 65 D4
Sînnicolau Mare . . . 114 C1
Sinopoli 67 E4
Sinsheim 55 D2
Sintra 38 A4
Sinzig 51 E4
Siófok 112 B4
Sion 27 E3
Sioule 26 A4
Šipan 75 F2
Šipanska Luka 75 F2
Šipka 115 D2
Šipovo. 71 E4
Sipoo 107 F2
Sipoonselkä 107 F2
Šiprage 71 E4
Sira 104 A4
Sira R 104 A4
Siracusa 69 D4
Sirdalen 104 B4
Sirdalvatn 104 A4

Siret 113 D3
Siret R. 113 D3
Sirevåg 104 A4
Sirig 72 C2
Sirino, Mte. 65 D4
Širitovci 75 D1
Sirkka 95 E1
Sirma 95 E2
Sirmione 60 C1
Sirna, N 92 C1
Široko Polje 71 F2
Sirolo 61 F4
Síros, N 88 B2
Siruela 39 F4
Sisak 71 D2
Šišan 70 A4
Sisante 40 C4
Šišljavić. 70 C2
Sissa 60 B2
Sissach 27 F2
Sissonne 20 B3
Sisteron 31 D3
Sistiana 59 F3
Sistranda 100 C1
Sitges 32 A4
Sithonía. 80 B4
Sitia 91 F4
Sitjar, Emb de 41 E3
Sitnica 77 D2
Sittard 17 D4
Sittensen 48 A3
Sittingbourne 11 D2
Siuntio. 107 E3
Siuro 107 E2
Siurua 99 D3
Siuruanjoki 99 D3
Siusi 59 D3
Sivac 72 B2
Sivaslı 115 F4
Siviri 80 A4
Sivota 82 B2
Sivros 82 B3
Siziano 60 A1
Sizun 22 B3
Sjælland 108 C3
Sjællands Odde . . . 108 B3
Sjenica 76 C1
Sjeništa 76 A1
Sjøåsen 97 D4
Sjöbo 109 D3
Sjøholt 100 B2
Sjona 97 E2
Sjötorp. 105 E4
Sjoutnäset 97 E4
Sjøvegan 94 B3
Sjulsmark 102 B1
Sjundea 107 E3
Sjusjøen 104 D2
Skåbu 100 C3
Skäckerfjällen 101 D1
Skadarsko jez. 76 B3
Skadovs'k 113 F4
Skafidiá 86 B2
Skaftá 96 B2
Skaftafell 96 C2
Skagafjörður 96 B1
Skage 97 D4
Skagen 108 B1
Skagern 105 E4
Skagerrak 108 A1
Skaill 3 E1
Skjálfandi. 96 B1
Skála (Kefaloniá) . . 86 A1
Skála (Lésvos) 85 F2
Skála (Pátmos) . . . 89 E2
Skála
  (Pelopónissos) . . . 87 E4
Skála (Stereá Eláda) 83 F4
Skála Eressoú 85 E2
Skála Kaliráhis. . . . 80 C3
Skaland. 94 B2
Skála Oropoú 84 B4
Skála Potamiás . . . 81 D3
Skála Rahoníou . . . 80 C3
Skalavík 96 A4
Skálfandafljót. 96 B2
Skalka 98 A2
Skalohóri (Lésvos) . 85 E2
Skalohóri
  (Makedonía) 79 D3
Skaloti. 80 C1

Skælskør 108 B4
Skamnéli 78 C4
Skandáli 85 D1
Skandári, Akr . . 89 F3
Skanderborg 108 B3
Skandzoúra, N. . . 84 B3
Skåne 109 D3
Skånevik 104 A3
Skåningsbukt. . . . 94 C2
Skånland 94 B3
Skänninge 106 A4
Skanör Falsterbo . . 108 C4
Skara 109 D1
Skaraborgs Län. . . 109 D1
Skaramangás 87 F1
Skærbæk 108 A4
Skarberget 94 B4
Skarda 74 B1
Skåre 105 E3
Skárfia 83 F3
Skärgårdshavet . . . 107 D3
Skärhamn 108 C1
Skarnes 105 D3
Skarplinge 106 B2
Skarsvåg 95 E1
Skärvången 101 E1
Skarżysko-
 Kamienna 112 B2
Skattungbyn 101 E4
Skatval 100 C2
Skaulo 94 C4
Skaun 100 C2
Skee 105 D4
Skegness 7 E3
Skei (Møre og
 Romsdal) 100 B2
Skei (Sogn og
 Fjordane) 100 A3
Skeiðarársandur . . 96 B2
Skela 72 C3
Skellefteå 98 B4
Skellefteälven 98 B4
Skelleftehamn . . . 98 B4
Skellig 14 A4
Skelmersdale 6 B2
Skenderbeut, M i . . 76 C4
Skender Vakuf . . . 71 E4
Skepastó 80 B2
Skerries 13 E3
Ski 105 D3
Skiathos 84 A2
Skiáthos, N. 84 A2
Skibbereen 14 B4
Skibby 108 C3
Skibotn 94 C2
Skiddaw 5 D4
Skidra 79 E3
Skien 104 C3
Skierniewice 112 B2
Skillingaryd 109 D2
Skiloundia 86 C2
Skinári, Akr 86 A1
Skiniás. 91 E4
Skinnarbu 104 B3
Skinnskatteberg . . . 105 F3
Skipagurra 95 F1
Skipton 6 C2
Skiros 84 C3
Skíros, N. 84 C3
Skíti 83 F1
Skive 108 A2
Skivjane 76 C2
Skjeberg 105 D3
Skjelvik 97 E2
Skjern 108 A3
Skjersholmane 104 A3
Skjerstad 97 E2
Skjerstadfjorden . . . 97 E2
Skjervøy 94 C2
Skjønhaug 105 D3
Sklavopoúla 90 B3
Sklithro. 83 F1
Šklov 111 E3
Škočivir 77 E4
Škocjanske jame . . 70 A3
Škodje 100 B2
Škofja Loka 70 A2
Škofljica. 70 B2
Skog (Gävleborgs
 Län) 101 F4
Skog (Västernorrlands
 Län) 102 A2
Skógafoss 96 B3
Skogerøya 95 F2

Skoghall 105 E3
Skogstorp 105 F4
Skokloster 106 B3
Skólis 86 B1
Skópelos (Lésvos) . . 85 F3
Skópelos (Skópelos) . 84 B2
Skópelos, N 84 B3
Skopí 91 F4
Skopiá 83 E2
Skopje 77 E3
Skopós 79 E2
Skopun. 96 A4
Skorenovac 73 D3
Skorovatn 97 E4
Skorped 101 F2
Skotina 79 F4
Skotterud 105 D3
Skoulikariá. 82 C2
Skoúra 87 D3
Skoúrta 87 F1
Skoútari
 (Makedonía) . . . 80 B2
Skoútari
 (Pelopónissos) . . 87 D4
Skoutáros 85 E2
Skövde 109 D1
Skrá 79 E2
Skrad 70 B3

Skradin 75 D1
Skradinski buk 75 D1
Skreia 105 D2
Skrim 104 C3
Skrolsvik 94 B3
Skrydstrup 108 A4
Skudeneshavn 104 A3
Skuleskogen 102 A2
Skull 14 A4
Skultuna 106 A3
Skuodas 110 B3
Skuov'gilraš'ša . . . 95 D2
Skurup. 109 D3
Skutskär 106 B2
Skutvik 94 A4
Skvyra 113 E2
Skye 2 B3
Skýros →
Slagelse 108 B3
Slagnäs 98 A3
Slånčev Brjag 115 E2
Slancy 111 D1
Slane 13 D3
Slaney 15 D3
Slangerup 108 C3
Slano 75 F2
Šlapanice 57 F1
Slapská přehr nádrž 53 F4

Slapy 53 F4
Šląsk 112 A2
Slatina (Bor) 73 E3
Slatina (BH) 71 E3
Slatina (Kraljevo) . . 73 D4
Slatina
 (Makedonija) . . . 77 D3
Slatina (RO) 115 D1
Slatine 75 D2
Slatinski Drenovac . . 71 E2
Slavgorod 111 E4
Slavinja 77 F1
Slavkovica 72 C4
Slavkov u Brna . . . 57 F1
Slavnik 70 A3
Slavonice 57 E1
Slavonska Požega . . 71 E2
Slavonski Brod . . . 71 E3
Slavonski Kobaš . . 71 E3
Slavuta 113 D2
Sławno 110 A4
Sławoborze 49 F2
Sleaford 7 D3
Slea Head 14 A3
Sleat, Sd of 2 B4
Slettfjellet 94 C2
Sliedrecht 16 C3
Sliema 68 B4

Slieve Bloom Mts . . 12 C4
Slieve Donard 13 E3
Slieve Mish Mts . . . 14 A3
Slievenamon 14 C3
Slieve Snaght 13 D1
Sligachan 2 B3
Sligeach 12 C2
Sligo 12 C2
Sligo (Co) 12 B3
Sligo B 12 C2
Slišane 77 D1
Slite 109 F4
Sliven 115 E2
Sljeme 70 C2
Šljivovica 72 C4
Slobozia 115 E1
Slonim 112 C1
Sloten 16 C1
Slough 9 F2
Slovac 72 C3
Slovenska Bistrica . . 70 A1
Slovenija 70 A2
Slovenj Gradec . . . 70 B1
Slovenske Konjice . . 70 B1
Slovenské
 Rudohorie 112 B3
Slovinci 71 D3
Słubice 49 F4

Sluck 111 D4
Sluderno 58 C3
Sluis 16 A4
Sluknov 53 F2
Slunj 70 C3
Słupsk 110 A4
Slyne Head 12 A3
Småland 109 D2
Smålandsfarvandet 108 B4
Smålands-stenar . . 109 D2
Šmarje 70 C2
Šmarješke Toplice . . 70 B2
Šmartin 70 B2
Smedby 109 E2
Smederevo 73 D3
Smedjebacken . . . 105 F3
Smederevska
 Palanka 73 D3
Smigáda 81 E2
Smila 113 F2
Smilčič 74 C1
Smilde 17 D1
Smiltene 110 C2
Smojmirovo 77 F3
Smokovec 112 B3
Smokovljan 75 D2
Smøla 100 B1

Smolensk 111 E3
Smolevicì 111 D4
Smólikas, Óros. 78 C4
Smoljan 115 D3
Smorgon 111 D4
Smørhamn 104 A1
Smygehamn 109 D4
Snaefell 6 A1
Snæfellsnes 96 A2
Snaith 7 D2
Snåsa 101 D1
Snasahögarna 101 D2
Snåsavatnet. 101 D1
Sneek 16 C1
Sneem 14 A4
Snežnik 70 B3
Śniardwy, Jez 110 B4
Snihurivka 113 F3
Snillfjord 100 C2
Snizort, L 2 B3
Šnjegotina Velika . . 71 E3
Snøfjord 95 D1
Snøhetta 100 C3
Snøtinden 97 E2
Snowdon 6 A3
Snowdonia Forest
 and Nat Pk 6 A3
Soave 60 C1

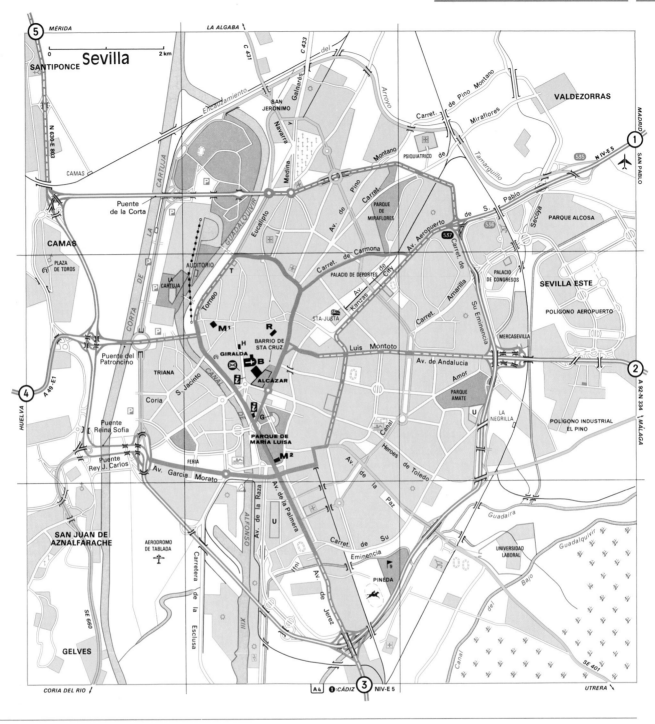

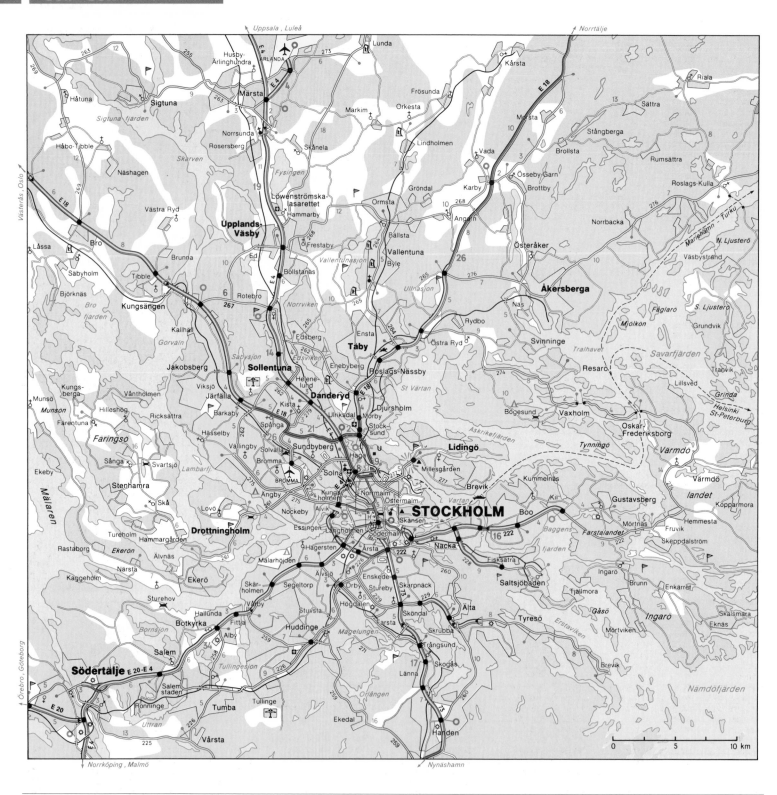

Sobeslav 57 D1	Söderbärke 105 F3	Soglio 58 B3	Sola (Rogaland).... 104 A3	Solholmen 100 B2	Solofra 64 B4	Somes 112 C4
Sobra 75 F2	Söderfors 106 B3	Sogndal 100 B3	Sola (Sogn og	Solignac (Haute-	Solosancho 39 F2	Somiedo, Pto de ... 35 D2
Sobrado de los	Söderhamn 101 F4	Søgne 104 B4	Fjordane) 104 A1	Loire) 29 F2	Solothurn 27 E2	Sommarøy 94 B2
Monjes 34 B2	Söderköping 106 A4	Sognefjell 100 B3	Solana de los	Solignac (Haute-	Solre-le-Château ... 20 B2	Sommatino 68 C4
Sobral da Adiça 42 C1	Södermanlands	Sognefjorden 104 A1	Barros 39 D4	Vienne) 29 D1	Solrød 108 C3	Somme 19 E2
Sobral de Monte	Län 106 A4	Sognesjøen 104 A1	Solana del Pino ... 43 F1	Soligorsk 111 D4	Solsona 32 A3	Somme (Dépt) 19 F2
Agraço 38 A3	Söderskog 109 D3	Sogn og	Solares 35 F2	Solihull 9 E1	Šolta 75 D2	Sommen 109 E1
Sobreira Formosa .. 38 C2	Södertälje 106 B4	Fjordane 100 A3	Solberg 101 F1	Solin 75 D1	Soltau 48 A3	Sömmerda 52 C2
Sobrón, Emb. de ... 36 B2	Sodražica 70 B2	Soham 11 D1	Solbergfjorden 94 B3	Soline 74 B1	Solunska Glava 77 E3	Sommesous 20 B4
Søby 108 B4	Sodupe 36 B1	Sohós 80 A2	Sol'cy 111 D2	Solunto 68 B3	Solvay 60 C4	Sommières 30 B3
Soča 70 A2	Soest (D) 17 F3	Soignies 50 B4	Solda 58 C3	Söll 59 D1	Sölvesborg 109 D3	Sømna 97 D3
Soča R. 70 A2	Soest (NL) 16 C2	Soini 102 C2	Sölden 58 C2	Sollana 41 E4	Sölvorn 100 B3	Somolinos 36 A4
Sočanica 77 D1	Soestdijk 16 C2	Soinlahti 103 D1	Soldeu 32 A2	Sollefteå 101 F2	Solvychegodsk .... No entry	Somosierra, Pto
Soccia 33 F3	Sofádes 83 E2	Soissons 20 A3	Solent, The 9 E3	Sollenau 57 F3	Solway Firth 4 C4	de 36 A4
Sochaczew 112 B1	Sofia 115 D2	Söke 115 E4	Solenzara 33 F4	Sollentuna 106 B3	Solynieve 44 A3	Sompio 95 F3
Sochaux 27 E2	Sofiero 108 C3	Sokna 104 C2	Solesmes (Nord) ... 20 A2	Sóller 45 E2	Soma 115 E4	Somport, Pto de ... 37 D2
Socol 73 D2	Sofikó 87 E1	Soko Banja 73 E4	Solesmes (Sarthe) .. 23 E3	Solleròn 101 E4	Sombernon 26 C2	Šomrda 73 E3
Socovos 44 C1	Sofó 83 E2	Sokolac 72 B4	Solevåg 100 A2	Sombor 72 B2	Soncillo 35 F2
Socuéllamos 40 B4	Sögel 17 E1	Sokolov 53 D4	Solf 102 B2	Søllested 108 B4	Someren 17 D4	Soncino 60 B1
Sodankylä 95 E4	Sogliano al	Sokołów Podlaski .. 112 C1	Solferino 60 C1	Solliès-Pont 31 D4	Somero 107 E2	Søndeled 104 C4
Söderåkra 109 E3	Rubicone 61 E3	Sokosti 95 F3	Solnečnogorsk 111 F2	Solnhofen .... No entry	Somerset 9 D3	Sønderborg 108 B4

Sønderby 108 B4
Sønder Felding.... 108 A3
Sondershausen.... 52 C2
Søndersø 108 B3
Sondrio 58 B3
Songeons 19 E3
Sonkajärvi 103 E1
Sonnblick 59 E2
Sonneberg 52 C4
Sonnewalde 53 E1
Sonogno 58 A3
Sonsbeck 17 D3
Sonseca 40 A3
Son Servera 45 F3
Sonta 72 B2
Sonthofen 55 E4
Sontra 52 B3
Soome Laht 110 C1
Sopeira 37 F3
Sopilja 76 A1
Sopište 77 D3
Sopoćani 76 C1
Sopot (PL) 110 A4
Sopot (Srbija) 73 D3
Sopotnica 77 D4
Sopron 112 A4
Sora 64 A3
Soragna 60 B2
Söråker 101 F3
Sørarnøy 97 E2
Sorbas 44 C3
Sorbe, R 40 B1
Sore 28 B3
Soresina 60 B1
Sørfjorden 104 B2
Sør-Flatanger 96 C4
Sørfolda 94 A4
Sörfors 102 A1
Sorga 52 B3
Sorgono 66 B3
Sorgues 30 B3
Sørgutvik 97 D4
Soria 36 B3
Sørkjosen 94 C2
Sorø 108 B3
Soroca 113 E3
Soro, M 69 D3
Soroní 93 E1
Sørøya 95 D1
Sørøysundet 95 D1
Sorraia, R 38 A4
Sørreisa 94 B3
Sorrento 64 B4
Sor, Rib de 38 B3
Sørrollnes 94 B3
Sorsakoski 103 E2
Sorsele 98 A3
Sorso 66 A2
Sort 37 F2
Sortino 69 D4
Sortland 94 A3
Sortlandsundet.... 94 A3
Sør Trøndelag 100 C2
Sorunda 106 B4
Sørvågen 97 E1
Sørvågur 96 A4
Sørvær 94 C1
Sørværøy 97 E1
Sörvattnet 101 D3
Sos del Rey
  Católico 37 D2
Soses 37 E4
Sosnovyj Bor 111 D1
Sosnowiec 112 B2
Sospel 31 E3
Šoštanj 70 B1
Sóstis 81 D2
Šostka 111 F4
Sotaseter 100 B3
Sotillo de la Adrada . 39 F2
Sotin 72 B2
Sotira 79 E2
Sotkamo 99 E4
Soto del Barco .. 35 D1
Soto de los
  Infantes 35 D1
Soto de Luiña 35 D1
Soto de Sajambre .. 35 E2
Sotogrande 43 E4
Sotopalacios 35 F3
Sottomarina 61 D1
Sottunga 106 C3
Sotuélamos 40 C4

Soúda 90 C3
Souesmes 25 F2
Soufflenheim. 21 F3
Soufli 81 F2
Soúgia 90 B4
Souillac 29 D2
Souilly 20 C3
Soulac 28 A1
Soulaines-Dhuys .. 20 C4
Soulinári 86 C3
Souliou, Óri. 82 B2
Soulópoulo 82 B1
Soultz (Bas-Rhin) . 21 E3
Soultz (Haut-Rhin) . 27 E1
Soúnio 88 A2
Soúnio, Akr. 88 A2
Souppes 25 F1
Sourdeval 18 C4
Soure 38 B2
Sournia 32 B2
Souroti 80 A3
Soúrpi 83 F2
Sousceyrac 29 D2
Sousel 38 C4
Soustons 28 A4
Soutelo 34 B2
Souterraine, la .. 25 E4
Southam 9 E1
Southampton 9 E3
Southborough 10 C3
South Downs 9 F3
Southend 4 B3
Southend-on-Sea .. 11 D2
Southern Uplands .. 4 C3
South Esk 3 D4
South Foreland .. 11 D3
South Molten 8 C3
Southport 6 B2
South Queensferry . 5 D2
South Ronaldsay .. 3 E1
Southsea 9 F3
South Shields 5 E3
South Tyne 5 D3
South Uist 2 A3
Southwell 7 D3
Southwold 11 E1
Souvála 87 F2
Souvigny 26 A3
Sovata 113 D4
Sövdeborg 109 D3
Soverato 67 F3
Soveria Mannelli .. 67 F3
Søvik 100 A2
Sož 111 E4
Sozopol 115 E2
Spa 51 D4
Spaichingen 55 D3
Spakenburg 16 C2
Spalding 7 E3
Spánda, Akr. 90 B3
Spandau 49 E3
Spangenberg 52 B3
Spanish Pt. 12 B4
Sparlösa 108 C1
Spárta 87 E1
Spárti 87 D3
Spartivento, C
  (Calabria) 67 E4
Spartivento, C
  (Sardegna) 66 B4
Spárto 82 C3
Spas-Demensk 111 F3
Spáta 87 F1
Spatharéï 89 E2
Spathí, Akr (Kíthira) . 90 A1
Spathí, Akr
  (Pelopónissos) .. 87 F2
Spodniji Brnik .. 70 B2
Spean Bridge 2 C4
Speikkogel 57 E4
Spello 63 E1
Spennymoor 5 E4
Sperhiáda 83 E3
Sperhiós 83 E3
Sperillen 104 C2
Sperlonga 63 F3
Sperrin Mts 13 D1
Spétses 87 E3
Spétses, N. 87 E3
Spetsopoúla, N .. 87 E3
Speyer 54 C2
Spey, R 3 D3
Spezzano Albanese . 67 E2
Spezzano della Sila . 67 E2

Spiddal 12 B3
Spiekeroog 47 E2
Spielfeld 70 C1
Spiez 27 F3
Spijkenisse 16 B3
Spilea Diroú 87 D4
Spili 90 C4
Spiliá 83 E1
Spilimbergo 59 E3
Spilsby 7 E3
Spinalónga 91 E3
Spinazzola 65 D3
Spincourt 20 C3
Spišić Bukovica .. 71 E2
Spišská-Nová Ves.. 112 B3
Spital 57 D3
Spittal 59 F2
Spitz 57 E2
Spjelkavik 100 A2
Split 75 D2
Spluga, Pso dello . 58 B3
Splügen 58 B3
Splügenpass 58 B3
Spodsbjerg 108 B4
Špola 113 F2
Spoleto 63 E1
Spornitz 48 C3
Spotorno 60 A3
Spreča 71 F3
Spree 49 E4
Spreewald 53 E1
Spremberg 53 F1
Spresiano 59 E4
Springe 52 A1
Sprogø 108 B4
Spurn Head 7 E2
Spuž 76 B2
Squillace, Golfo di . 67 F3
Squinzano 65 F4
Srb 71 D4
Srbac 71 E3
Srbica 77 D2
Srbija 73 D3
Srbobran 72 C2
Srđevići 75 E1
Srebrenica 72 C4
Središče 70 C1
Sredna Gora 115 D2
Srednje 71 F4
Srednji kanal 74 C1
Srednogorie 115 D2
Sredska 77 D3
Sremska Kamenica . 72 C2
Sremska Mitrovica . 72 C3
Sremska Rača 72 B3
Sremski Karlovci .. 72 C2
Srnetica 71 D4
Srnice Donje 71 F3
Środa
  Wielkopolska .. 112 A1
Srpska Crnja 72 C1
Srpske Moravice .. 70 B3
Srpski Itebej 72 C1
Srpski Miletić .. 72 C2
Stabbursdalen 95 D2
Stade 48 A3
Stádio 87 D2
Stadskanaal 17 E1
Stadthagen 52 A1
Stadtilm 52 C3
Stadtkyll 51 D4
Stadtlohn 17 E3
Stadtoldendorf .. 52 A2
Stadtroda 52 C3
Stadtsteinach 52 C4
Stadt Wehlen 53 F2
Staffa 4 A1
Staffanstorp 108 C3
Staffelsee 56 A4
Staffelstein 52 C4
Staffin 2 B3
Stafford 6 C3
Staffordshire 6 C3
Stágira 80 B3
Stahle 52 A2
Stahovica 70 B2
Stainach 57 D4
Stainz 57 E4
Stajovce 77 E2
Stalać 73 E4
Štalcerji 70 B3
Stalida 91 E3
Stall 59 E2

Stalle, Pso di 59 E2
Stallersattel. 59 E2
Stalowa Wola 112 C2
Stamford 9 F1
Stamnes 104 A2
Stams 58 C4
Stamsund 94 A4
Stange 105 D2
Stanišić 72 B1
Stanišinci 73 D4
Štanjel 70 A2
Stanke Dimitrov.. 115 D3
Staňkov 56 B1
Stankovci 74 C1
Stanley 5 E4
Stanós 80 B3
Stanós 82 C3
Stans 27 F2
Stansstad 27 F2
Stansted 10 C2
Stapar 72 B2
Starachowice 112 B2
Stara Gradina .. 71 E2
Staraja Russa .. 111 E2
Stara Moravica .. 72 B1
Stara Novalja .. 70 B4
Stara Pazova 72 C2

Stara Pl (BG) 115 D2
Stara Pl (Srbija) .. 73 F4
Stará Role 53 E4
Staravina 77 E4
Stara Vrata 70 C4
Stara Zagora 115 D2
Staretina 75 D1
Stargard
  Szczeciński .. 49 F2
Stårheim 100 A3
Stari 77 F3
Stari Bar 76 B3
Stari Begej 72 C2
Starica 111 F2
Starigrad (Hvar) .. 75 D2
Starigrad (Velebit) . 70 B4
Stari Gradac 71 E2
Starigrad Paklenica . 70 C4
Stari Jankovci .. 72 B2
Stari Log 70 B2
Stari Majdan 71 D3
Stari Mikanovci .. 71 F2
Starnberg 56 A3
Starnberger See .. 56 A3
Starodub 111 F4
Starogard Gdański . 110 A4
Starokostjantyniv . 113 D2

Staro Nagoričane .. 77 E2
Staro Petrovo Selo . 71 E3
Staro Slano 76 A2
Start Pt. 8 C4
Starý Smokovec... 112 B3
Staßfurt 52 C1
Statland 97 D4
Staußfurt. 52 C2
Stavanger 104 A3
Staveley 7 D3
Stavelot 51 D4
Stavenisse 16 B3
Staveren 16 C1
Stavern 104 C4
Stavrí, Akr 88 C3
Stavrodrómi 86 C1
Stavrohóri 91 F4
Stavrós (Évia) .. 84 B3
Stavrós (Imathía).. 79 E3
Stavrós (Ithákí) .. 82 B4
Stavrós (Kríti) .. 90 C3
Stavrós (Thessalía) . 83 E2
Stavrós
  (Thessaloníki) .. 80 B3
Stavrós, Akr (Kríti) . 91 D3
Stavrós, Akr
  (Thássos) 81 D3

Stavroúpoli 80 C2
Steblevë 77 D4
Štěchovice 53 F4
Steckborn 58 A1
Steeg 58 C2
Steenbergen 16 B3
Steenvoorde 19 F1
Steenwijk 17 D2
Stefání (Ípiros) .. 82 B2
Stefáni (Stereá
  Eláda) 87 F1
Stefaniná 80 B3
Stefanovikío 83 F2
Stege 108 C4
Stegérsbach 57 F4
Steibis 55 E4
Steiermark 57 E4
Steigen 97 E1
Stein (A) 57 E2
Steinach (A). 59 D2
Steinach (D) 52 C3
Steinau 52 A4
Steinbach-
  Hallenberg 52 B3
Stein (Baden-
  Württemberg) .. 55 D4

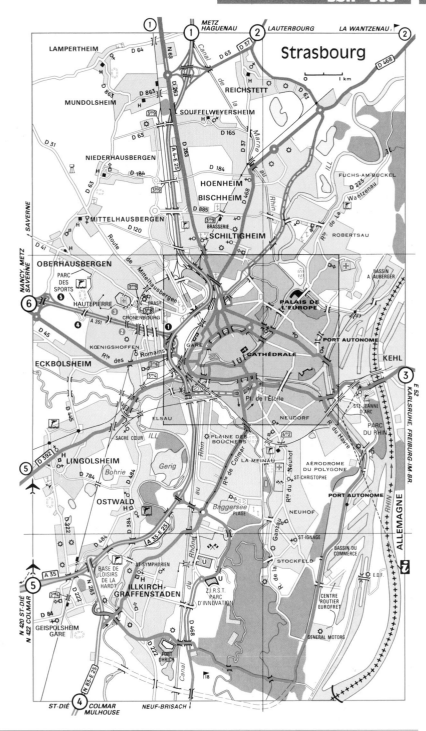

Strasbourg

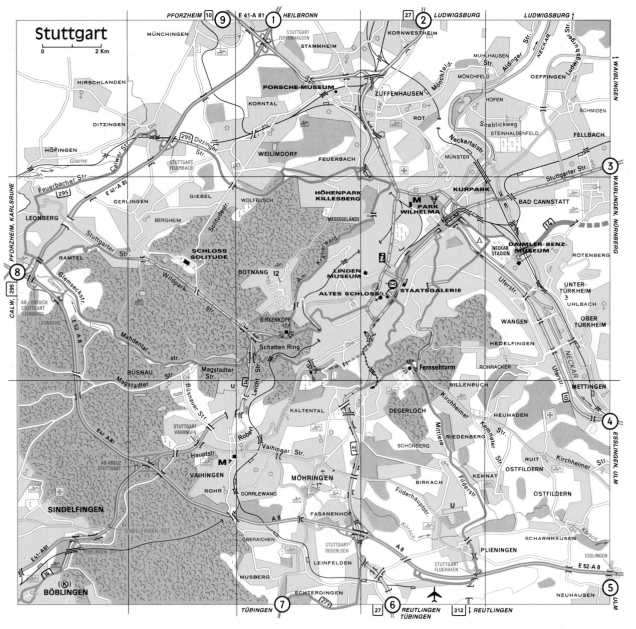

Stuttgart

Strasbourg 21 E4
Strasburg 49 E2
Straßburg 70 A1
Straßwalchen 56 C3
Stratford-upon-
Avon 9 E1
Strathaven 4 C2
Strathclyde 4 C2
Strathy Pt 3 D2
Stratóni 80 B3
Stratoníki 80 B3
Strátos 82 C3
Stratton 8 B3
Straubing 56 B2
Straumen (Bodø) 97 E2
Straumen
(Fauske) 97 F1
Straumen (Nord
Trøndelag) 101 D1
Straumsjøen 94 A3
Straumsnes
(Nordland) 97 E1
Straumsnes
(Troms) 94 C3
Straupitz 53 E1
Strausberg 49 E4
Straža (Srbija) 73 E4
Straža (Vojvodina) .. 73 D2
Straža, G. 70 B2
Stražbenica 76 B1
Strážný 56 C2
Streatley 9 E2
Street 9 D3
Strehaia 114 C1
Strehla 53 E2
Streitberg 52 C2
Strengberg 57 D3
Stresa 58 A4
Streymoy 96 A3
Strezimirovci 77 E1
Strezovce 77 D2
Stříbro 53 E4
Strimónas 80 B2
Strimonikó 80 A2
Strimonikós
Kólpos 80 B3
Strmac 71 E2
Strmica 75 D1
Strobl 56, C3
Strofádes, N. 86 A3
Strofiliá 84 A3
Strojkovce 77 E1
Strokestown 12 C3
Stromberg 54 B1
Stromboli, I 69 D1
Stromeferry 2 B3
Strömfors 107 F2
Stromness 3 D1
Strömsbruk 101 F3
Strömsnäsbruk 109 D2
Strömstad 105 D4
Strömsund 101 F1
Ströms vattudal .. 101 E1
Strongoli 67 F2
Stronsay 3 E1
Stronsay Firth 3 E1
Strontian 2 B4
Stroud 9 D2
Strovlés 90 B3
Strub, Paß 59 E1
Struer 108 A2
Struga 77 D4
Struge 70 B2
Struma 115 D3
Strumble Head 8 B3
Strumica 77 E3
Strumica R. 77 F3
Stryj. 112 C2
Stryn 100 A3
Strzelce
Krajeńskie 49 E3
Stubalpe 57 D4
Stubbekøbing 108 C4
Stubbenkammer .. 49 D1
Stubej 73 E3
Štubik 73 F3
Stubline 72 C3
Stuckenborstel .. 48 A3
Studena 77 E1
Studenci 75 E1
Studenica 76 C1
Stugun 101 F2
Stühlingen 54 C4

Stein (Bayern) 55 E1
Steine 104 A1
Steinestø 104 A2
Steinfeld (A) 59 F2
Steinfeld (D) 17 F2
Steinfurt 17 E2
Steingaden 55 E4
Steinhaus 59 D2
Steinhausen 55 D3
Steinheim (Baden-
Württemberg) ... 55 E2
Steinheim (Bayern) . 55 E2
Steinheim (Nordrhein-
Westfalen) 52 A2
Steinkjer 101 D1
Steinnuder Meer . 48 A4
Steinpaß 59 E1
Steinshamn 100 A2
Steinsland 104 A2
Stekene 50 B3
Stelvio, Parco Naz
della 58 C3
Stelvio, Pso dello . 58 C3
Stená Klissoúras . 79 D3
Stenay 20 C3
Stendal 48 C4
Steni 84 B4
Stenlille 108 C4
Stenløse 108 C4
Stenness 3 D1
Stenó 87 D2
Stenó, Akr. 88 B2
Stenó Itháris 82 B4

Sténoma 83 D3
Stenudden 98 A2
Stenungsund 108 C1
Stepanci 77 E3
Stepnica 49 E2
Stepojevac 72 C3
Stereá Eláda 83 D3
Sterkrade 17 E3
Stérna (Makedonía) 80 C2
Stérna
(Pelopónissos) . 87 D2
Stérna (Thráki) .. 81 F1
Sternberg 48 C2
Stérnes 90 C3
Sterup 48 A1
Sterza, la 60 C4
Sterzing 59 D2
Stevenage 9 F2
Stevns 108 C4
Stevns Klint 108 C4
Stewarton 4 C2
Steyr 57 D3
Steyrermühl. 56 C3
Stia 61 D3
Stigliano 65 D4
Stigtomta 106 A4
Stilfserjoch 58 C3
Stilida 83 E3
Stilo 67 F4
Stimánga 87 D1
Stimfalía, L 87 D1
Stímlje 77 D2
Stintino 66 A1

Štip. 77 E3
Stípsi 85 F2
Stíra 84 C4
Stirling 4 C2
Štirovača 70 C4
Štitar 72 C3
Štivan 70 B4
Stolice 72 B3
Stolice Mt 73 E4
Stjärnhov 106 B4
Stjärnsund 105 F4
Stjørnøya 95 D2
Stjernsund 95 D2
Stjørdal 100 C2
Stjørdalselva 101 D2
Stjørnfjorden 100 C1
Stobi 77 E3
Stockach 55 D4
Stockbridge 9 E3
Stockelsdorf 48 B2
Stockerau 57 F2
Stockholm 106 B4
Stockholms Län . 106 B3
Stockport 6 C2
Stocksbridge 6 C2
Stockton-on-Tees. . 5 E4
Stod 53 E4
Stöde 101 F3
Stogovo 77 D4
Stoke-on-Trent .. 6 C3
Stokke 104 C3
Stokkmarknes 94 A3
Stol. 73 E3
Stolac 75 F2
Stolac Mt. 72 C4

Stolbcy 111 D4
Stolberg (Nordrhein-
Westfalen) 51 D3
Stolberg (Sachsen-
Anhalt) 52 C2
Stolice 72 B3
Stolin 113 D1
Stollberg 53 E3
Stöllet 105 E2
Stolpen 53 F2
Stølsheimen 104 B2
Stolzenau 48 A4
Stómio 83 F1
Ston 75 F2
Stone 6 C3
Stonehaven 3 E4
Stonehenge 9 E3
Stonglandet 94 B3
Stopanja 73 E4
Stör 48 A2
Storå 105 F3
Stora Alvaret 109 E3
Stora Blåsjön 97 E3
Stora Lulevatten . 98 A2
Stora Sjöfallet 94 B4
Stora Sjöfallet
(National park) .. 94 B4
Stora Skedvi 105 F2
Stora Sundby 105 F4
Storavan 98 A3
Storby 106 C3
StStorlett 94 C2
Stord 104 A2

Stordal 100 B2
Store Bælt 108 B3
Store 104 A2
Storebø 104 A2
Storebro 109 E2
Store Heddinge .. 108 C4
Store Molvik 95 F1
Store Mosse 109 D2
Støren 100 C2
Storfjellet 97 F2
Storfjorden 100 B2
Storfors 105 E3
Storforsen 98 B3
Storforshei 97 E2
Storglomvatnet .. 97 E2
Storkow 49 E4
Storlien 101 D2
Stormi 107 D2
Stornoway 2 B2
Storo 58 C4
Storožynec' 113 D3
Storr, The 2 B3
Storsjö 101 D2
Storsjøen 105 D1
Storsjön (Gävleborgs
Län) 106 B2
Storsjön
(Ljungdalen) .. 101 D2
Storsjön
(Östersund) .. 101 E2
Storsjouten 97 E4
Storskarven 101 D2
Storslett 94 C2
Storsteinnes 94 C3

Storstrømmen 108 C4
Storuman 97 F4
Storuman L. 97 F3
Storvik (N). 95 D2
Storvik (S) 106 A2
Storvindeln 97 F3
Stotel 47 F3
Stoúpa 86 C3
Stour 11 D2
Stourbridge 9 E1
Stournaréika 83 D2
Stourport 9 D1
Støvring 108 B2
Stowmarket 11 D1
Stow-on-the-Wold . 9 E2
Strå 61 D1
Strabane 13 D1
Stracin 77 E2
Stradella 60 A2
Stradsett 11 D1
Straelen 17 D3
Stragari 73 D4
Strakonice 56 C1
Stralsund 49 D1
Stranda 100 B2
Strandebarm 104 A2
Strandhill 12 C2
Strangford 13 E2
Strangford L. 13 E2
Strängnäs 106 B3
Stranice 70 B1
Stranorlar 12 C1
Stranraer 4 B3

Stuhr-Brinkum 17 F1
Stupnik........... 70 C2
Stura di Demonte ... 31 E3
Sturehov......... 106 B4
Sturminster
Newton........... 9 D3
Sturup........... 108 C3
Stuttgart 55 D2
Stykkishólmur ... 96 A2
Styr 113 F2
Suances 35 F1
Subbiano........ 61 D4
Subiaco 63 F2
Subijana 36 B2
Subotica 72 B1
Subotište........ 72 C3
Suc-au-May 29 D1
Suceava 113 E3
Sučevici 71 D4
Suceviţa 113 D3
Suchań 49 F2
Suchiniči 111 F3
Süchteln 17 D4
Sucina........ 45 D2
Suck 12 C3
Sućuraj 75 E2
Sudbury (Derbys) .. 6 C3
Sudbury (Suffolk) .. 11 D2
Suddesjaur 98 A3
Sude 48 B3
Süderbrarup 48 A1
Suðuroy.......... 96 A4
Suðuroyarfjørður.. 96 A4
Sueca 41 E4
Sueros 35 D2
Suffolk 11 D1
Suhl 52 C3
Suhopolje 71 E2
Suho Polje 72 B3
Šuica 75 E1
Suinula........... 102 C3

Suippes 20 B3
Suir, R 14 C3
Sukeva 103 E1
Sukobin........ 76 B3
Sukošan........ 74 C1
Sukovo 77 E1
Sukth 76 C4
Sula 113 F2
Suldal........... 104 B3
Suldalsvatn....... 104 B3
Sulden 58 C3
Sulęcin 49 F4
Sulina 113 F4
Sulingen 17 F2
Sulitjelma........ 97 F2
Sulitjelma Mt 97 F2
Sulkava 103 E3
Sully 25 F2
Sulmona 64 A2
Sultanhisar 115 F4
Sulz 54 C3
Sulzbach (Baden-
Württemberg)... 55 D2
Sulzbach
(Saarland) 54 B2
Sulzbach-
Rosenberg....... 55 F1
Sulzemoos 55 F3
Sumartin 75 E2
Sumba 96 A4
Sumburgh 3 F2
Sumburgh Head 3 F2
Sümeg 112 A4
Šumen 115 E2
Sumiainen 103 E2
Sumiswald....... 27 F2
Šumperk 112 A3
Sumy 113 F1
Sunart, L. 2 B4
Sund 106 C3
Sunde (Hordaland) 104 A2

Sunde (Sør
Trøndelag) ... 100 C1
Sunderland 5 E4
Sundern...... 17 F4
Sundini 96 A3
Sundom 102 B2
Sundsvall 101 F3
Sundsvallsbukten.. 101 F3
Suni 66 B2
Sunja 71 D3
Sunnansjö 105 F3
Sunndalen 100 C2
Sunndalsøra..... 100 B2
Sunne
(Jämtlands Län) . 101 E2
Sunne (Värmlands
Län)........... 105 E3
Sunnemo 105 E3
Sunnylvsfjorden... 100 B3
Suodenniemi 107 D1
Suolahti 103 D2
Suolijärvet....... 99 E2
Suolijoki 99 D2
Suomenlinna 107 D2
Suomenniemi 103 E3
Suomusjärvi..... 107 E2
Suomussalmi 99 F3
Suomutunturi 99 E1
Suonenjoki 103 E2
Suontee 103 D3
Suopelto
(Kuopion Lääni) . 103 D2
Suopelto
(Mikkelin Lääni) . 103 D3
Super-Besse 29 E1
Super-Molina 32 A3
Supetar........ 75 D2
Supetarska Draga . 70 B4
Supino 63 F2
Šuplja-Stijena ... 76 B1
Surahammar 105 F3

Suraž........... 111 E4
Surbo 65 F4
Surčin 72 C3
Surduc 114 C1
Surdulica 77 E1
Surdup 76 B2
Sûre 21 D2
Surgères 24 C4
Surnadalsøra..... 100 C2
Surrey 10 C3
Sursee 27 F2
Survilliers 19 F3
Susa 31 E1
Suså 108 C4
Sušac........ 75 E3
Susak 70 B4
Susak I 70 B4
Susch 58 B2
Susek 72 B2
Sušice 56 C1
Suspiro del Moro,
Pto del 44 A3
Susqueda, Emb
de 32 B3
Süßen 55 D2
Sustenpass 58 A3
Susurluk 115 F3
Sutinjske Toplice.. 70 C2
Sutivan 75 D2
Sutjeska 73 D2
Sutjeska nac park.. 76 A1
Sutomore 76 B3
Sutri 63 E2
Sutterton 7 E1
Sutton 9 F2
Sutton Coldfield .. 9 E1
Sutton-in-Ashfield.. 7 D3
Sutton-on-Sea ... 7 E3
Suva gora 77 D3
Suva pl 77 E1

Suva Reka 77 D2
Suvasvesi 103 E2
Suvereto 62 C1
Suvobor 72 C4
Suvodol 77 D3
Suvorov 77 D3
Suwałki 110 C4
Suze, la 23 F4
Suzzara 60 C2
Svaljava 112 C3
Svalöv 108 C3
Svaneke 109 D4
Svanstein 98 C2
Svanvik 95 F2
Svappavaara 94 C4
Svärdsjö 105 F2
Svarstad 104 C3
Svarta 105 E4
Svartevatn 104 B3
Svartevatn L. 104 B3
Svartisen 97 E2
Sværvolthalvøya .. 95 E1
Svattälven....... 105 F3
Svedala 108 C3
Sveg 101 E3
Svelgen 100 A3
Svelvik 104 C3
Svendborg 108 B4
Svenljunga 108 C2
Svensby 94 C2
Svenstavik 101 E2
Švermov 53 F3
Svetac 75 D2
Sveti Andrija 77 D3
Sveti Ilija 75 E2
Sveti Janez 70 A2
Sveti Jovan
Bigorski 77 D3
Sveti Naum 77 D4
Sveti Nikita 77 D2
Sveti Nikola 76 B3
Sveti Nikole 77 E3

Sveti Pantelejmon.. 77 D3
Sveti Rok 70 C4
Sveti Stefan 76 B3
Svetlogorsk
(RB) 111 E4
Svetlogorsk
(ROS) 110 B4
Svetozarevo...... 73 D4
Svetozar Miletić .. 72 B1
Svidnik 112 C3
Švihov 56 B1
Svilaja 75 D1
Svilajnac 73 E3
Svilengrad 115 E3
Svingvoll 104 C1
Svinjar 71 E3
Svinoy 96 A3
Svištov 115 D2
Svitavy 112 A3
Svitlovods'k 113 F2
Svodđe 77 E1
Svolvær 94 A4
Svor 53 F3
Svorkmo 100 C2
Svoronáta 86 A1
Svorónos 79 F4
Svrljig 73 E3
Swadlincote 6 C3
Swaffham 11 D1
Swale 6 C1
Swalmen 17 D4
Swanage 9 E4
Swanley 10 C2
Swanlinbar 12 C2
Swansea 8 C1
Świdnica 112 A2
Świdwin 49 F2
Świebodzin 112 A2
Świecie 112 A1
Świecko 49 F4
Świerzno 49 F1

Swilly, L 13 D1
Swindon 9 E2
Swinford 12 B3
Świnoujscie........ 49 E2
Swords 13 D3
Sybil Head 14 A3
Syčovka 111 F3
Sykäräinen 102 C1
Syke 17 F1
Sykkylven 100 A2
Sylene 101 D2
Sylling 104 C3
Sylt 47 F1
Sylt Ost 47 F1
Sylvenstein-
Stausee 56 A4
Synod Inn 8 C1
Syötekylä 99 E3
Syre 3 D2
Sysmä 103 D3
Sysslebäck 101 D4
Syväjärvi 99 D1
Syväri 103 E2
Syvde 100 A3
Syvdsnes 100 A2
Syyspohja 103 E3
Szarvas 112 B4
Szczecin 49 E2
Szczecinek 110 A4
Szczeciński, Zalew . 49 E2
Szczytno 110 B4
Szécsény 112 B3
Szeged 114 B1
Székesfehérvár... 112 B4
Szekszárd 114 B1
Szentendre 112 B4
Szentes 112 B4
Szigetvár 114 B1
Szolnok 112 B4
Szombathely 112 A4

T

Tabanovce........ 77 E2
Tábara........ 35 D4
Tabarca, I de... 45 E2
Taberg 109 D1
Tabernas........ 44 B3
Taboada 34 B2
Tábor 57 D1
Tábua 38 B2
Tabuaço 34 B4
Tabuenca 36 C3
Täby 106 B3
Tachov 53 E4
Tadcaster 7 D2
Tafalla 36 C2
Tafjord 100 B3
Taganheira 42 A1
Taggia 31 F3
Tagliacozzo 63 F2
Tagliamento 59 E3
Taglio di Po 61 D2
Tahal 44 C3
Tahkvuori 103 E2
Taibilla, Sa de .. 44 C2
Taigetos, Óros..... 87 D3
Tain 3 D2
Tain-l'Hermitage.. 30 B2
Taipadas 38 A4
Taipalsaari 103 E4
Taivalkoski 99 E3
Taivassalo 107 D2
Tajera, Emb de la . 40 C1
Tajo, R. 40 B2
Tajuña, R 40 B2
Takovo 73 D4
Taktikoúpoli 87 E2
Tálanda 87 E4
Talarrubias 39 E4
Talaván 39 D3
Talavera de la Reina. 39 F3

Talavera la Real 39 D4
Talayuela 39 E2
Talayuelas 41 D3
Taldom 111 F2
Talgarth 9 D1
Talkkunapää 95 F3
Talla 61 D4
Tallante 45 D3
Tallard 31 D2
Tällberg 101 E4
Tallinn 110 C1
Talloires 27 D4
Tallow 14 C4
Talluskylä 103 D2
Talmont 24 B3
Tal'ne 113 E2
Talsi 110 B2
Talvik 95 D2
Tamames 39 E1
Tamar 8 B3
Támara 35 F3
Tamarite de Litera . 37 E3
Tamási 112 B4
Tambre, R. 34 A2
Tâmega, R. 34 A4
Tamélos, Akr 88 A2
Tamiš. 72 C2
Tammela 107 E2
Tammisaari 107 E3
Tamnava 72 C3
Tampere 107 E1
Tamsweg 56 C4
Tamworth 9 E1
Tana 95 E1
Tana R. 95 E1
Tanafjorden 95 E1
Tanágra 84 A4
Tanagro 64 C4
Tanamea, Pso di .. 59 F3
Tanaro 31 F2
Tancarville, Pont de. 19 D3
Tandådalen 101 D4
Tandragee 13 D2

Tandsbyn 101 E2
Tandsjöborg 101 E3
Tangerhütte 48 C4
Tangermünde 48 C4
Tanhua 95 F4
Taninges 27 E4
Tanlay 26 B1
Tann 52 B3
Tännäs 101 D3
Tanndalen 101 D3
Tannheim 58 C1
Tannila 99 D3
Tanumshede 105 D4
Taormina 69 D3
Tapa 110 C1
Tapia de
Casariego 34 C1
Tar 70 A3
Tara 72 C4
Tara R 76 B1
Taracena 40 B2
Tara klisura 76 B2
Tarancón 40 B3
Taranto 65 E4
Taranto, Golfo di . 65 E4
Tarare 26 B4
Taraš 72 C2
Tarašča 113 E2
Tarascon (Ariège) . 32 A2
Tarascon
(Vaucluse) 30 B3
Taravo 33 F3
Tarayuela 41 E2
Tarazona 36 C3
Tarazona de la
Mancha 40 C4
Tarbat Ness...... 3 D3
Tarbert (IRL) 14 B3
Tarbert
(Strathclyde) 4 B2
Tarbert (Western Is). 2 B2
Tarbes 37 E1
Tarbet 4 C1

Tarcento 59 F3
Tarčin 75 F1
Tardets-Sorholus . 37 D1
Tardienta 37 D3
Tärendo 98 C2
Tärendöälven..... 98 C1
Targon 28 B2
Târgovişte 115 E2
Tarifa 43 D4
Tarm 108 A3
Tarmstedt 47 F3
Tärn 29 D3
Tarn (Dépt) 29 E3
Tärnaby 97 E3
Tarna, Pto de 35 E2
Tärnäsjön..... 97 E3
Tarn-et-Garonne . 29 D3
Tarn, Gges du 29 F3
Tarnobrzeg 112 C2
Tarnos 28 A4
Tarnów 112 B2
Taro 60 B2
Tarouca 38 C1
Tarporley 6 B3
Tarqinia 63 D2
Tarragona 37 F4
Tarrasa 32 A4
Tàrrega 37 F4
Tarrekaise 98 A2
Tårs 108 B4
Tartas 28 B3
Tartu 110 C2
Tarvasjoki 107 D2
Tarvisio 59 F2
Täsch 27 F4
Tåsinge 108 B4
Tåsjo 101 F1
Tåsjön 101 F1
Tåstrup 108 C3
Tata 112 B4

Tatabánya 112 B4
Tatarbunary 113 E4
Tatry 112 B3
Tau 104 A3
Tauber 55 D1
Tauberbischofsheim
..... 55 D1
Taucha 53 D2
Tauerntal 59 E2
Tauerntunnel 59 E2
Taufers i. M. 58 C3
Taufkirchen 56 B3
Taulé 22 B2
Taunton 9 D3
Taunus 51 F4
Taunusstein 51 F4
Tauplitz 57 D4
Tauragė 110 B3
Taurianova 67 E4
Taurion 25 E4
Tauste 36 C3
Tauves 29 E1
Tavankut 72 B1
Tavannes 27 E2
Tavarnelle Val di
Pesa 60 C4
Tavastila 103 E4
Tavaux 26 C2
Taverna 67 F3
Tavernelle 63 E1
Tavernes 31 D4
Tavernes de la
Valldigna 41 E4
Tavignano 33 F3
Tavira 42 B3
Tavistock 8 C3
Tavolara, I 66 C1
Tavropós 83 D2
Tavropoú, Teh L .. 83 D2
Tavşanli 115 F3
Taw 8 C3
Taxenbach 59 E1
Taxiárhis 80 B3

Tay 5 D1
Tayinloan 4 B2
Tay, L 4 C1
Taynuilt 4 B1
Tayport 5 D1
Tayside 3 D4
Tazones 35 E1
Tczew 110 A4
Teano 64 C4
Teba 43 E3
Tebay 5 D4
Tech 32 B3
Techendorf 59 F2
Tecklenburg 17 E2
Tecuci 113 E4
Tees 5 E4
Teesside 5 E4
Teféli 91 D4
Tegéa 87 D2
Tegel 49 E4
Tegelen 17 D4
Tegernsee 56 A4
Teggiano 64 C4
Teguise 42 C2
Teide 42 B4
Teide Mt. 42 A4
Teide, Pque Nac
del. 42 B4
Teignmouth 8 C4
Teijo 107 D3
Teil, le. 30 B2
Teilleul, le 18 C4
Teisendorf 56 B3
Teisko 102 C3
Teixeiro 34 B1
Teixoso 38 C2
Tejeda, Sa de .. 43 F3
Tejo, R. 38 A3
Tekeriš 72 C3
Tekija 73 E2
Tekirdağ. 115 E3
Telč. 57 E1
Telde 42 B4

Telemark 104 C3
Télendos, N 89 E3
Teleno 34 C3
Telese 64 B3
Telford 6 C3
Telfs 58 C2
Telgte 17 E3
Tellingstedt..... 48 A2
Telti 66 B2
Teltow 49 D4
Témbi 83 E1
Tembleque 40 B3
Temerin 72 C2
Temmes 99 D4
Tempelhof 49 E4
Tempio
Pausania 66 B2
Templemore 12 C4
Templin 49 D3
Temse 50 B3
Temska 73 E3
Tenala 107 E3
Ténaro, Akr. 87 D4
Tenbury Wells .. 9 D1
Tenby 8 B2
Tence 30 B2
Tende 31 E3
Tende, Col de .. 31 E3
Tende, Colle di. .. 31 E3
Tendilla 40 B2
Tenerife 42 A4
Tenja 71 F2
Tennes 94 B3
Tenniöjoki 95 F4
Teno 95 E2
Tensta 106 B3
Tenterden 11 D3
Tentudia 43 D1
Teolo 61 D1
Teovo 77 E3
Tepelenë 114 C4
Teplá 53 E4

Torino

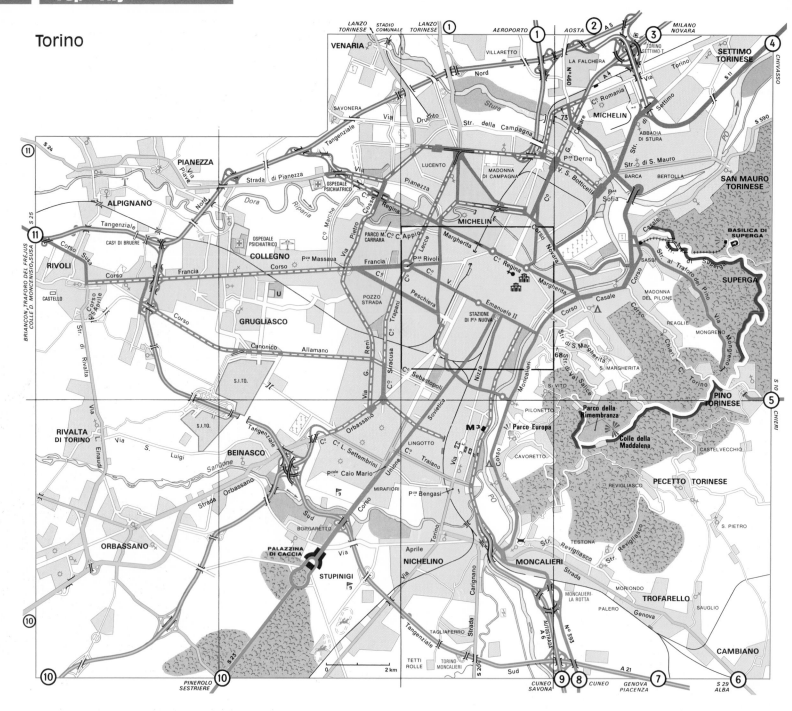

Teplice	53 E3	Ter, R.	32 B3	Teste, la	28 A2	Thann	27 E1	Thérmi	79 F3	Thillot, le	27 E1	Thouarcé	24 C2
Tepsa	95 E4	Terracina	63 F3	Tetbury	9 E2	Thannhausen	55 E3	Thermi	85 F2	Thimariá	81 F2	Thouars	24 C3
Teramo	63 F1	Terra de Basto	34 B4	Teteriv	113 E2	Thaon	27 D1	Thermissía	87 E2	Thimena	89 E2	Thouet	24 C2
Ter Apel	17 E1	Terradets, Emb		Teterow	49 D2	Tharandt	53 E2	Thérmo	83 D4	Thimena, N.	89 E2	Thouría	86 C3
Tera, R.	35 D3	dels	37 F3	Tetica	44 B3	Tharsis	42 C2	Thermopiles	83 E3	Thini, Akr	87 E2	Thoúrio	81 F1
Terebovlja	113 D3	Terråk	97 D4	Tetiïv	113 E2	Thássos	80 C3	Thérouanne	19 F1	Thionville	21 D3	Thráki	81 E2
Terena	38 C4	Terralba	66 B3	Tetovo	77 D3	Thássos, N	81 D3	Thespiés	83 F4	Thira	91 E1	Thrakikó
Terespol	112 C1	Terranova di		Tetrákomo	82 C2	Thatē, Mal i	77 D4	Thesprotía	82 B2	Thíra, N.	91 E1	Pélagos	81 D3
Terezino Polje	71 E2	Pollino	67 E2	Tettnang	55 D4	Thau, Bessin de	30 A4	Thesprotikó	82 B2	Thirassía, N	91 E1	Thrapston	9 F1
Terges, Rib de	42 B2	Terranuova Braccio		Teuchern	53 D2	Thaya	57 F1	Thessalía	83 E2	Thirsk	7 D1	Threshfield	6 C1
Tergnier	20 A2	lini	61 D4	Teufen	58 B2	Thégonnec	22 B2	Thessaloníki	79 F3	Thisted	108 A2	Thueyts	30 B2
Terjärv	102 C2	Terras de Bouro	34 A3	Teulada	66 B4	Theil, le	23 F3	Thessaloníki		Thíva	84 A4	Thuile, la	27 E4
Terlizzi	65 D3	Terrassa	32 A4	Teupitz	53 E1	Themar	52 C2	(Nomos)	80 A3	Thiviers	28 C1	Thuin	50 B4
Termas de		Terrasson-la-		Teuva	102 B3	Thenon	29 D2	Thetford	11 D1	Thizy	26 B4	Thuir	32 B2
Monfortinho	39 D2	Villedieu	29 D2	Tevere	63 E2	Theológos (Stereá		Theux	51 D4	Thoissey	26 C4	Thum	53 E3
Terme Luigiane	67 E2	Terrenoire	30 B1	Teviot	5 D3	Eláda)	83 F3	The Wash	7 E3	Tholen	16 B3	Thun	27 E3
Termini Imerese	68 B3	Terriente	41 D2	Tewkesbury	9 E2	Thèze	28 B4	Thèze	31 D3	Tholey	54 B1	Thur	58 A1
Terminillo	63 F2	Terschelling	16 C1	Texel	16 C1	Theológos		Thézenay	24 C3	Thollon	27 E3	Thüringen	58 B2
Terminillo, Mte	63 F2	Teruel	41 D2	Thabor, Mt	31 D1	(Thássos)	80 C3	Thiamis	82 B1	Tholó	86 C2	Thüringen (Land)	52 C3
Termoli	64 B2	Tervakoski	107 E2	Thale	52 C2	Théoule	31 E4	Thiaucourt	21 D3	Tholopotámi	85 E4	Thüringer Wald	52 B3
Terneuzen	16 B4	Tervo	103 D2	Thalfang	54 B1	Thérain	19 F3	Thiberville	19 D3	Thólos	80 B2	Thurles	14 C3
Terni	63 E2	Tervola	99 D2	Thalgau	56 C3	Thérma (Ikaría)	89 D2	Thiéblemont-		Thomastown	15 D3	Thurn, Paß	59 E1
Ternitz	57 E3	Tervuren	50 C3	Thalheim	53 E3	Thermá		Farémont	20 C4	Thônes	27 D4	Thursby	5 D4
Ternopil'	113 D2	Terzaga	40 C2	Thalmässing	55 F2	(Makedonía)	80 B2	Thiendorf	53 E2	Thonon	27 D3	Thurso	3 D2
Těrovo	82 C2	Tešanj	71 E3	Thalwil	58 A2	Thérma		Thiene	59 D4	Thorens-Glières	27 D4	Thury-Harcourt	18 C3
Térpilos	80 A2	Teslić	71 E3	Thame	9 F2	(Samothráki)	81 E3	Thiers	26 B4	Thorikó	88 A2	Thusis	58 B3
Terpní	80 B2	Tessin	48 C2	Thames, R.	11 D2	Thermaïkós		Thiesi	66 B2	Thorne	7 D2	Thy	108 A2
Terpsithéa	83 D4	Tessy	18 C3	Thanes, K e	76 C4	Kólpos	80 A4	Thérma Lefkádas	89 D2	Thiessow	49 D1	Thornhill	4 C3	Thyborøn	108 A2

Tibro 109 D1
Tichvin 111 E1
Ticino 60 A1
Ticino R 58 A3
Tidaholm 109 D1
Tidö 106 A3
Tiefenbronn 54 C2
Tiefencastel 58 B3
Tiefensee 49 E4
Tiel 16 C3
Tielt 50 A3
Tienen 50 C3
Tiengen 54 C4
Tierbmesvarri 94 C3
Tiercé 23 E4
Tierga 36 C3
Tierp 106 B3
Tiétar, R 39 E2
Tigharry 2 A3
Tighnabruaich 4 B2
Tignes 31 D1
Tignes, Bge de 31 E1
Tiheró 81 F2
Tihio 79 D3
Tihuţa 113 D4
Tiilikkajärvi 103 E1
Tiistenjoki 102 C2
Tijesno 74 C1
Tijola 44 B3
Tikkakoski 103 D3
Tikkala 103 F2
Tikveš, Ez 77 E3
Tilburg 16 C3
Tilbury 10 C2
Tilissos 91 D3
Tillberga 106 A3
Tillières 19 E4
Tilly-sur-Seulles 18 C3
Tilsit 110 B3
Tilos, N 89 F4
Timanfaya, Parque
   Nac. de 42 C3
Timbáki 91 D4
Timbano 81 D2
Timfi, Óros 78 C4
Timfristós 83 D3
Timfristós Mt 83 D3
Timiş 114 C1
Timişoara 114 C1
Timmelsjoch 58 C2
Timmendorfer
   Strand 48 B2
Timok 73 F3
Timoleague 14 B4
Timrå 101 F3
Timv. Peristéria 86 C3
Tinahely 13 D4
Tinchebray 18 C4
Tindari 69 D2
Tinée 31 E3
Tineo 35 D1
Tingáki 89 F3
Tinglev 108 A4
Tingsryd 109 E2
Tingvoll 100 B2
Tingvollfjorden 100 B2
Tinja 71 F3
Tinn 104 C3
Tinnsj 104 C3
Tinos 88 C2
Tiñosillos 39 F1
Tinos, N 88 C2
Tiñoso, C 45 D3
Tintagel 8 B3
Tinténiac 23 D3
Tinto, R 42 C2
Tiobraid Árann 14 C3
Tione di Trento 58 C3
Tipasoja 103 E1
Tipperary 14 C3
Tipperary (Co) 12 C4
Tiranë 76 C4
Tirano 58 C3
Tiraspol' 113 E3
Tire 115 F4
Tiree 2 A4
Tirgo-Neamt 113 D4
Tirgovişte 115 D1
Tîrgu Frumos 113 E3
Tîrgu Jiu 114 C1
Tîrgu Mureş 113 D4
Tîrgu Secuiesc 113 D4
Tirig 41 F2
Tirintha 87 D2

Tiriolo 67 F3
Tirnavos 83 E1
Tirol 58 C2
Tirós 87 D3
Tirrenia 60 C4
Tirreno, Mare 68 B2
Tirschenreuth 53 D4
Tirso 66 B2
Tirstrup 108 B3
Tirteafuera, R. 39 F4
Tisa 72 C2
Tiscar, Pto de 44 B2
Tisnaren 105 F4
Tišnov 57 E1
Tisvildeleje 108 C3
Tisza 112 B4
Tiszafüred 112 B4
Tiszavasvári 112 C3
Titaguas 41 D3
Titaríssios 83 E1
Titel 72 C2
Titisee 54 C4
Titlis 58 A3
Tito 64 C4
Titova Korenica 70 C4
Titov Drvar 71 D4
Titov Veles 77 E3
Titov vrh 77 D3
Titran 100 B1
Tittmoning 56 B3
Tiumpan Head 2 B2
Tivat 76 B3
Tiveden 105 E4
Tivenys 41 F2
Tiverton 8 C3
Tivissa 41 F1
Tivoli 63 E2
Tjaktjajaure 98 A2
Tjällmo 105 F4
Tjeggelvas 98 A2
Tjeldøya 94 B3
Tjeldstø 104 A2
Tjentište 76 A1
Tjøme 104 C4
Tjong 97 E2
Tjørnuvik 96 A3
Tjøtta 97 D3
Tkon 74 C1
Tobarra 44 C1
Tobercurry 12 C2
Tobermore 13 D2
Tobermory 2 B4
Toberonochy 4 B1
Toblach 59 E2
Toce 58 A3
Tocha 38 B2
Tocina 43 D2
Todi 63 E1
Todmorden 6 C2
Todorići 71 E4
Todtmoos 54 C4
Todtnau 54 C4
Toe Head (GB) 2 A2
Toe Head (IRL) 14 B4
Töfsingdalen 101 D3
Toft 3 F1
Tofte 104 C3
Toftir 96 A4
Toftlund 108 A4
Tohmajärvi 103 F2
Toholampi 102 C1
Toijala 107 E2
Toivakka 103 D3
Toivala 103 E2
Tojšici 72 B3
Tok 53 F4
Tokaj 112 C3
Toledo 40 A3
Toledo, Mts de 40 A3
Tolentino 61 F4
Tolfa 63 D2
Tolga 100 C3
Tollarp 109 D3
Tollense 49 D2
Tølløse 108 C3
Tolmezzo 59 E3
Tolmin 70 A2
Toló 87 D2
Tolosa (E) 36 C1
Tolosa (P) 38 C3
Tolox 43 E4
Tolva 99 E2
Tolve 65 D4
Tomar 38 B3

Tomaševac 73 D2
Tomaševo 76 B2
Tomašica 71 D3
Tomaszów
   Lubelski 112 C2
Tomaszów
   Mazowiecki 112 B2
Tombebœuf 28 C3
Tomelilla 109 D3
Tomelloso 40 B4
Tomiño 34 A3

Tomintoul 3 D4
Tomma 97 D2
Tømmervåg 100 B2
Tomra 100 B2
Tomtabacken 109 D2
Tona 32 B3
Tonale, Pso del 58 C3
Tonara 66 B3
Tonbridge 10 C3
Tondela 38 B1
Tønder 108 A4
Tongeren 50 C3
Tongue 2 C2
Tonnay-
   Boutonne 24 C4
Tonnay-Charente 24 C4
Tonneins 28 C3
Tonnerre 26 B1
Tönning 47 F2
Tønsberg 104 C3
Tonstad 104 B4
Töpen 53 D3
Topeno 107 E2

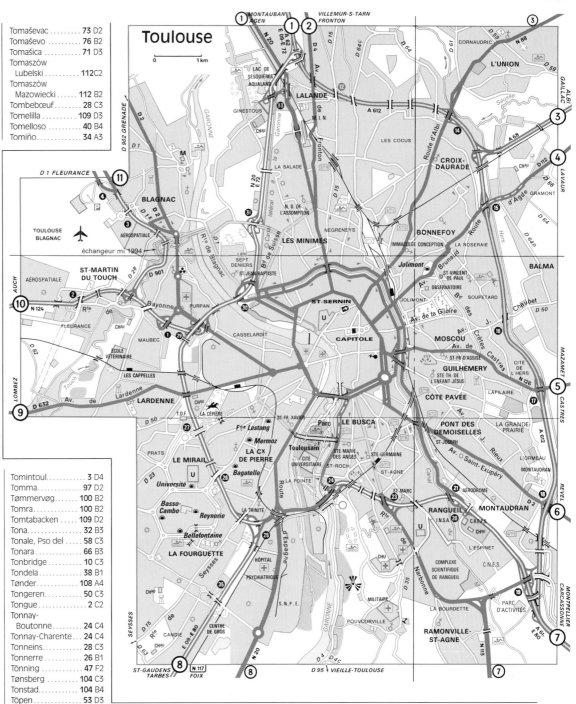

Toulouse

Topla 70 B1
Toplica 77 D1
Topli Do 73 F4
Topliţa 113 D4
Toploú 91 F4
Topola 73 D3
Topolčani 77 E3
Topol'čany 112 B3
Topólia 90 B3
Topolovnik 73 E3
Topusko 70 C3
Torà de
   Riubregòs 32 A3
Torano Castello 67 E2
Torbay 8 C4
Torbole 58 C4
Torcello 61 D1
Torchiarolo 65 F3
Tordera 32 B4
Tordesillas 35 E4
Tordesilos 41 D2
Tore 2 C3
Töre 98 C3
Töreboda 105 E4
Torella d. Sannio 64 B3
Toreno 34 C2
Torgau 53 E2
Torgelow 49 E2
Torhout 50 A3

Torigni 18 C3
Torija 40 B2
Torino 31 E1
Torio, R. 35 D2
Torla 37 E2
Törmänen 95 F3
Törmänmäki 99 E4
Tormes, R 39 E4
Tormos 37 D3
Tornavacas 39 E2
Tornavacas, Pto de . 39 E2
Torneälven 94 C4
Torneträsk 94 C3
Tornik 76 B1
Tornio 98 C3
Tornionjoki 98 C3
Tornjoš 72 C1
Törökszentmiklós . 112 B4
Toro, Monte 45 F1
Toróni 80 B4
Toropec 111 E2
Torpo 104 C2
Torpoint 8 C4
Torpshammar 101 F3
Torquay 8 C4
Torquemada 35 F3
Torralba de
   Calatrava 40 A4

Torrão 42 B1
Torre 38 C2
Torre Annunziata 64 B4
Torrebaja 41 D3
Torre Beretti 60 A2
Torreblanca 41 F3
Torrecaballeros 40 A1
Torrecampo 43 F1
Torre Canne 65 E3
Torrecilla 43 E4
Torrecilla en
   Cameros 36 B2
Torrecillas de la
   Tiesa 39 E3
Torre de Abraham,
   Emb de 40 A3
Torre de D. Chama . 34 C4
Torre de
   Embesora 41 E2
Torre de Juan
   Abad 44 B1
Torre del Aguila,
   Emb de 43 D3
Torre de la
   Higuera 42 C3
Torre del Bierzo 35 D2
Torre del Campo 44 A2
Torre del Greco 64 B4
Torre del Mar 43 F4

Torredembarra 37 F4
Torre de
   Moncorvo 34 C4
Torre de Passeri 64 A2
Torre d. Impiso 68 A3
Torredonjimeno 43 F2
Torre Faro 69 D2
Torre Grande 66 A3
Torregrossa 37 F4
Torreira 38 B1
Torrejoncillo 39 D2
Torrejoncillo del
   Rey 40 C3
Torrejón de Ardoz . 40 B2
Torrejón de la
   Calzada 40 A2
Torrejón el Rubio 39 E3
Torrejón-Tajo, Emb
   de 39 E3
Torre la Carcel 41 D2
Torrelaguna 40 B1
Torrelapaja 36 C3
Torrelavega 35 F2
Torrellano 45 E2
Torrelobatón 35 E4
Torrelodones 40 A2
Torremaggiore 64 B2
Torremegía 39 D4
Torre Mileto 64 C2

Torre Miró, Pto de . 41 E2
Torremocha 39 D3
Torremolinos 43 F4
Torrent 41 E4
Torrente de
   Cinca 37 E4
Torrenueva 44 B1
Torre Orsáia 67 D1
Torre-Pacheco 45 D2
Torre Pellice 31 E2
Torreperogil 44 B2
Torres del Rio 36 B2
Torres Novas 38 B3
Torres Vedras 38 A3
Torrevieja 45 D2
Torrico de San
   Pedro 38 C3
Torri del Benaco 60 C1
Torridon 2 B3
Torridon, L 2 B3
Torriglia 60 A3
Torrijas 41 D3
Torrijo 36 C4
Torrijos 40 A3
Tørring 108 A3
Torrita di Siena 61 D4
Torroella de
   Montgri 32 C3
Torröjen 101 D1

Unari L 99 D1	Unstrut 52 C2	Urbasa, Sa de 36 C2	Urnäsch 58 B2	Uskoplje 76 A2	Usťužna 111 F1	Utting 56 A3
Uncastillo 37 D2	Unterach 56 C3	Urbe 60 A3	Urnes 100 B3	Üsküdar 115 F3	Utajärvi 99 D4	Uttoxeter 6 C3
Unden 105 E4	Unterhaching 56 A3	Urbino 61 E3	Uroševac 77 D2	Uslar 52 B2	Utåker 104 A3	Uudenmaan
Undersåker 101 D2	Unter-	Urbión, Sa de 36 B3	Urovica 73 F3	Ussat-les-Bains 32 A2	Utbjoa 104 A3	Lääni 107 F2
Undredal 104 B2	Schleissheim 55 F3	Urdos 37 D2	Urquiola, Pto 36 B1	Ussé 25 D2	Utebo 37 D2	Uukuniemi 103 E3
Uneča 111 F4	Unterwalden 27 F3	Ure 6 C1	Urshult 109 D3	Usseglio 31 E1	Utelle 31 E3	Uurainen 103 D2
Unešić 75 D1	Unterwasser 58 B2	Uredakke 97 E4	Ursprungpaß 59 D1	Ussel 29 E1	Utena 110 C3	Uusikaarlepyy 102 B2
Úněšov 53 E4	Unterweißenbach 57 D2	Urepel 36 C1	Urtivaara 95 D3	Usseln 17 F4	Utiel 41 D3	Uusikaupunki 107 D2
Ungheni 113 E3	Upavon 9 E3	Urfahr 57 D2	Ururi 64 B2	Ustaoset 104 B2	Utne 104 B2	Uvac 76 B1
Ungilde 34 C3	Upinniemi 107 E3	Urfeld 56 A4	Ury 25 F1	Ustaritz 28 A4	Utrecht 16 C3	Uvac R 76 B1
Unhais da Serra 38 C2	Upper L Erne 13 D2	Urho Kekkosen	Urziceni 115 E1	Uster 58 A2	Utrecht (Prov) 16 C3	Uvdal 104 C2
Unhošt 53 F4	Uppingham 9 F1	kansallispuisto 95 F3	Usagre 43 D1	Ustevatn 104 B2	Utrera 43 D3	Uzdin 72 C2
Unije 70 B4	Upplands-Väsby 106 B3	Uri (CH) 58 A3	Uşak 115 F4	Ustibar 76 B1	Utrillas 41 E2	Uzel 22 C3
Universales, Mts 41 D2	Uppsala 106 B3	Uri (I) 66 A2	Uše 73 D4	Ustica, I di 68 B2	Utsjoki 95 E2	Uzerche 29 D1
Unna 17 E3	Uppsala Län 106 B3	Uriage 30 C1	Usedom 49 E2	Ustikolina 76 A1	Utsjoki R. 95 E2	Uzès 30 B3
Unnaryd 109 D2	Upton 9 E1	Urjala 107 E2	Usedom I. 49 E1	Ústí nad Labem 53 F3	Uttendorf	Užhorod 112 C3
Unnukka 103 E2	Uras 66 B3	Urk 16 C2	Usingen 51 F4	Ustiprača 76 B1	(Oberösterreich) 56 C3	Uzice 72 C4
Unquera 35 F1	Urbania 61 E3	Urla 115 E4	Usk 9 D2	Ustka 110 A4	Uttendorf	Uzyn 113 E2
Unst 3 F1	Urbasa, Pto de 36 C2	Urlingford 14 C3	Usk R. 9 D2	Ustronie Morskie 49 F1	(Salzburg) 59 E1	Uzunköprü 115 E3

V

Vä 109 D3	Valax 107 F2	Valdelacasa de	Valdobbiadene 59 D3	Valenciennes 20 A1	Valko 107 F2	Valloire 31 D1
Vaajakoski 103 D3	Valberg 31 E3	Tajo 39 E3	Valdosa 36 A3	Valensole 31 D3	Valladolid 35 E4	Vallombrosa 61 D3
Vääkiö 99 E3	Vålberg 105 E3	Valdelinares 41 E2	Valdres 104 C2	Valentano 63 D2	Vallata 64 C3	Vallon-en-Sully 25 F3
Vaala 99 E4	Valbiska 70 B3	Valdemarsvik 109 E1	Valdres Flya 100 B3	Valentigney 27 E2	Vallbo 101 D2	Vallon-Pont-d'arc 30 B3
Vaalajärvi 95 E4	Valbo 106 B2	Valdemeca 41 D2	Vale de Açor 42 B2	Valenza 60 A2	Valldal 100 B2	Vallorbe 27 D3
Vaalimaa 103 F4	Valbondione 58 B3	Valdemorillo 40 A2	Vale de Cambra 38 B1	Våler (Hedmark) 105 D2	Vall d'Alba 41 E3	Vallorcine 27 E4
Vaals 51 D3	Valbonë 76 C2	Valdemoro 40 A2	Vale de Estrela 38 C2	Våler (Østfold) 105 D3	Valldemossa 45 E2	Valls 37 F4
Vaaraslahti 103 D2	Valbonnais 31 D2	Valdenoceda 36 A2	Vale de Prazeres 38 C2	Valeria 40 C3	Vall de Uxó 41 E3	Vallsta 101 F4
Vaasa 102 B2	Val Camonica 58 C4	Valdeobispo, Emb	Vale, Emb de 37 F2	Valevåg 104 A3	Valle 104 B2	Valmiera 110 C2
Vaasan Lääni 102 C2	Valcarlos 36 C1	de 39 D2	Valeggio sul	Valfabbrica 61 E4	Valleberga 109 D4	Valmojado 40 A2
Vaassen 17 D2	Valdagno 59 D4	Valdepeñas 44 A1	Mincio 60 C1	Valga 110 C2	Valle Castellana 63 F1	Valmont 19 D2
Vabre 32 B1	Valdahon 27 D2	Valdepeñas da	Valença do Minho 34 A3	Val Gardena 59 D3	Valle d'Aosta 27 E4	Valmontone 63 F3
Vác 112 B4	Valdaj 111 E1	Jaén 44 A2	Valençay 25 E2	Valgorge 30 B2	Valle de Abdalajis 43 E3	Valogne 18 B3
Vaccarès, Etang	Valdajskaja	Valderaduey, R 35 D4	Valence-	Valgrisenche 31 E1	Valle de la Serena 39 E4	Valongo 34 A4
de 30 B4	Vozvyšennosť 111 E2	Valderas 35 E3	d'Albigeois 29 E3	Valguarnera	Valle de los Caidos 40 A2	Valoria la Buena 35 E4
Vacha 52 B3	Valdavia, R. 35 E3	Val de Reuil 19 E3	Valence (Drôme) 30 C2	Caropepe 68 C3	Valle de	Valpaços 34 b4
Väddö 106 B3	Valdeazogues, R. 43 F1	Valderiès 29 E3	Valence (Gers) 28 C3	Valhelhas 38 C2	Matamoros 42 C1	Valpalmas 37 D3
Vadehavet 108 A4	Valdecaballeros 39 E4	Valderøy 100 A2	Valencia 41 E4	Valico della	Vallehermoso 42 A4	Val Passiria 59 D2
Vadheim 100 A3	Valdecabras 40 C3	Valderrepisa, Pto	Valencia (Prov) 41 D4	Forchetta 64 A2	Vallejera, Pto de 39 E2	Valpovo 71 F2
Vado Ligure 60 A3	Valdecañas, Emb	de 43 F1	Valencia de	Valimitika 83 E4	Valle-Mosso 31 F1	Valprato Soana 31 E1
Vadsø 95 F1	de 39 E3	Valderrobres 41 F2	Alcántara 38 C3	Valira 86 C3	Vallentuna 106 B3	Valras-Plage 30 A4
Vadstena 109 D1	Valdecarros 39 E1	Valdestillas 35 E4	Valencia de Don	Valjevo 72 C3	Valleraugue 29 F3	Valréas 30 C3
Vaduz 58 B2	Valdecebollas 35 F2	Valdeverdeja 39 E3	Juan 35 D3	Valjok 95 E2	Vallet 24 B2	Valsamónero 91 D4
Vadvetjåkka 94 B3	Valdediós 35 E1	Valdevimbre 35 D3	Valencia de las	Valjunquera 41 F1	Valletta 68 B4	Valsavarenche 31 E1
Vaféika 81 E2	Valdeganga 41 D4	Valdezcaray 36 B2	Torres 43 D1	Valkeakoski 107 E2	Vallgrund 102 B2	Valserine 27 D4
Vafiohóri 79 F2	Valdeinfierno, Emb	Valdieri 31 E3	Valencia del	Valkeala 107 F2	Valli di Comacchio 61 D2	Valset 100 C1
Vågaholmen 97 E2	de 44 C2	Valdihuela 39 F2	Ventoso 43 D1	Valkenburg 51 D3	Vallø 108 C3	Valsjöbyn 101 E1
Vågåmo 100 B3		Val-d'Isère 31 D1	Valencia I 14 A4	Valkenswaard 16 C4	Vallo della Lucania 67 D1	
Vågan 97 E1						
Vaganj 75 E1						
Vaganski vrh 70 C4						
Vágar 96 A3						
Våge 104 A2						
Væggerløse 108 C4						
Vaggeryd 109 D2						
Vágia 83 F4						
Vagioniá 91 D4						
Vagnhärad 106 B4						
Vagos 38 B1						
Vågsfjorden 94 B3						
Vågsøy 100 A3						
Vágur 96 A4						
Váh 112 B3						
Vähäkyrö 102 B2						
Vahto 107 D2						
Vái 91 F3						
Vaiano 60 C3						
Vaiges 23 E3						
Vaihingen 55 D2						
Vailly (Aisne) 20 A3						
Vailly (Cher) 26 A2						
Vainikkala 103 F4						
Vaisaluokta 94 B4						
Vaison-la-						
Romaine 30 C3						
Vaksdal 104 A2						
Vålådalen 101 D2						
Valadares 34 A4						
Valais 27 E4						
Valalta 70 A3						
Valamen 103 E2						
Valandovo 77 F3						
Val-Andrè, le 22 C2						
Valareña 36 C3						
Valašské Meziříčí 112 B3						

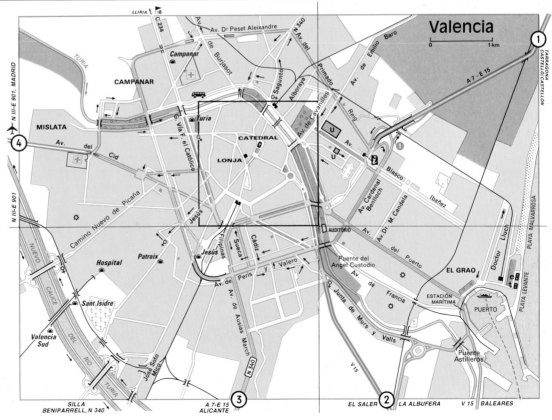

Valencia

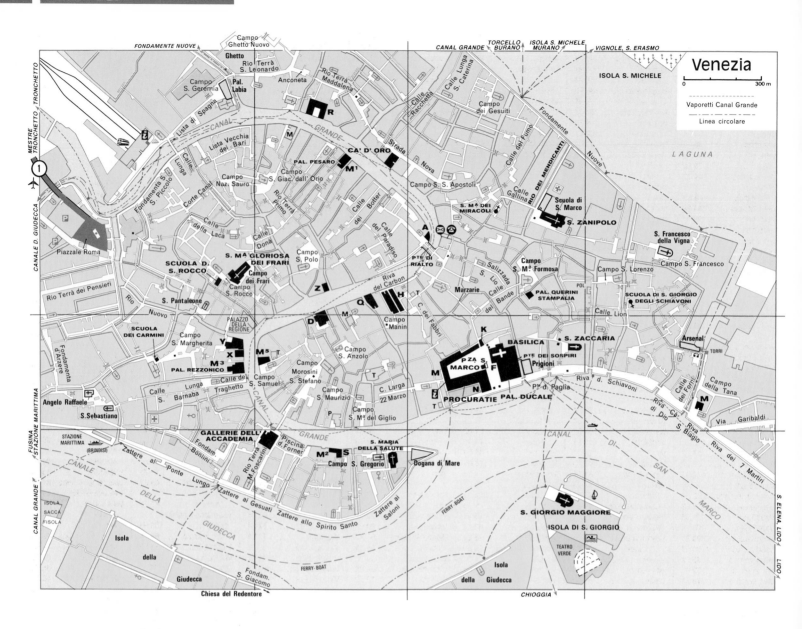

Vals-les-Bains........ 30 B2	Vandellòs........... 41 F1	Varazze........... 60 A3	Värmlands Län 105 E3	Vassiliká
Valtellina 58 B3	Vänern 105 E4	Varberg 108 C2	Varmo........ 59 E3	(Makedonía)...... 80 A3
Valtessiniko........ 86 C2	Vänersborg 108 C1	Vårbica 115 E2	Varna (BG)...... 115 E2	Vathilakos
Val-Thorens 31 D1	Vangshylla 101 D1	Varda 72 C4	Varna (Srbija) .. 72 C3	(Thessaloníki).. 79 F3
Valtierra 36 C3	Vangsnes 104 B1	Vårda 86 B1	Varnamo 109 D2	Vathípetro 91 D4
Valtimo 103 E1	Vangsvik 94 B3	Vardar 77 E3	Varnhem 109 D1	Vathís 89 F3
Váltos 81 F1	Vanha Vaasa.. 102 B2	Varde 108 A3	Varnsdorf 53 F2	Vatin 73 D2
Valtotópi 80 B2	Vanna 94 C2	Vardenik 77 E2	Värö 108 C2	Vega de
Váltou, Óri 82 C2	Vännäs 102 A1	Vardø 95 F1	Varoš Selo 77 D2	Espinareda....... 34 C2
Valtournenche ... 27 F4	Vannavålen 94 C2	Vårdö 106 C3	Varpaisjärvi .. 103 E1	Vegadeo......... 34 C1
Valun 70 B4	Vannes 22 C4	Vardoússia, Óri .. 83 D3	Várpalota 112 B4	Vega de Valcarce .. 34 C2
Valvasone 59 E3	Vannsjø 105 D3	Varel 47 F3	Värriötunturit .. 95 F4	Vegafjorden....... 97 D3
Valverde (Is	Vannsundet 94 C2	Vareleli 84 C4	Vars 31 D2	Vegarienza 35 D2
Canarias) 42 A4	Vanoise, Massif de	Varengeville 19 D2	Vars, Col de 31 D2	Vegårshei 104 C4
Valverde (La Rioja) .. 36 C3	la 31 D1	Varenna 58 B4	Vartdalsfjorden .. 100 A2	Vegas 35 E2
Valverde del	Vanoise, Parc Nat	Varennes-en-	Vartholomió 20 .. 86 B1	Vegas del
Camino 42 C2	de la 31 D1	Argonne 20 C3	Vartius 99 F4	Condado 35 E2
Valverde de	Vansbro 105 E2	Varennes-sur-	Värtsilä 103 F2	Vegesack 47 F3
Leganés........ 38 C4	Vans, les 30 B3	Allier 26 A4	Västerdalälven .. 101 D4	Veghel 16 C3
Valverde del	Vantaa 107 E2	Varennes-sur-	Väster Haninge.. 106 B4	Vegoritída, L. .. 79 E3
Fresno......... 39 D2	Vanttauskoski .. 99 D2	Amance 26 C1	Västernorrlands	Vehkalahti 103 F4
Valverde del Júcar .. 40 C3	Vaour 29 D3	Vareš 71 F4	Län 101 F2	Vehmaa 101 D4
Valøya 97 D4	Vaqueira 37 F2	Varese 58 A4	Västervik 109 E1	Vehmersalmi .. 103 E2
Våmb 109 D1	Var 31 D4	Varese Ligure .. 60 B3	Västmanlands	Veidnesklubben .. 95 E1
Våmhus 101 E4	Vara 108 C1	Vårgårda 108 C1	Län 105 F3	Veikkola 107 E2
Vamlingbo 109 F4	Varades 23 E4	Vargas 35 F2	Våvdos 80 A3	Veines 95 F1
Vammala 107 D1	Varallo 58 A4	Vargsund 95 D1	Växjö 109 D2	Veinge 108 C2
Vampula 107 D2	Varangerbotn .. 95 F1	Varhaug 104 A4	Våxtorp 108 C3	Vejen 108 A3
Vamvakás, Akr .. 85 F4	Varangerfjorden .. 95 F1	Varimbómbi .. 87 F1	Vayrac......... 29 D2	Vejer de la
Vamvakoú	Varangerhalvøya.. 95 F1	Váris 79 D4	V'az'ma 111 F3	Frontera 43 D4
(Pelopónissos) .. 87 D3	Varano de'	Varilhes 32 A2	Vaterá 85 F3	Vejle 108 A3
Vamvakoú	Melegari 60 B2	Varís 79 D4	Vateró 79 D4	Velada 39 F3
(Thessalía) ... 83 E2	Varano, L di 64 C2	Vássès 86 C2	Váthia 87 D4	Velagići....... 71 D4
Vanajavesi 107 E2	Varaždin 70 C1	Varkaus 103 E3	Vathi	Vela Luka 75 E2
Vanån 101 D4	Varaždinske	Várkiza 87 F2	(Dodekánissa) .. 84 B4	Velanídia 87 E4
Vanda 107 E2	Toplice 71 D1	Varmahlíð 96 B1	Váthi (Lefkáda) .. 79 F2	Velate, Pto de .. 36 C1
			Vathi (Makedonía) .. 92 C1	Velayos 39 F1
			Vathi (Stereá	Velbert 17 E4
			Eláda) 82 B3	
			Vassiliká (Évia) .. 84 A3	
			Vassiliká (Lésvos) .. 85 F2	

Velburg 55 F1
Velde 101 D1
Velden (A) 70 A1
Velden (München) . . 56 B3
Velden (Nürnberg) . . 55 F1
Veldhoven 16 C4
Velebit 70 C4
Velebitski kanal 70 B4
Velenje 70 B1
Velešta 77 D4
Velestino 83 F2
Veleta, Pico 44 A3
Velež 75 F2
Vélez Blanco 44 C2
Vélez de
  Benaudalla 44 A3
Vélez-Málaga 43 F3
Vélez Rubio 44 C2
Velfjorden 97 D3
Veličani 75 F2
Veliés 87 E4
Velika 71 E2
Velika Drenova 73 E4
Velika Gorica 70 C2
Velikaja 111 D2
Velika Jablanica . . . 76 C2
Velika Jamnička . . . 70 C2
Velika Kapela 70 B3
Velika Kladuša 70 C3
Velika Kopanica . . . 71 F3
Velika Kruša 77 D2
Velika Morava 73 D3
Velika Mučna 71 D1
Velika Plana
  (Morava) 73 D3
Velika Plana
  (Prokuplje) 77 D1
Velika Tresta 73 E3
Veliki Alan 70 B4
Veliki Bastaji 71 E2
Veliki Gaj 73 D2
Veliki Grddevac . . . 71 D2
Veliki Izvor 73 F3
Veliki Jastrebac 77 D1
Velikije Luki 111 E2
Veliki kanal 72 B2
Veliki Krš 73 E3
Veliki Popović 73 E3
Veliki Prolog 75 E2
Veliki Radinci 72 C2
Veliki Trnovac 77 E2
Veliki Vitao 76 A2
Veliki Zdenci 71 D2
Veliko Gradište 73 D2
Veliko Lašče 70 B2
Veliko Orašje 73 D3
Veliko Tărnovo 115 D2
Velilla del R Carrion . 35 E2
Veli Lošinj 70 B4
Velimlje 76 A2
Vélines 28 C2
Velingrad 115 D3
Velino 63 F2
Velino, Mte 63 F2
Veliž 111 E3
Veljun 70 C3
Velká Biteš 57 E1
Velké Meziříči 57 E1
Velkua 107 D2
Vellahn 48 B3
Velletri 63 E3
Vellinge 108 C3
Velopoúla 87 F3
Vélos 84 B4
Velpke 48 B4
Velten 49 D4
Velvendós 79 E4
Vemdalen 101 E3
Vemdalsskalet 101 E3
Vemhån 101 E3
Véna 81 E2
Venaco 33 F3
Venafro 64 A3
Venarey-les-
  Laumes 26 B2
Venaria 31 E1
Venčani 73 D3
Vence 31 E3
Venda Nova 34 B4
Vendas Novas 38 B4
Vendée 24 B3
Vendel 106 B3
Vendeuvre 26 B1
Vendôme 25 E2

Vendsyssel 108 B2
Veneheitto 99 D4
Veneta, Laguna 61 D1
Veneto 61 D1
Venezia 61 D1
Vengjaneset 104 A2
Venialbo 35 D4
Venjan 101 E4
Venjansjön 101 E4
Venlo 17 D4
Vennesla 104 B4
Vennesund 97 D3
Venosa 64 C3
Venosta 58 C3
Venray 17 D3
Venta 110 B3
Venta de Cruce 43 D3
Venta de Don
  Quijote 40 B3
Ventana, Pto de . . 35 D2
Venta Nueva 34 C2
Ventas de Huelma . . 44 A3
Ventimiglia 31 E3
Ventnor 9 E4
Ventotene, I. 63 F4
Ventoux, Mt. 30 C3
Ventspils 110 B2
Venturina 62 C1
Vera (E) 44 C3
Vera (N) 101 D1
Vera de Bidasoa . . . 36 C1
Verbania-Pallanza . . 58 A4
Verberie 19 F3
Verbicaro 67 E2
Verbier 27 E4
Vercelli 31 F1
Vercel-Villedieu . . . 27 D2
Verchnedvinsk . . . 111 D3
Verdalsøra 101 D1
Verde, Col de 33 F3
Verden 48 A4
Verdikoússa 83 D1
Verdon 31 D3
Verdon, le 28 A1
Verdun (Meuse) . . . 20 C3
Verdun (Saône-et-
  Loire) 26 C3
Verdun (Tarn-et-
  Garonne) 29 D3
Verfeil 29 D4
Vergato 60 C3
Vérgi 80 A2
Vergiate 60 A1
Vergina 79 E3
Vergio, Col de 33 F3
Vergt 28 C2
Véria 79 E3
Verin 34 B3
Verl 17 F3
Vermand 20 A2
Vermenton 26 B2
Vérmio, Óros 79 E3
Verna, Pzo di 69 D2
Vernet-les-Bains . . . 32 B2
Verneuil 19 D4
Vernon 19 E3
Vérno, Óros 79 D3
Vernoux-en-
  Vivarais 30 B2
Verny 21 D3
Veroli 63 F3
Verona 60 C1
Verpillière 30 C1
Verran 101 D1
Verrès 27 F4
Versailles 19 F4
Versmold 17 F2
Verteillac 28 C1
Vertiskos, Óros 80 A2
Vertus 20 B4
Verucchio 61 E3
Veruela 36 C3
Verviers 51 D4
Vervins 20 B2
Verzuolo 31 E2
Verzy 20 B3
Vesanto 103 D2
Veseli 57 D1
Vesijärvi 107 F2
Vesilahti 107 E1
Vesivehmaa 107 F2
Vesjegonsk 111 F1
Veskoniemi 95 F3

Vesle 20 B3
Vesoul 27 D2
Véssa 85 E4
Vest-Agder 104 B4
Vestby 105 D3
Vestbygda 104 A4
Vesterålen 94 A3
Vesterø Havn 108 B2
Vestertana 95 E1
Vestfjorden 97 E1
Vestfold 104 C3
Vestmanna 96 A3
Vestmannaeyjar . . . 96 B3
Vestnes 100 B2
Vestone 58 C4
Vestre Jakobselv . . . 95 F1
Vestvågøy 94 A4
Vesubie, Gorges de
  la 31 E3
Vesuvio 64 B4
Veszprém 112 B4
Veteli 102 C2
Veternica 77 E1
Vetlanda 109 E2
Vetralla 63 E2
Vetriolo Terme 59 D3
Vetschau 53 E1
Vettore, M. 63 F1
Veules-les-Roses . . 19 D2
Veulettes 19 D2
Veurne 50 A3
Vevey 27 E3
Vévi 79 D3
Veynes 30 C2
Veyre 29 F1
Veyrier 27 D4
Vezdemarbán 35 D4
Vézelay 26 B2
Vézelise 21 D4
Vézénobres 30 B3
Vézère 29 D2
Vézins-de-
  Lévézou 29 E3
Vezzani 33 F3
Vezzano 58 C3
Via Appia 63 E3
Via Aurelia 60 C4
Via Casilina 63 E2
Via Cassia 63 D1
Viadana 60 C2
Via Emilia 61 D3
Via Flaminia 61 E3
Viana 36 B2
Viana do Bolo 34 C3
Viana do Castelo . . 34 A4
Vianden 21 D2
Viano do Alentejo . . 42 B1
Viareggio 60 B3
Viar, R 43 D2
Vias 30 A4
Via Salaria 63 E2
Via Tiburtina
  Valeria 63 F2
Viaur 29 E3
Viborg 108 A2
Vibo Valentia 67 E3
Vibraye 23 F3
Vič 70 B1
Vic (E) 32 A3
Vic (F) 19 F3
Vicálvaro 40 B2
Vicdessos 37 F2
Vic-en-Bigorre 28 B4
Vicenza 59 D4
Vic-Fézensac 28 C4
Vich 32 A3
Vichy 26 A4
Vic-le-Comte 29 F1
Vico 33 E3
Vico del Gargano . . 64 C2
Vico Equense 64 B4
Vico, Lago di 63 E2
Vic-sur-Cère 29 E2
Victoria 68 B4
Vidå 108 A4
Vidago 34 B4
Viðareiði 96 A3
Vidauban 31 D4
Viddal 100 A3
Videbæk 108 A3
Vidiákhi 86 C1
Vidigueira 42 B1
Vidin 114 C2
Vídio, C. 35 D1

Viðoy 96 A3
Vidreres 32 B4
Vidrovan 76 B2
Vidsel 98 B3
Viduša 76 A2
Viechtach 56 B2
Viechtwang 56 C3
Vieira 38 A2
Vieira do Minho . . . 34 B4
Viejo, Pto. 39 D2
Viekinjärvi 103 F1
Vielha 37 F2
Vielle-Aure 37 E2
Vielmur 32 A1
Vielsalm 51 D4
Vienenburg 52 B1
Vienne 30 B1
Vienne (Dépt) 25 D3
Vienne R. 25 D4
Vieremä 103 D1
Viernheim 54 C1
Vierraden 49 E3
Viersen 17 D4
Vierumäki 107 F2
Vierzehnheiligen . . . 52 C4
Vierzon 25 F2
Vieste 64 C2
Vietas 94 B4
Vietri di Potenza . . . 64 C4
Vietri sul Mare 64 B4
Vieux-Boucau 28 A3
Vieux Chaillol 31 D2
Vif 30 C2
Vig 108 C3
Vigan, le 29 F3
Vigeland 104 B4
Vigeois 29 D1
Vigevano 60 A1
Viggiano 65 D4
Vigla 82 C2
Vigla, Akr. 91 D1
Vignale 31 F1
Vignanello 63 E2
Vignemale 37 E2
Vignes, les 29 F3
Vigneulles 21 D3
Vignola 60 C2
Vignole Borbera . . . 60 A2
Vignory 26 C1
Vigo 34 A3
Vigo di Fassa 59 D3
Vigone 31 E2
Vigonza 61 D1
Vigrestad 104 A4
Vihanti 99 D4
Vihiers 24 C2
Vihtavuori 103 D3
Vihteljärvi 102 C3
Vihti 107 E2
Viiala 107 E2
Viinijärvi 103 F2
Viipustunturit 95 E3
Viitasaari 103 D2
Vik (Aust-Agder) . . 104 B4
Vik (IS) 96 B3
Vik (Nordland) 97 D3
Vik (Sogn og
  Fjordane) 104 B1
Vika 105 F2
Vikajärvi 99 D2
Vikanes 104 A2
Vikebukt 100 B2
Vikedal 104 A3
Vikersund 104 C3
Vikeså 104 A4
Vikevåg 104 A3
Vikingstad 106 A4
Vikna 97 D4
Vikoč 76 A1
Vikran 94 B2
Viksdalen 100 A3
Viksjö 101 F2
Viksjøfjell 95 F2
Viksta 106 B3
Vila Boim 38 C4
Vilada 32 A3
Viladamat 32 B3
Vila de Cruces 34 B2
Vila de Rei 38 B3
Vila do Bispo 42 A2
Vila do Conde 34 A4
Viladrau 32 B3
Vilafamès 41 E3
Vila Fernando 38 C4

Vila Flor 34 C4
Vila Franca das
  Naves 38 C1
Vilafranca del
  Penedès 32 A4
Vila Franca de Xira . 38 A4
Vila Fresca de
  Azeitão 38 A4
Vilagarcia de
  Arosa 34 A2
Vilaine 22 C4
Vilaller 37 F2
Vilamarxant 41 E3
Vilán, C. 34 A1
Vilanova 34 C1
Vila Nova da
  Barquinha 38 B3
Vilanova d'
  Alcolea 41 F3
Vilanova de.
  Arousa 34 A2
Vila Nova de
  Cerveira 34 A3
Vila Nova de
  Famalicão 34 A4
Vila Nova de Foz
  Côa 39 D1
Vila Nova de Gaia . . 34 A4
Vila Nova de
  Milfontes 42 A2
Vila Nova de
  Ourém 38 B3
Vila Nova de Paiva . 38 C1
Vila Nova de
  Poiares 38 B2
Vilanova de Sau . . . 32 B3
Vilanova i la Geltrú . 32 A4
Vila Pouca de
  Aguiar 34 B3
Vila Praia de
  Âncora 34 A3
Vilar de Barrio 34 B3
Vilar de Barrio 34 B3
Vilar Real 34 B4
Vila-réal 41 E3
Vila Real de Santo
  António 42 B3
Vila-rodona 37 F4
Vila-seca 37 F4
Vila Velha de
  Ródão 38 C3
Vila Verde 34 A3
Vila Verde de
  Ficalho 42 C1
Vila Verde de Raia . 34 B3
Vila Viçosa 38 C4
Vilches 44 A2
Vilejka 111 D4
Vilhelmina 97 F4
Vilia 87 E1
Viljakkala 102 C3
Viljandi 110 C1
Vilkaviškis 110 C4
Villa Adriana 63 E2
Villa Bartolomea . . 60 C1
Villablanca 42 C3
Villablino 35 D2
Villabona 36 C1
Villabrágima 35 E4
Villabuena del
  Puente 35 D4
Villacañas 40 B3
Villacarriedo 35 F2
Villacarrillo 44 B2
Villacastin 40 A1
Villach 59 F2
Villacidro 66 B4
Villada 35 E3
Villa del Prado 40 A2
Villa del Río 43 F2
Villadiego 35 F3
Villadossola 27 F4
Villaescusa de Haro . 40 C4
Villafáfila 35 D4
Villaflores 39 F1
Villafranca 36 C2
Villafranca del
  Bierzo 34 C2
Villafranca del Cid . 41 E2
Villafranca de los
  Barros 43 D1
Villafranca de los
  Caballeros 40 B3
Villafranca di
  Verona 60 C1

Villafranca in
  Lunigiana 60 B3
Villafranca-Montes
  de Oca 36 A2
Villafranca
  Piemonte 31 E2
Villafranca Tirrena . 69 D2
Villafranco del
  Guadalquivir 43 D3
Villafrati 68 B3
Villafrechos 35 E4
Villafruela 35 F4
Villafuerte 35 F4
Villagarcia del
  Llano 40 C4
Villager 35 D2
Villaggio Mancuso . 67 F3
Villagonzalo 39 D4
Villaharta 43 E1
Villahermosa 44 B1
Villahoz 35 F3
Villaines-la-Juhel . . 23 E3
Villajoyosa 45 E1
Villala 103 F3
Villalba 34 B1
Villalba de Guardo . 35 E2
Villalba de la Sierra . 40 C2
Villalba de los
  Barros 43 D1
Villalba del Rey . . . 40 C2
Villalcampo, Emb
  de 35 D4
Villalcázar de Sirga . 35 E3
Villalenga 36 C3
Villa Literno 64 A4
Villalón de
  Campos 35 E3
Villalonga 45 E1
Villalpando 35 E4
Villalpardo 41 D4
Villamañán 35 D3
Villamanrique 44 B1
Villamartín
  (Andalucía) 43 D3
Villamartín (Castilla-
  León) 35 E3
Villamassargia 66 B4
Villamayor 37 D3
Villamayor de
  Campos 35 E3
Villamayor de
  Santiago 40 B3
Villameca, Emb de . 35 D2
Villa Minozzo 60 C3
Villandraut 28 B3
Villandry 25 D2
Villanova
  Monteleone 66 A2
Villanubla 35 E4
Villanueva de
  Alcardete 40 B3
Villanueva de
  Alcorón 40 C2
Villanueva de
  Algaidas 43 F3
Villanueva de
  Argaño 35 F3
Villanueva de
  Arzobispo 44 B2
Villanueva de
  Bogas 40 A3
Villanueva de
  Cameros 36 B3
Villanueva de
  Córdoba 43 F1
Villanueva de
  Franco 40 B4
Villanueva de
  Gállego 37 D3
Villanueva de la
  Concepción 43 F3
Villanueva de la
  Fuente 44 B1
Villanueva de la
  Jara 40 C4
Villanueva de la
  Reina 44 A2
Villanueva de la
  Serena 39 E4
Villanueva de la
  Sierra 39 D2
Villanueva de las
  Torres 44 B2

Villanueva de la
  Vera 39 E2
Villanueva del
  Campo 35 D3
Villanueva del
  Duque 43 E1
Villanueva del
  Fresno 42 C1
Villanueva del
  Huerva 37 D4
Villanueva de los
  Castillejos 42 C2
Villanueva de los
  Infantes 44 B1
Villanueva del Rey . 43 E1
Villanueva del Río y
  Minas 43 D2
Villanueva del
  Trabuco 43 F3
Villanueva de San
  Carlos 44 A1
Villa Opicina 59 F3
Villa Potenza 61 F4
Villaquejida 35 D3
Villaquilambre 35 D2
Villarcayo 36 A1
Villard-de-Lans . . . 30 C2
Villar de Cañas . . . 40 C3
Villardeciervos 35 D3
Villar de Domingo
  García 40 C2
Villardefrades 35 E4
Villar del
  Arzobispo 41 E3
Villar del Rey 39 D4
Villar de Peralonso . 39 E1
Villarejo de
  Fuentes 40 C3
Villarejo de Orbigo . 35 D3
Villarejo de
  Salvanés 40 B2
Villarente 35 D3
Villares de la Reina . 39 E1
Villares del Saz . . . 40 C3
Villargordo de
  Cabriel 41 D4
Villaricos 44 C3
Villarín de Campos . 35 D4
Villarino 34 C4
Villarquemado 41 D2
Villarramiel 35 E3
Villarrobledo 40 C4
Villarroya de la
  Sierra 36 C4
Villarroya de los
  Pinares 41 E2
Villarroya, Pto de . . 41 E2
Villarrubia de
  Santiago 40 B3
Villars 27 E3
Villars-les-Dombes . 26 C4
Villarta de San
  Juan 40 B4
Villarubia de los
  Ojos 40 A4
Villarubio 40 B3
Villasalto 66 C3
Villasana de Mena . 36 A1
Villasandino 35 F3
Villa San Giovanni . 67 E4
Villa Santa Maria . . 64 A2
Villasante 36 A1
Villa Santina 59 E3
Villasarracino 35 E3
Villasayas, Pto de . . 36 B4
Villaseco de los
  Reyes 39 E1
Villasequilla de
  Yepes 40 A3
Villasimius 66 C4
Villasor 66 B4
Villatobas 40 B3
Villatoro, Pto de . . . 39 F2
Villatoya 41 D4
Villava 36 C2
Villavaara 95 F3
Villaverde del Río . . 43 D2
Villaviciosa 35 E1
Villaviciosa de
  Córdoba 43 E2
Villaviciosa de
  Odón 40 A2
Villavieja de Yeltes . 39 D1

Villa Vomano 63 F1
Villè 21 E4
Villebois-Lavalette .. 28 C1
Villedieu, la .. 25 D3
Villedieu-les-
Poêles 18 B4
Ville-en-Tardenois .. 20 B3
Villefagnan 24 C4
Villefort 29 F3
Villefranche-
d'Albigeois.. 29 E3
Villefranche-de-
Lauragais........ 29 D4
Villefranche-de-
Lonchat .. 28 C2
Villefranche-de-
Rouergue .. 29 E3
Villefranche-du-
Périgord .. 29 D2
Villefranche-sur-
Cher .. 25 E2
Villefranche-sur-
Mer .. 31 E3
Villefranche-sur-
Saône.. 26 C4
Villel .. 41 D2
Villemur .. 29 D3
Villena .. 45 D1
Villenauxe-la-
Grande .. 20 A4
Villeneuve.. 30 B3
Villeneuve-d'Asq.. 19 F1
Villeneuve-de-
Berg .. 30 B2
Villeneuve-de-
Marsan .. 28 B3
Villeneuve-
l'Archevêque.. 26 A1
Villeneuve-sur-Lot.. 28 C3
Villeneuve-sur-
Yonne .. 26 A1
Villeréal .. 28 C2
Villers .. 19 D3
Villers-Bocage
(Calvados).. 18 C3
Villers-Bocage
(Somme).. 19 F2
Villers-
Bretonneux.. 19 F2
Villers-Cotterêts .. 19 F3
Villers-devant-
Orval .. 20 C2
Villersexel .. 27 D2
Villers-Farlay .. 27 D2
Villers la Ville.. 50 C4
Villers-le-Lac .. 27 E2
Villerupt.. 21 D3
Villerville .. 19 D3
Ville-sur-Tourbe .. 20 C3
Villeta Barrea .. 64 A2
Villiers-St-Georges.. 20 A4
Villingen-
Schwenningen.. 54 C3
Villoldo .. 35 E3
Villoria.. 39 E1
Villotta .. 59 E3
Villuercas .. 39 E3
Vilnius .. 110 C3
Vilppula .. 102 C3
Vils (Bayern) .. 55 F1
Vils (Bayern) .. 56 B2
Vilsbiburg.. 56 B2
Vilseck .. 55 F1
Vilshofen.. 56 C2

Vilusi .. 76 A2
Vilvoorde.. 50 B3
Vimercate .. 60 A1
Vimianzo .. 34 A1
Vimieiro .. 38 B4
Vimioso .. 34 C4
Vimoutiers .. 19 D4
Vimpeli .. 102 C2
Vimperk .. 56 C1
Vinac .. 71 E4
Vinadio .. 31 E3
Vinaixa .. 37 F4
Vinalapó, R .. 45 D2
Vinarós .. 41 F2
Vinay .. 30 C1
Vinça .. 32 B2
Vinča .. 73 D3
Vinchiaturo.. 64 B3
Vinci .. 60 C3
Vindafjorden .. 104 A3
Vindelälven .. 102 A1
Vindelfjällens N.R... 97 E3
Vindeln .. 102 A1
Vinderup.. 108 A2
Vindsvik .. 104 A3
Vingåker .. 105 F4
Vingelen .. 100 C3
Vingeveien .. 100 C3
Vinhais.. 34 C4
Vinica
(Makedonija) 77 F3
Vinica (SLO) .. 70 C3
Viničani.. 77 E3
Vinje .. 104 B3
Vinkovci .. 71 F2
Vinnycja.. 113 E2
Vinsternes .. 100 B2
Vinstra .. 100 C3
Vinstri.. 104 C1
Vintilänkaira .. 95 F4
Viñuelas .. 40 B2
Vinuesa .. 36 B3
Viotia.. 83 F4
Vipava .. 70 A2
Vipava R... 70 A2
Vipiteno .. 59 D2
Vir (BH) .. 75 E1
Vir (HRV) .. 70 C4
Vir I .. 70 C4
Vira .. 75 D2
Vire .. 18 C4
Virgen .. 59 E2
Virgen de la
Cabeza.. 43 F2
Virginia .. 13 D3
Virieu .. 30 C1
Virieu-le-Grand .. 27 D4
Virihaure .. 97 F1
Virkby .. 107 E3
Virkkala .. 107 E3
Virkkula .. 99 E2
Virksund .. 108 A2
Virmasvesi .. 103 D2
Virmutjoki .. 103 F3
Virolahti .. 103 F4
Virónia .. 80 A2
Virovitica .. 71 E2
Virpazar .. 76 B3
Virrat .. 102 C3
Virsbo.. 105 F3
Virserum .. 109 E2
Virsko more .. 70 C4
Virtasalmi .. 103 E3

Virton .. 20 C3
Virtsu.. 110 B2
Vis .. 75 D2
Vis I .. 75 D2
Visaurin .. 37 D2
Visby .. 109 F4
Visé .. 51 D3
Višegrad .. 72 C4
Višegradska Banja .. 72 C4
Viserba .. 61 E3
Viseu .. 38 C1
Viševica .. 70 B3
Viškan .. 108 C2
Viški kan .. 75 D2
Višnja Gora .. 70 B2
Višnjica .. 73 D3
Visočica .. 75 F1
Visočica R... 73 F4
Viso del Marqués .. 44 A1
Visoki Dečani .. 76 C2
Visoko.. 71 F4
Visovac.. 75 D1
Visp .. 27 F3
Vissani .. 78 B4
Visselhövede .. 48 A3
Vissenbjerg .. 108 B3
Vissiniá .. 79 D3
Visso .. 63 F1
Vistabella del
Maestrazgo .. 41 E2
Vistasvaggi .. 94 B4
Vistheden .. 98 B3
Vistonída, L .. 81 D2
Visuvesi .. 102 C3
Vitaby .. 109 D3
Vitala .. 84 B4
Vitanovac .. 73 D4
Vitebsk .. 111 E3
Viterbo .. 63 E2
Vitez .. 71 E4
Vitigudino .. 39 D1
Vitina .. 86 C2
Vitina (BH) ..75E2
Vitina (Kosovo) .. 77 D2
Vitlycke .. 105 D4
Vito d'Asio .. 59 E3
Vitoli .. 83 D3
Vitolište .. 77 E4
Vitomirica .. 76 C2
Vitoria-Gasteiz .. 36 B2
Vitorog .. 71 E4
Vitoša .. 115 D2
Vitovlje .. 71 E4
Vitré .. 23 D3
Vitry-en-Artois .. 19 F2
Vitry-le-François .. 20 B4
Vitsa .. 78 C4
Vitsand .. 105 E2
Vittangi .. 94 C4
Vittangijälven .. 94 C4
Vitteaux .. 26 B2
Vittel .. 27 D1
Vittoria .. 69 D4
Vittoriosa .. 68 B4
Vittorio Veneto .. 59 E3
Vittsjö .. 109 D3
Vitznau .. 58 A2
Viù .. 31 E1
Vivaro .. 59 E3
Vivel del R Martin .. 41 E2
Viver .. 41 E3
Viverio .. 34 B1
Viverols .. 29 F1

Viveros .. 44 B1
Vivier, le .. 18 B4
Viviers .. 30 B2
Vivonne .. 25 D4
Vizille .. 30 C2
Vižinada .. 70 A3
Viži .. 83 E2
Vizzavona .. 33 F3
Vizzavona, Col de.. 33 F3
Vizzini .. 69 D4
Vjosë .. 114 B4
Vlaardingen .. 16 B3
Vladičin Han .. 77 E1
Vladimirci .. 72 C3
Vladimirovac .. 73 D2
Vladimirovo .. 77 F3
Vlagtwedde .. 17 E1
Vlaháva .. 83 D1
Vlahérna (Ipiros) .. 82 C2
Vlahérna
(Pelopónissos) .. 86 C2
Vlahiótis .. 87 D3
Vlahokerassiá .. 87 D2
Vlahomándra .. 83 D4
Vlahópoulo .. 86 C3
Vlanen .. 16 C2
Vlasenica .. 72 B4
Vlašić (BH) .. 71 E4
Vlašić (Srbija) .. 72 C3
Vlasina Okruglica .. 77 E1
Vlasinsko jez... 77 E1
Vlasotince .. 77 E1
Vlássio .. 83 D2
Vlásti .. 79 D3
Vlieland .. 16 C1
Vlihó .. 82 B3
Vlissingen .. 16 B3
Vloré .. 114 B4
Vlotho.. 17 F2
Vltava .. 53 F3
Vobbia .. 60 A2
Voćin .. 71 E2
Vöcklabruck .. 56 C3
Vodice (Rijeka) .. 70 A3
Vodice (Šibenik) .. 74 C1
Vodna .. 73 E3
Vodňany .. 56 C1
Vodnjan .. 70 A4
Voe .. 3 F1
Vogatsikó .. 79 D3
Vogel .. 70 A2
Vogelsberg .. 52 A4
Vogelsdorf .. 49 E4
Voghera .. 60 A2
Vogošća .. 72 B4
Vohenstrauß .. 56 B1
Vöhringen .. 55 E3
Void .. 20 C4
Voikoski .. 107 F1
Vóïo, Óros .. 78 C3
Voiron .. 30 C1
Voiteur .. 26 C4
Voitsberg .. 57 E4
Vojens .. 108 A3
Vojka .. 72 C3
Vojmsjön .. 97 F4
Vojnić .. 70 C3
Vojnik .. 70 B1
Vojsko .. 73 D3
Vojtanov .. 53 D4
Vojvodina .. 72 C2
Vólakas .. 80 B1
Volary .. 56 C2

Volchov .. 111 E1
Volchov R .. 111 E1
Volda .. 100 A3
Voldafjorden .. 100 A2
Volders .. 59 D2
Volendam .. 16 C2
Volga .. 111 F1
Volímes .. 86 A1
Volissós .. 85 E4
Volkach .. 52 B4
Völkermarkt .. 70 B1
Volkmarsen .. 52 A2
Volkovija .. 77 D3
Volkovysk .. 110 C4
Volmunster .. 21 E3
Voločys'k .. 113 D2
Volodymyr-
Volyns'kyj .. 112 C2
Volokolamsk .. 111 F2
Volonne .. 31 D3
Vólos .. 83 F2
Voložin .. 111 D4
Volpiano .. 31 E1
Volta .. 60 C1
Volterra .. 60 C4
Voltri .. 60 A3
Volturara Appula .. 64 B3
Volturino, Mte.. 64 C4
Volturno .. 64 A3
Volvic .. 26 A4
Völvi, L .. 80 B3
Volyn' .. 113 D2
Volyné .. 56 C1
Vónitsa .. 82 C3
Vonnas .. 26 C4
Voors .. 17 D2
Voorschoten .. 16 B3
Voorthuizen .. 16 C2
Vopnafjörður .. 96 C1
Vorå .. 102 B2
Voralberg .. 58 B2
Vóras, Óros .. 79 E2
Vorau .. 57 E3
Vorchdorf .. 56 C3
Vorderberg .. 57 E4
Vorderrhein .. 58 A3
Vorderriß .. 56 A4
Vordingborg .. 108 C4
Vorë .. 76 C4
Voreppe .. 30 C1
Vorey .. 30 A1
Vóri .. 91 D4
Vória Píndos .. 78 C4
Vóries Sporádes .. 84 C2
Vøringfossen .. 104 B2
Vórios Evoïkós
Kólpos .. 83 F3
Vório Stenó
Kerkiras .. 82 A1
Vorivs'kyj Pereval .. 112 C3
Vorma .. 105 D3
Vormsi .. 110 B1
Vorna .. 99 D4
Voronet .. 113 D3
Vorsfelde .. 48 B4
Vorskla .. 113 F2
Võrtsjärv .. 110 C2
Võru .. 110 C2
Vosges (Dépt) .. 27 D1
Voss .. 104 B2
Votice .. 53 F4
Votonóssi .. 82 C1
Voúdia .. 88 B4

Vouga, R .. 38 C1
Vouglans, Lac de .. 27 D3
Vouhorína .. 79 D4
Vouillé .. 25 D3
Voukoliés .. 90 B3
Voúla .. 87 F1
Voulgára .. 83 D2
Vouliagméni .. 87 F1
Voúlpi .. 83 D3
Voulte, la .. 30 B2
Vouná Goúras .. 83 E2
Vouraïkós .. 86 C1
Voúrinos, Óros .. 79 D4
Vourkári .. 88 A2
Vourliótes .. 89 E1
Voúrvoura .. 87 D2
Vourvourioú .. 80 B4
Voutás .. 83 F3
Vouvant .. 24 C3
Vouvray .. 25 D2
Voúxa, Akr .. 90 B3
Vouziers .. 20 B3
Vouzela .. 38 B1
Voves .. 25 E1
Vovoússa .. 78 C4
Voxnan .. 101 E4
Vöyri .. 102 B2
Voz .. 70 B3
Vozarci .. 77 E3
Voznesens'k .. 113 F3
Vrå .. 108 B2
Vraca .. 115 D2
Vraca pl .. 77 D3
Vračev Gaj .. 73 D2
Vračevšnica .. 73 D4
Vrådal .. 104 B3
Vraháti .. 87 D1
Vrahiónas, Óros .. 86 A2
Vrahnéika .. 86 C1
Vrams-
Gunnarstorp.. 108 C3
Vrana .. 70 B4
Vrancei, M .. 113 D4
Vranduk .. 71 F4
Vranica .. 71 E4
Vranja .. 70 A3
Vranjak .. 75 F2
Vranje .. 77 E2
Vranjska Banja .. 77 E2
Vranovská přehr
nádrž.. 57 E1
Vran pl .. 75 E1
Vransko .. 70 B2
Vransko jezero .. 74 C1
Vrástama .. 80 B3
Vratarnica .. 73 F4
Vratnica .. 77 D2
Vratnik .. 70 B3
Vratno .. 70 C1
Vravróna .. 88 A1
Vražogrnac .. 73 F3
Vrbanja .. 72 B3
Vrbanja R .. 71 E3
Vrbas .. 72 B2
Vrbas R .. 71 E3
Vrbaška .. 71 E3
Vrbas klisura .. 71 E4
Vrbljani .. 71 D4
Vrbnica .. 77 D3
Vrbnik .. 70 B3
Vrboska .. 75 E2
Vrbovec .. 71 D2
Vrbovsko .. 70 B3

Vrčin .. 73 D3
Vrdnik .. 72 C2
Vreden .. 17 E3
Vrela .. 76 C2
Vrelo (HR) .. 70 C4
Vrelo (Srbija) .. 73 E4
Vreoci .. 72 C3
Vresse .. 20 C2
Vrésthena .. 87 D3
Vreta Kloster .. 106 A4
Vrginmost .. 70 C3
Vrhnika .. 70 A2
Vrhpolje .. 71 D4
Vría .. 79 E4
Vrínena .. 83 F3
Vríssa .. 85 F3
Vrisses .. 90 C3
Vrissiá .. 83 E2
Vrissoúla .. 82 B2
Vrla .. 75 D1
Vrlika .. 70 A2
Vrnjačka Banja.. 73 D4
Vrnograč .. 70 C3
Vrondádos .. 85 F4
Vrondamás .. 87 D3
Vronderó .. 78 C3
Vrondissí .. 91 E4
Vrondoú .. 79 E4
Vrondoús, Óri .. 80 B2
Vrossina .. 82 B1
Vrouhás .. 91 F4
Vrsar .. 70 A3
Vrsi .. 70 C4
Vrška Čuka .. 73 F4
Vrtac .. 76 B2
Vrtoče .. 71 D4
Vrutok .. 77 D3
Vučitrn .. 77 F3
Vučjak .. 71 F3
Vučje .. 77 E1
Vučkovica .. 73 D4
Vue des Alpes .. 27 E2
Vuka .. 71 F2
Vukovar .. 72 B2
Vulcano, I.. 69 D2
Vulture, Mte .. 64 C3
Vuohijärvi .. 107 F2
Vuohijärvi L .. 107 F1
Vuokatti .. 99 E4
Vuokkijärvi .. 99 F3
Vuokojaure .. 94 C3
Vuoksenniska .. 103 F3
Vuolijoki .. 99 E4
Vuollerim .. 98 B2
Vuolvojaure .. 98 A2
Vuonislahti .. 103 F2
Vuorji .. 95 D2
Vuosjärvi .. 103 D2
Vuoskuvarri .. 95 D3
Vuostimo .. 99 E2
Vuotso .. 95 E3
Vylkove .. 113 E4
Vyškov .. 57 F1
Vyšnij Voločok .. 111 E2
Vyžnica .. 113 D3

W

Waal .. 16 C3
Waalwijk .. 16 C3
Waasmunster .. 50 B3
Wabern .. 52 A3
Wachau .. 57 E2
Wachow .. 49 D4
Wächtersbach .. 52 A4
Waddeneilanden .. 16 C1
Wadebridge .. 8 B3
Wädenswil .. 58 A2

Wagenfeld .. 17 F2
Wageningen .. 17 D3
Waging .. 56 B3
Wagrain .. 59 E1
Wągrowiec .. 112 A1
Wahlstedt .. 48 A2
Waiblingen .. 55 D2
Waidhaus .. 56 B1
Waidhofen (Ybbs) .. 57 D3
Waidhofen (Thaya).. 57 E2
Waidring .. 59 E1
Waischenfeld .. 52 C4
Waizenkirchen .. 56 C2

Wakefield .. 7 D2
Wałbrzych .. 112 A2
Walchensee .. 56 A4
Walcheren .. 16 B3
Walchsee .. 59 D1
Wałcz .. 112 A1
Wald .. 58 A2
Waldbröl .. 17 E4
Waldeck .. 52 A2
Waldenbuch .. 55 D3
Waldenburg .. 53 D3
Waldfischbach-
Burgalben .. 54 B2

Waldheim .. 53 E2
Waldkappel .. 52 B3
Waldkirch .. 54 C3
Waldkirchen .. 56 C2
Waldkraiburg .. 56 B3
Wald-Michelbach .. 54 C1
Waldmünchen .. 56 B1
Waldsassen .. 53 D4
Waldshut .. 54 C4
Walensee .. 58 B2
Walenstadt .. 58 B2
Wales .. 8 C1
Wallasey .. 6 B2

Walldorf .. 54 C2
Walldürn .. 55 D1
Wallenfels .. 52 C4
Wallersdorf .. 56 B2
Wallerstein .. 55 E2
Wallingford .. 9 E2
Walls .. 3 F2
Walsall .. 9 E1
Walsrode .. 48 A4
Walsum .. 17 D3
Waltershausen .. 52 B3
Walton-on-the-
Naze.. 11 D2

Waltrop .. 17 E3
Wanderup .. 48 A1
Wandlitz .. 49 E3
Wanfried .. 52 B2
Wangen .. 55 E4
Wangenbourg .. 21 E4
Wangerland-
Hooksiel .. 47 E3
Wangerooge .. 47 E2
Wängi .. 58 A1
Wanna .. 47 F2
Wanne-Eickel .. 17 E3
Wantage .. 9 E2

Wantzenau, la .. 21 F4
Wanzleben .. 52 C1
Warburg .. 52 A2
Wardenburg .. 47 F3
Ware .. 9 F2
Waregem .. 50 B3
Wareham .. 9 D3
Waremme .. 50 C3
Waren .. 49 D2
Warendorf .. 17 F3
Warin .. 48 C2
Warkworth .. 5 E3
Warmensteinach .. 53 D4

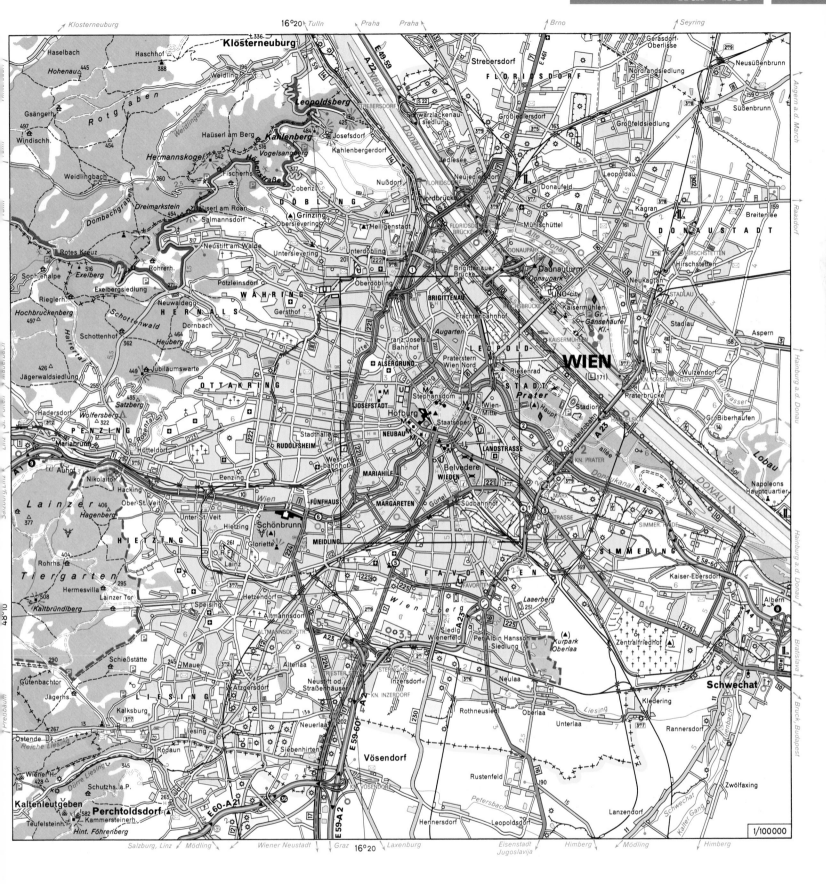

Warminster 9 E3	Warwick 9 E1	Wasser-Kuppe 52 B3	Waterloo 50 B3	Waxweiler 51 D4	Weggis 27 F2	Weil der Stadt 55 D2
Warnemunde 48 C2	Warwickshire 9 E1	Wassertrüdingen . . . 55 E2	Waternish Pt 2 B3	Wear 5 E4	Węgorzewo 110 B4	Weilheim (Baden-
Warnow 48 C2	Washington 5 E4	Wassigny 20 A2	Waterville 14 A4	Wechsel 57 E3	Węgorzyno 49 F2	Württemberg) . . . 55 D3
Warrenpoint 13 E3	Wash, The 7 E3	Wassy 20 C4	Watford 9 F2	Wedel 48 A3	Wegscheid 56 C2	Weilheim (Bayern) . . 56 A3
Warrington 6 B2	Wasselonne 21 E4	Wassen 58 A3	Wattens 59 D2	Wedemark-	Wehr 54 C4	Weimar 52 C3
Warstein 17 F3	Wassenaar 16 B3	Wassenberg 17 D4	Watchet 8 C3	Watton 11 D1	Mellendorf 48 A4	Weibersbrunn 52 A4	Weinfelden 58 A1
Warszawa 112 B1	Wassenaar 16 B3	Wasseralfingen 55 E2	Waterfoot 13 E1	Weener 47 E3	Weichshofen 56 B2	Weingarten 55 D4
Warszów 49 E2	Wassenberg 17 D4	Wasserbillig 21 D2	Waterford 15 D4	Watzmann 56 C4	Weert 17 D4	Weida 53 D3	Weinheim 54 C1
Warta 49 F3	Wasseralfingen 55 E2	Waterford (Co) 14 C4	Waulsort 50 C4	Weferlingen 48 C4	Weiden 56 A1	Weinsberg 55 D1
Warth 58 B2	Wasserbillig 21 D2	Waterford	Waveney 11 D1	Wavre 50 C3	Wegberg 17 D4	Weikersheim 55 D1	Weismain 52 C4
Wartha 52 B3	Wasserburg 56 B3	Harbour 15 D4	Wavre 50 C3	Wegeleben 52 C1	Weilburg 51 F4	Weißbriach 59 F2

Weiße Elster 53 D3
Weißenbach 58 C1
Weißenberg 53 F2
Weißenburg 55 F2
Weißenfels 53 D2
Weißenhorn 55 E3
Weißenkirchen . . . 57 E2
Weißensee 52 C2
Weißensee (L) 59 F2
Weissenstadt 53 D4
Weissenstein 27 E2
Weissfluhgipfel . . 58 B2
Weißkirchen 57 D4
Weißkugel 58 C2
Weißwasser 53 F1
Weitra 57 D2
Weiz 57 E4
Wejherowo 110 A4
Weldon 9 F1
Welgetschlag . . . 57 D2
Welland 9 F1
Wellin 20 C2
Wellingborough . . 9 F1
Wellington 9 D3
Wellington Bridge . 15 D4
Wells 9 D3
Wells-next-the-Sea . 7 E3
Wels 56 C3
Welsberg 59 D2
Welschnofen 59 D3
Welshpool 9 D1
Weltenburg 55 F2
Welwyn Garden City . 9 F2
Welzheim 55 D2
Wem 6 B3
Wemding 55 E2
Wemyss Bay 4 C2
Wendelstein 56 B4
Wenden 52 B1
Wengen 27 F3
Wenns 58 C2
Werbellinsee 49 E3
Werben 48 C3
Werdau 53 D3
Werder 49 D4
Werdohl 17 E4
Werfen 59 E1
Werl 17 F3
Werlte 17 E1
Wermelskirchen . . 17 E4

Wermsdorf 53 E2
Wernberg 56 B1
Werne 17 E3
Werneck 52 B4
Werneuchen 49 E4
Wernigerode 52 C1
Werra 52 B3
Wertach 55 E4
Wertach (R) 55 E3
Wertheim 55 D1
Werther 17 F2
Wertingen 55 E3
Wervik 50 A3
Wesel 17 D3
Wesenberg 49 D3
Wesendorf 48 B4
Weser 47 F3
Weser-Elbe-Kanal . . 48 C4
Wesselburen 47 F2
Wessobrunn 56 A3
West Auckland 5 E4
West Bridgford 7 D3
Westbury 9 D3
Westendorf 59 D1
Westenholz 48 A4
Westerburg 51 F4
Westerholt 47 E3
Westerland 47 F1
Westerlo 50 C3
Westernbödefeld . . 17 F4
Western Isles 2 B2
Wester Ross 2 C3
Westerstede 47 E3
Westerwald 51 E3
Westhofen 54 C1
West Kilbride 4 C2
West Linton 5 D2
West Loch Tarbert . . 2 A2
Westmeath 12 C3
West Mersea 11 D2
Weston-super-
  Mare 9 D2
Westport 12 B3
Westray 3 E1
Westray Firth 3 E1
West Sussex 9 F3
West-Terschelling . . 16 C1
West-Vlaanderen . . 50 A3
Wetherby 7 D2
Wetter 17 E3

Wetteren 50 B3
Wettin 52 C2
Wettringen 17 E2
Wetwang 7 D1
Wetzikon 58 A2
Wetzlar 51 F3
Wexford 15 D3
Wexford (Co) 15 D3
Weyer-Markt 57 D3
Weyhausen 48 B4
Weyhill 9 E3
Weymouth 9 D3
Weyregg 56 C3
Whaley Bridge 6 C2
Whalsay 3 F1
Wharfe 6 C1
Whernside 6 C1
Whitburn 5 D2
Whitby 5 F4
Whitchurch 6 B3
Whitebridge 2 C4
Whitehaven 5 D4
Whitehead 13 E2
Whiteness 3 F2
Whiten Head 2 C2
Whithorn 4 C4
Whitland 8 B2
Whitley Bay 5 E3
Whitstable 11 D3
Whittlesey 9 F1
Wick 3 D2
Wickford 11 D2
Wicklow 13 E4
Wicklow (Co) 13 D4
Wicklow Head . . . 13 E4
Wicklow Mts 13 D4
Widnes 6 B2
Wiehe 52 C2
Wiek 49 D1
Wieliczka 112 B3
Wieluń 112 B2
Wien 57 F2
Wiener-Neudorf . . 57 F2
Wiener Neustadt . . 57 F3
Wienerwald 57 E3
Wies (A) 70 B1
Wies (D) 56 A4
Wiesau 53 D4
Wiesbaden 51 F4
Wieselburg 57 E3

Wiesenburg 53 D1
Wiesensteig 55 D3
Wiesentheid 55 E1
Wiesenttal 52 C4
Wiesing 59 D1
Wiesloch 54 C2
Wiesmath 57 F3
Wiesmoor 47 E3
Wigan 6 C2
Wight, I of 9 E4
Wigton 5 D4
Wigtown 4 C3
Wigtown B 4 C4
Wijhe 17 D2
Wil 58 A2
Wildalpen 57 D3
Wildbad 54 C2
Wildeck 52 B3
Wildeshausen . . . 17 F1
Wildon 57 E4
Wildspitze 58 C2
Wildstrubel 27 E3
Wilfersdorf 57 F2
Wilhelmina kan . . 16 C3
Wilhelm Pieck-
  Stadt. 53 F1
Wilhelmsburg (A) . 57 E3
Wilhelmsburg (D) . 48 A3
Wilhelmshaven . . 47 F3
Wilkau-Haßlau . . 53 D3
Willebroek 50 B3
Willemstad 16 B3
Willingen 17 F4
Williton 8 C3
Wilmslow 6 C2
Wilnsdorf 17 F4
Wilster 48 A2
Wilton 9 E3
Wiltshire 9 E3
Wiltz 21 D2
Wimborne Minster . 9 E3
Wimereux 19 E1
Wincanton 9 D3
Winchcombe 9 E2
Winchelsea 11 D3
Winchester 9 E3
Windeck 51 E3

Windermere 5 D4
Windischeschenbach
  . . . . 53 D4
Windischgarsten . . 57 D3
Windsbach 55 E1
Windsor 9 F2
Winkleigh 8 C3
Winklern 59 E2
Winnenden 55 D2
Winnigstedt 52 B1
Winnweiler 54 B1
Winschoten 47 E3
Winsen (Celle) . . 48 A4
Winsen
  (Lüneburg) . . . 48 B3
Winsford 6 C3
Winsum 47 D3
Winterberg 17 F4
Winterswijk 17 D3
Winterthur 58 A2
Wintzenheim . . . 27 E1
Wipper 52 C2
Wipperfürth 17 E4
Wisbech 10 C1
Wischhafen 48 A2
Wiselka 49 E2
Wishaw 4 C2
Wisła 110 B4
Wismar 48 C2
Wissant 19 E1
Wissembourg . . . 21 F3
Wissen 51 E3
Witham R 7 D3
Witham 11 D2
Withernsea 7 E2
Witney 9 E2
Witnica 49 F3
Wittdün 47 F1
Witte 49 D1
Witten 17 E3
Wittenberg 53 D1
Wittenberge 48 C3
Wittenburg 48 B3
Wittichenau 53 F2
Wittingen 48 B4
Wittlich 51 E4
Wittmund 47 E3
Wittow 49 D1
Wittstock 49 D3
Witzenhausen . . . 52 B2

Władysławowo . . 110 A4
Włocławek 112 B1
Włodawa 112 C2
Wöbbelin 48 C3
Woburn 9 F2
Woburn Abbey . . . 9 F2
Woensdrecht . . . 16 B4
Woerden 16 C3
Wohlen 27 F2
Woippy 21 D3
Woking 9 F3
Wokingham 9 F3
Wołczenica 49 F2
Woldegk 49 E2
Wolfach 54 C3
Wolfegg 55 E4
Wolfen 53 D2
Wolfenbüttel . . . 52 B1
Wolfhagen 52 A2
Wolfratshausen . . 56 A3
Wolfsberg 70 B1
Wolfsburg 48 B4
Wolgast 49 E2
Wolin 49 E2
Wolin (Reg) 49 E2
Woliński Park
  Narodowy 49 E2
Wolkenstein 59 D3
Wolkersdorf 57 F2
Wöllersdorf 57 F3
Wollersheim 51 D3
Wollin 49 D4
Wolmirstedt 48 C4
Wolsingham 5 E4
Wolsztyn 112 A2
Wolvega 17 D1
Wolverhampton . . 9 E1
Wolverton 9 F1
Wolznach 55 F2
Woodbridge 11 D1
Woodhall Spa . . . 7 E3
Woodstock 9 E2
Wooler 5 E3
Worb 27 E2
Worbis 52 B2
Worcester 9 D1
Wörgl 59 D1
Workington 5 D4
Worksop 7 D2
Workum 16 C1

Wörlitz 53 D1
Wormerveer 16 C2
Wormhout 19 F1
Worms 54 C1
Worms Head 8 C3
Wörnitz 55 E2
Wörrstadt 54 C1
Wörth 21 E3
Wörth (Donau) . . 56 B2
Wörth (Main) . . . 55 D1
Wörth (Rheinland-
  Pfalz) 54 C2
Worther See 70 A1
Worthing 10 C3
Woświn, Jez 49 F2
Wragby 7 D3
Wrath, Cape 2 C2
Wrecsam 6 B3
Wrexham 6 B3
Wriezen 49 E3
Wrocław 112 A2
Wroughton 9 E2
Września 112 A1
Wulfen 17 D3
Wullowitz 57 D2
Wümme 48 A3
Wümme R 48 A3
Wünnenberg . . . 17 F3
Wünsdorf 49 E4
Wunsiedel 53 D4
Wunstorf 48 A4
Wuppertal 17 E4
Würzburg 55 D1
Wurzen 53 D2
Wurzen-Paß 59 F2
Wusterhausen . . 49 D3
Wustrow
  (Rostock) 48 C1
Wustrow
  (Wismar) 48 C2
Wuustwezel 50 C2
Wye, R 9 D2
Wyk 47 F1
Wymondham . . . 11 D1

X

Xallas, R 34 A2
Xanten 17 D3
Xánthi 81 D2

Xánthi (Nomos) . . . 81 D2
Xarrama, R 42 B1
Xàtiva 41 E4
Xeresa 41 E4
Xerovoúni 82 C2
Xerta 41 F2

Xertigny. 27 D1
Xesta, Pto de la . . 34 C1
Xifianí 79 E2
Xilópoli 80 A2
Xilaganí 81 E2
Xiliki 83 E3
Xilís, Akr 87 D4

Xilókastro 87 D1
Xilopáriko 83 D2
Xilókambi 87 D3
Xilóskalo 90 B3
Xiniáda 83 E3
Xinó Neró 79 D3

Xinzo de Limia . . . 34 B3
Xiró 83 F3
Xirokámbi 87 D3
Xirókambos 89 E3
Xirolímni 79 D3
Xistral 34 B1

Xixona 45 E1
Xódoto, Akr 89 D3
Xubia 34 B1
Xunqueira de
  Ambía 34 B3
Xúquer, R 41 E4

Y

Yaiza 42 C4
Yalova 115 F3
Yanguas 36 B3
Yare 7 F4
Yarmouth 9 E3
Yarmouth, Great . . 7 F4
Ybbs 57 D2
Ybbs R 57 D3

Yebra 40 B2
Yecla 45 D1
Yeguas, Emb de . . 43 F2
Yeguas, R de las . . 43 F1
Yell 3 F1
Yell Sd 3 F1
Yelmo 44 B2
Yeltes, R. 39 D1
Yenne 27 D4
Yeovil. 9 D3
Yepes 40 B3

Yerville 19 D3
Yesa 36 C2
Yesa, Emb de . . . 37 D2
Yeşilova 115 F4
Yeste 44 C1
Yeu, I d' 24 A3
Yèvre 26 A2
Y-Fenni 9 D2
Yıldız Dağları . . . 115 E3
Ylämaa 103 F4
Ylämylly 103 F2

Yläne 107 D2
Ylihärmä 102 C2
Yli-Kärppä 99 D3
Ylikiiminki 99 D3
Yli-Kitka 99 E2
Yli-Ii 99 D3
Yli-Muonio 95 D4
Yli-Nampa 99 D2
Yli-Olhava 99 D3
Ylistaro. 102 B2
Ylitornio 98 C2
Youghal 14 C4

Ylivieska 102 C1
Ylläs 95 D4
Ylläsjärvi 95 D4
Ylöjärvi 102 C3
Yngaren 106 A4
Yonne 20 A4
Yonne (Dépt) . . . 26 A1
York 7 D2
Yorkshire Dales
  Nat Pk 6 C1
Youghal 14 C4

Youghal B 14 C4
Yoxford 11 E1
Ypäjä 107 D2
Yport 19 D2
Yppäri 99 D4
Ypres 50 A3
Yr Wyddgrug 6 B3
Yser 19 F1
Yssingeaux 30 B1
Ystad 109 D4
Y Trallwng 9 D1

Ytterhogdal 101 E3
Yttermalung . . . 105 E2
Yuncos 40 A2
Yunquera 43 E4
Yunquera de
  Henares 40 B2
Yuste 39 E2
Yverdon 27 E3
Yvetot 19 D3
Yvoir 50 C4
Yvoire 27 D3

Z

Zaandam 16 C2
Žabali............. 72 C2
Žabari 73 D3
Zablaće........... 75 D1
Žabljak (Durmitor) . . 76 B1
Žabljak (Podgorica) . 76 B3
Žabno 71 D2
Zabok 70 C2
Zabrddde 72 B3
Zadar 74 C1
Zadarski kanal ... 70 B4
Zadvarje 75 E2
Zafarraya 43 F3
Zafóra, Ni 92 C2
Zafra 43 D1
Žaga 70 A2
Žagań 112 A2
Zaglavak 72 C4
Zagorá 83 F2
Zagória 82 C1
Zagorje 70 B2
Zagreb 70 C2
Žagubica 73 E3
Zagvozd 75 E2
Zahara de los
  Atunes 43 D4
Zahara, Emb de.... 43 E3
Zaháro 86 B2
Zahinos 42 C1
Zahna 53 D1
Záhony 112 C3
Zaidin 37 E4
Zajas 77 D3
Zaječar 73 F3
Zákinthos 86 A1
Zákinthos, N. 86 A1
Zakopane 112 B3
Zákros 91 F4
Zala 112 A4
Zalaegerszeg 112 A4
Zalamea de la
  Serena 43 E1
Zalamea la Real 42 C2
Zalău 112 C4
Žalec 70 B2
Zalew Wiślany 110 B4
Zališčyky 113 D3
Zalla 36 A1
Zálongo........... 82 B2
Zaltbommel 16 C3
Zalužnica 70 C4
Zambrana 36 B2
Zamora 35 D4
Zamość 112 C2
Záncara, R 40 B4
Zandvoort......... 16 B2
Zángano, Pto del .. 39 D4
Zanglivéri........ 80 A3
Zannone, I 63 F4
Zaorejas 40 C2
Zaostrog 75 E2
Zaovine Vežanja ... 72 C4
Zapadnaja Dvina ... 111 E2
Zapadnaja Dvina
  R 111 E2
Zapadna Morava ... 73 D4
Zapardiel, R 39 F1
Zapatón, R 39 D3
Zápio 83 E2
Zapponeta 64 C3
Zaprešić 70 C2
Zaragoza 37 D3
Zárakes 84 B4
Zaratán........... 35 E4

Zarautz............. 36 C1
Zarcilla de Ramos .. 44 C2
Zárkos 83 E1
Zarós............. 91 D4
Zaroúhla 87 D1
Zarrentin 48 B3
Žary 112 A2
Zarza la Mayor. ... 39 D2
Zasieki 53 F1
Zaškiv 113 E2
Žatec 53 E3
Zatoka Gdańska .. 110 B4
Zaton 75 F2
Zavala 75 F2
Zavattarello 60 A2
Zavidovići 71 F4
Zavlaka 72 C3
Zavratnica 70 B4
Zawiercie 112 B2
Žažina 71 D2
Zbaraž 113 D2
Zbraslav 53 F4
Ždár nad
  Sázavou 112 A3
Zdenac 70 C3
Zdice 53 F4
Ždrelac 74 C1
Ždrelo 73 E3
Zdunje 77 D3
Zduńska Wola ... 112 B2
Zebë, Maj'e 76 C3
Zebreira 38 C2
Žednik 72 B1
Zeebrugge 50 A3
Zeeland 16 B3
Zefiria 88 A4
Žegovac 77 D2
Žegra 77 D2
Žegulja 75 F2
Zehdenick 49 D3
Zeist 16 C3
Zeitz 53 D2
Zejtun 68 B4
Žekovec 70 B1
Zele 50 B3
Zelengora 76 A1
Zelengora (Reg) .. 76 A1
Zelenika 76 A3
Zelenogorsk..... 111 D1
Železná Ruda ... 56 C1
Železnik 72 C3
Železniki 70 A2
Železnogorsk.... 111 F4
Zelina 70 C2
Zélio 83 F3
Željezno Polje ... 71 F4
Željin 73 D4
Zell (D)......... 54 B1
Zell
  (Oberösterreich) . 56 C2
Zell (Tirol)...... 59 D2
Zella-Mehlis 52 C3
Zell am See 59 E1
Zellerrain 57 E3
Zeltweg 57 D4
Zelzate 50 B3
Zemun 72 C3
Zenica 71 F4
Žep 72 B4
Žepče 71 F4
Zerbst 53 D1
Zeri 60 B3
Zermatt 27 F4
Zernez 58 B3
Zerqan 77 D4
Zestoa......... 36 B1
Zeta.......... 76 B2

Zetel 47 E3
Zeulenroda........ 53 D3
Zeven 48 A3
Zevenaar 17 D3
Zevgaráki......... 82 C4
Zevgolatio 86 C3
Zevio 60 C1
Zêzere, R 38 C2
Žiča 73 D4
Zicavo 33 F4
Židlochovice 57 F1
Ziefsdorf 57 E2
Ziegenrück 52 C3
Zielona Góra 112 A2
Zierikzee 16 B3
Zierzow 48 C3
Ziesar 49 D4
Zi, Guri i 77 D4
Zijemlje 75 F1
Žilina 112 B3
Žilindar 76 C1
Ziller 59 D2
Zillertal 59 D2
Zimnicea 115 D2
Zinal 27 F4
Zingst 49 D1
Zin'kiv 113 F2
Zinnowitz 49 E1
Zinnwald 53 E3
Zirbitzkogel 57 D4
Zirchow 49 E2
Žiri 70 A2
Žirje 74 C1
Zirl 58 C2
Zirndorf 55 E1
Ziros 91 E4
Zistersdorf 57 F2
Žitište 72 C2
Žitkovac 73 E4
Žitkoviči 113 E1
Žitomisliči 75 F2
Žitoradđa 77 D1
Zittau 53 F2
Živinice 71 F3
Živogošče 75 E2
Žizdra 111 F3
Zjum 77 D2
Zlarin 75 D1
Zlarin / 75 D1
Zlata 77 D1
Zlatar 76 B1
Zlatar Bistrica .. 70 B2
Zlatarevo 77 F3
Zlatari 77 D1
Zlatarsko jez .. 76 B1
Zlatibor 72 C4
Zlatica 72 C4
Zlatni Pjasáci . 115 E2
Zletovo 77 E2
Zlin 112 A3
Žljebovi 72 B4
Zlobin 111 E4
Zlot 73 E3
Žlutice 53 E4
Zmajevo 72 C2
Zmerynka 113 E2
Žminj 70 A3
Znam"janka ... 113 F2
Znojmo 57 E1
Zöblitz 53 E3
Zoetermeer ... 16 B3
Zogaj 76 C2
Zollikofen 27 E2
Zoločiv 113 D2
Zolotonoša ... 113 F2

Zonári, Akr 93 F1
Zóni 81 F1
Zonianá 91 D3
Zonza 33 F4
Zoodóhos Pigi
  (Makedonía)..... 79 E3
Zoodóhos Pigii
  (Pelopónissos) ... 87 F2
Zörbig.......... 53 D2
Zorita 39 E3
Zossen 49 E4
Zoúrvas, Akr 87 F2
Zoutkamp 47 D3
Zoutleeuw 50 C3
Zoúzouli 78 C4
Žovti Vody ... 113 F2
Zrenjanin 72 C2
Zrin 71 D3
Zrinska gora ... 71 D3
Zrmanja R 74 C1
Zrmanja 75 D1
Žrnovnica 75 D2
Zrze 77 D2
Zschopau 53 E3
Zschopau R. ... 53 E3
Zubcov....... 111 F2

Zubin Potoku... 76 C2
Žuč 77 D1
Zucaina 41 E3
Zuckerhütl 58 C2
Zudar 49 D1
Zuera 37 D3
Zufre 43 D2
Zufre, Emb de .. 43 D2
Zug 58 A2
Zugspitze 55 F4
Zuid Beveland .. 16 B4
Zuidelijk-
  Flevoland 16 C2
Zuid Holland ... 16 B3
Zuidlaren 17 D1
Zújar 44 B3
Zújar, Emb del .. 39 E4
Zújar, R 43 E1
Žukovka 111 F3
Zuljana 75 E2
Zülpich 51 D3
Zumaia 36 B1
Zumárraga ... 36 B1
Zundert 16 C3
Zuoz 58 B3
Županja 71 F4

Žur 77 D3
Zürich 58 A2
Zurrieq 68 B4
Zürs 58 B2
Zurzach 58 A1
Zusmarshausen .. 55 E3
Žut 74 C1
Žuta Lokva 70 C3
Zvečan 77 D1
Zvenyhorodka .. 113 E2
Zvijezda nac park . 72 C4
Zvikovec 53 E4
Zvolen 112 B3
Zvonce 77 E1
Zvorničko jez .. 72 B4
Zvornik 72 B4
Zweibrücken ... 54 B2
Zweisimmen ... 27 E3
Zwenkau 53 D2
Zwettl (Nieder-
  österreich)..... 57 D2
Zwettl
  (Oberösterreich).. 57 D2
Zwickau 53 D3

Zwickauer Mulde ... 53 D3
Zwiefalten.......... 55 D3
Zwiesel 56 C2
Zwijndrecht 16 C3
Zwolle 17 D2
Żyrardów 112 B1
Žytomyr 113 E2
Żywiec 112 B3

Þ

Þingeyri 96 A1
Þingvallavatn 96 A2
Þingvellir 96 A2
Þistilfjörður 96 C1
Þjórsá 96 B2
Þórlákshöfn 96 A2
Þórshöfn 96 C1
Þórsmörk 96 B3